THE PUBLIC PAPERS OF
THE GOVERNORS OF KENTUCKY

Robert F. Sexton
General Editor

SPONSORED BY THE
Kentucky Advisory Commission
on Public Documents
and the
Kentucky Historical Society

THE PUBLIC PAPERS OF

GOVERNOR EDWARD T. BREATHITT

1963-1967

Kenneth E. Harrell, *Editor*

THE UNIVERSITY PRESS OF KENTUCKY

Library of Congress Cataloging in Publication Data

Breathitt, Edward T., 1924-

The public papers of Governor Edward T. Breathitt, 1963-1967.

(The Public papers of the Governors of Kentucky)

Sponsored by the Kentucky Advisory Commission on Public Documents and the Kentucky Historical Society.

Includes index.

1. Kentucky—Politics and government—1951- —Addresses, essays, lectures. I. Kentucky. Governor (1963-1967: Breathitt) II. Harrell, Kenneth E., 1932- III. Kentucky Advisory Commission on Public Documents. IV. Kentucky Historical Society. V. Title. VI. Series.

F456.2.B74 1983 976.9'043 83-25968

ISBN 0-8131-0603-6

Scholarly publisher for the Commonwealth, serving Bellarmine College, Berea College, Centre College of Kentucky, Eastern Kentucky University, The Filson Club, Georgetown College, Kentucky Historical Society, Kentucky State University, Morehead State University, Murray State University, Northern Kentucky University, Transylvania University, University of Kentucky, University of Louisville, and Western Kentucky University.

Editorial and Sales Offices: Lexington, Kentucky 40506-0024

CONTENTS

CONTENTS

CONTENTS

CONTENTS

TOURISM & RECREATION [235]

NATURAL RESOURCES [261]

CONTENTS

CONTENTS

CORRECTIONS, CRIME, & THE LAW [461]

STATE GOVERNMENT [496]

CONTENTS

GENERAL EDITOR'S PREFACE

THE Public Papers of the Governors of Kentucky is a series of volumes which preserves and disseminates the public record of Kentucky's chief executives. The need to make these records available was articulated by a number of persons interested in Kentucky history, government, and politics. In 1971 the Kentucky Advisory Commission on Public Documents, created by executive order, recommended the publication of the Public Papers of the Governors of Kentucky. The commission oversees and manages all aspects of the project in cooperation with the Kentucky Historical Society.

Approximately every four years the public papers of the last governor and one earlier governor will appear in separate volumes, each designed to provide a convenient record of that executive's administration. While the organization of the material may vary from volume to volume with differences in the styles of the governors, available materials, and historical circumstances, the volumes share an overall guiding philosophy and general format.

It is our hope that the series will prove useful to all those interested in Kentucky government, including citizens, scholars, journalists, and public servants. Not in themselves interpretations of Kentucky government and history, the volumes in this series will be the basis for serious analysis by future historians.

R.F.S.

EDITOR'S PREFACE

THIS volume contains 169 public statements made by Governor Edward T. Breathitt between December 10, 1963 and December 12, 1967. For the most part the statements are speeches; however, when appropriate to the organizational arrangement and topical content of the papers, press conferences and statements issued from the governor's office have been included. The precedent established in preceeding volumes of this series of excluding veto messages and executive orders has been followed here. Governor Breathitt vetoed nineteen senate bills, twenty-two house bills, and one joint resolution of the legislature. Those statements are published in the respective journals of the two houses of the General Assembly. Executive orders are available in the office of the secretary of state.

The papers are organized by topic, with chronological arrangement under each heading. This procedure reversed an earlier editorial decision to organize the papers chronologically. There were obvious merits to that choice, as other volumes in this series will attest; however, as the work progressed a topical structure for Governor Breathitt's papers seemed more appropriate. The topics—education, economic development, agriculture, highways, civil rights, natural resources, etc.—reflect the principal issues with which his administration was concerned. To be sure, the arrangement fails to provide absolute topical demarcation because Governor Breathitt saw significant interrelationships between many of the problems of his administration. Thus, economic development was dependent upon the expansion of educational opportunity, and improved highway and park systems were dependent upon passage of the bond issue. Yet, despite his tendency to reflect these interrelationships in his addresses, the topical ordering retains its integrity. Although it was impossible to eliminate all repetitious statements, duplicative sections of many speeches have been omitted and notes have been included to cite those omissions.

The speeches were originally prepared for public delivery rather than publication. Many were printed in speech-size type, with paragraphing designed for oral delivery; others contained penned-in notes, typographical errors, and awkward lists. Editorial attention was limited to corrections necessary for publication. In no case has the meaning of Governor Breathitt's statements been disturbed. Notes have been included identifying individuals the first time they are mentioned. Other notes, either explanatory or citing a source of information, have been included when appropriate. A complete chronological list of Governor Breathitt's speeches is located in Appendix 2.

Governor Breathitt donated his papers to Murray State University shortly after he left office. They include press releases, approximately 175 of his speeches, newspaper clippings, limited correspondence, executive orders, pictures, and a variety of other materials. The collection is housed in the Forrest C. Pogue Special Collections Library, and the university continues to add to the collection.

A number of people have provided invaluable assistance in the preparation of these papers. Mr. Don Mills, a member of Governor Breathitt's staff, assisted in the location of almost two-thirds of the governor's speeches. Without his assistance the speeches would no longer be available. The *Louisville Courier-Journal* generously agreed to allow the inclusion of Allan Trout's essay "The Breathitt Years. 'You have to Lead.'" Mr. Danny Gilkey, a graduate student in history at Murray State University, assisted in the initial work. A special debt is owed to Mr. Larry Sykes, a former graduate student at Murray State University now enrolled in the University of Kentucky College of Law. Mr. Sykes researched and wrote the original drafts of many of the notes. The Kentucky Historical Society provided funds for research assistance and typing. Governor Breathitt was invariably helpful in providing information when it was requested.

In the preparation of these papers I have attempted to avoid critical judgments of Governor Breathitt and his administration. That task belongs to the student who will at some future date write a definitive evaluation of this important period in Kentucky history. I hope these papers will encourage someone to undertake that project.

K.E.H.

GOVERNOR EDWARD T. BREATHITT
December 10, 1963, to December 12, 1967

EDWARD THOMPSON BREATHITT, JR., the only child of Edward Thompson and Mary Wallace Breathitt, was born November 26, 1924, in Hopkinsville, Kentucky. The Breathitt family had a long tradition of Kentucky political activity. A distant ancestor, John Breathitt, was elected governor in 1832; James Breathitt, Sr., Governor Breathitt's grandfather, won election as attorney general in 1907; and James Breathitt, Jr., an uncle, was elected lieutenant governor in 1937.

Breathitt was educated in the public schools of Hopkinsville. Following his graduation in 1942 he served three years in the United States Army Air Force. After the war he enrolled at the University of Kentucky, completing requirements for the Bachelor of Science in the College of Commerce in 1948 and the L.L.B. in the College of Law in 1950. He was a member of Sigma Alpha Epsilon social fraternity and president of Lamp and Cross and Omicron Delta Kappa, national leadership and scholarship fraternity. Breathitt's involvement in Kentucky government began early. In 1947, while he was a student at the University of Kentucky, Dr. Jack Reeves of the Political Science Department and Dr. Thomas Clark, chairman of the History Department, persuaded him to chair the campus campaign for a new state constitution. Breathitt accepted the position and became actively involved in the state-wide campaign. Although the effort failed, it was an issue to which he would return.

Following his admission to the bar Breathitt returned to Hopkinsville and began law practice as a member of the firm of Trimble, Soyars, and Breathitt. Active in commumity service as a Jaycee, Kiwanian, member of the chamber of commerce, and attorney for the Christian County School Board, Breathitt shortly launched his political career. In 1951 he was elected to the Kentucky House of Representatives from the Ninth District. He served in that capacity from 1952 to 1958. In the 1952 presidential campaign he was Adlai Stevenson's speaker chairman for the Commonwealth, and two years later he worked on the state campaign staff that successfully returned former Vice President Alben Barkley to the United States Senate. From 1952 to 1954 he served as president of the Young Democratic Clubs of Kentucky and was a member of the national committee of the Young Democrats of America.

As a member of the state legislature Breathitt supported passage of the Commonwealth's first strip mining legislation and improved registration and election laws. He joined with Representative Bart Peak of Lexington in an unsuccessful effort to secure adoption of a merit system for state employees. Although the legislature rejected their initial efforts, Breathitt and Peak persuaded Bert Combs to include the proposal in his 1959 platform. After Combs was elected he appointed Breathitt commissioner of personnel and requested that he draft the legislation and guide it through the legislature. Following passage of the bill Breathitt resigned as commissioner of personnel to accept membership on the Kentucky Public Service Commission. Implementation of the merit system then fell under the direcion of Felix Joyner and Walter Gattis.

In 1963 Breathitt challenged former Governor A.B. Chandler for the Democratic nomination for governor. He defeated Chandler in the Democratic primary; however, his running mate, John Breckinridge, was defeated by Harry Lee Waterfield. Breathitt and Waterfield then narrowly defeated the Republican ticket headed by Louie B. Nunn.

As Governor, Breathitt led successful campaigns for economic and industrial development, civil rights legislation, increased support for education, a $176 million bond issue, and expansion and improvement of the state highway and park systems. His most significant defeat was the rejection in 1966 of a new state constitution. During his tenure as governor Breathitt was appointed to the executive committee of the National Governors' Conference and named chairman of its natural resources committee, an area of considerable concern to him. His administration won several national awards, including: a Lincoln Key Award (1966) for leadership in the passage of state civil rights legislation; Society of Industrial Investors' award (1964) for the best industrial development program; the Midwest Travel Writers Association Award (1965) for the best travel promotion program; the U.S. Department of Interior Distinguished Service Award (1967) for contributions in the field of conservation. Breathitt was personally recognized as Conservationist of the Year by *Outdoor Life* magazine in 1967.

Following his term as governor Breathitt briefly returned to law practice in Hopkinsville, serving as special counsel to the Southern Railroad. In 1968 the Ford Foundation named him director of the Institute for Rural America to continue the work he had begun as chairman of President Lyndon Johnson's Commission on Rural Poverty. The institute drafted model legislation to assist states in establishing area development districts, conducted studies on rural problems, and suggested legislative remedies. Breathitt then served as chairman of the Coalition for Rural America, an organization he helped found and which was designed to implement the work of the Institute for Rural America. He also was president of American Child Centers, a company formed to establish and promote private preschool education.

In March, 1972, he was appointed vice president of the Southern Railway System, the position he currently holds. He has remained active in

Democratic party affairs and has served as a member of the Democratic National Committee and the Democratic Finance Council. He is currently a member of the Kentucky Council on Higher Education.

Governor Breathitt is married to the former Frances Holleman, and they are the parents of four children: Mary Fran, Linda, Susan, and Edward III. They reside in Washington, D.C.

INAUGURAL ADDRESS
Frankfort / December 10, 1963

THIS is not a day of exultation. This is not a day of triumph. This is not a day of unseemly rejoicing. This is a day of soul-searching. This is a day of dedication. Such words, coming as they do from the depths of a full heart, would be true under all circumstances. They are even truer as we stand under a flag at half staff, taking to ourselves in gratitude and humility the wounds and scars of a fallen leader who, in the prime of a brave young manhood, laid down his life not merely for his country but for all mankind.

It is written that the blood of martyrs is the seed of the church. It is also true that the blood of martyrs is the seed of liberty, the seed of compassion, the seed of equal opportunity for all of God's children, the seed of government by reason and law—the seed of all those moods and qualities which make for greatness in a people. In a very real sense, our liberty, our opportunity has been bought with the blood of John F. Kennedy.[1]

For us, the truest homage we can pay to his heroic example is to be reborn of his spirit. What is that spirit? It is a spirit of deep concern, compassionate concern, practical concern for the dignity, the selfhood, the personality of individual people. For John F. Kennedy there were no races, no geographical sections, no inferior classes. For him there was no rest of body, mind, or spirit so long as the accidents of color, of geographical isolation, of economic heritage, served to isolate or to alienate individual Americans from the fullness, the richness, the vast opportunities of American life.

It is a spirit of realism and detachment. No matter how deeply he might have been involved in causes or in struggles, John Kennedy never lost his capacity to see the world, the nation, and himself under the eye of eternity, from the vantage point of history. It is a spirit of courage, of willingness to assume the risks of personal and political disaster in order to keep peace in a troubled world and get on with the unfinished business of a great nation.

Let us today, in this historic and splendid Commonwealth, troubled with unhappy divisions, afflicted with grave difficulties, blessed with great resources, and challenged by unimagined opportunities, undergo a humble and hopeful baptism in that spirit of concern, that spirit of detachment, that spirit of courage. Let the pulse of our confidence quicken from the strong, steady, calming leadership which President Lyndon B. Johnson has given to all America in an hour of tragedy and trial. And at this time—grateful for the honor you have done me and for the kindnesses you have bestowed upon me and my family—I ask for your help, your prayers, and your understanding during the four years ahead.

This is not the appropriate occasion to discuss in detail the specific items of Kentucky's unfinished business, or our proposals for dealing with these items. When the General Assembly convenes in January, we shall present such a program—and we shall present it in a spirit of cooperation and nonpartisanship. Meanwhile, we can summarize the objectives of Kentucky's government during the next four years in a single phrase—a better opportunity for every Kentuckian to realize his full potential, whether he lives in the city or on the farm, whether he be white or black, whether he be rich or poor, whether his lot be cast in the north, south, east, or west. As to the means of attaining those goals, we shall, I am sure, have differences of opinion as to methods and measures.

There will be few, however, to deny or minimize the primary importances of education in any major effort to keep Kentucky moving forward. There can be little doubt that educational disadvantage is today the greatest single factor which restricts the opportunities of individual Kentuckians for a fuller and more productive life. Equally, there can be little doubt that the educational advances which Kentucky has made in recent years will, during the future, contribute immeasurably to the attainment of our economic goals. Kentucky cannot afford to halt or to slow down the onward march of educational progress. Even the dramatic breakthroughs of the past few years must be measured against the forward movement which has been taking place in our sister states—so that we must move ahead just to stay where we are.

Already, we are facing the need for critically important decisions in the field of higher education. Increasing numbers of boys and girls are knocking at the doors of these institutions, so that the sheer pressure of numbers alone is almost overwhelming. To this pressure we must add the demand for ever higher quality of instruction in an age of unparalleled advances in scientific and other fields of knowledge.

The crisis in higher education will call for bold and even risky decisions upon the part of Kentucky's leadership, both in education and in government. Let us all cast away the demons of parochialism, the temptations of empire building, the fetters of local and special interest, and arrive at a solution based on the dictates of reason and common sense, recognizing both the needs and the limitations which Kentucky faces in adapting her program of higher education to the requirements of a difficult decade.

Education contributes greatly to the economic advancement of the Commonwealth, and by the same token, only the expansion of Kentucky's economy can make possible the continued improvement of our schools, colleges, and university. Our economy is a seamless web, and no one sector can be separated from the other sectors without ripping the fabric of the whole structure.

Kentucky's economy, during the past decade, has been expanding faster than the economy of the nation as a whole. This means that Kentucky has been moving ahead at a faster pace than most of the other states. This is cause for cheer but not for self-satisfaction. Kentucky still rates below, and well below, the national average in per capita income. Kentucky still rates higher than the national average in total unemployment.[2] These facts are a challenge to the enterprise, the ingenuity, and the capacity of all Kentuckians, in and out of government.

We are committed to use all the tools at our command in stepping up the pace of Kentucky's expanding economy. The goals to which we are pledged, 75,000 new jobs and a billion-dollar annual farm income, are no mere campaign oratory. They are serious objectives—but they are not easy objectives, and we shall take them seriously. We cannot attain these goals by some magic formula, or by simply wishing for their realization. Government alone, and certainly a governor alone, cannot do the job. Every group in our Commonwealth—management, labor, agriculture, and government—must make a total commitment. As for me, I make that commitment to you today, in a spirit of complete dedication.

We must also recognize that Kentucky's economic progress cannot be built upon firm foundations so long as our Appalachian counties are tightly bound by the chains of isolation, poverty, and inaccessibility. Last week, had he lived, John F. Kennedy had planned to visit these areas, bringing to their people a message of hope and help, and I am sure that President Johnson will sometime soon be making the visit which President Kennedy had planned—a visit for which I shall extend him in your name a warm and urgent invitation.

The problems of eastern Kentucky, like so many of Kentucky's other problems, point to the fact that our state's resources, financial and otherwise, are limited resources. During the past four years, increasing revenues from a broad-based tax structure have made possible unusual progress.[3] For the next four years, we must rely for extended progress on that same tax structure—with no new taxes.[4] This makes it an absolute necessity for us to use our financial resources in accordance with priorities which put at the head of the list those things which are truly important—those things which promise the greater dividends in human and economic progress. We must learn in Kentucky's government to make every penny count. Every drone on the payroll is depriving some child of a better education. Every padded expense account is taking a bag of groceries away from some needy old person. Every wasteful expenditure is postponing the blacktopping of a much-needed rural road. I cannot promise you everything you want for the next four years, but this I can promise you—that the taxpayers of

Kentucky will get a dollar's worth of service for every dollar spent out of the public treasury—or heads will roll.

I am confident that, with the help of Almighty God and the cooperation of a free people, we can keep Kentucky moving ahead for the next four years. I cannot promise you that in four short years Kentucky can be first in all things. But at least in one thing Kentuckians can be first in all this land—first in nobility of spirit; first in their determination to cast away hate, bigotry, and prejudice; first in their willingness to forswear the ugly weapons of smear, suspicion, and slander in the discussion of public issues; first in their aspiration for a Commonwealth rooted in brotherhood, free from discrimination based upon any factor except individual character and capacity.

In that determination, and asking for the guidance and the blessing of Him who holds us all in the hollow of His hand, let us set sail together on a voyage of discovery and hope, determined like Ulysses of old, "To strive, to seek, to find/And not to yield."

---

1. John Fitzgerald Kennedy, thirty-fifth president of the United States, was assassinated on November 22, 1963 in Dallas, Texas. He was succeeded by Lyndon Baines Johnson. Governor Breathitt's tribute to the slain president was typical of remarks of public officials in the weeks following the assassination. President Kennedy telephoned Governor Breathitt shortly after the general election in Kentucky, extended his congratulations to the governor, and indicated that after a political fence-mending trip to Texas he would call again to discuss the Appalachia program. Interview with Governor Edward T. Breathitt, Washington, D.C., June 10, 1980. Hereafter cited as Breathitt interview.

2. The national average income in 1963 was $5,174 and the unemployment rate was 5.7 percent. The Commonwealth's per capita income was $1,792 compared to $2,449 for the nation. U.S. Bureau of the Census, *Statistical Abstract of the United States: 1965* (Washington, D.C., 1965) p. 334. Accurate data on unemployment in Kentucky in 1963 [are] unavailable; however, it is clear that the rate exceeded the national average. See Don M. Soule, "Economic Changes in Kentucky in Recent Years," typescript in the Papers of Governor Edward T. Breathitt, Pogue Special Collections Library, Murray State University, Murray, Kentucky, pp. 1-5. Hereafter cited as Breathitt papers.

3. General state revenue increased from $357 million in 1959 to $543 million in 1963. U.S. Bureau of the Census, *Statistical Abstract of the United States: 1961* (Washington, D.C., 1961), p. 426 and Ibid, *1964,* pp. 428-29.

4. During the primary and general election campaigns Governor Breathitt consistently made a commitment that his administration would levy no additional taxes.

LEGISLATIVE MESSAGES & STATEMENTS

STATE OF THE COMMONWEALTH MESSAGE
Frankfort / January 7, 1964

I AM pleased to be with you here today as you open the 1964 regular session of the General Assembly—a session that will have great bearing on the future course of our Commonwealth. First of all, it is gratifying to me that we function under a system of government that, although it separates the executive and legislative branches, provides opportunity for the chief executive to report to the legislature and to lay before both its houses his recommendations on needed law.

This system—which provides separation, but allows and promotes cooperation—is the best ever devised, and I intend to respect and advance it. I will not appear before you often, and there will be a minimum number of bills carrying the administration label. But I will not hesitate to follow custom and my constitutional privilege in presenting and helping guide those measures which I think are important to the people of Kentucky.

This opportunity to be with you today is also pleasing to me for a personal reason. It was here in this chamber twelve years ago this week that I first entered state government. I took my oath of office as a freshman member of the House of Representatives on a day such as this. I will always remember that day and will cherish those years I spent in that great deliberative body.

It is saddening to note today that a great legislative leader of that time and a great friend to me has recently passed from the scene. I refer, of course, to Dick Moloney.[1] It is with equal sadness that I pay my respects to the memory of a distinguished senator, Broadus Hickerson.[2] I pay tribute to both of these Kentuckians. We shall miss them greatly.

My legislative experience will, I believe, as no other experience could, help me understand your problems, your actions, and the job we have to do together in the days ahead. I am also glad to be with you today to make this report on the state of the Commonwealth because there are many good things to report.

Kentucky has advanced in the last four years as in no similar period of our recent history. For this I pay tribute to former Governor Bert Combs, to those of you who served in the legislature during that period, and to many, many other imaginative, skilled, and dedicated public servants who have helped bring about this better day.[3] During this period gains have been made in education, highways, jobs, parks, and vacation facilities, farm income, health facilities, and welfare programs. Our children are being taught by better qualified teachers than ever before and in better physical surroundings. Teachers are better paid than they have ever been.[4] More students are enrolling in and being graduated from our university and state colleges than ever before in history. More and better jobs are available for them and for other qualified persons. New highways stretch into all corners of the Commonwealth, and Kentucky, long called a detour state, is being honored not only for these new miles of road, but for its imaginative approach toward obtaining a highway system that is truly systematized and total in its coverage.

New parks and construction at existing facilities have given Kentucky the finest state parks system in the nation—a source of recreation for our citizens and a lure for the vacation money of out-of-staters. Industrial jobs are on the increase, and new industry that utilizes the products of our farms is making a new contribution in our rural areas. Per capita income in Kentucky is rising faster than in the nation as a whole. Services relating to the health of Kentuckians are more adequate than in previous years, and those persons dependent on welfare programs are being better taken care of.

We are cheered by and thankful for progress that has come to our Commonwealth, but it is one of the ironies of the modern, dynamic age in which we live that the state of progress we reached yesterday is not adequate to the needs of today—that once we pause in satisfaction or complacency the world moves on beyond us. And so, while we count the milestones we have passed, we must look ahead to those yet to come, to new horizons in service to Kentucky. You and I must set new goals for ourselves and for those we represent.

The people of Kentucky did not choose me as their governor to preside over a caretaker administration, a standstill government. If those in positions of leadership are content simply to tidy up the dust in state government, and trim the rough edges of existing programs, then we shall fail, and fail miserably, to meet our responsibilities. There are no rest stops on the road to progress. In recent years, the people of Kentucky have learned that stagnation and inaction are not the necessary or predestined lot of Kentucky and Kentuckians. The people of our state have discovered that Kentucky and Kentuckians can, if they will, move ahead not as stragglers but as leaders in the attainment of a better life for our people.

Let there be no misunderstanding of my position, my policies, my hopes and intentions for the next four years. In education, in highways, in the development of our natural and human resources, in building a virile, dynamic economy, both industrial and agricultural, in ending the isolation and poverty to which thousands of our fellow Kentuckians have been condemned, in recognizing the basic dignity and human personality of all Kentuckians, in whatever color, whatever class, whatever religious persuasion—in moving toward all these objectives I do not intend that Kentucky shall slow down her rate of advancement, but that we move ahead at an ever quickening pace.

As I survey Kentucky's needs and Kentucky's goals for the next two years, and indeed for the next four years and the next generation, I see six great challenges to which we must respond if Kentucky is to answer her call to greatness:

1. Education is the passkey to a better life and a better living for Kentuckians, both now and in the future. In an age which has brought to perfection the marvels of mechanization—in warfare, in industry, in agriculture, and in all aspects of our life, the human brain reigns more supreme than ever. Only men and women with basic skills and basic learning will be able to find employment or enjoyment in an age which has developed machines and problems, a way of life and a challenge to life, more complicated than human beings have ever known before.

Kentucky is committed to continued, rapid educational progress. We shall continue to build new classrooms, to buy better buses, to provide more laboratories, better physical facilities for our schools. But the teacher is and will remain the heart of the educational system—and quality instruction will come first in our program of progress. To retain our qualified teachers, and to attract more and better teachers for our children, we have pledged a $500 annual increase in the average teacher's salary under the foundation program, to be attained in two successive annual steps over the coming biennium. My budget message will provide for these increases, as well as for other needed improvement in the educational system.

We shall be facing a crisis in higher education during the coming biennium. Applicants for admission to our institutions of higher learning are increasing in number each semester, and we must face boldly the need for progress in higher education equivalent to that which Kentucky achieved in primary and secondary education with the enactment and improvement of the foundation program in 1954, 1956, and 1960.[5] If we are to make a commitment of this character and magnitude, then we must make certain that our system of higher education is organized along proper lines, to assure the wisest possible investment of the funds required and the greatest possible return in the form of top quality education at the college and graduate level. Higher education is recognized in legislation I am recommending to you today by a bill to formalize financial aid being given to the University of Louisville.[6]

The requirements of industry in an age of automation have raised our system of vocational education to a position of highest importance. Old-fashioned methods and old-fashioned skills have become outdated and outmoded. Fortunately, Kentucky has, in its system of area vocational schools, pioneered in the field of progressive vocational education. We must complete our plans for the construction and expansion of area vocational schools. Generous assistance from government will make it possible to retrain many of our unemployed and displaced workers for new job opportunities. Unfortunately, there are many of our unemployed who do not possess the basic literacy to enable them to take advantage of these opportunities. We must, therefore, launch a long-range attack on adult illiteracy, through a comprehensive program of adult education over a period of years. Moving ahead in all these sectors of educational effort, Kentuckians can look forward to the day when all our people, children and adults, will be equipped with the best that quality education can offer in preparing them to make a good living and live a good life.

2. Human rights. Democracy and the democratic philosophy are based upon two propositions which may seem contradictory but which are in fact complementary: all men are equal and all men are different. Men are not inherently equal in talent, in tastes, in opinions, in mental capacity, or in many other attributes. It is these differences which make for the richness, the variety, and the unpredictable possibilities of life. Underlying, and indeed making possible all these differences, is a common humanity which belongs to man not because of government, or law, but because, as we believe, he is created in the image of God. Whatever denies the fundamental dignity which belongs to that common humanity affronts the Creator and denies the basic brotherhood which we have affirmed down the centuries in the Declaration of Independence and the Constitution of the United States.

All social and economic institutions, including that of private property, operate as a part of the total community and depend for their continuing vitality upon their service and benefit to the community, a community of human beings. The rights of property are essential to provide a safeguard for the integrity and independence of the individual in a world where ungoverned government is a threat to the liberty of the citizen. Yet we must face the fact that in a complex and highly mobile society, property carries with it power to influence and sometimes to govern the lives and liberties of others.

It is for this reason that, throughout our history, but especially during the last century, property rights have been subject to reasonable regulation by the people's representatives in the interest of the public welfare. Health and safety codes, zoning ordinances, minimum wages, and many similar regulatory measures have restricted the rights of property whenever property has been used to injure or to degrade human beings.

Discrimination against individual citizens, or their exclusion from places of public accommodation, is a denial of basic human dignity. If a respectable, orderly, law-abiding citizen and his family are refused ordinary service in a restaurant, hotel, or motel, then property becomes supreme over people—and that is not consistent with either the fundamental assumptions of a democratic society or the fundamental principles of the Hebrew-Christian ethic. The Constitution of the United States provides that all persons born or naturalized in the United States shall be citizens, and we cannot set apart, upon grounds of race or color, a single class of citizens and permit them to be excluded from the simplest and most basic part of our common life.

The difficulty comes when society and government seek to secure observance of basic human rights in the most practical way, without undue turmoil and friction. Since 1960, our Human Rights Commission has operated in Kentucky on a voluntary basis—with much success, with great benefit, and without appreciable hardship to the proprietors of places of public accommodation.[7] Despite the success of these efforts, Kentuckians are still in many communities denied service in places of public accommodation, solely for reasons of race or color. This presents a challenge, and a serious challenge, to the conscience of Kentucky. I know not what course others may take, but as for me, I intend to meet that challenge.

The right of all citizens to equal treatment in places of public accommodation, regardless of race or color, is one which must find vindication through legislative action. The Congress of the United States, which has broad authority in this field, is now considering legislation in this area.[8] You will, I am sure, want to know, if possible, what federal legislation is likely to be enacted in the field of public accommodations before acting yourselves. Certainly I should like to know what federal legislation is likely to be enacted before recommending legislation to you on the state level. This does not mean that Kentucky is shirking her responsibility, that you will be shirking your responsibility, or that I shall be shirking my responsibility. Let me make it clear that, if the federal Congress has not enacted civil rights legislation before the last fifteen days of your session, I shall at that time recommend legislation to you for the protection of basic human rights in the field of public accommodations, and you will have ample time to act upon my recommendations.[9]

3. After the longest era of uninterrupted economic expansion in this nation's history, after a twenty-five year boom, one-fifth of a nation is still ill-nourished, ill-clad, ill-housed, ill-educated, ill-cared for. This is not the occasion for a detailed discussion of the problem of poverty in all its complicated aspects. Nevertheless, it is a fact that geographical isolation is one of the potent causes of persistent poverty, and that the Appalachian region in particular is one of the tragic centers of unyielding poverty in the United States. Many of Kentucky's eastern counties lie in this region.[10]

In these counties, thousands of families are cold, hungry, jobless, seemingly condemned to a dreary life in an economic and social backwash. Hope itself seems shredded and frayed to these people, and their children are growing up—many of them—as a generation who have known only the bread of welfare, for whom the handout is a way of life. For these Kentuckians, who are the equal of us all in true potential, poverty is worse than poverty—it is an aching, life-destroying emptiness which kills the soul. I wish that I could tell you that the problems of our Appalachian counties could be solved by Kentucky's own actions and policies. But Appalachia covers portions of ten states, and its problems require regional solutions and resources beyond the command of a single state.

Our late and beloved President Kennedy was deeply concerned with the problems and the opportunities of the people of the Appalachian region. The area redevelopment program, the accelerated public works program, the food stamp plan, and above all the long-range plans of the Roosevelt commission owe their inspiration to this leadership.[11]

Thankfully, I can report to you from personal conversations that President Lyndon B. Johnson is dedicated to completing the work and carrying forward the plans of President Kennedy in this area. Already, we have instituted a massive retraining program for the unemployed in the Appalachian counties, and we are confident that other federal programs, some of them on a pilot level and some on a large scale, will be announced in future weeks.

Long ago, however, I concluded that it is not enough for Kentucky to stand, hat in hand, waiting for federal initiative. In the first place, most federal programs require state participation both financially and administratively. Secondly, federal programs are responsive to initiative and leadership from the state level. It was Kentucky's foresight which made it possible to obtain, for the first time, Area Redevelopment Administration money for highway construction. It was Kentucky's progressive system of vocational education which made it possible for us to obtain a $9 million allocation for retraining unemployed Kentuckians. It was Kentucky's influence and prodding which paved the way for the creation of the Roosevelt commission. In my budget message, and in other messages, I shall recommend to you plans and measures to provide help, jobs, and economic stimulation for the Appalachian counties of eastern Kentucky.

4. I cannot give up the conviction that Kentucky's constitution needs revision. This charter has been in effect longer than any of the four constitutions under which our state government has operated. Our 1891 constitution contains a multitude of detailed restrictions and prescriptions which are more legislative than constitutional in nature, and which make it difficult to operate our government in an age of space. Indeed, some of our older constitutions, and especially the 1799 charter, seem better fitted to the needs of today than does our present fundamental law.

In the past, Kentuckians have been reluctant to authorize the calling of a constitutional convention—largely, I think because of uncertainty as to the changes which might be made. Section 4 of the present constitution preserves the basic right of the people to alter their fundamental law in any way which they see fit, and the Court of Appeals has upheld the right of two successive sessions of the legislature to call a limited convention. In 1962, the General Assembly created a Constitutional Revision Commission, with delegates selected from each senatorial district.[12]

I propose to activate this commission immediately for the purpose of drafting a model constitution which you could consider submitting to the people of Kentucky by vote of two successive sessions of the General Assembly or for the consideration of a future voted constitutional convention. I suggest to you that the statute be amended to make all living elected governors members at large of the commission. By this means we can, in the full glare of publicity, discuss the problems of constitutional revision and hammer out solutions which are acceptable to the people. The final document can be debated and discussed fully and freely, then submitted to the people, who will retain the supreme power to accept or reject it.

5. Highways are the arteries which carry the bloodstream of Kentucky's economy. During the past few years, Kentucky has ranked among the nation's leaders in highway construction. Not only must we complete the planned network of high-speed roads ribboning from one end of the state to the other, but we must emphasize to an ever greater extent the rural and secondary roads which pierce the barriers of isolation which hem in so many of Kentucky's communities and families.

Increasing revenues from tourists and other traffic on our main highways make additional funds available for maintenance, and for improvement of secondary roads. We are pledged to and we shall double the rural highway fund this biennium. We are pledged to and we shall make every road fund dollar do double duty in the service of the people rather than politics. We are pledged to and we shall push completion of our parkway system with all planned extensions.

In the budget message I shall discuss in greater detail the financial requirements of our highway program. At this time, I recommend that you submit to the people another bond issue to make it possible to thrust forward with our highway program without increasing road fund taxes or license fees this biennium. It may be possible to save substantial outlays of interest and amortization on our turnpike bonds by refinancing them on better and more favorable terms. Legislation permitting such refinancing will be presented to you today.[13] Also to be presented to you today is a measure to change the distribution of rural highway funds to conform to the distribution of rural secondary funds.[14] I ask your help on both of these bills.

6. Economy. We have set as our goals for an expanding economy 75,000 new jobs and a billion-dollar annual farm income. Attainment of these goals will require a monumental effort, will require the selfless and far-sighted cooperation of Kentuckians in all walks of life, but I am convinced that we can do the job. Already we are surveying the organization and operation of our economic development program to make it more flexible and even better fitted for the need of the coming years.

Today I shall submit for your consideration a proposed change in our state income tax law to permit accelerated depreciation for new capital investment.[15] We are considering the more effective mobilization of our research institutions, including Spindletop and the University of Kentucky, for such programs as the establishment of better facilities in the field of water research and the more effective utilization of our trained technical and scientific personnel.[16]

Soon I shall appoint the Agricultural Development Commission which will establish goals and recommend means of meeting those goals on a local, voluntary basis in the farm economy. There is no question but that, with proper organization and the cooperation of those who realize the basic importance of an expanding agriculture, we can make Kentucky's grasslands the source of increased production and increased income for our farmers and farm communities.

These six challenges will occupy your time and energies and mine, but there will be other items of importance to face you this session. One of the most important will be the passage of a budget adequate to meet the needs of our government for the next biennium. I will come to you later with a suggested budget. It will represent the best thinking of the executive branch of government, having been tightened and trimmed to give the people the very best services possible for the least amount of money. It will not exceed the revenue anticipated for the period under the present tax structure and present tax rates.

An urgent need of the Commonwealth is a better system of corrections. This will require more money and additional personnel as well as possible new methods of operation. I shall have recommendations on this subject for you later on.

For the last ten years Kentucky has sought to control and regulate the extraction of minerals by stripping and augering operations so as to reclaim the land that is mined and protect surrounding land and streams. This regulation has not been as successful as was hoped when the first strip-mining law went on the books, and today vast areas of our state are scarred and rendered desolate and many of our finest streams are polluted because of poorly controlled mining operations. I shall recommend new legislation on this vital matter later in this session.

I have previously cited several bills on which I will ask early action—bills that will be introduced today. In addition I am asking immediate passage of four other measures. They are for the most part legislation that will increase the efficiency of state government and enable us to get the greatest service for the money we spend. I call for:

1. A model purchasing law. Under this bill present statutes relating to purchasing would be revised so as to improve product specifications, enlarge the number of bidders, and schedule purchasing so as to get more favorable prices. Such a law is basic to the determination of this administration that the people of Kentucky will get the most for their money when state purchases are made. But even the best of laws must be administered properly if they are to have their best results. I pledge to you that this law will be used wisely and effectively by those in charge of the state's buying.[17]

2. A resolution establishing a commission on economy and efficiency in government. I pledged such a commission during my campaign for governor because I thought it would make the conduct of government more responsive to the needs of Kentucky and put it under closer control of its citizens.[18] Since I became governor I have come to believe more and more in the desirability of such a commission. In those few days, we have taken measures to improve the economy and efficiency of your government, and it is our plan to take more such measures. Each department head has been asked to study all personnel positions in his agency to see what positions might be abolished without hampering his operation. At this time they have taken action on personnel reductions that will result in annual savings of some $700,000, and not all departments have acted yet. Personnel is only only one place in which I feel savings can be made, and it will greatly help me and other officials of my administration if you will establish this commission. If you act on this request favorably, I will ask one of Kentucky's most distinguished public servants to be commission chairman. He is Dr. James Martin, who has served Kentucky as commissioner of finance, revenue, and highways and who for many years was a professor of public finance at the University of Kentucky.[19]

3. A debt consolidation law. This would restrict the ability to issue revenue bonds for capital construction and centralize their issuance in the State Building Commission.[20] Such a law would enable the Commonwealth to keep a closer tab on its obligations and take a more immediate look at the amount of its bonded indebtedness, its ability to refund and refinance, and its ability to borrow.

4. A law making the Kentucky Tax Commission an independent agency. This measure would take the commission out of the Department of Revenue and remove the commissioner of revenue as a member.[21] Its purpose is to make it easier for taxpayers to appeal what they consider unfair assessments and to assure them a fair hearing.

I submit these measures to you with the belief that endorsement of them will presage a constructive and profitable legislative session. I submit them to you with all the respect I feel for your position as legislators and for this great body to which I once had the honor of belonging. I submit these recommendations and I will submit further recommendations with the conviction that the legislative and executive branches of Kentucky's government have a solemn obligation to the people of Kentucky to work together to make that government the best possible and to provide the best possible life for each of our citizens. To these ends I pledge my cooperation and I solicit yours.

---

1. Richard Patrick Moloney, Sr. (1902-1963), Lexington attorney; member of the state Senate (1944-1956); eight years as Democratic floor leader. From 1960 until his death he served as a member of the House of Representatives. As majority floor leader in 1962 Moloney was instrumental in guiding Governor Bert Combs's legislative program through the House. Governor Breathitt expected Moloney to serve as an administration leader in the 1964 session; his death, coupled with slender administration majorities in the legislature, was a severe blow. *Louisville Courier-Journal,* December 24, 1963.

2. Broadus E. Hickerson (1896-1964), of Lebanon in Marion County, was killed in an automobile accident January 6, 1964 enroute to Frankfort. He had served in the state Senate since 1958. *Louisville Courier-Journal,* January 7, 1964.

3. Bert Thomas Combs (1911-), Louisville attorney; city attorney, Prestonsburg (1950); judge, Kentucky Court of Appeals (1951-1955); governor of Kentucky (1959-1963); judge, United States Court of Appeals, 6th Circuit (1967-1970); practicing attorney, Louisville (1970-). *Who's Who in America 1976-1977,* 39th ed. (Chicago, 1976). Governor Breathitt, a close political associate of Governor Combs, continued most of the programs initiated by Combs. In Breathitt's campaigns against A.B. Chandler in the Democratic primary and Louie B. Nunn in the general election, Combs actively supported Breathitt. Governor Breathitt considered the continuation of the Combs programs, providing eight years of continuity in civil rights, transportation, parks, economic development, and education, among the more important contributions of his administration. Breathitt

interview, June 10, 1980. For further information on the Combs-Breathitt political relationship, see Malcolm E. Jewell and Everett W. Cunningham, *Kentucky Politics* (Lexington, Ky., 1968), pp. 137-38, 157-78, 231-32, 237-44.

4. In 1963 Kentucky employed 26,678 instructional staff in the public elementary and secondary schools at an average annual salary of $4,531. The average annual salary for 24,333 classroom teachers was $4,347. U.S. Bureau of the Census, *Statistical Abstract of the U.S., 1964* (Washington, D.C., 1964), p. 126. In a series of actions between 1954 and 1960 the General Assembly enacted legislation implementing and funding a 1953 amendment to the constitution permitting "distribution of the public school fund on a basis other than per capita." Under the new legislation the distribution of state funds to schools was based upon school enrollment and average daily attendance. Full financing of the Minimum Foundation Program in 1956 resulted in improved teachers salaries, a decrease in one-room schools, a minimum nine-month school term for all students, more classrooms, and an expanded curriculum. State Department of Education, *History of Education in Kentucky 1939-1964* (Frankfort, Ky. 1963), pp. 118, 124, 172.

5. In the early 1960s Kentucky, like most other states, experienced an explosion in public college and university enrollment. Enrollment increases arose largely from the World War II and postwar "baby boom," although general prosperity, a growing public appreciation for the value of higher education, and job opportunities for college graduates were important contributing factors. Colleges and universities were unprepared for the onslaught. Shortages of dormitories, classroom and library facilities, and instruction staff were everywhere apparent. Nationwide, enrollment at public institutions of higher education increased 22.2 percent between 1961 and 1963. During the same period in Kentucky total enrollment increased 10.3 percent. U.S. Department of Health, Education and Welfare, *Opening Enrollment in Higher Education, 1961* (Washington, 1961), p. 45 and Ibid., *1963,* pp. 3, 20. Governor Bert Combs responded by increased appropriations for higher education; however, the largest growth in enrollment occurred during the administration of Governor Breathitt. Between 1963 and 1967 enrollment in Kentucky's public institutions increased from 57,391 to 90,211 students. Meeting the constant demand for more state resources for higher education was a continuing challenge for the Breathitt administration, especially in view of his commitment not to increase taxes.

6. Legislation supported by Cooper Gardner, Democrat for Owensboro, enabled the state to provide financial aid to the private medical and dental schools at the University of Louisville. *Acts of the General Assembly of the Commonwealth of Kentucky, 1964,* Chapter 8 (S.B. 4), pp. 13-14. Hereafter referred to as *Acts.*

7. The Kentucky Commission on Human Rights was established by House Bill 163 in 1960 in an effort to "discourage discrimination" and improve race relations. The commission's powers were limited, however. It was authorized to conduct studies; receive, investigate, and report on complaints; hold public hearings (without the authority to compel testimony). However, the commission was specifically denied the authority to take action to force the integration of private businesses, facilities, or organizations. *Acts, 1960,* Chapter 76 (H.B. 163), pp. 332-34. In 1962 the General Assembly authorized all cities in the Commonwealth to create city commissions on human rights and affirmed their legal authority to forbid discrimi-

nation in places of public accommodation. *Acts, 1962,* Chapter 171 (H.B. 193), pp. 608-09.

8. Governor Breathitt referred to civil rights legislation introduced in Congress during the summer of 1963. At the time of the State of the Commonwealth address the future of the bill was uncertain. *Louisville Courier-Journal,* December 20, 1963. For additional information see the section of these papers entitled "Civil Rights."

9. The public accommodations legislation to which Governor Breathitt referred was introduced in the senate by Shelby C. Kinkead, a Democrat from Lexington.

10. The Appalachian region, which included forty-four eastern Kentucky counties, comprised an area the size of the state of California containing 357 counties in ten states, from Pennsylvania and Ohio in the North to Alabama and Georgia in the South. In 1963 the population of the region was 15,500,000. During the same year the region's income was 30 percent below the national average, its welfare rolls were 50 percent higher than the national average, and illiteracy was 45 percent above the national average. *Louisville Courier-Journal,* February 9, 1964. For additional information on the Appalachian region see the section of these papers entitled "Appalachia."

11. The Area Redevelopment Act (ARA) of May 1, 1961, was a product of President Kennedy's commitment to West Virginia in the election of 1960 and a series of factors at work on the national level since the mid-1950s. The law allows considerable discretion in choosing redevelopment areas and provided $394 million over a four-year period for loans and grants to depressed areas. In order to qualify for assistance an area was required to develop an overall economic development program. Appalachia received approximately 30 percent of Area Redevelopment Act funds. The Accelerated Public Works Act (APW) of 1962 authorized grants up to 75 percent for local public works projects. Placed under ARA jurisdiction, the more flexible APW program spent approximately 23 percent of its funds in Appalachia. The Accelerated Public Works Act expired on June 30, 1964, and the Area Redevelopment Act ceased to function on September 1, 1965. Many of its functions, however, were absorbed by the Public Works and Economic Development Act of 1965. Donald N. Rothblatt, *Regional Planning: The Appalachian Experience* (Lexington, Mass., 1971), pp. 39-42, and Rupert P. Vance, "The Region's Future, A National Challenge," in Thomas R. Ford, ed., *The Southern Appalachian Region* (Lexington, Ky., 1962), p. 291. The Roosevelt Commission established April 9, 1963, was the President's Appalachian Regional Council (PARC), a joint federal-state commission championed by the Conference of Appalachian Governors. Chaired by Under Secretary of Commerce Franklin Delano Roosevelt, Jr., it represented an effort to develop a comprehensive development program for Appalachia. Rothblatt, *Regional Planning,* pp. 51-52. The food stamp program began as a small pilot project established by executive order in 1961. In 1964 the Johnson administration received congressional approval for a bill authorizing $375 million over a two-year period to expand the pilot project into a nationwide program. Under the terms of the act, low-income families were allowed to purchase at a discount food stamps of sufficient value to obtain a nutritionally adequate diet. The discount rate was determined by a formula based on the amount a person at the individual's income level normally spent on food. *Congressional Quarterly Almanac,* vol. 20 (1964), pp. 110-15.

12. Senate Bill 232 reconstituted the Constitution Revision Committee into a thirty-eight member body appointed jointly by the governor, lieutenant governor, speaker of the house of representatives, and chief justice of the Court of Appeals. The Legislative Research Commission was directed to conduct research for the committee, and the committee was required to report to the governor and General Assembly biennially. *Acts, 1962,* Chapter 110 (S.B. 232), pp. 452-55.

13. Senate Bill 5 empowered the Kentucky Turnpike Authority to refund revenue bonds in advance of maturity. The ultimate aim of the bill was to secure lower interest rates on bonds that financed the Kentucky turnpikes. *Louisville Courier-Journal,* January 23, 1964, and *Acts, 1964,* Chapter 9 (J.R. 5), pp. 14-16.

14. *Acts, 1964,* Chapter 10 (S.B. 6), pp. 16-17.

15. *Acts, 1964,* Chapter 140 (H.B. 2), p. 502.

16. Spindletop, a private research firm modeled on the concept of the North Carolina Research Triangle, was established in Lexington in 1961. It served as an independent research organization and provided professional, scientific, and management services to clients on a contractual basis.

17. The purpose of the model purchasing bill was to create a division of purchases, give the purchasing director more control over state buying, gain more favorable prices through better scheduling, require all departments and agencies to submit budgets, permit the director to write standards and specifications for buying, induce competitive bidding, and place a twenty-dollar maximum on items bought without bidding. The effect of the legislation was to centralize purchasing activity in the Department of Finance. Both houses of the legislature approved the bill unanimously. *Acts, 1964,* Chapter 16 (H.B. 1), pp. 40-47. In 1967 Breathitt reported that improved purchasing procedures had saved the Commonwealth $1,259,088 since 1964 on eight commonly purchased items. Press release, July 1, 1967, Breathitt papers.

18. The Commission on Economy and Efficiency in Government was created by a joint resolution of the legislature. The purpose of the commission was to advise the General Assembly and governor on means to increase efficiency and decrease governmental expenditures. Fifteen members appointed by the governor for a two-year term were to review the total governmental system and recommend to him methods to eliminate waste. It passed both houses by substantial majorities. *Acts, 1964,* Chapter 3 (H.J.R. 7), pp. 2-3.

19. James W. Martin (1893-   ), Lexington economist; professor of economics, University of Kentucky (1928-1948); distinguished professor (1948-1964); commissioner of revenue, Kentucky (1936-1939); commissioner of finance (1955-1957); commissioner of highways (1957-1958). *American Men of Science: The Social and Behavioral Sciences,* 11th ed. (New York, 1968), p. 1056.

20. The debt consolidation law broadened the power of the state Property and Building Commission to issue bonds, required commission approval preliminary to universities or colleges making financial commitments, and amended several state laws relating to expenditures. *Acts, 1964,* Chapter 7 (S.B. 3), pp. 7-13.

21. *Acts, 1964,* Chapter 141 (H.B. 3), pp. 502-33.

EXECUTIVE BUDGET MESSAGE TO THE GENERAL ASSEMBLY
Frankfort / February 10, 1964

NOTHING indicates more clearly the nature of an administration, the goals toward which it strives, or the course it intends to follow than its budget, and I hope I may be excused a measure of gratification and even of pride in the budget which I present to you today.

I realize that the timing of this budget message represents a break with recent tradition, but I chose to devote extraordinary time and effort to this budget because I feel that no session of the General Assembly has ever been asked to consider a fiscal document of more critical importance to Kentucky and the shape of her future, or one that required a more delicate balancing of limited resources and pressing human needs.

This budget reflects a businesslike approach to the operation of government, with economy foremost in its framing. It is a budget geared to speeding up the rate of Kentucky progress, a budget that keeps faith with the future without neglecting the demands of today. It is a balanced budget, and it is balanced without higher taxes, without new taxes, without hidden taxes, without tricks or gimmicks. It reflects the expansive, progressive mood of our state. It is an optimistic budget based on optimistic economic forecasts, a federal tax cut, a growing state economy and the most diligent economy in the management of your state's government.

I am confident that the optimism reflected in this budget is justified. For we have broken with the old, tired, unsure ways of the past. Ours is a mood of growth and vigor and confidence, and the mood is being felt throughout the state in every aspect of our society and economy. With the adoption of this budget, which represents the soundest thinking of our state's most expert public servants, we will not only keep Kentucky marching forward, but we will quicken the pace of that march.

At the same time I must advise you that this is a most precisely balanced document, and I can carry out my pledge to finance it without new or higher taxes only if the Assembly resists the temptation to indulge in costly measures not contained in this budget, or to expand programs contained herein beyond their proposed boundaries.

The commissioner of revenue has estimated that our General Fund income should total approximately $274 million in the coming fiscal year and $292 million in the following year. The General Fund income, Road Fund receipts, departmental fees, and federal grants—supplemented by surpluses and savings made possible by a continuing economy program—

should enable us to finance our total budget of $695,700,000 in the coming fiscal year and $725,500,000 in 1965-66.

During the election campaign I promised the people of Kentucky that I would step up the rate of our educational progress by increasing teacher salaries by $500 a year, that I would increase funds to our university and colleges, continue development of our community colleges and expand our regional libraries, accelerate Kentucky's major highway program, expand the rural road program by doubling the state's annual appropriation, increase funds and services to our depressed counties, modernize our correctional system, and improve programs for the mentally ill and retarded. I also pledged a campaign to strengthen Kentucky's farm economy, to broaden our tourist industry, and to provide 75,000 new jobs in the next four years.

Each and every one of these pledges is recognized by this budget. And let me repeat that this is achieved without new taxes, without higher taxes, and without hidden taxes. I am determined that Kentuckians shall not pay one cent more than is absolutely and inescapably necessary to keep the state on the high road of progress and to bring them and their children the kind of state, the type of tomorrow, that is their rightful heritage.

The budget I am presenting for your consideration today gives first priority to the education of our children. Good teachers are the backbone of any school system, and this budget will help us to get good teachers and to keep the good ones we have. Salaries of qualified teachers will be raised $300 the first year and $200 the second year in accordance with the Kentucky Education Association program. The teachers' retirement system is strengthened.

This budget also puts new muscle into vocational education. One million dollars is provided during the next two years to match the new funds available under recent federal legislation. This budget expands the program for adult education and places particular emphasis on the problems of the functionally illiterate. Funds for these classes are included in the grants to local school districts.

The foundation program is fully financed, and funds are included in the foundation program to provide 100 new classroom units for exceptional children.

This year we are spending slightly more than $11 million at our five state colleges, which have an enrollment of about 17,000 students. This budget will enable the colleges to admit an additional 4,000 students during the next biennium, and to improve the quality of education available to these larger student bodies by providing $32,800,000 for the next two years. It allows each college to employ more professors and associate professors and to pay all professors better.

At the University of Kentucky we must anticipate more than a 30 percent increase in the number of students during the next two years, both at Lexington and at our community colleges. The budget gives the university $39 million this biennium. I propose today to give the university $57,200,000 over the next two years. This includes funds for operation of the Elizabethtown and Prestonsburg community colleges beginning in 1964 and the community colleges at Somerset and Hopkinsville in 1965.

This will enable the university to grow in quality as well as quantity. Provision for higher salaries will enable the university to recruit and keep the best possible faculty. Major departments of the university can be placed on an academic year basis. A badly needed retirement system for faculty members is established and fully funded. The budget will permit the university to step up its agricultural research and service functions. It will permit the colleges of medicine, dentistry, and nursing to reach maximum planned size by the end of this biennium.

The budget also increases the state grant to the University of Louisville medical and dental schools by $200,000 each year of the biennium, increasing state support from $500,000 a year now to $900,000 in 1965.

The budget provides funds for continued planning for a statewide educational television network, looking toward 1966 for activation of the system. Finally, in the field of education, this budget provides for expansion of the library extension program throughout the state.

In recent years Kentucky's gigantic highway program has pushed roads into all parts of the Commonwealth. Our splendid roads have attracted nationwide attention, aided our tourist industry and other commercial and industrial activities, and made travel safer and more convenient for our citizens. Today's budget makes it certain that this construction will continue and at a faster rate in all its phases—interstate, primary, secondary, and rural highways. The rural road appropriation is doubled for each of the years of the biennium, bringing the total to $10 million each year.

I believe that no section of the budget is more significant than the appropriation of $113 million for the health and welfare needs of Kentuckians during the coming biennium. This represents an increase of $14 million available for the benefit of those whose future welfare depends so directly on the increasing excellence of our welfare programs.

A major area of unmet need concerns the welfare of the many children in our state who are deprived due to the inability of their fathers to find employment. Our public assistance program presently provides help to children when there is no longer a father or a wage earner in the home. But we are not helping the hungry children whose father cannot support his family because he can find no job. These children need food, clothing, shelter, medical attention—the opportunity to attend school to make them productive citizens. The fathers need a chance for a job or training.

The federal government last month allocated a million dollars for a pilot program to put parents of dependent children to work in seven of our chronically depressed eastern Kentucky counties. Beginning July 1, 1964, this program will be extended to more of the Appalachian area, and on July 1, 1965, the program will be implemented on a statewide basis. The budget includes $1,100,000 for the first year of the biennium to match 3,340,000 federal dollars. The statewide program for the second year will be financed by 1,460,000 state dollars and 4,690,000 federal dollars.

Almost every dollar requested by the Department of Corrections to assure a first-class probation and parole system is provided in this budget. These funds will make it possible to employ additional probation and parole workers, improve existing salaries, and finance a modern in-service training program. The budget also provides for a limited number of professional personnel who will develop rehabilitation and treatment programs in our institutions during the next two years.

I also ask you to appropriate $120,000 to finance immediate reforms in Kentucky's penal system. This sum will make possible the employment of a medical director and a director of training for the Corrections Department, a psychologist at Eddyville, twenty-eight new guards at LaGrange and an associate warden for treatment programs, a training officer, a physician, and a supervisor at each institution. Failure to vote these funds will mean a delay of six months or more for the start of the vital reform program promised for both LaGrange and Eddyville.

The budget also includes funds for the operation of three new camps for delinquent boys. Each camp will accommodate forty boys and will relieve overcrowding in Kentucky Village. Funds are also included in this budget for the care of 100 additional children in foster homes in each year of this biennium.

The budget makes possible the improvement and expansion of the programs for the mentally ill and the mentally retarded that have brought Kentucky national recognition during the past six years. It includes additional funds which will permit Outwood State Hospital to increase its patient load from 100 to 500, making possible the care and training of some unfortunates now neglected, and serving to relieve some of the deplorable overcrowded conditions of the facilities here at Frankfort.

With funds afforded by this budget, the commissioner of mental health has assured me that the phased activation of the new $4,100,000 facility at Central State Hospital can be undertaken and that the facility can be staffed and equipped within the time schedule established by the department. This will make available radically new programs of mental care and treatment which experts predict will be of unprecedented success in returning mental patients to normal productive life and in effective savings not only of tax dollars but of human resources of value impossible to calculate.

The budget includes funds to take the Minimum Foundation Program for county health departments to three additional counties in 1964 and three more the following year. It will continue present support to the eighty-two counties now participating in this matching program.

The budget calls for $2,325,000 for Kentucky's nationally famous system of state parks and shrines which are the core of our state's valuable tourist industry. Not only will these funds provide for further expansion of tourist and vacation attractions but for an extensive publicity and advertising program to make sure that our expanding parks will be utilized to the maximum.

I am also asking you to make a supplementary appropriation of $1,500,000 for the Department of Parks. During the past three years the department has put into operation a vast system of facilities made possible by the $20-million building program. It has undertaken services, programs, and a scale of service never before attempted on a state level, and it has effected this nationally recognized achievement without impropriety or relaxation of standards. As any businessman who has ever started a big new business will tell you, it was inevitable that during the early phases of such an operation, costs would exceed income. Indeed, when we consider that this parks system is the heart of the tourist industry that last year brought Kentucky more than $304 million and paid more than $17 million in tax revenue alone, this $1,500,000 is shown to be a very sound investment, one that will continue to pay returns to Kentucky and her taxpayers.

Kentucky greatly needs additional job opportunities, and one of the goals of this administration is the development of 75,000 new jobs within the next four years. This budget takes into account the responsibility of state government in seeking new industry by increasing the industrial development function of the Department of Commerce.

It also recognizes the contribution that research can make to industry and employment and provides that the department will continue to support Spindletop Research through contractual arrangements for specific projects. The budget recommends a campaign of advertising Kentucky's industrial advantages, and it contains funds for the Kentucky Industrial Finance Authority, a unit that lends money for development of industry.

We have started a campaign in Kentucky that we hope will push our state's farm economy to a billion dollars a year within the next few years. This budget, in its support to the College of Agriculture, the State Fair, and the Departments of Agriculture and Conservation, recognizes the needs of this campaign.

The State Fair Board requests a supplemental appropriation of $220,000, and I urge you to grant the request. It is true that the board has been obliged to request such supplementary assistance in a majority of the years since the new fairgrounds and exposition center was opened; but we have in the center an asset of such value to Kentucky, its farmers, and business concerns, that the funds needed for its operation represent an investment whose soundness I know you will appreciate.

The proposal which is being presented today makes no provision for major needs of the state in terms of major new construction of facilities. I shall submit within the next few days a proposal for the financing of capital outlay programs for those agencies which receive their primary support from the General Fund. At the same time I shall submit to you a proposal regarding financing the federal aid highway program.

I know that you will want sufficient time to consider the details and ramifications of this budget. Yet I am confident that, after careful and conscientious deliberation, you will decide that it deserves your support and approval. It is, I know, not a document whose primary appeal will be to the timid or overcautious. It challenges our imagination and our courage as well as our old fiscal boundaries. It is a concrete expression of our determination to brush aside our limitations and hindrances and to push forward with increased imagination and courage, energy, and determination, into the newer and better day in which we must live.[1]

---

1. Governor Breathitt's budget passed the House, without changes, on February 19, 1964, by a vote of 95-5. On February 25 the Senate approved the budget 37-1 with two amendments. One amendment cut $500,000 from the Kentucky Industrial Development Finance Authority. This agency loaned money for industrial construction and subdivision projects in an effort to create jobs. Lending capital for the authority was to come from portions of funds in the state employee and teacher retirement systems. A second amendment prevented overdrafts of deficits if revenue failed to meet expectations. Governor Breathitt reported that the extra $500,000 would be used for a new facility at the Danville School for the Deaf. The House approved the revised budget 94-0. *Louisville Courier-Journal,* February 20, 26, 1964. Governor Breathitt discussed the budget changes in an address to the House on February 25, 1964. That address is included in these papers.

STATEMENT TO THE HOUSE OF REPRESENTATIVES
Frankfort / February 25, 1964

I APPRECIATE the invitation that you have extended to me to appear before you again. I want to congratulate the House on the responsible manner in which it has considered the budget. I agree with your suggestion that the budget be amended to include the de-escalator clause contained in previous budgets as a further clarification of the basic law on the subject. This budget tested the sense of responsibility and statesmanship of all of us who have been charged by the people to plan the expenditure of our state revenue in the wisest possible manner in order to help solve the great problems which face our state.

The leadership and members of the Senate, with my approval, worked out a sound method to finance the Kentucky Industrial Finance Authority, through loans from the retirement systems supported by the state. This makes it possible to transfer the $500,000 previously allocated to the authority to the contingent fund.

Before you are asked to concur in these amendments, I think that it is only proper that I indicate to you and the people of Kentucky how I intend to use this addition to the contingency fund. During my campaign for governor, I became very concerned about the condition of the dormitories at the School for the Deaf in Danville. I visited this institution with members of the Danville Business and Professional Women's Club and was distressed to see that a number of the children who lived on the fourth floor had to use toilet facilities in the basement. I share the concern of these women and the other citizens of Kentucky for the safety of these children because of the danger from fire. I promised, during my campaign for governor and in the House caucus of my own party last week, to construct new dormitories to relieve this condition during this administration. I pledge to you today, unequivocally, that this additional $500,000 in the contingent fund will be used to construct new facilities at the School for the Deaf.

I want to pay tribute to both the House and the Senate for making these recommendations which will enable us to more adequately finance the lending agency which is so important in achieving our goal of 75,000 new jobs and in relieving the dangerous situation at the School for the Deaf. I am confident that every member of this honorable body is just as concerned with the safety of our deaf children as I am, and I hope and pray that all of you will concur in these two amendments which, in my judgment, will make a good budget even better.

CAPITAL CONSTRUCTION MESSAGE TO THE GENERAL ASSEMBLY

Frankfort / March 9, 1964

On February 10 I appeared in this chamber and presented to you for your approval an operating budget for state government for the next two years. This budget was conceived in discussions with hundreds of Kentuckians from all parts of the state, representing all segments of our citizenry. It was sharpened in conferences with prominent leaders knowledgeable in the needs and desires of our people and in what is best for our Commonwealth.

The plan I presented stood the test of your further evaluation and extensive public discussion and has become law. The budget you passed sets us upon a course of action I believe to be the most desirable for state government and for all Kentuckians in the four years that lie ahead.

I said at the time that I delivered the operating budget message that I would have a message for you later concerning capital construction for those agencies which receive their primary support from the General Fund and also a proposal regarding the financing of new highways. My message to you today is on these subjects.

My election in November was a directive from the people to proceed with the program contained in the Democratic platform. The mandate was well defined. The course of action was clear. This course of action was reflected in the operating budget which I presented and which passed the General Assembly. In a very real sense, the people of Kentucky wrote the operating budget for the Commonwealth when they voted in November, and we have simply ratified their decisions. The people have not had, to my satisfaction, however, an opportunity to speak clearly on the matter of a capital improvement budget. I want them to have an opportunity to do so. I am asking, therefore, for your consent to present to the voters in November of 1965 a referendum on the sale of $176 million in general obligation bonds for highway construction and other capital outlay programs. In this fashion we will be guided directly by the wishes of the people.

Tax revenues are not presently available to support the capital requirements of state government. If we are to meet those needs, therefore, our only alternatives are to issue general obligation bonds and revenue bonds. Our experience with both these sources of income is good, and the credit of the Commonwealth is excellent. They enable us to do those things which are necessary but which we cannot otherwise afford immediately. The principal outstanding on revenue bonds issued by the state totals $400,583,612 to date.[1] These bonds will be retired by people utilizing the facilities for which the bonds were issued and will not require tax revenue. Highway tolls, for example, will retire turnpike bonds; room rentals will retire dormitory bonds at our colleges, and rents charged to guests will retire park bonds.

General obligation bonds are of a completely different nature. They must be voted by a majority of the people, and they pledge the full faith and credit of the Commonwealth in repaying the bonds through normal tax channels. A favorable vote on a referendum to issue $176 million in general obligation bonds will be a decision by the public to build in the same way that an expanding industrial corporation will borrow funds to build a new plant or buy new machinery.

The general obligation debt of Kentucky today totals $319,335,000. The proposed borrowing would raise this figure to $495,335,000. This total is approximately $204,665,000 less than one year's income for state government. Not many major businesses have total obligations that could be retired with only one year's income.

An additional bond issue of $176 million in no way approaches the point of endangering the state's strong financial position. Based on the current interest rate, bonds could be sold for a thirty-year period at an interest rate of only about 3.5 percent. At this rate of interest about $9.5 million will be required annually to retire the debt. I believe that the growth in our economy will be adequate to take care of the additional obligation which we will assume by this bond issue. Consistent with my pledge to exercise fiscal responsibility, should there be changes in economic conditions which would require additional state income, I would recommend an increase in motor vehicle registration fees on a graduated basis.

The bond issue which I recommend that the General Assembly present to the people of Kentucky for their approval would be for these purposes.

1. Highways. One hundred thirty-nine million dollars would be dedicated to the construction of highways and would assure us that Kentucky continues to take advantage of every federal dollar available for completing our interstate system and for pushing primary road construction in all parts of the state. The interstate highway program provides nine federal dollars for every state dollar and is a bargain we cannot turn down. Another bargain may be forthcoming in the development of an improved road system for the Appalachian area of Kentucky. President Johnson will soon submit to Congress a comprehensive proposal for development of this region, and improved highways will be a cornerstone of his proposal. Kentucky will certainly want to take full advantage of this opportunity to make basic advances in eastern Kentucky.

2. Education. Twenty-two million, five hundred ninety-five thousand dollars would be dedicated to education. This would include $14,110,000 for the construction of classroom buildings and dormitories at the University of Kentucky, and for construction at the five state colleges. Three

million dollars would go toward construction of the medical center at the University of Louisville. The continuing critical shortage of doctors and dentists in Kentucky warrants the inclusion of this project in the bond issue. The School for the Deaf would get $425,000 for improvement of its facilities; the School for the Blind would receive $425,000; and $550,000 would go for a building to house the Industries for the Blind in Louisville. Construction of new vocational school facilities and expansion of old facilities would require $3,440,000. A state library to serve as the center of the statewide library extension program is proposed at an estimated $645,000.

3. Parks. Our state park system would get $4,500,000 for construction of new facilities designed to keep it in its position of preeminence among all state park systems. This amount will not only help assure us our place of leadership but will contribute substantially to our economic growth by helping continue the expansion of our tourist industry.

4. Health and welfare. Seven million, one hundred thousand dollars is proposed for capital improvements which would provide facilities to care for the mentally ill and the mentally retarded and to help speed the rehabilitation of those in our penal institutions. Planned are a crib case facility for severe cases of mental retardation; community facilities for both the mentally ill and the mentally retarded; new centers for receiving, diagnosing, and rehabilitating both adult and juvenile offenders; new farm dormitories at each of our two major penal institutions; two forestry camps for the rehabilitation of adult prisoners; and county health centers in twenty Kentucky counties.

5. Conservation. To continue the progress we have made in developing a chain of lakes across Kentucky, $1 million is suggested for the construction of additional lakes to provide a local water supply for industry, recreation, and flood control. One hundred thousand dollars is included for forest fire control facilities.

6. Agriculture. Seven hundred thousand dollars is asked for construction of an animal disease diagnostic laboratory, and $200,000 for construction of livestock show and sale facilities at Murray State College and the state fairgrounds.

7. Airports. In order to continue the airport development program which has been so successful during the last few years, I am asking $505,000 to match federal and local funds for airport construction and for improvement of existing airports.

8. Public safety. Three state police barracks are included at an estimated cost of $100,000 each.

The construction which I have described for General Fund agencies will require $37 million of the bond issue. When this amount is matched with federal, local, and revenue bond funds it will provide facilities worth

$108,053,290 to the people of Kentucky. The $139 million set aside in the issue for highway construction will be matched by federal funds in ratios ranging from fifty-fifty to ninety-ten and will make possible highways worth many times the amount acquired by the bond sale.

I think you will agree that the objectives of this bond issue are sound—that they are commendable. This proposal has been developed in consultation with those responsible for the programs it would help advance. It does not provide all the funds for all the construction that is desired either by those concerned with the programs or by me. It does, however, strike a balance between our capital needs and the amount of borrowing it is wise to attempt during this biennium.

I respectfully request that you give the people an opportunity to vote on these recommendations. Their approval will contribute significantly, I believe, toward the continued and orderly progress of Kentucky during the next few years.[2]

---

1. Shortly before Governor Breathitt's inauguration a report entitled "Kentucky's Debt—Something to Think About" appeared in the *Courier-Journal.* Prepared by the Kentucky Government Council, a nonpartisan, nonprofit organization of professional persons, the report called Governor Breathitt's "attention" to what the organization obviously regarded an alarming situation. The report concluded: (1) Kentucky's bonded debt had risen from $10,306,000 in 1952 to $550,182,000 in 1963—a fifty-three fold increase and greater than that of any state during the same period. (2) In 1952 Kentucky ranked thirty-ninth in outstanding debt, but ranked tenth in 1962. (3) Of the outstanding debt only 46.3 percent was covered by restrictions imposed by the state constitution, while 53.7 percent of the debt was in nonvoted revenue bonds with no tax guarantees imposed by the constitution. (4) Tax revenues were twelve and one-half times the state debt in 1952, but revenue was only 57.9 percent of the debt in 1963. (5) Interest payments rose from .2 percent of total revenue in 1952 to 6.3 percent in 1962—well above the average of 3.1 percent in other states. (6) In 1952 Kentucky's per capita debt of $3.53 was far below the $42.85 average of all the states. By 1962 Kentucky's $178.51 ranked above other states' average of $116.52. *Louisville Courier-Journal,* December 8, 1963.

2. The bond issue bill passed the House on March 13, 1964, by a vote of 74-10. Six days later the senate approved it 27-8. Accordingly it was placed on the November 2 ballot for public consideration. *Acts, 1964,* Chapter 188 (H.B. 474), pp. 662-72 and the *Louisville Courier-Journal,* March 14, 20, 1964.

PUBLIC ACCOMMODATIONS BILL MESSAGE

House of Representatives
Frankfort / March 10, 1964

ON this occasion I am grateful for the opportunity to ask your help in resolving a great moral issue—the right of every Kentuckian to have access to public accommodations without regard for the color of his skin.[1] This is an issue which the people's representatives should decide, and it is an issue upon which the people are entitled to an answer in both houses of the General Assembly.

As a candidate for governor, I pledged myself to submit this matter to the General Assembly and to abide by their decision. There is now in effect an executive order issued by my predecessor.[2] I have stated, and I state again, that when the two houses of the General Assembly act on the question of public accommodations, I shall rescind the executive order.

My predecessor intended his order as a temporary rather than a permanent solution to the problem. So do I. But I think, indeed I deeply believe, that those who must daily suffer humiliation and the denial of basic human rights have a right to ask you and to ask me to protect their basic rights. I have not shirked this challenge, and I do not believe that you will shirk it. I recommend that the House and Senate set the amended Kinkead bill for a special order of business for the same hour this week.[3] This action will insure a fair hearing on this bill, and I will rescind the executive order prior to the vote.

Kentucky's constitution states that arbitrary power exists nowhere in a republic, not even in the largest majority. We must face the fact that some of our fellow Kentuckians are born, grow up, live out their lives, and die without ever having known what it is to be free from arbitrary power—a power to exclude them from the basic decencies and amenities of our community life—simply because their skins are dark. When decent, respectable, law-abiding Kentuckians cannot eat a meal in a good restaurant, cannot lodge in a decent motel, cannot enjoy themselves as others do, then they are not, in any meaningful sense, free men and women.

The legislation which is before you for consideration does not give to our fellow citizens any new rights. It simply protects those rights which they already possess because they are human beings, created in the image of a good God. The Declaration of Independence stated in 1776 that all men are created equal, and that they are endowed by their Creator with certain inalienable rights—including life, liberty, and the pursuit of happiness. Thomas Jefferson and his associates did not proclaim the rights of white men, or black men, or yellow men. They proclaimed the rights of all men. Today, in America and in Kentucky, we are seeking to make good on the promises of Thomas Jefferson and the Declaration of Independence.

In recent years we have heard a great deal about states' rights. We must recognize that states' rights also involve state responsibilities, and that a failure upon the part of Kentucky to protect the basic human rights of her citizens is but an open invitation to the federal government to intervene in this area to an ever increasing extent. State legislation pending before you would make it possible for state tribunals to deal with discrimination in places of public accommodation. I do not believe that those who believe in states' rights will relish a situation in which the attorney general of the United States and the federal courts will be charged with the sole responsibility for enforcing human rights in Kentucky.

I have no desire at this time to engage in a labored or extended discussion of these issues. Repeatedly I have made my sentiments known. In good conscience, however, I must appeal to you to join with me in facing up to one of the great moral challenges of our time. The scores of letters and calls which I have received from clergymen, priests, rabbis, and devoted religious laymen have etched upon my heart a moral imperative to make this appeal.

Let me put it as simply as I know how. Suppose that any one of you, along with the members of your family, were compelled to live your daily life under the awful shadow of exclusion and discrimination in your own home town. Suppose that any one of you were compelled to face the daily shame and humiliation of service denied in eating places, sleeping places, and other places of public accommodations. Under such circumstances, you would, as I would, feel wounded and violated, caught in the toils of an arbitrary power.

I say to you, from the deepest convictions of my heart, that you and I cannot claim for ourselves rights and opportunities which we will not claim for all of our fellow citizens, regardless of race or color. Let us not hide behind the shelters of anonymity. Let us not duck or dodge this great moral challenge. Let us tell the whole world that in Kentucky the golden rule is written on the books of law and in the hearts of men. Once we have mustered the courage to make this decision, the mists of prejudice will clear away, the kind and generous people of this state will accept our decision, and our children will point to this hour as a landmark for human decency in the history of a great Commonwealth.[4]

---

1. This speech, which was addressed only to the House, was delivered one hour after a public accommodation bill was killed in the House Rules Committee. In the Senate the Kinkead bill had survived two readings and awaited only a final report from the Senate Rules Committee to reach the floor for final passage. The Senate

refused to call up the bill until one of two similar bills was brought out for first and second readings in the House. The House Rules Committee refused, thus killing chances for the passage of public accommodations legislation. *Louisville Courier-Journal,* March 11, 1964.

2. The executive order to which Governor Breathitt referred was issued by Governor Bert Combs on June 26, 1963. Issued in response to pressure from civil rights leaders in Louisville to amend the call of the 1963 special session of the legislature to permit consideration of legislation banning racial discrimination in public accommodations, the order aimed to end racial discrimination in establishments and professions licensed by the state. George W. Robinson, ed., *The Public Papers of Governor Bert T. Combs* (Lexington, Ky., 1980), pp. 417-18 and *Louisville Courier-Journal,* June 27, 1963. Breathitt's retention of the order and his own efforts to secure stronger civil rights legislation in the 1964 General Assembly attest to his commitment to racial justice. Nonetheless, politically the Combs executive order came at an inopportune time. Issued during Breathitt's campaign against Louie B. Nunn, the order produced ugly racial overtones and nearly defeated him in the general election. Breathitt interview, June 10, 1980.

3. The Kinkead bill was introduced February 27, 1964, by Shelby Kinkead, a Democrat from Lexington. The bill as drafted banned racial discrimination in public accommodations defined as any inn, motel, or establishment that provided lodging to transient guests other than an establishment located in a building of not more than five rooms for rent or occupied by the proprietor as his residence. Also included were retail establishments engaged in selling food eaten on the premises, gasoline stations, theaters, stadiums, and other places of public entertainment. Private clubs, barber shops, and beauty shops were not included. *Louisville Courier-Journal,* February 28, 1964.

4. The press reported legislative reaction to Breathitt's address as noncommital. Republican Whip Harold DeMarcus labeled the speech "politics of the worst kind." Louis Peniston, Democratic caucus chairman, thought it was well received by most legislators and praised the speech for its expressiveness, but adopted a "wait-and-see attitude." *Louisville Courier-Journal,* March 11, 1964, and Civil Rights file, Breathitt papers. The feelings of the legislators were more clearly apparent when two days later the House rejected a move to wrest the bill from the rules committee by a margin of 21-38. A similar effort was defeated in the Senate 9-18. *Louisville Courier-Journal,* March 13, 1964.

PRESS CONFERENCE—REVIEW OF 1964 GENERAL ASSEMBLY
Frankfort / March 20, 1964

THIS has been a good session of the General Assembly—a constructive session, a session which has brought real benefits to Kentucky. I congratulate the members of both houses on their accomplishments. Perhaps the outstanding achievements of this session have been the budget and the bond issues. The budget bill did more than continue existing programs: it charted new paths of progress—in education, in health, in conservation, in welfare. It is neither a caretaker budget nor a standstill budget. It is, however, a balanced budget—balanced without new taxes or higher taxes.

Second only to the budget among the accomplishments of this session I should list the submission of a bond issue for Kentucky's needs in the field of highway and capital construction. This bond issue will be a wise investment in Kentucky's expanding future. It will bring us new and better highways, improvements in our institutions of higher learning, more human correctional facilities, a complete and outstanding park system, a network of modern airports, and many other facilities to bring a better life to Kentuckians and Kentucky communities. The capital facilities which the bond issue will make possible are tools for a growing, thriving economy which will produce added revenues for state and local government.

This has been a good session for honest government. We have passed a model purchasing law, and we have created a Commission on Economy and Efficiency in Government—redeeming thereby two planks in our partnership for progress platform.

This has been a good session for farm people and for agriculture. We have provided for additional laboratory facilities to test livestock and diagnose livestock disease. We have provided funds for the Agricultural Science Center. We have doubled the rural highway fund from $5 million to $10 million per year. We have kept our promises to farm people.

This has been a good session for education. We have increased teachers' salaries by $500 over the period of the biennium exactly as contained in the Kentucky Education Association program, have financed the expanded foundation program, have made available record sums for higher education, have strengthened the teachers' retirement program and the teacher tenure laws.[1] We have kept our promises to the school people, to the parents and the children of Kentucky.

This has been a good session for conservation of our natural resources. We have passed a strong strip-mine bill. This bill was carefully prepared after a four-year study, including consultation with the Farm Bureau, the Association of Soil Conservation Districts, the League of Women Voters, and the garden clubs of Kentucky. The Berea study was used in its preparation, and a comparative analysis was made of all strip-mine laws in the country. We also called in national experts to assist in the preparation of the bill—experts who have drafted and participated in the administration of strip-mine laws.[2] We have strengthened and reorganized our forestry program, we have given additional financial tools to the watershed conservancy districts, and continued the valuable small lake program. We have kept our promises to conserve Kentucky's natural heritage.

Another area in which we have made significant progress because of legislative action is constitution revision. The assembly has already had its first meeting, and further organization is now underway. By the means we are employing we can, in the full glare of publicity, discuss the problems of constitutional revision and hammer out solutions which are acceptable to the people.[3]

I make no apologies for the session of the General Assembly which concludes today. The record of this session speaks for itself, and it is a record which has brought substantial benefits to Kentucky. Naturally, I am disappointed at the General Assembly's failure to act in the field of human rights. I believe, as so long as I live I shall always believe, that every citizen is entitled to obtain equal treatment in places of public accommodation regardless of the color of his skin. I shall continue to fight for adequate human rights legislation with all the strength at my command, and I urge upon all Kentuckians a campaign of continued public education in this field.

Of course, no session of the General Assembly can solve all of Kentucky's problems in a period of sixty days. Much has been done, and there is much which remains to be done. Meanwhile, let me express the people's thanks and my thanks to the members of the assembly. I pledge the best efforts of my administration in carrying forward the partnership for progress which has made such a good beginning during this session.

---

1. For details on changes in the Minimum Foundation Program, teacher retirement system, and tenure regulations see *Acts, 1964,* Chapter 41 (H.B. 52), pp. 150-64; Chapter 171 (H.B. 419), pp. 623-28; and Chapter 43 (H.B. 72), pp. 166-92.

2. The strip-mine law included a series of provisions relating to application permits to strip mine, reclamation plans, forfeiture of bond for failure to reclaim land, and a time limit to complete reclamation work following the expiration of the permit. During the 1964 session of the legislature Governor Breathitt worked to secure legislation strip miners "could live with." In the 1966 session he pursued

a stronger law. Breathitt interview, June 10, 1980. See also *Acts, 1964,* Chapter 61 (H.B. 145), pp. 228-37.

3. The act creating the Constitution Revision Assembly was signed into law February 7, 1964. *Acts, 1964,* Chapter 4 (H.B. 39), pp. 3-6.

LEGISLATIVE MEETING
Frankfort / July 20, 1964

TODAY we face again a task we have faced before, that I have spoken to you about before, that you have pondered in your legislative halls before —but a task that is still with us.[1] This task that we face is—simply put— the task of providing equality for all Kentuckians in the service they receive in places of public accommodation, the task of assuring all our citizens that places open to the public are open to all the public on a fair and equal basis.

Circumstances surrounding the whole subject of a public accommodations law have been modified considerably since I last spoke to you last March. At that time we were expecting the Congress to enact a civil rights bill that would include a public accommodations section, and my feeling was that we should have a state law prior to federal legislation. I felt that regardless of the action of Congress, there was a state responsibility in this field and I wanted Kentucky to stand up to that responsibility. I felt, further, that Kentucky should take advantage of provisions of the federal law that allow states to implement and administer portions of it.

Now we have the federal civil rights law, and it is my belief that the great majority of Kentuckians respect it and abide by it. We have a federal law, but there still remains the state responsibility that I spoke of earlier. I hope that you are here today prepared to say that you will do something about that responsibility.

I realize that the problem of providing equal rights for all Kentuckians is not a simple or an easy one. I realize that the problem will not be solved once we have a state law on the books, just as it is not solved by the fact that we have a federal law. But you and I as leaders—while we cannot solve the entire problem—can take a big step in the direction of fairness and equality by passing a state law that will complement and bolster the federal law and at the same time give Kentuckians the right to administer it in Kentucky.

Such action on our part would be notice to all our citizens and to all the world that we believe in principles of justice and fair play and that we are ready, willing, and able to promote these principles without outside help. Such action on our part would be in keeping with Kentucky traditions of calmly and sensibly solving our own problems in the sensitive—often emotional—field of civil rights. We have integrated our public transportation facilities without outside help. We have integrated our schools and colleges without outside help. No outside help has been necessary for any Kentucky citizen who desires to exercise his privilege to register to vote and to vote. No outside help was needed when the decision was made to throw open our state parks and other areas of recreation to all citizens.

The federal Civil Rights Act of 1964 provides that there will be outside help for those who are denied rights to places of public accommodation unless the states have laws to reserve to themselves the right to administer the act. I hope you will pass such a law.

I am asking you to pledge yourselves to vote for a bill as a condition of my calling a special session because I do not believe the cause of human rights in Kentucky would be served by a long, noisy, expensive session concerning a matter on which we have already had extensive debate and to which I am convinced you have already given much sober thought, much weighing of pros and cons, much soul-searching and much prayerful consideration.

In return for this pledge, I give you my pledge that I will continue to be vitally concerned with the whole subject of human rights and that I will do all I can to see that the law is enforced equitably and fairly for the benefit of the public and for the benefit of those who own businesses serving the public. While you must be responsible for passing the law, I will be responsible for its administration—along with my Human Rights Commission, similar local bodies and courts and officials throughout the Commonwealth.

You will recall that mayors of the first four classes of Kentucky cities meeting here last spring called unanimously for such a bill as that to be explained to you here today. This action came with no prompting from me and was based wholly on their belief that such a measure would be good for Kentucky.

Within the last few weeks I have found much additional sentiment for Kentucky passing its own law. A survey reported to me within the last few days indicated that a great majority of Kentuckians would rather have the state administer the provisions of the federal law than leave it to the federal courts. This sentiment was followed regardless of whether those answering were happy or unhappy that the federal law has passed.

I hope that those members of the General Assembly who were ready to vote for a public accommodations law last March will be ready to now. I hope that those who did not favor a bill last March will favor one now. I would remind them that the question before them in July is different from the one before them in March. The question in March was, shall we have a bill? This is no longer a question because the Congress has passed and the president has signed a bill. The question now is, shall Kentucky or the federal courts administer and enforce that bill?

This seems to me to be a good time to speak directly to all citizens of Kentucky as well as to the members of the General Assembly and say that I recognize that this is a time of trial, a time of readjustment for many of our citizens. I hope it does not also become a time of turmoil or a time of strife.

I know that there are many Kentuckians who do not agree with provisions of the civil rights law that has just been passed and who would not agree with provisions of the state act I am proposing here today. Of them I beg understanding as they adjust to social changes brought about by the law. Of them I beg compassion and understanding for those who will benefit by the law. Of them I beg peaceful compliance and respect for the law.

To those Kentuckians to whom the new law means added opportunity as citizens and new self-respect as the result of the abolition of degrading and debasing customs and practices, I say that I hope this transition into fuller citizenship will go smoothly for you. I hope you will do all you can to make the changes the law involves easier for those who must change, that you will have full faith in the law and will use the law rather than physical displays or demonstrations to acquire the rights it grants.

While I expect each citizen to proclaim the federal law or to criticize it as he sees fit, I also expect each citizen to recognize it and obey it, and I am hopeful that we can count on the good sense and the good citizenship that Kentuckians have displayed in the past. Any Kentuckian who does less, any Kentuckian who seeks to inflame rather than becalm the issue not only does a disservice to his own cause—whatever his beliefs may be—he does a disservice to himself and to the state in which he lives—the state he loves. And now, distinguished members of the Kentucky General Assembly, I conclude my part on this program. I leave this most important question to the conscience and wisdom of this group.

---

1. Following his failure to secure civil rights legislation in the 1964 regular session, Governor Breathitt suggested that after federal action on civil rights he might call a special session. On July 2, President Johnson signed the Civil Rights Act of 1964. The act banned discrimination by establishments offering food, lodging, gas, or public entertainment; prohibited discrimination by employees or unions in hiring, firing, promotion, job referral, or apprenticeship training; autho-

rized federal agencies to withhold funds from programs found discriminating; authorized the attorney general to file suit to force public parks, playgrounds, libraries, pools, and schools to comply with desegregation orders; tightened procedures aimed at eliminating discriminatory denial of voting rights; and extended the Civil Rights Commission to 1968, giving it broader powers to collect national information to check compliance with the law. The Breathitt administration drafted a state public accommodation bill, presented it to the July 20 legislative meeting, and announced that if sufficient support was apparent the governor would call a special session of the legislature to enact the bill. One hundred and three of 137 legislators attended what proved to be a stormy meeting. Many legislators, angry about the federal law, questioned its constitutionality; others objected to the specific bill the Breathitt administration drafted; and some civil rights advocates accused Breathitt of playing politics with the issue. When the votes were counted, thirty-five legislators agreed to support the bill, thirty opposed it, and thirty-seven refused to vote. Breathitt had earlier announced he would call a special session only if "he had reasonable assurance from the members of the legislature that they would pass a bill." *U.S. Statutes at Large*, vol. 78 (Washington, 1964), pp. 241-45 and *Louisville Courier-Journal*, July 3, 24, 1964. Following the meeting, Breathitt announced he would not call a special session. "I think the sentiment of the membership is clear and unmistakable and that sentiment is that the majority does not favor a bill. I think this, despite the various excuses and lines of reasoning given by various members who voted no. Any member who really and truly wanted a public accommodations law could have voted in the affirmative." Press conference, July 20, 1964, Civil Rights file, Breathitt papers.

SPECIAL LEGISLATIVE SESSION
Frankfort / August 23, 1965

YOU meet in extraordinary session to deal with extraordinary issues—issues which affect the well-being, the prosperity, and the future opportunities of every Kentuckian. I scarcely need to tell you what those issues are. They have been on the minds and on the tongues and pens of countless Kentuckians during the past two months. You are met here to make certain that the property owners of Kentucky may find reassurance against the widespread fear of unbearable increase in their property taxes.[1]

"Taxes," as the late Justice Holmes once said, "are the price we pay for civilization."[2] The education of our children, the protection of our lives and property against crime and disorder, the streets over which we travel, the measures which we use to protect the health and welfare of our people are foundations of our society which would crumble without taxes to provide the necessary funds. Those in public life who will not face the fact that the increasing quantity and quality of public services can be paid for only out of taxes are simply unable or unwilling to face the facts of fiscal life. Let me make it clear, however, that our purpose in meeting here tonight is not to increase taxes but to reduce them; not to add to the taxpayers' burdens, but to relieve those burdens.

As President Grover Cleveland once said, "It is a condition and not a theory which we face." What is that condition, what are its causes, and what do we propose to do about it? These are the questions which we, working together, must answer, not only to the satisfaction of the people of Kentucky, but to the satisfaction of our consciences and the needs of our children.

These needs are not mutually exclusive. The finest educational system which we could plan would topple and crumble if our farmers, our homeowners, and our business enterprises were so crushed by high taxes that our prosperity and sovereignty are threatened. But, by the same token, even if we could reduce taxes to the barest minimum, the wealth of our Commonwealth would rust and rot if we did not provide good schools and improved educational opportunities for the boys and girls who will produce the wealth that pays the taxes of the next generation. In this, as in most difficult decisions which we are called upon to make in public life, we must adjust, we must reconcile, we must piece together the conflicting needs and conflicting pressures from which must emerge laws and policies which can keep our educational system on the upward path without bankrupting the taxpayer.

The Constitution of Kentucky was written in 1891. The framers of that document wrote into it a clear command that all property not exempt from taxation should be assessed at and taxed on the basis of its fair cash value. The framers of our constitution went even further than this. They wrote into our basic law a definition of fair cash value as the price which property would bring at a voluntary sale. Our constitution says nothing about assessment ratios, about percentages of value, about fractional assessments, or any of the other complications which have crept stealthily, but surely, into the field of tax assessment.

Constitutions are not easy to write and their language must sometimes seem vague or obscure by the very necessity of the case. But those provisions of our state constitution dealing with the assessment of property for purposes of taxes are as plain as the English language can be.

Despite the clarity and vigor of our constitution, it was evaded, ignored, and disobeyed almost from the day it became law. This failure we cannot lay at the door of any one man or group. St. Paul said, "All have sinned and come short of the glory of God." I think it is fair that in the assessment of property for tax purposes, over a period of seventy-five years, all of us —governors, legislators, commissioners, assessors, and just plain taxpayers —all of us have sinned and come short of our responsibility in living up to the requirements of our constitution.

This has resulted in two very serious practical difficulties in the administration of taxes at local levels of government. In this connection, we must remember that the property tax has ceased to be a basic source of revenue for state government. Since 1891 we in Kentucky have come to rely upon the income tax, the sales tax, and the various excise taxes for the support of government programs at the state level. But the property tax has continued, and in all probability will continue, to remain a basic and perhaps the basic source of revenue for cities, for counties, and for local school districts.

Our failure to assess property at its fair cash value has inflicted two deep wounds on our fiscal system in the area of local government. First, it has confused and mixed up the function of assessment with the responsibility for setting tax rates. The fundamental policy of our constitution was designed to place responsibility for determining the total tax bite on the elected representatives of the people—the city councils, the fiscal courts, the local school boards—subject, of course, to the restrictive power of the General Assembly. But the people's representatives could not meet this responsibility so long as assessments were variable, unequal, and unrealistic.

Secondly, the failure to assess property as required by the constitution has resulted in an unequal and unfair distribution of the total property tax burden. The property tax cannot afford a workable basis for financing local government when the assessment procedure is riddled with injustice and discrimination.

What, then, has happened to change all this during the last two months? The answer is simple, though the problem may be difficult. Some months ago a group of citizens and taxpayers went to the courts and asked the courts to compel the Department of Revenue and the local tax assessors to assess all property at its fair cash value, as the constitution commands. Let me make one thing clear: I did not start this lawsuit, the Department of Revenue did not start this lawsuit, and the tax commissioners did not start this lawsuit. On the contrary, we defended the suit. We had no control over those who did bring it. When the lawsuit reached the Court of Appeals, our highest court, without a single judge dissenting, granted the relief sought by these citizens and directed that beginning January 1, 1966, all property be assessed at its fair cash value.

This is what I mean when I say that it is a condition and not a theory which confronts us. Existing tax rates have been set, for the most part, on the basis of assessments at a level much lower than fair cash value. If property is now to be assessed in accordance with the constitution and the court's decision, existing tax rates would produce in many cases astronomical and unbearable increases in the burden of taxation.

Of course, you and I know that our local governing bodies—our fiscal courts, our city councils, and our school boards—will not continue existing rates in the face of 100 percent assessments. These bodies are all elected by the people in the various communities, and they are composed of sane and sensible citizens. I simply do not believe that the magistrates, the county commissioners, the mayors and councilmen, and the school board members in Kentucky will act irresponsibly and recklessly.

I believe, however, that the uncertainties which have followed in the wake of the recent decision by the Court of Appeals have produced widespread fear and insecurity among our people; and this fear is a fact of life which you and I must face. Until property has been reassessed in accordance with the court's decision, and until local governing bodies have given tangible evidence of their firm desire to protect the taxpayer against unjust burdens, I believe that action by the General Assembly is urgently necessary to relieve the fears of our people.

This is why I have called upon you to convene in this extraordinary session. What, then, shall we do about it all? So far as property tax rates at the state level are concerned, the answer seems to me to be clear. We can simply reduce all state property tax rates to a point at which tax receipts, under 100 percent assessment, remain at the same level now prevailing. Indeed, as to livestock and farm machinery, which are extremely difficult to assess, and which produce less than $600,000 of revenue each year, I think we can go further and reduce rates to the point of a practical exemption. This I recommend to you.

This leaves to be considered the all-important matter of local tax rates and the limitations to be placed upon them by the General Assembly in the light of changed assessments. As to this, I have sought information, have sought advice, have sought enlightenment, from every possible source, from every group and every individual. I have conducted this inquiry without preconceived opinions, without respect to politics, and solely in a spirit of searching for the right answer—the answer which will protect the greatest number of taxpayers against unjust burdens and at the same time permit adequate local support for education and the other necessary activities of local government.

To discuss and analyze each suggestion made, with all possible variations on a particular theme, would keep you here in session all night. Most proposals, however, have gone under a few broad categories, and with one or two of these I should like to deal for a moment.

The proposal which we have heard perhaps most frequently is a deceptively simple one—to reduce the maximum tax rate for local schools from the present level of $1.50 to a flat lower level, the figure of fifty cents being frequently mentioned, and for comparable reductions in the maximum level allowed for other local units of government. This proposal I do not believe would be workable or practical. It would see some of our cities, counties, and school districts, where assessment ratios have been highest, actually reduce revenues below the existing level.

The effect of such a policy would be to destroy some of our finest local school systems and to cripple city and county government by compelling reduction in government services. On the other hand, in those counties, cities, and school districts where assessment ratios have been lowest, a fifty-cent maximum school rate or its equivalent for other local units of government would permit very substantial and in some cases almost inconceivable increases in taxes.

For example, a fifty-cent maximum school tax rate on the basis of 100 percent assessment would reduce revenue in Jefferson County by more than $600,000 per year; in Bullitt County by nearly $35,000 per year; in Bellevue by more than $60,000 per year; in Fort Thomas by more than $200,000 per year; in Newport by $35,000 per year; in Lexington by almost $200,000 per year; in the city of Henderson by $84,000 per year; in the city of Covington by nearly $300,000 per year; in Lee County by $4,000 per year; in the city of Paducah by more than $20,000 per year.

On the other hand, a fifty-cent maximum rate would permit increases of substantial nature in every school district where assessment ratios are now below average. A fifty-cent tax rate, on the basis of 100 percent assessment, would increase revenue in Barren County by more than $160,000, or 58 percent; in Hickman County by more than $75,000, or 57 percent; in Owen County by more than $80,000, or 40 percent; in Morgan County by almost $60,000, or 67 percent; in Breckinridge County by nearly $100,000, or 43 percent.

It would, of course, be possible to lessen the destructive impact of the fifty-cent maximum proposal in those counties with high ratios by permitting higher rates where necessary to preserve existing levels of revenue, but this would still make possible substantial increases in the tax burden in many school districts.

I am convinced that the better plan would be a rollback in rates to compensate for increased assessments; in other words, legislation which would freeze the tax burden on existing property at the existing level. This would guarantee the average local taxpayer against any increase in his tax bill resulting from the reassessment of property at fair cash value.

It would not and could not prevent the taxpayer whose property is underassessed in comparison with that of his neighbors from having some increase in his tax burden, just as it would result in a reduction in taxes for those taxpayers whose property is now assessed at a higher ratio than that of his neighbors.

After all, the very purpose of requiring assessment at full cash value is to equalize the tax burden, and this will naturally result in some increases and some decreases in individual tax bills. Our objective is to equalize assessments—to distribute the burden fairly among taxpayers, but to prevent the total burden from rising as a result of reassessment.

The proposal which I recommend to you, I repeat, is that you, the General Assembly, require local taxing districts to roll back their tax rates so that the average person in the local district does not suffer a tax increase as a result of reassessment. This result cannot be accomplished under the fifty-cent maximum rate proposal, but it can be accomplished under the rollback proposal.

After we have achieved this result, we must face the fact that some, though by no means all, of our local school districts and other local taxing districts may be faced with special, urgent and pressing needs for modest additional revenue. I do not think we can, in fairness to our children, place every local school board and every local governing body in a complete straitjacket. Therefore, I suggest to the General Assembly that, in addition to the rollback of tax rates, you provide a moderate safety valve which will allow any local school board or fiscal court, after full notice and public hearing, to increase local tax rates by not more than 10 percent in any one year.

These recommendations are based in part upon the experience of the state of Florida. In Florida, as in Kentucky, the highest state court ordered the assessment of property at full cash value. In Florida, as in Kentucky, the legislature was called upon to act for the protection of taxpayers against crushing burdens which might have resulted from increased assessments under existing rates. In Florida, as I hope will be the case in Kentucky, the legislature did not set arbitrary numerical maximum rates but directed a rollback in local tax rates to compensate for increased assessments. In Florida, as I hope will be the case in Kentucky, the legislature provided a safety valve by permitting an increase of not more than 10 percent in rates fixed by local government bodies after notice to the public and after a full public hearing.

The recommendations which I make to you provide greater protection to the taxpayer than does the Florida law, because Florida made provision for an additional 5 percent emergency increase in local tax rates, which I am not recommending to you. This is not to say that Florida, in her legislation, has found the answer to the questions which Kentucky must face, but Florida's situation more nearly resembles that of Kentucky in respect to these matters than does any other state, and I believe we may find her experience useful in solving our problems.

I have included three other matters in the proclamation which has brought you here. One relates to a permissive occupational tax for educational purposes in Louisville and Jefferson County. It is recommended by the educational leadership in that community, is endorsed by both political parties, and contains a provision for referendum if that be desired by sufficient percentage of the voters. This is nothing more or less than a home-rule proposition, and it has not been requested on a similar basis by other school districts.

I have also proposed for your consideration the ratification of the proposed amendment to the Constitution of the United States relating to presidential succession and presidential disability. This amendment was submitted by vote of both houses of Congress, where it passed by overwhelming majorities with bipartisan support. In my opinion, this nation cannot afford the risk of doubt as to who is at the head of its government and as to how the affairs of the nation are to be conducted where the president may be physically or otherwise disabled from exercising the powers of his office.[3]

The Constitution Revision Assembly is nearing the completion of its work. The regular session of the General Assembly which convenes in 1966 will want to consider the submission of its handiwork for the consideration and judgment of the people. Three methods of submission have been suggested: (1) the calling of an unlimited constitutional convention, (2) the calling of a limited constitutional convention, and (3) the direct submission of a revised constitution to the vote of the people.

The regular session in 1964 took necessary action to permit the first of these alternatives to be considered in 1966, and the third alternative did not require preliminary action prior to the 1966 session. In order to keep alternative methods of submission open for consideration in 1966, I recommend that you take steps for the calling of a limited convention.[4]

As to the main problem which has brought you here, I can only say that the inherent difficulties of the subject are sufficiently great without the addition of partisanship or quest for political advantage. Without a surrender of self-interest, without a willingness to listen to all points of view, without a determination to reach a sound and workable solution regardless of all else, we shall simply dissolve into a confusion of tongues, a senseless furor of clamoring voices, full of sound and fury signifying nothing.

This I do not believe would be the spirit of this General Assembly, nor the spirit which will appeal to the sober second thought of our constituents. At the first impulses of insecurity and discontent, which have not unnaturally followed in the wake of a fundamental change, those who talk loud and think little may believe that they have discovered a demagogue's paradise.

But the people are not all that feckless. As they listen, as they think, as they face the facts, Kentuckians will realize that the answer is best which will best fit the facts and best stand the test of experience. And when those to whom you and I must answer are ready to make their enduring judgment, they will give the accolade of confidence and approval to those who are ready to stand the heat and who refuse to be led off the main highway by the noisy clamor of each passing moment. I am confident that you, in facing up to your responsibilities, will earn that accolade in the work which you are about to do.

---

1. In November, 1964, Jefferson County voters turned down a proposal to increase property taxes and occupational taxes (on salaries, wages, and net profits) which were to have provided additional revenue for the city and county school systems. The relatively underpaid Louisville teachers were demanding salary increases, and county schools were being forced into split sessions for lack of funds. Though Jefferson County's financial problems appeared to be the most pressing, school districts throughout the state were experiencing similar difficulties. Following the November elections, Louisville teachers demanded that Governor Breathitt call a special session of the General Assembly to deal with school finances in Jefferson County. The governor resisted such pressures until a prior agreement on a basic solution could be reached. He stated that any agreement must have bipartisan political support, be approved by educators, avoid an increase in state taxes, and be acceptable to the public. By March, 1965, an acceptable proposal was formulated by Jefferson County political and educational leaders, and the governor announced that he would call for a special legislative session in June, thereby avoiding a strike by Jefferson County teachers projected for April. Breathitt further promised to expand the business of the special session to consider school financing throughout Kentucky, provided the same conditions of prior agreement could be met in the rest of the state. Eleven regional meetings were held to develop funding proposals. Three potential solutions emerged from these discussions. One was the Jefferson County plan for imposing an occupational school tax of up to 1 percent. Another was the Kentucky Educational Association plan to increase the tax rate which school boards could invoke without specific voter approval from the prevailing $1.50 per $100 of assessed value to $2.00 per $100. The third solution entailed the restoration of the 1956 assessment ratio (about ⅓ of property's real value). The then current ratio varied throughout the state but averaged 27 percent. Individual school districts were to be allowed one 10 percent rate increase should revenue from the new assessment ratio prove insufficient. The special session was projected for late June, but the Kentucky Court of Appeals forced a change in the governor's plans. Following the November, 1964, referendum, a Louisville educational group filed suit in the Kentucky courts requesting the enforcement of the Kentucky constitutional provisions stipulating 100 percent assessment of property for tax purposes. On June 8, 1965, the Court of Appeals ruled that the 100 percent ratio must be observed, throwing Kentucky taxpayers into a virtual panic and putting Breathitt under immediate and heavy pressure to reduce its impact on an angry electorate. Breathitt therefore postponed the special session in order to fashion a response to the radically altered circumstances created by the court's decision. When the call for a special session came in July, 1965, the Jefferson County school

problem was not included. Rather, the session was initially intended only to deal with the property tax issue raised by the new assessment ratio. However, on August 11, at the request of Jefferson County legislators and school board officials, Breathitt expanded his call to include the Jefferson County occupational tax plan proposed in June. At the special session Breathitt found his proposal for reducing property tax rates challenged by Lieutenant Governor Waterfield's advocacy of his own alternative legislation. Jefferson County senators provided the decisive votes which tipped the scales in favor of the Breathitt forces, ensuring in return Breathitt's support for a modified version of their occupational tax proposal. In its final form, the tax legislation enacted by the special session of the legislature contained three main features. First, property tax rates throughout the state were to be reduced in proportion to the increased assessment ratio, thereby leaving the actual amount paid by the taxpayer virtually unchanged. However, 10 percent increases in maximum school tax rates were authorized for 1966 and 1967. Second, an occupational tax of up to .5 percent for Jefferson County schools was approved, with a provision exempting nonresidents. Finally, the legislation established a process whereby Jefferson County voters could repeal the new tax through petition and referendum. See *Louisville Courier-Journal,* March, June-September, 1965, December 10, 1967, and *Acts, First Extraordinary Session of 1965,* Chapter 2 (H.B. 1), pp. 3-27.

2. Oliver Wendell Holmes, Jr. (1841-1935), American jurist; appointed to U.S. Supreme Court by Theodore Roosevelt in 1902. Holmes served until his retirement in 1932. Richard B. Morris, ed. *Encyclopedia of American History* (New York, 1953), p. 677.

3. The 1965 special session of the legislature ratified the proposed amendment, making Kentucky one of the first states to do so. It was ratified by the requisite number of states and became the Twenty-fifth Amendment to the Constitution of the United States on February 10, 1967. *Acts, First Extraordinary Session of 1965,* Chapter 4 (S.R. 4), pp. 30-32.

4. The special session voted for the required steps preliminary to a limited convention; however, the 1966 General Assembly decided to submit the revised document directly to the electorate in the elections of 1966. *Acts, First Extraordinary Session of 1965,* Chapter 3 (S.R. 2), pp. 28-29.

PRESS CONFERENCE ON AMENDMENT TO HOUSE BILL 1
Frankfort / September 1, 1965

ON Friday the permissive occupation tax for Louisville and Jefferson County will be offered as an amendment to House Bill 1. I am confident that the rules committee will adopt this as a committee amendment, and that the House will back up the judgment of the rules committee. Both personally, and as head of the administration, I stand 100 percent for the occupational tax amendment, with nonresidents excluded, and for the speedy adoption of House Bill 1 as amended on Friday.

The boys and girls of Louisville and Jefferson County, the teachers of Louisville and Jefferson County, the entire metropolitan community, need the help and sympathy of our whole state. We cannot allow double session, sanctions and all the other symptoms of a decaying educational system to cripple the health and growth of Kentucky's largest urban community.

If there have been any misunderstandings between the governor and the senators and representatives from Jefferson County, I accept my share of the responsibility—but I want to make it clear that at all times I have favored quick and decisive action to relieve the educational crisis in Louisville and Jefferson County.

Likewise, the taxpayers, the children, the parents of Kentucky are looking to this special session for speedy action on property taxes. House Bill 1 protects the taxpayers against confiscatory tax increases and provides a needed margin of safety for our local school systems. It is the only measure now before the special session which meets this test. It ought to pass, and I shall do all in my power to see that it passes.

I called this session to take care of the taxpayers and the children of Kentucky. I did not call the legislature here to loaf or to play politics. I am sure that there is no political advantage for me personally in anything which will come out of this session. It is the duty of both houses to stay in session and to keep at work until a sound, workable bill is placed on the statute books.

That is my aim, and I think a great majority of the legislators share that aim. I do not believe that a majority of either house will be led astray by political mischief makers seeking a chance to fish for cheap political advantage in troubled waters. Any effort to adjourn this session for a prolonged period of time, or to keep this legislature from working on Friday, is nothing but petty politics and deserves the condemnation of all straight-thinking Kentuckians.[1]

---

1. The complex circumstances surrounding tax assessment and the Louisville occupational tax at the special session of 1965 produced one of the more public political conflicts between Breathitt and Waterfield supporters. For details of the struggle see the *Louisville Courier-Journal,* August 24, September 1, 2, 3, 4, 1965.

HOUSE BILL 1 SIGNING
Frankfort / September 16, 1965

THIS bill to which I am about to place my signature represents the best thinking and best judgment of many, many Kentuckians and many groups who have met and discussed all aspects of the Court of Appeals ruling that property must be assessed at its fair cash value, beginning January 1, 1966.

First, and foremost in importance, is the fact that this bill protects the taxpayer from a skyrocketing of his local property taxes—that it places a tight lid on local governing bodies so that they cannot increase the local tax burden unjustly or irresponsibly. Had this bill not been enacted into law, local governing bodies could have increased taxes anywhere from 200 to 500 percent in every single Kentucky county.

Moreover, the bill actually provides an overall tax decrease in state levies on property. The rates are rolled back sharply to the point where revenue collected from these levies is reduced by at least $500,000 and perhaps as much as $750,000. This, I know, is welcomed relief.

As a safety valve, the bill permits a 1 to 10 percent increase in budget revenue in 1966 and 1967 if local authorities think such increases are necessary, but only after a full public hearing. The thinking of the majority of legislators was to allow this permissive increase of 1 to 10 percent in those districts where the local taxpayers themselves deem it absolutely necessary. It is highly unlikely that any school board, any fiscal court or any city council would ask for an increase in taxes if it met strong and vocal opposition at a public hearing.

Another provision in the bill provides the remedy, at long last, for the end to double and triple school sessions in Jefferson County. This part of the bill is for, more than anyone else, the children of our greatest metropolitan area. It will give every boy and girl in Jefferson County a better chance for an adequate education. It will enable them to receive quality instruction from properly paid teachers during a normal and safer school day. In return, it places a greater responsibility on the teachers and school administrators to make sure that for each education dollar spent, the citizens of Jefferson County receive a full dollar's value.

The permissive half-cent occupational tax, which must be imposed by the Jefferson Fiscal Court and which is subject to recall referendum if 15 percent of the citizens petition, was supported by a majority of the members of both political parties and by practically all the political, business, and community leaders of Louisville and Jefferson County. For this support, I am grateful. The bipartisan leadership they displayed is a real credit to the community.

The people of Jefferson County also owe a debt of gratitude to those senators and representatives from outside Jefferson County who came to their assistance in this time of crisis. These senators and representatives are to be applauded for their progressive, sympathetic attitude. They demonstrated their appreciation that our state is a seamless web, and that no one sector can be separated from the other sectors without ripping the fabric of the whole structure.

To all the senators and representatives who contributed to the writing, debate, and enactment of House Bill 1, I express my appreciation. It is a good bill and one that is in the best interest of our Commonwealth. As far as the Senate proceedings, the constitutional majority of the senators did, in my judgment, what was right and that was to go ahead with the people's business at hand without undue delay.[1]

This session has been long and tiring, but it has been productive and helpful. When I addressed the opening meeting of this special session of the General Assembly last month, I said that I thought it imperative that we take action to protect Kentuckians against the possibility of skyrocketing property taxes and, at the same time, to preserve the ability of schools and other governmental services to function properly. Today we complete that action as I sign House Bill 1.

---

1. Breathitt is referring to a controversial attempt by Waterfield to delay the progress of House Bill 1 through the Senate. On Thursday, September 9, Waterfield used his parliamentary powers as presiding officer of the Senate to enable his supporters to pass a motion to adjourn the Senate until 7:30 P.M., Monday, September 13. Administration supporters appealed and overturned the ruling of the chair and continued the session without Waterfield and his supporters, who maintained that the Senate had already adjourned and therefore they refused to participate. House Bill 1 was reported favorably out of committee and received the required first reading by the remaining senators. On Friday, with the Waterfield forces again absent, the bill was read a second time, preparing the stage for a final vote. The Senate approved the measure by a 23-12 vote on Tuesday, September 14, despite Waterfield's continued insistence that the Thursday and Friday sessions were illegal. *Louisville Courier-Journal,* September 10, 11, 14, 15, 1965.

PRELEGISLATIVE SESSION
Gilbertsville / December 6, 1965

I AM pleased to welcome you and be with you this morning as you begin work for the 1966 regular session of the General Assembly—a session that will have great bearing on the future course of our Commonwealth. You constitute the chosen leadership of a modern people, in a modern state, during a modern time. Some of you are first timers, just as I was fourteen years ago when I entered state government as a member of the House; and others of you are veteran members, many of you with several sessions behind you.

Our system of government—which provides separation between the executive and legislative branches, but allows and promotes cooperation—is the best ever devised, and I intend to respect and advance it. I appreciate the problems, the pressures, and the aspirations of the membership of the General Assembly.

To those of you who were in Frankfort in 1964 and during the special session of the legislature in August and September, I am grateful for your help and support, and I solicit your continued support in the future. I assure you and all the new members that you have my wholehearted assistance and understanding as you perform the duties entrusted to you by the people of Kentucky.

There have been times in the past when the first half of an administration was devoted to the people, the second half to politics. This is not going to happen this time. This administration will become a lame-duck administration the day a new governor is inaugurated in December of 1967 and not one minute before.

Legislative sessions, I know, are never completely devoid of political implications. Let me urge you, however, to join with me in declaring, so far as is possible, a moratorium on politics during the next session on many issues that are vital to the progress of Kentucky and its people. You and I have been entrusted by the people with the heavy responsibility of administering the affairs of their government for the next two years.

It is our responsibility—yours and mine—to work together to manage these affairs the best we can and to solve unfinished business. I am proud that Democrats and Republicans worked together to solve the Jefferson County school crisis. I am proud that we worked together to give our taxpayers protection from high and burdensome property levies once the Court of Appeals made its decision to assess all property at its fair cash value as the constitution requires. I am proud that Kentuckians, both

Republican and Democrat, from east and west, urban and rural areas, joined to give overwhelming approval to the state bond issue.

These examples demonstrate loudly and clearly what we can do if we put our shoulders to the wheel, cast aside our personal differences, and work for the good of our people and our children. It shows what we can do when we put first the fact that we are Kentuckians and second our political affiliation. At the next session of the legislature, there will be still other issues that will command a moratorium on politics.

I will propose to you legislation to provide stricter control of strip and auger mining to assure that our beautiful hillsides and rolling land are preserved for our children and our children's children. I will ask you to enact civil rights legislation to strengthen the federal law and make certain that every Kentuckian gets equal access to all public accommodations and equal treatment in job opportunities. You probably will want to give your attention to the senseless slaughter on our highways and the growing need to conserve our water. Our election laws are totally inadequate and unrealistic. They need to be rewritten so that they will provide a full and honest disclosure of campaign expenditures.

The writing of a new state constitution and the procedure to follow in placing it before the people for a vote should also be bipartisan. There will be changes in our insurance laws—a tightening of our laws to make certain that policyholders have greater protection. Our bailbond system is antiquated and needs modernization and reform. I personally believe that we should limit the use of capital punishment. And there are other issues that you will want to give your attention.

Many of these programs that I will propose will not be advanced without protest. But some small sacrifice is required if Kentucky is to maintain its place as a progressive state in this great nation. All of us must be prepared to take some punishment in order that our children may have the opportunities to which they are entitled.

In a message, on opening night at your invitation, I will present to you a budget to cover the needs of government for the next two years. It will be a balanced budget. There will be no fat in the budget, and it will not require new taxes or an increase in present taxes.

Receiving top priority will be our children and the schools they attend. Kentucky cannot afford to halt or to slow down the onward march of educational progress. Even the dramatic breakthroughs of the past few years must be measured against the forward movement which has been taking place in our sister states—so that we must move ahead just to stay where we are.

Today there is a new spirit in Kentucky. People are beginning to see that we can solve our problems. Neighboring states are beginning to regard us with new and greater respect. We no longer live in the past. And if we do what we can and should do at the next session, we will advance up the ladder of progress. We have taken the offensive and we can keep it.

Our rate of growth in personal income is running way ahead of the national average. In highway construction, school building, in seeking industry—we are making rapid progress. It will be our task in January to consolidate the gains that have been registered and see to it that our state moves ahead, steadily and unceasingly.

I believe, indeed, I know, that when the record of accomplishment is written, it will show that this membership comprises the best and the most productive General Assembly in our modern history.

During the next two days various commissioners and other persons who are working on programs that are vital to our progress will discuss them in detail with you. If between now and January you desire additional information on any aspect of these programs, please do not hesitate to contact my office or the appropriate agency in Frankfort. . . .[1]

---

1. At the conclusion of his speech Governor Breathitt introduced J.O. Matlick, commissioner of natural resources, the first of a series of speakers.

STATE OF THE COMMONWEALTH MESSAGE

Kentucky General Assembly
Frankfort / January 4, 1966

TONIGHT I come to you in a mood of both confidence and concern—confidence in reporting to you that never in the history of this Commonwealth has the path of our progress been so true, the future of our Commonwealth so bright, the economy of our Commonwealth so vigorous, or the state of our Commonwealth so sound.[1]

But confidence is not enough. Confidence without concern is a mental lotus land, where we grow deaf to the urgency of our unfinished business. Concern for that unfinished business is the dominant and pervasive theme of this occasion. Tonight you and I must join forces to establish new goals, take new measures, and mark new milestones in a partnership for progress.

Two years ago on this very spot I spoke in a similar vein. I proclaimed to this honorable body that the people of Kentucky did not choose me as their governor to preside over a standstill government or a caretaker administration. Tonight I say to you, as I said then, that there are no rest stops on the road to progress—and we have not rested.

As we proceed tonight to chart our compass for a voyage of further advancement, I think it both fair and helpful that we recognize the accomplishments—yes, the dramatic and unexcelled accomplishments—which vigorous leadership has brought to Kentucky during the past two years. We have unfinished business, we have serious problems, we have heavy responsibilities. All this you and I recognize fully. But let me make it clear that I do not come to apologize for, to extenuate or to obscure the record of the past two years—but rather to proclaim that record and to build upon it.

That record is already a part of Kentucky's experience and Kentucky's history. This is not the occasion to expound it in detail, but merely to summarize it with the broadest stroke:

The growth of our economy—more than a quarter of a billion dollars invested in new and expanded industry; our four-year goal of 75,000 new jobs more than met in less than two years; a more than 14 percent increase in personal income, and unemployment at the lowest level since records have been kept; agricultural production and the per capita increase of farm income at an all-time high.

In the education of our children—a substantial reduction in our high school dropout rate; an increase of more than 5,000 high school graduates in a single year; more than 2,800 new and modern classrooms constructed and under contract; teachers' salaries up approximately $500; nearly 50 percent of our college-age youth in institutions of higher learning; one-third of our first grade children graduates of the head start program; a solution for the school crisis in Louisville and Jefferson County; and a greater percentage increase in state appropriation for public education than any state in the nation during the past decade.

In the construction of a modern highway system—completion of the Blue Grass Parkway; construction of more than 145 miles of superhighways; commencement of the Appalachian program, including quick-start contracts to begin completion of the east Kentucky road system; improvement of 2,500 miles of additional roads, most of them farm-to-market and secondary arteries.

In meeting human needs and in building a happier, healthier Commonwealth—construction of fifty-five new hospitals; revamping our penal system with emphasis on rehabilitation rather than punishment, and the establishment of a professional career service in these institutions; the vocational rehabilitation of more than 4,000 handicapped Kentuckians.

These are not all the monuments for progress to which we could point, but they are enough to prove that the covenant between this General

Assembly and this governor made two years ago has pointed the way to the rest of the journey.

Tonight I shall outline to you our budget for the next biennium—a balanced budget, a prudent budget, a budgetary blueprint for further greatness in Kentucky. And a budget which calls for no new taxes.

Two years ago I submitted to this body a budget calling for biennial expenditures of $1.4 billion. The General Assembly accepted and approved that budget, demonstrating then its faith in the sincerity and accuracy of the executive branch of your state government. I told you, and my advisers told you, that our estimates of the revenue were responsible and realistic, and that we could achieve growth and progress without adding to the burden of Kentucky's taxpayers and without fiscal deficits.

There were those who told the 1964 General Assembly that the 1964 budget was unreasonable, fantastic, and irresponsible, and that our revenue estimates were politically padded. Tonight I am here to tell you that history has already proved us to have been right and our critics to have been wrong. Revenues have exceeded our estimates and our state has prospered even beyond what we thought she could do. The budget which I offer for your consideration tonight for the coming biennium is a $2.5 billion budget—a big budget for a big state.

It makes possible a substantial increase in the financing of many of our important governmental programs. It is both an indication of Kentucky's growth and an investment in Kentucky's growth. It will make possible better lives and better living for our people. But it is a careful budget, a well-planned budget, a budget designed to give priority to those things which are most vital to the growth and the vitality of an expanding Commonwealth.

Those who prepared this budget did not do so on a haphazard or scattergun basis. They did not simply look at the revenue estimates and then devise a plan to scatter dollars like confetti to a joyful populace. If the resources had been available, it would have been possible to spend three billion dollars or perhaps even four billion on the activities of your state government without fundamental waste and without unduly pampering needed programs.

This is not the way government operates. We are limited by the revenues which are available from our existing tax structures, because we are pledged not to impose new or increased taxes during this administration. Our problem, therefore, is to allocate limited resources to those activities which are most essential and which will provide the biggest dividends in progress for our people.

Let me assure you, as one who has sat through countless hours of budget hearings and who has worn out many lead pencils in this difficult task, that the decisions involved in the budget-making process are hard and painful; and that it is simply not possible to divert all of our limited resources to any one or two of our vital programs.

Take education, for example. There is little doubt that, if the money were available, we could justify increases in funds and education well beyond those which are contained in the proposed budget. But we could not ignore the needs of our old people, our sick people, and those suffering from mental illness. Likewise, I have no doubt that we could, without undue generosity, provide increases in old-age pensions larger than those which we have recommended in this budget. But we could not ignore the needs of education. What we have tried to do is to make the best possible allocation of available funds in the light of all of our most important needs.

We have not proposed to spend more than the existing revenues will provide. Neither have we left any cushion beyond that which prudence always dictates to avoid the danger of a deficit. Thus, I must point out to those who might be tempted to expand any one item in this budget that you can do so only at the expense of some other item or by the imposition of new or increased taxes. This budget contains no fat to be trimmed.

Having spoken in this cautious vein, I hasten to assure you that the proposed budget does provide for the expansion and the fuller financing of all our basic and essential programs. It is not a standstill budget. It is not a mark-time budget. It is a budget for progress, for growth—but for balanced progress and balanced growth.

I have said many times that education is the passkey to progress for Kentucky, both now and in the future. We have given it first place in our thinking and in our recommendations.

First, a substantial increase in teachers' salaries: $400 per classroom unit over the biennium; $200 for the first year and an additional $200 for the second. This marks a notable addition to the $500 salary increases which I pledged as a candidate in 1963. When added to the $500 increase voted in 1964, it marks a total increase of $900 in basic salaries during this administration, the second largest increase in any four-year period in the history of the Commonwealth, and the largest increase ever granted without new or higher taxes.

We also propose to place in operation a statewide educational television network during 1968, to accelerate rapidly our present vocational education program, to build twenty new vocational schools, to expand eight existing schools, and to relocate five others. This is a vital investment in job opportunities for both young people and adults, for Kentuckians of all races in the war against poverty and inequality.

We have recommended 110 additional classroom units for exceptional children, most all of them for the mentally retarded, which will provide facilities for 1,650 additional children; conversion of the Lincoln Institute into a secondary school for gifted youth so that the ablest young people shall not be barred from the fullest attainment by poverty; better salaries and more teachers at our School for the Blind and our School for the Deaf.

The dramatic increase in enrollments in our state-supported institutions of higher learning presents us with a great challenge and great opportunity. We have recommended an increase of approximately $45 million for higher education—including our university, our five state colleges, and our community colleges. This represents an increase in funds for higher education of 49 percent and, when taken in connection with the increase made in the last budget, represents an expansion of 120 percent, by far the largest increase in any four-year period.

Enrollments are expanding far more rapidly in our institutions of higher learning than in our elementary and secondary schools. We anticipate an increase of nearly 30 percent in the number of students at our state-supported colleges and universities through the next two years. Consequently, large increases and appropriations are necessary merely to provide facilities and personnel for expanded enrollment.

We propose three new community colleges: in the Hazard-Blackey area, in Maysville, and in Jefferson County, thus giving evidence of our purpose and goal of bringing this type of education within the reach of an ever greater number of our young people and a greater number of communities.[2] We recommend a scholarship program to supplement the federal program so that more students will be able to further their education.[3]

Kentucky's highway program for the next biennium will total more than $500 million for the first time in history. We shall move on to complete the interstate system; to carry out the Appalachian program; to meet the regular federal-aid highway matching funds; and to improve more than 2,000 miles of important rural and secondary roads. In addition, we plan construction of two new toll roads: the Jackson Purchase Parkway and the Pennyrile Parkway.

During the coming biennium we anticipate a graduated substantial increase in revenue for the Road Fund from existing sources. Our construction program alone will exceed $300 million; the costs of maintaining our highways will exceed $50 million, all provided from state funds. Nearly $69 million will be spent on rural, secondary, and county road aid programs. Our highway program is not only an important contribution to the comfort and convenience of our citizens, but an indispensable tool in economic, industrial, and agricultural development, providing access to our communities for new industries, additional mobility for our labor force, and better markets for the products of our farms.

In the preparation of this budget, we have not been deaf to the call of human needs—our senior citizens, the mentally ill, our retarded children, the blind, the sick, and those imprisoned by poverty. We intend to increase old-age pensions by an average between four and six dollars per month—two dollars of which will begin with the checks for this month and the remainder of which will commence on July 1, 1966. State funds should be provided to implement fully the 1965 Medicare program so that an additional 60,000 Kentucky senior citizens may qualify for participation in it. And we intend to broaden Medicare services to include cost of care by physicians in hospitals, for x-ray services, and to expand the Kerr-Mills program. We are proposing increases in the monthly payments for the blind and the totally disabled similar to those recommended for old-age pensions.

Likewise, the budget will expand the food stamp program to include thirty-nine counties—twenty-four in addition to the fifteen counties where the plan is now in operation. When the expanded proposal is in full operation, the food stamp plan, financed largely with federal funds, would buy groceries worth $13 million per year. We also propose to extend the program for unemployed parents to include thirty-nine counties—an additional twenty counties added to the nineteen where the program is now in effect. This program also is financed almost entirely by federal funds.

In the vital field of public health, we are recommending increased appropriations to permit over 40,000 tests designed to detect cancer in its early stages among women who are unable to pay for such tests; to expand tuberculosis skin tests for 440,000 persons; and to expand activities in protecting our people against water pollution and air pollution.

In the field of mental health, we are recommending an increase of 27 percent over the sum budgeted by the 1964 General Assembly—the largest appropriation for mental health in the history of our Commonwealth. This will make it possible for us to establish and operate twenty new centers for the mentally ill, permitting many hundreds of patients suffering from mental illness to remain at home and receive treatment from their own communities. We are also providing funds for two small residential units for retarded children in Jefferson County; to hire new psychiatrists for our state mental hospitals; and to improve the care for all patients in our institutions assisting the mentally ill.

We are also recommending bigger appropriations for the Department of Public Safety: to start a ten-year program for 500 additional troopers, adding 50 during the coming fiscal year and another 50 in the second year of the biennium; to increase beginning salaries for troopers to $415 per month; and to put radio operators on a five-day week.

Our correctional programs must also be upgraded. We must add to the professional staff of our institutions; put our correctional officers on a five-day week; increase the number of probation and parole officers; open a new forestry camp, a new farm dormitory at LaGrange, and another at Eddyville.

In the area of child welfare, funds are provided to increase the number of placements in foster homes by 250. Funds are also recommended for activating a new camp for boys and a new camp for girls.

Construction costs for park facilities total an estimated $12 million. Funds also are provided to staff two new parks and accelerate tourist and industrial promotion. Funds for all these proposals are recommended in the budget.

This is but a summary of the high spots in our proposed budget. I am submitting to you at the same time a more extended discussion which we call the "Budget in Brief." It explains in some detail the contents of the executive budget which I am also submitting, and in turn which forms the basis of the biennial appropriation bill which will be introduced tonight.

In addition to the budget there are some legislative matters which are so important that I must discuss them with you briefly at this time.

Throughout the nation there is a growing awareness of the priceless value of our natural resources—the earth and its waters, its minerals and vegetation and scenery. Just as Kentucky is second to no state in the richness of its earth, so must we be second to none in our concern for it and protection of it. We are fortunate in having a strong foundation of conservation laws on which to build, and I will ask you to strengthen these with significant but carefully designed new approaches to the old problems of conservation.

Foremost among the matters requiring your consideration is that of strip-mine regulation. Experience over the past two years has shown that, despite the most conscientious and energetic efforts at enforcement, our present laws are not adequate to protect the people or their land and to deal fairly with the coal industry. I want, and I know you want, the coal industry, like all industries, to flourish in Kentucky. But people deserve protection from the adverse effects of any industry, just as the owners of industry deserve fair, clear and consistent regulation, and I assure you that the bill I shall propose to you will be as strict but as fair as any in the United States.[4]

It will protect a man's rights upon his own land. It will require restoration to useful surface of land disturbed by area stripping, and the terracing of cuts made by contour stripping. And it will require of operators no measure not demanded by other states where operators have complied without going out of business.

Aside from the regulation of strip mining, I will ask you to create a Water Resources Authority, which will insure an adequate supply of clean water for our growing population and industrial complex.[5] I hope you will tighten our antilitter laws to make it illegal to dump trash and litter, not only on roadways but in waterways and on all lands, public and private, not designated for that purpose.[6]

I will also propose to you a bill regulating access roads used in logging operations, in order to make our access road regulations uniform for all industries.[7] And I will ask you to effect changes in our present laws to make Kentucky conform with provisions of the Interstate Compact on Strip Mining which I have championed, specifically those provisions dealing with surface disturbance.[8]

Let me repeat: It is not the intention of this administration to put any industry out of business, or deprive our people of jobs. On the contrary, it is the purpose of this legislation to create jobs and job opportunities, and to avert disasters which have blighted the economies of regions where natural resources were not protected. Jobs need not be created at the expense of the earth which holds the key to today's prosperity and tomorrow's promise, nor should they be used as an excuse for men who would ravage our hills, spoil our streams, and dim Kentucky's bright legacy of natural beauty.

Now, finally, I am compelled to state to you my conviction that all of our programs, all the activities of our government, all the aims of our public policy are based upon the fundamental proposition that all men—black, white, brown, or yellow—must stand equal under God and the law. We mock the fatherhood of God and the brotherhood of man, we scorn the Declaration of Independence and the Constitution of the United States, we compromise the position of our nation and our state before the world, and we belie all the prompting of our consciences so long as our fellow citizens are subject to humiliation, discrimination and economic or social penalties based on color.

The Congress of the United States in 1964 enacted federal legislation. The Civil Rights Act of 1964 makes it possible for the states, by enacting laws of their own, to participate in the enforcement of federal policy. This alone would justify the enactment of state legislation. However, there are additional and important reasons which impel me to recommend the passage of a state civil rights law. Certain types of public accommodations in which many of our citizens suffer from discrimination are not governed by federal statutes. Similarly, the limitations contained in the fair employment provisions of the federal law deprive a large number of Kentuckians of its protection.

I feel strongly that we should fill both these gaps in the Civil Rights Act of 1964 by the passage of state legislation based upon the same fundamental principles as the federal law by extending additional protection to our fellow Kentuckians.[9] There is now, I believe, a general and widespread acceptance of the basic philosophy of the Civil Rights Act of 1964 and of the moral imperative which undergirded it. So as long as the states fail to meet their responsibility in this field, there will be ever increasing determination for more and stronger federal intervention.[10]

I feel, and feel most deeply, that it is time for us in Kentucky to meet our responsibilities, and to let each one of our fellow Kentuckians feel no doubt that we accept him fully and freely as a citizen of this Commonwealth not because of or in spite of the color of his skin, but because he is a human being entitled to all the fullness of humanity.

There will be introduced tonight a civil rights act, a bill for the better control of strip and auger mining, and a budget bill. I urge upon you immediate consideration of all three. Additional legislation will be offered shortly dealing with many other needs, and I may from time to time communicate with you in regard to such measures, including the elimination of gambling on pinball machines, the inspection of motor vehicles to protect the public safety, more adequate provisions for unemployment compensation, the reform of our bail bond system, the strengthening of our insurance laws, as well as other matters.[11]

We have much work to do. Our unfinished business is big business and cannot be dealt with easily or lightly. We can reach our goals only by cooperative effort. We have a joint responsibility which we must jointly discharge. Since I last sat where you are now sitting, ten years ago, I have watched the legislative branch of our government with pride and appreciation. The quality of its membership and the quality of its work have steadily improved. The people of this Commonwealth have a right to be proud, and they are proud, of the manner in which their senators and representatives have contributed, especially during the recent decade, to the extension of the frontiers of Kentucky's progress in all aspects of government.

It is both the difficulty and the glory of progress that it never stops, that its goals are always incomplete, that those who work forward are never allowed to be at ease in Zion. The more we do the more there is left for us to do. The more successfully we struggle, the more we are involved in newly and ever more complex struggles to realize the promise of a future which we can sometimes perceive only in a dim and uncertain light.

Because those who have sat in your seats, and those who have stood in my place have accepted those challenges in past years, we have moved ahead in this Commonwealth and we are moving steadily ahead today. Let us tonight rededicate ourselves to the spirit which has made possible the gains of the past, the gains of the present, and which will open the door to a future which will make our children and those who come after them rejoice that we were given a part in the march of Kentucky's progress.

---

1. In 1964 Governor Breathitt delivered separate budget and State of the Commonwealth addresses. Two years later he combined the messages. By 1966 Breathitt, who admitted political shortcomings in the 1964 session, had consoli-

dated his power and he dominated the 1966 session. The budget was designed by the governor and his executive departments alone and was submitted to the House in summary form only two days before it was voted upon. Administration supporters were successful in limiting debate and preventing amendments. A Chandler supporter, obviously irritated with the proceedings of the 1966 session, complained "we have one-man government in Frankfort." The consolidation of Breathitt's power reflected both his political skill and the success of his economic development program. His handling of the thorny tax issue in the 1965 special session reflected a growing political effectiveness that would be unpleasantly apparent to administration opponents in 1966. The economic development program, spurred by an upturn in the national economy and the infusion of federal money into the state, generated approximately $100 million in increased state revenue between 1963 and 1966. The 1966 $2 billion budget, 27 percent higher than the 1964 outlay, included appropriations for most political districts that made it difficult for their representatives to oppose. Clearly, Breathitt's increased political power was instrumental in the passage of civil rights legislation and a strict strip-mine bill in the 1966 legislature. For an excellent analysis of the political circumstances of the 1966 legislative session, see James Ott, "Kentucky's Bullfighter," undated clipping from the *Cincinnati Enquirer* in the Press Release file, Breathitt papers.

2. An act of the 1966 General Assembly gave the University of Kentucky control of the community college system and mandated that community colleges be maintained in Ashland, Covington, Cumberland, Elizabethtown, Henderson, Hopkinsville, Prestonsburg, Somerset, Blackey-Hazard, Jefferson County, and Mason County. *Acts, 1966,* Chapter 6 (H.B. 238), pp. 99-104. Paducah Junior College, a well-established two-year institution, was authorized to be included in the University of Kentucky Community College System under separate legislation. See *Acts, 1966,* Chapter 189 (H.B. 501), pp. 821-22.

3. See "An act relating to higher education assistance," *Acts, 1966,* Chapter 93 (S.B. 294), pp. 513-22.

4. The 1966 strip-mine law created in the Department of Natural Resources a Strip Mining and Reclamation Commission empowered to adopt rules and regulations pertaining to strip mining; conduct hearings under the act on regulations adopted by the commission; subpoena witnesses; require production of "books, papers, correspondence, memoranda, agreements or other documents of records" which the commission deemed relevant to its inquiry; issue orders, after hearings, to operators to comply with provisions of the 1966 law or regulations adopted by the commission; and revoke the permit of an operation. *Acts, 1966,* Chapter 4 (H.B. 36), pp. 63-96.

5. The 1966 General Assembly enacted legislation creating the Water Resources Authority of Kentucky. The authority consisted of the governor; the commissioners of natural resources, finance, health, commerce, agriculture; and the attorney general. It was authorized to construct water resource projects and acquire lands deemed necessary to accomplish the purposes of the authority. See "an act relating to the conservation, development and wise use of the water, soil, forest, and other natural resources of the Commonwealth." *Acts, 1966,* Chapter 23 (H.B. 260), pp. 178-226.

6. In keeping with the "Keep America Beautiful" campaign of the Johnson administration, the legislature adopted a series of laws relating to abandoned automobiles, junkyards, and advertising adjacent to interstate highways. *Acts, 1966,* Chapter 105 (H.B. 59), pp. 532-33; Chapter 162 (H.B. 337), pp. 689-93; and Chapter 76 (S.B. 192), pp. 446-49.

7. "An act providing for the construction of industrial access roads" empowered fiscal courts, upon the recommendation of the county road engineer, to construct access roads that "would serve as an inducement to industrial location or a substantial expansion of industry. . . ." *Acts, 1966,* Chapter 191 (H.B. 512), pp. 822-23.

8. Although Governor Breathitt, in several speeches, made a strong appeal for the necessity of effective interstate cooperation to control strip mining, the 1966 legislation authorizing Kentucky's participation in an interstate mining compact provided for cooperation, fact finding, and technical assistance rather than regulation. *Acts, 1966,* Chapter 4 (H.B. 36), pp. 63-96.

9. See "an act to prevent discrimination in employment and public accommodations within the Commonwealth of Kentucky," *Acts, 1966,* Chapter 2 (H.B. 2), pp. 43-62. In a related and little-noticed action, the General Assembly amended a series of sections of the Kentucky Revised Statutes requiring discrimination on the basis of race. *Acts, 1966,* Chapter 184 (H.B. 475), pp. 800-03.

10. Governor Breathitt frequently emphasized his opinion that the surest guarantee of federal intervention into areas normally under state jurisdiction was the failure of states to exercise their responsibility.

11. See "an act relating to gambling," *Acts, 1966,* Chapter 5 (S.B. 104), pp. 96-99; "an act relating to motor vehicle inspection," Chapter 115 (H.B. 256), pp. 550-56; and "an act relating to unemployment insurance," Chapter 28 (H.B. 111), pp. 246-48. Reform of the bail bond system awaited the administration of Governor Julian Carroll. The 1966 General Assembly passed several acts relating to the insurance industry.

ADDRESS TO JOINT SESSION OF THE 1966 LEGISLATURE
Frankfort / February 23, 1966

MORE than four weeks ago, on January 21, I appointed a Commission to Help Education. I named myself as chairman of this commission because I believe that the governor of this Commonwealth has a basic responsibility for leadership in providing better educational opportunities for our young people.[1]

In the budget which I submitted to your bodies, my recommendation for increased educational appropriations was the largest sum which I could conscientiously recommend in the light of then existing revenue estimates. Those recommendations, taken with the increased appropriations which I recommended and which the 1964 General Assembly provided, made possible the second largest increase in teachers' salaries in any administration in the history of the Commonwealth—exceeded only by the increases provided in the administration of Governor Combs at the time when the 3 percent sales tax became effective.

As a candidate for governor in 1963, I made certain commitments and pledges to the children, parents, teachers, and school administrators of Kentucky. Every promise, every commitment which I made as a candidate, has been met and more than met. At the same time, as a candidate, I committed myself to oppose any new taxes or any increase in existing taxes by state government. That commitment, like all other pledges which I made, was public, open, and unequivocal. Everyone who supported me and everyone who opposed me knew of that commitment—including the friends of education. That commitment also has been kept. Despite this, some individuals—perhaps from honest misunderstanding, perhaps from a yearning to muddy political waters—have repeatedly sought to confuse and befuddle the people of Kentucky with respect to this promise. Let me repeat that my pledge was a pledge of opposition to new or increased state taxes. I did not promise that all property would be assessed, or continue to be assessed, at valuations far below those prescribed by our state constitution. I did not promise that no fiscal court, no city council, no local school board would change the rates or the forms of taxation at the local level. I could not have made this promise because our fiscal courts, our city councils, and our school boards are elected by the people of the various districts, and they are not subject to the governor's dictation in the exercise of their independent powers.

On the contrary, both as a candidate for governor and during the entire period of my administration, I have constantly emphasized the importance of a better balance between state and local contributions to the financing of our educational progress. When the Court of Appeals, members of which were all elected by the people and not a single one of whom was appointed by me, decided that the plain language of the constitution with respect to property assessments must be followed, I called a special session of the General Assembly to prevent the skyrocketing of local taxes as a result of the court's decision. At this special session, we achieved what seems to me—and I think to most of the thinking people of our state—a workable balance: legislation which on the one hand guarantees the taxpayer against punitive and crushing burdens, and on the other hand made available substantial increases in local revenue for our local school districts if the elected members of our local school boards chose to avail themselves of it. Let me remind you and the people of our state that the total additional resources made available to local school districts under the legislation enacted at the special session in 1965 could amount to almost $25 million during the years 1966 and 1967. This, of course, is in addition to the increased funds provided in the budget which I recommended and which you have already enacted into law. Yet I should be the first to admit that sometimes even our best is not good enough.

Despite all the efforts which we have made in recent years and which we have made in the recent budget to improve the lot of our teachers, we have still fallen behind other states which have also recognized the importance of well-qualified, well-paid teachers.[2] Here in Kentucky, we have been increasing, and consistently increasing, teachers' salaries. Most of this increase, indeed practically all of it, has come from state support, while at the same time local effort has been lagging and dragging. In the percentage of state support for education Kentucky ranks twelfth from the top among all the states, but in the percentage of local support we rank very low. I realize that even many of our school people are inclined to assume that it is easier to obtain additional funds on the state level and are disinclined to face the sometimes unpleasant task of seeking additional local support for educational progress. For the long pull, we simply cannot afford to continue or to accentuate the imbalance between state and local support for education. We must revitalize a partnership between state and local government, with each shouldering a fair share of total educational cost.

These are the problems which faced our commission: First, a dramatic and well-based demonstration of the inadequacies of current salary levels even after the increases provided in the 1966 budget. Second, the need for additional funds for capital outlay, in ending one-room schools, in providing new classrooms in areas of growing population and replacing obsolete buildings. Third, an unbalanced fiscal situation as between state and local effort. And, fourth, a commitment by this administration against new taxes at the state level.

The commission was made up of twenty outstanding Kentuckians: six members of the General Assembly, six educators, three of whom are classroom teachers, and six representative citizens. Dr. Harry Sparks, our able superintendent of public instruction, served as vicechairman.[3]

Our commission undertook to determine, with as much thoroughness as possible in a short time, the adequacy of our existing salary schedules both in terms of overall salary and in terms of the proper incentive and reward for competent, experienced teachers. Second, the [commission considered the] means available to finance such additional salary increases and expenditures for new classrooms and other operating costs as might prove necessary at this time.

The commission has completed its labors, or at least the first phase of its labors, and on behalf of the commission I bring you their report and their recommendations tonight for your consideration. I believe that the recommendations which the commission has made can and will bring about a remarkable improvement in Kentucky's school system, can and will mark a historical advancement in our educational progress.

The commission has thoroughly reviewed teachers' salaries in Kentucky and has compared the salary levels with those prevailing in other states. Among all the states of the nation, we found that Kentucky ranks forty-sixth in average annual salaries for our teachers. This situation we felt to be intolerable. It may be a long time before we attain front rank or even the national average in this respect, but we cannot be content with forty-sixth place. Furthermore, the commission discovered that while we are first among all the states in the southeastern region in salaries for beginning teachers, we are next to the bottom even among southern states in average salaries.

The commission, therefore, recommends substantial additional increases in teachers' salaries and especially a better break for our experienced and more highly trained teachers. The members of the commission have recommended that, in addition to the increases provided in the current budget, we appropriate $24 million in the next biennium in order to provide, over a two-year period, the amount requested by the Kentucky Education Association Delegate Assembly last December. The commission concluded that these funds would necessarily have to come primarily, if not entirely, from state revenue.

We have found that this can be done, that these salary increases can be provided out of anticipated current revenue from an economy expanded at a much faster rate than we had realized in December and early January, and by a speedup in the collection of corporation income taxes. I do not recommend that any part of this plan be financed at the expense of the teacher retirement benefits provided in House Bill 104, which I hope will be promptly passed.[4]

Let me make it clear that these are not financial gimmicks, that our revenue estimates are—as they have always been—carefully considered and not based upon political considerations or upon dictation from the governor. When I addressed you in January, our then existing revenue estimates were based upon the situation as it appeared early in December. Since that time, the pace of financial support for the war in Viet Nam has accelerated.[5] Since that time the president has submitted his budget to the Congress. Since that time the Council of Economic Advisors has revealed its prognosis for the national economy during the coming year. Since that time agency after agency and individual after individual, both public and private, have projected and predicted an economic growth for 1966 which is markedly in excess of what they had predicted and what we had anticipated. On the basis of those estimates, together with the technical change which I have mentioned before, I am prepared to recommend that you appropriate the additional sums recommended by our Commission to Help Education, and I am prepared to give you my opinion that this can be done within the existing revenue structure.

Since our Department of Revenue was established in 1936, its staff and its personnel have earned and enjoyed a nationwide reputation for care and accuracy in estimating the revenues. Two years ago, I based my budget, and the General Assembly based its budget, on the predictions and estimates of the Department of Revenue. And there were those political scoffers who said that the estimates were padded and that the budget was a political makeshift. But the proof of the pudding is in the eating, and the revenue estimates of 1964 have proved conservative and accurate. The budget of 1964 has proved to be a balanced budget, and we shall end the current fiscal year with a surplus. The change in estimates which has come since early December and on which our present recommendations are based is due to the quickened pace of our economy and to the moderate inflationary pressures which have been evident in recent months. All of us can be gratified that our teachers will obtain the full benefit of this stepped-up economic growth and that we can give them a well-deserved, well-earned, overdue break out of the dividends from a dynamic economy.

Our commission has not limited its recommendations to a request for more money for our teachers. The members of the commission have unanimously agreed that quality education requires a change in the method of distributing appropriations to our school districts and in the method by which our salary scales are established.

We want two basic safeguards to assure that the money which you appropriate for salaries will in effect go to our teachers, and that money will have the greatest possible impact in improving the quality of our education. First, the commission unanimously recommends that an index system be used in distributing state appropriations for teachers' salaries. This system, which will give greater reward for teaching experience as well as academic progress, is endorsed by the Kentucky Education Association Delegate Assembly and the National Education Association. Under our present ranking system, the commission has discovered that Kentucky is at the top among all southeastern states in salary scales paid to beginning teachers, and at the bottom in salaries paid to teachers with ten years' experience. This has caused many of our able young teachers to start in a Kentucky school system but to leave our state after having gained experience in order to go to some other state where that experience is more adequately compensated.

The commission has also requested that appropriate bills and legislation provide assurance that the budgets of local school districts, before being approved by the state Department of Education, maintain existing salary schedules and fund them in such a way that the money provided by the legislature for teachers' salaries will actually find its way into the teachers' pockets.

The commission has also recognized that, in addition to better salaries for our teachers, we must have additional resources to eliminate our 481 one-room schools and to build the 3,749 new classrooms which are required. The commission recommended that responsibility for this additional effort should be laid primarily upon local school districts; but the commission has felt that local districts must be provided with new sources of revenue to meet such needs—sources at the local level to be drawn on by local decision.

If you adopt the recommendations of the commission, local school districts will have access to three alternate sources of additional revenue for the purpose of meeting requirements for classroom construction and general operating expenses. Let me make it clear once more that each of these sources of revenue would be available, but could only be drawn upon by decision of the local school board itself; that only one of the three new sources could be utilized; and that all these new sources would be subject to a recall referendum on petition of 15 percent of the voters in the local school district similar to the provision contained in the legislation authorizing the occupational tax for education in Louisville and Jefferson County. These three new sources of revenue are: (1) a license tax measured by net income of individuals; (2) an occupational license tax measured by wages, salaries, and profits; and (3) a license tax based upon furnishing telephone and telegraphic, gas, water, and electric service.[6]

In addition, of course, local school boards already have it within their power, if they choose to exercise that power, to levy up to 10 percent increases in property taxes authorized at the special session in 1965. The commission believes that use of these sources of revenue, and with the growth in property values and property improvement in many of our local areas, it will be possible to finance the more urgent need for classroom construction and operating expense in the overwhelming majority of our school districts.

I believe that all of you will agree with me that the members of the commission have made recommendations which will assist in the solution of our current crisis and will make possible dramatic educational progress in our state in the immediate future. However, the commission has wisely recognized that this is a long-range problem which cannot be solved overnight and that many vexing issues will arise in the future even after you have acted upon the recommendations of the commission. I therefore join the other members of the commission in recommending that it be established as a permanent statutory body to advise the governor, the General Assembly, and the Department of Education with respect to all the problems, financial and otherwise, which are involved in an effort to provide education of ever increasing quality for our young men and women at the elementary and secondary level.

Let me say one final word to those who have been inclined toward impatience with the pace at which we have been proceeding toward objectives with which we all agree. The people of Kentucky and the legislators of Kentucky have not been stingy or niggardly with our teachers and with our educational system. We are not at the top of the states in wealth or in per capita income, any more than we are at the top in teachers' salaries or in total education expenditures. Within the past decade Kentuckians have twice accepted, and cheerfully accepted, substantial increases in their tax burdens, most of the revenue of which has gone to education. Let me point out that, if you accept my recommendations, our teachers will have received during this administration the largest salary increases ever provided during any administration in the history of this Commonwealth—and all this without an increase in our state taxes.

We are making progress in Kentucky—industrial progress, agricultural progress, progress in solving the problems of Appalachia, progress in our highway system, progress in meeting human needs. In accepting these recommendations, you will once more demonstrate to the people of Kentucky and of the nation that education comes first with Kentuckians and that we are determined that our children and those responsible for the training of our future leaders and citizens will receive the recognition and the reward which is due to their efforts and due to the magnitude of their responsibilities, insofar as that lies within our power.

---

1. The Commission to Help Education, appointed by Governor Breathitt on January 21, 1966, included the governor as chairman, Dr. Harry M. Sparks, state superintendent of public instruction as vice chairman, Martha Comer, Maurice Henry, Jack Tankersley, Dr. John Bell, Martha Dell Sanders, Mrs. Carl Reeves, Newton Thomas, Conrad Ott, Maurice Dodson, J.T. Clifton, Durham Howard, Tom Garrett, Norbert Blume, Phillip King, Burl St. Clair, Alex McIntyre, and Terry McBrayer. The appointment of the committee came in response to a vote by the 600 teacher-member Kentucky Education Association Delegate Assembly to stage a one-day walkout on February 3 and to seek "severe sanctions" if additional funding for education was not forthcoming. *Louisville Courier-Journal,* January 22, 1966.

2. In 1966 the average teacher salary in Kentucky was $4,930. Only Arkansas, Mississippi, South Carolina, and South Dakota paid lower salaries. U.S. Depart-

ment of Commerce, *Statistical Abstract of the United States, 1966* (Washington, D.C., 1966), p. 127.

3. Harry Magee Sparks (1907-), A.B., Transylvania College (1930); E.D., University of Kentucky (1954); teacher, coach, principal, Kentucky public schools (1930-1948); professor of education, Murray State University (1948-1952); chairman of department (1952-1964); superintendent of public instruction, Commonwealth of Kentucky (1964-1968); president, Murray State University (1968-1973). *Who's Who in American Education 1967-68* (Nashville, Tenn., 1968).

4. See "an act relating to the teacher's retirement system of the state of Kentucky," *Acts, 1966,* Chapter 16 (H.B. 104), pp. 124-37. The act was approved March 4, 1966.

5. By early 1966 the cost of the war in Vietnam was forcing the Johnson administration to make choices between continued social programs and the ever increasing demands for more men and supplies in Southeast Asia.

6. See "an act relating to education and the financing thereof," *Acts, 1966,* Chapter 24 (H.B. 471), pp. 226-40.

ECONOMIC & INDUSTRIAL DEVELOPMENT

BOWLING GREEN–WARREN COUNTY CHAMBER OF COMMERCE
Bowling Green / January 15, 1964

It is a pleasure to be here tonight to visit with leaders of one of Kentucky's most progressive communities and one that holds such great promise for the future.[1] The growth of your area is among the fastest in the state. Your industry thrives. You are an important trading center for a large segment of Kentucky. You are among our state's leaders in education and culture. Your farms are prosperous and productive. Your leadership is active and imaginative. Your landscape has great natural beauty and your streets and buildings are inviting. You live in a place that is a good place to live. This you believe and this you tell your industrial prospects and other prospective new residents.

Many things have happened in Bowling Green and Warren County and throughout Kentucky to make life better within the last few years. Not the least of these, I believe, is the coming into being of new awareness of possibilities for progress within our state and our communities. You have this awareness and you have a determination to achieve that progress. I salute you for it.

Kentucky has prospered generally during the last several years, and tonight I would like to review some of the reasons for that prosperity and explore some of the things we must do to build even greater prosperity and happiness in the future. I am acutely aware, of course, that not all of our state is as fortunate as this community, my home communiity of Hopkinsville, and other cities where business is good, people have jobs, and living is at a high standard.

A vast area of our state is depressed—chronically depressed—people are hungry, jobless, cold, and bordering on despair. They have lived for years only on government relief and handouts from charitable groups. These areas and these people must have priority on whatever abilities the state will have to institute new programs to improve the economy during the present administration. This is not true simply because of a feeling of humanitarianism, although compassion certainly enters into it. It is true because no section, no community in Kentucky—Bowling Green, Hopkinsville, the Bluegrass, Louisville or any other—can reach its highest level of prosperity or achieve its potential as a place to live happily while neighboring communities and neighboring Kentuckians suffer from want and neglect.

What are some of the things that have happened during the last few years to advance Kentucky, to give us a better base on which to build tomorrow's prosperity? First, our schools have become better than ever before. Education—and good education—is a requisite for successful execution of today's jobs in industry and business. Today we have more people who are better educated—more people who are thus eligible for employment. Gains have been made not only in our elementary and secondary schools but in higher education and in vocational schools. Kentucky's system of vocational schools is one of the finest in the nation and is improving. It is possible today for a prospective employer to find skilled or trainable help in practically any part of Kentucky.

Our highway system has set records for construction, bringing all sections of the Commonwealth closer together and tying us more firmly to our sister states. Good transportation is a necessity for industry, and each mile of our interstate system or parkways system completed has meant jobs and payrolls not only for the communities served directly but for the state as a whole.

We have established the outstanding state parks system in the United States and are using it as a means of promoting a rapidly expanding tourist industry that pays money into our gasoline stations, our grocery and clothing stores, our hotels and motels, and our places of amusement, and pays taxes into our state treasury. Our tax base has been broadened to induce new industry and industrial expansion, and our taxation is more equitable than ever before.

And, certainly not least, Kentucky has gone all out in its effort to promote new and expanded industry, to show the advantages of our state as a place to live, to do business, and to prosper. We have advertised our advantages all over this nation. We have sent our emissaries wherever interest in Kentucky has been indicated, and we have instigated and nurtured interest where it did not exist. The results of these programs—and others not quite so major or so evident—are more industries, more jobs, bigger payrolls, and a per capita income that is rising faster than that of the nation as a whole.

I speak of progress made before the start of this administration. I pay tribute to that progress and to those who had a hand in it, but I would like to look to the future for a few minutes and to the things we must do to continue our upward journey. First, we will persist in our efforts to publicize Kentucky as a good place for industry to locate. Our advertising and promotion may take a little different form from previous procedures, but it will be no less dedicated, no less intense. As your governor, I intend to do some of this promoting. Where I am needed, I will go. Where I can profitably put in a word, I will do so.

Second, we will keep our present tax structure and our present tax rates. We will always try to improve our tax administration and our internal procedures to make our taxes more equitable for all our citizens, however.

We will boost our support to Kentucky's school system. You and all Kentuckians are no doubt aware of my pledge to that portion of the Kentucky Education Association program that calls for a $500 raise in teachers' salaries during this biennium. That pledge will be honored, and I am confident it will result in higher standards of teaching and better opportunities for our children.

We will continue and expand our vocational training program. The federal government has recently given us a big boost in this effort through a $9 million grant for job training in our Appalachian counties.[2] This massive undertaking will benefit not only those counties directly involved but the state as a whole.

We will continue our support of higher education, including your own great college of which we are all so proud. We will not give our colleges all we would like to give them, but we will do our best within budget limitations.

Our highway program will continue at all levels—interstate, turnpikes, primary, secondary, and rural. We will double the rural highway fund, as promised, during this biennium. Soon Bowling Green will be served directly by an interstate highway, and soon you will have easier access to the Western Kentucky Parkway via a new bridge at Honaker's Ferry. I am not able at this time to say exactly when this will be, but it will be as soon as possible.

Our park and tourist promotion program will continue and expand. The full impact of our park construction of the last two or three years will only be felt this year, and we look for 1964 to set a new record for tourist dollars.

We plan to promote agriculture as never before as we push toward a billion-dollar farm economy. Agriculture-based industries have shown a big gain in Kentucky during the last few years, and we plan to sustain and accelerate that rate of growth.

It is a fond hope of mine that we will be able to write and pass a new constitution that will replace the old, outmoded, restrictive one we have now. I fully believe that such a move will help business and industry in Kentucky and will help all our citizens by providing a better base for statutory law. Just before this meeting I visited with one of your most distinguished citizens—indeed one of the most distinguished of all Kentuckians—Judge John B. Rodes.[3] I discussed the matter of a new constitution with him and found him as interested and imaginative as ever concerning this subject. I would like to say tonight that if I have my way as one of those who appoint delegates to the constitutional convention we plan, and if he is willing to serve, Judge Rodes will represent this district at the convention.

I am sure you are aware that this administration hopes to help Kentucky acquire 75,000 new jobs during the next four years. I have outlined some of the programs we plan that will boost our economy and provide new jobs and payrolls—improvement of schools and highways, tourist and industrial promotion, vocational training, constitutional reform, equitable taxation, and promotion of agriculture. All these programs will help, but they will not be enough. We can reach our goal of 75,000 new jobs only through the concerted effort and the complete dedication of individuals such as you and of organizations such as yours all over Kentucky.

This is the first speech I have delivered to a group of this type since I have been governor, and so it is the first opportunity I have had to implore a civic club or a chamber of commerce to get behind this job expansion program. I ask you to look around you, to use your imagination, to be challenged by this goal. Think hard of things that can be done in Bowling Green and Warren County to expand your economy, to build your industrial base, to create more jobs.

I do not imply by this that you have not been thinking—certainly it is the business of organizations such as yours to think and promote. But I would like for you to take a second thought, for you to go a little beyond your usual promotional efforts, effective as they may be.

For this is a special and extraordinary project we are undertaking—one that will mean greater prosperity for all our citizens, an easing of the chronic depression in parts of our state, a reversal of the population trend that has us now losing a representative in Congress every ten years.[4] It is a project I am going to ask all Kentuckians to be a part of. After you have done your share of thinking, after you have employed your imagination to the fullest and the time has come to act, if we can be of service to you in Frankfort, let us know.

I pledge to you that we will be thinking, we will be planning, we will be working. Together we can reach our goal, together we can create 75,000 new jobs for Kentucky. Together we can make your city, your county—and all Kentucky—a better, more prosperous place to live.

---

1. Governor Breathitt's address to the Bowling Green-Warren County Chamber of Commerce was one of his earliest statements on economic development, and it set the tone for dozens more delivered across the Commonwealth between 1963 and 1967. In his campaign for governor he established several specific economic development goals, including 75,000 new jobs and an annual billion-dollar farm economy. His economic development speeches, which constitute approximately 30 percent of his public addresses, characteristically focused upon his administration's progress in meeting the goals outlined in his election campaign. Thus, most of his speeches relating to economic development reported developments of specific interest to his audience and progress on a variety of economic fronts. Only rarely did he devote an entire address to a single topic. Moreover, Governor Breathitt viewed most concerns of his administration to be directly or indirectly related to economic development. Therefore, although state support for education was intrinsically valuable, the governor frequently discussed education as a tool to provide the managerial and manpower skill to attract new industry. Similarly, the $176 million bond issue, highway development, parks and tourism, constitutional revision, and many other areas of administrative attention were often viewed from the perspective of their potential for economic development. Breathitt, reflecting this perspective, frequently employed the phrase "a seamless web" in describing economic development in the Commonwealth.

2. A program providing job training for residents of forty-four eastern Kentucky counties was announced December 23, 1963. The courses averaged forty-four weeks and included training in fifty job areas. The expenditure of $8,764,000 was authorized under the provisions of the Manpower Development Training Act of 1962. *Louisville Courier-Journal,* December 23, 1963.

3. John Barrett Rodes (1870-1970), Bowling Green attorney (1892-1964); master commissioner, Warren County Circuit Court (1898-1902); president, Kentucky Bar Association (1940); trustee, Ogden College (1898-1955); member, Board of Regents, Western Kentucky State College (1944-1948); judge, Warren County Circuit Court (1948-1963); cochairman, Advisory Commission on Constitutional Revision (1960). *Louisville Courier-Journal,* March 26, 1970. Judge Rodes declined appointment to the Constitutional Revision Assembly because of age. Telephone interview with Sarah Rodes Graham, January 30, 1981.

4. Although Kentucky's population had grown from 2,845,627 in 1940 to 3,038,156 in 1960, the rate of growth fell behind the growth rate of the nation. In 1940 the Commonwealth had nine members in the House of Representatives. By Breathitt's administration the number had been reduced to seven. P.P. Karan and Cotton Mather, eds., *Atlas of Kentucky* (Lexington, Ky., 1977), p. 17.

CHEMICAL BANK NEW YORK TRUST COMPANY
New York, New York / June 3, 1964

EVERYONE is familiar with the popular imagine of Kentucky—an easygoing, hospitable place noted for thoroughbred horse farms in the Bluegrass, My Old Kentucky Home at Bardstown, the mint julep, the Kentucky Derby, and as an area where someone saying, "I'll be there directly," means in a little while.[1]

This view of Kentucky is a very pleasant one, but it is not at all the full picture of Kentucky as it is today. The landscape is changing as new industrial plants take shape, as superhighways are pushed through, and as flood control and navigation projects are developed.

Recently, the free world's largest blast furnace went into operation in Kentucky as an expression of Armco Steel's satisfaction with its Kentucky employees and the many advantages Kentucky offers Industry. Ground was broken on May 23 in Bowling Green for a new Cutler-Hammer electrical controls plant. In picking the site—Bowling Green's industrial park—Cutler-Hammer's president, Edmund B. Fitzgerald, said that the decision was motivated by the many economic advantages the area offers.[2]

Farther west in Kentucky, at Elkton, Rockwell Manufacturing Company is erecting an industrial facility where plastic meter parts will be manufactured. "You are our kind of people," a Rockwell official said when ground was broken for the plant.

Recent dedication of a Kellwood Company subsidiary clothing plant at Brownsville, in central Kentucky, attracted an enthusiastic crowd of some 3,000 persons. In northern Kentucky the Divco-Wayne Company is building a specialized automotive vehicle plant. It will be the seventh manufacturing operation in the Northern Kentucky Industrial Foundation Park. These are but a few examples of the new upsurge of industrial growth in Kentucky. These are facilities of some of the most highly respected and forward-looking industrial firms in the nation.

Behind these and the many other recent plant locations in Kentucky are a variety of factors. Our good business climate, favorable to industrial expansion; strategic geographical location in relation to consumer and industrial markets; excellent transportation facilities; and a large pool of intelligent and easily trained men and women eager for jobs in industry are several of the "plus factors" which Kentucky offers the industrial prospect.

It is not our purpose to seek to uproot established industries in other states and to transport them to Kentucky. But industries which are looking around for profitable locations in which to expand operations interest us greatly, and I believe they will be interested in the many choice sites set aside for industrial development by Kentucky communities.

We are interested in new jobs and new payrolls for Kentuckians from any worthwhile source, and we welcome branch plants as well as home-owned industries. The nation's industrial giants—110 at last count—have manufacturing facilities in the Bluegrass State. We are justifiably proud of this confidence they show in Kentucky, just as we are proud of the new industrial enterprises which are Kentucky based and are an important part of our recent economic growth.

The new Kentucky, a land of industrial opportunity, a land of tomorrow built on the charm, skilled workmanship, and sincerity of yesterday, issues you and your industrial clients an invitation to visit us and let us show you what we have to offer.

---

1. While in New York Governor Breathitt also delivered addresses to the board of directors of the First National City Bank and at the New York World's Fair. These speeches are not included in this volume. In addition to his business recruiting trip to New York, Breathitt also traveled to San Francisco, Chicago, Detroit, Los Angeles, and Dallas in attempts to persuade business and industry to locate in Kentucky. Although the governor personally made no recruiting trips to Europe, several missions were dispatched to promote international trade and investment.

2. Edmund B. Fitzgerald (1926-), educated University of Michigan; vice president in charge of engineering, Cutler-Hammer Incorporated (1959-1961); administrative vice president (1961-1963); president (1964-1968); chairman and chief executive officer (1969-). *Who's Who in Finance and Industry, 1977-1978*, 20th ed. (Chicago, 1977).

SPINDLETOP RESEARCH ANNUAL MEETING
Lexington / October 21, 1964

WE can all agree, I'm sure, that today's brief review of Spindletop's activities, over only two full years of operations, indicates the breadth and variety of the contributions Spindletop can make to Kentucky's future and the leadership and economic stimulus its research can give. Since taking office, I have received several of Spindletop's reports. Each of them is thoroughly professional and each is geared directly to a facet of regional economic development of very real importance to public and private enterprise alike.

All of Spindletop's work is not in Kentucky or for Kentucky, but every bit of it is to Kentucky's interest. When such firms as Time, Inc., Sears Roebuck, Philco, General Electric, and CBS come to Kentucky for technical planning assistance—and they have come to Spindletop for it—all of Kentucky benefits.

This point has been brought home to me strongly during the last few months in meetings with numerous out-of-state industrialists and bankers, both here and in visits to Chicago, Detroit, and other cities. The reaction to my description of Spindletop's work is quick and it is positive. These men know what good research can accomplish. The Spindletop experiment is showing great promise and is being favorably observed in many places.

Many of you here today have been closely associated with Spindletop Research from the beginning. In fact, several of you are personally responsible for the ideas, planning, and effort that made it possible to begin at all. The creation of Spindletop was the creation of a vital resource. There is much pride to be shared among you. The concept of Spindletop as an independent organization has assured its professional integrity and its freedom to develop programs consistent with, and often in the vanguard of, advancing technologies.

The concept of Spindletop as a private corporation has served to restrain any attempt at control by either the state or the university. Spindletop could not fulfill even a fraction of its potential if it had a state affiliation. And the experience of others demonstrates clearly that such an organization's true value could not be realized if it was part of the university system. But it should be emphasized here that, although the university and Spindletop are separate entities, their interests and activities are complementary. Full cooperation between the two institutions can and will be significantly beneficial to Spindletop, the university, and Kentucky.

Finally, the concept of Spindletop as a profit-oriented organization with its first financial nourishment from state government—and state government only—was the making of a new tradition. Governor Combs, Lieutenant Governor Wyatt, and the state legislature fully supported the principle of investing public funds for launching a new institution which would serve primarily private interests.[1] The previous administration, and the legislature, committed over three million tax dollars to support this private venture. This concept was a unique first in Kentucky, and is the leading feature of Spindletop's history.

Today, the state will vest in Spindletop's board of directors clear title to 130 acres, the administration building and furnishings, physical assets amounting to over $2 million. With this event the state's obligations, initiated and carried out by two successive administrations, will have been met. I should now like to call forward Mr. Grant McDonald, the newly elected chairman of the board of directors of Spindletop Research.[2]

It is with great pleasure that I present you with this deed. The existence of Spindletop Research is a tribute to the desire and ability of government enterprise and private enterprise alike to work together for common purposes. The state has set Spindletop in motion. Commonwealth funds have created an asset for the benefit of business and industry in Kentucky and for the economic well-being of our entire state and region. It is the business community of our state, however, that will benefit most immediately and substantially from this asset.[3]

---

1. Wilson Watkins Wyatt (1905-), J.D., University of Louisville (1927); practiced law in Louisville (1927-1935); trial attorney for Louisville (1934); mayor of Louisville (1941-1945); lieutenant governor of Kentucky (1959-1963); Democratic national committeeman for Kentucky (1960-1964). *Who's Who in America, 1980-1981,* 41st ed., (Chicago, 1980).

2. Grant McDonald (1909-), born, Mt. Pleasant, Michigan; employed by Square D Corporation (1929-1973); engineering degree from Lawrence University (1938); assigned to Lexington, Kentucky by Square D (1957); chairman of the board, Spindletop Research; president, Kentucky Chamber of Commerce; currently resides in Boca Raton, Florida. Henry Hornsby, "Success Story: Grant McDonald," *Kentucky Business,* May 1965, pp. 14-15.

3. In May, 1966, Spindletop opened an office in Washington, D.C., designed to establish and maintain an information link between the nation's capital and Frankfort. Specifically, the office provided information relating to contemporary trends affecting state-federal relationships, pending federal legislation affecting Kentucky's economic development, federal budget decisions, important committee hearings, and changes in criteria under which federal funds were administered. The announcement was made by Governor Breathitt in a speech delivered in Washington, D.C., May 12, 1966. This speech is not included in this volume.

KENTUCKY BANKERS ASSOCIATION
Louisville / November 17, 1964

IT is a pleasure to be with you today as you have your annual meeting and to talk to you briefly about Kentucky's business and industrial outlook and about steps the state administration is taking to find jobs for every man and woman who wants to work.

First of all, let me say that I come to you in a spirit of great optimism for the future of Kentucky business, for rapid expansion of our industry, for the growth of individual income, for the continued expansion of our tourist trade, for an increased agricultural income, for a growing confidence in Kentucky as a place to do business on the part of our nation's industrial and commerical leaders.

This is not mere oratory or wishful thinking. Kentucky's economy is on the move, and it is up to us to hasten the expansion, to quicken the growth. As much as any other single group, the bankers of Kentucky are demonstrating their confidence in Kentucky's future economic expansion.

As I travel over Kentucky from Mills' Point to the Big Sandy, I see banks modernizing their facilities, providing new services in new and expanding quarters. This construction provides, not only employment, but more importantly, encouragement to other businessmen to invest in the economic future of their area. Further evidence of the banks' belief in the growth of our state is demonstrated by the fact that twenty-five of Kentucky's state-chartered banks have increased their capitalization by a total of some $2 million during the past year.

On June 30 of this year, at the end of the fiscal year, assets in our state-chartered banks totaled $1,798 million compared to $1,682 million a year ago—a growth of more than $100 million. During the same period, loans increased from $743 million to $849 million—money that was invested in Kentucky's industry, business, farms, and homes. I call these figures a tremendous vote of confidence in our state's economic future.

At the same time, Kentucky's state banks invested $20 million in municipal bonds for increased services in schools, highways, water and sewer districts, and utilities.

Within the Department of Banking, we are making every effort to work with your association in order that we may have one of the finest banking systems in the country. We have and we will continue to encourage and cooperate with the association's school of banking. We have and we will continue to upgrade the professional standards of our department.

I think bankers would be the first to agree that our Kentucky economy is operating at a very high level as we near the end of 1964. More Kentuckians are working, earning more, than ever before in the history of the Commonwealth.

Nonagricultural employment is hovering around the 735,000 mark. Each month we have a gain over the same month in 1963. Unemployment has dropped to 3.2 percent of the labor force. Profits are up. Wages are higher than ever. . . .[1]

We are striving for growth in all phases of our economy. However, we are fully aware that industrial growth is necessary to trigger gains in other areas. Consequently, great emphasis has been placed on our program to develop new industrial jobs. So far this year our success has been spectacular. From January 1, 1964, to the first of November, we have recorded announcements of eighty new industrial firms which will provide 6,093 new jobs and a plant investment of $47,645,000.

Equally important to a rising economy is the expansion of our existing industry which is taking place concurrently. One hundred and twenty of our fine Kentucky industries have begun or plan to begin expansion of facilities, which will mean an investment total of $49,798,000 and 4,188 additional jobs. Some of the investment figures have not been released by the companies, indicating that the total has probably passed $100 million. With a continuation of the national economic surge, which economists are predicting, our future looks bright indeed.

The industry which we are acquiring today will inevitably breed new satellite industry and the expenditure of additional dollars for further expansion of present operations. One firm which started construction early this year has already revealed plans for a $14 million addition. Another which began operations in Princeton two years ago has since expanded twice and now employs over 800 persons, from a starting work force of 170.

I believe this will clearly indicate that the companies being attracted to Kentucky are not "fly-by-nights" seeking the largest subsidies which are offered. On the contrary, many of them are among the nation's largest and oldest industrial powers. The products they make are diversified.

The list for this year alone has included such names as Gates Rubber Company, SKF Industries, General American Transportation Corporation, Cutler-Hammer, Inc., Rockwell Manufacturing Company, Air Reduction Chemical & Carbide Company, A.O. Smith Corporation, National Casket Company, Pennsalt Chemicals Company, P.R. Mallory & Company, and Divco-Wayne Corporation.

What are we doing to maintain and accelerate this economic growth? Our Kentucky Department of Commerce and the other development groups which we are fortunate to have in Kentucky—our railroad and utility firms and our many local chambers of commerce and industrial foundations—are making a concerted effort to reach those expansion-minded companies and to sell them the advantages which our state can offer—sell them with facts and figures which will prove the economic practicality of a location in our state. And, of course, the banks of Kentucky are playing a great role in this effort.

I have attempted to lend the assistance of the office of Kentucky's chief executive by personally talking with groups of industrialists in Detroit,

Chicago, and New York—at meetings which have been set up by our friends and former Kentucky residents in those cities. Trips of this nature are planned for the West Coast—Los Angeles and San Francisco—next month. Incidentally, these meetings have been arranged by key members of the banking fraternity in these cities and this has added to their effectiveness.

All of state government has been alerted to the vital importance of this industrial development phase of our program, and all departments are giving full cooperation, in the routing of highways, scheduling of vocational training programs, industrial advertising, and in numerous other ways. In one very recent successful plant location project, we had to call upon the services of our Department of Highways, attorney general, adjutant general, and Departments of Finance and Health before all problems were resolved and the way cleared for an announcement.

In seeking new industry and new jobs, we are not confining our efforts to New York, Chicago, Detroit, and other of the nation's industrial centers. We have representatives of the Department of Commerce daily engaged in contacting our existing industry to learn how we can help solve their problems and to inquire of their plans for future expansion. One recent endeavor along these lines was a week-long schedule of visits with our major Lousville, Kentucky, industry, with the active participation of representatives of railroads and utility companies serving the Louisville area.

Kentucky is definitely on the move and we are trying to add to the momentum. We have a fine state and we have a good program. By every means at our command we are simply attempting to communicate this enthusiasm to prospective new industry. We want growth and we will have growth.

We have only begun to realize our potential in Kentucky—only begun to glimpse the greatness that can be ours. Let us work together to reach that place of eminence to which we aspire and to which our energy, our ambition, our devotion to Kentucky can carry us.

---

1. In this speech, in which Governor Breathitt reviews economic development in Kentucky in 1964, remarks relating to the commitment of the administration to job creation and farm economy development have been deleted.

1964 PROFESSIONAL TROPHY AWARD LUNCHEON OF THE SOCIETY OF INDUSTRIAL REALTORS

Houston, Texas / January 29, 1965

It is with great pleasure that I accept the 1964 Professional Trophy Award of the Society of Industrial Realtors for Kentucky's industrial development program. I accept this award in behalf of the many Kentuckians whose work and dedication have made possible the industrial growth of the Commonwealth and the national recognition our state has achieved.

Governor Connally, it is a great honor for Kentucky to follow in the footsteps of Texas in winning this award.[1] Kentucky shares with Texas a pioneer heritage and a history rich with the names of men whose ideas and action have paved our nation's upward struggle to the threshold of the "Great Society." Kentucky isn't as rich in tax revenue and personal income as many states. But Kentucky is trying harder than many states to fulfill the great potential of its rapidly growing economy. Few states, however, can rival Kentucky's old and colorful image as a land of Daniel Boone, bourbon whiskey, burley tobacco, the Kentucky Derby, Bluegrass horse farms, and traditional hospitality.

The image is changing, for Kentucky has entered a new era of economic expansion and industrial growth. A border state during the Civil War, Kentucky today is competing successfully in the "War Between the States" to attract industry. Kentucky offers industry the economic climate and assets needed for profit and growth. Over half the population of the nation lives within 400 miles of Kentucky's borders. A Kentucky plant site is only a day away by rail and motor freight service from 27 percent of the nation's markets. And plentiful supplies of power and fuel—electricity, coal, oil and natural gas—are available to industry.

National advertising and promotional efforts have been intensified during the past year to spotlight Kentucky's many advantages for industry. As chairman of the Kentucky Economic Development Commission, I have joined Commissioner of Commerce Katherine Peden in personally contacting top industrial and financial executives during trips to Chicago, Detroit, New York, Los Angeles, and San Francisco.[2] Yesterday we met with Texas leaders of business and industry in Dallas. The Department of Commerce which heads up the industrial development program of Kentucky state government has opened branch offices in New York and Chicago to provide industrial prospects in the East and Midwest with full details on profit opportunities in the Bluegrass State.

These opportunities are growing because of a unique climate of cooperation in Kentucky which produces a teamwork effort for progress on the state and community level. There is a new awareness of the importance of business and industry and a new dedication to community improvement. Leaders of state and local governments, chambers of commerce, civic organizations, and the business community are working together for a common goal.

Investments in new manufacturing plants and the expansion of existing facilities announced in Kentucky during 1964 exceed $113 million—almost triple the total for 1963. The number of industrial foundations, which have attracted new manufacturing plants to communities throughout Kentucky, rose to 125 during 1964—as compared to forty in 1960. Many of these local development organizations offer choice plant sites in industrial parks and subdivisions. More than $107 million in industrial revenue and general obligation bonds have been issued by thirty-seven Kentucky cities and one county to finance or equip new plants.

The Harvey Aluminum Company is building a giant rolling mill near Lewisport which will employ 1,000 persons. The plant is being financed by a $50 million industrial revenue bond issue sold by the small community of 700 residents. This is the largest single municiple bond issue of its kind ever marketed in the nation.

There are many examples of "bootstrap" improvement efforts by Kentucky communities. Four years ago the economy of Dawson Springs was declining. Residents formed a nonprofit development agency, purchased land for an industrial park, and sold an industrial revenue bond issue. Expansion of the $750,000 plastics plant that Dawson Springs obtained was announced at its dedication recently. All Kentuckians share in the honor of this award, for it recognizes the importance of an industrial development effort that is benefiting every segment of our state's economy.

---

1. John Bowden Connally (1917-), educated University of Texas School of Law, L.L.B. (1941); secretary to U.S. Representative Lyndon B. Johnson (1949); Secretary of the Navy (1961); governor of Texas (1963-1969); partner, Houston, Texas law firm (1969-). *Who's Who in American Politics, 1975-1976,* 5th ed. (New York, 1975). Connally, originally a Democrat, moved to the Republican party during the 1970s and was an unsuccessful candidate for the Republican nomination for the presidency in 1980.

2. Katherine Graham Peden (1926-), vice president, radio station WHOP, Hopkinsville (1944-1968); commissioner of commerce for Kentucky (1963-1967); president, Katherine G. Peden and Associates, Incorporated; President's Commission on the Status of Women (1961-1962); member, President's Commission on Civil Disorders (1967); Democratic nominee United States Senate (1968). *Who's Who of American Women, 1975-1976,* 9th ed. (Chicago, 1975). In 1964 Commissioner Peden accompanied thirty-one other Kentuckians on a trade mis-

sion to Brazil, Peru, Ecuador, and Columbia. The following year she was a member of the Kentucky economic development delegation that visited the Ruhr Valley. In 1967 the United States Agency for International Development (AID), in recognition of her achievements in industrial development, selected Commissioner Peden to assist in its Inter-American Development Seminar held in Agrequipe, Peru. Press release, July 6, 1967, Economic Development file, Breathitt papers.

LABORATORY DEDICATION: PUBLIC SERVICE COMMISSION
Lexington / April 28, 1965

TODAY we join to participate in the dedication of a meter standards laboratory—one more piece of evidence that Kentucky is on the move, looking ahead. For me it is a unique pleasure to participate in this dedication because the authorization for and much of the initial planning of this facility came about while I was a member of the Kentucky Public Service Commission during the administration of Governor Bert T. Combs.

I am proud to have been able to take a part in bringing about the construction of this facility for the people of the state of Kentucky and to be able to participate in its dedication during my term as governor. I am particularly pleased to have the Southeastern Association of Railroad and Utilities Commissioners present at this dedication. I know from personal experience that through the meetings, committee work, and exchange of ideas of this great association our Public Service Commission people have been able to do a far better job of regulation in Kentucky. Chairman Francis has told us something of the purpose and development of this meter standards laboratory. I would like to take this opportunity to give you my idea of how it will benefit the people of our great Commonwealth.

We believe that the future of Kentucky lies in progress, through industrial and commercial development. By such development increased and better job opportunities will be available to our citizens, and we hope more of our young people will be able to remain here and prosper. If our people are producers, they will become self-reliant and contribute not only to their own personal advancement but to the advancement of our state as well. To expand our present industry, to construct new industry, and to encourage our young people to stay here and develop Kentucky, we must be progressive.

Kentucky's industrial growth so far this year is running well ahead of last year. Industrial investments in new and expanded manufacturing plants totaled $43.3 million for the first three months of this year, and these facilities will create 5,100 new jobs. This compares to $28.6 million in industrial investments announced through April 30 of 1964—a four-month period. This means that, not counting Sundays, Kentucky has obtained a new plant or industrial expansion for each of the ninety days through April 1.

The construction and operation of this meter standards laboratory, perhaps the first in the United States, to be operated by a state commission, is progress, and I believe will demonstrate to commerce and industry that we expect safe, adequate, and accurately measured utility service here in Kentucky. I believe that providing safe, accurate, adequate, and reliable utility service is a vital element in providing a favorable climate for commercial and industrial development in this state. This laboratory will be an important tool in the hands of the Public Service Commission in continuing its fine job of insuring such a climate, and we want our public agencies to have the best possible tools for carrying out their duties to the public. This facility, I believe, is timely and necessary. This is evident because of the tremendous growth of utility service in our state.

Kentucky is fortunate in having abundant supplies of the cheapest known fuel for electric generation, bituminous coal. Water power, as a by-product of flood control and irrigation has also been extensively developed here. We are still a large producer of natural gas, and water supplies are abundant in our many streams, lakes, and rivers. The possibility of gasification of our abundant coal deposits will take on increasing importance over the years, particularly if the demand for natural gas should catch up with other available supplies.

The growth of utility service provided by our privately owned utilities and cooperatives, operating under the able regulatory jurisdiction of our Public Service Commission, is continuing at a rapid rate. For the ten-year period, 1952 through 1962, the number of individual services of electric, gas, and water utilities increased some 300,000, or approximately 30 percent.

Increase in consumption of utility service, however, has been much greater. For example, over this ten-year period, annual consumption of electric energy has increased from 3,921,000,000 kilowatt hours to 8,331,000,000 kilowatt hours, over 100 percent. Annual electrical revenues have increased from some $82 million to $163 million in the same period. I see no reason why this rate of growth should not continue into the future. Indeed, we hope to increase it as we improve the living standards of our citizens in Kentucky.

Certainly, the consuming public must put forth great faith in its Public Service Commission to take all reasonable diligence to see that fair and impartial measurement is made of service used by the individual consumer. It also expects its Public Service Commission to take all reasonable care to insure that utility service, potentially hazardous as it must be, is rendered in such a manner as to insure the safety of the consuming public.

It is estimated that there are close to 1,400,000 individual metered gas, electric, and water services in Kentucky that are operated under the jurisdiction of our Public Service Commission. It is obvious that the work of this facility in setting the standards for uniform measurement of utility service will touch almost every household in Kentucky. Our private utilities and cooperatives regulated by the Public Service Commission here in Kentucky have done a fine job in the past in meeting the needs of our citizens for utility service, and their record of providing safe service has been an outstanding one.

This facility, we believe, will provide for them a conveniently located place in Kentucky where, under the supervision of the Public Service Commission, they will be able to calibrate their meter standards. We hope it will be of assistance to them in carrying on the excellent standards of service that they have rendered in the past.

I wish at this time to thank Chairman Dave Francis, Commissioner Woodrow Burchett, and Commissioner Wells Lovett of the Public Service Commission for their perseverance and industry in making this facility possible and the commission's engineering staff for their foresight and resourcefulness in recommending, planning, and getting it ready for operation.[1] I also wish to thank Dr. Oswald and his staff at the university for their most generous assistance in locating and planning the facility.[2]

---

1. J. David Francis (1919-), member Public Service Commission (1959-1965, 1966-1967); chairman, Public Service Commission (1967-1968); currently circuit court judge in Warren County, Kentucky. Woodrow W. Burchett (1911-), attorney from Prestonsburg, Kentucky; member Public Service Commission (1959 -1965, 1967-1968); chairman, Public Service Commission (1965-1967). Wells T. Lovett (1923-), attorney from Owensboro, Kentucky; member Public Service Commission (1963-1967, 1967-1968); chairman, Public Service Commission (1967). Information provided by Harold Greenwood, director, Division of Administrative Services, Energy and Utilities Regulatory Commissions.

2. John Wieland Oswald (1917-), Ph.D., University of California at Berkeley (1942); faculty member, University of California at Berkeley (1945-1963); chairman, Department of Plant Pathology (1954-1959); vice president and executive assistant to the president (1961-1962); president, University of Kentucky (1963-1968); executive vice president, University of California (1968-1970); pres-

ident, Pennsylvania State University (1970-). *Who's Who in America, 1976-1977,* 39th ed. (Chicago, 1976).

SOUTHERN INDUSTRIAL DEVELOPMENT COUNCIL
Louisville / October 25, 1965

IT is a great privilege to participate in the annual conference of the Southern Industrial Development Council. First, let me say how delighted we are that you chose Kentucky for this year's meeting. The people of Louisville have done everything possible to make your visit pleasant, and we know you're going to enjoy it. I have met some old friends and colleagues from other southern states and we've had a regular family reunion. This is, in a sense, a family of industrial development experts, a gifted family whose every member has his own special field and talents and his own list of achievements for the improvement of his hometown, his state, and the entire South. The members of this organization are, in fact, the "builders of the South." Just a few short years ago, the southern states were linked with agriculture and the gracious life. Today we are taking our place with our northern neighbors in the manufacturing field. Our industrial revolution is in progress now. And you are playing a major role in the battle to gain new industry and employment for the people of the South.

We are proud of the fact that so many Kentuckians are members of this fine organization. Glover Cary, manager of industrial development with Texas Gas Transmission Corporation, was your president last year before handing over the reins to another of our friends and colleagues, Allen Douglas, vice president of industrial development of the Southern Railway.[1] Both the Southern Railway and Texas Gas have been major contributors to the success of the industrial development program in Kentucky.

Our state is fortunate to have many organizations such as these working together for our overall economic development. We are fortunate to be the location of the home offices of Texas Gas and the Louisville and Nashville Railroad and to have the services of their industrial development personnel. The Kentucky Chamber of Commerce, the "old pros" in the industrial development game, had the foresight many years ago to bring together the knowledge and talents that we have here in Kentucky and to form an industrial team, composed of the director of industrial development of the chamber and the heads of industrial development departments of all of our railroads and utility companies. This team has been successful as a working unit and as a means of bringing about the intended results—new industry for Kentucky.

The Kentucky Department of Commerce, an agency of state government, is a segment of the state industrial team. And I would like to commend the job that this department, under the leadership of Katherine Peden as commissioner, has done and is doing. Apparently, some other people agree, since last year we received the Society of Industrial Realtors Professional Trophy Award for our program, after being runner-up the three previous years. We are very proud, indeed, to be the recipients of this honor.

Actual statistics on what is taking place in Kentucky point up unequivocally the success of the efforts of Kentucky's industrial development program. In June of 1965, manufacturing employment in our state reached an all-time high, with 201,500 workers in industrial jobs. In this same month total nonagricultural employment also set a record, with 764,700 in nonfarm jobs, an increase of 40,300 over the same month of 1964. In 1964 and the first nine months of 1965, Kentucky has gained a total of 149 new plants, to provide 13,494 new jobs. Cost of the new facilities will exceed $117 million. Equally important in depicting our industrial growth is the number of expansions of existing plants which, in this same period of time, total 238 companies expanding employment by 10,939 and spending over $108 million in new plant facilities. Over 24,000 new industrial jobs have been created in this less than two-year period, and we think that's a pretty good record.

Many of our southern states can cite records equally impressive, some perhaps more so. This does not diminish in any way the pride each of us feels in witnessing the results of his own efforts. Statistics for the sixteen-state southern region show an increase from 1958 to 1963 of 314,851 persons in production employment, and a gain of $650 million in capital expenditures. Value added by manufacture during the same period showed a phenomenal rise from $28,484,000,000 to $40,269,000,000. And this is something we can all point to with pride.

Kentucky's growth in the last two years is not luck or accident. A dynamic program has been put into effect which is creating a new image and putting the message across to the nation's industrialists. Operating under the slogan "Come to Kentucky—It's a Profitable Move," our advertising has undergone a face-lifting designed to first attract attention and then provoke the reader to examining the hard-hitting facts. We now have figures to pinpoint locations where savings in operation can be effected, and these cost factors are being placed in the hands of thousands of the country's major industrialists.

Our Department of Commerce has established three branch offices—in New York, Chicago, and Los Angeles. The foreign element is being explored, as well, starting with a trade mission to Germany and Belgium in May, 1965, to study the German economic development, the European Common Market, and opportunities for attracting German investments to Kentucky. An early result of this trip is the proposed visit of a prominent German industrialist to Kentucky next month.

While we are making an all-out effort to attract outside interests, internal building and improvements programs necessary to keep pace with constant growth are not being neglected. Here, too, we have had the able and invaluable assistance of some of Kentucky's leading citizens. Jack Tankersley, president of Western Kentucky Gas Company, as Kentucky Chamber of Commerce president last year devoted many hours of his valuable time to this vital cause.[2] Grant McDonald, vice president of Square D Company and this year's president of the chamber, is equally active and effective. Our Kentucky bankers are other valuable participants in the industrial and community development program.

Taking a page from the Southern Industrial Development Council book and the establishment of the Industrial Development Institute at Norman, Oklahoma, we have started our own annual institutes for the education of local leaders in industrial development practices. Sessions were held in three cities in the eastern, central, and western sections of the state in July, and attendance exceeded all expectations for a first venture.

Our Kentucky Economic Development Commission, a group of twenty top-level executives representing industry, labor, education, financing, agriculture, retail businesses, just about every field of endeavor, is working as five subcommittees designed for pinpointing weaknesses and finding workable solutions to problems affecting industrial development. Through a sixty-eight-member advisory committee, our Department of Commerce is utilizing the technical knowledge and abilities of a wide representation of business interests concerned with the state's development. Many of these people are members of your council as well.

Last year we inaugurated the practice of bringing together community leaders and local industry officials in an "Industry Appreciation Week," for public expressions of appreciation to Kentucky industry. The week was kicked off by a luncheon for officials of new plants announced during the year, and was then carried on throughout the week by local functions honoring existing industry.

We cannot ever adequately express our full appreciation to our industry, both new and old, and to the people who are helping to bring industry to Kentucky. Our affiliation with the Southern Industrial Development Council, the exchange of ideas and discussions of problems of mutual interest with our counterparts in other southern states, has done much to influence the thinking and broaden the outlook of the people of Kentucky. The members of this organization are a vital force in shaping the ideas of the citizens of southern states and projecting the image of the entire South for future development of this region of our country. This is a weighty responsibility, but every individual here possesses the capabilities for handling the task. While feeling and displaying a justifiable pride, we must fight complacency. While confident that we are exerting our fullest effort, we should not shun innovations. Working together as an organization devoted to a common goal, we can assure an even greater South of the future.

---

1. Glover H. Cary, Jr. (1923-), attended Western Kentucky State College; U.S. Marine Corps (1943-1945); employed by Texas Gas in Owensboro, Kentucky (1950-); operations and housing (1950-1955); safety engineer (1955-1956); industrial development (1956-1969); manager of public affairs (1969-). Telephone interview, February 4, 1981. Allen Douglas (1923-1977), born Savanah, Georgia; B.A., University of Georgia; industrial development department, Trust Company of Georgia; assistant vice president for industrial development, Southern Railroad System (1964-1968); vice president (1968-1977). Information provided by Jack Howard, Atlanta, Georgia.

2. George Jack Tankersley (1921-), born, Ruston, Louisiana; president, Western Kentucky Gas Company, Owensboro, Kentucky (1957-1966); resigned Western Kentucky Gas Company to assume presidency of East Ohio Gas Company, Cleveland, Ohio; currently chairman of the board, Consolidated Natural Gas Company, Pittsburgh, Pennsylvania. Information provided by Mr. Ed Davis, director of personnel, Western Kentucky Gas Company, Owensboro, Kentucky.

AEC TEAM BRIEFING
Louisville / November 30, 1965

As the chief executive of the Commonwealth of Kentucky, and as the elected representative of more than three million Kentuckians, it is my pleasure here today to welcome to Louisville the representatives of the Atomic Energy Commission who are in Kentucky to study proposed sites for a giant nuclear accelerator.[1]

To Mr. John Vinciguerra, executive assistant to the Atomic Energy Commission and team leader to Kentucky; Mr. Duane Turner of the AEC

Research Division; Mr. Robert Cooper of the AEC Construction Division; and Dr. Ronald Rau of the Brookhaven Long Island Laboratory, I say—in the name of all Kentuckians—"Welcome to the Bluegrass State, the land of new industrial opportunity."[2]

All of us know that there are but three sources of new wealth and new dollars: agriculture, mining, and manufacturing. But we, in Kentucky, are keenly interested in a catalytic agent—research—which stimulates development in all three of these primary sources of new wealth. For this reason, it is my hope that the Atomic Energy Commission will determine that one of our Kentucky sites—whether in the areas of Paducah, Murray, Louisville, West Point, Lexington, or northern Kentucky—is the logical place for construction of the 200-billion electron volt accelerator.

I have been informed by our Kentucky experts, who have studied the locational needs of such a huge research facility, that each of these sites meets the criteria outlined by the Atomic Energy Commission. One site may be a better choice than another on certain points, but each fulfills the requirements for such an establishment.

Kentucky has been accused in some jealous quarters of "pirating" industry. If what we are doing to build a better Kentucky through industrial expansion is pirating, then I agree with my commerce commissioner, Miss Katherine Peden, who has said that "If this is pirating, then let's hoist the Jolly Roger and full speed ahead!" Of course, pirating is not involved when it comes to the location of the nuclear accelerator. Plans for this tremendously important research facility are still on the drawing board. Therefore, we Kentuckians cannot be accused of trying to "steal a plant" when we offer two inducements to the Atomic Energy Commission to select Kentucky as the site of the accelerator.

One of these inducements is a commitment by the state of Kentucky to provide a site free of cost to the Atomic Energy Commission. The other is the assurance that a "companion piece"—an institute for advanced physics and engineering—will be established and operated by the University of Kentucky if a Kentucky site is chosen for the National Accelerator Laboratory regardless of where it is located in our state.

I have made a commitment, as governor, for an appropriation of $5 million for establishment of this institute. The primary mission of the institute would be the conduct of research in elementary particle physics and related areas. It would be the organization through which the scientists in the universities and colleges in this immediate area, and possibly beyond, might make most effective use of the facilities of the National Accelerator Laboratory and would also be the organization through which the laboratory might work to utilize the educational programs and facilities in these institutions.

The advice and counsel of laboratory personnel would be sought in the development of final plans for the institute in order that there might be maximum coordination of effort and that the organization might render the greatest service to both the laboratory and the educational institutions. In developing these preliminary plans, a faculty committee of the University of Kentucky has had the benefit of advice from professors of Harvard, Wisconsin, Notre Dame, and Duke. There have been more brief consultations with several high-energy physicists from other universities and laboratories.

While the institute would be valuable to our institutions of higher learning, providing the scientists with an organization to expedite participation in the research activities of the laboratory and support for the graduate students in high-energy physics and related areas, it would prove of special value to the laboratory. It would serve as the liaison and coordinating unit between the laboratory and the universities for the graduate education programs offered for laboratory personnel, and as one means for providing adjunct professor appointments for laboratory scientists who might desire to participate in the academic programs of the University of Kentucky or the University of Louisville.

There would also be a special opportunity for the institute personnel to make contributions to the programs of the laboratory as a "support group" if such participation was desired by the laboratory. In this context the institute personnel, in addition to the usual "user group" research utilizing laboratory facilities, might concern themselves with bubble chamber or other hardware design and construction, with problems of beam design, and with other matters of equipment or technique of consequence to the total laboratory.

Beyond these two inducements—a free site for the laboratory and creation of an institute for advanced physics and engineering—Kentucky offers to the Atomic Energy Commission many solid locational factors which are of major importance in considering Kentucky for the home of this new and tremendously important nuclear research tool.

Our central location, reinforced with easy access by land and air stemming from a growing network of interstate and toll roads and an upsurge in airport development, would put the National Accelerator Laboratory in the mainstream of U.S. and international travel by visiting physicists.

We are taking a great forward stride in expansion of educational facilities. Between 1960 and 1965, $165 [million] has been used or committed to construct new classroom, library, research, dormitory, and other facilities at the University of Kentucky, its community colleges, and at the five state colleges. State financial support for local school districts has risen 102 percent since 1959.

In the fall of last year, 62,497 undergraduate and graduate students were enrolled in the Commonwealth's public and private institutes of higher education. This reflects a growth of 14.4 percent over the previous year.

Kentucky, long noted for "bourbon, burley and bluegrass," is now emerging as a state with a significant industrial base. This year, for example, 193 manufacturing companies have announced plans to build $131,034,000 worth of new facilities, which, when in full operation, will provide 11,500 more jobs for Kentuckians.

For our own citizens, and for the growing millions of tourists who visit us each year, we are rapidly expanding the state's system of parks and recreational areas. We are also currently cooperating with the Tennessee Valley Authority to make the vast Kentucky section of the 170,000-acre area between Kentucky Lake and new Barkley Lake in western Kentucky a prime mid-America recreational paradise.

Other Kentucky attractions are found on the cultural side. The Louisville Orchestra and the "Book of Job" drama, presented each summer at Pine Mountain State Park, are internationally known, as are other Kentucky productions in the fields of drama and the arts. We say in Kentucky, "Come to Kentucky—It's a Profitable Move." I invite, here and now, the U.S. Atomic Energy Commission to build the National Accelerator Laboratory in the Bluegrass State. It will be a profitable move for the nation—and for Kentucky.

---

1. One hundred and seventeen communities in forty-six states vied for the projected 200-BEV particle accelerator, which Governor Branigan of Indiana termed "the scientific prize of the century." The reason for the governor's statement and the intense competition among contending communities can be seen from the following facts: the building cost for the accelerator was projected as high as $348 million; annual operating cost would be $58.7 million; the accelerator would employ approximately 2,000 highly paid scientists and technicians on a permanent basis, as well as attract visiting scientists from many countries to use its facilities. Governor Breathitt joined with his colleagues in the Southern Governors' Conference to promote a southern city as the site for the accelerator; however, a panel from the National Academy of Science selected Weston, Illinois, a suburb of Chicago as the location of the accelerator. *New York Times,* April 29, 1965, September 13, 1965; March 23, 1966, and December 17, 1966.

2. John Vincent Vinciguerra (1916-), government official (1941-); Atomic Energy Commission (1947-); member, Division of International Affairs (1960); assistant director, Safeguards Division of International Affairs (1960); director, Division of Contracts (1960-1962); executive assistant to general manager (1962-). *Who's Who in Government, 1972-1973* (Chicago, 1972). Duane Turner, no data available. Robert F. Cooper, B.S., civil engineering, University of Maryland (1950); various engineering assignments, Division of Construction, U.S. Atomic Energy Commission (1962-1971); chief, Construction and

Engineering Branch (1971-). Information provided by historian's office, U.S. Department of Energy, Washington, D.C. Ronald R. Rau (1920-), Ph.D. in physics, California Institute of Technology (1948); instructor, Princeton University (1947-1950); senior physicist and chairman of the Department of Physics, Brookhaven National Laboratory (1956-). *American Men of Science: The Physical and Behavioral Sciences,* 11th ed. (New York, 1967), p. 4342.

LOUISVILLE CHAMBER OF COMMERCE
Louisville / January 1, 1966

IN looking about me here today I find that the leadership of every major segment of Louisville's and Kentucky's economy is well represented. I am sure that I could not find a better or more receptive audience for reporting on the progress made in our state during the past twelve months.

This also is a very appropriate day on which to make such a report. New Year's Day is a time for taking stock of accomplishments, and, in the light of these accomplishments, to forecast what the new year will bring to our people in the way of many more productive jobs, a strengthened educational program, highway improvements, expanded recreational opportunities, and beneficial changes in other areas vital to growth, prosperity, and living conditions.

I would like to stress that the accomplishments of the past year are firmly rooted in the fine spirit of cooperation found at every level of our society. This cooperation stems from the earnest desire of community leaders to build a better Kentucky through community development. Without this cooperation many of our state programs would have little lasting effect.

One of the best barometers of progress is found in the rate of growth of new industry and the expansion of existing industry. I am pleased to be able to report that we have just closed out a banner year in this area. In 1965 there were 206 announcements of major manufacturing plant construction activity. When these projects are completed and in full operation it will mean more than 13,900 new jobs for Kentuckians. All told, these construction projects call for capital outlay well in excess of $208 million. That sum is $91 million over the total for all of 1964. However, within a few days I expect another announcement that will total about $70 million. This means Kentucky's industrial growth will be $278 million for this past year—a remarkable boom.

Let us take a look at another important progress indicator. Nonfarm employment in Kentucky reached a record high of 797,800 in November. This is 47,900 more than in the same month of 1964. While campaigning for the governorship, I pledged 75,000 new jobs for Kentuckians in the next four years. We have reached and passed that goal in only two years. If I am to be accused of underestimating Kentucky's economic growth potential, then the blame should actually be laid at the doors of all the good people of Kentucky who worked so hard and long to bring in new industry and encourage expansion of existing Kentucky plants.

An analysis of our recent industrial growth shows that new and expanded manufacturing facilities are springing up in all sections of the Commonwealth. Every area is sharing in this industrial boom. Last year, for example, six new manufacturing plants began operations or took shape in eastern Kentucky. And in the far west, on the bank of the Mississippi River, two major developments will provide hundreds of industrial jobs for local people. In the past these areas have been off the mainstream of industrial progress. They are now beginning to get their fair share of the nation's upsurge in the production of consumer and industrial goods.

Again, I would like to point out that these developments rest firmly on local effort. Without the dedication and interest of local leadership, the state—through its intensified program of industrial development—could only "lead the horse to water." When the horse drinks, the credit goes to the community which has drive and initiative; the willingness to meet and surmount the problems of industrial expansion. And can convince the industrial prospect that a particular Kentucky town or city is the place in which to sink deep roots and develop an operation firmly based on the profit motive.

Before turning to other indices of Kentucky's growth, I wish to compliment the voters of Kentucky on their expressed desire to see the Bluegrass State move ahead in the years to come. Their overwhelming endorsement of the $176 million state bond issue on November 2 means that we can progress on many fronts. It means that Kentucky can continue to develop a vitally needed interstate program; can expand its overtaxed higher education complex; develop new state parks; upgrade and expand vocational training; and push ahead with these and other programs which will put us in the forefront of the nation's development.

Business Week magazine, which monthly gauges the personal income rise and fall by states, shows that for the first nine months of 1965 the personal income of Kentuckians rose 9.4 percent over the comparable period in 1964, and was well above the national average.

It is heartening to know that "King Burley"—Kentucky's top money crop—still wears a firm crown. When the market closed for the holiday season, prices were running around five dollars per hundred pounds above the average of last year. Also, less than one-third as much of the poundage was going into the price support program, thus indicating a healthy outlook and a willingness of the buyers to pay premium prices for a top-quality crop.

On the agricultural front there is another sign of progress. Last year, in the January-September period, the Kentucky farmer's cash receipts from marketings of livestock and products advanced $22,345,000 over the same period in 1964. This increase was due largely to sales of beef cattle and hogs. Our rolling pasture lands, advantageous cattle-watering situation, and good climate are now paying off under a drive by the state to achieve leadership in this important category of agricultural production and to realize a better balance between crops and livestock.

State financial support of public colleges and the University of Kentucky, an advance of 186 percent—highest in the South—has been achieved between 1960 and 1965. The state financial support for Kentucky public school districts in the same period jumped 102 percent. These are impressive figures. But it is my hope, and it is the determination of schoolmen and awakened parents, to change percentage figures to the actuality of adequate educational facilities for all the youth of Kentucky. In speaking of financial support for education and for the other areas of progress in Kentucky, I wish to make it clear that the new dollars needed for these projects will come from increased prosperity in our state.

When the General Assembly convenes this week the progressive program which I shall place before that body for consideration will require no new taxes nor increases in present taxes. The cost of forward-looking programs will be borne by increased revenues derived from a healthy, advancing economy. In this connection, a report from the Department of Revenue shows that for the first eleven months of 1965 state tax collections were running $36,400,000 ahead of the same period in 1964. New taxes are not in the cards. Our advances on all the economic fronts, coincident with a national picture which has never been better, mean that every envisioned plan for betterment can be carried out within the framework of expanded revenue from existing sources.

It has often been said—and with truth—that Kentucky has a long way to go in realizing her full potential for growth and for providing the "good life" for her citizens. This is, and has been, an interior problem. But let us not forget that we face another problem from outside our borders. That is the hardening competition from other states—many more wealthy than Kentucky—for the new industrial dollar, for the growing tourist dollar, and for the business dollar represented by shifting headquartering of distribution and service companies.

It has also been said—and again with truth—that in the light of this tough competition Kentucky must run fast in order to stand still. I believe, and I hope that you will agree with me, that the state's present aggressive development efforts, coupled with the fine cooperation we have experienced, will result in a "runaway race"—that Kentucky will forge ahead of competing states and build an economy second to none.

AREA DEVELOPMENT MEETING, PRESTONSBURG COMMUNITY COLLEGE
Prestonsburg / July 28, 1966

WE have known in Kentucky for some time now that the way not to get something done locally is for each and every community to strike off on its own separate path, oblivious to the needs and resources of the area surrounding it. Instead, we have begun to travel common paths, ones that will lead whole multicounty areas to better, more efficient, in fact, total, social and economic development. And we know these common paths will not slight the individual county or town. The greater resources of an area, we have learned, can be focused on individual local problems as well as on area ones.

Only a few years ago individual counties conducted tooth and nail battles with one another to attract industry, to gain new public facilities, or to get roads. But now, through area organizations such as the Big Sandy Development Council, closely cooperating multicountry groups offer industrial prospects several towns to select from instead of just one. We in Kentucky have learned to lift our sights, to take the wider, broader view. Consequently, we are getting more done.[1]

Prior to 1958 few, if any, federal development programs were in force here in eastern Kentucky. We couldn't meet the criteria. When we applied for a federal grant, we found we didn't have enough matching money. When we went for a new road we found the existing traffic count wouldn't justify it. So, we built a courthouse here and a sewerage system there, projects that were swallowed up by the enormity of problems much greater than those small, one-at-a-time projects could handle.

But, thanks to people like yourselves, things began to change. Your awareness of, and your organizations for, development on a larger scale began to attract the attention of Washington lawmakers through citizen action. You demonstrated, like no one else could, that democracy is something done every day of the year and not something just talked about in Fourth of July speeches.

As a result, we now have federal programs either designed, or malleable enough in design, to meet our needs. The three most broadly based of these new programs—the Appalachian Act, the Economic Opportunity Act, and the Public Works and Economic Development Act—are built around the area development concept. In fact, two of them established special provisions to make this concept into reality.

Coupled with your state government's initiative at Frankfort, these programs are doing a good job for us. Let's take a moment to look at what has been gained from these programs in this one six-county area in a little over a year-and-a-half's time. Let's begin with the Economic Development Act.

As most of you know, Jenny Wiley State Park received a $618,600 EDA grant for expansion and improvement. In other counties in this area, $466,400 went to the Big Sandy Industrial Foundation in Johnson County for the purchase and development of 190 acres' worth of industrial sites; $69,000 went into Martin County for the improvement and construction of a doctors' clinic; $59,000 went to Louisa for an extension of that community's water line; $379,000 in grants and loans were made available for a water treatment plant in Louisa; and Martin County received $868,000 in grants and loans for a similar purpose. In this area, the Economic Development Administration has invested, so far, a total of $2,062,000 in grants and has loaned $493,000.

The Economic Opportunity Act, a program aimed entirely at the problems of impoverished people, also works for you on an area basis. You have an area-wide effort administered by a full-time paid director.

As of July 1 a huge number of projects had been approved for funding here in the Big Sandy. I won't try to cite all of them now except to give you the total amounts invested by OEO in each county. These projects cover such things as headstart, the neighborhood youth corps program, adult basic education programs, rural loans, and others. (Pike County, $547,631; Magoffin County, $162,372; Martin County, $559,318; Lawrence County, $97,334; Johnson County, $327,062; Floyd County, $845,103.)

The Appalachian Redevelopment Act has benefited your area in the following ways:

1. As part of a region-wide program to build and improve thirteen vocational schools across eastern Kentucky, this area will gain two new schools. Bids are ready to let on a $250,000 building in Inez, and by August 1 bids will be let on a $300,000 facility in Belfry in Pike County.

2. In this area, again as a part of a region-wide effort, five landholders have gotten the nod from the Appalachian Regional Commission for land stablization and conservation projects.

3. Roads are a principal part of the program's economic investment in Appalachia, and in this area this will mean the widening and straightening of roads such as Highway 119 and Highway 23.

4. We are also hopeful of obtaining a federal grant to help in the construction of an educational television network for eastern Kentucky. Transmitters in Hazard and Ashland will beam into this area the best in educational and informational programs.

As I said, this represents funding activities covering only the last year and a half. Before these programs were born other programs, such as the Area Redevelopment Act and the Accelerated Public Works Act, also did much for us. But this is only the beginning, I assure you. There are more programs, some on the drawing board, others ready for passage, that will require heavy emphasis on the area approach.

A prime example is the Rural Community Development District bill now being proposed by the agriculture people. Already passed by one house, it is now being considered by the second, and final approval is said to be probable.[2] You will hear more about this later from one of our panel members, but I would like to point out at this time that this new program is built entirely around the idea of multicounty districts.

Existing programs, such as those under health and mental health, already work on an area basis. So does the state's tourist development matching program. The state's land use planning assistance program is administered on an area basis, and I understand you are now contemplating an area-wide land use plan here in the Big Sandy.

Now, all this is good. All of this spells benefits to our state. It also spells some problems for us. Because in spite of the fact everybody is eager to work on an area basis, they don't necessarily want to work with area groupings used by the other fellow.

Everyone wants to draw lines of cooperation on the map, but they want them to be their lines and not lines drawn previously by someone else. This means that for one program your county might be required to work with one grouping of counties, but that to take advantage of another program you might find yourselves working with an entirely different set of counties.

If we allow this to happen, and it has already begun to happen, the whole idea of multicounty cooperation will go up in smoke. Although there will be limited cooperation on an individual program basis, there will be little, if any, cooperation on a multiprogram or overall basis.

And this presents another problem, one I know touches all of you. As each new program arrives on the scene demanding new procedures, new area boundaries, and new organization, local people find themselves attending more and more meetings. They find that in order to keep up on all the new information on the myriad of new programs being developed, they are "meeting more and enjoying it less." The lessening of enjoyment, of course, comes from the fact that this increase in meeting time is biting into their action time—the time they need to actually get these programs going.

I don't feel, and I don't believe you do, either, that we can successfully tackle our problems on a one-program-at-a-time basis. We have tried that approach and it has not worked. No one program can stand alone. Each must be backed up and supplemented by another so that the impact of both can be more fully realized.

Does it make sense for the economic opportunity people to train folks for jobs when we have not provided industrial development or job-building projects using, say, the resources of the economic development program? Does it make sense for the Appalachian program to build roads to spur tourism when we have made no provision to build or upgrade tourist facilities along that road?

In order to coordinate job training with job building or road building with tourism development, we need to keep the geographic areas through which these programs are administered the same. And this, I warn you, is going to take some doing.

Many of the tools we keep in our development kit are federal ones, and therefore many of the problems we have in making them work for us come from the federal level. Less than two weeks ago, I received a letter from a federal official advising me that his agency had mapped out a development area for us, a geographic area through which this agency was planning to work and dispense funds. There are several things about the way this one area was drawn that made me hesitate to accept it as a bona fide development district.

In the first place, their area designation agreed with no other grouping of counties ever set up for any program for that area of the state. Secondly, their area was much too large to allow for practical area-wide citizen participation. Thirdly, their area took in three counties of another state, which could turn out to be practically and legally unworkable.

The problem, then, is clear: either we begin penciling our own map or someone else will mark it for us. It is important, however, that we do this job intelligently with sureness and unity. A few years ago, when he was still commander of the NATO forces, General Norstad remarked that "The enemy that worries me most is the one that knows exactly what he's doing."[3] Certainly, we do not want to give those in the federal government any cause to feel that we view them as enemies—but just as certainly we need to show them that we know what we are doing.

Because I feel this to be the vital issue that it is, I urge you to begin thinking of how a consistent, across-the-board, all-program grouping of counties can be obtained in this area. For my part, I pledge to do three things to assist this effort:

1. Work to achieve unanimity in Frankfort on coalignment of those multicounty groupings used by state agencies.

2. Work as "Your Man In Washington," to see that whatever difficulties we might have there are ironed out.

3. Work with you, through my area development office, to see that your wishes and preferences in the matter are also represented.

In the process of our working with you on this problem, you may find that you have some re-evaluating of your own to do, to reassess the boundary lines of the councils, committees, and other organizations through which you already work. There are three good reasons why you might do this: first, you may discover that the boundary lines you set some years ago are now simply out of date and that a new pattern needs to be cut. Second, you will discover that state programs, with criteria of their own, will have to be taken into consideration if you are to take full advantage of them. Third, I know you will discover that the new federal programs have their own sets of boundary line criteria and that these will certainly have to be looked at when you assess the manner in which your area groups are organized at the present time.

In order to succeed in our developmental efforts we need the tools offered us by the federal government. What we don't need are those influences and regulations that will prevent us from coordinating those programs in the most efficient, useful, and economic way possible. Organization of work at the local and area level must be handled by local and area people. If it is handled in any other way—if direction of these programs is to be purely a from-the-top-down situation—we will find ourselves weakened and less able to take care of our own problems.

---

1. The Area Development Districts in Kentucky were an outgrowth of a variety of "Great Society" federal aid legislation requiring local districts and local planning groups. During the Breathitt administration Robert A. Cornett, area development director, communicated with local officials and citizens' committees across Kentucky to select the most workable boundaries for federal programs. In early 1967 Cornett released an area development district plan dividing the Commonwealth into fifteen major economic development districts. The districts ranged in size from five to seventeen counties. Noting that nearly all federal programs required multicounty districts, Cornett aimed at establishing boundaries consistent for as many programs as possible. Although the major emphasis was upon federal programs, Cornett correctly predicted that many state activities would follow the proposed boundaries. Press release, March 14, 1967, Area Development Office file, Breathitt papers.

2. The Rural Community Development District Act was recommended to the Congress as another element of Lyndon Johnson's "Great Society" legislative program in 1966. The measure was to provide grants to establish central planning agencies in rural areas consisting of a regional trade center and its economic hinterlands. The agencies were to coordinate planning for investment in public services and to secure available federal aid. The measure passed the Senate on April 25 but expired in the House without coming to a vote. *Congressional Quarterly Weekly Report*, January 21, 1966, p. 280.

3. Lauris Norstad (1903-), graduated U.S. Military Academy (1930); promoted to general (1952); air deputy, S.H.A.P.E. (1953-1956); Supreme Allied Commander, Europe, S.H.A.P.E. (1956-1963); president, Owens-Corning Fiberglass Company (1964-). *Who's Who in America, 1976-1977*, 39th ed. (Chicago, 1976).

HARVEY ALUMINUM DEDICATION
Lewisport / August 12, 1966

THIS dedication is an important event in Kentucky's economic history. This new Harvey Aluminum Company facility is Kentucky's first primary producer of aluminum. As such, it is of particular significance to Kentucky's economic growth. The 1,000 jobs to be created here are the first of what will undoubtedly be thousands of additional jobs in an expanding Kentucky aluminum industry.

The location of Harvey in Lewisport did not just happen. Hard work by many citizens and organizations in Hancock County was necessary to cause this event to take place. And, in addition, there was interest, work, and cooperation in great measure from neighboring communities and counties. This type of area cooperation was in a sense unique and points the way to greater development effectiveness in the future. Our development effort and teamwork must not stop at the county line. We must blend our efforts on a broader geographic basis for maximum success.

The assistance given by Owensboro to this endeavor deserves special mention. This larger community, realizing that what benefits Lewisport benefits Owensboro, gave full support in all ways. A joint effort made feasible the solution of the many problems always inherent in an enterprise of this magnitude.

Harvey Aluminum's decision to locate in Lewisport stimulated considerable national comment on a number of counts. The decision of Lewisport to finance this $50 million facility through issuance of municipal industrial revenue bonds aroused undue interest in this form of financing. Use of revenue bond financing for industrial plans has been criticized by certain special interest groups for a number of years. This criticism has reached a new intensity in recent months. In my opinion, it is unjustified.

Industrial revenue bonds issued by localities of this state have been good for Kentucky. They have financed the suppliers of the jobs so badly needed by our citizens. The officials and citizens of Lewisport exhibited vision and courage in the decision to finance Harvey Aluminum through this means. They have provided on their own initiative a local economic base from which future growth and expansion will spring.

The facts tell us clearly that industrial revenue bonds have added strength to the Kentucky economy. Plants so financed and in operation had 17,000 employees in December, 1965, and annual payrolls of $75 million. And this does not include Harvey and a number of other major firms not yet in production. Let those who frown on this method of financing argue their case with those 17,000 workers and their families. And they should not neglect those in thousands of new secondary jobs, the merchants, and those working in service occupations.

The location of Lewisport on the Ohio River is a strong positive factor for future growth to Lewisport and Hancock County. The Ohio River is destined to be one of the chief catalysts for growth in Kentucky in the years ahead. The potential of this valley for industrial purposes has been realized, and significant growth has already been recorded in this sector of the economy. Hancock County became fully aware of the value of the Ohio with the location of Harvey, and this was reaffirmed recently by the announcement of Wes Cor Corporation to build a pulp facility at Hawesville. This, incidentally, will be the first pulp facility constructed in Kentucky during the past 100 years.

There is awareness of the industrial importance of the river, but less attention has been given to its recreational possibilities. These, in my opinion, are unbounded and will be extremely important to Kentucky and her neighboring states in the years to come.

The Lewisport Economic Area, which includes Daviess, McLean, Ohio, Breckinridge, and Hancock counties, has been a steadily growing area over the past several years. Population has increased in these five counties about 5 percent since the 1960 census. There are about 38,000 nonfarm jobs in the area, and these, of course, are heavily concentrated in Daviess County. There are indications that total nonagricultural employment has increased by 15 percent during the past five years. Manufacturing furnishes approximately 11,500 jobs and seems destined for appreciable gains in the future.

Hancock County's two new firms and the location of Cowden and Thomas Industries in Ohio County are optimistic signs for the area's more rural sector. Owensboro's growth momentum will inevitably continue.

Even more important than what has happened in past growth is the potential for the future. This area, in my opinion, will continue to grow and prosper at a greater rate than has been experienced. My thinking in this respect is based on the fact that local organization and leadership for development is strong in most of the area's communities.

There is a substantial labor supply of easily trainable persons who can be recruited for industrial jobs. Two major rivers are available for transportation and for processing water. Transportation is also adequate by road and rail. Electric power, a prime ingredient of many growth industries, is available in large quantity at reasonable rates. Two institutions of higher learning and a major area vocational school are located at Owensboro. Vocational facilities will continue to be improved in the future to meet the needs of industry and business. In fact, a $1,200,000 expansion program will be completed next year at the Owensboro Area Vocational School. One-half the funds will come from the bond issue, and one-half from federal funds.

The area is near major recreational complexes. There are a variety of industrial sites available throughout the area to meet the needs of many types of industry. These factors very simply add to growth.

Again, let me stress the importance of Harvey, not only to this area but to all of Kentucky. This is another first in our industrial structure. Not only do we continue to grow, but our diversity and quality is satisfying. During the past two and one-half years twenty-two firms listed in *Fortune*'s top 500 have located in Kentucky, and our growth is widespread geographically.

Kentucky's industrial and economic future is exceptionally promising. However, progress will not occur automatically. You at the local and we at the state level must continue our efforts and cooperation if we are to produce the future we desire. I am confident that this will be ours.

KENTUCKY CHAMBER OF COMMERCE TOUR
Elizabethtown / September 27, 1966

THE Dow-Corning Corporation has built a $275,000 addition to its plant here this year. This is just a small part, of course, of the $15 million in new and expanded industry that has been added to the economy of Elizabethtown during the nearly three years of this administration.

Some $14 million of the total expenditure may be attributed to the Gates Rubber Company, which started here in 1964 with a $2 million investment and soon effected a $12 million expansion.

Your older industries here are reflecting success by their expansions. Last year, Crucible Steel constructed $600,000 worth of new facilities. Also last year, the Coca Cola Bottling Company added $300,000 of production power, and the Ingraham Company had a $150,000 expansion.

Throughout Kentucky, I might add, progress is being made in such areas of service provided by state government as health, welfare, safety, and highways. We have underway at this time the largest building and construction program in the history of the Commonwealth.[1]

---

1. Governor Breathitt delivered similar addresses, each focusing on local economic development, in Hodgenville, Munfordville, Mammoth Cave, Glasgow, Scottsville, Franklin, Bardstown, Bowling Green, Hopkinsville, Russellville, Guthrie, Elkton, Madisonville, Henderson, and Owensboro. The tour began September 27 and concluded September 29. He made a similar tour to several eastern Kentucky communities September 26-29, 1967.

KENTUCKY SCIENCE AND TECHNOLOGY ADVISORY COUNCIL
Frankfort / October 10, 1966

I WANT to express my appreciation to you, the members of the state's first statutory Advisory Council on Science and Technology, for having agreed to undertake the momentous and difficult tasks ahead, in addition to your other heavy responsibilities of your individual jobs and personal interests.[1] There is little, if any, personal reward for the public service you are about to perform. But were it not for such service, given freely by dedicated leaders such as you, our great free enterprise society would not exist today.

Each of you [has] achieved success in your particular field; you represent the best leadership Kentucky has to offer for the advancement of science and technology in the state. You are a pioneer body in that you have been constituted for a purpose never before attempted by the Commonwealth, and probably only by a few states in the Union. You are a unique body. I am convinced you will achieve a degree of success that will gain the attention of our sister southern states—indeed from the rest of the nation.

The people of our Commonwealth may today take little note of your purpose, as our generation will not be the great benefactors of what we may accomplish. But we cannot place a value on the rewards our children and their children stand to gain from the accomplishments of this newly established council and commission.

During my term as governor, I have had the privilege to name many special study groups and commissions directed toward solutions of specific critical problems—and all have been very important. But none have been more important, or needed more, than this council which the 1966 legislature established. I regret that it wasn't established at least twenty years ago. But we in Kentucky have had many other social and economic problems to overcome before such a body as this could be effective.

I believe we have now progressed to a point in our socio-economic structure where this body can become an effective force in the future economic development of Kentucky. I view this as another first step being taken by Kentucky in achieving the highest economic level our capabilities will permit. And one of our major goals is to extend our capabilities year by year and decade by decade.

Each of you well understands the impact technology is making on our society today. It is an established fact that the society which chooses not to accept leadership as dictated by this age of technology will become a society of the past. It will become the society on the lower end of the economic and cultural level, for such a society cannot compete for long with those who take the initiative in developing new and better programs in all fields for the betterment of mankind, whether it be in education, health, agriculture, or science and technology.

The degree of progress achieved in one field is dependent upon the degree of progress achieved in others. And lest we lose all the worthwhile gains made in Kentucky in recent years we must become truly a leader in the complex and ever changing field of science and technology. We must not only be a producer of the products of science but we must have a greater role in developing those products which are yet to come from the test tube.

This is a role essential to Kentucky if she is to achieve and maintain a totally balanced economy. It is essential to our nation's welfare that we meet this challenge. The vast federal programs for economic development now being implemented in the state will be meaningless in years ahead unless we today take appropriate steps at the state level to build upon those programs. We must view these programs as temporary measures to relieve economic deprivations and not as the total solution. Otherwise we shall continue to depend upon the federal government for the leadership which is rightfully our responsibility. I say the states have a responsibility to assume joint leadership with the federal government in giving meaningful direction to federal-state programs, rather than allowing the federal government to lead alone. And I intend for Kentucky to become a leader—not separately from the federal government, but with it.

Kentucky has already taken an initial step in assuming leadership in the field of science. We are the first state to have established an authority on atomic energy. And we are among the first of our fifty states to establish a Council and Commission on Science and Technology for the purpose of directing and developing overall strategy in scientific research on a statewide basis. Your goal essentially is to assess our resources and capabilities and to develop a unified plan for using these resources and capabilities in a scientific research program.

Though Kentucky is making progress in scientific research facilities, Kentucky still is among some forty states which are doing no more than 30 percent of the nation's total scientific research. This is an imbalance which must be corrected for the good of our nation, and we in Kentucky must help correct it for the betterment of Kentucky's economic posture.

Though we are increasing our per capita income in Kentucky, we shall never be able to reach the per capita income of our richest states unless we obtain a greater percent of the nation's scientific research. We cannot expect to reach the economic level of those states having great centers of scientific research unless we too broaden our scientific research program. I am convinced we have the capabilities to become a leader in the scientific research field. However, the task ahead may be difficult, as we must enter into an accelerated program in order to merely catch up. Great scientific research centers are well established in the eastern states and on the West Coast. These centers will continue to be depended upon for major scientific advancements until other centers are developed. This is the challenge we in Kentucky face, and one we will meet.

We now have five state universities and the University of Louisville through which we can start developing a comprehensive scientific research program. We have a nucleus of independent and industrial research centers. Industry must be induced to expand its existing centers in the state and establish others. We must entice good scientific teams to come to Kentucky, convince our science students to remain in Kentucky, and provide them with the needed facilities. An immediate goal is to obtain more federal research grants for projects which may be successfully conducted in existing facilities.

Your job is a challenging one—the opportunities are unlimited—the rewards in knowledge of public service and self-satisfaction are to be envied by others and cherished by you. We are grateful for this contribution you are making to the people of Kentucky.

---

1. The 1966 General Assembly created the Kentucky Science and Technology Commission to replace the Kentucky Atomic Energy Authority and the Kentucky Science and Technology advisory committee on Nuclear Energy. See "an act relating to science and technology," *Acts, 1966;* Chapter 220 (S.B. 298), pp. 916-29.

1966 ECONOMIC DEVELOPMENT STATEMENT
Frankfort / December 31, 1966

I AM pleased to report that the major indices of industrial and economic growth continued to reflect an upward turn in Kentucky during 1966. Kentucky's economy is at its healthiest and unemployment is at its lowest in many years. Today some 41,200 more Kentuckians are in nonagricultural jobs than a year ago. The November total approached 823,000, an all-time high.

Manufacturing wages alone have jumped 12.5 percent between 1965 and 1966. The 1966 total is estimated to be $1,318,000,000, as contrasted with $1,171, 735,000 in 1965. Profits and corporate income also are up.

Since I took office in December, 1963, the flood of announcements of new or expanded manufacturing facilities has passed the 600 mark. These new plants and additions mean that new job openings are being filled rapidly by some 37,000 Kentuckians. Capital investment in these new facilities will exceed $500 million.

And it means that many nationally known companies, as well as locally sponsored operations, are putting their dollars and their faith in Kentucky's improved business climate, and in the locational factors which are the keys to industrial and economic growth in the Commonwealth.

These "plus" factors include availability of ample and trainable manpower, central location in relation to industrial and consumer markets, abundant water supplies, adequate power and fuels to turn the wheels of industry, and a growing network of interstate highways and state parkways to speed inbound shipment of raw materials and outbound cargoes of finished products.

Industry likes Kentucky and the Kentucky program of gearing for development on all economic fronts. This was demonstrated in 1966 as many new industrial facilities went into operation from Louisa on the Big Sandy River in eastern Kentucky to Clinton in the far western part of the state.

Many other industrial operations, announced in 1966, are now either in production, under construction, or on the drawing board. When all are in place, it will mean something like $300 million more of investment in Kentucky's industrial future compared to $212,402,000 in 1965. This 1966 figure includes two electric power generating stations: one under construction on the Big Sandy River by the Kentucky Power Company, a subsidiary of American Electric Power Company, which will cost $100 million, and the other—to cost $25 million—going up in Hancock County as a facility of the Big Rivers Rural Electric Cooperative Corporation.

When these new power plants are "on stream," plus others now under construction in the state, it will mean that there will be better than a 50 percent hike in electric power generation in Kentucky.

Our state also in 1966 enjoyed its greatest year ever in highway construction as $194,527,639 in road construction was put under contract, setting an all-time record. By the end of September this year, the latest reporting period by the U. S. Bureau of Public Roads, Kentucky was third in the nation in number of miles under highway construction contracts, surpassed only by Texas and North Carolina. There are other indications that 1966 was a banner year of economic growth in Kentucky.

The Department of Revenue reports that there was an 11.5 percent increase in combined General Fund and Road Fund tax revenues for the fiscal year ending June 30, 1966, as compared with the previous fiscal year. The total revenue for the year ending last June was $427,233,019. The money increase was $43,997,969. Receipts for the second half of 1966 will not be complete until the end of January, but every indication shows that revenue is up sharply and the state is meeting its revenue estimates.

Coal production was up in 1966, with an estimated 89,800,000 tons taken from mines in eastern and western Kentucky coalfields. This is a 3 percent increase over 1965.

Gasoline consumption increased 6.5 percent, with the estimated gallonage this year pegged at 1,190,000,000. This reflects, in part, the tremendous growth of the tourist industry, sparked largely by national advertising and publicity about Kentucky's excellent state park system.

For the first nine months of this year, farm marketings showed a heartening 19.7 percent jump over the same period in 1965. Farm income was $444,421,000, compared to $371,198,000 for a comparable period in 1965. The total picture will not be known until the remainder of the 1966 tobacco crop is marketed early next year. Prospects are good that the 1966 farm income will set an all-time record despite the fact that the pre-

Christmas tobacco sales were lower than anticipated and much of the crop will be sold in 1967.

There is every indication that Kentucky will move ahead on industrial and other economic fronts in 1967. According to economists, the national outlook is bright and 1967 will be prosperous. Wages and profits will reach new highs. There will be more jobs than ever, especially for skilled workers. The unskilled and semiskilled will find employment harder to come by. The Gross National Product will soar to somewhere between $780 and $783 billion compared to $738 billion in 1966. Kentucky, now gaining stature as a state with significant industrial output and potential, will certainly share in the manufacturing and other economic developments which lie ahead in the new year.

As we usher in the new year, permit me to remind you that Kentucky will celebrate its 175th birthday this year—a history that has been filled with great tradition and color. Building on the solid foundations developed in 1966, we can, by working together, make 1967 the best year Kentucky has ever known.

PRESS CONFERENCE
Frankfort / February 24, 1967

I AM today announcing, along with Mr. Roy Richards, president of the company, that Kentucky's first aluminum reduction plant will be built in Hancock County by the Southwire Company of Carrollton, Georgia.[1] The 120,000-ton capacity plant will be built at a cost of approximately $90 million—making it one of the largest investments ever made in Kentucky. The plant, which will ultimately employ 600 persons with an annual payroll of $5 million, will be located on the Ohio River near Hawesville.

Operation is scheduled for 60,000 tons of production by late 1969, with the production of the remainder to be underway in late 1970. Southwire will break ground in April, 1967, for its first facility.

The first stage in the giant Southwire Aluminum plant will consume approximately seventy million kilowatt-hours of electricity each month. This power will be purchased from the Green River Rural Electric Cooperative Corporation in Owensboro. One of the chief reasons for the company's decision to locate in Kentucky was the fact that Rural Electric could provide ample power at a reasonable cost.

This announcement represents another major development in the aluminum industry, which is attaining paramount importance in Kentucky's industrial future. The location of a new Kentucky plant of this magnitude by a firm as prominent in its field as Southwire Company will create a far-reaching effect upon the economy of Kentucky.

I know that I speak for all of our three million citizens when I say, Mr. Richards, that Kentucky greatly appreciates this investment on your company's part in our state. It demonstrates clearly that you have faith in Kentucky and its future, that you believe that our state is a good place to do business and to make a profit.

Here in Kentucky we are putting forth every effort to develop our economy, to provide good-paying jobs for our people, and to put our economy on a sound, solid base. This industrial revolution we are experiencing will affect not only the take-home pay of our people but also the development of our schools, our colleges and universities, our highways and other public facilities and services. As our industrial economy grows, so will our social and cultural opportunities.

This announcement today culminates more than a year's negotiations and work carried on between Southwire, Mr. J.R. Miller, and state officials.[2] It was Christmas week of last year that I sat down with representatives of the company to talk about the advantages of locating such a plant in Kentucky and the assistance that we could provide at the state level in building this huge plant. These efforts are more than rewarded with this announcement.

This new plant will put Kentucky in the heavy metals business from the start of the product to its finish. It is an important breakthrough for our state and should bring about the location of many satellite industries in Kentucky.

To Commissioner Peden and her staff and especially J.R. Miller of Owensboro, I express my immense appreciation for the work and effort you have done in securing this plant. To Mr. Richards and other company officials, I say welcome. We deeply appreciate your decision to locate in Kentucky.

---

1. Roy Richards (1911-), corporation executive; president, Roy Richards Realty Corporation, Carrolton, Georgia (1950-); Southwire Realty Company, Carrolton (1950-); National Southwire Aluminum Company, Hawesville, Kentucky (1968-). *Who's Who in America, 1976-1977,* 39th ed. (Chicago, 1976).

2. James R. Miller (1916-), public utility executive, Owensboro, Kentucky. President of Miller Construction Company (1944-1946); general manager of Green River Rural Electric Coop Corporation (1946-); member of several state advi-

sory boards and active in Democratic party politics. Hambleton Tapp, ed., *Kentucky Lives* (Hopkinsville, Ky. 1966), p. 361.

CARBORUNDUM COMPANY DEDICATION
Hickman / March 30, 1967

DEDICATION of this major facility of the Graphite Products Division of the Carborundum Company is a particularly gratifying event. Carborundum is a major producer in one of the nation's real growth industries. This firm will upgrade Kentucky's industrial complex through its modern production techniques and management competence. Then, too, it is always satisfying to witness sound industrial growth in my native western Kentucky. In my opinion, the economic future of the entire Purchase is particularly bright. You have the resources that will guarantee progress if the proper decisions for allocation and employment of these resources are made.

We in state government appreciate the fine publicity which Carborundum has given the Commonwealth and Hickman through a double-page color spread in *Business Week* calling attention to this new plant and distribution to national news media of pictures and description of this facility located, as they stated, in "the new dynamic Mississippi Valley." We bid a warm welcome to members of the Carborundum board of directors and hope that they are enjoying the livability and beauty of the Purchase. Now, let both state government and Hickman reciprocate by dedicating ourselves to seeing that this operation is successful. All promises to Carborundum must be kept; all obligations must be honored.

This major plant location, in a cornfield here at Hickman, was a true team effort involving full cooperation by many groups and organizations. Your chamber of commerce and industrial commission were motivated and organized for effective performance. Leadership from men such as Ardel Fields, Elbert Burcham, and Dr. R.H. White was an essential ingredient for success.[1] And there are many other unsung heroes in your industrial program who have a right to feel pride today.

The Kentucky Department of Commerce provided strong support in this project. I am very proud of Kentucky's industrial record of the past three years and three months, which totaled 700 announcements of new and expanded facilities to employ 45,000 industrial workers and with a new capital investment of $750 million. And I am proud of the commissioner of commerce and her staff.

Your resources for additional growth in Hickman are imposing:

•your labor supply is bountiful;

•land for additional commerce and industry is available;

•rail service is adequate;

•the potential from the Mississippi River is great;

•Murray State University is only fifty miles to the east;

•the "Land Between the Lakes" complex is within easy driving distance; and

•the terminus of the Purchase Parkway is only ten miles away.

Yet, the existence of a potential for growth does not ensure growth. You must be willing to organize, plan, and then act to convert potential to actuality. Your community attitude must be that of cooperation and progress. Past accomplishments indicate that this sort of organization, desire, and willingness to work for growth is found today in Hickman. School improvements, utility extension, a summer recreation program, and other improvements are indicators of a community with pride, leadership, and concern for the future.

Here in the Purchase—bounded on the east by the Tennessee River, the north by the Ohio, and the west by the Mississippi—I am vividly reminded of the economic importance to Kentucky of our rivers. These are truly major growth assets for the future. The Mississippi was important in Carborundum's decision to produce at Hickman. It is also of great interest to West Virginia Pulp and Paper in their consideration of a location near Wickliffe. Harvey Aluminum, Southwire Aluminum, and Wescor would not have decided on Hancock County as a point to produce had the Ohio River not been there.

Our rivers have been of importance in our past—they are of importance in our present—they will be of even greater importance in our future, if developed. The mere existence of a river system does not guarantee that development will take place. Rather, the means must exist whereby potential can be transformed into reality if this resource is to have maximum impact.

The 1966 General Assembly enacted farsighted legislation in this respect. Creation of the Kentucky Port and River Development Commission was a giant step forward toward maximum utilization of our river-related resources.[2] This commission is directed to:

(1) Aid in the promotion and development of river-related industry, agriculture, and commerce in Kentucky.

(2) Aid in the promotion and development of local riverport authorities.

(3) Aid in promotion and development of industrial districts, parks, and sites for complexes that utilize the rivers and river-related resources.

(4) Analyze, plan, and aid in systematically developing river-related resources by the development of services and facilities.
(5) Promote the development of industrial parks and terminal facilities for manufacturing and distribution industries for attracting and serving private and public enterprises that are river oriented.
(6) Promote the exportation of Kentucky-made products in foreign commerce.

This same legislature also improved legislation relating to local "riverport authorities" which was first enacted in 1964. And I am pleased to note that Hickman was the first city to form a "riverport authority" under the 1964 legislation. The Kentucky Port and River Development Commission was activated in mid-1966, with your fellow townsman Elbert Burcham as a member. Although funds for operation are scarce, the commission is active today and working in close cooperation with your local port authority.

Here are some things that the commission has underway:
(1) The needs for a public port within a 100-mile radius of Hickman are being surveyed.
(2) The 700 largest industries in the United States are being surveyed regarding their use and needs for ports in Kentucky and the importance of ports to their expansion plans. Hickman, with the only slack water port between St. Louis and Memphis, is given prominence in this survey.
(3) A proposal to the Economic Development Administration to analyze (a) the feasibility and design of a major public port plus marinas to serve the sixty-mile stretch of the Kentucky-Mississippi and (b) port facilities on Lake Barkley is in the process of formulation.

And entirely consistent with these efforts, which will affect our future world trade, was approval by the Economic Development Administration of a technical study of the feasibility of a "Latin American Friendship Center" at Fulton. We in Kentucky have taken the firm initial steps for fuller development and utilization of our river resources. These are important actions toward future growth.

---

1. Ardel Fields (1927-), resident of Hickman, Kentucky, and presently employed by United States Postal Service. Elbert Burcham, Jr. (1927-), owner and operator of Burcham Chevrolet Company in Hickman, Kentucky. Dr. R. H. White (1922-), employed by West Kentucky Allied Services in Mayfield, Kentucky. Information provided by Angie Lawson of the *Hickman Courier.*

2. See "an act relating to the port and river development and the taxation thereof," *Acts, 1966,* Chapter 64 (S.B. 127), pp. 409-15.

INDUSTRIAL APPRECIATION LUNCHEON
New York, New York / September 22, 1967

HERE in the twilight days of my term as governor of Kentucky, I am particularly aware that during the four years of my administration Kentucky has been undergoing a major social and economic transition. Kentucky has made progress on practically all fronts during the past four years. Our economic progress has been facilitated by the actions of many of you to locate new plants or expand existing facilities in Kentucky. For those decisions we are truly grateful. I feel that in Kentucky we created an atmosphere which is conducive to industrial and business expansion and growth.

By your actions you registered approval of our governmental programs and your confidence in Kentucky as a sound and profitable place in which to do business. I've come here to express the deep appreciation of three million Kentuckians for your millions and millions of dollars in investments in our state. This luncheaon is for you and is symbolic of our gratitude.

I am very proud of the economic growth of Kentucky during the past four years. By the end of 1967 we will have created a minimum of 140, 000 new nonagricultural jobs during this administration through your help. This increase of 20 percent in job opportunities for Kentuckians was a rate of gain substantially in excess of any similar period in our state's history.

A particularly brilliant chapter in our story of growth during the past four years has been industrial location and expansion which resulted—as of the end of August—in 749 announcements by manufacturing concerns of location of new plants or the expansion of existing facilities in our state. The 57,000 new manufacturing jobs created when full production is reached will inject a stimulant into all phases of Kentucky's economy.

By the end of this year we fully expect announced new plant investment for the past four years to exceed $1.25 billion. During the past four years we have witnessed a $1.9 billion jump in personal income of Kentuckians. Unemployment is down to just about 4 percent of the labor force thanks to many of you.

This expanding economy certainly was not the result of actions by state government alone. True, we have carried out an economic development program spearheaded by what I consider to be the nation's best Department of Commerce. But we have also had the full cooperation and support of hundreds of organizations throughout the state. These organizations, particularly those at the local level, have provided a strong foundation on which we have built. Not only did we operate an aggressive, imaginative program for economic development in Kentucky, but we made a concerted effort to provide a state governmental environment which was good for business operations. We have tried to be fair to all segments of the economy, and in this I feel that we have succeeded.

In looking back, I feel that some of our policies and programs which are of particular significance to business growth are: (1) We have maintained an equitable, stable, balanced tax system. Kentucky has had no increase in state taxes since the 1960 session of our General Assembly. Few states, if any, can match this record of tax stability.

(2) We have made massive expenditures in education at all levels in full awareness that we must provide an intelligent, educated work force if the needs of our industries are to be met in the future. Vocational education has undergone tremendous expansion both in facilities and numbers of students. We are making every effort to ensure that the curriculum of our vocational-educational schools is adequate to meet the needs of business and industry. We have made startling improvements in the staff and facilities of our universities. We realize that industry's need for managers, professionals, and technicians must be met to ensure future growth.

(3) Kentucky is rapidly completing a modern highway system adequate to handle the goods of commerce and industry. Our highway program of the past four years has been based on economics rather than expediency. We have deliberately planned our system of highways to stimulate development and to meet the needs of growing industry. Today there are few manufacturing concerns who are not within thirty-five miles of a modern four-lane highway.

(4) We have taken strong action for the conservation and proper utilization of our natural resources. A modern strip-mining law has been put on the books and is now being enforced. We improved our water pollution legislation and created a new air pollution commission. A new water resources authority was created in 1966 to plan for the future water needs of Kentucky and to see that these needs are met.

(5) State government has been operated efficiently, with a strong trend toward the use of more and more professional personnel and the professional approach to problem solving.

There have been other actions taken in Kentucky, while not directly related to industrial development, that have considerable indirect significance. In 1966 we passed a very broad-based civil rights act. In the same year a corrupt practices act was passed tightening state laws regulating political campaign contributions. We enacted a modern purchasing law to make our purchasing procedures more effective in order to ensure that the taxpayer gets more for his dollar. Congressional redistricting was accomplished in 1966 without difficulty. These actions reflect the progressive outlook of Kentucky and of state government.

Kentucky today, as you know, is a good place to invest and make a profit. Our communities are eager to get new plants. Our people are eager to work, to do a good job in whatever they undertake. We have the skilled workers, the proximity to markets, the modern transportation system, cheap and adequate power. All the basic ingredients of a great industrial state. When you choose to expand your plants, I hope you will look to Kentucky as the place to do business.

Kentuckians today are holding their heads high. No longer are we considered a backward state. We are on the move, and thanks to industrialists and businessmen like you, we are fast becoming a highly industrialized state. Daniel Boone long ago, when he first came through Cumberland Gap, said, "Heaven must be a Kaintuck of a place." Today, more than ever before, Daniel Boone's description fits the Bluegrass State.

KENTUCKY ECONOMIC DEVELOPMENT COMMISSION

Gilbertsville / October 4, 1967

SINCE this will probably be the last official meeting of the Economic Development Commission during my administration, I want to express to you my wholehearted appreciation for your support of our economic development program and your willing and able assistance and cooperation in carrying out this program. I know we are all proud of the results we have achieved. We are deeply indebted to all of you, but at the same time we know you have attained a large measure of gratification from your participation in a highly successful undertaking. I am very pleased to have this opportunity to spend some time with each of you, and perhaps discuss courses of action to sustain and perpetuate those portions of our program which we know are important to the future growth of Kentucky.

Since your terms do not expire until July of 1968, you will have an opportunity, as some of us will not, to help assure a continuation of some of the programs which you have seen initiated. Later on today we will, I hope, hear your recommendations on new programs of action and measures for strengthening some of those programs already in effect.

Whether Kentucky continues to grow, whether we pursue a course of innovation or become stale in our approach, whether our business climate continues to improve or whether it deteriorates, whether we will have in Kentucky 250 of the nation's top industrial firms or will be content with the present 150—these things depend upon individuals such as the members of this commission.

Recently I had an opportunity to meet and talk with industrialists from the New York and New England states who had established operations in Kentucky. We invited these business executives to a luncheon for the express purpose of thanking them for the faith they have had in Kentucky and for pledging to them our continued interest and lasting efforts to prove that this faith is justified. Some of you were at this luncheon.

Some of you were at a similar affair four years ago when I sought the help of many of these same executives in fulfilling a promise of 75,000 new nonagricultural jobs for Kentucky. Since that time fifty-four of the New York area firms have located new plants or expanded operations in Kentucky.

A similar luncheon will be held in Chicago later this month, and in Los Angeles the following month. We have actively sought expanded facilities of these firms. Obviously we have been able to sell them on the advantages of locating in Kentucky. I think it is only fitting that we now express our appreciation by doing everything in our power to fulfill our obligation to these companies, to insure a healthy business climate in Kentucky where they can enjoy profitable business operation.

The impetus of the past four years' growth alone could and should assure continued manufacturing expansion in the years ahead if we continue to provide the atmosphere that industry wants and requires to survive in a highly competitive field. Some of the new industries which we have gained—the aluminum plants, the paper mills, the wire and cable plants—are completely new fields of production for Kentucky, and their impact upon our future development will be great.

The over one billion dollars in plant investment in Kentucky since January, 1964, is unmatched in any similar period of our state's history. This is an indication that we are on the move—that we are on the way to attaining a prominent place in the industrial world.

Today we have in Kentucky about forty more of the nation's largest manufacturing firms than we had four years ago. Our industrial growth has become more widespread, encompassing a greater area of the state than ever before. We are achieving what every Kentuckian wants and needs.

The groundwork has been laid and the momentum can carry us far. Our biggest concern is to maintain our enthusiasm, to continue our program of development with further improvements, both in this program and in our business climate. We're going to depend upon you and others like you to carry forward this program.

AGRICULTURE & RURAL DEVELOPMENT

KENTUCKY COOPERATIVE COUNCIL
Lexington / February 11, 1964

THIS is one of many speaking appearances I expect to make during the four years of my administration to a group that has a primary concern for Kentucky agriculture and an ability to make a major contribution to it. I appreciate the opportunity to be with you this morning, not only because your invitation gives me a chance to be among many old friends but because it gives me a chance to enlist your support in a program that I hope will make a lasting impression on the farm economy of our state.[1]

It is a program that is designed to put money in the pockets of Kentucky's farmers, processors, manufacturers, merchants, and, indeed, all citizens of our state. It will give state and local governments additional money for services without additional taxes. It will help raise our standards of education, our standards of health, our standards of living. This program will, we hope, raise the income of Kentucky farmers by 50 percent during the next few years. It will result in a billion dollar agricultural economy for our state.

I talked about a billion dollar farm economy for Kentucky throughout my campaign for governor last year. I consulted with the most knowledgeable agricultural leaders I could find—including many of you—and I was assured this level could be reached. I have had a few preliminary meetings within the last few weeks on the organization we will need to promote this increased economy, and we are about ready to move.

I will announce, I hope sometime this week, a fifteen-man Agricultural Development Commission which will be attached to the governor's office.[2] Some of the members are in this room this morning. I will be chairman of the commission and the lieutenant governor will be vice chairman.[3] This will be, to my knowledge, the first time that agriculture has been given such attention within the office organization of any Kentucky governor.

In addition to the commission, we will have many committees and subcommittees serving in support of the commission. These will be specialized groups devoted to various segments of agriculture and working with and advising the commission on these subjects. In addition to the committees and subcommittees, we will have local organization and local participation devoted to needs and potentials of the counties and the various farming communities.

This entire organization will not be set up to function independently of other organizations or other agriculture efforts. Its duties will be to set the pace, to select the objectives, to help direct and channel the efforts of other groups and organizations.

The goal we have set for it is a difficult one. The work it will require is massive in scope and is unprecedented in the history of the Commonwealth. But the work when done, the goal when reached, will establish Kentucky as a leader in agriculture and will make our state a better, happier place for us and our children.

I am not here to tell you this morning that we will have a billion dollar farm economy while I am governor—I have never predicted that we will and I do not make this prediction now. Four years is too short a time in which to expect gains of this magnitude. But four years is plenty of time in which to launch the campaign that will give us those gains and in which to make significant progress toward the billion dollar goal.

What must Kentucky do to reach the billion dollar mark in agriculture? What would such an accomplishment mean related to today's figures? If we look for this goal to be reached simply by taking today's crops and products and applying the proper percentages to them in order to reach a billion dollar total, it might mean we would need to get $150 million more from our tobacco crop, $45 million more from dairy products, $30 million more from hogs, and $60 million more from cattle and calves. That is the magnitude of the task that faces us, but these examples do not really describe or define the task. They merely extend accomplishments of today, to reach the limits sought for tomorrow.

In my opinion, the task we face cannot be met with such a simple, quantitative extension. It requires a whole new approach to agriculture, the best and most imaginative plans we can formulate, unrestricted by today's or yesterday's notions of what our farms should be or do.

Certainly, we know that we are going to have to raise more and better cattle and hogs, produce more milk, and increase the crops we now produce. But this is not the entire answer. We are going to have to find new crops and new activities for our farms. We are going to have to render productive land that is not now producing. We are going to have to derive new products and new practices that use our agricultural output. We are going to have to develop new markets and methods of distribution. We are going to have to enlist new people in the cause of agriculture.

The commission will develop an overall plan for the campaign we must conduct and will set some goals relating to production of individual agricultural items—with the guidance and counsel of the committee and subcommittee organization. They are going to call on many of you here to help, to serve, to let them take advantage of your good nature and your good citizenship by piling assignments on you. They are going to solicit your thoughts, your energy, your imagination, your persuasive and leadership abilities.

My request of you is that you respond to them. That you give your interest and your strength and the talents that you possess. And that you spread the word of this effort to all of those who may provide similar assistance.

As I said earlier, this is only one of many speeches I plan to make before agricultural groups while I am governor. I believe there is no better way of launching ourselves on this great mission we have before us than to solicit the services of those who have both the best interests of Kentucky and of agriculture at heart. Yours is an organization with the inclination and the ability to push toward the goals we seek. I respectfully petition you, individually and as a group, to give us your help.

---

1. In 1964 Kentucky reported 133,038 farms covering 16,265,180 acres. The value of all farm products sold was $591,598,210. Persons involved in farm production totaled 449,353 in farm-operator households and 14,245 regular hired workers (150 days or more). U.S. Bureau of the Census, *Census of Agriculture, 1964: Statistics for States and Counties, Kentucky,* (Washington, 1965), pp. 7, 11, 35.

2. The Agriculture Development Commission was established on March 2, 1964. Commission members were Governor Breathitt, chairman, Lieutenant Governor Harry Lee Waterfield, vice chairman, Dr. William Seay, Wendell P. Butler, J.O. Matlick, William C. Johnstone, Samuel R. Guard, Hiliary Deweese, Robert Green, John Dixon, Charles Gatton, Lewis Allen, George Busey, John Moser, Henry Beserden, Sr., Barney Tucker, and R.O. Wilson. *Louisville Courier-Journal,* March 3, 1964.

3. Harry Lee Waterfield (1911-), member, Kentucky House of Representatives (1938-1950), speaker, (1944-1946); lieutenant governor of Kentucky (1955 -1959, 1963-1967); presently chairman of the board, Investors Heritage Incorporated. *Who's Who in the South and Southwest, 1965-1966,* 9th ed. (Chicago, 1965).

BURLEY DARK-LEAF EXPORT CONVENTION
Gilbertsville / September 28, 1964

It is a pleasure to be with you today and to talk with you briefly about Kentucky's agricultural outlook and about steps the state administration is taking to promote the prosperity of our rural economy and the well-being of our farmers. First of all, let me say that I come to you today in a spirit of great optimism for the economic future of Kentucky, for rapid expansion of our industry and for an increased agricultural income.

Last week I appointed a nineteen-member committee, as part of the Kentucky Agricultural Development Commission, to explore ways to step up the income of our tobacco farmers.[1] Some of you are on this committee. Next week we plan to call to Frankfort all committee members of the Agricultural Development Commission—somewhere in the neighborhood of two hundred Kentucky farm leaders—to discuss methods and programs whereby we can raise the state's annual farm income.

I feel that the commission and its committee members can be of great help in giving direction to Kentucky's agricultural development in the years ahead. The job they have undertaken will not be an easy one. We have not set a definite date for achieving that goal—let's just say that we hope to get there as soon as possible.

The Agricultural Development Commission already is working closely with the tobacco researchers at the University of Kentucky to encourage our tobacco producers to improve the quality of our product so that we can expand our domestic and export markets. Just as we find new markets for tourists, I am confident we can find new markets for Kentucky tobacco.

The efforts on your part—the ingenuity and energy put forth by you and the work being done by the Burley Tobacco Growers Cooperative Association—to expand the use of the American blended cigarette deserve the praise of all Kentuckians. After all, our economy is a seamless web. When the income of the tobacco farmer increases, so do the sales of the merchant, the miller, the trucker, and the restaurant owner.

Certainly, many countries in the Near East and the Middle East will buy more of our burley if they know how to make this desirably blended cigarette and if it can be purchased at a reasonable price. This means that our tobacco must be produced efficiently—a goal the Agricultural Development Commission will stress in order to reduce production costs while keeping the quality of the burley high.

The recent appropriation by Congress of $1.5 million, to be used in starting at the University of Kentucky an integrated agricultural-medical research program on smoking and health, provides the state with a unique opportunity.[2] Not only will it help the tobacco grower by hastening the day when people may smoke with maximum assurance of health, but it also enhances the state's prestige as a tobacco producing state. I assure you that the project has my full support and will receive the cooperation of all departments of the University of Kentucky and of all agencies of the Commonwealth of Kentucky in making it successful.

I do not need to tell you that I have been interested in tobacco all my life. I come from a tobacco community and a tobacco family. Income from tobacco fed me, clothed me, and educated me as I grew up. I feel I know firsthand the serious economic consequences that would result in Kentucky from any action to alter restrictively the present practices and methods of growing and distributing any tobacco product.

That is why I made appearances in Washington this past year to testify before the Federal Trade Commission and the House Committee on Interstate and Foreign Commerce at a time when tobacco faced its greatest crisis in several decades. I feel that we are winning the war to preserve our state's number one cash crop, but all the battles are not won. At a time when we are trying to increase our state's farm income, we must not let this goal blind us to the dangers that face tobacco.

Some political critics advocate the repeal of the farm price support program. You and I know that such action would bring the death knell to many of our state's tobacco growers. We can no more afford ten-cent tobacco than we can afford to shut the doors of our schools. As you know, tobacco accounts for about $300 million, or 45 percent, of Kentucky's farm income each year. It is by far Kentucky's chief cash crop, producing 82 percent of the receipts from all crops. As you know, 21 percent of all tobacco and about 70 percent of all burley grown in the United States is grown in Kentucky. Some 150,000 farms were engaged last year in producing burley on 226,000 acres of Kentucky land. If the price for tobacco falters, not only will Kentucky fail to reach its billion dollar farm goal; there will be danger that its agricultural income will actually fall below today's level and that many thousands of small farmers, already hard pressed to make a living, will be threatened with a marginal existence.

Farmers are not the only Kentuckians who would be affected directly. Sooner or later, some 12,000 jobs in processing and manufacturing in Kentucky and some $50 million in wages and salaries would be affected. This does not include those who profit from the transportation of tobacco or those who distribute or merchandise it. So this, then, is the stake that Kentucky has in protecting its tobacco economy.

The production and marketing program designed for tobacco has enabled price supports under which each farmer's lot of tobacco is priced at a profitable level. This system and the repetition with which it is continuously adopted by vote is evidence of the farmers' desire to work with the government in developing their economy. Our tobacco price support program has been operated at a relatively small cost, and it has established stability throughout the industry.

We cannot tolerate substandard conditions on the farm any more than we can in industry. A fair return is a necessity for the laborer and the owner in business. It is also necessary for those who farm our land. I pledge to you that, as long as I am governor, I will do all in my power to protect tobacco and to expand its production and price.

I am confident that, with the cooperation of farm and nonfarm people and with proper guidance, we can increase Kentucky's farm income substantially during the next three years. In that determination, let us sail together on a voyage of exploration, hope, and hard work.

---

1. The tobacco committee established by Governor Breathitt was one of several special product advisory committees to function under the overall direction of the Agricultural Development Commission. Its membership included Freeman Showalter, S.J. Stokes, Jr., John Berry, Louis Payne, Louis Ison, Ted Barnes, Emmett Walton, Joe Frank Ferguson, Jack Griffith, Holmes Ellis, Albert Clay, Clarence Maloney, Garner Hancock, T.H. Ruggles, Wayne Stewart, and Julian Walden. Press release, September 25, 1964, Agriculture file, Breathitt papers.

2. In the mid-1960s the surgeon general of the United States released a report linking smoking to the incidence of lung cancer and heart disease. Representatives of the tobacco industry and political figures from tobacco producing states contended no absolute evidence existed proving smoking was hazardous to health. Nonetheless, the industry and several states funded research programs to produce safer cigarettes. The agricultural-medical research program established at the University of Kentucky was a part of that effort. For a thorough statement of the tobacco industry position, see telegram from Frank Dryden of the Tobacco Institute to Don Mills, August 11, 1967 in Agriculture file, Breathitt papers. Governor Breathitt, in testimony before the Federal Trade Commission in Washington, D.C., on March 18, 1964, outlined the importance of the tobacco industry to Kentucky and attacked proposed regulations on advertising and labeling. "Such labeling and advertising regulations are not needed," he said. "Who among us does not know that if he smokes, eats or drinks to excess that he runs the danger of physical discomfort and physical harm. Do we need to label with a skull and crossbones all materials ingested by the human body because of the risk of unwise use or overindulgence. I feel very strongly that government agencies set up to protect the public should provide the strongest protection possible from those who would abuse or prey upon the public. I do not believe it is the duty of these agencies to try to scare the public or try to regulate a legitimate product to death." This address is not included in these papers.

KENTUCKY DAIRY PRODUCTS ASSOCIATION
Louisville / March 15, 1965

I AM glad to have this opportunity to meet with a group of Kentucky businessmen who have a vitally important part to play in developing one of this state's largest industries—the production, processing, and marketing of milk and its related products. We are making exciting progress in dairying today and there is every reason to believe we can make even greater progress in the future. If this appraisal of the future of the Kentucky dairyman appears optimistic, then I can only say that it is an accurate description of my views.

I am optimistic—very optimistic—and I am happy to say that my enthusiasm is shared by some of our leading farm experts who are most intimately familiar with our resources to expand this industry. This optimism is, I believe, shared by the majority of you here. You have, individually and as an organization, indicated your awareness of what we can achieve in this field, and you have demonstrated your desire to cooperate fully in our billion dollar farm program to insure success.

Actually, if we can all work together on this program, if we can cooperate on the many complex and interwoven details of this operation, if we can reach the point where we are beginning to realize a significant portion of the benefits suggested by the potential that exists, then there will be ample rewards reaped by all concerned. We want everyone to feel that he is an important part of a growing farm industry, that he has responsibilities to each of the other parts, responsibilities that transcend any one area of interest. And I want to make it clear that this responsibility rests just as heavily on the man who produces the product as it does on the man who sells it.

We have the opportunity today to become mid-America's horn of plenty for dairy products—with all the economic advantages that accrue to that status. We have the people, the plants, the know-how, the research facilities, the proximity to markets, the incentive—everything that is required. All we have to do now is accelerate our progress in building on the momentum that has been established. The opportunities will unfold in increasing numbers, and if we are prepared to seize them, we can confidently expect an era of unimagined prosperity.

Two years ago, Kentucky ranked second among the states in evaporated milk production. We ranked third in American cheese, nineteenth in butter, and thirteenth in total milk production. Although the figures for 1964 are not official yet, it appears that Kentucky's total value of milk produced last year will exceed $105 million. This means that dairying is second only to tobacco as the Kentucky farmer's cash crop.[1]

As processors, you have a profound impact on our state's economy. Our cheese operations illustrate this point. Cheese plants buy milk from more than 15,000 Kentucky farmers and they put some $20 million annually in their pockets. The plants employ about 1,000 persons and have a yearly payroll of about $5 million.

We have made a good start in building the Kentucky cheese processing industry. But we need to do much more. One way the state can help this industry as well as other milk and other food processors is to sponsor a nationwide advertising program calling attention to the high quality of Kentucky's farm products. This is the way to get the housewife to look for Kentucky products when she shops. The success of such an advertising program depends, to an extent, on the advertising campaign itself. There is one other thing, however, that we must keep in mind as we move forward in any comprehensive program designed to promote Kentucky's food industry. That one thing is the continuing need for improving the quality.

There will be a need, of course, for improving the basic product. The best processing, packaging, and marketing facilities in the world cannot compensate for an inferior product. Today's consumer is discriminating. Better than anyone you know this, and as a result you should insist on quality raw material.

By the same token, a quality product, even when properly processed, will stand little chance of wide acceptance unless it is properly marketed —and in many instances, the thing that sells in the first place is packaging. This is vitally important, not only because it is a primary factor in selling the product, but because, as you know, it is the third ranking cost in the average processing operation. I have asked the state Department of Agriculture and our Department of Public Information to prepare a plan to promote Kentucky's high-quality products in an effort to get more of them in the housewives' shopping baskets and more dollars in the pockets of producers and processors.

The great majority of us share the conviction that Kentucky's agricultural potential is practically limitless—and we base that conviction in large part on our knowledge of the obvious opportunities available to us in food production, processing, and marketing.

Today, there are 192 million Americans. In fifteen years there will be 250 million. Each of them is a potential market, a customer for the Kentucky milk industry, a step up the economic ladder for every citizen of this state. In production, in processing, in packaging, in marketing, in management, in research and in all other phases of this business—we will need vision, we will need intelligent leadership, we will need hard work, and we will need close cooperation. If we neglect one phase of the industry, all phases will suffer. Products are no good to us without markets. And markets are no good to us without products of sufficient quantity and quality to compete. Processing plants are useless without the highly trained people needed to run them and the broad research program needed to back them up.

By the same token, we have an informational job to do here. And, I believe that we all have a responsibility for seeing that this job gets done. We must get to the farmer with the message. For instance, the manufacturing milk plants in Kentucky can handle, without expanding their facilities, an additional 3,807,000 pounds of milk daily during the flush season and 8,865,000 pounds of milk daily during the winter months. To operate the existing plants for six additional months at the same rates as in the flush season would require approximately 800 million pounds of milk more per year, or an increased output of 75 percent by those farms who sell manufactured milk in Kentucky. At 1963 prices this would mean $26.8 million more income yearly for our dairy farmers. The market for this milk is already available. All we have to do is take advantage of this need.

To accomplish a higher dairy income, we must explore additional ways to reach our farmers and our potential dairymen with information and visual aids. We must encourage record keeping, production testing, dairy management, production efficiency, and proper handling. We must give high priority to adequate training and research, utilizing the facilities at the University of Kentucky fully.

This administration intends to give major emphasis to our farm economy and its related industries during the next three years. Let me say the door to the governor's office is open to your advice. I want your ideas, and I will help you put them to work. So long as people need milk to drink, so long as they eat cheese and butter, so long as they need cream and evaporated milk, then dairying can be a major industry in our state.

Let us use our imagination to develop our resources, to improve our income, to widen our opportunities. To increase farm income, this administration will back research, promote financing, encourage any projects, assist any group. The opportunity is ours![2]

---

1. Kentucky was a leading source of dairy products among the south-central states in 1965, ranking second in milk production and first in the production of butter and nonfat dry milk. Within the nation as a whole, Kentucky ranked thirteenth in milk production, fifth in production of American cheese, and second in the production of evaporated whole milk. Two long-term trends were notable in 1965: an increasing percentage of milk production was intended for marketing

to dealers and plants as opposed to direct retailing or home use; and Kentucky dairy farmers were becoming more efficient, increasing milk production while the total number of dairy cows declined. U.S. Department of Agriculture and Kentucky Department of Agriculture, *Kentucky Agricultural Statistics,* 1965 (Louisville, Ky., 1966), pp. 104–08.

2. In an effort to improve the growing dairy industry in Kentucky, Governor Breathitt, in August, 1964, appointed a nineteen-member state committee on dairying to serve as an advisory body to the Agricultural Development Commission. Members included John A. Moser, chairman, Robert Barkman, Charles D. Bennett, R. Vernon Fiers, Herbert T. Glynn, Frank E. Gunn, Ernest Harris, Tom Harris, Boyd Hart, John Housden, E. B. Howton, William B. Hughes, Kenneth E. Mennen, Hubert F. Shelton, Charles W. Speers, Jr., Robert Thoke, William G. Anderson, Billy Adams, and Raul Hays. Press release, August 20, 1964, Agricultural Development Commission file, Breathitt papers.

KENTUCKY FARM PRODUCTS WEEK
Frankfort / April 27, 1965

FOR several months now, many of you here this morning have been hearing about "potential"—potential in this, and potential in that for Kentucky farmers. Potential, you know, is what you can achieve if you work at it. We all know that rural leaders all over Kentucky are working hard toward a billion dollar annual income goal for Kentucky agriculture.[1] Many of you here are on the governor's Commission on Agriculture which has that goal as its objective. I told you in Louisville at the first state-wide Conference on Agriculture, and I reminded you a month ago in Lexington at the joint agriculture meeting, that we have the potential in Kentucky, we have the soil, and we have the climate and the water.

Distribution and markets are the big problems facing us. And this gets us to this farm product week promotion—to why we want people to buy Kentucky farm products. Even before May 3—when this special promotion week gets underway—we have already realized some achievements. I want to detail just one of these achievements.

Winn-Dixie Stores, Inc., our hosts this morning, which are cooperating so helpfully with us in this special week, made an extensive study of Kentucky manufacturers. And C.E. Schmidt, vice president of Winn-Dixie, tells me that the Owensboro Canning Company is the only full-time cannery in the state.[2] Of course, we have dairies, meat packers, manufacturers of pickles, preserves, and other farm products; but the Winn-Dixie study revealed that the Owensboro company is the only cannery in Kentucky. The Owensboro company joined forces with us by sending a bulletin to its distributors throughout the state. This bulletin emphasized the economic advantages to Kentuckians of buying Kentucky farm products.

George Panagos, Jr., vice president of the Owensboro Canning Company, in a letter to me pointed out that his company had used as much as 80 percent of snap beans, one of the company's major products, from out of state.[3] But this year—and I quote from Mr. Panagos's letter—"through the cooperation of state agencies and the efforts of local farmers and ourselves, we plan to use approximately 60 percent of our total green bean production from Daviess County farmers. We already have contracted for 483 acres of green beans in Daviess County."

The Owensboro cannery also plans to buy its cardboard packaging from a Louisville source in a further attempt to stimulate Kentucky sales. Until this "Buy Kentucky Farm Products Week" promotion started, the Owensboro company did not even know this Louisville packaging firm existed. So, you see, one of our big objectives must be one of education, letting the people of Kentucky—producer, processor, and consumer—know what is grown and what is manufactured in Kentucky. I sincerely believe that the result will be spiraling in effect—just as it was with the Owensboro cannery, Daviess County farmers, and the Louisville packaging firm. I ask you agriculture leaders here today—isn't it good, sound business to stock Kentucky stores as much as possible with Kentucky labels, rather than buying from outside sources who spend their money elsewhere? Wouldn't you rather buy Kentucky products?

You here at this breakfast seemed to enjoy the menu this morning. Only Kentucky farm products were served. The whole purpose behind "Buy Kentucky Farm Products Week" is to point up the high quality of farm products produced in Kentucky and what the Kentucky farmer contributes to the well-being of Kentuckians—both economically and nutritionally.

I'm convinced that all Kentuckians would buy more Kentucky products, if we point out these economic advantages. And there's no better financial focus than somebody's pocketbook. In Kentucky, we have 151,000 farms providing a livelihood for over 600,000 people. That's a mighty big captive market to talk to, as a beginning, in addition to the two and one-half million other Kentucky residents not living on the farm.

We're grateful to Mr. Schmidt of Winn-Dixie for the idea of this week. He suggested it at the agriculture conference in Louisville. And he pledged then, and is making available now, the support of the thirty-one retail outlets in Kentucky which he supervises. Winn-Dixie also has been giving a large part of its newspaper, radio, and television advertising to "Buy Kentucky Farm Products Week." The company has been making prominent store displays of Kentucky products. Clerks and other employees are wearing Kentucky Colonel hats and ties.

But neither Winn-Dixie nor we in state government can do it by ourselves. We need the help and the constant plugging by you in your communities and in your different parts of Kentucky. We need the teamwork which has been so obvious in our Commission on Agriculture—the teamwork which is so obvious in progress now in all areas of Kentucky's economy. For too long in Kentucky we've depended on tobacco. It still is our biggest cash crop by far—about 40 percent of the cash crop, to be specific. Of course, we're proud that Kentucky is the leading burley tobacco producer in the world and that Lexington is the biggest burley tobacco market in the world. Scientific farming has helped us increase our tobacco yields and thereby increase our net. And, along with promotion such as this, it can help us realize similar potentials in all farm markets.

Last year cash receipts from Kentucky farm marketings totaled $732.7 million. This was 13 percent above the 1963 figure and is particularly significant when compared to the national average, which was a decrease of 2.5 percent. Another feather in the cap of Kentucky farmers is the 1964 increase in net income. After all, net income is what we are most interested in. Kentucky farmers last year increased their net income by 30 percent per farm over the year before, going from an average of $2,100 to $2,800.

Agriculture Commissioner Butler has pointed out several times that our biggest room for expansion is in livestock.[4] Dairy income continues to increase despite the fact that we have fewer dairy cows in Kentucky. This means we are doing a more efficient job in production. Our state-supported dairy shows and sales in six different breeds are attracting the nation's top herds. And more and more of the best stock in the nation sold at these shows and sales are being bought by Kentuckians and kept in Kentucky. The success we have had in these shows and sales—higher yields and increase in net farm income—more scientific farming in many areas of Kentucky—all these point up the many possibilities. And, as I said before, we have the potential in everything, including the know-how, the soil, and the climate.

Even our geographic location favors Kentucky. We are located within a day's drive of nearly half the nation's population. We must take advantage of this in marketing our farm products. We must find these markets in neighboring states. Why import so much beef, for example, when it can be grown and processed in Kentucky? Why import so much canned goods, when they can be grown and processed in Kentucky—as the Owensboro Canning Company already is proving? We must begin here at home in this educational and promotional campaign.

Research to some people sounds like a bookish word. But we must have research and current studies in today's competitive market. We must know what the other fellow is doing, where we can sell these Kentucky products, and how we can best advertise them. And, of course, we must know how we can best produce and grow them—quality- and quantity-wise. In Kentucky, we have the university's nationally recognized extension service. Also at the University of Kentucky, we have the Agricultural Research Center helping us by continuing research. These are just two of the excellent agencies available to us for research and education.

From the results we've already enjoyed after just getting under way in this "Buy Kentucky Farm Products Week" promotion, from the attendance and enthusiasm of the statewide Conference on Agriculture in Louisville, from the planning and programs of the Commission on Agriculture, we know now we have something concrete to work toward. In fact, we already have those results I mentioned earlier. Let's continue this teamwork and carry the message to all Kentuckians. What benefits some Kentuckians, benefits all Kentuckians.

The success of this special week, May 3-8, for farm products can lead to another special week this fall. This fall we can push for the sale of all products made in Kentucky—such things as furniture, farm tractors, automobiles, household appliances, and electric typewriters. During any of these special weeks, we can tie in Kentucky's built-in attractions of historic and scenic opportunities and the promotional possibilities for Kentucky food products. Look what Colonel Sanders did with Kentucky Fried Chicken.[5] Just think what a similar promotion could do for Kentucky country ham. So you see, the possibilities are endless. Let's meet the challenge of this "Buy Kentucky Farm Products Week" the same way in which we have started the other agricultural challenges in recent months.

---

1. Governor Breathitt's campaign to improve farm income enjoyed considerable success in 1964. In that year Kentucky farmers received $732.6 million from the sale of farm products—a 13 percent increase over 1963. In 1963 Kentucky ranked twenty-fifth among the states in farm income. The following year it ranked nineteenth. Realized net income per farm jumped 30 percent in 1964 to $2,823; however, that figure remained well below the $3,642 per farm for the country. *Louisville Courier-Journal,* March 15, 1965.

2. C.E. Schmidt (1911-), division manager and vice president, Winn-Dixie of Louisville, Incorporated. Retired December, 1972. Information provided by Winn-Dixie of Louisville, Incorporated, telephone interview July 11, 1980.

3. George Panagos, Jr. (1936-), employed by Owensboro Canning Company (1959-); vice president for manufacturing (1963-); member, Kentucky Agriculture Commission (1964-1968). *Who's Who in Finance and Industry, 1974-1975,* 18th ed. (New York, 1971).

4. Wendell Pace Butler (1912-), teacher, public schools, Metcalfe County, Kentucky (1931-1936); superintendent of schools (1938-1942); superintendent of

public instruction, Commonwealth of Kentucky (1952-1955, 1960-1963); commissioner of agriculture, Commonwealth of Kentucky (1964-1967, 1972-). *Who's Who in America, 1976-1977,* 39th ed. (Chicago, 1976).

5. Harland Sanders (1890-1980), food franchising company executive. Initiated franchise operations of Kentucky Fried Chicken (1956); owner (1956-1964); good will ambassador, Kentucky Fried Chicken (1964-1980). *Who's Who in America, 1978-1979,* 40th ed. (Chicago, 1978).

KENTUCKY SEED DEALERS ASSOCIATION
Louisville / May 20, 1965

THANK you for inviting me here tonight and giving me an opportunity to meet with a group of people who, as individuals and as an organization, can exert tremendous influence on the future of this state. There can be no doubt that the days ahead offer unprecedented opportunities for the seedsmen. And there can be even less doubt that these opportunities impose upon you a comparable number of unprecedented responsibilities.

Agriculture, in the future as in the past, is vital to Kentucky economic stability and overall prosperity. And the membership of this association certainly occupies an extremely important position in the agriculture picture. Your position, in fact, is far more important than the average person realizes. It is important because high-quality seeds are essential to high-quality production. And it is important because your industry itself is a major factor in the state's economy.[1] The production and marketing of seeds is a multi-million dollar enterprise in Kentucky. By any standards, this is a big business—affecting directly the well-being of many thousands of our people. In fescue seed alone we produced 68,000 acres last year, valued at nearly $2.5 million.

But even more important is the fact that you are obviously conscientious in your efforts to provide the Kentucky farmer with the kind of seeds needed to facilitate both quality and quantity in production. This is not an assumption. It is a proven fact. A study made by Murray State College several years ago in the Jackson Purchase area clearly established that seeds purchased from seedsmen are superior in almost every way to homegrown seeds.

In another instance, it was shocking what a farmer found in a single pound of lespedeza seed purchased from a neighbor at 8.7 cents a pound. This pound of seed was only 77 percent pure, and it contained 583 noxious weed seeds per ounce. And, the germination test was only 26 percent—all of which means, to put it in dollars-and-cents figures, the cost of a pound of pure live seed would have been forty-three cents. But, if the farmer had bought certified seed at the beginning, it would have cost only eighteen cents per pound, would have contained no weed seed, would have been 99.9 percent pure and had a 94 percent germination figure.

My feeling is that this is a form of neighborliness that the average Kentucky farmer can ill afford. This case illustrates one of the disadvantages the farmer encounters when he goes bargain hunting at planting time. Even when he produces his own seed, he must accept a lower quality than he could acquire from the seedsman. Studies show that commercial seeds are superior on all quality counts and that germination is practically always higher than the homegrown variety.

The conclusion I draw from this is that the farmer who does not acknowledge the importance of certification and does not avail himself of the service and advice of the qualified seedsman is penalizing himself at the most crucial point in many of his farm operations. Yet, this is exactly what surprisingly large numbers of our farmers are doing today in Kentucky. When one figures that quality seed only averages 1.5 to 2 percent of the total production cost of most crops and that the seed can mean the difference between success and failure, one can readily see why this is a matter of concern for all of us who are interested in and fascinated by the future of Kentucky agriculture.

Seed quality is an essential factor in both the quality and quantity of the crop produced. There has long been an indication that many Kentucky farmers are not taking advantage of the high-quality seed available to them. By not doing so, they fail to achieve the full yield potential from their efforts and from their investment in production materials.

No one in Kentucky works harder for his livelihood than the farmer. Far too frequently he is required to operate on the borderline between profit and loss. He knows that he must produce a quality product because he is in a competitive business. He must lay his tobacco, his corn, his small grains, his cotton, and his other crops on the line for the high dollar he needs to make a profit. For this reason, it is inconceivable to me that he would knowingly stack the deck against himself right from the beginning. Yet the evidence would seem to indicate that this is exactly what he is doing in far too many cases. He is shortchanging the state's agricultural economy. Even worse, he is shortchanging himself.

I believe that we have an educational job to do here. And I believe that we all have a responsibility for seeing that this job gets done. We've got to get to the farmer with the message. And we have to do more than tell him that high-quality certified seeds mean money in the bank. We've got to show him. The state Department of Agriculture, the University of

Kentucky and our other state colleges, and the governor's Commission on Agriculture are moving in the right direction. But we need to do much more.

And yet the sole responsibility does not rest with the state. A large share rests with the membership of this association. And that job does not end with the production and marketing of top-quality seeds. You have a responsibility to yourselves and to the people who plant your seeds to really get out and sell the importance of quality seeds. This responsibility will increase in the days ahead. Kentucky agriculture is in a period of transition that holds out the promise of almost limitless opportunities in the future. This is an exciting time in the agricultural history of this state. Most of you, I am sure, are familiar with our billion dollar farm program. This is a carefully thought out, realistic program that is designed to raise the state's total farm income by more than $250 million in the next few years. The key to the success of this program is income gains resulting from increased production of presently grown farm commodities, and the development of new income sources on new products.

Seed will most certainly be a vitally important factor in this program. Agriculture officials are well aware of this fact and, while they intend to do everything possible, they are counting heavily on the enthusiastic support of the seedsmen.

I would also like to urge your interest in the drive to greatly expand the food production and processing industry in Kentucky. There are many who feel that this is the most profitable facet of the agricultural changes taking place in our state today. Farm officials and businessmen are excited about the possibilities in this field, and most important of all, the farmers themselves are encouraged about it.

I realize, of course, that we are limited in the kind of seed we can produce in Kentucky for the food crop producer. Our climate is such that we simply cannot produce top-quality seed for certain crops. For example, we have to go as far away as Colorado for watermelon seed. But you do occupy a key position in insuring that the farmer, engaged in the production of foods, has the best possible seed. If the seed can be produced in Kentucky, I would hope that you would place it on the market. If it cannot be produced here, then you have the responsibility of finding top-quality seed from whatever source and making it available to our farmers.

The future holds a big challenge for the seedsman, but it is a challenge that I am sure you will face with enthusiasm. The record shows that you can get the job done. Our farmers are counting on you. Kentucky is counting on you. Enough seed can be produced in Kentucky to plant every acre of commercial crops with certified seed if we can get the message to the farmers and if the demand is sufficient. You will continue to have the close cooperation of all the state agencies working in your field, and I urge you to take advantage of the services available. We are all working for the same thing—a more prosperous Kentucky and a more abundant life for our people. The opportunities are there. Our job is to seize them.

---

1. In 1965 Kentucky ranked first in the nation in the production of fescue seed and second in the production of lespedeza and orchard grass seed. U.S. Department of Agriculture and Kentucky Department of Agriculture, *Kentucky Agricultural Statistics, 1965* (Louisville, Ky., 1966), p. 17.

NATIONAL FARM MACHINERY SHOW
Louisville / February 15, 1966

It is a great pleasure to be here with you tonight to open this National Farm Machinery Show. During the remainder of this week we look forward to having thousands of farmers from Kentucky and neighboring states look at the latest machines and equipment for producing food and fiber. I extend a hearty, old-fashioned, Kentucky-type welcome to you all. We Kentuckians are mighty proud of this exposition center—proud that we can have an exhibition of this size under roof, so that you can take your time and enjoy inspecting these modern miracles of the farming industry.

As I look at this huge display of machinery, equipment, chemicals, and all the other items that make the American farmer the most efficient in the world, I am impressed with the hard work and perseverance that made it possible. This is a great tribute to those who had the foresight to see the untold educational benefits of such a show, and the myriad other possibilities it affords the agribusiness industry.

We are especially grateful to you exhibitors who are making the American farmer the best producer of food and fiber in the world. You play an important part in keeping this nation better fed, better clothed, and better housed, at a smaller percentage of the disposable income dollar, than any nation on earth. We salute you for it!

No better place could have been selected for this event—Louisville being within a one-day drive of 68 percent of the population of the United States. With the exception of citrus fruit production, no type of agriculture is foreign to Kentucky and her neighbors. Approximately 30 percent of the nation's farms are located in Kentucky and the seven other states surrounding us.

During the first ten months of last year, farmers in Kentucky, Tennessee, Indiana, Ohio, Illinois, Virginia, West Virginia, and Missouri bought nearly 50,000 tractors at an estimated cost of $170 million. Those 50,000 tractors represented about one-third of all the tractors sold in all fifty states. During the same period of time machinery firms sold $60 million worth of combines, or one-third of all sold in the United States; $22 million worth of hay balers, or one-fourth of all sold in the United States; and $11 million worth of corn pickers, one-third of all sold in the United States.

Some of the people in farming tell me that agricultural practices are changing so fast that they can hardly keep track of them. This further points up the need for this show and for a national exhibit for everyone to see all the new innovations at one time at one place. The day of the straw-chewing farmer is over. Today he is a big businessman with production assets per farm totaling $65,000, or $32,000 per farm worker. Even industry with their record-breaking earnings this year doesn't have such an investment. Total United States farm assets are $253 billion—equal to about half the total market value of all corporation stocks sold on the New York Stock Exchange. Farmers' investments in tractors and trucks alone now total $26 billion.

Farm machinery manufacturers and research scientists have been hard put to keep ahead of the demands of changing times. Consider just one fact. From 1880 to 1960, the labor requirements to produce an acre of corn declined from forty-six hours to just seven hours. Good farmers now are doing it in less than two hours, and scientists say it will go to 1.3 hours in a matter of a few years.

There was a time when Bill Johnstone and his fellow extension workers started a corn derby at the University of Kentucky to raise corn yields from about twenty-five bushels per acre.[1] Now the average is sixty-nine bushels and still climbing. But farmers found out they could get more from their corn crops than just the grain, so the machinery manufacturers helped them by designing silage choppers so they could utilize the entire stalks for more economical gains on their livestock, and greater milk output.

What does the future hold? I'm told that scientists now are thinking of even heavier-duty nuclear-powered tractors which will be fueled at the factory and run a lifetime with only yearly recharging. Controlled vibrations to energize the cutting edges of plows may be in the not-too-distant future, some scientists say.

The statistics of agriculture stagger the imagination. The United States Agricultural Yearbook this year says farmers own four and one-half million tractors and all the equipment that goes with them. They replaced twenty-two million work animals and seventy-six million acres that would have been needed to grow feed for them. Contrast, if you will, the advent of the steel plow in 1870, when 85 percent of the population of the United States lived on farms and produced to feed themselves almost alone, with the 7.5 percent of the population today feeding a much greater population. Contrast the farmer in the early 1900s feeding a few animals by hand, with the fact that today, with proper equipment, six men are feeding and caring for feed lots with 25,000 head each. Remember the turning of the churn by hand and the pumping of water of the early 1900s; now it is being done by electricity, which in 1934 served only 11 percent of the farms, and today nearly 100 percent of our farms are electrified.

An economic theory almost unheard of in this country surrounds the fact that mechanization actually might not be the most practical and sensible way of farming for some. In India and China, the populations are so large and labor so cheap, farmers actually have to consider if they can utilize hand labor more economically than they can mechanical devices. While we in the United States are highly mechanized on our farms, more than 90 percent of the power on the farms of the world is still being generated by human beings and by animals.

Our success story in agriculture begins with the advent of the tractor in 1903 and built-in power takeoffs in 1919, followed by the tricycle-type tractor with mounted implements and the rubber-tired tractor. Despite the giant strides of agriculture in mechanization, improved varieties, cultivation, fertilization, use of chemicals, and all the other improved practices, farming still has a long way to go. Kentucky aims to be a part of that growth.

We have launched a program in our state, through our Commission on Agriculture, to increase farm income to one billion dollars a year, and to increase net income and efficiency. This farm machinery show will help us accomplish our goal. Let us build this show into an annual event that will attract people from all over the country to see the latest and best in agriculture. Again, we welcome you to Louisville and Kentucky and hope you enjoy the show.

---

1. William Clarkson Johnstone (1895-1978), born in Georgetown, South Carolina; B.S. in agriculture, University of Kentucky (1916); horticulturist, government of Brazil (1916-1922); county agricultural agent for the College of Agriculture Extension Service, University of Kentucky (1923-1937); agronomist at University of Kentucky Agriculture Experimental Station (1937-1952); agricultural consultant, Kentucky Bankers Association (1952-1978); promoter of Kentucky 31 fescue and hybrid corn. Information provided by Edward Johnstone.

TOBACCO ASSOCIATION OF THE UNITED STATES
White Sulphur Springs, West Virginia
June 27, 1966

I AM highly honored by your invitation to participate in this joint convention of the Tobacco Association of the United States and the Leaf Tobacco Exporters Association. Coming from the largest burley tobacco producing state, I welcome the opportunity to praise the merits of burley and all other varieties—especially all those which Kentucky produces.

I note that Kentucky Senator John Sherman Cooper was your speaker several years ago—the last "burley man" to speak to you.[1] We want to be sure that burley, this important ingredient of the widely sought "American blend," is not neglected—we hope you will continue to keep burley properly "blended" into your discussions and activities.

We Kentuckians are proud of our tobacco heritage just as all of us here today are proud of what tobacco contributed to our great American heritage. I come here today not to apologize for tobacco, nor to defend it. I come to proclaim its virtues from the housetops and to assert that tobacco has an important affirmative mission in adding to the happiness and peace of mind of those who enjoy it.

Since that day in 1612 when John Rolfe assured the success of the Jamestown settlement and gave the New World its first export commodity —tobacco has contributed to this nation's success.[2] In *Narrative and Critical History of America* Justin Winsor reported, "It may be added as an indisputable fact, that the culture of tobacco constituted the basis of the present unrivalled prosperity of the United States."[3]

And since in 1787, when General James Wilkinson left Louisville, Kentucky, with a cargo including some hogsheads of tobacco produced in the virgin soils of Kentucky, on his momentous flatboat trip down the Mississippi River—outmaneuvered the Spanish export barrier at New Orleans and established a trade outlet for Kentucky tobacco—our Commonwealth has been known as the "Tobacco State."[4]

For almost a century now, Kentucky has maintained its place as the foremost producer of burley tobacco. Burley now is grown in most of our 120 counties. And I might add, with not a little pride, that blended cigarettes would taste different—and not nearly as good as they do—if they lacked burley leaf. If anyone doubts this statement, let him submit it to the free choice of the world's consumers. Whenever the smoker is free to buy, he buys the burley blends.

Personally, my family has been associated with the tobacco industry for many years. So you can see why I feel a strong kinship with this important industry that has meant so much to my family, to the heritage of my state, and to the economy of this nation.

The area of Kentucky from which I come is a producer of diversified types of tobacco. In addition to burley, we grow dark-fired, one-sucker, and green river types, which are important in the heavier smoking and chewing products.

Since the days of General Wilkinson when tobacco was one of the few commodities this new nation could export, till today when tobacco ranks third in the value of U.S. farm exports—the tobacco industry has been vital to our economy. The importance of tobacco to the economy of our individual states, to the nation, and to the world, cannot be overlooked or taken lightly. The fact that 750,000 farm families in twenty-two states depend on tobacco as a cash crop and as a major source of income is significant. That income amounts to more than $1.3 billion annually. But add to that the fact that tobacco provides employment in whole or in part for seventeen million people—9 percent of our entire population—and you have an industry of major significance.

Retail tobacco sales amounting to more than $8 billion a year provide more than $3 billion annually in federal, state, and local government revenues. In fact, taxes on tobacco and tobacco products alone more than offset the cost of all price support programs since 1933. During that time these taxes have amounted to some $52 billion, more than three times as much as the Commodity Credit Corporation has spent on all support crops.

The contributions made by this industry to growers and government are only a beginning. Consider the total economic impact felt in the employment and trade generated by warehousemen, dealers and merchants, and manufacturers. Add to that the value of tobacco to the fertilizer, chemical, petroleum, and machinery industries—to the paper, aluminum foil, plastics, and transportation industries—and the economic stimulus of tobacco becomes great enough to stagger the imagination.

As governor of the second largest tobacco growing state, I have an overriding interest also in the export market for it. Since tobacco contributes 40 percent of Kentucky's annual cash farm income, we want to see our exports continue to grow. Just two weeks ago I attended the Poznan International Trade Fair in Poland as President Johnson's representative and met with Polish officials about the possibility of buying more American tobacco.[5] Even the Poles admit that our tobacco is far superior in quality to that they are buying from Eastern Europe.

But it is interesting to note that from 1957 to 1965 imports of tobacco by the Common Market countries increased by 232 million pounds. However, United States' exports to the Common Market increased only nineteen million pounds. Thus, on balance, we have fallen far behind. Part of our failure may be laid to the ad valorem duties levied on imported tobacco, combined with the relatively high price of U. S. tobacco. We hope that the president's special representative for trade negotiations, former Secretary of State Christian A. Herter, will closely monitor trade restrictions in this area, and aid us in keeping this important market open for exportation of U.S. tobacco.[6]

I believe our farmers should seriously consider some form of a "checkoff" system, similar to that used by the National Livestock and Meat Board, to finance an educational and promotional program for tobacco not only in this country but abroad as well.

We are proud that burley, principally Kentucky burley, plays such an important part of the "American blend" for cigarettes and pipe tobaccos so much in demand throughout the world. This has kept our export picture relatively bright. We intend to continue to stress the production of high-quality burley that will be an asset to foreign and domestic manufacturers.

When I became governor I appointed a Commission on Agriculture to find realistic routes to increase income for all areas of Kentucky agriculture. The tobacco committee of this commission has defined its primary responsibility as increasing efficiencies in producing, handling, and marketing a quality product that will increase the demand for tobacco.

But despite our problems of exports, acreage allotments and other difficulties, there is a far more serious matter today concerning the welfare of the tobacco industry. This is the series of attacks against the product, which seem to be growing more widespread and more punitive in nature. These attacks stem from charges that cigarettes cause certain diseases. However, these charges are still based almost entirely on statistical studies. And there are many scientists and doctors who question the extreme statements being made about tobacco. Statistics can be made to support many different conclusions. Statistics are—in the last analysis—statistics. But statistics cannot prove cause and effect. Only patient, expensive, never-ending research—medical and scientific research—can establish the medical facts on a basis of demonstrable scientific proof.

The critics are at work across the land. They have many projects afoot, ranging from prohibitive tax proposals to schemes that would curtail smoking by changing human behavior. There have been warning statements on cigarette packages since the beginning of this year. But critics of tobacco will not be satisfied unless they can eliminate cigarette smoking and other forms of tobacco use. Even now, there is growing pressure to get Congress to require warnings in all cigarette advertising—to make cigarette advertising "self-defeating" in the words of one critic.

This effort to destroy the tobacco industry must be opposed by all who know and love the industry. On behalf of the millions in my state and other states—millions who depend on tobacco to feed and rear their families—I claim for our historic crop the right to be pronounced innocent until proved guilty beyond a doubt.

Certainly, you, the members of the Tobacco Association of the United States and the Leaf Tobacco Exporters Association, are more aware of the stakes involved than many others. I know that you can be counted on to see that the facts are known about the responsible attitude our industry is taking, the research which is under way, and the self-imposed restraints being enforced through the Tobacco Advertising Code.

To do our part in this research, we have launched at the University of Kentucky a comprehensive research program on tobacco and health, working in cooperation with the scientists of the United States Department of Agriculture. Three of our units at the university—agriculture, medicine, and chemistry—are directly involved in an interdisciplinary research program related to this very important matter. In the agricultural part of the program alone, twenty senior scientists and at least sixty junior scientists, technicians, and aides are studying the metabolic systems of the plant, breeding and genetics, disease and insect control, fertility and cultural practices, biochemical characteristics of the plant, mechanical harvesting and new curing and housing procedures. The close working relationship between agriculturists and medical personnel offers a unique opportunity to get answers not available to this point.

And this is only a part of the millions of dollars that are being spent by all segments of this giant industry for one purpose—to find the truth. Find it in the quiet, unprejudiced laboratory of exact science, find it in the test tube, not in a computer. We must not accept a sentence based on circumstantial evidence, but demand judgment by an impartial, objective, qualified jury in a court of medical inquiry. We do not intend to take these attacks lying down. We do not intend to accept an economic death sentence for millions of Americans without exhausting every available means of self-defense. Thank you for inviting me here. You may depend on me and my state to stand up and be counted in defense of our precious amber weed.

---

1. John Sherman Cooper (1901-), attorney from Somerset. Kentucky House of Representatives (1928-1930); judge, Pulaski County (1930-1938); circuit judge (1945-1946); United States Senator (1947-1949, 1953-1955, 1957-1973); U.S. ambassador to East Germany (1974-1976). *Who's Who in American Politics, 1965-1976,* 5th ed. (New York, 1975).

2. John Rolfe (1585-1622), a colonist noted for his production of a tobacco favored by Europeans, making tobacco the staple crop of Virginia in the colonial period. Dumas Malone, ed., *Dictionary of American Biography* (New York, 1935), vol. 16, pp. 117-18.

3. Justin Winsor (1831-1897), a noted historian and librarian at the Boston Public Library and Harvard College. He compiled *A Narrative and Critical History of America,* an important eight-volume work especially significant for information regarding North America before 1787. *Concise Dictionary of American Biography* (New York, 1964), p. 1234.

4. James Wilkinson (1757-1825), moved to Kentucky following service as an officer during War for Independence and quickly became a powerful political figure in the new state. Wilkinson is best remembered for his involvement in the "Burr conspiracy" of the early nineteenth century. Dumas Malone, ed., *Dictionary of American Biography* (New York, 1936), vol. 20, pp. 222-26.

5. In his remarks to the International Trade Fair Governor Breathitt said: "Over the past decade our trade exchange has regularly increased and as part of this effort we have extended the most favored nation treatment to imports from Poland and have sold over one half-million dollars worth of agricultural products to Poland on easy credit terms. Poland's goods, from ham to horses, have found a receptive market in the United States and not even the governor of America's most famous horse breeding state really objects to the import of fine horses. I should say, however, that I would be glad to match Kentucky's horses with yours at the race track some time. So far, we have progressed far, I think, in the development of our trade and this progression has been built on the firm foundation of historic Polish-American ties. We hope, of course, that we can go further for trade by itself does not necessarily mean that our relations are as developed as they could be and should be and so, on our part, we hope for more than just expanded trade ties with Poland. We hope for greater exchanges of scientists and scholars; greater cooperative programs in health and education; and greater and never ending efforts to find peace and independence and development for all nations on this earth. This is the message which President Johnson has asked me to bring to you in Poznan today." This speech is not included in these papers.

6. Christian A. Herter (1895-), representative, Massachusetts legislature (1931-1943); U.S. House of Representatives (1943-1953); governor, Commonwealth of Massachusetts (1953-1957); undersecretary, Department of State (1957-1959); secretary of state (1959-1961). *Who's Who in America, 1966-1967,* 34th ed. (Chicago, 1966).

UNIVERSITY OF KENTUCKY AGRICULTURE EXTENSION CONFERENCE
Lexington / December 5, 1966

I DEEPLY appreciate this opportunity to attend your extension conference. It is always a pleasure to express appreciation to folks for doing a good job, and that is one of my purposes during this visit. But I think you know me well enough to know that I would not miss the opportunity to challenge you to even greater achievements in the field of extension education. And I hope that the rewards of your accomplishments will serve as an inspiration for the future.

When I became governor three years ago I pledged to the farmers of Kentucky that I would exert the full influence of my office and this administration to help them reach a one billion dollar annual cash income. We have fulfilled that pledge to work more closely with our farmers. I appointed fifteen outstanding farmers and farm leaders to the governor's Commission on Agriculture. And this is the hardest working commission that I have appointed.

With the leadership of men like your dean, Dr. Seay, along with Bill Johnstone, Jack Matlick, Wendell Butler, and all the farmer members, the Commission on Agriculture has developed a plan and program of work that will result in a billion dollar farm income for our state.[1]

When I charged the commission to develop this program, with your help, I also charged them to implement it as rapidly as possible. To my great delight, and to the surprise of many people, the program has been implemented at all levels, also with your assistance.

The most effective and lasting way to reach an objective is to provide existing forces with new approaches and tools that will help them accelerate their programs. This is the philosophy of our commission—to develop tools that can be used by our present agricultural agencies, farm organizations, and farmers—and then to coordinate all these activities to achieve our purpose. That purpose is for our farmers to make more money.

This is the reason we have solicited your close cooperation and assistance—we feel that the commission can help you make your program more effective, and reach more farmers. This is the reason we are extremely grateful to the Cooperative Extension Service for the key role you have assumed in implementing this program, especially at the local level. This is the reason we feel that the production potential study for Kentucky agriculture is the "roadmap" by which we will reach our goal—it shows us the direction we must travel if Kentucky is to continue to be a major farm state.

And continue we must, not for our benefit alone, but for the benefit of our children. World population is expected to double in the next thirty-four years. In less than two generations more than three billion more people will inhabit this earth. Increased production of food is not only desirable, for our farmers to make more money—it is imperative because these people must be fed. And they will not be well fed unless we continue to intensify our efforts. Last year alone, world population increased seventy million, but food production was static. The big question now is whether we can continue to increase food production as rapidly as the population grows. It is professionals in agriculture, in research, teaching, and extension like yourselves, here and throughout much of the world, who must answer that question.

Yours is the greatest challenge that has ever been handed to man. The challenges to be "first" in scientific or economic fields of endeavor are insignificant when compared to this one. Our very survival depends on it! We must not let succeeding generations say that we let them down! Our challenge closer to home is easier to visualize. It is to help our farmers see the economic benefits of more intensive use of our land and other resources, and then assist them in reaching the individual goals they set for themselves.

The job of the governor's Commission on Agriculture is just beginning. Continued "follow-through" will bring our billion dollar goal into reality. We can already see results of our work. Cash farm income is expected to set an all-time record this year. Income for the first nine months of this year was 20 percent above the same period in 1965, and 12 percent above the national average. This is due to improvement in farm prices, and expanded production. And since much of this year's tobacco crop will not be sold until after the Christmas market recess, I'm sure the 1966 income figures will not reflect the true production picture. I believe we should start figuring farm income in Kentucky on a March-to-March basis, which would give a truer picture of our annual production and income.

I pledge to you and all the people of Kentucky that this administration will continue to work for the farmers of our state. We will continue to work to make farming the second largest income producer, surpassed only by manufacturing. We entreat you to continue your key role in this program. All of us, working together, can reach our goal. I realize that your role as county extension agent is changing rather rapidly these days. You must spread your talents and energies over wider areas. You must raise your level of specialization to meet the demands of a more specialized, more technical agriculture.

Your sphere of influence is also widening beyond agriculture. You find yourself involved in programs for the total development of your community. This not only broadens your area of influence, it keeps the rural and the urban segments of the community working together for the common good. This balance of leadership is urgently needed, and you are in the position to supply it.

And speaking of total development—we are very proud of the fine working relationship between our area program office and you folks. I know that Bob Cornett, director of our development program, will be on your program tomorrow morning.[2] I'm sure that he will discuss ways we can work together even more closely, but I deeply appreciate your cooperation.

These two areas of work, agriculture and overall development, are among the many vital areas of social and economic opportunity in which states must assume greater responsibility. And they also are the concern of our federal government.

On September 28, President Johnson named me chairman of the National Advisory Commission on Rural Poverty, whose task it will be to make recommendations, within one year, on the most efficient and promising means of assuring proper development of rural America. This commission was named because we have a rapidly changing society—one in which more and more Americans are moving to the cities to find employment and social advances. The president believes, and the commission believes, that our rural life must be preserved. This means we must provide jobs in our smaller communities in new industries, that there must be an adequacy of good schools, of housing, health, and cultural opportunities for rural families. The fact that I was named chairman of this group, I feel, is a compliment to Kentucky.

For we in Kentucky—the community leaders and our state leadership—are moving aggressively to develop this Commonwealth—to make certain that the small community and our rural areas are not neglected. The fact that nearly eighty of our counties have gotten either a new or expanded industry during the past three years is evidence of this concern and wise development.

At the same time we in Kentucky are working to get new water systems, to get new vocational schools, to establish new libraries, to raise farm income, to improve our schools, to develop public housing, to assure our older citizens of proper care.

I do not know what this twenty-six-member commission will recommend, for our purpose is to make an in-depth study of the problems of rural proverty across this country and then advise. We have been asked to develop ways of combating rural poverty and of eliminating the continued migration from rural areas to urban ghettos. This is a challenging assignment.

Dr. C.E. Bishop, vice president of the University of North Carolina, has been named executive director of the commission.[3] A staff of competent research personnel has been assembled to assist the director and the commission in its study. I am announcing today that the first meeting of this commission will be held at 10 A.M. December 17 at the Executive Inn in Louisville. At the meeting we shall review the plans of the staff for carrying out its study and make recommendations concerning the work which we will undertake. We shall also make plans for conducting public hearings in several locations in the United States during January and February.

During the year, we will be evaluating the means by which existing programs, policies, and activities relating to the economic status and community welfare of rural people may be coordinated or better directed or redirected to achieve the elimination of underemployment and low incomes of rural people and to obtain higher levels of community facilities and services. We also will develop recommendations for action by local, state, or federal government or private enterprise as to the most efficient and promising means of providing opportunities for the rural population to share in America's abundance. We are going to propose what is needed in order to make the rural future brighter for people who live in our rural areas. The first step in that journey is the pooling of the common resources of rural Americans—joining them in a common planning effort that will magnify the resources of each.

As county agents, home demonstration agents, and extension specialists you have been working in this area for a long time. You will play an even greater role in the future as your services are expanded. You have the experience to make a valuable contribution in this overall effort. Thank you for this opportunity to come here today, and best wishes for a successful conference.

---

1. William Albert Seay (1920-), Ph.D., University of Wisconsin (1949); associate professor, University of Kentucky (1953-1954); administrative assistant, College of Agriculture (1956-1957); dean and director of Agriculture Experimental Station, (1962-). *Who's Who in American College and University Administration, 1970-1971* (New York, 1970). Jack O. Matlick (1911-), editor and general manager of *Kentucky Farmer* (1940-1960); manager of Kentucky State Fair (1945, 1947, 1948); commissioner, Department of Natural Resources (1960-1968). George W. Robinson, ed., *The Public Papers of Governor Bert T. Combs, 1959-1963* (Lexington, Ky., 1979), p. 475.

2. Robert M. Cornett (1929-), budget director, Commonwealth of Kentucky (1959-1966); director of special projects, Council on State Government, Lexington, Kentucky (1976-1978). George W. Robinson, ed., *The Public Papers of Governor Bert T. Combs, 1959-1963* (Lexington, Ky., 1979), p. 59.

3. Charles Edwin Bishop (1921-), economist; B.S., Berea College (1946); M.S., University of Kentucky (1948); research assistant in agricultural economics, University of Kentucky (1947-1948); faculty member, North Carolina State University (1950-1967); head of Department of Agricultural Economics (1957-1965); chancellor, University of Maryland (1970-); member, various government agriculture advisory organizations (1960-). *Who's Who in America, 1972-1973*, 37th ed. (Chicago, 1972).

NATIONAL ADVISORY COMMISSION ON RURAL POVERTY

Louisville / December 17, 1966

I AM pleased to welcome you to this first meeting of the National Advisory Commission on Rural Poverty.[1] Our assignment is a difficult one. Each of you has a copy of the executive order establishing the commission. The president has requested that we make a study and recommendations to him to combat rural poverty. Specifically, he has charged us to:

(1) Make a comprehensive study and appraisal of the current economic situation and trends in American rural life, as they relate to the existence of income and community problems of rural areas, including problems of low income, the status of rural labor, including farm labor, unemployment and underemployment and retraining in usable skills; rural economic development and expanding opportunities; sources of additional rural employment; availability of land and other resources; adequacy of food, nutrition, housing, health, and cultural opportunities for rural families; the condition of children and youth in rural areas and their status in an expanding national economy; the impact of population and demographic changes, including rural migration; adequacy of rural community facilities and services; exploration of new and better means of eliminating the causes which perpetuate rural unemployment and underemployment, low income and poor facilities; and any other related matters.

(2) Evaluate the means by which existing programs, policies, and activities relating to the economic status and community welfare of rural people may be coordinated or better directed or redirected to achieve the elimination of underemployment and low incomes of rural people and to obtain higher levels of community facilities and services.

(3) Develop recommendations for action by local, state or federal governments or private enterprise as to the most efficient and promising means of providing opportunities for the rural population to share in America's abundance.

This is a responsibility which I am pleased to accept because I am convinced that the problems of poverty are among the most challenging and difficult problems faced by our nation today. I am convinced that the future of our nation will be determined in large measure by our effectiveness in coping with these problems.

In fact, we are not the first commission to be charged with the responsibility for coping with these problems. In transmitting the report of the Country Life Commission to the Congress in 1909, President Theodore Roosevelt said, "one of the chief difficulties is the failure of country life, as it exists at present, to satisfy the higher social and intellectual aspirations of country people."

The commission report concluded that "Broadly speaking, agriculture in the United States is prosperous and the conditions in many of the great farming regions are improving. . . . There is marked improvement, in many of the agricultural regions, in the character of the farm home and its surroundings. . . . Many institutions are also serving the agricultural needs of the open country with great effectiveness, as the United States Department of Agriculture, the land-grant colleges and experiment stations, and the many kinds of extension work that directly or indirectly emanate from them.

"There has never been a time when the American farmer was as well off as he is today—yet the real efficiency in farm life, and in country life as a whole, is not to be measured by historical standards, but in terms of its possibilities. . . . There has been a complete and fundamental change in our whole economic system within the past century.

"This has resulted in profound social changes and the redirection of our point of view on life. In some occupations the readjustment to the new conditions has been rapid and complete; in others it has come with difficulty. In all the great series of farm occupations the readjustment has been the most tardy. . . . It is not strange, therefore, that development is still arrested in certain respects; that marked inequalities have arisen; or that positive injustice may prevail even to a very marked and widespread extent. . . .

"All this may come about without any intention on the part of anyone that it should be so. The problems are nevertheless just as real, and they must be studied and remedies must be found."

These excerpts from the Country Life Commission are equally appropriate to 1966. You are familiar with the general scope of poverty problems in this country. I need not bother you with extensive statistics concerning the incidence of poverty. Let me simply remind you, however, that nearly half the poor in the United States live in rural areas and almost one in every two rural families has a cash income of less than $3,000.

However, the number of poor in rural nonfarm villages exceeds the number of poor living on farms. The impact of poverty upon our rural citizens is manifested in many ways. Not only are money incomes low, but the purchasing power of the rural people is low. Consequently, rural families receive less medical attention, have poor health facilities, have poorer schools, and lag behind urban residents in educational attainment. Moreover, the direct association between rural poverty has become strikingly obvious to us as we have watched millions of ill-trained, poorly educated American citizens move from rural America to low-income areas in our large cities.

In fact, it would be foolhardy to attempt to compartmentalize poverty into farm, rural nonfarm, and urban components. In our deliberations, therefore, we must make our studies and recommendations sufficiently comprehensive to cope effectively with the problems of rural poverty, giving due consideration to the interrelationship which exists between poverty in rural and urban areas.

Here in Kentucky we have taken steps to help our farmers and other rural citizens toward a level of income more nearly in line with that in urban areas. One of the most effective programs we have developed has been the Kentucky Commission on Agriculture. This commission was charged with developing a program that would fully utilize farm resources, increase efficiencies in production and marketing of farm products to assure the farmer a higher gross and net income. This commission has developed a keen awareness of the opportunities available to increase Kentucky farm income among all agricultural agencies, organizations, and individual farmers. This coordination of effort has motivated an expansion in Kentucky farm production.

In 1966, Kentucky is one of the few states in the nation showing an increase in milk production. We are one of the leading states in increases in swine, and feed grain production also expanded this year. Prospects are bright that gross cash income this year will set a new record. This increase in income to the farmer himself creates a total turnover of money far greater than that received by the farmer. It has been said by an economist that every dollar the farmer receives turns over 2.59 times in his community before it leaves, thus creating a total money volume 2.59 times greater. We feel that "do it yourself" programs to raise levels of living must necessarily complement and supplement those initiated and executed by government.

Another effort to boost the economy of our rural communities has been Kentucky's aggressive campaign to lure new industries into our smaller towns. Since January 1, 1964, there have been announcements of approximately 600 new or expanded manufacturing facilities in Kentucky, located in 79 of our 120 counties, which shows the healthy diversity of this drive. These will employ about 37,000 workers directly in manufacturing, and capital investment will approach $600 million.

Kentucky Appalachia has not been bypassed in Kentucky's growth surge. This is a strong note of encouragement for our future. Since January 1, 1964, there have been announcements of 131 new or expanded manufacturing facilities in eastern Kentucky.

For as long as most Kentuckians can remember, one of our state's most serious problems has been the heavy migration of its young people to other states, and especially our larger cities. As an example, federal statistics show that approximately 400,000 Kentuckians moved to other states in the 1950s. Now, however, through our own bootstrap efforts, there are hopeful signs that this migration has virtually halted. Experts estimate that 15,000 to 18,000 new jobs a year in Kentucky would halt the migration of our young people. Recent U.S. Labor Department reports show that well over 100,000 new jobs have been created in our state during the past three years.

I do not mean to imply that we are doing enough in Kentucky or that everything is all rosy. We still have many communities and many individuals who have been bypassed by this growth and the better living conditions which come with it. What I am saying is that, I think, we are heading in the right direction. We must do much more for our people, and especially our farmers, to assure all of them a fair share in our American prosperity.

---

1. In September, 1966, President Johnson established by executive order the President's Committee on Rural Poverty. Composed of the secretaries of agriculture, interior, commerce, labor, health, education and welfare, and housing and urban development, the director of the Office of Economic Opportunity, and the chief administrator of the Small Business Administration, the committee was to develop formulas for coordinating private and governmental programs to "achieve for the rural population the quality of living and levels of opportunity available to other segments of the population." Governor Breathitt was named chairman of a twenty-six member advisory committee which was instructed to assess existing economic conditions in rural America, the probable course of future change, and ways government could direct change toward the goals established by the president's commission. *Louisville Courier-Journal,* December 18, 1966.

GOVERNOR'S CONFERENCE ON AGRICULTURE
Louisville / January 25, 1967

I WANT to add another word of welcome to what I have already said. We are deeply grateful to you for participating in this third Conference on Agriculture. Your attendance here is proof of the confidence we have in the bright future of Kentucky's number one industry. It is proof that all farm and agribusiness leaders believe in working together to bring the greatest possible results in the shortest possible time.

About four years ago, one of Kentucky's most respected and beloved farm leaders, the late Samuel R. Guard, made me acutely aware of the great opportunities we have in agriculture.[1] Mr. Guard was so enthusiastic about his idea that cash farm income could reach a billion dollars a year, that he and others like Bill Johnstone and Jack Matlick talked me into making this goal a part of my campaign platform. I have always had great admiration for Sam Guard, and I am indeed grateful for the chance to help carry out one of the many progressive ideas of this great man. We all owe Mr. Guard a debt of gratitude.

Kentucky farm income set a new record in 1966. Early estimates from agricultural economists at the University of Kentucky place cash receipts at $760 million, conservatively, possibly even higher—which is an 8 percent increase over 1965. During the last decade the increase in farm income has averaged 3.7 percent, so, as you can see, this is quite a gain. I'm sure Secretary Freeman will have more conclusive figures tonight.[2] This estimate is based on official United States Department of Agriculture reports for the first ten months of the year, plus tobacco sales before the Christmas recess, plus 1965 figures for November and December on other crops and livestock. Since monthly receipts during 1966 have been approximately 20 percent higher than 1965, we feel that the $760 million figure is conservative. When we add government payments, value of food consumed at home, and rental value of farm dwellings to the $760 million, we have an estimated realized gross income figure of $920 million.

Even more important than this is the realized net income per farm, which rose 8 percent in 1966 to $2,850 per farm. In 1963 cash receipts were only $644 million. Further evidence of the progressive, optimistic trend in the Kentucky farm picture is that 1967 income is also expected to increase. U.S. farm income is expected to decline about 5 percent this year. One of the reasons for this expected increase is that a larger than normal part of the 1966 tobacco crop is being sold in 1967—about 38 percent, in fact. Of course, if this tobacco had been sold in 1966, farm income would have been about $90 million more.

Other reasons why we expect the 1967 income to be greater are higher prices for many farm products, and expanded production. For example, winter wheat acreage is up 25 percent this year over last year. Beef cattle and hog numbers are also expected to grow. Government payments may be lower in 1967 than in 1966, and production expenses will not rise as much as in 1966. If our farmers apply the technology becoming available daily, intensify the use of their land, and upgrade management skills, we will continue to make rapid progress toward our billion dollar goal, and beyond.

We realize that not all areas in Kentucky have the same agricultural potential. This is evident as we travel about the state, and is pointed out in the production potential study. Some areas and counties could double farm income; others could not. An example of an area that could at least double its farm income is the central Pennyrile area of Simpson, Logan, Todd, Christian, and Trigg counties. Income in these counties was $41.6 million in 1963 and could reach $84 million, according to the production potential study.

According to a recent study by Dr. John Bondurant at the University of Kentucky, this area is probably making the most rapid advance in agricultural technology of any of the major agricultural areas in Kentucky.[3] Net income per farm for typical tobacco-dairy farms averaged $6,859 in 1965, up 35 percent from 1964. Typical tobacco-beef cattle farms had net incomes of $6,150, up 31 percent. The net incomes for 1965 were also above the average net incomes for the period 1957-59 by 49 and 66 percent respectively. Since 1954 net incomes have doubled for both types of farms. Also, the total production for the tobacco-dairy farms doubled during the same period, and the production for the tobacco-beef farms increased slightly more than 50 percent. The total acreage per farm was 238 acres for the tobacco-dairy farms and 324 acres for the tobacco-beef farms in 1965. I commend the farmers in this area for this phenomenal growth in income during the past several years. I feel they have taken the recommendations of the Commission on Agriculture seriously and are moving ahead.

While this particular area shows great potential for grain-livestock farming, other areas show similar opportunities for other systems of farming. This area approach to increasing our farm income has considerable merit. Where there is similar land, topography, transportation, and specific market outlets, as well as common interests, certain enterprises will flourish.

Another case in point is the Lake Cumberland area, which is making rapid progress in swine production. An intensive educational program was carried out in this nine-county area last year, involving extension, vocational agriculture, and all other agencies, agribusiness people, and interested farmers. This project has already shown significant increases in hog numbers, better quality fed hogs and feeder pigs, and higher income for the area. I know that the progress reports we hear from our committees will have other examples of accomplishment—and they probably will name some problems that are being faced. Someone has said that "problems are only unsolved opportunities," so I am confident that these problems will be turned into opportunities if we all work together.

The wholehearted, enthusiastic support and assistance given this program by commission members, by those serving on committees, and by the hundreds of people we have called on from time to time has been one of the most gratifying experiences of my term as governor. When I appointed these commission members, I told them I wanted them to work hard, and that I would work hard with them. Well, they haven't let me forget it! They keep me busy.

One of our members, Mr. Albert Cash, of Fancy Farm, has resigned recently because of increased commitments at home.[4] I am today appointing Mr. Elton Noel, an outstanding young farmer from Christian County, to the commission, and asking him to serve as chairman of the processing and marketing committee.[5] I'd like for Elton to stand. Because of the increasing work load, we are expanding the commission by one member. I am also appointing today, Mr. Eddie Moore of Hyden, and asking him to serve as chairman of the forestry committee.[6] Eddie, would you stand? Mr. Barney Tucker has been chairman of the forestry committee, but because of his wide interests and experience, I have asked him to chair the promotion committee.[7]

Two years ago, from this platform, I said that "the real work of this conference cannot be done at meetings in Louisville. It must be accomplished by action on the farms in the counties you represent. What the conference does establish is that such action is possible, feasible, and desirable—and that even one individual farmer can accomplish a great deal." The concrete results of the past three years have strengthened this belief. They are positive proof that agriculture is a dynamic industry in our state. We now have a full head of steam—let's keep the throttle wide open until we top this grade and reach a one billion dollar annual farm income; then set our sights on even greater things for Kentucky agriculture.

---

1. Samuel R. Guard (1890-1966), editor of *Breeder's Gazette* (1927-1958); farm columnist, *Louisville Courier-Journal* (1958-1966); graduate of Ohio State University; president, Friends of Kentucky Libraries, Inc.; Associated Sheep Farmers of America; Kentucky Farm Press and Radio Association; member President Dwight D. Eisenhower's Commission on Judicial and Congressional Salaries. *Louisville Courier-Journal*, September 16, 1966.

2. Orville Lothrop Freeman (1918-), attorney from Minneapolis, Minnesota; chairman, Civil Service Commission, Minneapolis (1946-1949); state chairman, Democratic-Farmer-Labor party (1948-1950); governor of Minnesota (1956 -1960); U.S. secretary of agriculture (1961-1969). *Who's Who in American Politics, 1975-1976.* 5th ed. (New York, 1975).

3. John Harvey Bondurant (1900-1973), a native of Lexington, Kentucky. B.S., University of Kentucky (1926); M.S., Cornell University (1932); Ph.D. (1942); teacher of agriculture and principal, Sharpe, Kentucky (1926-1930); professor of agricultural economics, University of Kentucky (1932-1971). Information provided in telephone interview with Mrs. John H. Bondurant, February 4, 1981.

4. Albert Cash (1915-), born and educated in Fancy Farm, Kentucky. Farmer and businessman, Graves County (1935-1941); U.S. Army (1941-1945); farmer in Graves County (1946-1966); chairman, Graves County Farm Bureau

(1962-1963); county chairman, Breathitt campaign for governor (1963); postmaster, Fancy Farm (1966-). Telephone interview, February 4, 1981.

5. Elton Noel (1934-), farmer, Christian County, Kentucky. Active in Kentucky Young Farmers Association (1966-1967); associated with West Kentucky Production Credit Association (1972-). Telephone interview, February 6, 1981.

6. Eddie J. Moore (1921-), born, Hazard, Kentucky; educated public schools, Morehead; employed as machine operator, Springfield, Ohio (1940-1945); engaged in lumber business in Hyden, Kentucky (1946-); chairman of Forestry Committee, Commission on Agriculture (1965-1967). Telephone interview, February 4, 1981.

7. Barney Tucker (1915-), temporary executive director, Kentucky Agriculture Development Commission (1969); member, Commission on Agriculture (1968). Tucker is a businessman from London. Robert F. Sexton, ed., *The Public Papers of Governor Louie B. Nunn, 1967-1971* (Lexington, Ky., 1975), p. 275.

NATIONAL ADVISORY COMMISSION ON RURAL POVERTY
Natural Bridge State Park / May 3, 1967

It is a pleasure to greet you once again as we get on with this most important work, and it is especially good to greet you here in Kentucky. We like to think that there is nothing that compares with springtime in this part of the country, and it does us good to be able to share it with a distinguished group such as this. So, welcome to Appalachia, welcome to Kentucky, welcome to our state park system, and welcome to Natural Bridge. If there is anything you need to make your stay more pleasant and it has not been offered to you, ask one of our staff members. They will do their best to comply with your requests—within reason, of course.

At the risk of being elementary at a time when the work of this commission must be technical and driving toward some conclusions, I would like to summarize some attitudes I think we must have if we are to make our work here meaningful and lasting. These are attitudes that affect us individually and as a group—attitudes that I believe will influence both the personal dedication and the team play that will go into the remaining months of our labors and that will have a profound impact on the report that we produce.

I would like, incidentally, to congratulate and commend each person in this room for his interest and his dedication. This has been and is a hard-working commission, and I know that President Johnson will be pleased with your contribution and that your fellow Americans will owe you great thanks upon the completion of our work.

I think first that we must be dedicated to the idea that this great country can provide the opportunity for good living to all its citizens. This includes the tenant farmer as well as the landowner; the migrant worker as well as the suburbanite; the small town resident as well as the big city dweller; the Indian on the reservation as well as the white man in the subdivision. This opportunity must be present in the coal fields of Appalachia, in the deserts of the Southwest, on the Mississippi delta, in the ghettos of our large cities, in the wilderness settlements of Alaska. It will manifest itself in different ways in all of these localities, of course, but it must consist of the basic ingredients of good housing, good schools, good health services, and a chance at employment that will make it possible to utilize these resources. This attitude—this premise—is simply a belief that America can take care of its own, that our democracy is strong enough to let everyone participate in its benefits and dynamic enough to always provide those benefits as the character of national life changes.

A second attitude I believe we must have—and this will certainly seem basic to you who have worked so many hard months on this commission—is that the preservation and development of healthy rural areas and small towns is vital to the strength of our country. Today we find many millions of our citizens being swallowed up and straitjacketed by our large cities. They are the prisoners of our freeways, the elevators in our apartment and office buildings, our bus stops and subways. They are pushed, shoved, stepped on, and run over. Their faces are soiled by the soot that falls, their lungs are fouled by exhaust fumes, their complexion is paled by the constant shadow of the high walls around them. They have little privacy and almost as little freedom as the dogs they lead around on leashes.

This may be an extreme view of city life today, but it is accurate for the purpose of illustrating what is one of the greatest ironies of our time. That irony is that there is less need for large cities today than at any time in our history. Good highways, such as the one you drove on coming to this park, are all over the American landscape, making small towns and countryside easily reached. Cultural activities are no longer confined to large cities. Conveniences of modern living are available practically everywhere. It has been shown that industries thrive when transplanted to rural or small town locations.

The individual's pride is heightened and his spirit is awakened when he is freed from our city fortresses. Yet, with all this being true, we are still piling people layer upon layer in a few square miles of our great country while much of it remains unpopulated. I see our job, then, not only as one of combating the poverty of rural America and stemming its importation to the city but also, hopefully, of finding ways in which many of our city prisoners may find new opportunity on the outside — in rural America.

A third attitude which I think is basic to our deliberations is that of true interest and compassion for those who are now the victims of poverty, that cruel and tyrannous master that presently holds so many Americans as its victims. We must, as we consider the plight of these people, be able to put ourselves in our brother's place. We must, somehow, be able to feel the despair, the loss of dignity, the overpowering loneliness, the hunger of those we seek to help.

In the three hearings you have held you have seen them and heard from them. They have told you their story—from the lady in Tucson who quit school and got married at fourteen and lived in a migrant worker camp with nine children, to the unemployed miner in Memphis, to the lady in Washington who had moved to the city and longed to get back to the country. These are real people and their problems are real. Our concern must be equally real and geared to the helping of individuals as well as to proposing large national policy. I feel deeply that if we concern ourselves only with dealing in charts and graphs and abstractions relating to this complex subject, we will lose its flavor and our report will be flat and devoid of human feeling.

These, then, are some of the attitudes and ideas which I hope we are following and that I believe should permeate our work. Again, I hope that you will forgive me for being so elementary this late in the game.

If I were permitted one more observation—and I assume that I would be —I would like to make the observation that the poverty that we speak of is all around us, and if we but look for it we will find it to be quite a serious raveling in our national fabric. For instance, in this county and the four counties that surround it per capita income ranges from $467 a year in the lowest county to $945 a year in the highest. The percentage of families with income under $3,000 a year ranges from 57 percent to 80 percent. More than 15 percent of the total population is on public assistance. Approximately half of the children who start the ninth grade do not finish high school. I do not cite these statistics to in any way demean or denigrate the people of this area. I would, in fact, like to observe that these counties have progressed greatly within the last few years. Most of their citizens are simply victims of an environment which is not conducive to prosperity and most have simply had little chance to find the better things that are the promise of this great nation.

The point I make is that any one of you can find similar pockets of poverty and deprivation in the rural areas of your own state, that the target we seek to hit is all around us. It does not surprise you and it does not surprise anyone else that we would find poverty in this part of Appalachia, but it may be surprising to many how much indigence and want is scattered throughout an otherwise prosperous and thriving land.

It was a disappointment to me that I was unable to attend the hearings of this commission, so that I might personally have heard from some of the people who are the subject of our efforts and from some of the people who are seeking to help them. I know the hearings were in good hands, however, and I thank all of you for seeing that they were so fruitful.

I know that you, having seen and heard from those who testified, have a much greater appreciation for our problem and I know that you are eager to get to working toward its solution. Dr. Bishop, we have a lot of work before us. We have a dedicated commission and a competent staff. Let us get on with the agenda and seek the answers the president is counting on us to come up with.

NATIONAL RURAL SOCIOLOGICAL SOCIETY
San Francisco, California / August 27, 1967

It is an honor to have been invited to speak before such a learned and distinguished group as this. I feel humbled by the presence of so many scholars—particularly so many who are scholarly in what is one of the most important fields of study and endeavor in our nation today. In fact, if I had realized the caliber of this crowd a little earlier I might have turned the business of the commission over to you for the last two or three days and let the commission members go sightseeing, go fishing or whatever else you do to entertain yourself in this delightful city where we are meeting. I am certain you would come as close to having the answers the commission is seeking as any group in the United States.

The problem the commission is studying—which I would like to discuss a little with you here tonight—is one that pervades all parts of our society, spreads across all cultural, racial, and religious divisions, permeates all sectors of the economy, knows no geographical barriers, affects all educational and scientific pursuits, is in the purview of all levels of government, and touches the daily lives of all two hundred million Americans.

Leaving the word "poverty" out for a moment, the problem simply stated is: How do we make rural and small town life productive, comfortable, and meaningful? Implicit in this problem are related sub-problems: How do we provide an economic base in rural America sufficient to support those who live there or would like to live there? How do we assure proper rural housing and attractive rural neighborhoods? How do we improve our transportation systems to end the isolation that is in itself often the cause of rural poverty? How do we upgrade health services so that rural Americans have the same advantages as anyone else? How do we take the opportunities of good schools, good libraries, and other institutions of culture and education to each neighborhood in rural America? How do we structure our units of government and motivate our officials at all levels of government to do the best job of fighting poverty? How do we husband and develop our natural resources so as to keep rural America attractive and also keep it productive? And—perhaps most important of all—how do we battle and finally eradicate the attitude of hopelessness, the feeling of despair, the mood of defeat, the pessimism that afflicts a large segment of America's people—those who have been poor so long they have fallen into a culture of poverty?

If we can find answers—or partial answers—to these problems we will have also helped answer the problems of our inner cities, now wracked and tortured by the explosive unhappiness of those confined there. For the cities are the product of the countryside. Poverty is a transportable item and it particularly likes to go to town. If we had given greater thought and taken wiser action in fighting the problems of rural America within past generations, the slums of our cities would not now reverberate with warfare.

Vice President Humphrey said in a speech last week that the slums and the ghettos of our cities are a repudiation of the Statue of Liberty, a denial of our great American Constitution.[1] I am sure that the vice president would agree that poverty and hopelessness and lack of opportunity in rural America—those conditions which helped spawn the slums and ghettos—constitute just as great a denial and repudiation of the things our country stands for. . . .[2]

It is unthinkable but true that today—in the richest nation on earth—we have some thirteen million rural Americans living in poverty—some of them in desperate poverty. The South has the greatest concentration of rural poverty, although the rural poor live in all parts of the nation. The incidence of poverty among Negroes is higher than among whites, although there are more total whites living in poverty. Our Indian reservations usually are poverty areas. The very young and the very old constitute an unusually high proportion of the rural poor.

The rural poor are generally unskilled and have little education. Their children are unlikely to acquire more education than the parents. Families are larger than those in the city. Housing is inadequate if not pitiful. The level of health care is low. Disease is often prevalent. Malnutrition is widespread. Starvation is not unheard of. Families who are at the $3,000 a year income, generally considered the threshold of poverty, are often among the more fortunate in poor rural areas. Seventy percent of rural poor families live on less than $2,000, and one family in four gets by on less than $1,000 a year. This is a brief description of rural poverty. Add the defeat, the despair, the hopelessness that I mentioned earlier and the picture emerges more clearly, if more depressingly.

I do not think it would be proper for me to report on any of the commission's conclusions here tonight or even to speculate on what the final report may contain. This is a presidential commission, and the president and those cabinet officers involved are the proprietors of the report once the commission has concluded its work.

I would, however, like to make a point or two that I believe do not violate the restricted nature of the report and that I do believe reflect pretty well the feelings of the commission. First, I would like to say that the commission does not believe that it is enough to establish antipoverty programs designed to just lift persons above the threshold of poverty. We must, of course, help those with the greatest need first. We want to do what we can to help a family that is improperly fed, improperly housed, sick or lacking in clothing.

But our goal is not simply to suggest or devise measures which raise incomes above $3,000 a year. Our goal is to give our rural poor an opportunity to rise as far as their ambitions and their abilities will permit. The man educated or motivated to earn only $3,000 a year today will most assuredly be below the poverty level again tomorrow as our economy advances and as our culture develops the need and the appetite for greater human fulfillment.

This leads me to a second point that I have already touched on. It is that the commission considers it part of its charge from the president to combat the presence of a "poverty culture" in this country. This is the culture that knows only the defeat, the despair, and the hopelessness that I mentioned earlier. This is the culture or the conditioning that leads a poor man to expect his children to be poor and not to do the things which would give them fuller lives. This is the tendency to give up and make poverty a companion for life. This is the attitude that causes the poor individual to withdraw and denies society the benefits of any aptitudes or talents he may possess.

We could stop poverty—for a short period of time—by instituting a system of payments to those who are below the poverty level and putting a minimum amount of money into the pocket of every citizen. But removing the symptoms would not cure the disease. This can only be done by removing the causes of poverty and by eradicating the culture of poverty.

Third, we of the commission want our society to attack the whole problem of poverty—and it really cannot be done by isolating rural poverty from poverty in other areas—with the attitude that poverty is not only uncomfortable and degrading, but with the attitude that the presence of poverty is a mark against our national honor and the sufferance of conditions that create poverty is sinful.

Surely a nation that can find it within its ability to reach the planets, that leads the world in technology, that was founded and has progressed on a spiritual base that proclaims the nobility of man has it within its means and has it within its heart to end the want and the suffering of its own citizens.

And last, the commission does not consider the job of doing something about rural poverty to be one for the federal government alone. Surely we will have to depend on federal help—massive federal help—if we are to be successful, but we cannot forget that there are other layers of government also serving the people. Speaking now as a governor rather than as chairman of the National Advisory Commission on Rural Poverty, I would like to say—and say with some emphasis—that the states must be partners in this endeavor and, in turn, must see that local governments are involved. To me this means that states must be willing to share in the effort, and it means that the federal government must not bypass them. It also means that local government must be functional enough and skilled enough to do its share.

Two developments of recent years lead to the conclusion that the states are not dead—have not been strangled by the strength of Washington—and are still able to function. One is the success of the concept put forth in the Appalachian Regional Development Commission, where the member states are partners with the federal government and determine the program to be followed.

The other is the creation of multicounty development districts within states. We have recently designated these areas in Kentucky, have told departments of state government and federal agencies that serve the state that they are to follow the designated district lines in their field organizations, and are in [the] process of making the districts functional.

The first development—the Appalachian region concept—establishes federal-state ties that use the best abilities of both levels of government. The second development—the organization of multicounty districts within states—gives both state and federal agencies a better working arrangement with areas of a state and gives local governments—often too weak and too poor to function well by themselves—a unit to tie to in dealing with state government.

I believe that both of the developments are significant, but they are only two instances of governmental innovation designed to make government more responsive to the people. I believe we can devise others—or else turn over all problems, all functions, all rights to our national government.

I hope that federal, state and local governments working together—and involving massive citizen support—can soon do something about the problems of rural poverty, the problems that I outlined at the start of this talk. We must develop the economic base that will support jobs for our people in rural and small town environments. We must improve our rural education, our rural health services, our rural transportation, and our rural housing.

When we do these things we will not only have started to solve the problem that I stated earlier: "How do we make rural and small town life productive, comfortable, and meaningful?" We will have also helped make the dream on which America was founded come true for countless thousands of our fellow citizens.

You who are in convention here tonight, who have given years of thought and study to the subjects I have talked about, can do more to help us reach these goals than can the members of the National Advisory Commission on Rural Poverty. We can only advise, as the name of the commission indicates, and try to indicate what we think are some preferred goals, priorities and devices, as determined by a year of study, hearings, and consultation. You who are the professionals and the scholars will be the real innovators and the real movers as we try to change the structure of our society, particularly our rural society, to accommodate to the needs of those who have been so long neglected. That is, you will if you are the activists I hope you are.

With your help, and the help of thousands of others like you—motivated professionals who believe it is within our power to lift the burden from our poor—we will make of rural America a place that is productive, that is comfortable, that is healthy, that is fulfilling, and that is a happy place to live.[3]

---

1. Hubert Horatio Humphrey (1911-1978), was a leading figure in the Democratic party for three decades. He represented Minnesota in the United States Senate from 1949 to 1964. During that time he was noted for his strong and effective support of civil rights legislation. From 1964 to 1969 he served as Lyndon Johnson's vice president and in 1968 was the unsuccessful Democratic nominee for the presidency. In 1970 he returned to the Senate, where he served until his death in 1978. *Current Biography, 1978,* p. 470.

2. A section of this speech, repetitious of Governor Breathitt's remarks on May 3, 1967, to the National Advisory Commission on Rural Poverty, has been deleted. That speech is included in these papers.

3. The advisory committee's final report was presented to the president's commission in September of 1967. The report found existing rural poverty programs to be severely inadequate. The primary focus for the committee's recommendation was underemployment in rural areas. The lack of jobs drove large numbers of rural

Americans to the already overcrowded cities, where they contributed to the urban problems of the 1960s. For those that remained in the countryside, the lack of job opportunities often meant low-income subsistence. Breathitt's committee recommended a "thorough overhauling of our manpower policies and programs" and federal efforts to encourage the establishment of industry in smaller cities to stem the out-migration of workers and raise income levels in the surrounding rural areas. Eventually, the report envisioned an expensive program of guaranteed federal employment. Furthermore, the report urged expanded efforts in education, housing, food stamps, and birth control programs. *Louisville Courier-Journal,* August 2, December 10, 1967.

TRANSPORTATION

KENTUCKY HIGHWAY CONFERENCE
Lexington / March 11, 1964

ADEQUATE transportation is a cornerstone of any thriving, progressive society; and the people of the United States and other nations of the civilized world are, as they become more mobile, growing increasingly dependent on modern, safe systems of highways. Every state in the United States, every city and every county in every state spends a substantial portion of its income to build and maintain good highways and streets. Every family and every business is affected by the social and economic ramifications of our expanding highway systems and most contribute monetarily to their building and their upkeep. Linked inextricably with the highways industry is the automobile industry—that mammoth indicator and influencer of our economy—the petroleum and rubber industries, and many others.

Highways are a modifying and determining force in the lives of all of us and it is both fitting and commendable that you, the leaders of highway building in Kentucky—the designers, the engineers, the contractors, the administrators—should schedule such a conference as this to exchange ideas and information that you may provide a better product for the public you serve. I hope that your sessions have been rewarding. I know that they have been interesting because I have attended conferences such as this before, and I regret my inability to sit in on more of your meetings today.

I feel that I am a nonexpert in the midst of experts, and looking over your schedule of distinguished speakers does not comfort me that I may add appreciably to your knowledge or to what has transpired here. But I would like to express to you some ideas on Kentucky's highway needs of the future and on the course I think we should follow in meeting those needs.

We have in recent years been leaders in highway construction as we have pushed our turnpikes, our interstate, primary, and secondary systems into all parts of the Commonwealth.[1] Kentucky has at last become respectable in the matter of highways offered to the driving public and no longer suffers under the onus of being a detour state. For the first time Kentucky has a system of highways that is truly systematized—a plan for roads that is based on need, not personality or political consideration.

For this I give credit to Henry Ward, whose tenure as highway commissioner is among the longest in the history of the job, his staff and his department.[2] This organization has grown in proficiency and professionalism as our new miles of highways have extended across the state. Without this growth and without this leadership those new miles and the many that we hope will follow would have been much more difficult to obtain. I also give credit to those in private enterprise who have helped us make recent progress—the engineers, the construction crews, the suppliers. Their ability is attested to by the record of the last few years.

The progress of yesterday or today will not be sufficient to the needs of tomorrow, however, and if we are to meet those needs, if we are to keep the construction momentum we have gained, we must make our plans now—we must recognize those needs today.

Thousands of new automobiles and thousands of new drivers are appearing on Kentucky's highways each year. An expanding population, in itself, means greater traffic in the years ahead. An expanding economy has made the two-car family commonplace and has introduced the three-car family. Shorter work hours, more vacation time, and earlier retirement will put additional millions of vehicles on our highways.

I do not think it is an overstatement to say that the highway needs of today would have astounded the highway planners of a generation ago—the World War II period—and that the needs of a generation from now challenge our best abilities of foresight. There are many of you here today who were planning highways twenty and twenty-five years ago. I wonder if you were able to predict our present need for expressways, the trend toward turnpikes and the interstate system—which is being built as an addition to what was being planned then. And who foretold ten years ago that the number of motor vehicles in Kentucky would increase by more than 50 percent in the decade that was to follow?

I am not looking twenty-five, twenty, or even ten years ahead, however, when I say we must be prepared for increased highway use. I am looking to the more immediate future, and I am sure that Mr. Ward and his planners, while they have an eye out for 1990, are more concerned now with 1970 and the years between now and then; and I am sure they are concerned with how we shall pay for our highways during those years.

In 1970 our portion of the interstate system is scheduled to be completed.[3] But in 1966 the bond money that Kentucky has used to match federal funds to build the system will be exhausted. We face the prospect of curtailed construction and roads inadequate to meet the traffic of the years ahead unless more money can be obtained. It is for this reason that I have recommended to the General Assembly that they present to the voters a referendum on a general obligation bond sale which would include $139 million in highway construction funds. The vote would be in the fall of 1965 and subsequent sale of the bonds would enable us to continue scheduled construction.

The bond money would be used not only for interstate construction but for regular federal aid highways. It would also provide funds for us to take advantage of a new, special program for the Appalachian area which Congress is being asked to consider. If the program is approved, the federal government would provide money to the states in the area on an eighty-twenty matching basis. This is no small program. It has been recommended that a minimum of $90 million a year be allocated for trunkline highways to Appalachia, and of this total Kentucky may get as much as $25 million. I do not think that we can afford to pass up such a bargain for eastern Kentucky. I do not think that we can allow our interstate program to falter. I do not think that we can cut back on our highways under regular federal aid.

The requirements of the years ahead dictate that we build now—not when the money would come to us through normal tax channels. If we wait, we have no chance for a safe, modern highway system adequate to carry the heavy traffic we anticipate as our state grows, as our tourist industry expands, and as an ever more mobile public takes to the highways in increasing numbers.

The excellent highways we now drive on were made possible in large part by bond issues voted by the people in 1956 and 1960. If we had waited then until we got the money through taxes we would still be driving on highways that were not adequate ten or even twenty years ago.

Kentucky has had good experience with past bond issues and the credit of the Commonwealth is excellent. We will get a favorable rate of interest on the bonds we sell, and I confidently predict that an expanding economy—helped in no small part by good highways—will provide enough new money to retire the issue. These new general obligation bonds—both for highways and for other construction—are vital to the progress of Kentucky. I hope the General Assembly will agree to take this matter to the people, and I hope that you will give the measure your unqualified support when it appears on the ballot.

There is one other matter I would like to talk you to about and for which I solicit your interest and your support. It is a matter that most of you have been directly concerned with for years and that every citizen talks about. Yet it is a matter on which we do not seem to make the progress we should make. I am talking about highway safety. Last year 841 people died in traffic accidents on Kentucky highways. I am today asking the General Assembly to adopt the most important Kentucky highway safety legislation since the organization of the Kentucky State Police in 1948. It is a known fact that lives can be saved on our highways if motor vehicles are given periodic safety inspections. Experience in other states has proven this. States with good auto safety inspection programs have about a 15 percent better safety record than states without auto safety inspections. I am therefore urging the General Assembly to enact into law Senate Bill 190 providing for the annual inspection of all motor vehicles in the Commonwealth.[4]

Seat belts can also save lives. If all occupants of vehicles involved in traffic accidents in Kentucky last year had worn seat belts, eighty lives would have been saved. Senator Mann has introduced Senate Bill 1 providing for the installation of two front seat belts in all new cars sold in Kentucky.[5] The Senate has passed this bill. I urge the House of Representatives to do so. It is also my hope that the legislature will adopt House Bill 455 providing for Kentucky's participation in the vehicle equipment safety compact, to help establish uniform vehicle safety standards throughout the nation.[6]

Seat belts can save lives. Periodic inspection of automobiles to see that brakes, lights, and other safety equipment are in working order can save lives. I recommend these measures to the General Assembly in behalf of the safety of the citizens of Kentucky. I hope you will do all you can in support of these measures and that through their adoption we can save some lives. It has been an honor to meet with you today. I thank you for the opportunity to bring these thoughts on highway financing and highway safety to you and I wish you much success for the rest of your conference.

---

1. The completion and expansion of the highway program of the Combs administration was a major thrust of the Breathitt administration. As of April, 1964, the following sections of interstate and parkways were completed: Western Kentucky Parkway from Princeton to Elizabethtown, Mountain Parkway from Winchester to Campton, I-64 from Louisville to Frankfort and Lexington to Mount Sterling, I-65 from Upton to Louisville, and I-75 from Lexington to Cincinnati. Under construction or planned were I-24 from Paducah to the Tennessee border near Hopkinsville, I-64 from Frankfort to Lexington and Mt. Sterling to Ashland, I-65 from Elizabethtown to the border near Franklin, I-71 from Louisville to Cincinnati, the Central Kentucky Parkway from Elizabethtown to Versailles, and the Mountain Parkway from Campton to Pikeville and Whitesburg. *Louisville Courier-Journal,* April 16, 1964.

2. Henry Ward (1909-), reporter, columnist, and editor of *Paducah Sun-Democrat* (1928-1948); Kentucky House of Representatives (1934-1943); majority

leader (1942-1943); Kentucky Senate (1946-1948); commissioner of conservation (1948-1955); commissioner of highways (1960-1966); unsuccessful Democratic nominee for governor (1967). See Henry Ward "Recollections of Forty-Five Years in Kentucky Government and Politics," Oral History Collection manuscripts, Murray State University, Murray, Kentucky.

3. The completion of the interstate system fell far behind schedule in Kentucky and the nation and remained uncompleted in 1980.

4. Senate Bill 190, introduced by Shelby Kinkead, provided for inspection of motor vehicles. The bill died in committee without a reading in the Senate. *Journal of the Senate of the General Assembly of the Commonwealth of Kentucky, 1964,* (Louisville, Ky., 1964), pp. 286, 664.

5. William C. Mann (1908-1971), physician from Marrowbone, Kentucky; Kentucky House of Representatives (1954-1956); Kentucky Senate (1962-1968). Information provided by Mrs. William C. Mann. Senate Bill 1 required front seat belts before a new passenger car could be sold, leased, traded, transferred or registered in Kentucky. It passed the Senate on February 5, 1964, by a vote of 32-2; however, it died in the House of Representatives for lack of a third reading. *Journal of the House of Representatives of the General Assembly of the Commonwealth of Kentucky, 1964* (Louisville, Ky., 1964), p. 1656, and *Journal of the Senate of the General Assembly of the Commonwealth of Kentucky, 1964* (Louisville, Ky., 1964), pp. 99, 125.

6. See "an act relating to motor vehicle equipment," *Acts, 1964* (H.B. 455), pp. 348-59.

AMERICAN BRIDGE, TUNNEL, AND TURNPIKE ASSOCIATION

French Lick, Indiana / April 19, 1964

IT'S a pleasure and an honor to appear before you this evening and to relate some of the experiences Kentucky has had with toll roads and bridges—and to report at the same time that our Commonwealth has had an enjoyable experience with the system that all of you represent and support. While Kentucky is new to the toll road industry—if you wish to call it that—we do have a kinship with your association that goes back at least a decade. One of our highway commissioners, a man still active in highway construction work, a highly regarded engineer and administrator—Bill Curlin—was a member of your board of directors about the time Kentucky built its first major toll road—the highly successful Kentucky Turnpike which runs from Louisville to Elizabethtown.[1] Since that beginning—a task undertaken, I must admit, with a great deal of fear—Kentucky has taken giant strides.

Another step is in the making—a step to be taken with some finality—in about seventy-two hours. On Thursday of this week local and state officials will gather near historic Bardstown, the site of My Old Kentucky Home, and we shall break ground for the Central Kentucky Turnpike. That road will serve one of the most heavily populated areas of our state. It will serve, when completed, a section that has attracted thousands of tourists. It will serve the land the great Stephen Collins Foster visited and immortalized in song, where Lincoln was born and spent a portion of his boyhood, a section where much of Kentucky's great history was fashioned.[2]

But more than that—the Central Kentucky will bring together the east and the west of our Commonwealth. Sectionalism will disappear as we drive back and forth. We shall, on its completion, fashion a strong, modern highway system of toll roads that has one end anchored in the vastness of our Kentucky mountains, not too far from the borders of West Virginia, and the other end anchored not too many miles from the banks of the Mississippi. Thus visitors to our Commonwealth—and you are all welcome to come and see us—can go from the mountains on the east nearly to the delta land on the west, and all of it will be on turnpikes with the exception of a short distance around Lexington.

Let me give you some background—the story of how and why Kentucky embarked on its program of toll roads and modern turnpikes. For many a generation Kentucky was plagued by a lack of finances—a situation not a stranger to any state government. We would build ten miles of modern road in one section of the state. We would construct another section of, say, five miles in still another area. A curve was straightened out. A passing lane was built. But before we could construct a highway of any major proportions the improvements already made had become obsolete. Thus Kentucky, as other states, turned to the turnpike method of construction. We issued revenue bonds which found a ready market.

I would be less than honest if I said that we undertook the program without a great deal of doubt. Critics declared that the first road would never pay out, that the Kentucky Turnpike from Louisville to Elizabethtown would be forever a drain on the regular highway appropriation. The first few years were anxious years. Revenues increased month by month, but there was still not enough in the till.

Today—and I make this report with a great deal of satisfaction—that first toll road is in such shape that we shall pay off the bonds twenty-two years ahead of schedule. Critics and doubters have become supporters of the program; and with an increase in traffic and the tourist trade, we confidently expect the Mountain Parkway, the turnpike through some of the most beautiful scenery in the eastern half of the nation, to eventually pay for itself. We also expect to pay out with the Western Kentucky Parkway as more visitors as well as Kentuckians make their way to the recreational areas of Kentucky Lake and Barkley Lake and to other areas of western Kentucky. And with the Central Kentucky Turnpike still to get its formal name, the entire system will be tied together, one section generating traffic and revenue for the other.

Now, I want to make myself completely clear. Neither the Mountain Parkway nor the Western Kentucky Parkway has reached that happy state. But the pattern of increased revenue follows that of the Kentucky Turnpike. And we hope that within a few years we shall be able to make similar reports on the early retirement of bonds. In the meantime Kentuckians will have the use of those facilities which under the orthodox method of construction might never have been made available. More than that, the state highway fund is getting a return in revenue that under other conditions might not have flowed into the treasury. All this, of course, did not just happen. It was planned.

We have a turnpike authority and those officials, together with the Highway department, constantly worked to increase toll road traffic and, it follows, revenue.[3] Perhaps as important as any one angle was the development of Kentucky's great tourist potential. We built new parks, we constructed new lakes, we dammed flowing streams. We put up new lodges to house visitors. We gave strong encouragement to private enterprise to join us in providing entertainment and housing and food for the vacationer. And close to all these areas were the turnpikes.

In our efforts—successful ones I can report—we went to industry and told them of new plant sites and pointed to the proximity of turnpikes. We gathered in local conferences the businessmen and officials of the area and discussed the problems and the opportunities.

Within the past few months our people hit upon another revenue-generating project. We recognized the convenience of credit cards, and so we issued credit cards to major consumers—consumers of toll road mileage. Sixty-four firms now use those credit cards—a total of more than 1,200 cards. And more such cards are being issued. A single card in the hands of the commercial driver is good for all such roads—and the Shawneetown Bridge across the Ohio River. You might say that we are going to make it as easy as possible to use our toll roads and bridges—short of forgetting to collect the toll.

We did other things to make people aware of the roads. We discarded the unimaginative noun turnpike. We asked citizens to suggest new names. And out of that suggestion came the names Mountain Parkway and Western Kentucky Parkway. And our landscape people attempted to make the highways conform—true parkways through a beautiful and hospitable land. Shortly we shall take a similar step for the new turnpike through the central Kentucky area.

Let's bring up to date the story of revenue collections. Last month collections on the Kentucky Turnpike topped the $300,000 mark. This is the first time that that amount has been reached so early in the year. And it was the first $300,000 income month since the height of the tourist season last summer. The Mountain Parkway and the Western Kentucky Parkway produced lesser sums, but all such collections increased over comparable periods. In brief, Kentucky's experience with toll road development, while not as extensive as that of some other states, has been a pleasant experience, and if the past is prologue we can look forward to other successes and more converts to the system of building modern, adequate highways in as short a period of time as possible.

We in Kentucky look upon the turnpike system as a conveyor belt for industry—bringing factories into close proximity to mass markets. We look upon it as a pleasant avenue down which visitors and Kentuckians can ride in safety to a vacation destination in any part of the state. If you need testimony as to the effectiveness of turnpikes, call upon those who have been charged with their construction and promotion. They'll bear witness.

---

1. William P. Curlin, Jr. (1933-), born in Paducah; engineering aide with Department of Highways (1951-1954); legal aide, attorney, and special administrative assistant to the commissioner of revenue (1960-1963). Information provided by Division of Personnel, Frankfort.

2. Stephen Collins Foster (1826-1864), composer famous for his Negro ballads and songs about the South, despite the fact that he spent his entire life north of the Ohio River, primarily in Pittsburgh and New York. He is best remembered by Kentuckians for "My Old Kentucky Home." David Ewen, ed., *Popular American Composers* (New York, 1965), pp. 62-65.

3. The Kentucky Turnpike Authority was created by the General Assembly in 1960 as a means of circumventing constitutional limitations in the ability of the state to finance the construction of turnpikes. The Turnpike Authority was designed as "an independent corporate agency and instrumentality of the Commonwealth." It was given the authority to issue and retire bonds and to build and operate turnpikes in conjunction with the department of Highways. *Acts, 1960,* Chapter 173 (S.B. 223), pp. 753-80.

GREATER CINCINNATI AIRPORT
Covington / September 28, 1964

THIS, I think, is a day to mark with an accent in the history of Greater Cincinnati Airport. It is a day on which those with narrow viewpoints have been pushed aside by those whose imagination and vision focus on a wider scope. For the benefits of the Greater Cincinnati Airport do not stop at the edge of the Boone County line—or at the state line of Kentucky. The benefits are regional, not confined by a political boundary. What we are doing here today recognizes this by adding to the Kenton County Airport Board six citizens of Cincinnati—six persons from Ohio who will help guide the destiny of this airport in the years ahead.

It is true that these six men will serve the board in an advisory capacity and not be voting members. In the last session of the legislature we considered a bill which would have put Cincinnatians on the Kenton County Airport Board as full-fledged members. But it was decided that this would have violated Kentucky's constitution.

This is a fault which needs mending. For although Greater Cincinnati Airport is geographically in Kentucky, it serves a region which extends beyond the state boundary. It is reasonable then that the management of the airport should be representative of the region and the financing of capital improvements should be the responsibility of the region. I would like to see the creation of an interstate airport authority for greater Cincinnati. I would like to see representatives of both our states take places on this authority. And I would like to see a portion of Ohio's allocation of federal aid to airports spent on this facility.

There are still some in southern Ohio who would spend millions and millions of dollars on a regional airport. Such an airport would be merely a duplicate to the regional facility we already have here. And with I-75 connecting Cincinnati to this airport the air travelers of that city have an ideal access.

I have with me today an executive order in which I have appointed an advisory commission to the Kenton County Airport Board. It is composed of six Cincinnatians. They are Paul W. Christensen, Jr., William B. Schroeder, John M. Lodhart, David F. Shaw, William S. Rowe, and John Hilberg.[1] This action was taken at the request of the Kenton County Airport Board and County Judge James A. Dressman, Jr.[2] Gentlemen, I congratulate you on your vision.

Let us make this a beginning and go on from here.

---

1. Paul Walter Christensen, Jr. (1925-), gear manufacturing company executive with Cincinnati Gear Company (1946-); president (1947-1958); chairman of the board, Cincinnati Steel Treating Company (1961-); director, Ohmart Corporation. *Who's Who in America, 1964-1965,* 33rd ed. (Chicago, 1964). William B. Schroeder, member, Kenton County Airport Board (1964-1967). Information provided by Kenton County Airport Board. John M. Lodhart (1911-), independent financial consultant; member, Kenton County Airport Board (1964-). Information provided by Kenton County Airport Board. David Frederick Shaw (1913-), engineer and executive; plant engineer and inspector, Tennessee Valley Authority (1934-1939); engineer for Birmingham Slag Company (1939-1941); director of security, Manhattan Engineering District (1946-1947); U.S. Atomic Energy Commission (1947-1955); assistant general manager of manufacturing (1955-1957); vice president, Henry J. Kaiser Company (1957-1960); General Electric Company, Cincinnati (1960-). *Who's Who in America, 1964-1965,* 33rd ed. (Chicago, 1964). William S. Rowe (1916-), president, Fifth Third Bank of Cincinnati (1963-1979); chairman of the board (1979-); chairman of the board, Fifth Third Bank and Fifth Third Bank Corporation (1980-); member, Kenton County Airport Board (1964-). Information provided by Fifth Third Bank of Cincinnati. John Hilberg, member Kenton County Airport Board (1964-1974). Information provided by Kenton County Airport Board.

2. James A. Dressman, Jr. (1922-), born in Covington, Kentucky; educated at St. Gregory's Seminary, Cincinnati, and Xavier University; L.L.B., Salmon P. Chase Law School; practicing attorney in Covington (1949-); member, Kentucky House of Representatives (1952-1954); member, Kenton County Airport Board. Hambleton Tapp, ed., *Who's Who in Kentucky* (Hopkinsville, Ky., 1966), and telephone interview with James A. Dressman, III, March 5, 1981.

HIGHWAY CONSTRUCTION STATEMENT
Frankfort / June 9, 1965

A PLAN of financing that would provide for early completion of a modern four-lane highway from Hopkinsville to Henderson, replacing old U.S. 41, and would free millions of state and federal funds to accelerate modernization of highways in the Owensboro area is being developed by the state of Kentucky.[1] This plan would include the issuance of revenue bonds to finance the new highway work between Hopkinsville and Henderson.

Under the plan new highways would be built to replace outmoded sections of U.S. 41 both north and south of the recently completed Madisonville bypass. These would include a 33.8 mile section between the end of the new bypass at Henderson and the Madisonville bypass, and an 18.5 mile section between the Madisonville bypass and Hopkinsville. It would also include the construction of a modern bypass around the east side of Hopkinsville connecting with the four-lane section of U.S. 41-A immediately south of Hopkinsville.

The use of revenue bonds to finance this construction would free a total of $24 million of state and federal funds which could be utilized to accelerate modernization of highways U.S. 60, U.S. 431, U.S. 231, and KY 54, which are the major highways serving Owensboro and that area. The key to early construction of modern highways to replace old U.S. 41 and to serve the Owensboro area is financing.

Even with approval of the bond issue in the November 2 election, the only funds which would be available under the regular state and federal programs for modernization of these highways would be the annual regular federal aid primary allocation which can be expended on the basis of 50 percent of the cost being borne out of federal funds and 50 percent out of state funds. The total amount of the state and federal allocation under this program for primary highways is only $15 million a year. This is the gross amount available for expenditure annually on the entire primary system in Kentucky. Therefore, only a reasonable portion of that total could be allocated for the improvement of highways in this area. It is obvious at a glance that modern highways to serve these areas could not be achieved at an early date.

Every study made by the Kentucky Department of Highways has demonstrated that there is now and will continue to be a very heavy volume of traffic that wants to follow U.S. 41 north-south. These studies indicate that revenue bonds could be issued to complete modernization of the substitute for U.S. 41 in the immediate future and that tolls which could be collected on the new sections would be more than adequate to retire the bonds.

Under this plan Kentucky could expedite attention to the major problem of highway improvements in this area. It could give the cities interested in U.S. 41 a modern highway in the very near future. Otherwise many years obviously would elapse before four-laning of the present route could be accomplished. The use of revenue bonds for the improvement of U.S. 41 would make possible the transfer to highways serving the Owensboro area the regular state and federal funds which otherwise would be required on U.S. 41. This would mean improvement of these routes at a date much earlier than otherwise could be achieved.

This plan would not interfere with the efforts being made by Kentucky in cooperation with Indiana to secure another route of the Interstate Highway System running north-south, east of U.S. 41. It has always been recognized that there is no possibility of securing this new interstate route unless present efforts are successful in getting additional interstate miles before 1972.

Traffic studies clearly indicate that there is going to be enough traffic on U.S. 41 to justify the construction of an interstate route nearby in the future. Kentucky would continue to press for this route. Modernization of U.S. 41 would be helpful to Kentucky in its efforts to secure the location of an interstate route that would cross the Ohio River near Owensboro.

To supplement its own planning efforts, the Kentucky Department of Highways has already engaged the internationally known firm of Wilbur Smith and Associates to conduct additional studies indicating long-range traffic on U.S. 41 and the proposed additional north-south corridor. This study also is designed to show future traffic movements relating to Owensboro both north-south and east-west.

The Wilbur Smith firm has been given specific instructions to consider Owensboro as the hub of a highway system and to make studies which would develop projected traffic needs on major arterial highways that radiate from and through Owensboro in all directions. The firm, by its contract, has been directed to ascertain the feasibility of construction of any of these major routes as a toll facility.

Every study that has been made by the Kentucky Department of Highways, particularly in the last four years, has demonstrated conclusively that there needs to be modernization of a major highway along U.S. 41 from Hopkinsville to Henderson and that modern highways are needed to serve the growing economy of Owensboro. These studies definitely indicate that U.S. 41 will continue to be a major north-south highway because it clears a traffic corridor from Chicago south and penetrates in an area not served by any section of the interstate system. Furthermore, this corridor serves Evansville, Indiana, which is the largest city in the United States not served by a section of the highway. The combination of the population of Evansville and Henderson, Kentucky, which is just across the Ohio River from Evansville, totals 156,892. Traffic studies show that any metropolitan area with this type of population constitutes a traffic generator that not only needs to be served but also will provide permanent guarantees that traffic will be continued. In addition, Madisonville and Hopkinsville are important communities and also make a major contribution to the traffic volumes that utilize this route.

U.S. 41 several years ago was four-laned from Hopkinsville to the Tennessee line, serving the Fort Campbell area. In 1962 a sixteen-mile section of U.S. 41 was completely rebuilt, bypassing Madisonville. A new bypass of U.S. 41 around Henderson was opened to traffic in 1962, and at the present time U.S. 41 is being six-laned from U.S. 60 at Henderson to the approaches to the bridges across the Ohio River. A new bridge is under construction which will make U.S. 41 four lanes across the Ohio River to Evansville. The state of Indiana has plans to continue modernization of U.S. 41 north of Evansville.

In a recent meeting which we had with Governor Roger Branigin and Indiana Highway Department officials at Indianapolis, they indicated a great interest in working with Kentucky for the modernization of U.S. 41 and to secure a new route for the Interstate Highway System needed for the future to carry the heavy volume of traffic that studies indicate this corridor will develop.[2]

All of these studies demonstrate conclusively that highway improvements are needed desperately. Studies also conclusively demonstrate that the means of financing these improvements are not immediately available. It is for this reason that we have concluded that this program can be expedited by the issuance of revenue bonds which would release regular federal aid for other purposes in the area. We are continuing these studies with the definite objective of being in a position to consider issuance of revenue bonds for the modernization of the U.S. 41 substitute at the same time we go to the market to sell revenue bonds for the Purchase Parkway. We have explored this plan with New York financial advisors, and they encourage it with enthusiasm.

This enthusiasm is based on the fact that projected traffic volumes which can be anticipated for U.S. 41 demonstrate that revenue bonds issued to finance construction of the short section as a toll road could be retired easily from the revenue that could be anticipated. At the present time the average daily traffic on U.S. 41 between Hopkinsville and Henderson is 6,000 vehicles. The Kentucky Department of Highways estimates that traffic on the same sections forty years from now will average 20,000 vehicles per day. Under this plan there can be a modern substitute for the antiquated U.S. 41 now. It is obvious that under any other plan a number of years would be required to secure funds necessary to provide for modernization of U.S. 41.

Even by utilizing the present two-lane U.S. 41 between Hopkinsville and the Madisonville bypass and between the northern end of the Madisonville bypass and Henderson, it is estimated that it would cost $17 million to build another two lanes. In addition, it is estimated that it would cost $6 million to build a bypass around Hopkinsville.

We need to be reminded again that Kentucky has a total of $15 million a year of both state and federal funds for improvement of the primary highway system, and this fund must be distributed over the entire state to meet the needs. The availability of federal money, the cost of improvements which are anticipated as necessary in the Owensboro area, and completion of the modernization of U.S. 41, constitute a problem for Kentucky that must be recognized.

Kentucky is in a competitive situation with other states in the nation and must move forward. We must be aggressive in determining the needs of our state and then providing the solution for these financing problems. The particular plan that we are now exploring represents an acceptance of responsibility by the state to move now rather than delay economic progress until some uncertain future date.

---

1. The planned highway was the Pennyrile Parkway.

2. Roger Douglas Branigin (1902-), attorney; deputy prosecuting attorney, Franklin, Indiana (1926-1929), counsel, Federal Land Bank and F.C.A., Louisville (1930-1938); governor of Indiana (1965-1969); law practice, Lafayette, Indiana (1969-). *Who's Who in America, 1976-1977,* 39th ed. (Chicago, 1976).

U.S. 119 GROUNDBREAKING
Baxter, Harlan County / September 30, 1965

WITH dynamite and bulldozer, we break ground here today in the Cumberland Valley for what would ordinarily be just a highway. But our action here today is far more than the beginning of a highway construction job. As we begin to build this highway we are beginning the foundation for the building of a complete development program and a new economy for the Cumberland Valley area of Kentucky.

In the first place, this project is unusual even as a highway building project. Seldom in the history of Kentucky—with the exception of our recent experience on the Interstate Highway System—have we been able to break ground on one highway project with the full knowledge that further construction would proceed forward without stopping until the entire highway was complete. While we start this road here in Harlan County today, we are ready now to build the highway from one end of the Cumberland Valley to the other.

Even more than that, however, this highway will connect with a system of highways which we know will be built by the same schedule. Therefore, this highway, when completed, will connect with highways out of the Cumberland Valley and into the interstate system itself. The road we begin building here today will connect all parts of your area with all parts of the United States. This is one of the reasons we call this a development highway.[1] It is not built just to serve traffic, although we have certainly needed this road desperately and for a long time for this purpose alone. But this road is built in such a fashion as to tie the economy of the Cumberland Valley of Kentucky to the prosperous economy of the United States. Tourists and commercial travelers from all over the country will now be able to travel directly from their homes to Harlan, Kentucky, without traveling on any bad roads in their journey. This means this highway will begin to open up great opportunities for this valley, and it is in taking advantage of these opportunities that this highway can give us that the rest of the program becomes important.

The second reason that we call this road a development highway is that it is built as part of a complete development program. We know that the highway can carry commercial traffic—but it is therefore necessary for us to build the commerce and the industry in this valley to do business with the commerce and the industry in our entire nation. We know that this highway will serve tourists and we know that this great area has the potential to be a major attraction for tourists. But in other parts of our development program it will be necessary for us to make this valley into a major national recreation area so that the tourists who can get here on good roads will be encouraged to make this their destination. We firmly believe that the tourists of America will come to know the Cumberland Valley of Kentucky, as well as other parts of eastern Kentucky, as a major vacation land of fun and variety with pleasant accommodations and excellent services to care for the travelers' needs.

Thus, today, we look forward to the development program which will unfold rapidly in this area. Our Kentucky area development office is working closely with the Appalachian Regional Commission and with many other agencies who will be working directly with your Cumberland Valley Area Development Council to prepare the plans over the next few months to paint the picture of a new future for this valley. These plans will be action plans spelled out in separate action projects like the building of this highway. All together these action projects will bring new jobs, new businesses, new homes, and new opportunities to the people of this valley.

It is important to note, for instance, that under other aspects of the overall program, great progress is being made in education and in health programs in this area. The Head Start programs and the Youth Corps and Job Corps programs already at work in this valley have been highly successful.[2] The recent announcement by the president—only last week—of approval for additional funds for aid to education amounts to many thousands of new dollars for each county in this valley and will allow great improvements in the educational systems of all parts of this area.

We have just presented to the Appalachian Regional Commission a comprehensive plan for the construction of vocational education schools in the entire region of eastern Kentucky. The system has been planned so that it will provide vocational education facilities within reasonable reach of all of the youngsters—and of many adults in need of such training—in each county of eastern Kentucky. We believe that the Appalachian commission will approve this program which has already been described as the most comprehensive single project ever prepared in the Appalachian program with the exception of the comprehensive highway system which we recognize here today.

We are about to undertake, over the next few months, the planning of what will be described as the nation's most advanced health program, and in this process we will be bringing new health services to all parts of our area.

The new Economic Development Act, recently passed by Congress, will mean that we have the tools at hand to work on industrial sites and community facilities and on the improvement of industrial and commercial jobs throughout this area.

This afternoon I leave here to go to Middlesboro, where we will be celebrating the addition of a new industry in that community. This new industry is just an example of the new progress which is beginning to show itself in this area and which holds great promise for the future.

As all of you know, the approval of the construction of U.S. 119 and U.S. 25E to provide a good road through this valley did not come easily—even within the Appalachian regional development program. Now that the road has been approved, I think that we need to recognize that there are two important meanings to this road.

First, we need to know that the approval of the road required a great deal of hard work and concentration on the part of a great many people to prepare the evidence that was required to justify the construction of this road under the new Appalachian criteria. As you know, I personally presented this evidence directly to the commission. You see, in establishing the Appalachian regional program, Congress determined that these investments in highways and in other facilities could be made only where we could prove that they would show a payoff in growth and development. There were some who thought we could not show this growth potential in the Cumberland Valley. The study and the hard work that was carried out by a great many people on a crash basis has now indicated that this valley does have a potential for growth and development. We have known that all along, but we had to prove it. Now that we have proven that the potential is there, however, we have to prove that we can do the job.

The second reason that approval of this road has great meaning for us is that it means that this area has been placed on trial—but we have also been given a great opportunity. The first major investment in the growth of this valley has now been assured. Other investments can follow if we can prove that our development program will be successful—if we can prove that we can develop this area as we have insisted we can do.

We will be looking to your Area Development Council and through that council to all the organizations and all the citizens of this valley to make the plans and to carry out the projects. Our Kentucky area development office will be working side by side with you in making these plans possible and in expediting your projects in the various programs. You will find that our state agencies—as well as the federal agencies involved—will respond as rapidly as possible to the projects that are developed to the action stage. But much will be asked of you through your local governments and through your local organizations. You will need to take a look at the future of your area in a new light as you work toward a new day. I personally believe that the nation is due for a surprise in the response that will come from the Cumberland Valley as its development program goes into high gear.

Our argument of the case for approval of your highway was aided greatly by the surprising and exciting pace of progress we discovered is already under way in many of your communities. We found that the pace of new industrial and commercial development in the western end of the valley—where we dedicate another new plant this afternoon—exceeds that of most all parts of the state. We have not only found that the Cumberland Valley has a potential to grow—we have discovered that great parts of this valley are already growing at a faster pace than many other parts of Kentucky and than many other parts of the United States. We believe that you have the potential to bring about this kind of growth throughout the valley. You have needed the tools to do the job in the past. Today the tools are available. Action is under way. The rest is up to us to work together to complete the job.

As your governor, I would be derelict in duty if I talked to you today in celebrating this new project for your valley without mentioning the important action we all must take in Kentucky to keep projects like this one on the move. I am sure you know that I am referring to the bond issue which will be before the citizens of Kentucky on November 2.

Surely no one can see more clearly than you the reasons why we must choose this wise and prudent way to invest in the facilities we must have for development. You of the Cumberland Valley are already seeing the benefits of the leadership Kentucky has shown in going ahead and planning the Appalachian program—in going ahead to press for its adoption—and in constantly attempting to be prepared to meet this program once it was ready for action.

As you know, in the earliest days of the Appalachian program, Henry Ward—the greatest highway commissioner in Kentucky's history—announced that the Highway Department was prepared to meet the matching fund requirements for the Appalachian program immediately in this year. The project we dedicate here today is a result of Kentucky's strong leadership in the building of the Appalachian program and of the Kentucky Highway Department's readiness to build the highways under this program.

But we must clearly face the fact that the remainder of this highway—the sections of the highways adjoining this one that could be built in the future—will not and cannot be built unless the bond issue is passed. The only alternative to the bond issue, of course, is some other and less desirable means of providing the money we must have to build for Kentucky.

I'm sure you know that the congressmen and other leaders from across the United States who supported the Appalachian program are watching to see how eastern Kentucky supports this bond issue. They need to assure their belief that we will do our part to make the Appalachian program work.

When I campaigned to become your governor, I listened closely to what you had to say. More than anything else, I was told in all parts of Kentucky—and especially in eastern Kentucky—that you wanted to continue the great development program . . . to keep up the great progress . . . that was begun in the term of my predecessor, Governor Bert Combs. I vowed that we would keep that progress moving and that we would build even more and with increasing speed to our destiny in the development of Kentucky. I have hoped that I could keep pace with the ambitions of Kentuckians and build as strong as the strength of our Commonwealth.

During this administration of your state government I have never yet known one project which, by itself, so clearly signaled that we are keeping the pace; that we are building toward strength; and that we are on our way to success. This project exemplifies the newest in development ideas—a true investment in the future, a foundation of action on which to build a whole new pattern of development. This project exemplifies the newest in the policies of government—an act of faith in the worth of people who love their homeland and a belief that government and private enterprise together can use the technology of today to build a better life. This project exemplifies the key strength of the Kentucky development concept—that by working together we can achieve the impossible. Never was one project produced with such complete cooperation and dedication of so many people in many government agencies and in all walks of private life. And this project stands as the perfect example of what we know we can do, based on what we have already accomplished. Knowing that we have proven that this highway should be built is to know that we can build the Cumberland Valley. It is time to begin, together, here, today, to do the job.

---

1. U.S. 119 was a part of the Developmental Highway System approved by the Appalachian Regional Commission. The purpose of the system was to provide transportation and communication corridors to and through the isolated areas of Appalachia, thereby integrating the region into the more prosperous national economy. Henry Ward, "Reasons for Recommending Corridor 5 (U.S. 25-E and U.S. 119) for the Appalachian Development Highway System," typescript in Appalachia file, Breathitt papers. Ideally, remote areas with the greatest potential for economic development were to be selected for the new highways. In practice, however, ideals of the plan were altered by the circumstances in which it was applied. The time required to begin construction of a road, political considerations, and bargaining between states frequently were deciding factors in funding. In the final analysis the Developmental Highway System filled in gaps in the interstate system. Kentucky, a founder and leader of the Appalachian development movement, received a relatively larger share of highway funds than other states. Donald N. Rothblatt, *Regional Planning: The Appalachian Experience* (Lexington, Mass., 1971), pp. 83-87, 131-36.

2. Head Start, Youth Corps, and Job Corps were components of President Johnson's war on poverty. The programs were administered under the general direction of the Office of Economic Opportunity. Job Corps and Youth Corps programs established urban and rural camps for economically deprived young people and school dropouts. Camp participants received job training and remedial education and worked at what were often their first regular jobs. The Head Start program began during the winter of 1964-65 and quickly attracted more interest than its planners anticipated. The program was based on the premise that children from poor families entered school at a disadvantage arising from their preschool environment. The program provided preschool children from economically deprived backgrounds an eight-week summer session designed to give them intensive individual attention and intellectual stimulation. *Time,* March 5, 1965, p. 21; *Newsweek,* July 19, 1965, pp. 80-81; and *Business Week,* March 20, 1965, p. 156.

PURCHASE PARKWAY GROUNDBREAKING
Mayfield / August 30, 1966

I AM proud to be here today for this occasion. It is a matter of deep satisfaction to me as your governor to be able to bring you a major public facility which will give you a tool for continuing the development of this part of the Commonwealth—the Jackson Purchase.

When we break ground here at Mayfield this afternoon for the Purchase Parkway, we are making the first outward, physical move in a project which has been in my heart and in my mind since I was a candidate in 1963.[1] When you elected me to serve as your governor, I committed myself to expanding the system of major highways on which the motor transportation of Kentucky depends. What we are starting to build today is solid evidence of the kind of progress that has been characteristic of our administration to date.

Your new road is a part of all that is being done by your state in the way of increasing the development of Kentucky through building a system of fine, modern highways. So far this year, the Highway Department has awarded contracts for improvements in the amount of $146 million. This program covers all sorts of roads in all parts of the state. In size, it will be the greatest highway construction year in the history of our Commonwealth. An important part of this year's program, not only to the people of the Purchase, but to the entire state system, is this road we are starting here today. When these men who have contracts to build this road have finished their job, the people of the Purchase will have a highway that is as fine as any in this part of the world.

We live in a time of movement. On this movement depends the development of all the resources that are in the Purchase—the water, the agriculture, the recreation, the education. It is characteristic of our age that much of this movement takes place on highways. Its nature is such that it cannot very well take place on the kind of highways that were built early in this century. This superhighway will help boost the economy of every county in this area because new industry needs adequate transportation and because tourists go where the good roads are located.

What we are starting to build here today is a road for the second half of the twentieth century—one that is built with the capacity to serve the people of the Purchase and their needs for many years to come. Around it can be evolved a road transportation system that will contribute mightily to the development of this region of Kentucky.

This road, at its inception, does not stand alone. It is a part of a superhighway system that is being built to tie together all parts of the Commonwealth, and to link Kentucky with all other areas of the nation. At its northern end, the Purchase Parkway will connect with Interstate 24, a major part of the country's national system of interstate and defense highways. At its southern end, it will connect to an interstate bridge across the Mississippi River at Hayti, Missouri, opening up traffic from I-55 and all of the Southwest to Kentucky and points east.

These superhighways reach from coast to coast and from border to border. They are being built—41,000 miles of them—to carry the large volumes of traffic that are growing all across the land. Interstate 24 will pass through this area on its way from St. Louis to Chattanooga by way of Paducah, Hopkinsville, and Nashville. Along its course, it will connect with Interstate routes 75, 59, 65, 40, 64, 55, 57, 70, and 44. This makes the people of the Purchase near neighbors with about half the people in the country. And this fact will give them an even greater opportunity to develop the place where they live.

Furthermore, completion of this parkway and the Appalachian program will give Kentucky an east-west superhighway all the way from Fulton to the Virginia line. A Kentuckian will be able to drive 381 miles from Fulton all the way to Prestonsburg, then travel U.S. 23 some fifty miles through Pikeville on to the Virginia border, all by superhighway.

Such is my faith in the people of the Purchase and in the potential of the area that we chose the revenue bond route to build this road. And it wasn't hard to get the money either. I took this course of action because I knew that you people didn't want to wait ten or twenty years, or maybe longer, to get a road like this. The only other way to have built this 52.5 mile superhighway at one time would have been to totally ignore the fact that nearly 5,000 miles of the state's primary roads are in need of improvements, and to spend all of the available money for two or three years on this one road. And during that time, the rest of the state would have had to do without improvements that are needed in their areas. Borrowing money to build a toll road is the course that I have chosen to serve you. I believe it is a wise one, and I trust that you will share my belief and that you will use this road, enjoy it, and reap benefits from it for many years to come.

Kentucky, all over this nation, is receiving plaudits for its remarkable progress in highway construction. Last year, only four states—Texas, North Carolina, Louisiana, and Iowa—built and improved more roads than Kentucky. This year we should do even better. All of these roads mean progress for Kentucky. Today we break ground for another road that will open up this region to new opportunity, new jobs, and higher income. It means that all Kentucky will have a greater future.

---

1. The Purchase Parkway was designed to link Fulton, Kentucky, with I-24 near Gilbertsville. Interstate 24 provided a four-lane connection with the West Kentucky Parkway.

PENNYRILE PARKWAY GROUNDBREAKING
Hopkinsville / October 25, 1966

TODAY is one of those rare days in the life of a governor. It is not often that a public official has the opportunity to bring good news to his old home town. Today I am able to do just that. Before we leave here this afternoon, we are going to turn over some of this Christian County soil to signal the builders that they can get started with the construction of the Pennyrile Parkway.[1] This is a day that many of us have been looking forward to for longer than we care to remember. This modern highway, which will soon be a reality, is an undertaking which is close to my heart. Before I took office, the need for this kind of travel facility in this part of the state had become clear to many citizens. I am proud of the fact that what is so clearly needed is becoming a reality while I am serving as your governor.

The 56.6-mile Pennyrile Parkway is this administration's answer to a problem that has been vexing the people of this part of Kentucky for a good many years. Ever since they started selling new automobiles again in 1946, all of us who live along U.S. 41—from the Tennessee line to the Indiana border—have had a front row seat at one of the spectacles of the midtwentieth century, the very rapid expansion of highway travel.

I could cite statistics that would describe in detail this modern phenomenon—the Kentucky Highway Department and the United States Bureau of Public Roads have yards and yards of them—but you people don't need statistics to tell you what has been going on right before your eyes.

There is one pertinent fact I would like to call to your attention. The fact is this: we are not at the end of the period of expansion of highway transportation. We are somewhere nearer the beginning, according to the best forecasts that I have seen. In Kentucky this past summer, travel on highways outside of cities was increasing at a rate that was greater than that shown in all except four of the other states. The actual increase was calculated by the highway engineers to be 6.9 percent for the month of July, 1966, compared with the same month of 1965. We can expect, then, that more and more cars and trucks are going to be rolling along this traditional and nationally important north-south travelway. And that's all to the good—up to a point. But, as with most anything else, we can have too much of a good thing, and not room enough to put it.

When we get through building the Pennyrile Parkway, there will be plenty of room for whatever kinds of traffic are generated in this area and whatever else comes in from other parts of the country. If you want to travel up to Madisonville for a football game or visit Audubon State Park up by the Ohio River, or if the folks from up that way want to come down here and enjoy Christian County hospitality or go on over to Lake Barkley State Park for a holiday—there will be plenty of room for all. You share with your fellow Kentuckians from all over the state this need for more room—more room to travel, more room to work, more room to educate your children, more room to build up your communities. A modern road, like the Pennyrile Parkway is going to be, goes a long way toward giving you more of the room you need.

When this toll road is completed, I predict that it will be the second highest revenue producer in our toll system because of its unusually heavy traffic—taking second place only to the Kentucky Turnpike. This prediction is even more phenomenal when you consider that toll revenue from all turnpikes through September of 1966 is running some 24 percent ahead of the consultant's estimate. If the revenue trend continues through the last three months of the year, revenue from toll facilities this year will be about 30 percent higher than for 1965. This revenue growth is fantastic and indicative of a wisely planned toll system. . . .[2]

Already, we have awarded contracts for approximately nineteen miles of this road. Others will be let soon. As a matter of fact, the entire parkway from here to the Madisonville bypass and from the bypass to Henderson will be under construction by early next spring. Here in the Hopkinsville area we are planning diamond interchanges for the parkway at U.S. 41 and U.S. 68. Exit loops also will be constructed at KY 107. And U.S. 41-A, where the southern terminus of the parkway joins, will be extended to Interstate 24 so that the heavy traffic traveling on this major, north-south interstate can be routed onto the parkway if motorists desire to travel north through Evansville.

As many of you know, the state of Indiana now has under way a traffic and revenue feasibility study on the possible construction of a 200-mile toll road from the Pennyrile's northern terminus near Evansville to Interstate 65, which runs generally northwest from Louisville to Chicago. The study is being made by Wilbur Smith and Associates and should be ready next month. Should such a road prove feasible, and I'm sure it will either now or sometime in the near future, traffic on the Pennyrile Parkway will get a substantial boost.

The pattern that is developing here in western Kentucky, with this new Pennyrile Parkway, the West Kentucky Parkway, and the soon-to-be-constructed I-24 to carry the rapidly growing volumes of traffic, is being repeated all across the state. We now have completed and opened to traffic 347 miles of interstate highways and 275 miles of parkways—a total distance of 622 miles of our planned 1,100-mile interstate and parkway system.

The superhighway network is laid out in a way that is making travel into, out of, or through most any part of Kentucky easier than you or I would have believed possible as short a time as fifteen years ago. And, what is even more important, our modern highway network is giving Kentucky the economic stimulus in industrial growth and tourism that we've so badly needed.

William James said many years ago that what the world needs is a moral equivalent for war—a peaceful and constructive goal which will enlist the spirit of self-sacrifice, the spirit of dedication, the sense of being swept up in a great crusade.[3] I say to you that for the Kentuckians of this age the moral equivalent of war is the great midcentury crusade for economic development which we are now experiencing throughout our great Commonwealth.

In some far-off future day, these boys and girls in this audience and all young people throughout this state will look back. Looking back, they will pass judgment on the decisions that we are making in 1966. I'm confident that they will say, in gratitude and respect, that we did not fail them.

---

1. The Pennyrile Parkway, a north-south toll road, connected Hopkinsville and Henderson.
2. A brief section of the speech, in which Governor Breathitt reviewed preliminary figures on 1966 Kentucky highway construction, has been deleted. A more complete review is contained in his address to the Kentucky Highway Conference in Lexington on November 15, 1966, which is included in these papers.
3. William James (1842-1910), noted American psychologist and philosopher; teacher and author at Harvard University (1872-1907). *Concise Dictionary of American Biography* (New York, 1964), pp. 487-88.

INTERSTATE 75 DEDICATION
Richmond / November 23, 1966

TODAY, as Kentucky approaches the end of what has been a record highway construction year, we are opening and putting into use another dozen-mile link of Interstate 75.[1] Its completion comes at an opportune time. Hopefully by this time tomorrow afternoon, the action we take here today will have saved the lives of some motorists.

Coming on the eve of a national holiday, the traffic has already begun from the north southward and from the south northward as happy families in a holiday spirit make preparations to spend Thanksgiving with families and other loved ones. Unfortunately—even tragically—many of them will never reach their destinations. However, those who are able to travel on our interstate highways have a better statistical chance to enjoy the holiday alive and uninjured.

The twelve new miles which we put into use today is more than just another key segment in the 190 miles of I-75 through Kentucky. It is a key segment in the 1,500 miles of this major north-south route which extends from Sault Ste. Marie, Michigan, to St. Petersburg, Florida. The mileage opened in Kentucky this year has pushed to more than 1,000 the total miles of this route now being used in the six states through which it passes. Interstate 75 in Kentucky is now open for 132 miles—almost 70 percent completed through the state. Another twenty miles are under construction. Other sections will be put under construction early next year. All of the proposed route is well advanced in design and right of way acquisition.

Kentucky is keeping pace with the rest of the nation with its interstate and toll road program. At the end of September, 22,100 miles of the 41,000-mile National System of Interstate and Defense Highways were open to traffic. Construction was underway on another 6,382 miles.

We in Kentucky have about 350 miles of interstate open—about 47 percent of the state's allotted total. But, bear in mind that during the same period of time we have been building interstate, we also have built and opened 275 miles of toll roads to supplement the interstate system.

In a recent speech in Lexington I called attention to the fact that our small roads complement the larger roads and that during this fiscal year about $33 million in state funds is being spent on the small roads. This is nearly a third of the Highway Department's annual budget and really has significance when you realize this is more than three times the amount of state funds it will take during the same period to match federal funds for interstate highway construction.

We are building a system of roads and highways in Kentucky for the first time in its history—roads to serve the greatest traffic needs within our state and roads which connect with similar logical systems in other states. The fact that we have spent $550 million during the past three years attests to the effort we are making. National statistics prove we are doing a good job. These statistics have placed Kentucky in the top five states in road building since 1960.

Here in Madison County road expenditures for all purposes since January 1, 1960, have totaled $28,084,229. So we feel we have done a good job in this particular county. Roads are important to your institutions of higher learning—the university here at Richmond and the world-renowned college at Berea. The interstate we are opening today will make travel much easier to both institutions. Next year and the year following it will be even easier as we push toward completion of this route through Kentucky. By 1969 we hope to have it completed in its entirety.

As of today, here is the schedule we hope to meet for its completion. Twenty-seven miles of the remaining sixty-one miles to be built between Berea and Goldbug in Whitley County are now under construction. The section from KY 21 at Berea to Conway will be paved and opened next year, as will more than nine miles of the route coming northward from Goldbug to U.S. 25-W south of Corbin. We hope next to give some construction priority to the section around Corbin in order to relieve the bad traffic situation in Corbin's downtown area caused by the through traffic. One section around Corbin is scheduled to be let to grade and drain contract in April of next year, and the other section and the U.S. 25 connector north of Corbin will be let next summer. Grade and drain construction on the twenty-mile section between the north Corbin interchange and the Rockcastle River is scheduled for letting in the fall of 1967. From the Rockcastle River to near Sand Hill School in Rockcastle County is scheduled for grade and drain letting in March, 1967.

This leaves a 3.4-mile gap from near Green Hills School to Renfro Valley in Rockcastle County which has been delayed to allow Mt. Vernon authorities to complete negotiations for a federal loan with which to form a lake from a "fill" dam in construction of the route at that point. The loan, we understand, has been approved in Washington, but the paperwork actually authorizing it is still being processed. The Highway Department has plans completed and will be able to let a grade and drain contract for this section within a few weeks after the loan is formally received. And, there you have it. If all goes well by Thanksgiving Day, 1969, motorists will be able to travel border to border through Kentucky on Interstate 75.

---

1. The section of Interstate 75 opened on this occasion was from Richmond to Berea. When completed I-75, a north-south interstate route, linked Covington and the northern Tennessee line near Williamsburg. Interstate 75 was part of the National System for Interstate and Defense Highways, a $50 billion highway program legislated by Congress in 1956. The program included construction of approximately 41,000 miles of interstate highways and improvement of more than 700,000 miles of primary and feeder roads. *U.S. News and World Report,* October 26, 1956, pp. 96-97.

SOUTHERN REGIONAL HIGHWAY SAFETY CONFERENCE

New Orleans, Louisiana / December 19, 1966

I SINCERELY regret being unable to attend what I am certain will be a fine, worthwhile, and most rewarding conference on highway safety.[1] This subject is of intense interest and concern—yes, alarm—to me, and it is one to which my administration in Kentucky has devoted much time and attention and stepped-up outlays of money. I am determined that we shall do even more during the remaining months of my four-year term, which ends next December.

May I say at the outset, I regard the challenge to the states today, in the field of traffic safety, as our greatest for the foreseeable future. May I hasten to add, I believe this deeply, and not from any fear of encroachment into this field by the federal government. We have received reassurance on this score from the recently announced guidelines and statements by U.S. officials on the 1966 federal motor and highways safety acts.[2]

As I see it, there will be a measure of performance by the states, rather than any rigid set of rules. But the measure of our performance by federal officials is not the most important test. That, in my opinion, is how we measure up in the eyes of our people, for we state officials are their servants.

And, as I reported at our Southern Governors' Conference last September, when Kentucky was honored to be host for this great annual event, the major responsibility for traffic safety rests with the states. And we, as representatives of various individual states, must see to it that we provide the leadership in this war. Yes, it is a war. And I am reminded that in a new traffic safety campaign we have under way in Kentucky, there are eye-catching ads captioned "Viet Nam Is Safer!"

Critical? Alarming? Certainly, this situation is all that—for we are killing at the rate of 50,000 persons a year on the highways and close to two million are being injured. In my own state, despite our increased efforts to improve traffic safety, for the first time in history we have recorded more than 1,000 traffic deaths this year. The record high had been 916, set in 1965.

More shocking is the rate of increase in injuries, many permanently disabling. In Kentucky, injuries have more than doubled in a ten-year period. Back in 1955, when there were 862 traffic deaths compared with last year's 916, we had 12,555 persons hurt in highway accidents. In 1965 the total was 26,557.

Of course, there are more vehicles and drivers today, around 1.5 million of each, for instance, in my state. Vehicle registration is increasing about 5 percent annually. But the sobering fact is that Kentucky's death rate per 100 million vehicle miles traveled has soared this year. The latest figure I've seen was above seven, up 1.1 from the comparable 1965 period.

All of you are fully aware of the magnitude of our problems. And I frankly do not believe they can be solved until we have an aroused citizenry. Citizen support is the most important ingredient, and we must exert greater efforts along many fronts to earn and keep such support. Perhaps this crisis in traffic safety, disastrous as we consider the present situation, will, in the end, result in enough people determining that they will become involved and do something about it. I firmly believe that will occur.

I think, too, the congressional hearings and other publicity about traffic and vehicle safety in recent months have been healthy from the standpoint of getting people worked up. For we all know what great good Americans have accomplished in times of crisis during our rich past. And they can—indeed, I believe, they will—rise to the occasion in this traffic crisis.

Some of us are of the opinion the hearings and other statements on our traffic problems should have put more emphasis on the drivers' role. But, be that as it may, there is more being written and spoken today on traffic safety than ever before. And we cannot get too safety conscious.

In the past, we all know, the federal government's policy has been to leave the major responsibility for traffic safety to states and local authorities. I see a continuation of that policy, so far, in the Washington pronouncements. But, while the federal officials are, I believe, gently prodding the states now, we may expect greater pressure, from the Congress and the people, if we, on the state level, fail to assume our rightful and required responsibilities and perform our duty in the traffic safety field. We, in Kentucky, think we are in a relatively good position, as of now, toward meeting the federal requirements. But I intend to exert all the leadership of which I am capable to see to it that we do more than just the minimum—for that's not enough!

The 1966 Kentucky General Assembly enacted a compulsory motor vehicle inspection law, under which all vehicles will have to be inspected annually, beginning in 1968.[3] Some of our authorities believe our present statutes will allow periodic examination of drivers, another requirement under the federal acts. But, if legislation is needed, I have confidence that it will be approved by our 1968 legislature—when I will have returned to private life, since Kentucky governors cannot succeed themselves.

While Kentucky will be the twenty-first state to have compulsory vehicle inspection, along with the District of Columbia, it now is the only state with a driver limitation program requiring a driver having three accidents in a two-year period to appear before a medical review board. This is a cooperative program, now in its third year, involving the Kentucky Medical Association—doctors serving without pay—the Kentucky Department of Health and the state Department of Public Safety. The purpose is to provide the driver licensing administrator with sound medical advice concerning the licensing or nonlicensing of special risk drivers. This group includes those with physical handicaps, mental problems, chronic conditions; and those suffering with lapses of consciousness or control. Our present program may not be broad enough to meet the federal criteria of denying licenses to applicants nearly blind, but it, too, could be amended.

Kentucky, like many other states, will need legislation to cover other items in the new federal requirements, such as separate categories of licenses for motorcyclists, school-bus operators and others; expanded driver education programs; helmets for motorcyclists and their passengers, and examination of fatally injured motorists and pedestrians for blood alcohol content. We now require checking of drivers' past records before issuing new licenses, but I am of the opinion our records and data processing systems should be further modernized and expanded. These steps are necessary to provide information more quickly and give us more raw material for research.

States should provide more money for research—for through it we can discover problems we are not aware of now, confirm or reject some of our present theories, and find new avenues of approach to current problems. We have a new law enforcement school, established this past school year at Eastern Kentucky University, awarding bachelor's degrees. Eastern's Traffic Safety Institute now is cooperating closely with our Department of Public Safety in implementing our new programs and preparing proposals for aid under the 1966 federal safety legislation. In addition, the University of Kentucky and Spindletop Research have been conducting, and will continue to do, much needed research.

Highway design has been vastly improved over the years, but I urge strenuous steps to make it better, along with more modern signs and traffic control devices. We must keep in mind that the roads and signs are so constructed that they will minimize the chances for the average, or below par, driver to have accidents, as well as the so-called good drivers.

Another objective toward which I've worked hard, is better enforcement of our traffic laws. Kentucky has a program to add 50 state troopers annually for the next ten years, at increased pay and benefits. But today, while our authorized strength is about 525, we have in uniform only about 450 men, approximately the same as in 1960, to cope with the rapidly increasing traffic—this despite a vigorous recruiting campaign. Thus, we find that new and even greater efforts are needed along this line, to provide incentive to young men to make careers in traffic safety and police work.

As a move in this direction, we have just started a program that might be likened to internship, employing youngsters to perform functions other than those of police officers and attend college in their off-duty hours.

Kentucky's driver education programs are being expanded under 1966 legislation requiring a five dollar reinstatement fee for drivers losing their licenses before they can qualify for new permits.[4] Thus these license losers are helping those who haven't quite lost. For the income helps finance driver-improvement clinics for those who have accumulated points, but not the total of twelve, which results in license loss under Kentucky's point system. These problem drivers get points deducted for successfully completing the improvement course.

I, perhaps, have dwelt upon our Kentucky problems and programs too much, but after all, they are the ones with which I am most familiar. And I believe this discussion shows we're doing something, although admittedly not enough. Each of us has some similar problems, and yet some have problems no one else faces. Don't we learn that every day in the discharge of our official duties!

However, I am encouraged by our increasing awareness and that of the public of the real seriousness of this business of trying to save lives and prevent injuries and huge economic losses caused by traffic accidents. This dynamic new federal program can be the stepping-off place for us to achieve, with the states leading the way, our greatest strides ever in improved traffic safety. I urge expanded public information programs everywhere, to bring home to the people vividly that the final solution rests with them—until each individual driver knows and practices, at least, the rule that he is his brother's keeper. He also must know and do all he can to insure that this safety rule is followed: a good driver in a safety checked car is a much better risk than a bad driver in a unsafe car.

But how to reach all drivers—especially those problem drivers—to impress this upon them and get them to care and then be careful? That is one of the most critical of all our problems. And that's the basic reason I want bigger and better public information-education programs for which we must seek new ways to "get through" to the people. It is an integral part of the overall challenge. And, every day in every way possible, each of us must preach and practice good safety rules, in meeting the challenge—not to just the states, or the federal government, or local governments—but to all our people, of improving traffic safety.

---

1. This speech was delivered for Governor Breathitt by Shelby McCallum, speaker of the Kentucky House of Representatives.

2. In September, 1966, President Johnson signed into law legislation giving the federal government a significant role in promoting highway safety. The National

Traffic and Motor Vehicle Safety Act authorized a three-year, $41 million program to establish federal motor vehicle safety standards for new cars, buses, and trucks beginning with the 1968 model year. The legislation also required a uniform quality grading system for tires. The Highway Safety Act, specifically referred to here by Governor Breathitt, required each state to generate highway safety programs following standards established by the future secretary of transportation (the Department of Transportation had just been created by the 89th Congress). The standards were to apply to such areas as driver education, licensing, accident record-keeping and investigation, vehicle registration and inspection, and highway design and maintenance. The act also authorized $322 million over a three-year period to provide matching funds for the state programs. Failure to comply with the congressional mandate by December 31, 1968, would cost the offending state 10 percent of its federal highway funds as well as the money distributed under the act itself. *Congressional Quarterly Almanac,* Vol. 23 (1966), pp. 71, 281-85, 269-78, and U.S. *Statutes at Large,* Vol. 80 (Washington, 1967), pp. 718-30.

3. The 1966 General Assembly enacted legislation requiring every motor vehicle, trailer, semitrailer, and pole trailer registered in Kentucky to have an annual inspection. The inspections were to be conducted by qualified stations (garages and service stations) operating under permits issued by the Department of Public Safety. *Acts, 1966,* Chapter 115 (H.B. 256), pp. 550-56.

4. See *Acts, 1966,* Chapter 78 (S.B. 208), pp. 450-51.

HIGHWAY STATEMENT
Frankfort / May 26, 1967

I AM today recommending to the Kentucky Turnpike Authority that it authorize the construction and financing of two toll roads—one to run between Henderson and Owensboro and the second to link London and Hazard.[1] The design engineering on the Owensboro-Henderson road is now underway and, if the Turnpike Authority approves, the final engineering on the London-Hazard road would begin immediately. Bonds will be sold for financing the two proposed roads between now and early fall, the exact timing dependent upon completion of engineering plans and the state of the bond market. We are hopeful that construction contracts can be let in winter and construction started in early spring.

The 23.4-mile Henderson-Owensboro road, a spur from the Pennyrile Parkway which is presently under construction, will link Owensboro to the interstate-parkway system. Owensboro is the only city of its size in the Commonwealth not now tied into the major four-lane system. Dense traffic on existing routes in this area, plus rapid industrial growth, show that four lanes are presently needed.

The 62.4-mile London-Hazard road will be a developmental highway—designed to spur the economy of this area through industrial development and increased tourism. The developmental concept, first used in the Mountain Parkway, has been accepted nationally and is the basis for the Appalachian highway program. This road will connect Interstate 75 at London with the southern leg of the Mountain Parkway. It will tie the Appalachian system of highways into the interstate system, and it is part of a long-range improvement of KY 80—a major east-west highway that runs the entire length of Kentucky.

The London to Manchester to Hyden section of this highway has been called "hell's highway" because it is one of the worst roads in the state. What we've got to do is remake KY 80, building a major federal aid highway, connecting all towns between London, Pikeville and Hazard to Interstate 75 and tying the entire southern and eastern part of Kentucky into a highway system reaching from Ashland to the Mississippi River.

The London-Hazard road also will become a vital link in the scenic highways system established by the United States Department of Commerce earlier this year. This highway will cut through some of Kentucky's most rugged and beautiful mountain area, opening up this underdeveloped region to new industry and additional tourism. The new industries that have located in the area of the Mountain Parkway prove the worth of such highway development.

The proposed corridor location of the London-Hazard road would begin at the planned Interstate 75-KY 192 interchange southwest of London and would extend eastward 2.7 miles as a free section to KY 80 southeast of London, intersecting at grade with KY 363, U.S. 25, and KY 80. From KY 80 southeast of London the toll road would be located north of and somewhat parallel to KY 80 and would cross KY 80 and U.S. 421 approximately 1.2 miles south of Manchester, with an interchange with U.S. 421 at this point.

From Manchester the toll road would extend eastward, crossing to the south side of KY 80, crossing back to the north side near Big Creek. It would then generally parallel KY 80 to near Hosea, where it would again cross to the south of KY 80 and proceed eastward to intersect and interchange with U.S. 421 approximately 2.3 miles south of Hyden. The corridor would then cross to the north of KY 80 south of Hyden, and generally parallel KY 80, and tie into new KY 15 north of Hazard, which is the southern leg of the Mountain Parkway.

The proposed corridor, which is 62.4 miles in length, would reduce the eighty-mile existing route between London and Hazard by 17.6 miles. Traffic in this corridor would require a high-type, two-lane highway similar to the Mountain Parkway extension with truck-climbing lanes where required, and cost estimates have been based on this type of facility.

Toll stations would be located at the Manchester and Hazard interchanges. As part of the toll road project, consideration also would be given to improving the connecting roads from the toll road to nearby cities of London, Manchester, and Hyden. New KY 15 will provide a new connection to Hazard. The connections would be reconstructed two-lane facilities except at London, where four lanes are proposed.

The total estimated cost of the proposed toll road and connecting roads is $79,109,000. Of this amount, $75,068,000 would be used to construct the toll road and $4,041,000 would be used to build the connecting roads.

The proposed corridor location of the Henderson-Owensboro road would begin on the Pennyrile Parkway with an interchange near the south city limits of Henderson. The corridor extends easterly, lying south of and generally parallel to KY 54. There will be an interchange and main line toll plaza at KY 416 south of Hebbardsville. The project continues easterly to cross Green River about one-half mile upstream and south of Hamilton Ferry, thence continuing easterly just north of Sargho and KY 54 to junction with the planned Owensoro belt line with an interchange just north of Fifth Street Road. This proposed road would be constructed as a four-lane, controlled access facility. Design standards would be similar to the Pennyrile Parkway and other toll roads in Kentucky. The estimated cost of the toll facility is $24,800,000.

---

1. The proposed toll roads were the Audubon Parkway linking Henderson and Owensboro and the Daniel Boone Parkway between London and Hazard.

STATEMENT ON HIGHWAY DEVELOPMENT CONCEPT

Midwestern Governors Conference
Lake of the Ozarks, Missouri / August 28, 1967

A HIGHWAY is not a development highway by itself. Only when it is built as part of a development program does it become a development highway. The highway itself represents a basic investment. The payoff is in the other developmental projects which the highway makes possible, such as industrial, commercial, recreational, or residential sites. And the highway does not produce the payoff projects; it only makes them possible for local development organizations to carry out.

The highway development concept now being implemented in the big Appalachian highway system was originated in our eastern Kentucky development program. It was first fully developed in the Appalachian regional development program. But it is not my purpose here to discuss the Appalachian program as such, but rather to discuss the concept of developmental highways as a concept which can well be applied to any part of the nation. Furthermore, the development concept also can be applied to general public investment policies for facilities other than highways.

Highway development concept now represents the change in public investment policy generally followed in the United States. As you know from experience in your own states, the concept no longer is based as extensively on "where the people are," but more and more on industrial, tourist, and other factors. In the new developmental investment approaches, we develop the high-type highway to bring the commerce from a developed area into an area which may be underdeveloped, but which has potenital. Instead of following the need, the development highway generates or creates the need.

For these reasons, the development highway must be incorporated in a complete system to be effective. The traffic must be induced from existing traffic generation points by the improved transportation which it affords to bring the traffic through the area which is to be developed.

The local area is developed when the developmental highway passes through an undeveloped area, providing that the same highway connects with terminal points which already are developed and growing. It is important that we learn more accurately how to gauge the location and the design of developmental highways, since the location and design must be related to development not in existence, but being planned. Therefore, it is extremely important that our highway departments involve area economics and community and regional planning principles more soundly in highway location activity, along with the sound engineering practices involved in such locations.

Developmental highway systems can help stabilize the unhealthy characteristics of the population mobility of our times. I refer to the too rapid growth of metropolitan centers. This is especially true if the highway links rural area communities with potential to the burgeoning commerce of larger urban and metropolitan areas. This will be avoided only if overall development is organized by state and local institutions to take place in the rural areas. If local development is not properly carried out, the developmental highway can become an easier conduit for the aimless—and often hopeless—out-migration.

We are just beginning to learn how to utilize the developmental highway in some specific ways. For instance, we have experimented with great success in the use of highway fills designed to serve as dams to create small lakes for municipal and industrial water, land conservation, recreation, and so on. We are now working on a particular project in Kentucky in which we can create a 900-acre lake in connection with the construction of an interstate highway at a major interchange point. The local development organization is planning and developing a major recreation area around the community at this interchange. The local development people there are utilizing shoreline lands on the new lake to gain further specific development benefits by establishing sites for recreation and summer residential developments. The local development organization coincidentally is serving as the water district management organization and will utilize the reservoir for municipal and industrial water supplies. They thereby will create local sites for industry.

By doing this, just enough has been added to the natural scenic resources this area already has to convert it from a beautiful area seen and enjoyed by only a few to a major scenic and recreational activity area accessible and usable by many. As a result, a base for economic development has been established in a small community which previously could not find the "take-off point" for development.

Obviously, residents of metropolitan areas at distant points along the interstate highway are served just as well by bringing together the factors of regional development at a point accessible to them from the new highway. So, even an interstate highway which was not designed originally as a developmental highway now serves a developmental process. It is important to note that most of our interstate highways have been designed almost exclusively to serve the function of moving traffic from one major urban area to another. And little thought was given in their early design to the tremendous developmental potential they can create when just a reasonable amount of sound economic planning enters into their design.

It is possible that we can convert the remaining sections of interstate highway to be built to greater developmental usage. But this will not happen accidentally. We must build the highway with developmental planning and by working with local developmental organizations in the projects and programs they must carry out.

In the small community I mentioned, both the full-time and part-time jobs which will result are particularly suitable to the near future needs of the people of this area. Many of the people prefer to and can more economically and comfortably continue to live in their farm homes. Their farm operations, however, in themselves would not continue to provide an adequate income base. Thus, this community becomes one which can grow and whose people can stay in place.

This is a great economic saving in the national interest, instead of the people using the highway to flee their home area and to migrate to already crowded metropolitan areas. It is obvious today that some such population movement should be recognized as healthy to the lives of our people and to our economy. But a large proportion of this forced migration is highly expensive in the cost related to depleted population of towns left behind and in the great costs of solving the problems of relocation.

We are just beginning to experiment in depth with the use of overall planning as a factor in highway location. We particularly are conducting some intensive work at this point in considering the use of the earth moving made necessary at the time of construction. And this is to be correlated in the development of industrial, commercial, and other level sites so critically needed along the developmental highways in our mountainous regions, such as Appalachia.

We have learned most about the concept of developmental highways in our Appalachian regional development program—which originated in Kentucky. Now we are going ahead to apply the principles of development highways in our comprehensive area development programs throughout Kentucky.

In addition, we must note that the "development concept as a basis for a new policy of public investment" should be carefully considered in relation to other major public investments. We must have in effect a practical, flexible, overall area developmental plan—the location, design, and financial justification of water resource development facilities, rural and urban water and sewerage systems, hospitals, airports, and many other kinds of facilities. Then these facilities can serve far more than the specific function for which they were designed. They can, indeed, serve as the basis for an entirely new and previously impossible approach to development.

We are finding in Kentucky a most encouraging and realistic trend to developmental location decisions by private enterprises. This trend is placing industrial and commercial operations in many of our small communities where there was virtually no industry prior to our current developmental period. This new concept of highway development and related planning is largely responsible not only for our record industrial growth, but also for our rapidly expanding tourist industry. Tourism, by the way, is Kentucky's fastest-growing business.

In the Appalachian section of Kentucky, where there was little or no industry previously, just since January 1, 1964, we have had announcements of 155 new or expanded industries. These have created nearly 15,000 jobs and represent a capital investment of nearly $254 million. It also is significant that of the 155 announcements, the new industries total

79 and the expansions 76. In our entire state during the same period of just over three and one-half years, we have had announcements of 743 new or expanded industries. These have created more than 52,000 jobs and represent a capital investment of more than $1.1 billion.

Our entire road building program in Kentucky—in which we never forget the importance of rural and secondary systems—has helped both industry and tourism as well as other segments of our economy. More than $600 million has been spent on Kentucky highways of all kinds in the first three years of this administration, more than in any previous four-year total. Last year Kentucky awarded contracts for more miles of highways than any state except Texas.

We have reaped benefits in tourism in many ways. Tourism in Kentucky has increased by $75 million in the last three years—with last year's figures at an all-time high of $425 million. In 1966 more than twenty-six million out-of-state tourists spent $295 million in Kentucky. Kentuckians themselves added another $130 million. Our tourist industry provides nearly 9 percent of total retail business receipts in the state; jobs for more than 74,000 persons employed to serve and assist travelers; some $25 million in direct taxes; and more than $90 million per year (directly) to personal incomes of Kentuckians.

It is highly significant that of our forty state parks and shrines and national parks in Kentucky, thirteen of these are in our Appalachian region. So the impact of developmental programs has been graphically reflected in tourism, as well as in industry.

As you know, both the Appalachian and interstate highway programs are scheduled for completion by 1972. Obviously, in the nation as a whole and in most of our local areas, the further development of highway systems will have an even higher priority than the need presently being met. It is most important and appropriate that we give strong consideration to the design of highway programs beyond 1970, to the end that they incorporate a maximum relationship to developmental potential.

INTERSTATE 24 GROUNDBREAKING
Eddyville / December 6, 1967

TODAY is one of the important days in the history of western Kentucky. I say this not merely because we are breaking ground for ninety miles of freeway through this section.[1] I say it because this road symbolizes the great strides your state government has taken to provide the people of western Kentucky with a roads system second to none.

Allan Trout, famed columnist and writer for the *Louisville Courier-Journal* who is retiring this year after some thirty-eight years on the Kentucky scene, recently was quoted in the Frankfort *State Journal* as saying: "Western Kentucky shows promise of becoming the most attractive region in the United States. Barkley and Kentucky Lakes are the greatest recreation complex in mid-America. It is supplied with cheap power which brings industry into that area and it will be crisscrossed with a fine road system." Trout continued: "When you impose the state toll system on the interstate, there won't be an area better served by roads. It is the garden of promise."[2]

This interstate is the road referred to by Allan Trout. It represents part of a freeway system, financed largely by the federal government, which in a few short years will stretch all the way from points south and Nashville through Lyon County, across the Tennessee and Cumberland Rivers, and on to St. Louis. Interstate 24 will be part of a modern road network for this area that also will include the Jackson Purchase Parkway and the Pennyrile Parkway. And, of course, it will provide an extension of the Western Kentucky Parkway on to Paducah.

By the addition of I-24 to our highway system, we give to western Kentucky additional opportunities for economic growth, for highway safety, and for the savings of time and money on the part of the motorists who will use this great highway. There can be no doubt that a direct connection exists between the modern highway and the growth of the area it serves. True, the popular concept of the new highway is that it simply provides immediate relief of traffic congestion.

But the long-range economic benefits of an interstate or expressway are far more important. First, the new expressway makes the trip safer and less expensive for the user. The latest figures for traffic fatalities show conclusively that limited access highways experience far less deaths than other type roads. Furthermore, expressways provide the motorists with a faster trip—a trip which is less expensive by about two cents per mile, according to extensive surveys by highway experts. The other great factor which provides economic values to the modern highway is accessibility. High-speed expressways open new areas to development. They provide a climate for growth where industry and commerce can expand, where more tourist dollars are spent, and, most important, where more jobs are created.

When this project is completed, the commerce and industry of many of your great southern and northern cities—cities like Nashville, Atlanta, Tampa, and Mobile in the South and cities like St. Louis and other markets of the North—will be closer to western Kentucky. This means that new factories, warehouses, and stores will locate within this area, bringing with them untold new wealth. It also means that western Kentucky will be within one day's journey from many of our larger metropolitan areas. Tourists and vacationers will find it easier to fill the lakes and motels of this region. Recreation itself will receive a great boost.

Today we will turn the spades of dirt for the approaches of this interstate for the Eddy Creek Bridge. Early next spring the Highway Department hopes to let the contract for the substructure of the giant bridge across the Ohio River near Paducah. Other sections of the route will follow the logical construction sequence.

This new facility, when completed, will comply fully with federal safety design criteria and will be one of the most carefully designed interstate roads in the state.

During the four years of this administration, we have tried to provide this area with a first-rate system of highways. In addition to the roads already mentioned, we've started the four-laning of U.S. 45 between Paducah and Mayfield and U.S. 641 between Murray and Benton. Both of these roads are in a position to have additional contracts let next spring. I am hopeful that the next administration will move forward with these two important highways.

While I feel we've made important strides in road construction in western Kentucky during this administration, we've not neglected other parts of the state. As a matter of fact, I am proud to announce today that 1967 has set an all-time high for road construction. Through November contracts awarded for all purposes reached a dollar volume of $198,599,103. This amount exceeds by $4 million last year's record amount of $194.5 million. The total volume for 1967 should reach $215 million by the end of this month.

If there be any doubters as to whether we've spent this money wisely and efficiently, then I'm also proud to announce that Kentucky this year is leading the nation among all states in the number of miles put under construction, according to the United States Department of Transportation. Kentucky has put under contract more than 3,000 miles of roads, including rural roads, which exceeds even the giant state of Texas.

While we have made and are making great strides toward giving all of Kentucky the roads it needs to have a transportation system which will permit and encourage growth, much remains to be done. As one who will become a private citizen again in a few days I pledge you my efforts in the future to see what needs to be done is done. Working together with community leaders like yourselves not only on roads but on other projects as well, we can make certain that the future we regard so hopefully today will be a bright reality tomorrow.

---

1. The original route of Interstate 24 was through the Jackson Purchase. It was to enter Kentucky in the vicinity of Paducah and follow a southeasterly course to the vicinity of Paris Landing, Tennessee. Design alterations to allow I-24 to serve as a four-lane connector between the Purchase Parkway and the West Kentucky Parkway moved most of the Kentucky mileage east of the Cumberland River.

2. Allan Trout (1903-1972), newspaperman and columnist for the *Louisville Courier-Journal* (1929-1967); after retirement from the *Courier-Journal* Trout became director of company relations with Investor's Heritage Life Insurance Company. See Sister Mary Carmel Browning, *Kentucky Authors* (Evansville, Ind., 1968), pp. 51-52.

APPALACHIA

U.S. DEPARTMENT OF INTERIOR NORTH CENTRAL FIELD MEETING
Whitesburg / May 13, 1964

THE Declaration of Independence 188 years ago set forth what we as Americans believe: that every man, woman, and child in this country has the right to life, liberty, and the pursuit of happiness. One-fifth of our population, however, is, in effect, barred from this pursuit by poverty. The abundance, the comforts, the opportunities they see all around them are beyond their reach and their children's reach.

Here in Kentucky, our Appalachian counties are tightly bound by the chains of isolation, poverty, and inaccessibility. The problems of eastern Kentucky, like so many of Kentucky's other problems, point to the fact that our state and our state government's resources, financial and otherwise, are limited resources. Here in this area, with its beautiful hills and rushing streams, we have the rich and the poor, we have the educated and uneducated, we have the happy and the hopeless. To those who are not so fortunate we must turn our attention. For as long as one citizen of this state is forced to go to bed hungry and cold, then all of us share the responsibility to do something about his misery.

As governor of Kentucky, I endorse 100 percent the Appalachian Recovery Act and the Economic Opportunity Act sponsored by President Johnson. Both of these bills before Congress are based on the conviction that our nation's great and continuing prosperity should bypass no one. These programs are not handouts, not just another way to support people who cannot support themselves, but realistic programs that will give people a chance to become self-supporting, productive citizens.

They will give all the people of Appalachia an opportunity to be participants in our free enterprise system. They offer a plan to create an economic base on which private enterprise can build.

The Appalachian bill, whose chief sponsor is Franklin D. Roosevelt, Jr., will strike at the very heart of the causes of poverty, not just the results. The highway construction portion of the bill, for example, will open up the area for industry, tourists, and general commerce. The flood control projects will help stop the devastation that has left much of Appalachia in shambles several times within the last few years. Vocational training will enable industry to find a pool of educated and skilled workers. Community development will make cities and towns more attractive and more prosperous and will also help to solve problems of health and substandard existence. Forest resources development provisions of this bill will enable our people to use our vast supply of forest products in a manner that will provide jobs and income throughout the area.

These are but some of the important provisions of this plan for Appalachia. The total program will all add up to one thing for Kentucky: transformation of an area that is rich in natural and human resources, but lacking in opportunity, into a prosperous region that is self-sustaining and capable of providing a happy place to live for its citizens and a region that can contribute its share to the well-being of our nation.

This program, if passed, will be a milestone in our continuing search for a better life for all Kentuckians. To President Johnson, Mr. Roosevelt, and the others, you and I owe a debt of gratitude for their tireless work and able assistance towards this goal.[1] Let us tonight, in this splendid and beautiful section of the Commonwealth, pledge ourselves to an all-out effort to drive poverty from history's richest nation. I urge every public official and private citizen to join me.

---

1. Franklin Delano Roosevelt, Jr. (1914-   ), member, 81st, 82d, and 83d Congress; chairman, Equal Employment Opportunity Commission (1965); Liberal party candidate for governor of New York (1966). *Who's Who in America, 1976-1977,* 39th ed.(Chicago, 1976).

EASTERN KENTUCKY DEVELOPMENT MEETING
Ashland / August 3, 1964

WE meet in eastern Kentucky today in a moment of greater hope than this region has known in our lifetime. Two great pieces of legislation which are now ready for the final decision of the Congress, can give us a basic and comprehensive development program for this region. When Congress gives its favorable action—and we have good reason to expect this to happen within the next few days—eastern Kentucky can expect to have the tools it needs, for the first time, to meet its critical problems; to build an economy of growth in the place of decline, and to create a new climate of fair opportunity for its people.

With the enactment of the Appalachian Regional Development Act and the national Economic Opportunity Act, we can begin with hope and confidence to work for ourselves to create a new era of development.[1] We have great confidence in this anticipated development program because it makes possible the kind of special action long dreamed of by eastern Kentucky's people, the action carefully planned by the Eastern Kentucky Regional Development Commission, the action already spearheaded by such state projects as the Mountain Parkway, by federal projects such as Fishtrap Dam, by state-federal and local programs such as the Accelerated Public Works, the ARA, or the Unemployed Parents Work and Training Program. And, of course, the overall development program will help us use all our existing programs much more effectively.

Our confidence, finally, rests on three things—strength, intelligence, and leadership. In terms of strength, for instance, we now look at a program which begins to measure up to the problem. Instead of just building a breakthrough road, such as the Mountain Parkway, we can now build a system of roads to serve the entire region and to serve development. But no matter how big the program is, it cannot be big enough unless it is carefully and intelligently focused on those objectives which will count for most in encouraging development. Great care has been given to bring human judgment to bear in this program at all levels, through the Appalachian Regional Commission, the East Kentucky Commission, the statewide Kentucky Development Committee, and the area development councils and various local organizations.

It will be through the intelligence of these groups that we will devise a regional development program instead of just a collection of projects, a road system instead of a road, full water resource utilization instead of just a dam, a Magic Mountain tourist complex instead of just a motel, a region-wide tourist industry and a full program of education, training, and permanent job opportunities rather than just temporary public works and welfare help.

Today we recognize the work and the accomplishments of all of you who have shown an interest in eastern Kentucky. I salute particularly our great Congressman Carl Perkins, who has been a major voice in spearheading the vital programs keyed to the needs of this region, and federal administrators like Ed Baxter and Ivan Nestigen and the fine people who work with them and who are here today at their own initiative to demonstrate—beyond the call of duty—their special interest in our people and our problems.[2]

The key leadership, which counts for most and without which no program will have real success, is that which you who are local officials and citizens will give in your communities. The most significant meaning in the attendance here today of so many of us who work for you in the state and federal governments is our total confidence in your work and leadership. We know that the demanding challenges you will meet will make our special efforts worthwhile.

State government in Kentucky is organized to serve you and to serve the anticipated new programs. All of our departments have geared their programs to the theme of development—what can best be done to create new growth, a stable economy, new jobs and opportunities. Many of our department heads and key staff members are here to work with you. Henry Ward later this morning will discuss with you our present Kentucky highway program which is keeping our state foremost among the states in this field and, of course, the prospects now before us for the Appalachian development highway program. In your discussion groups you will be working with many of the people who are helping Kentucky to lead and pioneer for the nation, especially in the several imaginative new programs you will be considering here.

In my office at Frankfort we are providing special organization to help you meet the demands and gain the greatest benefit from both existing and new programs in the forthcoming regional development effort. Our area program office and office of local affairs are both represented here. To give overall administration and coordination to the new Appalachia and economic opportunity programs, I have designated John Whisman, who is the administrator of our area program office.[3] As you know, John has been a principal architect of these new programs, and his knowledge and experience will be geared to making them work best in Kentucky. He will discuss with you the schedules and procedures being planned to begin working with you immediately after Congress acts on the pending legislation.

I think it may be fair to remind all of us here today that the special programs for this region have not been won easily and will not work easily to meet our goals. Even now—with all the demonstration of need for these programs—there are those who refuse to recognize the need for them and who oppose them while offering no others in their place. We must continue to fight to get the programs—to keep them—and to make them work.

In today's meeting you will be working with existing programs—and existing leadership—to use these programs in better ways. You will get new programs, but the leadership will stay the same. The challenge will rest upon all of us, and most especially upon you who lead in your own communities. It is the great attendance here today of state, federal, and local leadership which proves the presence of real enthusiasm, cooperation, ability, and enterprise. You, and your work, make up the best evidence of the expressions of new hope with which I began these remarks—and with which I close them in wishing you great success in the exciting and rewarding work ahead of you.

---

1. The Appalachia Regional Development Act (P.L. 89-4) was President Johnson's key legislation aimed at relieving the depressed area of Appalachia. It was introduced in the House of Representatives on April 29, 1964; however, Congress adjourned October 3, 1964 without voting on the bill. The 89th Congress resumed consideration of the bill and it passed the Senate 62-22 and the House 257-165. On March 7, 1965 President Johnson signed the bill into law. The act provided over one billion dollars for highway construction, construction of health facilities, conservation, mining area restoration, vocational education facilities, sewage plants, grants, and research for the Appalachian region. *U.S. Statutes at Large,* vol. 79 (Washington, 1966), pp. 5-22, and Donald N. Rothblatt, *Regional Planning: The Appalachian Experience* (Lexington, Mass., 1971), pp. 61-66. The Economic Opportunity Act of 1964 (P.L. 88-452) was the cornerstone of President Johnson's war on poverty. Administered by the Office of Economic Opportunity headed by Sargent Shriver, the act created a series of programs designed to provide training for young people (Job Corps), work-study opportunities for low income students in institutions of higher education, urban and rural community action programs to combat poverty, adult basic education programs, voluntary assistance programs for needy children, special programs to combat poverty in rural areas, and assistance to migrant workers and other seasonally employed agricultural workers. *U.S. Statutes at Large,* vol. 78 (Washington, 1965), pp. 508-34.

2. Carl D. Perkins (1912-), attorney from Knott County, Kentucky; counsel, Kentucky Department of Highways (1948); member United States House of Representatives (1949-); chairman, House Education and Labor Committee. *Who's Who in American Politics, 1975-1976,* 5th ed. (New York, 1975). Edmund Baxter (1913-), born Richmond, Kentucky; regional director for the U.S. Department of Health, Education and Welfare (1956-1966). *Who's Who in America, 1966-1967,* 34th ed. (Chicago, 1966). Irvin Nestigen (1921-), government official and attorney; mayor of Madison, Wisconsin (1956-1960); undersecretary of Health, Education and Welfare (1961-1965). *Who's Who in America, 1966-1967,* 34th ed. (Chicago, 1966).

3. John Whisman (1921-), executive director of Eastern Kentucky Regional Planning Commission (1960-1966); executive director, Appalachian Regional Planning Commission, Washington, D.C. (1966-1976). George W. Robinson, ed., *The Public Papers of Governor Bert T. Combs, 1959-1963* (Lexington, Ky., 1979), p. 158. John Whisman was an important figure in the evolution of the Appalachian regional development concept. In August, 1957, Bert Combs appointed him executive director of the newly created Eastern Kentucky Regional Planning Commission (KRPC), whose purpose was to devise long-term economic development plans

for Kentucky's Appalachia region. The commission's 1960 report went beyond parochial solutions and proposed an institutional arrangement for multistate regional development. This proposal provided a rallying point for the early efforts of Appalachian state governors to solve their common problems through cooperative action. In 1961 the governors of eight Appalachian states formed the Conference of Appalachian Governors (CAG). Whisman headed a staff committee responsible for the CAG's principal tasks: formulating detailed plans for regional development and establishing fruitful contacts with President Kennedy. In 1963 Kennedy was persuaded to create the President's Appalachian Regional Commission (PARC), a joint federal-state agency to study the region's problems and potential and to make recommendations to the president. Whisman was made executive secretary of the new agency and designated as the Washington representative for the Conference of Appalachian Governors. The Appalachian Regional Development Act was shaped largely by the PARC's recommendations. The Appalachian Regional Commission (ARC), created by the act to supervise its implementation, was based on the institutional arrangements generated under Whisman's direction for the KRPC and the CAG. The Appalachian Regional Commission was composed of representatives of the participating states and a federal cochairman. It eventually found itself unable to cope with the volume of project proposals it received and it delegated much of its authority to an executive committee with only two voting members, the federal cochairman and a state's regional representative selected by, paid by, and responsible to the Appalachian states. Whisman was one of the first men selected by the states for this powerful position, a reflection of both his personal contribution to Appalachian development and the strength of Kentucky within the ARC. Donald N. Rothblatt, *Regional Planning: The Appalachian Experience* (Lexington, Mass., 1971), pp. 45-71.

THE ECONOMIC OPPORTUNITY PROGRAM IN KENTUCKY
Frankfort / December 9, 1964

KENTUCKY'S work in the federal government's economic opportunity program is moving ahead at a brisk, progress-making pace.

Late last month, four projects were announced for Kentucky under the opportunity program—three Job Corps installations and a high school work-training project for one of our cities. These four projects were part of 120 granted to only two-thirds of the states of the Union. Only thirty other states were included in this first, program-opening move by the federal government.

And, just last week, the largest grant made yet in the economic opportunity program came to Kentucky in the form of a $7.5 million work and training program for unemployed fathers. Starting with nine eastern counties, this project will next year be phased into thirty others and, with the use of additional state and federal funds, will ultimately become statewide in scope. This grant, destined to become even larger, comes from work done last winter by John Whisman, administrator of our area program office, in cooperation with federal officials. The result was an unprecedented one million dollar grant announced by President Kennedy for a nine-county unemployed fathers work-training program—the pilot effort of the project awarded the Commonwealth last week.

But these five approved projects represent only a small part of the thinking and work that has been put into economic opportunity projects by Kentuckians. Since the act was approved by Congress late last July, more than seventy local projects have been channeled through Mr. Whisman's office and sent on to Washington. Many of these came in even before Congress had voted money to support the act. Nearly all were submitted before the newly formed Office of Economic Opportunity was able to establish program policies, guidelines, and project writing instructions.

Much of this energetic local activity stemmed from wide publicity, and attention given the economic opportunity program at the state level. In September and October information teams—sponsored by the Kentucky Development Committee and directed by the area program office—made more than fifty visits to towns across the state, presenting program information to over one thousand community leaders. Then, as early, informal information was made available from Washington it was immediately made available to these leaders.

To assist local communities in developing project ideas, nine advisory teams were set up at the state level, to suggest possible avenues of approach as well as guidelines for project selection for the economic opportunity program in Kentucky. The teams covered such important fields of interest as health, education, and conservation. In some cases, these teams wrote projects of their own. From one team came an ambitious project proposal formulated by our Department of Child Welfare. If approved, this $4.5 million project will provide aid to needy youngsters in sixty-two Kentucky counties.

By November administration of some specific parts of the Economic Opportunity Act had been given over by the Office of Economic Opportunity to other federal agencies, such as the Department of Labor and the Department of Education. Representatives of these agencies also began to traffic the state, spurring more activity.

So far, grants have been made mainly under Title I of the act—the section that deals with the enhancement of job and educational opportunities for our young people. Except for the program approved last week, all Kentucky projects were granted under this section. This is mostly true of the other states receiving Economic Opportunity Act grants.

Projects approved under Title II, or the community action program section, only went to nine states. None of these were for specific projects but went toward project development. Kentucky is now negotiating and will soon receive a program development grant at the state level that will enable the Commonwealth to employ technicians to help compile and draft additional opportunity projects.

Title III, which provides for small grants to low income farmers, has yet to be activated and no projects have been announced as approved under this title.

Title IV, which provides for loans to small businesses up to $25,000, has not been an active program either. As a matter of fact, only one such loan has been approved and this is to a cooperative in Louisiana.

Title V covers work experience projects for adults and is a program section of great interest to many Kentuckians. With its $7.5 million unemployed fathers program, Kentucky is one of the first states to receive aid under this section.[1]

Title VI of the act will establish the Voluntary Service Corps, or VISTA program.[2] So far, we've received no word that this program has been put to work anywhere in the country. However, Kentucky has had a pilot program in this area for a year now. I am referring to the Appalachian Volunteers program, one that uses college student volunteers to work "peace corps" fashion with local people in economically distressed sections of our state. This program is sponsored and financed by the Council of the Southern Mountains, which is headquartered at our own Berea College.

We should remember that the Economic Opportunity Act of 1964 was designed to lead to the permanent improvement of the economic plight of those persons in the United States who are in a position of poverty. There are nearly twelve million families in the nation whose annual incomes are less than $3,000. Kentucky's share of this number reaches almost 300,000. Twenty-one and four-tenths percent of all U.S. families are below the $3,000 mark. But in Kentucky this figure jumps to 38.5 percent. In some counties it's above 50 percent.

It should also be remembered that Kentucky's work in "economic opportunity" began long before the federal Economic Opportunity Act was even put on the drawing board. In fact, many of the concepts in the act had been previously tested in Kentucky. Many of these ideas came about as a result of Mr. Whisman's leadership and the work of the area program office, an agency attached to my office.

It was for this reason that I appointed Mr. Whisman as state coordinator for the opportunity program and the area program office as the program liaison agency for the Commonwealth. I want to continue to coordinate both the Economic Opportunity Act and, when passed, the Appalachian Regional Development Act, as well as other special area and community programs, through Mr. Whisman and his office. It's been suggested that we have two coordinators—one for the Economic Opportunity Act, another for the Appalachian program—but this would be in direct contradiction of a system that has already worked well in Kentucky for several years now, one which depends upon a unified, straight-line approach.

However, we are expanding the staff of the area program office so that it can give more intensive technical assistance to communities working on economic opportunity projects while at the same time maintaining the unified approach. This staff expansion is now under way.

The Economic Opportunity Act of 1964 is one of the best programs yet devised for the alleviation of the nation's poverty problems. It will be up to Kentuckians to use this resource so that it will have the best possible effect on the poverty situation in Kentucky. We're confident the opportunity program will work well in Kentucky because it has the support of all our state agencies as well as the support of the Kentucky Development Committee, a volunteer group which unifies the brainpower and work of both state and federal agencies, as well as many private organizations, in behalf of total development of the state.

---

1. Title V of the Economic Opportunity Act authorized the director of the Office of Economic Opportunity to transfer designated funds to the Department of Health, Education and Welfare to pay the full costs of pilot programs established by the states to train and employ heads of families receiving payments through Aid to Families With Dependent Children. Under the omnibus Public Welfare Amendment Act of 1962 the federal government had been authorized to share the costs of such programs within limits established by the act. Kentucky, taking advantage of the increased funding made available by the Economic Opportunity Act, initiated the Unemployed Parents Work and Training Program in December of 1964. *Congressional Quarterly Almanac,* vol. 20 (1964), pp. 208-12.

2. Volunteers in Service to America (VISTA), a domestic counterpart to the Peace Corps, was a product of the Economic Opportunity Act of 1964. Title VI of the act authorized the director of the Office of Economic Opportunity to recruit, select, and train volunteers who were to provide personal assistance to the urban and rural poor of the nation and generally "further the activities" and goals of the Economic Opportunity Act and President Johnson's war on poverty. *U.S. Statutes at Large,* vol. 78 (Washington, 1965), pp. 530-31.

COMMENTS TO THE GOVERNORS OF THE APPALACHIAN STATES
Washington, D.C. / April 19, 1965

I AM convinced that all thoughtful Americans are rooting for us to succeed in Appalachia—to show the way toward solutions of complex socio-economic problems that exist in every region. I am confident that we will succeed. My confidence is based, in large measure, upon the success that we in Kentucky have shared with you in creating development opportunities in each of our states.

But the Appalachian Regional Development Act has already been attacked as a regional pork barrel, limited in value and parochial in scope. It will continue to be attacked until our combined successes in Appalachia demonstrate that the type of problems found in Appalachia can be solved and that our solutions can be applied to other regions of the United States. If we falter in the face of criticism and fail to develop these solutions, it is doubtful that regional development programs will be launched for other regions—indeed, the whole idea of state-federal partnership in developing opportunities could die in our mountains. We in Kentucky are determined to not let this happen. To make sure it does not, we have taken many special actions, of which the following are typical, to prove the feasibility and value of the development approach.

We have clearly established development as the keynote of state government policy and as a recognized function in all of our programs. We redesigned and expanded our state parks system to stimulate tourism, which created dozens of new businesses and hundreds of new job opportunities in otherwise severely limited areas. We designed Kentucky's Mountain Parkway, which has become the first portion of the Appalachian highway system, and the West Kentucky Turnpike to be arteries to pump new opportunities into underdeveloped areas. We contributed $3 million to establish Spindletop Research Center as a major applied research institute for our region, in recognition of Kentucky's need to develop a technological base for our economy.

The Appalachian Regional Development Act articulates a new approach to bridging the gap between the federal and the state levels. In effect, it created a state-federal body, with a representative from each interpreting and fending for its parent group. Within each of our states there are significant regional differences that call for the same type of working relationship to be established within the state to assure recognition of the physical, social, political and economic forces of each area within the state's borders.

I know that each area of Kentucky has its particular local problems and each county wants to retain its autonomy. Also, my various department heads are oriented toward looking at the state as a whole from an operational point of view and in terms of a particular program. Thus, a real problem I see at this time is to utilize a mechanism similar to that of the Appalachian Regional Commission to operate at the state level that will weld together state and local interests and resources. We are working to develop a mechanism to deal with this problem effectively; to design a plan; to mobilize all of our resources in support of our goals; and to create criteria against which we can judge development programs.

To this end, by executive order, I have established a high priority throughout state government for support and implementation of the Appalachian program, and have set up Appalachian "desks" in each department of state government. In addition, I have designated the Kentucky Area Development Office as coordinator of the Appalachian program and of other area development programs in Kentucky. This office reports directly to me. I have designated the Kentucky area development administrator as Kentucky's representative to the Appalachian Regional Commission and as a member of the state planning committee.

Our state agencies are working closely with the statewide Kentucky Development Committee and the various area development councils throughout Kentucky, which we have recognized as major organizations through which we can achieve our interagency coordination and our state-local relationships. Also, Kentucky has set aside $7 million for our part of the Appalachian highway program, and we are taking steps to provide matching state funds for Kentucky's maximum participation in all other aspects of the Appalachian program. We are also strengthening all of our state sponsored programs in the Appalachian region to take advantage of the total development opportunity now uniquely available to this region.

In closing, I hope, gentlemen, that we will not restrict our thinking to the borders of our respective states. When I consider the recreational opportunities of the southeastern part of Kentucky, for example, I should not think of that region without thinking of West Virginia, Tennessee, or Virginia. Any major recreation development program in Appalachian Kentucky will have a significant impact on our neighbors. To do my job right, I feel I must look outside Kentucky's borders. We must look to each other for guidance, assistance, ideas, advice, and support if we are to develop regional programs that will have a maximum impact for the mutual benefit of our people. We have often referred in the past to the Appalachian problem. Today, as a result of the concerted initiative and action of local people, state and federal government agencies, and private interests, we are now on the threshold of the Appalachian opportunity. Our success can permanently change the outlook in Appalachia from that of problem to that of opportunity.

APPALACHIAN REGIONAL COMMISSION
Washington, D.C. / June 7, 1965

It is a pleasure for me to participate with the Appalachian Regional Commission again, and to recognize with you that in less than two months we have made tremendous progress toward achieving the real purpose for our existence—action for Appalachia. The Commonwealth of Kentucky has participated actively and earnestly in all of the efforts which culminated in the approval by Congress of the Appalachian Regional Development Act of 1965. Former Governor Bert T. Combs aided in the creation of the Appalachian Governors Conference and served as its chairman. When I succeeded Governor Combs in December, 1963, I proceeded immediately to provide continuity for Kentucky's participation in this program and endorsed the report by the president's Appalachian Regional Commission made to President Johnson a year ago.

As you know, I am here today to express my strong conviction that corridor five of the Appalachian Development Highway System is a keystone in our program for development of the Cumberland Valley region of Kentucky and Tennessee. This strong conviction stems from our extensive experience in area development in Kentucky. We have learned that a comprehensive approach to area development is the key to getting the maximum benefit and growth effects from public investments. We have learned that all programs—federal, state, and local—must be focused within the framework of an overall program for maximum development impact, and that development highways are the foundation for development if they relate to regional needs, and at the same time open up the areas where isolation is the prime frustration for development.

The Kentucky Mountain Parkway, opened in 1962—a development highway paid for entirely by Kentucky—is a living example of these convictions, now tested by experience. Usage has far exceeded expectations, and evidence of development has followed rapidly in the wake of this attack on isolation. This is the goal we all seek for the Appalachian region.

The Kentucky Department of Highways, after close cooperation with other states, the United States Bureau of Public Roads, and the president's Appalachian Regional Commission, made recommendations for corridors in Kentucky designed to create a sound regional developmental network. These recommendations by Kentucky were included in the map published as a part of the president's Appalachian Regional Commission report, and the Commonwealth of Kentucky has reaffirmed its support for these corridors on every occasion that has arisen since then. As a matter of fact, these corridors—identical to those now under consideration—were first recommended in Kentucky by the Eastern Kentucky Regional Planning Commission in their blueprint for eastern Kentucky regional development, published 1960.

The Commonwealth of Kentucky has acted in good faith and has made its recommendations for corridors on the developmental system with a genuine concern for sound reasoning in the regional program. We had understood that the corridor recommendations for the regional system, as planned by the president's commission, had been considered sound and were practically assured at the time the legislation was under consideration by Congress. The Commonwealth of Kentucky was gratified that the Appalachian Regional Commission approved a major portion of its corridor recommendations and "quickstart" projects at a meeting on May 11. Under no circumstances is Kentucky's position now an indication of any feeling that we have received anything other than fair treatment.

The point that I want to emphasize today is that it is vitally important to Kentucky that the Appalachian Regional Commission approve the remaining mileage of the corridors to be built in Kentucky as soon as possible so that Kentucky may proceed in an orderly way to develop plans, acquire rights of way, and achieve construction of these important highways. It requires a minimum of eighteen months to two years from the time a highway project is authorized until a contract for construction can be awarded. Since all of these projects must be completed or under contract by 1970, Kentucky cannot discharge its responsibilities in the building of this system if extensive delays are encountered in approval of corridors. I am sure this is true for each state.

The Commonwealth of Kentucky recommended corridors that we know will provide the greatest service to the economic development of mid-Appalachia, where severe past problems have limited real development but where significant potential for growth is present and can be generated by sound approach.

Since the highway system is essential to the total program, the deferral of approval of an important corridor, such as corridor five, stymies the activation of a truly comprehensive program in a key area. We appreciate the fact that the commission has already approved a portion of corridor five generally paralleling U.S. 119 from Jenkins, Kentucky, to Charleston, West Virginia. The remainder of the corridor extends along U.S. 119 from Jenkins to Pineville, Kentucky, and thence along U.S. 25-E to the Tennessee state line, where it would proceed to connect with Interstate 75 or Interstate 81, or both, in Tennessee.

The Kentucky Department of Highways, in response to our urging for fast action, has plans ready for "quickstart" projects on sixteen miles of the corridor in Bell and Harlan counties. Local citizens are greatly interested in these projects. It is vitally important to the success of the program that this corridor be approved at an early date so that Kentucky can take advantage of its head start in planning on these projects.

The Commonwealth of Kentucky based its original recommendations to the president's Appalachian Regional Commission on planning studies developed by the Department of Highways and the area development office over a period of years and on other facts gained by agencies of the Commonwealth which demonstrated the validity of this corridor and the developmental potential of the area it would traverse.

In addition, today, we are filing with the commission a presentation further outlining the development potential of the Cumberland area. This presentation, including a report by Spindletop Research, Inc., which clearly identifies an existing growth situation in the Cumberland Valley area, demonstrates that this corridor is essential to the Appalachian highway network.

I urge that the commission approve corridor five at the earliest possible date for the following reasons.

1. The people of Kentucky will vote on a $176 million bond issue this fall which, if passed, will make available matching funds for the Appalachian road program and those primary highways which connect to the Appalachian network.

2. Kentucky is ready to advertise for contracts for a number of these connecting highways during this construction season in anticipation of the expected approval of corridor five. Contracts have already been let on some of these sections, and other sections will unnecessarily be delayed if we do not have early approval.

3. Kentucky has approved other major capital construction programs in the area served by corridor five, including a community college in the Blackey-Hazard area, major capital improvements in our state parks system, and construction of vocational schools. In addition, the Hazard and Whitesburg communities have developed plans for a tourist complex center. The feasibility of all of these programs [is] dependent upon the early approval of corridor five.

The Kentucky Department of Highways has already advertised for the construction of three projects on approved corridors of the Appalachian system. It is the first state in the Appalachian area to achieve this goal. We are ready to advertise immediately two more construction projects on U.S. 119 in Bell and Harlan counties. We are convinced of the necessity of this program.

Our Cumberland Valley Area Development Council has committed itself to an aggressive program which will move forward as soon as they are assured of the approval of this corridor. We have the will and the state funds to move aggressively to build these highways. All we lack is the official approval of the Appalachian Regional Commission, and I urge that this action be taken at the earliest possible time.[1]

---

1. Governor Breathitt's address to the Appalachian Regional Commission was designed to win approval of a section of U.S. 119 in Harlan and Bell counties as a "quickstart" project. Residents of the area and Kentucky officials, including Highway Commissioner Henry Ward, had presumed the section would be funded. However, when the commission announced the eighty-seven miles of roads designated as "quickstart" projects, U.S. 119 was not included. *Louisville Courier-Journal*, June 6, 1965. For an excellent discussion of the problems associated with "quickstart" projects see Monroe Newman, *The Political Economy of Appalachia* (Lexington, Mass., 1972), p. 89.

GROUNDBREAKING KY 15
Isom / July 6, 1965

TRAILBLAZING is a heritage in Kentucky, and we Kentuckians are proud to be trailblazing today. Our pioneer forefathers blazed trails into the wilderness of Kentucky to seek the rich resources they knew were here. Today we seek to blaze new trails to tie our resource rich areas to the growing commerce and industry of the nation.

But we do more here today than blaze a trail. As we break new ground for a road which will cut through our mountains and guide commerce into our valleys, we do more than point the way. We build into this new road a basic foundation for total development action for our region and for new opportunities for our people. Truly, today, we begin action on the Appalachian regional development program. I was present in the White House when President Lyndon B. Johnson signed the Appalachian Regional Development Act into law, and I heard him say, "The dole is dead, the pork barrel is gone."

The deep satisfaction I felt that day is stronger today. The great feeling of that day was the knowledge that we had won a long fight to get an Appalachian program. Today we begin to see what we can do with this great program—how we can shape it and make it work for us. For the Appalachian program began right here in eastern Kentucky, beginning with the ideas of people all over this region, studied and shaped by the Eastern Kentucky Regional Planning Commission. With the administration of my predecessor, Bert T. Combs, these ideas were carried forward to the Conference of Appalachian Governors, who were organized just to move their program forward. Then the late President John F. Kennedy took the basic ideas and gave them his leadership when he established the president's Appalachian Regional Commission. Following the tragic loss of our great friend President Kennedy, the Appalachian program was taken by President Johnson, who gave it his personal and highest priority attention. It became the first major legislation passed by the current Congress. Kentucky's John Whisman, of course, has been deeply involved in this entire process. And thus this great program of regional development already being evaluated by other regions throughout the nation took its first ideas from eastern Kentucky and now returns to take its first action in eastern Kentucky.

The future of this program will be, of course, whatever we make it to be. The program provides for the special and best use of all programs working together in unusual cooperation to meet specific problems of our region. To increase the effective program tools for us to work with, the Congress has recently added the special new programs provided in the Economic Opportunity Act: the Manpower and Vocational Training Acts, the Federal Aid to Education Act, the Housing Act of 1965, the Land and Water Resources Act, the Economic Development Act, and, of course, the Appalachian Regional Development Act itself.[1]

With these new programs we can put together an overall eastern Kentucky action program for the first time good enough to do the job. Although we symbolize the beginning of development today with the breaking of ground for a regional highway network, I want to mention just briefly the effective steps we are taking in many other special programs. Some of these comments relate to federal programs, some to state programs. The keynote of the Appalachian program is its new and stronger relationship between our state and federal and local governments. We will be working carefully with your area development councils to help you design your own effective action for development in your own area in each of these fields.

Education, of course, comes first to our minds. To begin to meet the critical needs for better facilities and services we will seek progress and improvement at all levels. Our new community college program will help to bring higher education closer to aspiring and talented young people. We will be able to support an intensive expansion of vocational and technical schools. We will have special programs to help deserving students to meet the cost of training and even to gain subsistence income in some instances. Finally, with help from both the Economic Opportunity Act and the federal aid to education program, we will be able to bring increased funds to local school systems for many special activities to assist both the schools and the students at the elementary and high school levels.

In the important field of health care we can see dramatic and pioneering opportunities develop here in eastern Kentucky—a model of comprehensive health care programs. As you know, the Appalachian hospitals have been assisted recently so that they may continue their operation. However, keeping these hospitals in business to serve you has been only a first step. It will now be our purpose through a new joint effort between the federal Office of Economic Opportunity, the Appalachian Regional Commission, and state government to work with doctors, health officers, hospital administrators, and area leaders to build a great new health program in this region. We are now in the design phase of this program and we are working with all interests. We have been given assurance of the resources needed to put the program into action.

In the general field of conservation and physical resource development—and without going into detail here today—we will move forward with many new programs, including a new national forest in this general area; a new privately organized timber development organization to promote greater use of eastern Kentucky timber; rapid completion of the special studies of the strip-mine problems under both our state's own efforts and those of the Appalachian commission, plus my own and the efforts of others as necessary; strong action resulting thereafter to begin to deal effectively with the critical problems related to strip mining; a useful new program to aid small farmers in this area in carrying out a general land improvement program—an acceleration with Appalachian funds of all water resource development projects in this area; and even more important, the design of an entirely new water resource development program especially suited to the problems—and opportunities—of this area.

In important other fields, we will take special steps to create new jobs. We will get underway in the immediate future an overall program for new tourist facilities, both state parks and private facilities, to create a major new tourist industry here. We will use special actions, based on both the new Economic Development Act and the new Housing Act, to make gains in small industries and commercial development, as well as in housing and community facilities development.

Our great Kentucky interest in highways for this region stems from our longstanding conviction that all these important programs can be effective only if we break the bottleneck of isolation and free the commerce of men to move to and from our region. We advocate the solid position of the Appalachian program—to create real growth and development, rather than to foster aid and dependency—but we know we must base our growth on a solid foundation and a first-class highway system. We have long preached the certainness of what we have called a "developmental highway system" for Appalachia. We, in Kentucky, have practiced what we have preached.

The first true development highway in the country is the Kentucky Mountain Parkway—planned with the courage of Governor Combs as an act of faith in the region and its people and in the fact that we would be able to continue that great highway, as we do here today. Last week we added another section to the Mountain Parkway and we dedicated—just yesterday, as you know—the first section of development highway ever financed in part with federal funds. Kentucky proposed and received the only Accelerated Public Works grant for regional highway construction, for the Jackson to Van Cleve route. Therefore, you see, a part of the development highway network has already been planned even as we break ground here today. Our new situation today is that we may look forward to more than a few phases of highways. The project we dedicate here will grow into a complete system of great highways through eastern Kentucky and the other states of Appalachia. With this growth system, our development program can move ahead at an accelerated pace.

Here I should point out that, for those of us in Kentucky, this priority system will not be effective without the inclusion of the route from here to Cumberland, Harlan, Pikeville, Middlesboro, and on through Tennessee. As you know, I have made a special presentation concerning the development potential of the Cumberland Valley to the Appalachian commission. I feel confident that we will have approval of this highway corridor and its "quickstart" projects very soon.

It is a great testimonial to this program, which calls for all of us to work together as never before, to see so many counties represented here and to have the Appalachian regional representatives from several of our sister states with us today. While we break ground in Letcher County, there is just as surely a road for Perry County, and Breathitt County, for Leslie County, and for Harlan and Bell counties, as the Mountain Parkway is joined to serve Letcher County and all of us. By the same token, this groundbreaking, and the groundbreaking in West Virginia, begins work upon a road system to serve the development of all our states.

Now, so far, we have talked of what this road system and what the program will do for us. In the words of the late President Kennedy—who did so much for eastern Kentucky—"What can we do for our country?" I know we all will have many opportunities to grow in various projects of this vast program. But I want to take a moment to remind us all that we will have to take one action, facing us in the next few months, or virtually none of these great new programs for Appalachia will be available to us. I am sure you know that I am referring to the forthcoming bond issue. Without this the future of this entire program—the future of any new Appalachian highway projects beyond this year—the future of the overall health program, the community colleges, the vocational schools, and the other development projects—and, finally, the jobs and dollars we need, depend squarely upon the passage of the bond issue. With its passage, of course, can come a dramatic rate of development projects and dollars—at a rate of five to one, or better.

However, there is one more reason we must show the greatest majority in all the state on the bond issue for eastern Kentucky. It must be clear to all of us that, if congressmen for all of America are willing to vote for funds for eastern Kentucky, they will be watching closely to see whether we are willing to support our fair share. Our programs, our reputation, and our future depend upon the action on the bond issue. I deem the action we will take here this afternoon as we break ground, an action on the entire Appalachian regional development program, as one of the most important actions of my administration. It is a pleasure to share this event with all of you. Now I think it is time we got to work. Let us move the earth to make eastern Kentucky grow.

---

1. The 89th Congress amended and extended the Manpower Development and Training Act of 1962, authorizing $454 million for its continued operation in 1966 and additional funds as needed over the next two years. The new amendments increased benefits and eligibility in the training and employment programs established under the original act to reduce long-term unemployment. They also contained provisions for further experimental and demonstration projects and apportioned a greater share of the programs' costs to the federal government, thereby saving many existing and projected programs. *Congressional Quarterly Almanac,* vol. 21 (1965), pp. 810-16. The Elementary and Secondary Education Act of 1965 provided the first general federal school aid in U.S. history. Over $1 billion of the total package of $1.3 billion authorized by the bill was to be funneled through the states to individual school districts. The amount received by each district was determined by a formula based on the number of children from low-income families in the district and the average state expenditure per pupil for education. The rest of the authorization was alloted to improving library facilities, establishing supplementary public education centers and research facilities, and to state departments of education. *New York Times,* April 10, 1965, pp. 1, 12, and *U.S. Statutes at Large,* vol. 79 (Washington, 1966), pp. 27-58. The Housing and Urban Development Act of 1965 authorized the spending of $7.8 billion over a

four-year period on a long list of programs designed to expand housing in the United States and improve the living conditions of the poor. The most controversial program in the package authorized the payment of rent subsidies to low-income families otherwise unable to afford adequate housing. The bill included a number of additional new grant and loan programs for housing and urban development and extended or increased funding for many established programs, including urban renewal. *Congressional Quarterly Almanac,* vol. 21 (1965), pp. 358-81. The Water Resources Planning Act of 1965 promoted federal and regional coordination in planning water resource development. It provided statutory authority to the Federal Water Resources Council, authorized the establishment of a federal-state river basin planning commission, and authorized $5 million per year over a ten-year period to plan water resource programs. *U.S. Statutes at Large,* vol. 79 (Washington, 1966), pp. 244-53. The Public Works and Economic Development Act of 1965 was the successor to the 1961 Area Development Act and the 1962 Accelerated Public Works Act. It provided $3.25 billion in grants and loans over a five-year period for public works, development facilities, and other projects to attract business and industry to the nation's underdeveloped areas. The act also provided technical expertise and administrative mechanisms to promote developmental planning on a multicounty and multistate basis. It was, in many respects, an extension of the Appalachian act to the rest of the country. *Congressional Quarterly Weekly Report,* August 20, 1965, p. 1635, and *U.S. Statutes at Large*, vol. 79 (Washington, 1966), pp. 552-73.

OBO WORKSHOP BANQUET
Frankfort / June 28, 1966

TO you who are here working to improve the quality and to step up the speed of our fight against poverty, I bring good wishes and assurances of gratitude, not only as an individual but as the spokesman for Kentuckians who look hopefully to you and your efforts. Whenever a great leader breathes the breath of life into a new possibility for the improvement of human life, or for the defeat of some ancient evil, it becomes fashionable for armchair critics, political nitpickers, and viewers with alarm to embrace the basic objective but at the same time to destroy the actual program with a long series of detailed and destructive criticisms.

It is from this type of attack that our war against poverty is suffering today. It was only a few years ago that we affluent Americans were even willing to admit that such a thing as poverty existed in this rich and abundant land. Many of us were willing, consciously or unconsciously, to sweep not only the problem of poverty but the poor people themselves under the rug of invisibility.

Then, as imperceptibly as most great changes occur in history, the conscience of a great people began to assert itself. Perhaps, the single event to which historians will point as marking the shift in the historic tide was the publication of Michael Harrington's great book *The Other America* in 1962, and the review of that book by Dwight MacDonald in the *New Yorker* magazine.[1]

From this book, and this magazine article, came the sparks which lighted the war on poverty. Its conception was in the heart of John Kennedy, and it was born to reality under the action-oriented, driving leadership of Lyndon Johnson.

I am not here tonight to detail for you the accomplishments of the war on poverty, or to seek out and analyze its failures, if any. But I am here to tell you the basic objective of this war is not only a sound objective, a human objective, but that it is a moral imperative—and a moral imperative which can be realized, if we want to do it, in your lifetime and mine.

I am sure that there will be, as there have been, mistakes and missteps. Lincoln made mistakes in saving this Union. Franklin Roosevelt made mistakes in fighting the depression. And I am sure that there will always be mistakes, errors, and waste in any effort as great, as unprecedented, and as dependent upon trial and error as is the war on poverty.

Remember that this is a war we are fighting. And, to a degree, war always involves waste. There was waste in the New Deal effort of the thirties, but it saved this nation from despair and our free institutions from destruction. There was waste in World War II, but it saved mankind from the barbarous tyranny of Hitler. There was waste in our foreign aid program, but it saved Europe from communism. There was waste in the Korean War, but it saved the United Nations from the fate of its predecessors, saved Asia from unchecked aggression, and may well have prevented World War III. So, when the critics tell us that there is waste in the war on poverty, my reply is that if we can eliminate the vicious cycle of squalor, alienation, and dehumanization to which poverty has been condemning one-fifth of a nation, it is worth a little waste.

Let me say also that it is time we stopped taking the defensive on this issue and started taking the offensive. It is time we stopped analyzing our failure and started bragging about our successes. Many of these successes are right here in Kentucky. For example, permit me to announce to you tonight that 24,338 preschool youngsters will be enrolled in Head Start programs in 108 of our counties and will be attending clases for two months this summer. On the average last summer those young boys and girls added eight to ten points to their I.Q.s and fourteen months to their intellectual performances. Not least of Head Start's achievements has been to nip budding health problems by giving its children complete medical exams—their first in most cases.

Thus far in Kentucky some fifty-six neighborhood Youth Corps projects have been approved, providing thousands of needy teenagers with jobs in local libraries, parks, and other institutions so they could remain in school. Approximately 152 VISTA volunteers—commonly referred to as the "domestic Peace Corps"—have been assigned to Kentucky to live with our people and help them. They draw, as you know, fifty dollars a month plus a subsistence allowance, and have provided a real service in improving the lives of many Kentuckians.

Although there are many community action programs now underway in our state, let me cite two. The first is known as "Millstone" in Letcher County, and the area is made up of four creeks—Sergent, Thornton, Millstone, and Kona. The population is 1,603 persons, and over 50 percent of these families make less than $3,000 a year. The project involves the staffing of a sewing center that renovates donated clothes for needy children. Fourteen people are employed. Each year two or three trailer trucks deliver clothing donated by the Salvation Army. These clothes are remade and distributed to the needy children of the area. Because of this program, more of these children are staying in school, more of them are holding their heads high and mixing with their peers.

The second of these community projects is in Verda in Harlan County. The population is 1,350 and the average family income is less than $1,000 a year. The project is located at a community center and has three basic programs outside the center itself. There is a family development and service program, health education, and youth activity program. A fundamental goal of the community center program will be to provide activities which will directly increase the family incomes. This will be through the teaching of crafts, trades, and skills which will have income potential; through health and home management training which will offer persons more energy to devote to the making of an income by improved diet and family relations; and through cultural and enrichment activities which are so often necessary for income and financial management. These are but two of scores of programs that are helping Kentuckians enjoy a richer, fuller life.

There will come a time, in your lives and mine, when all this will be history. There was a time when men believed that disease was a scourge of God. Now we know better. There was a time when men believed that ignorance and illiteracy were the ordained lot of most men. Now we know better. There was a time when we believed that depressions, panics, and mass unemployment were a part of natural law. Now we know better. There was a time when men believed that destitution and expediency were the natural lot of the aged, the sick, and the unemployed. Now we know better.

Some day, not far off, we shall look back in pity and disbelief on a time when men believed that poverty, stark, grinding, soul-destroying poverty, was as much a part of the natural order as the sun, wind, and stars. Already we know better; soon we shall see better and do better. And when the victory comes, you may look back proudly on your part as combat veterans in another great war for the liberation of mankind.

---

1. Michael Harrington (1928-), noted political activist and author; associate editor of the *Catholic Worker* (1951-1952); organizational secretary of the Worker's Defense League (1953); professor of political science, Queens College, City University of New York (1972); member of national executive committee of the Socialist party (1960-1972). Harrington's most noted work, *The Other America,* was published in 1963. He examined poverty in the United States, devoting major attention to Appalachia. *Who's Who in America, 1976–1977,* 39th ed. (Chicago, 1976). Dwight McDonald (1906-), staff writer, *Fortune* (1929-1936); associate editor, *Partisan Review* (1937-1943); editor and publisher, *Politics* (1944-1949); staff writer, *New Yorker* magazine (1951-1971). *Who's Who in America, 1980-1981,* 41st ed. (Chicago, 1980).

RECOGNITION OF APPALACHIAN INDUSTRIES
Frankfort / February 2, 1967

THIS is an unusual gathering. Who would have dreamed a few years ago that in February, 1967, a special time would be set aside for recognition of the industries of Kentucky Appalachia. Then such an event would have been, to a marked degree, an empty gesture. Little of note in industrial growth had taken place in eastern Kentucky at that time. Today this recognition of new and expanded industry has real significance and bespeaks a bright promise for the future of eastern Kentucky. You, by your action to create a new industrial facility or to expand an existing one, have reacted in a positive manner to the resurgence of community spirit and leadership in Kentucky Appalachia. Your decision to produce here indicates an industrial future for eastern Kentucky well beyond our most optimistic expectations of the past.

Yesterday we had another gathering here at the state capitol. As you know, I invited the citizens of the Commonwealth to drop in and present to the governor and heads of departments their opinions, ideas, and gripes about state government. They came and it was quite a day. It was a day of real worth. Yesterday your state government, through personal contact, was responding to the needs and desires of the people. Today, in a real sense, we are responding to the needs of our industries. It is healthy that government do both.

During the past three years 133 industrial concerns have announced the location of new plants or the expansion of existing facilities in eastern Kentucky. The product range is wide and includes metals, transportation equipment, carpets, apparel, shoes, and flake board. These actions will create about 11,000 new jobs in manufacturing alone. Other jobs will, of course, be created in the supportive industries.

Total capital investment will total about $230 million, including the $100 million in new generating facilities by Kentucky Power Company. These 11,000 new jobs will generate at least $40 million annually in wages. This will mean in the neighborhood of $24 million in additional retail sales. This is big business. The most productive antipoverty program possible for Kentucky Appalachia is the creation of jobs. If there are adequate employment opportunities for our labor force at home, we can solve our problems.

People are, and have been for many years, the greatest resource for production in eastern Kentucky. This remains so despite heavy attrition by out-migration of population in past years. Today Kentucky Appalachia has a population of almost one million. The labor force totals about 225,000, which in terms of population is quite low. The area has about 25,000 manufacturing jobs at present, which is equal to less than 3 percent of the total population—a low ratio indeed. Now, in Kentucky as a whole 7 percent of the population is employed in manufacturing occupations. The figure for the nation is 10 percent. The relative scarcity of manufacturing activity in eastern Kentucky is a prime reason for low income and insufficient jobs. Your decision to locate here will be an important corrective measure in this regard.

Fantus Area Research in a recent evaluation, "Kentucky's Recruitable Labor Supply for Industry," estimated that in eastern Kentucky there is a current labor supply of about 50,000 men and 42,000 women between the ages of eighteen and forty-five who are available for industrial employment. During the school year there are also 50,000 students enrolled in high school. There are 1,500 from these counties enrolled in vocational education. College enrollment exceeds 12,000. Kentucky Appalachia today has manpower resources for greatly expanded industrial production;

and, furthermore, this current supply of labor will be augmented year by year by the entrance into the labor force of these youngsters now enrolled in high school, vocational, or college institutions. This resource is of particular significance in today's stringent labor market.

Every practical means will be used to carry the story of eastern Kentucky's labor supply to industrial leaders throughout the country. I am sure that you who are now in production in eastern Kentucky can attest to the productivity and trainability of your workers. You can be our most effective salesmen for the future.

Plentiful manpower resources, however, were not enough to create growth. The economic infrastructure of eastern Kentucky in years past was simply not adequate for efficient business and industrial operations. There was a scarcity of facilities—roads, streets, hospitals, schools, industrial sites—and also in local leadership and energy. But time has brought startling changes in this respect. There has been a resurgence and revitalization of local leadership for development throughout Kentucky Appalachia during the past few years. Local programs for growth have been formulated and aggressively implemented in numerous communities. These efforts have been given full support and assistance by Kentucky state government as well as by many agencies of the federal government. The result of this partnership between the governmental and private sectors has been creation of the framework and the basics for growth.

I don't have to elaborate in detail. You have seen the roads. You have seen the new and improved recreational facilities. You have seen the new schools—secondary, vocational, and community college. You have seen the new streets, the new sewers and water facilities that have been put in place. You have seen the construction of the basic infrastructure required for growth. You are aware that this has been possible only through concerted action of all segments of the economy. Federal programs—Economic Development Act, Appalachian Regional Commission, Hill-Burton—to mention just a few have been available to reinforce our state and local efforts. Forward planning and effective implementation have enabled Kentucky to effectively make use of this assistance.

Kentucky Appalchia during the past three years has participated in Kentucky's surge of growth to a gratifying extent. This has not always been the case. Your new plants operating there are proving to industrial leaders everywhere that eastern Kentucky is a good place in which to produce at a profit. We must be certain to take the steps necessary to fully consolidate and confirm this image.

Economic growth is a primary objective of Kentucky government. We are fully committed to legislative programs and departmental policies and procedures which facilitate growth and prosperity for business and industry. In keeping with the objective of growth and this philosophy, we intend to pay close attention to your problems of production and expansion. We will make available the full range of state government services in helping you arrive at solutions to your problems. I pledge to you, here and now, that this will be done. The Kentucky Department of Commerce, in particular, is available at all times to assist you and the communities in which you operate to develop the solutions required for your mutual advancement.

I have confidence in the economic future of eastern Kentucky. A noteworthy economic breakthrough has been made—but much yet remains to be done. We must have the wisdom, the vision, the courage to make the decisions for growth. Business and government working in partnership can do this. The choice is ours.

DEDICATION OF PUBLIC ASSISTANCE BUILDING

Jackson / February 6, 1967

BREATHITT County has benefited to the total amount of $3,860,021 in 1966 from programs administered by the Kentucky Department of Economic Security. Since the days in the 1930s when the federal and state government joined together to recognize that people are the ultimate asset this nation has, employees of this department have made available better health, better education and job opportunities to make possible the pursuit of happiness for all Americans as provided for by our founding fathers.

This building we dedicate today is a physical symbol of the cooperation between our national and state government in many programs conceived and put into action to actually help thousands and thousands of needy people to overcome their adversities and those who are now unable to help themselves.

Possibly there is no other single aspect of social legislation that has provided more needed help over the years than the program of public assistance, providing funds for buying food, paying rent, or buying clothes to keep children in school and to offer the less fortunate the advantages of medical services. That this program benefits Breathitt County is apparent to you, I'm sure.

In 1966 the average number of public assistance recipients in this county was 2,610 persons a month receiving a total of $1,404,900 per month, including $261,600 in medical assistance. This has provided funds to keep eligible families together as a unit, an objective with the most human of all motives, plus providing funds for better health.

Field workers from this office have crossed the creeks and gone up the hollows to work closely with the needy in order that the funds received are used in a wise and prudent way. The test of all programs reaching the people are the social workers' dedication to their responsibilities, and I know for sure that these in Breathitt County are meeting this test and making A plus for their effort.

Persons in need in Kentucky were remembered in 1966 through increases in the payments of public assistance, first in January with an average of $2 for adult cases and $4 for family cases, and again in July with average raises of $3 or $6 for adults and $16 for family cases.

This building represents an investment of some $155,000 in federal and state funds and has some 5,780 square feet of space. I want right here to congratulate William Blanton Moore, the architect, and Barco, Inc. of Lexington, the contractor, for planning and constructing this building.[1] It will be used wisely and well in serving this county.

I want to mention some of the other programs going on in this county that are administered by the Department of Economic Security and the Division of Public Assistance. The work experience and training program exists primarily to assist men who have been unemployed for ninety days or more to become more employable. The fathers or stepfathers must not be eligible for, nor be receiving any other public assistance payments nor unemployment insurance. They must be in reasonably good health and be available for and willing to accept a fair offer of employment. In this county there were an average of 489 unemployed parents being helped by the program in 1966, including 2,714 individuals in the entire families. While the training allowance is computed for each family on the amount of income compared with their real needs, the average payment during 1966 for all counties was $200, with another $15 worth of medical assistance services. The total of training allowances and medical assistance received here in 1966 was $1,426,200, including $1,256,200 in money payments and $170,000 in services to medical assistance vendors, such as doctors, hospitals, pharmacies, dentists, and nursing homes.

I don't want to remind you of all the projects these men finished in this county because of time. But some of the major highlights include some fourteen new forestry trails cut, and many more miles were maintained. More than 82,000 trees were planted; some 86 miles of county roads were built and 495 more were repaired. The fathers cleared another 1,340 miles of right of way in this county alone.

The food stamp program in Breathitt has provided fresh foods, a better choice of foods, plus protecting human dignity and using normal trade outlets, to an average of 4,125 persons per month during 1966. The total value of food stamps came to $767,100, with $292,500 of this a bonus to the food stamp recipients and to the local economy. A food stamp coupon will change hands many times just like cash before it is returned through the banking system of the federal government. Millions of dollars are being brought into Kentucky communities and spent locally because of the food stamp program. This is why a bonus of $292,500 is a stimulant to the local economy.

The Hazard office of the employment service, which has Breathitt County along with Knott, Leslie, Letcher and Perry, conducted 5,165 counseling interviews, 1,841 tests with 551 placements. Many of this total were from Breathitt County. Another service of the Department of Economic Security is finding the man to fit the job.

In an effort to bring the personnel of state government closer to the people, a full-time member of the employment service staff at Hazard is in this building to register those seeking employment, to file unemployment claims, and to screen applicants for the Job Corps and other training programs. Referrals are made to the Hazard office. This makes possible the full services of the employment service in Breathitt County. Also it serves residents of Lee, Owsley, Wolfe, and Powell counties who find this office closer than the one at Hazard.

Some $52,004 was paid to unemployed in this county in 1966 under direction of the unemployment insurance division. Also the Division of Personnel Security has administered social security payments and payments for the 420 employees in the five local agencies covered in this county. Wages totaled $297,825, and contributions were $25,017. The five local agencies of government [have] social security coverage contracts in the personnel security division in the Department of Economic Security.

The higher education program is finding high potential young persons from low income families and enrolling them in school. I am particularly pleased to state that of forty-four such students in Breathitt County last year six went on to college and one to vocational school. Looking to this year, surveys show that there are fifteen twelfth graders with excellent college potential; seventeen have average potential, and twenty-five have potential for and interest in vocational schools. The department has devised this joint federal-state program and has been able to convince federal agencies of its worth. In most instances each student going to college receives $70 per month, and those going to vocational school $30 per month. In many instances this is enough to keep the student in school or incentive enough for him to seek other sources of income while going to school.

---

1. William Blanton Moore (1919-), architect from Louisville, educated Massachusetts Institute of Technology, B.Arch. (1943); president of firm of William Blanton Moore and Associates (1955-). John F. Gane, ed., *American Architects Directory, 1970,* 3rd ed. (New York, 1970), p. 638.

TOURISM & RECREATION

DEDICATION OF NEW HEMLOCK LODGE
Natural Bridge State Park / June 24, 1964

THIS beautiful new lodge is a welcome addition to Kentucky's park system. It is a credit to the people of Kentucky. It is one more piece of evidence that Kentucky has the nation's outstanding state parks. New Hemlock Lodge is also a fitting and lasting tribute to the vision and the diligence of Bert Combs and to his administration of the affairs of Kentucky. While honoring Governor Combs, this building also honors those who were members of his state parks board—Henry Ward, John Ed Pearce, Herndon Evans, and Marvin Music—and those who guided the Department of Parks during the system's greatest period of expansion—Ed Fox, Tommy Nelson, and George Lyons.[1] I salute each of these gentlemen and others who had a part not only in the creation of this lodge but in the total park expansion that has taken place since 1960. Their work will be noted and cheered by Kentuckians for years to come.

I would also like at this time to offer my congratulations and thanks to the present commissioner of parks, Robert D. Bell, and to his staff for their work in getting this lodge in operation and for their work throughout the system to take care of an unprecedented number of guests this summer.[2]

The magnificent expansion of our facilities in the Kentucky park system was made possible by the general obligation bond issue of 1960 and the revenue bond issue of 1962. Together, these two issues provided $20 million dollars for capital development of our parks. These funds represent not only a wise investment which will benefit all Kentuckians as they use and enjoy these facilities; they also represent an investment which will repay our Commonwealth many times as we attract thousands upon thousands of visitors from other states to Kentucky.

Last year, the tourist and travel industry in Kentucky amounted to $320 million. Of this amount, $220 million came from visitors from out of state who also paid taxes into our state treasury which totaled $18.8 million. There is no doubt in my mind that the amount of funds spent on our state parks was a wise, a prudent, and a farseeing investment in Kentucky's future.

Temporarily, because of our fiscal position and because most of our building needs have been met for the present, we are in a period where an emphasis must be placed on operation and maintenance of existing parks. At the present time, there are no capital funds available for additional development of facilities within existing parks or for the development of new parks. This is a temporary condition. We will build again and we will build anew. The demand on the part of our citizens for recreational facilities is growing by leaps and bounds, and that demand must be met. If there is a doubt in anyone's mind that this demand will not grow and grow and grow, think about these statistics which recently appeared in a national report.

1. By the end of this century the population of the United States will nearly double—from 190 million persons today to 350 million in the year 2000.

2. By the end of this century people will have more time to spend on recreation. By the year 2000 it is estimated that the average workweek will be thirty-two hours and many Americans will work much shorter hours than this.

3. Americans will have more money to spend on recreation. Disposable consumer income will increase from $354 billion in 1960 to nearly one and a half trillion dollars in the year 2000.

4. Because of the increase of population, income, and free time, the recreation demands of Americans will more than triple in the next forty years.

5. The demands on facilities in Kentucky will be even greater than this because of its central location and its abundant water and because better roads and turnpikes will make Kentucky attractions more accessible to the population of the East and Middle West.

I have said that the fiscal limitation on building new park facilities is purely temporary. I can say this with confidence. There is presently pending before Congress, a land and water conservation fund which has excellent nationwide support and which, if passed, would provide federal funds to state and local governments for both planning and development of park and recreational facilities.[3] On May 5 of this year, I reaffirmed Kentucky's support of this act which Governor Combs had previously voiced. This bill would provide substantial funds to the Commonwealth of Kentucky for additional development of park and recreational facilities.

In November of 1965, the voters of Kentucky will be asked to approve a new general obligation bond issue in the total amount of $176 million. One hundred and forty million dollars of this would be devoted for highway purposes. The balance would be spread among several agencies—including the Department of Parks, which would gain an additional $4.5 million for park development from the proceeds of the bond issue. I am confident that the voters of Kentucky, when the advantages of the bond issue are explained to them, will approve this issue. As the events come to pass, Kentucky will move out again in park development and expansion. We are now the leading state and we intend to remain so.

In the meantime, we will plan and prepare ourselves for the park development which must occur if we are to keep up with the demands of Kentuckians and the out-of-state tourist. I have authorized the Department of Parks to enter into a contract with the Spindletop Research Center on at least two major studies. One of these studies will concern itself with the problem of lengthening our vacation, travel, and park season. Presently, 60 percent of the visitors to our parks and 70 percent of the receipts collected come in the three-month period from Memorial Day through Labor Day. If we are to maximize the use of our facilities and also make the maximum contribution to the tourist and travel industry in Kentucky, we must do everything in our power to lengthen the operating season within our parks. Spindletop will be asked to make a study in depth to see if there are programs or facilities which can be instituted to further this objective.

The provisions of the land and water conservation act I spoke of a minute ago will require any state, before it can obtain federal funds, to have a basic statewide recreational plan which properly assigns the responsibilities of various state and local agencies and spells out what facilities presently exist as well as what facilities will have to be added to meet the needs of the future. So as a second project Spindletop Research will be asked to work cooperatively with the various state agencies who are involved in this general program to develop such a study and a blueprint for our future needs.

Today has great significance for this section of Kentucky. To you who have lived near this beautiful park for many years and have supported it and loved it, I know that today's dedication is gratifying. Let me say that those of us from other parts of Kentucky are also pleased and thrilled that Natural Bridge State Park now has such a fine new facility and can do so much more to take care of its visitors. This building would never have come into being and this park would never have been the beautiful place it is now without the interest and perseverance of those of you who live in this neighborhood. I congratulate you and your friends and backers across the state. I thank you for your past interest and support; and I respectfully ask that this support, this interest, this love for Natural Bridge continue and that all of us help it live up to the possibilities presented by the building we dedicate today.

---

1. John Ed Pearce (1919-), newspaperman and author; graduate of the University of Kentucky; staff writer and columnist, *Louisville Courier-Journal* (1946 -); recipient of Nieman Fellowship for advanced study at Harvard University (1957); resident of Louisville. *Louisville Courier-Journal,* June 6, 1957. Herndon Evans (1895-1976), born Morehead, Kentucky; owner and editor, *Pineville Sun* (1923-1956); news editor for *Lexington Herald* (1956-1968). Information provided by *Lexington Herald.* Marvin Music (1914-), board member for public protection (1978-1979); resident of Prestonsburg, Kentucky. Information provided by Division of Personnel, Frankfort. Edward V. Fox (1918-), born Guthrie, Kentucky; business manager and assistant director with Department of Parks (1950-1956); commissioner and executive officer (1960-1969); resident of Frankfort. Information provided by Division of Personnel, Frankfort. Tommy Nelson (1907-), born Springfield, Ohio; architect, planner, assistant director, executive officer, and superintendent of operations, Department of Parks (1949-1968); resident of Frankfort. Information provided by Division of Personnel, Frankfort. George Lyons (1904-), served as city manager and city engineer, Covington, Kentucky; Kentucky Department of Highways (1939-1961); appointed to head Division of Construction and Maintenance (1961). *Louisville Courier-Journal,* December 30, 1961.

2. Robert D. Bell (1925-), executive assistant with Department of Conservation (1950-1954); executive assistant lieutenant governor's office (1959-1960); deputy commissioner of highways (1960-1963); commissioner of revenue (1963); commissioner of parks (1963-1967); commissioner of natural resources (1975-1976); board member, Council on Higher Education (1981-); currently a resident of Ashland. Information provided by Division of Personnel, Frankfort.

3. The Land and Water Conservation Fund Act established a special fund to promote rapid development of public recreational areas. Sixty percent of the fund would be distributed in matching grants to the states to help finance the acquisition of land and the construction of recreational facilities. The remaining 40 percent could be used by federal agencies to purchase land for recreation and conservation. The fund was to acquire revenues through the sale of federal property, through the federal motorboat fuel tax, and from newly authorized entrance and recreation user fees charged at federal land and recreation areas. In addition, for the first ten years of its twenty-five year statutory life, the fund was to receive special congressional appropriations. These were to be repaid in later years. The act also gave the secretary of the interior the authority to require states receiving fund grants to present a comprehensive statewide outdoor recreation plan and empowered the president to require coordination with federal projects. *Congressional Quarterly Almanac,* vol. 20 (1964), pp. 477-84.

KENTUCKY PETROLEUM CONVENTION
Gilbertsville / May 7, 1965

THIS is a fortunate time and an especially appropriate place to kick off the 1965 travel season. Kentucky has never been readier to welcome tourists. The Commonwealth is greener and cleaner than it has ever been before. We have many miles of magnificent interstate highways and a better state road system than we have ever known—including the Western Kentucky Parkway. We also have hundreds of first-rate tourist attractions and better accommodations to serve the travelers who come to see our great natural wonders, our historic shrines, and our prize recreation areas. And to top it off, this is "Kentucky Homecoming Year," when all of us are asking all our old Kentucky friends and kinfolks who wandered off to come back home and see us and see just how well we are doing.[1] Already more than sixty communities throughout the state are planning special homecoming celebrations.

I understand that the 101st Airborne Division at Fort Campbell has just announced its homecoming—and that should be a real big one on August 14. Another big one in this area will be held at the Fulton Banana Festival in October.[2] And Paducah has so much going on they can't hold it all to one date. Kentucky Lake itself will be the headquarters July 4 for the homecoming celebration for former residents of Birmingham, which, as you know, is now under the waters of the lake.

This is an especially appropriate place to kick off the travel season, too. The fifteen-county area comprising your Kenlake district is home of one of the outstanding stars in Kentucky's travel crown—this great Kentucky Lake recreation complex and its developing neighbor, Barkley Lake. And although it is still in the short pants stage, the 170,000-acre National Recreation Area Between the Lakes will open its Rushing Creek camping and day-use area next Saturday.[3]

To give you an idea of the tourist potential of this new spot, 12,000 visitors from twenty states last summer launched Rushing Creek's first season while it was still under construction, and this year Rushing Creek will have three times as many campsites. When the total lake and recreation area is fully developed there won't be a spot in America to top the vacation appeal of western Kentucky. Our big and still growing western Kentucky recreation area is one reason that the travel business in Kentucky is getting bigger every year—and still growing at a higher rate than other states. Last year travelers from other states spent $238 million in Kentucky, which was $18 million more than they spent the year before.

Another reason for Kentucky's increase in travel business is that we make it our business to get this business. We advertise nationally to promote our outstanding resort park system—our bounty of running waters—our famous attractions and our unique scenery. We set up travel booths just about anywhere they will let us in—as far away as Canada. We show films about Kentucky, we tell stories about Kentucky, we feed people Kentucky ham, we pass out folders; and we wind up making so much racket about Kentucky that a stranger might think he was wasting his entire honeymoon if he didn't take it at Kentucky Lake—and that's just what we want him to think. Because that's what we believe. Kentucky's tourist promotion is a vigorous program because it has to be. Like the Avis Company, our buttons read: "We Have to Try Harder."[4] Kentucky got off to a late start in competing for the tourist dollar. We're running strong now, but we still have a long way to go just to catch up.

We are pleased that visitors from other states now bring in an average of seventy-nine dollars a year for every Kentucky citizen; that's twice what they brought us thirteen years ago. But other states are now joining the pack. Indiana and Ohio, for instance, have been hurting so bad from their people coming down here that they are setting up a hue and cry of their own, and will soon be major competition for us. So we keep trying harder. The homecoming promotion is one of our efforts to keep ahead of the pack. Another way we try harder is to promote travelers off the interstate highways and off the turnpikes and get them out to see the numerous attractions distributed all over the state. Five information centers are already operating on the interstates. Twenty-two more will be built and put into operation.

The new travel matching advertising fund is another effort in this direction. The 1964 legislature allocated $115,000 to match regional money raised to promote local attractions. The program goes into effect July 1, and I understand the region centered here has already made an aggressive push; that you will be asking for all you are eligible for and more. That's good. That's the way the plan was designed to work. Each region needs its own program and literature because each region knows its own attractions best. New advertising materials produced from the matching fund can be placed in the rest areas and information centers on the interstate highways and parkways. From the results already in, it looks like the matching fund will have to stretch itself to keep up with the demand for material about off-highway attractions.

This demand for information is an encouraging sign that 1965 will be another banner year for Kentucky travel business. And as you members of the petroleum industry know, that means a banner year for the gasoline business because travel business and gasoline business go together like catfish and hushpuppies. As Kentucky travel business has grown, so has gasoline business: in 1963 your volume of $267 million was triple the 1948 volume. Surveys show that your business took another increase in 1964, 7.5 percent, up to a new total of $287 million. And since the travel end of your business represents 12 percent of your total sales, you have a heavy investment in Kentucky's travel future.

But if Kentucky travel and gasoline volume go up the hill together, like Jack and Jill, they can do down together, too. I have already pointed out that other states are coming on fast in the run for the tourist dollar. The warning is clear. If Kentucky slows down now, the competition will be ready to go out in front.

We do not intend to slow down. In fact, we intend to increase the pace. We are going to continue to go after this business. Our Commonwealth is within 500 miles of an estimated seventy million Americans. That is one-third of the nation's population—and we intend to make Kentucky boosters out of every one of them. I know that many of you are Kentucky's best salesmen and that you make a real effort to get travelers to stay in Kentucky longer. I particularly want to say what a fine, capable job Tom Maxedon is doing through the Kentucky Petroleum Council to bring more tourists.[5] I'm glad Kentucky has the benefit of Tom's efforts.

And as partners in Kentucky's travel business each of you can help by giving full support to your region's matching advertising fund plans; by telling everyone you know that this is homecoming year, and by working to get your communities to plan homecoming activities. And your project does not have to be elaborate, just sincere. You can also help by adding your personal voice to the promotion of Kentucky's tourist appeal. Countless Kentuckians travel out of state without ever having seen Kentucky Lake or Mammoth Cave. You can also help by supporting beautification and cleanup projects to keep Kentucky attractive. This is one of the best ways to insure that tourists will want to come back and see us again.

If we do these things together, the natural beauty of our Commonwealth and the inborn graciousness of our people will do the rest. If we do these things together, our tourist industry in Kentucky will grow as bountifully as Kentucky Lake bass. You and I know there is no better place to vacation in America than right here in Kentucky. Let's all go out and tell everyone we see.

---

1. Governor Breathitt declared 1965 as "Kentucky Homecoming Year" by executive order.

2. The annual Fulton Banana Festival was inaugurated in 1963 by the twin cities of Fulton, Kentucky, and South Fulton, Tennessee. The celebration's theme derived from Fulton's central role in the distribution of Central American bananas to mid-American markets. The railroads brought large banana shipments north

from importers in New Orleans to the rail center in Fulton, where they were stored and then distributed to the rest of the country. The festival was intended to bring national and international recognition of the city's role in commerce. Political and business leaders from Kentucky and Tennessee as well as representatives from foreign countries and the U.S. State Department have attended the festival, which featured parades, oratory, beauty pageants, cooking contests, and other activities. *The Fulton News,* September 5, 1963.

3. The Land Between the Lakes national recreation area occupies a narrow peninsula formed by the shores of Kentucky Lake and Lake Barkley and the canal which connects them. Kentucky Lake was created in 1944 by the construction of Kentucky Dam, the final dam located on the Tennessee River before it intersects the Ohio at Paducah, Kentucky. Lake Barkley was formed twenty years later by impounding a section of the Cumberland River which runs roughly parallel to the Tennessee in West Kentucky. Though both lakes were created for the purposes of flood control, improved navigation, and hydroelectric power generation, it became evident that the completion of Barkley Dam would make the already singular "Land 'Twixt the Rivers" area an unusually promising region for recreational and conservation programs. After much debate in the early sixties, the Tennessee Valley Authority assumed the task of developing the 170,000 acre area, which already contained approximately 70,000 acres of government-owned land, including the Kentucky Woodlands Wildlife Refuge. The Tennessee Valley Authority's plans for purchase included all private property in the area and the concommitant destruction of its small towns, such as Golden Pond. The relatively unspoiled land which was incorporated into the Land Between the Lakes has been employed by the Tennessee Valley Authority for conservation, wildlife management, educational and recreational purposes, and has become a major element in Kentucky's tourist industry. The economic value of the tourist industry to Kentucky was compared by Cattie Lou Miller, commissioner of the Department of Public Information in 1965, to "a second tobacco crop." Kentucky spent approximately $40 million from 1948 to 1965 to develop its state parks with the attraction of out-of-state tourists as a major goal. A 1965 report prepared for the Department of Public Information assessed the economic benefits of the park system. The report estimated during the previous year the state had attracted twenty-two million visitors who spent $238 million in Kentucky. Marguerite Owen, *The Tennessee Valley Authority* (New York, 1973), pp. 125, 140-141, 196. See also *Louisville Courier-Journal,* August 15, 1965.

4. Avis, Inc., lagging far behind Hertz in the car rental industry, struck a responsive cord with its advertising slogan "We're only number two: We have to try harder." The phrase became a common part of American speech, Avis became a household word, and the company quickly increased its rentals 28 percent. *Time,* July 24, 1964, pp. 77-78.

5. Thomas H. Maxedon (1924-), born in Alamo, Tennessee; reared in Paducah, Kentucky; B.A. University of Kentucky (1948); graduate study in economics, Michigan State University; motor fuel tax administrator, Kentucky Department of Revenue (1952-1958); executive director, Kentucky Petroleum Council (1958-); resident of Anchorage, Kentucky. Telephone inverview, March 1, 1981.

KENTUCKY TRAVEL COUNCIL
Louisville / February 16, 1966

On taking office two years ago, I pledged to you a partnership for progress between the state administration and all of you interested in the development and promotion of Kentucky's travel industry. I meet with you today in a spirit of rejoicing and of strong resolve: I rejoice that the past two years have brought the greatest increase in tourist spending in Kentucky in the state's history. I resolve that during the next two years we shall, with your cooperation, make the strongest effort Kentucky has ever made to attract the tourist to our state, and give him his full dollar's worth while he is here.

It is with great pleasure that I release today to you and to the press the seventh annual Kentucky Tourist Report, prepared by Dr. Lewis C. Copeland, University of Tennessee economist and travel industry expert.[1] This report shows that during 1965 Kentucky set new travel industry records. Kentucky has a 9 percent growth in spending in Kentucky by people from other states, and for the first time we passed the quarter-billion dollar mark in tourist income. Twenty-four million bona fide tourists—that is, travelers who come to Kentucky from other states—spent $260 million on their visits here in 1965. This increase of two million people and $22 million over 1964 exceeds any previous increase in Kentucky's tourist business.

For the fifth consecutive year the rate of growth of tourist spending in Kentucky has exceeded the national rate of growth. The tourist also paid a larger share of our tax burden, with travelers from other states contributing $22 million in Kentucky state taxes—6 percent of state revenue collections. The dollars tourists spend are "new" dollars. They are doubly welcome because they put new money into circulation.

Traveling in Kentucky by Kentuckians also increased last year. All travel spending—including Kentuckians and tourists from other states—rose to $378 million. The travel and transportation business for Kentucky rose to $876 million. It is safe to predict that the travel and transportation business (lodging, eating, recreation facilities, auto servicing, and rail, bus, and air passenger carriers) will become a billion-dollar industry in Kentucky by 1967. Doctor Copeland's statistics go on—but these are sufficient to tell you that the tidings are good. Kentucky's banner for the tourist industry is high, and for most of the 14,670 Kentucky firms serving travelers business was better in 1965 than it has ever been.

As beautiful as Kentucky is, this growth in our travel industry does not happen through accident. Tourists are choosing Kentucky because you, as business people, are getting them with warm hospitality and giving them full value for the money they spend. They are choosing Kentucky because

Kentucky is building a great road system, and because we have the nation's best parks system and are creating more parks and recreation areas, lakes, and other needed attractions. And they are choosing Kentucky because the Bluegrass State is thumping its drum effectively. I am as proud as you are that Kentucky's Department of Public Information won the Midwest Travel Writers' Association's top 1965 award for the best travel promotion job in America, and that they tied with the Bahamas News Bureau for the top international honor. In future years more tourists will come to Kentucky because of the action Kentucky has taken to protect our scenery and prevent damage caused by strip mining.

But the competition for the tourist dollar grows stronger, both in our nation and in the world. As Kentucky moves to retain and increase her share, let us decide together about where we go from here—what needs doing?—and how do we get it done? Looking at the future of our travel industry, I consider the strongest tool at our command to be the bond of cooperation and hard work between all who want to see the industry grow. Cooperation made the 1965 homecoming year a success, with more than 400,000 nonresident Kentuckians coming home, and more than 116 communities holding major homecoming events. I doubt that any promotion in America has produced more dollars and cost less than Kentucky's 1965 homecoming year. Cooperation has keyed the success of Kentucky's travel advertising matching fund program. Regions have gone together in united promotion efforts, and I am glad we can continue this program in the state budget for the remainder of my administration. The same sort of cooperation has worked effectively as we have joined with other governments in efforts such as the Lincoln Heritage Trail promotion. In 1965, 87,000 more people registered at Lincoln Memorial in Hodgenville than the record high of 284,585 chalked up in 1964.

Next, we need to keep pace with our growth. To this end, the state parks system opens the 1966 travel season with extensive renovations and new facilities completed and with plans for more to come. We have dedicated a new park at Fort Boonesborough, and plan $500,000 more in development there. We will move as quickly as possible with the new Barren River State Park and Lake Barkley State Park, both being developed as major resort park facilities. Perryville Battlefield will welcome visitors this year with a new museum. Audubon and Pine Mountain state parks will open new golf courses. Kenlake Hotel has been thoroughly modernized, as has the auditorium at Kentucky Dam Village. In total, we will put in use this spring eighty-eight new rooms at our resort lodges, 160 covered boat slips and 430 new sites for tents and trailers.

Private facilities are also growing and need to move at a greater rate to capitalize on the potential of our growing tourist industry. This is the year for Kentucky businessmen to work with each other and with the state and national parks to take full advantage of this growth. Let every lodging point any overflow of customers to some other Kentucky lodging. Don't let our customers drift across the borders and away from Kentucky cash registers.

Next, we need to get ready to greet—this year and every year—the influx of tourists with our grass the bluest, our fences the whitest, our signs the most inviting, and ourselves and our fellow Kentuckians the most knowledgeable we have ever been about Kentucky and its great attractions. Let's have Kentucky shining like a new penny before the Derby, and let's keep it that way all year, as we direct our best effort toward making each succeeding year a greater and better year for Kentucky.

---

1. Lewis C. Copeland, resident of Knoxville,Tennessee; associate professor of statistics, University of Tennessee (1953-); author of numerous works on tourism and the travel industry. W. Landis Jones, ed., *The Public Papers of Governor Wendell H. Ford, 1971-1974* (Lexington, Ky. 1978), p. 457. Copeland prepared a series of reports on tourism in Kentucky during the administrations of Governors Combs, Breathitt, Nunn, and Ford.

BARKLEY PARK STATEMENT
Fort Campbell / July 23, 1966

PRESIDENT JOHNSON's announcement today that a federal grant totaling more than $3.9 million has been approved by the Economic Development Administration to help Kentucky develop a major new resort complex at Barkley Lake State Park is good news for the Commonwealth.[1] It is one of the largest grants ever made by the Economic Development Administration.

State funds on a matching basis will be provided to build one of the most beautiful and finest parks in our system—a park to which all Kentuckians can point with pride. Total cost of the park project will be $7,945,000. The state's share will come from proceeds of the 1965 general obligation bond issue, a new revenue bond issue, the governor's contingency fund, and other state appropriations.

Much of the preliminary architectural and engineering work on the new lodge already has been done, and we also have obtained 1,800 acres of land for the park from the U.S. Army Corps of Engineers. We plan to have dirt flying and concrete being poured on the lodge before the summer is over.

To President Johnson and our federal government, we of Kentucky want to express our genuine appreciation. This new park will boost the economy of western Kentucky and will provide a fine resort complex for a growing United States population in need of recreational opportunities. With this new park, plus the many fine facilities already in this area surrounding Barkley and Kentucky lakes, both public and private, this region is rapidly becoming the greatest tourist attraction in mid-America.

The new park will feature a 124-unit, circular-shaped resort lodge designed by world-famous architect Edward Durrell Stone, fifteen modern vacation cottages, a multipurpose recreation building with outdoor game courts and square-dancing facilities, two golf courses, two beaches, picnicking and other day-use areas, all set in the scenic splendor on the shores of Lake Barkley.[2]

The main dining room will seat 300 guests with banquet accommodations for as many as 400 persons. Also to be available in the lodge are meeting rooms, lounges, and recreation rooms. Guests in each lodge room will have a lake view, and the lodge will feature a guest swimming pool. Two beaches will offer excellent swimming, including one which will serve day users and campers. The other will be for lodge and cottage guests. Also a bathhouse will be constructed to serve the day users.

The multiuse activity and recreation center will have a potential of seating 300 persons for meetings. It will also contain a snack bar, washroom facilities, and projection rooms for the showing of movies, slides, and educational exhibits. In addition, there will be an open-roofed pavilion for square dancing and other recreational activities. Also in the complex will be tennis courts, a multipurpose court for other outdoor games, shuffleboard courts, and a minature golf course. Two large picnic areas with four picnic shelters, each with sanitary facilities, are planned, along with necessary tables and grills. Abundant parking will be located near the picnic areas. Vacation cottages will balance out the lodge accommodations. Cottages will contain a living-dining room area, kitchen, bath, and minimum of two bedrooms.

It is proper that I pay tribute to Congressmen Stubblefield and Natcher and other members of our congressional delegation for their help in securing this grant.[3] Credit is due also to former Senator Earle C. Clements, who helped shape the idea for Barkley Dam, which impounds giant Barkley Lake.[4] Parks Commissioner Robert Bell and his deputy, Ed Fox, also should receive plaudits for their role in making this grant possible for what will be the showplace of our state park system.

The tourist industry in Kentucky is booming. Statistics bear this out. In studies made by Dr. Lewis C. Copeland, an economist, the tourist and travel industry in Kentucky was worth more than $375 million last year. This represents an increase in spending of $106 million since 1959, when the first Copeland report on tourist spending in Kentucky was published. Attendance to our state parks has more than tripled over this period, thanks to those who saw the need for a vigorous parks expansion program and pushed hard to win such a program. Attendance at all parks in 1959 was an estimated five million visitors. Last year the attendance figure had swelled to more than fifteen million.

---

1. The land for Barkley State Park was donated to the Commonwealth by the U.S. Corps of Engineers. President Johnson provided the Breathitt administration with funds to construct the park. State development of the Lake Barkley resort area was hotly contested by private interests in west Kentucky anxious to use the site for private development. Breathitt interview, June 10, 1980.

2. Edward Durell Stone, Jr. (1932-), B.A. in Architecture, Yale University (1954); president, Edward D. Stone, Jr. and Associates, Ft. Lauderdale, Florida (1960-); recipient of numerous awards in architecture. *Who's Who in America, 1980-1981,* 41st ed. (Chicago, 1980). Governor Breathitt first saw Stone's work on a visit to west Kentucky. Stone was the architect for Paducah's award-winning city hall. He was subsequently employed by the Breathitt administration to provide designs for several state buildings, leaving many structural and mechanical details to be worked out by state-employed engineers and architects. Breathitt interview, June 10, 1980.

3. Frank Albert Stubblefield (1907-1977), born in Calloway County, Kentucky; B.S., University of Kentucky (1932); retail drug business, Murray, Kentucky (1933-1977); U.S. Navy (1944-1945); Kentucky Railroad Commission (1951-1955); U.S. House of Representatives (1959-1976). *Biographical Directory of the American Congress, 1774-1971* (Washington, 1971), p. 1772. William H. Natcher, federal conciliation commission, western district of Kentucky (1936-1937); county attorney, Warren County, Kentucky (1937); U.S. House of Representatives (1953-). *Who's Who in American Politics, 1975-1976,* 5th ed. (New York, 1975).

4. Earle Chester Clements (1896-), teacher and coach Morganfield High School (1920-1931); judge, Union County (1934-1941); Kentucky Senate (1942-1944); U.S. House of Representatives (1944-1947); governor of Kentucky (1947-1950); U.S. Senate (1950-1956). Robert A. Powell, *Kentucky Governors* (Frankfort, Ky., 1976), p. 100.

BARKLEY DAM DEDICATION
Gilbertsville / August 20, 1966

ON behalf of three million Kentuckians, Mr. Vice President, I welcome you to Kentucky and to an area that is destined to become mid-America's greatest outdoor recreational region.[1] We are proud to join with you, the Corps of Engineers, and all the others who had a part in creating this magnificent Barkley Dam in dedication ceremonies here today. This occasion marks another great milestone in the progress of Kentucky.

This multiple-purpose project, costing approximately $145 million, has provided a giant lake extending some 118 miles into the neighboring state of Tennessee. The importance of this dam and lake to our economy cannot be stressed too much. Plentiful and cheap electric power to serve homes and businesses, and to turn the wheels of industry, is an essential for the growth and prosperity of Kentucky. Recreational use alone will bring hundreds of thousands of additional tourists to our Commonwealth, adding greatly to the business of those who deal with tourists.

Much untold human misery and financial disaster caused by uncontrolled and ravaging floods will be avoided in the future because of this dam and others like it in the Cumberland Valley. And, certainly, the navigation improvements provide a deeper and wider channel for shipping.

This is the kind of project to which Alben Barkley would want his name attached and remembered.[2] Alben Barkley understood that government has the express purpose of helping the people of America help themselves —"to promote the general welfare," as it says in the Constitution. No engineering structure is truly capable of symbolizing the greatness of the man Alben Barkley, but in a small way for generations to come this great dam and great lake will honor his life, which so ably served his state and nation in public office for more than fifty years.

It is fitting and proper that we also pay tribute to another man—a man with whom I share this platform. Without the strong support, the constant urging, and the hard work of Senator Earle Clements, this great dam might not be in existence today. To him, we express our gratitude. And, above all, we express our appreciation to our United States government and our democratic system which has been so generous to this entire area.

Now, my fellow Kentuckians, it is my great pleasure and honor to present to you our neighbor from the Volunteer State of Tennessee—a man who three times has served his state as governor, being elected first at the age of thirty-two, a chief executive who has done much for Tennessee, a man who has just won Democratic nomination to the United States Senate —my friend, the Honorable Frank Clement, governor of Tennessee.[3]

---

1. The reference is to Hubert H. Humphrey.
2. Alben William Barkley (1877-1956), lawyer from Graves County, Kentucky; prosecuting attorney, McCracken County, Kentucky (1905-1909); judge, McCracken County (1909-1913); member, U.S. House of Representatives (1913-1927); member, U.S. Senate (1927-1949); vice president of the United States (1949-1953). Robert Sobel, ed., Biographical *Directory of the United States Executive Branch, 1774-1977* (Westport, Conn., 1977), p. 17.
3. Frank Goad Clement (1920-), attorney in Nashville and Dickson, Tennessee (1946-1950); governor of Tennessee (1953-1959, 1963-1967). *Who's Who in America, 1966-1967,* 34th ed. (Chicago, 1966).

KENTUCKY TRAVEL CONFERENCE
Louisville / February 15, 1967

It is always a pleasure to meet with you at the annual Kentucky Travel Conference because I am always able to share good news with you. Travel in Kentucky today is big business. It is a pleasure for me to be able to report to you that the travel business in Kentucky is not only helping meet our needs for recreation, additional open space, preservation of our outstanding heritage, and improved use of our water supply—but is continuing to bring more and more millions in cash dollars for our economy from tourists from other states.

I have just received and am glad to share with you the eighth annual Kentucky tourist report on travel spending, prepared for us by Dr. Lewis C. Copeland, University of Tennessee economist and travel expert. I am pleased to announce that 1966 was a record year—a boom year for tourist spending in Kentucky. In 1966 twenty-six million tourists from other states spent $295 million in Kentucky. That's 13 percent more than in 1965. This increase of $35 million in a single year is a far greater increase than in any previous year. This year's increase was, in fact, equal to the amount of increase in any four-year period between 1954 and 1963. The report shows that increased efforts to bring tourists to Kentucky—an emphasis I promised during my campaign for governor—is paying off.

Here are a few of the highlights from Dr. Copeland's preliminary report on 1966 travel spending.

1. All travelers (including Kentuckians and tourists from other states) spent $425 million in 1966. This amounts to 9 percent of Kentucky's total retail business receipts.

2. Spending in Kentucky by tourists from other states has increased 119 percent since 1954.

3. In Kentucky 74,300 people are employed in serving and transporting travelers—that's about one-seventh of the total employment opportunities in Kentucky's private commerce.

4. Much of the income from tourists is paid out in salaries; tourists from other states contributed $98 million to Kentuckians' personal income; also, $24 million to Kentucky state revenue, which amounts to 6 percent of all state revenue collections. Another $5 million of county and city taxes also traces to the tourist trade.

5. The total travel service and transport industry reported receipts of $969 million during 1966, and it is obvious that this figure will reach one billion dollars before I leave office.

Those here at the Kentucky Travel Conference know that this growth took teamwork. It is the result of hard work on the part not only of your government but also on the part of private investors, civic organizations, and individual citizens who have joined efforts to develop the travel industry and tell the story of the wonders of Kentucky as far as the message can reach.

In 1966 Kentucky's national advertising and promotion program created the rather amazing total of over one billion reader impressions for Kentucky's vacation attractions. This program won for Kentucky's Department of Public Information the top award for the best travel promotion program in the United States from the National Association of Travel Organizations. The Midwest Travel Writers Association also gave us the national award for the most creative travel promotion ideas in the country. And they haven't seen anything yet. Wait until Kentucky gets a chance to show Kentucky's special brand of hospitality to the Midwest Travel Writers when they come to Kentucky Dam Village in May for their spring meeting.

We are pledging that 1967 is going to be even greater for travel in Kentucky than any year yet. As a candidate for governor I pledged to work for a goal of $300 million annual tourist spending in Kentucky before I leave office. We nearly reached it last year. We'll exceed it this year. Here are some of the plans for coming months. The state has approved $18.8 million in parks projects to be started during the year. This will include more than $3.4 million worth of major construction at Barren River State Park near Glasgow. This fine family resort park will have a fifty-room lodge and all the facilities that have made our parks known as the best in America. Another great new park—I think it will be the greatest in America—is being developed on the east shore of Lake Barkley. We are also air-conditioning all the guest cottages at the resort parks and at John James Audubon State Park. And we are adding more camping areas, particularly at Rough River, General Butler, and Levi Jackson. DuPont Lodge at Cumberland Falls will be completely renovated and the park there will get a large pool. A new lodge is also scheduled for Greenbo Lake.

Throughout the system the 1967 story is the same: new playgrounds, more golf courses, pools, museums, and a general expansion of the popular recreation program. We are painting up, fixing up, shining up, and building to keep this fine system of thirty-five parks and shrines up-to-date and up to snuff.

We are also adding lakes. With all the water Kentucky enjoys—more miles of navigable streams than any state excepting Alaska—you wouldn't think we'd need any more; but we do. Kentucky and other states south of the Ohio and east of the Mississippi will one day become the "water basket" for an increasingly parched American civilization. And of course, every time we add a reservoir of water we are adding to our recreation assets.

The U.S. Engineers expect to have the 20,000-acre Cave Run Reservoir filled in Kentucky's northeast gateway region by 1968. This will create Kentucky's fourth largest lake and provide for additional recreation opportunities for the state and economic development for the people of the area.

During the year the state will make several additions to its chain of small lakes. In our great "western waterland," where we are building Lake Barkley State Park, the Tennessee Valley Authority is doing an excellent job of developing the 170,000-acre Land Between the Lakes National Recreation Area. The Tennessee Valley Authority tells us that visitor response to the initial development indicates that this region will soon draw more tourists than the nation's most popular national park, Great Smoky Mountains. Five million, four hundred thousand people visited Land Between the Lakes in 1965, and TVA still has three years to go on their minimum plans. In addition to two camping areas open there now, one of the major facilities is the youth activities station where school groups can stay for up to two weeks to learn about nature and enjoy this unspoiled preserve.

Local governments, private groups, and individual citizens are working just as hard to develop the resources in their sections. In our Bluegrass region, tourists are visiting Shakertown at a growing rate even while the $2 million renovation is still going on. At Danville, where our government was launched, plans are under way for an expansion of Constitution Square. The enlarged attraction will encompass a major section of downtown Danville. The Bluegrass Trust in Lexington is working hard in cooperation with state government to acquire the home of Mary Todd Lincoln. And over at Richmond, we hope to add to the growing list of notable restored homes historic Whitehall, where our nineteenth century Cassius Clay lived out his famour life.

Historical societies throughout the Commonwealth are helping to bring Kentucky's colorful background into the foreground. The society at Harrodsburg has done a fine job to spur restoration of Morgan Row. They took one of the five row houses and restored it for their headquarters and a public museum. This step was followed by the public library obtaining two of the others for their headquarters. We all hope that the remaining two will be purchased by groups willing to share our heritage with the public. Colonel George Chinn, director of our state historical society, tells me that the historical society is going to reproduce a number of Paul Sawyier's works so that more and more people can enjoy color prints of his beautiful, nostalgic scenes of our state.[1] The Kentucky Historical Society will be looking for your cooperation in marking Kentucky's 175th anniversary year. Interesting events can, with proper publicity, bring added tourist money to our state.

The Kentucky Heritage Commission will this year begin its program for marking buildings of historic or architectural interest. Kentucky truly has a great tradition of eighteenth and nineteenth century culture and I am very glad to see these efforts to maintain our heritage.

The new travel world in Kentucky would be lost to all of us and the growing millions of tourists without the continued growth of our fine road system. In 1966 we ranked second in the nation in the number of miles of road construction let to contract. At year-end we had 470 miles of interstate open to traffic or under construction. We still have 270 miles to go in this system. In the Appalachian development highway program we have been approved for 413 miles, and we have already started on 51 more than any other participating state. We are also pushing forward with our parkway system, counting 70 miles under construction of the 107 miles in the two new toll roads we are building.

Important adjuncts of the road building and tourist promotion program are the information centers and rest areas we are constructing to encourage travelers to stay longer in Kentucky. These centers are effective tools which help increase the stay of the interstate traveler. The center at Shepherdsville on the Kentucky Turnpike registered over 30,000 people who came to the center to get travel information on Kentucky attractions last year. Over 25,000 registered at Pineville. Even the newest information center on the Western Kentucky Parkway is already getting heavy use. Another center at the intersection of the Mountain Parkway and U.S. 23 in Prestonsburg is 99 percent complete and will open this spring.

Next week we will open bids for an interstate highway information center and rest area in Boone County to serve tourists arriving in Kentucky by I-75 south through Cincinnati. Three other rest areas are under construction on I-75 now. These are in Boone County (northbound lane) and in Scott County (one northbound, one southbound). They are 90 percent complete and should open in about a month. Four rest areas on I-64 are already in operation. And the Highway Department expects to get at least three more centers in operation this year on interstate highways. Ken Arnold, who is director of roadside development for the Highway Department, is here, I believe.[2] He has furnished this drawing of the center to be built on I-75 in Boone County this spring.

Just as government is helping prepare for the traveler in Kentucky, so is private business. In four years private investors have added some 4,000 modern motel rooms to our hospitality picture—an investment in rooms alone of $24 million. This does not include the additional investment in new restaurants, swimming pools, and service facilities for the 106 new motels built by private capital during this period.

Kentucky's travel industry has never experienced a greater period of growth, development, and productivity. The belief shared by yourselves and many other far-sighted Kentuckians that our state could and should develop a substantial tourist industry has proven to be soundly based. So soundly based, in fact, that I nearly dropped my teeth when I read a January 18 news account of a report submitted to the Appalachian Regional Commission by two consulting firms assigned to explore the role of the recreation industry in economic development. According to the news account, the report amounts to a smear on the practicality and economic worth of the whole tourist industry. The news story quotes the report as concluding that development of the recreation industry in Appalachia would be a costly mistake. Such a report, if it goes unchallenged, could, in my opinion, discourage investment in the recreation industry both by the federal government and private capital. I have not yet seen the report. But if the news account is correct, I can tell you now that I sharply disagree with some of the conclusions it suggests, and I challenge those conclusions on behalf of Kentucky and our growing tourist industry.

I believe that such a study, were it fairly and properly done, absolutely must conclude that the development of Kentucky's tourist industry—including eastern Kentucky's tourist industry—is a positive must to the proper development of this region's economy. I fail to see, in fact, how such a report, if perceptive, could avoid a conclusion that recreational and industrial development of this area are so closely related as to be practically interdependent. We have learned from experience that just as sure as prospective industry asks about transportation and education it also asks what recreation facilities are available. We do not contend that tourism is the total answer for Appalachia—any more than industry alone, or mining alone, or agriculture alone, is the total answer. But it is an important part of the answer.

I am not encouraged to think that the report was either carefully drawn or perceptive when I am told that the newest Copeland report it considers on Kentucky was the report for 1961. This is downright difficult to understand when five annual economic surveys of Kentucky's tourist industry have been made by Dr. Copeland since 1961 and copies are immediately available and free for the asking. Why did consultants work from a dust-covered report from 1961—a year tourists from other states spent $193 million in Kentucky—when they could instead have considered 1966—the year in which the figure has already reached $295 million?

The news story of the report discounts the recreation industry as being seasonal. If we try to improve Appalachia's economy by discarding every enterprise that is seasonal, we will end up with a lot more hungry people than we have now. By such a line of reasoning, agriculture, for example, would be a discard. Certainly everyone agrees that, seasonal or not, agriculture is worth investing in and deserves to be developed to the fullest extent of our ability.

Tobacco has long ranked as Kentucky's number one cash crop and is properly valued as a vital part of our economy. Opining from their ivory tower, the consultants apparently did not discover that tourists from other states spent more in Kentucky in 1966 than the Kentucky farmer got for his entire tobacco crop—burley, dark fired, and all other varieties included. Nor did they discover, apparently, that the same thing had already become true in 1965.

The consultants' report, according to the same news story, brushes aside the tourist industry because wages are low. Certainly all of us recognize that wages should and will improve as the industry grows. The report, apparently, ignores the new federal minimum-wage law which provides immediate improvements in the salaries of many in the recreation and tourist industry. It apparently also ignores that one of the finest traits of the industry is that a great part (about one-third) of tourist dollars goes into salaries and provides personal income for Kentuckians.

If through the years Kentucky had taken the attitude the report apparently suggests, there could well be 23,000 fewer jobs in our state today. That is the number of jobs Dr. Copeland says are created by the $295 million tourists from other states spent in Kentucky in 1966. If Kentucky—and those of you who are expert in this field—had adopted that attitude you and I would not be in this room today. There would be no travel council and no travel industry.

If the report does indeed draw the rather amazing conclusions the news story describes, the report is one of the largest pieces of tommyrot that has come down the pike, and I shall urge the governors who are my fellow members of the Appalachian Regional Commission to refuse to accept its conclusions.

Today, as we look at the new world of travel in Kentucky, we must not think the job is done just because (other than some "leftfield" report) things look so good at this point. The success of our program has spurred other states in the midsouth and southeastern regions to give us some healthy competition. We cannot slow down. We have roads to build, motels to build, regional attractions to develop, lakes to create, open space to conserve, promotion to do—in short—plenty of work for all of us working together.

To help remind all Kentuckians how important it is to get ready for the 1967 tourist year, I will issue a proclamation soon declaring the week of April 16-22 Tourist Appreciation Week in Kentucky. We will emphasize our thanks to those who came to Kentucky to spend $295 million with us last year, and we will send a special "You folks come back" call to the twenty-six million visitors who came here from other states. And, most important of all, I hope all of us will dedicate our efforts to fixing up the welcome mat for the folks who will enjoy the new world of travel in Kentucky in 1967.

---

1. George Morgan Chinn, Jr., born in Mercer County, Kentucky; educated at Center College; retired U.S. Marine Corp officer; advanced ordnance course, Michigan State University; gage course, University of Cincinnati Gage Laboratory; director emeritus, Kentucky Historical Society; author of books on military weaponry and Kentucky history; resident of Harrodsburg. Information provided by Kentucky Historical Society. Paul Sawyier (1865-1917), American impressionist best known for nostalgic themes reflected in his paintings and drawings of old Frankfort and the Kentucky and Elkhorn rivers. John Wilson Townsend, "Paul Sawyier: Kentucky Artist: Some Recollections of Him," in Lowell Harrison and Nelson L. Dawson, eds., *A Kentucky Sampler: Essays From The Filson Club Quarterly, 1926-1976* (Lexington, Ky., 1977), pp. 423-27.

2. Kenneth Arnold (1929-), agronomist; executive officer with Kentucky Department of Highways (1962-1969); currently engaged in landscape business, Lexington, Kentucky. Telephone interview with Kenneth Arnold, Jr., March 2, 1981.

THE LEAGUE OF KENTUCKY SPORTSMEN
Covington / June 9, 1967

As your governor, it is a privilege and a pleasure to meet and mingle with you, in addition to sharing thoughts and ideas on conservation. But I feel a special kinship to this organization, because of the honor you bestowed upon me last year—"Conservationist of the Year." I appreciate and cherish that honor very much, and I will live up to its responsibility and challenge to the best of my ability.

Actually, your organization and your Kentucky state government have many things in common—including, of course, the conservation of our many natural resources throughout this great Commonwealth. The beauty of our state, plus its fish and its game, through the years have made this state a top tourist attraction. And now our state park system is recognized as the nation's best.

But Kentucky's heritage—historically, scenic-wise, and every-wise—is an attraction in itself. The name Kentucky itself goes a long way in luring tourists to our great Commonwealth. Last year alone, Kentucky's tourist industry totaled $425 million, including $295 million spent by more than twenty-six million visitors from out of state. Kentuckians themselves added another $130 million. In the last three years, this state's tourist industry has increased by $75 million. This tourist industry now provides nearly 9 percent of total retail business receipts in Kentucky; jobs for 74,300 persons employed to serve and assist travelers; some $25 million in direct taxes; and more than $90 million per year (directly) to personal incomes of Kentuckians.

I know, however, that as pleased as you are with this tourism and its contribution to the economy of our state, you are basically concerned with the conservation of the fish and wildlife resources in Kentucky, and the conservation of other resources. Not only in the forest and other lands in our fine state park system, but with all the forests and all the land in Kentucky and the natural resources thereon and therein—the waters, the wildlife, the fish, and the other components of our natural resources.

As you know, protection of public lands was the theme of National Wildlife Week in March. "This Is Your Land—Know It, Enjoy It and Protect It," the slogan read. Appropriately, this national observance is planned annually to include the first day of spring—and the original proclamation starting it was signed in 1938 by President Franklin D. Roosevelt. Every citizen is a part owner of local, state, and federal lands and should be interested in how they are being used. This means working with public and private organizations as well as public officials to ensure that we receive the maximum benefits from our public lands.

Many public lands which are presently underdeveloped could benefit campers, hikers, and sportsmen and provide for wildlife. Wise use of these public lands can be fostered by citizen interest and encouragement. Future needs for natural resources and recreation to meet both a growing demand and an increasing population are dependent upon wise land use planning today.

Most of you are familiar with your state government's emphasis on conservation of our natural resources in Kentucky—our efforts and the new legislation in the matters of water and air pollution and in other areas of related interest. I know of no better way to emphasize and to dramatize the vital importance of developing and protecting our natural resources than through gatherings such as the annual conservation congress we sponsor. And we emphasize and dramatize the specifics of hunting and fishing—which likewise are of such vital interest to you here tonight—by a separate department in your state government, the Department of Fish and Wildlife Resources.

Your League of Kentucky Sportsmen is a "live" organization. And your organization has been alive and active since it was started back in 1935. You know about a group of interested sportsmen meeting in Louisville in the interest of conservation, and in the interest of protecting and perpetuating game and fish in this state. That was the birth of the league, and that child has now grown to full manhood and a power in this state—not only in fish and wildlife conservation, but in the conservation of all other natural resources. This organization has been blessed throughout its existence by strong leadership, from Dr. B.W. Kelly of Louisville as the first president and through the years to tonight.[1] Some of the presidents through the years, plus others who contributed so much, are here tonight.

Your league's power is pinpointed by your action in the passage two years ago by the legislature of the strip-mine bill, the most restrictive one in the nation and a model since for many other states. Your league's power now is being demonstrated in the field of beautification; in the fight against air and water pollution; in the effort to curb the spoiling of our stream banks; in the effort to fight the spoiling of our rivers and our forests. Wherever there is a conservation movement, you are likely to find action by the League of Kentucky Sportsmen.

The Fish and Wildlife Department—with the cooperation of you sportsmen of Kentucky—has been able to achieve many things for sportsmen and all Kentucky. The fish and wildlife agency has stocked over 50,000 ponds with a balance of bass and bluegill for what we like to call "backyard fishing." Several years ago, also with your cooperation, we started stocking rainbow trout in a number of suitable streams. Success was almost immediate. Then a number of rainbow trout were placed in Lake Cumberland proper. This has paid off wonderfully well, since three-to five-pound rainbow in this lake are not unusual at all. The prediction is that this lake will become one of the finest rainbow trout producing lakes in the southeastern United States, when enough rainbow can be obtained from new hatcheries to stock it properly.

Most of you are familiar with the Land Between the Lakes development in southwest Kentucky—the huge family recreation area that also is serving so well in conservation education for our youngsters. Your Kentucky state government is cooperating in every way possible with this federal project. The deer herd in Kentucky now has been built up to 50,000 and already offers exciting hunting for both gun and bow-and-arrow marksmen. Each year you sportsmen all around the Commonwealth are given a total of some 80,000 day-old quail chicks. These are raised to six weeks of age, when they are released in the field.

The department and your league started a state-owned lakes program and constructed twenty-six lakes for Kentucky fishermen. This program became the small lakes program under Governor Combs and is being continued by this administration, with the cooperation of the Highway Department. The total of lakes from both programs now is forty-six, and all are fishable. There are many current projects of the Department of Fish and Wildlife Resources. You all are familiar with Harry Towles' fishing report weekly on television and his daily program heard on forty-two radio stations throughout the state.[2] And the department further uses Harry's talents by his editorship of "The Happy Hunting Ground." And the department, again with the cooperation of you sportsmen, has achieved a new $1.5 million federal trout hatchery below Wolfe Creek Dam. Bids are to be taken on this project next month.

The department's fisheries biologist this year is experimenting with a hybrid fish— a cross between the rock fish, native to the ocean, and our white bass and yellow bass. This hybrid is expected to grow about three times as fast as our pure white bass— or about two and one-half pounds the first year.

The folks at Fish and Wildlife also have stocked in Barren River Reservoir approximately eight million wall-eye fry. No fishing for them now is permitted in this lake. The lake is to be used for a wall-eye hatchery, from which eggs and fry are to be used to stock other suitable wall-eye waters in Kentucky. In addition, a warm-water fish hatchery now is in the planning stage, hopefully to be started in the next year. A number of sites have been studied, and the most suitable one will be announced in the near future. This hatchery will provide, in addition to bass and bluegill necessary in our stocking program, muskellunge.

In the middle of the department's growth and expansion always has been found your league. Your league has protected, at all times and with everything in your power, the department as it is today. Your league has cooperated with the department in the formation of far-reaching programs that have been of much benefit to Kentucky and to Kentuckians. Your league has been instrumental in the formation of the conservation education division, in which conservation education is taught in the classrooms of many Kentucky schools. And your league has supported other legislation necessary for the department's forward strides. And, in itself, your League of Kentucky Sportsmen has gained in prominence and in prestige. Today, your league is recognized as a progressive organization powerful in Kentucky lawmaking; powerful in your protection of the game and fish and other natural resources of our state.

You are proud, and rightfully so, that your League of Kentucky Sportsmen was the first affiliate in the nation of the National Wildlife Federation to enter the conservation contest sponsored by the national unit and the Sears-Roebuck Foundation. Two years ago, in Paducah at your annual meeting, I had the pleasure of making the first Governor's Conservation Awards.

Your current president, Willie Riehman from South Fort Mitchell, is continuing the fine leadership that has become a tradition in this organization throughout its thirty-two year history.[3] Again I say, some of the former presidents and other officials who steered your group through trying times are here tonight. And I know you appreciate the eleven-year service of Redmon Payne, of Franklin, as secretary and treasurer.[4] And you know the fine publication of John Murphy, of Covington, in his "Shield."[5] Then there are the vice presidents in each of the nine districts—and the various committeemen. All of you members, as well as officials, past and present, share in the prestigious position of the League of Kentucky Sportsmen.

I understand that league membership has increased from that handful who started in Louisville in 1935 to nearly 42,000 members this year in 314 clubs around the state. This is wonderful. But don't you think that it can be increased manyfold? Is there any reason why all hunters and fishermen should not be members of the League of Kentucky Sportsmen? In addition, you and I both know that women also are becoming more interested in fishing and hunting.

Your league is designed for fishermen and hunters. It should attract many thousands more, and tonight I issue this challenge to the league; enroll those many hunters and fishermen who are not now members of your organization. State government is doing—and will continue to do—everything it can to support the policies and the purposes of your league.

---

1. Brown Wilson Kelley (1899-), dentist from Irvine, Kentucky; graduate of the University of Kentucky and the University of Louisville (1925); member of the board of directors and president of the League of Kentucky Sportsmen. Hambleton Tapp, ed., *Kentucky Lives* (Hopkinsville, Ky., 1966), p. 295.

2. Harry Towles, public relations official for Department of Fish and Wildlife. Information provided by Division of Personnel, Frankfort.

3. Willie Riehman (1921-), buyer for machine tool company, Covington, Kentucky; president, League of Kentucky Sportsmen (1966-1967); board of directors (1961-1966); resident of South Fort Mitchell, Kentucky. Telephone interview, March 2, 1981.

4. Redmon Payne, no data available.

5. John Murphy, former newspaper reporter and sports editor of *Kentucky Post Times-Star,* Covington, Kentucky; retired and a resident of Park Hills, Kentucky. Information provided by Willie Riehman.

NATURAL RESOURCES

CONSERVATION CONGRESS
Louisville / October 15, 1964

I KNOW of no better way to emphasize and dramatize the vital importance of developing and protecting our natural resources than through gatherings such as the Conservation Congress. The fine attendance at this fourth annual congress speaks well for the goals we have set for doing the job that lies ahead. No job is more important, and your presence here—as delegates from all sections of Kentucky—is proof of your deep concern for the God-given treasures that are the Commonwealth's land, water, forest, and mineral resources.

When I was campaigning to be your governor, our platform pledged full cooperation with groups and individuals seeking to promote the development, wise use, and protection of our natural resources. We have kept faith with that pledge. Not only have we expanded and improved conservation activity on all fronts; we have strengthened this vital cause with new laws passed by the General Assembly.

The reclamation of strip-mined lands is no longer a hit-or-miss proposition. We have a new law that requires coal operators to plant and seed the land they disturb, or forfeit their performance bonds. The law is being rigidly enforced—and we play no favorites in doing it. All we ask is full compliance with the law, and the industry, with few exceptions, is cooperating. We do not want to destroy the industry. We merely want to protect our land and streams from the destructive aftermath of surface mining. Our water resources are protected, too, with other improved laws. A citizen can now go to court to stop the illegal practice of dumping waste and debris into streams and lakes.[1] Under another amended law, landowners may vote a special assessment on themselves to obtain additional revenues for local flood control structures.[2]

The organized protection of our forest resources is being expanded with increased appropriations. A new federal program of rural fire defense will ensure further safety for our woodlands. . . .[3]

I have summarized just some of the advancements in the interest of sound conservation practices. There are many more. And our efforts will continue to bear fruit so long as dedicated individuals and federal, state, and local agencies work together in harmony. You'll notice I mention individuals first because governmental bodies can do just so much—the main job remains for the individual.

Each of us has a responsibility that steadily grows larger and more exacting. Pressing against limited natural resources on all sides are the demands of an increasing population and the spreading requirements of a more complex society. More people want to use the resources at hand more often and for more things. And, from all indications, the trend will continue. Consider this, for a minute: with this nation's population already growing at a rate of about three million each year, we will need twice as much production from agricultural lands by 1980; by the year 2000, we'll have to double the production of wood from the forest resources of our state and nation; America will need 600 billion gallons of water a day by 1980—more than double the present requirement; each year about a million acres go out of agriculture, primarily to urban uses; and our requirements for recreational space and facilities are multiplying rapidly, especially near centers of population. You can see, then, that to serve the relentless forces of demand and necessity, we must nurture and protect the source of supply. And this can be done only through the concerted effort of every citizen. We are making progress, to be sure, but there are signs which point to the need for pulling the throttle wide open.

Consider that, as a nation, we are still losing 500,000 acres of topsoil each year as a result of erosion and other forms of land damage. Consider that, after a quarter-century of conservation effort, more than two-thirds of the job of conserving land remains to be done. And, consider that 90 percent of the development work for watershed protection and flood prevention is yet to be started.

In all instances, Kentucky lags badly, but we have achieved some results in the 121 soil conservation districts since 1960. No longer do these districts limit their programs to agricultural lands. More and more they include the "whole land"—highways, watersheds, flood control, and recreational and urban areas. This in no way detracts from the traditional "on the farm" program. If anything, it has made that phase even more effective in all respects. Some 90,000 landowners in Kentucky now cooperate with local soil conservation districts. Some 51,000 of these farmers have completed basic plans that establish good practices on nearly six million acres of land.

The United States Soil Conservation Service works with the local districts in conservation farm planning. The districts also receive invaluable assistance from the agricultural experiment station, the Agricultural Stabilization and Conservation Service, extension service, Farmers Home Administration, vocational agricultural departments, and many other agencies and organizations.

Outdoor recreation is the theme of this year's Conservation Congress—and the subject is both timely and appropriate. Recent surveys and studies show beyond doubt that increased leisure time will tax further the resources of our state and nation—particularly since many leisure activities are of the outdoor type. With a forty-hour work week or less, paid vacations and legal holidays, Americans who earn their living now spend less than one-quarter of their time actually working at paid jobs. Since increased leisure time and greater economic independence will place more people in outdoor activities, a direct relationship exists between such activities and the conservation of natural resources.

The kinds of outdoor recreation most people take part in today are relatively simple—walking and driving for pleasure, playing games, swimming, sightseeing, picnicking, fishing, bicycling, boating, and hunting. These lead the list—and it is readily apparent that water is the focal point in outdoor recreation. Because water is the focal point, outdoor recreation is even more significant in Kentucky, a state that has more miles of running water than any state except Alaska. Through the cooperation of federal, state, and local agencies, we are developing our water resources for flood control, recreation, industry, and agriculture.

The magnitude of the development is staggering. For example, the U.S. Corps of Engineers has some $770 million worth of authorized projects in the Commonwealth. About half of them have been completed and the remainder are being developed at the rate of $70 million a year. In addition, local soil conservation districts and private sources have built more than a thousand lakes ranging in size from five to 1,100 acres. Your state government has constructed forty-three lakes impounding more than 5,600 surface acres of water. Nine of these lakes were created by converting highway fills into dams. This economical way of creating lakes is being pioneered by the state of Kentucky.

Recreational use of these lakes alone will bring many more tourists into our state, adding greatly to the business of those who deal with tourists—restaurants, motel and hotel operators, service station owners, local merchants, and employees of all of them. Also, these new man-made lakes add to our industrial prospects. They offer new and replenishable sources of water to industries thinking about moving to Kentucky—and this is at a time when we are seeking 75,000 new jobs for our citizens.

I hope Kentucky can build more lakes—whether they are the large Corps of Engineers projects or the smaller links in our own chain of lakes. If the proposed $176 million bond issue is approved next fall, $1 million will be used for small lakes development. With this we can build many of the still needed dams and reservoirs to supply enough water for tourists, towns, farmers, industry, and sportsmen, and protect them from too much water.

The most economical use of resources requires joint effort from the scientist, the technician, and the citizen. We are faced with many decisions because there is no single use of a resource. Each use reflects different interests, and each question answered seems to bring an additional question. Facts are all too often not yet available. Where we do have facts we must have action rather than continue waste that results from greed and ignorance. The late President John F. Kennedy once said that "Conservation, in the real analysis, is the job of us all." With that being true, the solution of conflicting viewpoints toward conservation lies in an informed public. We must see—through meetings such as this—that the Kentucky citizen is aware of his dependence on these resources both for his and this nation's future.

President Kennedy has been designated as the proponent of a third wave of conservation in this country, following that of Theodore Roosevelt and Franklin Delano Roosevelt. President Johnson indicated his commitment to this policy when, in addressing the National Wildlife Federation, he said: "We must never neglect the future of nature's rich endowment for our country. We must constantly be vigilant and on the alert to keep our air clean, to keep our water pure, and keep our forests green, to keep our birdlife abundant and our wildlife plentiful or else we will lose a vital essential of what we love to call America."

In Kentucky, we have been making progress in conserving our natural resources; we are making progress; and we will continue—with your leadership—along the road to progress and occupy our rightful place in the Great Society.

---

1. See "an act relating to natural resource development," *Acts, 1964,* Chapter 67 (S.B. 136), p. 246. In addition to prohibiting dumping waste and debris into streams, the law created a Division of Flood Control and Water Resource Development within the Department of Conservation. The new division received greater authority to develop water resources than its predecessor, the Flood Control and Water Usage Board.

2. Under the new law the board of directors of a water conservancy district was empowered to determine the need for new water projects, their design and scope, and if the district had sufficient available taxing power to carry out the project. If funds were unavailable, the board, after appropriate hearings, was authorized to conduct an election on the issuance of watershed project assessment bonds. The

bonds were to be amortized through special tax assessments affecting only those property owners who benefited directly from the project. Only those property owners were eligible to vote in the election. *Acts, 1964,* Chapter 116 (S.B. 134), pp. 381-84.

3. A section of this speech, in which Governor Breathitt discussed his efforts to improve farm income, has been deleted.

GOVERNOR'S CONFERENCE ON FORESTRY
Lexington / February 18, 1965

THE late President John F. Kennedy once said that "Conservation, in the real analysis, is the job of us all." With that being true, I can think of no better way to emphasize and dramatize the importance of developing and protecting our forests than through such gatherings as this second annual Conference on Forestry. There must be the look ahead, there must be a realization of the fact that to waste, to destroy our timberland, to cut and exhaust our forests instead of using practices to restore their usefulness, will result in undermining in the days of our children the very prosperity which we ought by right to hand down to them amplified and developed.[1]

So rapid has been the rate of exhaustion of timber in the United States in the past, and so rapidly is the remainder being exhausted, that our nation is unquestionably on the verge of a timber famine which will be felt in every household in America. The present annual consumption of timber in this nation is certainly greater than the annual growth, and, if the consumption and growth continue unchanged, practically all our lumber will be exhausted like it is in so many countries of Europe where the people failed to practice conservation.

Happily for Kentucky, however, the conservation of forests not only fits into a standard pattern of life; it is conducted on a grand scale that has earned nationwide recognition for this Commonwealth. For the first 100 years of Kentucky's existence as a state, little attention was paid to conservation practices, particularly as they applied to our forests. Land was cleared for cultivation by cutting or burning, and the timber that was felled was generally wasted by being allowed to rot or was piled and set on fire. Forests to the pioneers were enemies to be attacked, not friends that could provide life and a living. But, then, timber was plentiful and who could have foreseen that by today more than half of our original forested area would have been cleared and devoted to other purposes.

Only in the last few years have we realized the dangers that exist for our forests. Only during the last few years have we awakened to the realization that the enemies of wooded areas—fire, disease, indiscriminate cutting and clearing—are robbing us of a precious heritage that can never be replaced. But today, here in Kentucky, we have instituted conservation measures that are designed not only to protect what we have but to increase our forest acreage at the same time that consumption of forest products is increasing.

Disease control programs are saving trees in our forests in all sections of Kentucky. Research into oak wilt gives promise of better control and, hopefully, eventual elimination. Studies of insect damage also hold out hope of improved control and better protection of our trees. Organized fire protection is now available in 101 counties, holding 10.4 million acres of Kentucky's 11.5 million acres of forest lands. Our Forestry Division detects and controls fires with a vast network of communications, manpower and equipment, including 154 lookout towers, four aircraft, and fifty-eight professional foresters who watch over the management of woodlands. And, because Kentucky was selected as one of five states by the federal government's forestry division for a pilot project to train volunteers for fire-fighting purposes, our state soon will have complete protection in all 120 counties. Over 1,500 volunteers already have been trained under this joint program.

Still another program, which was initiated by the Forestry Division, in cooperation with the state Department of Corrections, is the rehabilitation of prisoners at a camp in Kentucky Ridge State Forest. The camp, located on a 12,000-acre tract of mountainous land in Bell County, houses forty-four prisoners from LaGrange Reformatory; they build fire breaks and access roads and fight fires under the technical supervision of the Forestry Division. The camp has been so successful that a site in Harlan County has been chosen for a second camp.

The division also demonstrates good management practices and efficient methods of utilization and marketing in seven state-owned forests embracing 46,211 acres. The reforestation of idle and abandoned land is accomplished through the use of three nurseries with a total capacity of fifty million seedlings. These nurseries now produce twenty million seedlings yearly to meet the ever increasing demand for tree-planting stock.

We now have a new strip-mine law, passed by the 1964 General Assembly, that requires coal operators to plant and seed the land they disturb, or forfeit their performance bonds. I am 100 percent opposed to improper stripping or augering operations that do not restore the land to usable conditions, that leave an exposed surface of poison materials. Because of this feeling, I intend to see to it that our present law is strictly and rigidly enforced. And, before the 1966 General Assembly meets, I plan to review the present strip-mine law and its results to make sure that the law is suitably and properly protecting our land. Should another law be necessary, then I will not hesitate to call for its enactment when the legislature convenes in January.

Because of all these measures—these forward-looking programs—we have begun to conserve and perpetuate Kentucky's forests, which support our industries, which regulate our rivers, which prevent erosion of our soil, which provide beauty for our people. Kentucky now is in the unique position of maintaining its supply of wood, through these various programs and private efforts, while the nation's supply of wood dwindles. As the supply diminishes in our neighboring states, the demand for Kentucky wood and wood products will go up. As the demand increases, so will the price. Therefore, it is to our best interests from both a conservation viewpoint and an economical viewpoint that we redouble and rededicate our efforts to preserve and replant our forests. In the years ahead, we will find forestry becoming an even more profitable and bigger industry than it is today.

Last year farmers received more than $20 million from the sale of timber. In turn, this timber contributed more than $300 million to the state's economy through the allied businesses of harvesting, processing, transportation, marketing, and construction. Your state administration has been working hard to promote the development of the wood-processing industry across Kentucky. We are doing this because we feel that we have only scratched the surface in the wood-use business. We know that the door is wide open, and Kentucky intends to step through it. We know that it is one thing to talk about building a major wood-processing industry in Kentucky and still another thing to convert the talk into reality, but we are firmly convinced that we can accomplish this goal. The results of our initial efforts have been extremely gratifying.

The Forestry Committee of the governor's Commission on Agriculture, which is working towards a billion dollar annual farm income, has compiled a lengthy, commendable report with recommendations and ways to implement a program to bring about a major increase in forestry income. The Economic Opportunity Act—the so-called war on poverty program—makes it possible for Kentuckians to obtain low-interest loans for small business ventures into the wood-processing industry. And the Appalachian program, pending before Congress, is still another avenue of opportunity in forestry for the people of this great state.

Few states in this nation can match the volume or variety of timber that is here in Kentucky. Yet, we have settled for the meager profits to the producer in far too many cases. We have shipped our best timber to other states for processing and marketing. And, in so doing, we have also shipped away a major portion of the profit to be derived from our forests.

These are just a few of the more obvious examples of the opportunities we have been missing in the past—opportunities that we do not intend to miss in the future. Since those of you here tonight represent some of the best producers and customers of our timber in Kentucky, I am happy to join with your efforts to promote and develop Kentucky's forests.

There are many aspects to the wood-processing industry, stretching as it does from the seedling to the cutter to the factory to the household. I want you to know that we intend to develop the potential for this tremendous industry in our state and that we are developing this potential. The opportunity is ours. We know what must be done. Let's get on with the job.

---

1. Approximately 43 percent of the Commonwealth is woodland, principally in eastern Kentucky. Kentucky is a transition zone between northern and southern forests, and species characteristic of both regions, including red oak, short leaf pine, pecan, bald cypress, sweet birch, swamp white oak, and white pine, are found in the state. P.P. Karan and Cotton Mather, eds., *Atlas of Kentucky* (Lexington, Ky., 1977), pp. 122-23.

BOURBON COUNTY SOIL CONSERVATION DINNER
Paris / April 15, 1965

THANK you for inviting me here tonight to participate with you in your annual banquet and to join with you in recognizing persons who have achieved distinction in a conservation-related field. The Bourbon County Soil Conservation District has long been one of our most active districts in the state, and for this effort I applaud you and express my thanks and the thanks of all our citizens for the job you are doing.

I am told that in 1960 you were awarded the Goodyear Award for having the most active and complete program in the state. And tonight you are receiving the Master Conservationist Award for the sixteenth time—which is, needless to say, quite an achievement. Part of this honor, I am sure you will agree, must go to three of the original supervisors of this district who are still serving—Sam Clay, Roy Galloway, and Herman Kearns.[1]

Coming from Christian County, which has some of the best farm land in this state, I have long been interested in and appreciated the conservation of our soil and water. Floods which sweep over our farms and our towns, erosion which tears the heart out of our land—these primitive forces do not distinguish between sections in Kentucky. And the task of controlling our streams, of using and conserving our soil to make and keep it productive—this is a task which challenges the best thought and the most dedicated efforts of all good citizens, regardless of whether we're Democrats, Republicans, or independents.

Kentucky can be proud of the progress made during the last fiscal year with the technical assistance of the Soil Conservation Service. In that period 5,201 landowners completed the development of their conservation plans or revised them, an increase of about 12 percent over the previous year. Technical assistance was provided to 36,942 landowners—and this amounts to a 28 percent increase. In addition, our soil survey mapping program increased from 828,000 acres to 1,022,000 acres in the 1964 fiscal year. In Kentucky today—and I think these statistics are not only significant, but impressive as well—84,702 landowners cooperate with the soil conservation districts. Of these, 50,021 have completed the development of a conservation plan for their operating unit.

Encouraged as we all are with this kind of progress, of great concern to me—and certainly to you—is the federal government's Budget Bureau's present proposed cutback in appropriations essential to speed up land, water, forest, and wildlife conservation work on the privately owned lands of Kentucky and America. At issue are proposals to chop $100 million from the Agricultural Conservation Program cost-sharing funds and to establish a "revolving fund" through which landowners would be charged $20 million for Soil Conservation Service technical assistance to districts. These proposals would deal a crippling blow to conservation in Kentucky—and I have expressed strong opposition to them in Washington.

In a nutshell, here is what the revolving fund would do. It would put the brakes on vital conservation work on the nation's privately owned lands, which comprise more than 70 percent of the U.S. total; in Kentucky, 94 percent of our lands are in private hands. The revolving fund would result in dismissal of one out of every three Soil Conservation Service technicians. It would break faith with local and state governments now contributing $44 million annually in funds and services to the partnership effort. Landowners, including those least able to afford it, would be double taxed for technical assistance. And that's not all. Coupled with the proposed 40 percent cut in ACP funds—from $220 million to $120 million—the result would be: a reduction of about 50 percent in establishment of conservation measures; a reduction of employees who provide Soil Conservation Service technical assistance; and additional burdens on landowners least able to afford costs of conservation measures.

In Kentucky our part of this proposed revolving fund would amount to about $510,000 annually, not including the ACP 5 percent funds used to pay for technical assistance in the Agricultural Conservation Program. This amount would need to be raised to maintain the existing staff assisting districts. The possibility of raising additional funds to make up our part of this proposed revolving fund is very limited. In fact, it would be extremely difficult to raise more than 10 percent of the required amount. As you well know, farmers are in a tight financial condition and have very little unobligated cash that could be used for this purpose.

Soil conservation districts in Kentucky now receive funds and services estimated at $1,065,288 annually from local and state governments and from individuals and commercial concerns within the state. These funds pay for only a limited amount of technical assistance; however, they do provide services that facilitate the technical assistance of the Soil Conservation Service. To add another half-million dollars to the landowners and taxpayers of Kentucky would place a heavy burden on them. It would hit hardest, of course, in the depressed areas of the state where this type of assistance is needed most.

In the Commonwealth, the impact of the revolving fund would be to reduce the existing staff by 75 to 80 persons. We now have about 250 people working in the soil districts in Kentucky. A reduction in staff would seriously affect the amount of conservation work done by landowners. It is estimated that the practices requiring on-site technical assistance would be reduced by about 65 percent, and in terms of conservation practices applied, an overall reduction of about 50 percent. The economic impact of such a reduction would be drastic, indeed. The estimated reduction in earthmoving practices alone would amount to about $995,000 annually. The impact would be felt across the state largely by the conservation contractors and small businessmen.

It seems to me that now is the time to advance, rather than retreat. This is shown by the fact that: good land to grow food crops is dwindling at a time when our population is exploding at a rapid rate; more than 8,300 watersheds need land treatment and improvement structures; erosion remains the dominant conservation problem on some two-thirds of the nation's rural land; floods in the Northwest and Kentucky, dust storms in the Great Plains, and growing sedimentation and silt pollution problems in eastern urban areas plague the nation; conservation districts are already short technical assistance right now; and economic growth, water shortages, and the mounting population are increasing the demands on districts for assistance of every kind—in the towns, suburbs, and all across the countryside.

I believe—and I know you do, too—that the conservation and development of our soil and water resources is basic to any development program and to the economy of any area. Therefore, in the name of all that is right and necessary, I feel that we need to increase the amount of technical assistance rather than receive a reduction. An evaluation of the staffing needs in soil conservation districts reflects a need for additional employees nationally and fifty-four in Kentucky.

I endorse the recommendations set forth by the Kentucky Association of Soil Conservation Districts. These recommendations would eliminate the revolving fund proposed and restore the $20 million in the Soil Conservation Service budget and raise the budget estimate for conservation operations from $104 to $115 million. This would include funds for staffing twenty-five new soil conservation districts that are expected nationally next year and funds to provide additional employees to meet the existing workload in districts across the nation.[2]

---

1. Sam Clay (1917-), farmer and chairman, Board of Supervisors, Bourbon County Conservation District. Roy Galloway (1892-1974), farmer and secretary, Board of Supervisors, Bourbon County Conservation District. Herman Kearns (1909-1978), farmer and vice chairman, Board of Supervisors, Bourbon County Conservation District. Information provided by Mrs. Romona P. Hurst, district clerk, Bourbon County Conservation District.

2. The Agricultural Conservation Program (ACP) provided federal funds to cover approximately 50 percent of the costs of soil conservation programs on individual farms. Criticism of the ACP centered on the high proportion (approximately 40 percent) of program funds which were applied toward the purchase of limestone and fertilizers. These soil additives allowed farmers to bring depleted croplands back into production after a short fallow period, but did little to further permanent soil conservation. The practice, therefore, was criticized as a direct subsidy to farmers. The ACP had withstood such budgetary attacks frequently since the Eisenhower administration, and it weathered this one as well. The final legislation (H.R. 8370, P.L. 89-316) appropriated the full $220 million which the agency generally received. In contrast to the ACP, the Soil Conservation Service (SCS) did not make payments directly to farmers. Rather, the service provided individual technical assistance designed to develop integrated land management programs combining soil and water conservation with efficient use of resources. The Soil Conservation Service provided soil surveys and analysis, joint planning, provision of necessary designs and specifications, and supervisory aid. The SCS operated through soil conservative districts and local farmers' organizations chartered by the states. One SCS soil expert serviced each district. The revolving fund which Breathitt criticized in his speech was to accumulate slowly, taking up to ten years to reach the full $20 million level. During that time the SCS was to operate under a limited budget of $40 million plus the amount existing in the revolving fund in a particular year. Opposition to the revolving fund concept within Congress and among interested groups was so powerful that the legislation was never introduced and Congress appropriated the full $60 million to the SCS. *Congressional Quarterly Almanac,* Vol. 21 (1965), pp. 200-02.

NATIONAL GOVERNORS CONFERENCE: PRESS CONFERENCE

Minneapolis, Minnesota / July 26, 1965

I HAVE always believed, and continue to believe, that state problems should be handled by states. But in recent years the practice of open pit or strip mining has confronted Kentucky with a problem of such scope and gravity that it cannot adequately be handled by the state alone. It is a problem that demands interstate agreement and possibly the assistance of the federal government.

Kentucky is but one of a dozen states in which strip mining is already a major concern, and one of twenty-five in which it may soon become one. In no state have the problems attending strip mining grown more dramatically than in Kentucky, and no state has made a more determined effort to solve these problems.

Yet we cannot say with confidence that our efforts have been enough, and if they have not been not only Kentucky should be concerned. For the mountain that is destroyed robs tomorrow's generation of one bit of a scenic beauty, one recreation area, one source of timber and clean water. One river polluted by the strip miners makes all of America that much poorer.

Since the 1930s, coal has been produced by the open-pit method in the flat country of western Kentucky, and for the past fifteen years we have conducted contour and auger mining on the steep hillsides of eastern Kentucky's Appalachian Mountains. But recently firms mining in western Kentucky have developed giant drag lines and power shovels that can take 200 cubic yards of earth in a single bite. And in the mountains seven-foot augers that bore their way into coal seems at thirty tons a minute are but one of several machines that are literally tearing our hills to pieces.

A person has only to watch a strip-mine operation to appreciate the troubling problems it presents. In flat country the giant shovels rip off over 100 feet of earth to get at the coal seam beneath. The earth is piled into gigantic hedgerows, 100 feet or more in height. When the ripped earth hits the air, oxidation results in the formation of acids which form malodorous ponds between the spoil banks and seep off to pollute and poison nearby streams, wash out with rains to kill the nearest vegetation, and complicate the problem of getting anything to grow on the ugly, jagged spoil banks of disturbed earth.

On the steep mountainsides the problem is even greater. The earth is blasted from the top of the coal and then shoved with bulldozers down the side of the mountain. A high, vertical, barren wall is formed against the mountainside above the coal seam, perhaps ninety feet high, and a flat bench is left when the coal has been lifted out, often hundreds of feet wide, miles long, and consisting mainly of slate and rock. When the rains come the water cascades off this raw, acid earth, down the highwall, across the bench, washing the spoil down the mountainsides in massive earth slides and acid mud flows, covering and ruining forest, fields, homes, farms, roads, and rivers.

Kentucky has been as aggressive as any state in its efforts to control the damages of this industry. In 1954 we enacted a law designed for the flatland, open pit mining then practiced, requiring regrading and replanting of stripped land.[1] In 1960 we revised it to include regulations of the mountainside stripping then becoming a serious problem.[2] And last year, in 1964, Kentucky's General Assembly enacted into law what we consider the strictest and most scientifically sound strip-mine control law in the United States. It requires of the strip-mine operator not only the usual performance bond and acreage fee, but requires them, before they can get a permit, to submit to the director of the Division of Strip Mining a plan for reclaiming the stripped site, showing how they propose to remove the earth, what type of earth it will be, how it will be handled and replaced, how the water draining from the site will be managed to prevent erosion and pollution, and how the area will be replanted. All auger holes must be covered and the covering earth compacted.

The bench, from which the coal is removed, must be sloped toward the highwall to make sure that the water will drain along the bench and down the hillside through natural draws, not down the raw spoil banks, and no spoil may be dumped into draws or natural drain ways. Access and haul roads must be properly surfaced and drained, and shoulders planted as carefully as spoil banks once the operation is finished. Toxic material, metal, lumber, and other refuse must be covered, and no disturbed earth or other material may damage adjacent property.

In flat country strips, spoil banks must be leveled on top to a width of no less than fifty feet, and the sides graded to accessible slopes. Adequate drainage must be provided to assure that no acid pooling is allowed, and the area must be planted, to reduce visual blight and check erosion. No impoundments are permitted unless approved by the state authority.

Nor is this all. After a recent tour of strip mines in both eastern and western Kentucky, I directed the Division of Strip Mining to refuse permits for strips on hillsides so steep that erosion and sliding of spoil banks seemed possible, and to require operators to restore flatland spoil banks to a contour traversible by farm machinery. I intend to make every effort possible to save Kentucky's scenic land from destruction by this or any other industry, and to this end I expect to ask the legislature that convenes next January to tighten strip-mining controls still further.

But this is going to be a fight—possibly even a losing fight, due to the circumstances attending the growth of strip mining. A great part of our strip-mined coal goes to meet the growing demand of the steam plants that produce our electricity. In their modern furnaces, these plants can utilize low-grade coal for which they pay low prices. This has not only led to a drop in demand for the high-grade lump coal produced in our underground mines; it has made possible the exploitation of low-grade outcrop coal previously considered uneconomical, but which can now be profitably mined by strip and auger methods.

Nearly all of these seams occur in counties hard hit by dropping underground mine employment, and even though strip mines cause frightful damage to the earth, they provide jobs and income that the people of the area are often reluctant to lose. Thus the state authorities face a political, as well as an economic, problem when the strip-mine operators threaten to move their operations to more lenient states.

This, in fact, is one of the most common and consistent of our problems. As you know, our eastern Kentucky coal counties are some of the most severely depressed in the Appalachian region. Coal income is vital to them. And when coal operators threaten to move to Tennessee or Virginia—neither of which have regulatory laws—employees and commercial and business interests in the area become worried, and the resulting pressures are felt in the legislature as well as in our administrative agencies.

This is not the only reason we need more than state regulation. Rivers that flow into eastern Kentucky from Virginia are alternately black with coal washings and red with strip-mine erosion. The Cumberland River, which literally springs out of strip-mined hills, flows directly into Tennessee. The Kentucky River, which cuts through the heart of our strip territory, flows into the Ohio, which pours its silt into the Mississippi. And the worsening floods on each of these silted, polluted rivers increase the suffering and misery of a region that already survives on the charity of the rest of the nation.

For these reasons I propose that the governors of the coal-producing states meet at their earliest convenience to discuss avenues of greater cooperation in the control of strip mining and the enforcement of reclamation laws. I will further solicit the support of every governor at this conference for a statement of principle which I hope to have presented to Congress this year urging prompt legislation of minimum uniform standards for strip-mine reclamation. This legislation should include a provision encouraging interstate compacts for the control of strip mining, leaving regulation and enforcement in the hands of those states affected so long as they enforce the standards regarded as minimal by the federal government, but providing for federal enforcement of federal standards and regulations when the states fail to act.

I shall further propose that the Tennessee Valley Authority be authorized by Congress to require that its coal suppliers follow strict reclamation procedures and meet standards at least as high as the federal minimums. And I shall further propose the TVA be authorized and funded by Congress to conduct extensive reclamation projects on those stripped and auger-mined sites furnishing coal to the agency.

While the Tennessee Valley Authority clearly has an obligation to help in restoring earth damaged to produce cheap coal for its furnaces, it is patently unfair to place the whole blame, or even a major part of the blame, on this splendid agency which has contributed so much to the nation. Neither is it reasonable to expect TVA (and ultimately its power consumers) to pay higher costs for its coal in order to subsidize reclamation by their coal suppliers. For TVA is but one of many users of strip-mined coal, and while its practices in this field may have disturbed some of its long-time supporters, it has pursued far more enlightened policies than the private companies that consume the great majority of stripped coal.

Neither do I wish to encourage states to avoid their obligation to insure reclamation not only of land currently being stripped but that land that was damaged by stripping before protective laws were passed. To this end, I will also propose that Congress authorize a strip-mine restoration fund, in which states may participate on a fifty-fifty matching basis, for the restoration and reclamation of these "orphan" strip-mined banks that were stripped prior to passage of protective laws. This action may necessitate the individual states charging a tonage fee for all coal mined in open pits in order for states to pay their part of the reclamation costs. I believe that the actions I have outlined here are both desirable and necessary if we are to preserve our land for generations yet to come.

---

1. The 1954 law created a Strip Mining and Reclamation Commission, required operators to secure permits, established a fee from $100 to $250 per acre to assure the operation would carry out the provisions of the law and established general criteria for reclamation work. Most of the criteria gave considerable discretion to the judgment of the operator and the commission. *Acts, 1954,* Chapter 8 (S.B. 45), pp. 19-28.

2. For ammendments to the 1954 law, see *Acts, 1960,* Chapter 163 (H.B. 401), pp. 601-05.

FIFTH ANNUAL CONSERVATION CONGRESS
Louisville / October 14, 1965

THE theme of this Congress, "Economic and Social Aspects of Natural Resource Development," leaves little else to be considered in this vitally important program being carried out by our Department of Natural Resources. This is as it should be. It is high time we took a long, hard look at all our natural resources and how we can do a wiser job of utilizing them. I believe there is a spirit of reawakening throughout Kentucky and the nation as a whole for the protection and conservation of all our natural resources—soil, water, minerals, and forests. Examination and analysis of our present position and planning for the future cannot wait to be done by a future generation. This is especially true where the water supply is concerned.

You have already heard Commissioner Jack Matlick paint an alarming but true picture of the water problems facing us in the immediate future.[1] We cannot sit back and take our present abundant water resources for granted. It is true that the Corps of Engineers continues to build big dams in Kentucky, but these dams function primarily for flood control and navigation, which certainly is vital to our livelihood. But what about water for cities and industries? I say now is the time—not tomorrow or the next day—to protect and develop our water supply while the shortages in the East and misfortunes of others bear fresh on our minds. We must accelerate the development of water to provide ever increasing supplies of clean water for business, industry, municipalities, recreation, agriculture, and for individual use in our homes.

The reasons are simple enough—water is the most precious commodity on earth. Man can live without clothes, without shelter, and even for some time without food, but without water—he soon perishes. However, contaminated water does not contribute to his survival. Authorities estimate that during 1965 nearly five million children will die before their first birthday from dysentery and other diseases contracted through polluted water. More and more money will have to be spent on antipollution measures so that water can be used over and over on its way from headwaters to the sea.

We are blessed with an annual average rainfall of forty-five inches, which is far more than many other states. This fact, along with our many miles of fresh water streams, makes our Commonwealth one of the most sought-after states for industrial sites and recreation areas. We cannot shirk our responsibility to utilize this water to its fullest advantage. One big problem is the distribution of rainfall. We don't get water in the right amounts, in the right places, at the right time.

Therefore, we cannot stress strongly enough the absolute necessity for implementing a program by legislation or otherwise that will insure us a continuing, adequate flow of clean water. With this in mind, I have asked Jack Matlick and his staff to draft comprehensive legislation that will eventually solve our flood, drought, and pollution problems.

I will soon invite the governors of Illinois, Indiana, and Ohio to discuss with me our mutual interests in the development of water resources of the Ohio River to best serve all of the people affected by this tremendous resource which borders all our states.

I am sure I needn't remind you that we are interested in strip mining. Our recent trip to Pennsylvania surface-mining operations has proved to me that it is vitally important that the state act with responsibility in the whole area of strip and auger mining to protect the rights of the citizens of today as well as those of tomorrow. It is increasingly apparent that we must take further action in that direction in the 1966 legislature. I believe that regulations similar to those of Pennsylvania will work in Kentucky. And, because I believe this, I will introduce in the next General Assembly new and stronger strip-mining laws patterned after those now working to good advantage in Pennsylvania. Incidentally, the Pennsylvania law is recognized as the most rigid in the nation. However, it did not destroy the coal industry in that state as had been previously supposed. I am convinced, after talking to coal operators there, that they are pleased with the new law. The operators now feel they are doing reclamation that is acceptable to the public and that they are leaving the land in usable condition for this and future generations.

I believe that state problems should be handled by the states insofar as possible. But strip mining presents a problem of such scope that it cannot be adequately handled by the state alone. For this reason, I am working very hard for an interstate compact regarding uniform reclamation standards and regulations which I hope will be adopted by all states engaged in strip-mining operations. At the 1964 Southern Governors Conference, I cosponsored with Governor Bellmon of Oklahoma a resolution requesting the Countil of State Governments to assist representatives of the states in which strip mining takes place in exploring the role of such an interstate compact.[2] This compact is imperative if all states are to continue to progress both economically and in the conservation of natural resources. At the National Governors Conference in July, I presented a statement of principle that was signed by forty-six other governors. This statement, which was forwarded to Congress, called for more control and uniform legislation of strip mining through individual state regulations, interstate compacts, and federal participation.

I have, as chairman of the Natural Resources Committee of the National Governors Conference, called a meeting with other affected states in St. Louis, November 3-4, to write this compact. This is to be a working meeting, and I intend to press for a workable compact at the earliest possible moment. Such a compact will ease the competitive disadvantages suffered by Kentucky strip-mine operators at the hands of states which presently have less effective strip-mining laws.

Our package of resource legislation would not be complete without measures applying to the protection of our land and forest resources. It is important that we continue to accelerate the development of our forestry potential and the production of more high-quality lumber. Increased forestry management and fire protection are imperative if we are to realize this potential. The proposed bond issue to be voted on November 2 contains $100,000 for more forest fire towers and forestry personnel. This is a small price for this increased protection when we consider that one forest fire season recently destroyed $3 million worth of timber.

There are many acres of our steeper slopes that need to be reforested, as recommended by the Forestry Committee of our Commission on Agriculture. Proper land use according to the commission's proposals will not only bring us increased income but conserve our agricultural land.

And discussion of the wise use and development of our natural resources would necessarily include cleanup and beautification, the program that is gaining Kentucky national acclaim. For example, at a national beautification conference in New York recently, Lady Bird Johnson singled out Kentucky as a model state in this endeavor.[3] I understand the First Lady does this quite frequently. And advertising of this type is sure to make us new friends and help in tourist and industrial promotion.

Kentucky, blessed with some of the most scenic landscapes and beautiful streams in the world, has a singular responsibility in conserving its natural resources for this and future generations. We seek your support in our statewide and interstate endeavors—and we challenge you to accept individual responsibility in this vital matter.

---

1. In 1964 three years of poor rainfall in the northeastern United States produced the worst drought since 1930. Although conditions were most severe in New England, by late summer the midwestern and plains states were also suffering. Learning from the misfortune of other states, the Breathitt administration in 1965 conducted an examination of Kentucky's available water resources and the government's ability to manage them. To meet the growing demands on those resources and to mitigate the effects of any future droughts, the governor eventually

proposed to the 1966 General Assembly a new agency, the Water Resources Authority, designed to allow increased funding for the expansion of water resource development. *New York Times,* November 15, 1964 and *Louisville Courier-Journal,* January 2, 1966.

2. Henry Bellmon (1921-), farm operator, Billings, Oklahoma (1946-); Oklahoma House of Representatives (1946-1948); governor of Oklahoma (1962-1966); U.S. Senator (1968-). *Who's Who in the South and Southwest, 1971-1972,* 12th ed. (Chicago, 1971).

3. Lady Bird Johnson (1912-), wife of President Lyndon B. Johnson. During her tenure as First Lady Mrs. Johnson was a prominent advocate of environmental protection and beautification programs. *Who's Who in America, 1972-1973,* 37th ed. (Chicago, 1972).

NATURAL RESOURCES COMMITTEE OF THE NATIONAL GOVERNORS CONFERENCE

St. Louis, Missouri / November 4, 1965

As American citizens, we are privileged to live in a land of plenty, a land where nature's treasures have blessed us with the highest standard of living in the world. But with this citizenship goes a sacred obligation—that of developing, using wisely, and protecting our natural resources. No nobler cause could occupy the hearts and minds of mankind and this, in essence, is why we are gathered here today. We are going forth to observe, to perceive, to question, to challenge, and to decide how we can make life better in the trying years ahead.

A look at the past tells tragically what can happen if we continue to waste and abuse our God-given resources. Our most abused resource, water, always has dominated human life. Nations reached great heights and toppled in the dust because their water supply failed. Even though three-fourths of the earth's surface is covered by water, shortages are commonplace in our daily lives. The basic problem is one of distribution: we simply must have the right quantity, the right quality of water at the right time and in the right place.

But whatever the resource—water, land, forests, or minerals—each of us inherited a responsibility that steadily grows larger and more exacting. Pressing against limited natural resources on all sides are the demands of an exploding population and the requirements of a complex society on the threshold of journeying to the moon. There is no letup in sight, as borne out by these projections: with the human race doubling in numbers every thirty-five years, we will need twice as much production from agricultural lands by the year 2000; each year about a million acres of land go out of agriculture, primarily to urban and industrial uses; by the year 2000, we'll have to double the production of wood from the forest resources of our state and nation; the United States will need 600 billion gallons of water a day by 1980, an amount doubling the present daily requirement; and our requirements for recreational space and facilities are multiplying rapidly, especially near centers of population. From these statistics alone, it is readily apparent that to serve the relentless forces of demand and necessity, we must safeguard the source of supply through proper planning and management of our natural resources.

Whatever water shortage now exists is not a shortage of water, but a shortage of human foresight in planning and management. We can no longer take our natural resources for granted. Now is the time for a renaissance—a rebirth, if you will, in our thinking and action toward the conservation of natural resources. We must, in effect, strike a bargain with nature to provide that extra margin of safety for our children and their children's children.

Over the past century we have had conservation scandals that centered on our forests, wildlife, and soil. In each case, the American people reacted against plunder and waste. Farsighted conservation plans took shape to halt the erosion of vital national resources. As Secretary of the Interior Stewart Udall pointed out recently, water is the conservation scandal of our generation.[1] Industries and cities contaminate our waterways, while silt from stripped land, acid mine water, pesticides, and chemicals diminish the usefulness of our available water.

At the turn of this century the American people were forced by the facts—and by the dynamic leadership of men like Theodore Roosevelt and Gifford Pinchot—to put forest management on a planned, sustained-yield basis.[2] Similar water action is needed now. It was Teddy Roosevelt, by the way, who in 1908 called the nation's governors in for a conference on natural resources. The meeting gave birth to what is now the National Governors Conference and, fittingly enough, evolved into the modern effort on behalf of conservation.

The answer—as always in conservation crises—is acting with foresight that puts the future first. Long-range planning must be substituted for short-range local solutions; recycling must replace discharge; reclamation must supplement recovery; and research and technology must make new and dramatic contributions toward these ends.

In Kentucky we have launched an all-out offensive against the plunder and waste of our natural resources. Our immediate concern, coupled with efforts toward developing water resources, is that of curbing the destructive aftermath of strip and auger mining of coal. . . .[3]

We hear a great deal these days about the population explosion and its possible effect on natural resources throughout the United States and the world. There is no doubt in my mind but what this rapidly exploding population is the greatest problem in the world today. Startling facts dramatizing the problem have been brought to light by the International Industrial Conference. In the next thirty-five years, for example, the world population will skyrocket from 3.3 billions to about 6 billions—almost doubling by the year 2000. The biggest increase—more than 100 percent—will come in the less developed nations, where the food supply does not come up to even the bare essentials. In Asia, Africa, and most of Latin America, millions of people go to bed hungry every night.

The necessity for doubling the food supply by the year 2000 comes at a time when nearly all of the virgin lands in the world already have been brought into production. There is no assurance that the job can be done in time. In fact, there is a possibility that the world will face a great famine. As Dr. Earl L. Butz, dean of the College of Agriculture at Purdue University, and one-time chairman of the U.S. delegation to the Food and Agricultural Organization of the United Nations, has warned: "The world is on a collision course. When the massive force of an exploding population meets the much more stable trend of world food production, something must give. Unless we give increased attention now to the softening of the impending collision, many parts of the world, within a decade, will be skirting a disaster of such proportion as to threaten the people and stability of the western world."[4]

Another leading authority—Dr. George Borgstrom, professor of food science at Michigan State University—is in full agreement.[5] Nothing but an all-out attack by science and technology, he says, will halt the increasing lag between the population explosion and food production. "We are losing the race between the baby crop and the grain crop," he says. Dr. Borgstrom goes on to say that more than 600 million of the billion children now living on this earth will never reach adulthood, primarily due to the food shortage. "Starvation and malnutrition are their only fate," he says. They will not even have the privilege of a hearty, filling meal once in their lifetimes.

Gentlemen, these are chilling facts—startling to the point of disbelief. Even more so, perhaps, is the dilemma facing the entire western world. The communist countries, including Red China, will experience a smaller population explosion than will the noncommunist countries, the experts say. The outlook is for the population in the communist world to grow by only about 49 percent, while the free world population jumps by 98 percent between now and the year 2000.

Communist leaders recognize the importance of food in the face of an expanding world population. Their number one goal, in fact, is to surpass America in the production of this vital necessity of life. They realize that in the years ahead, a country's ability to produce huge quantities of food to feed their people and their allies, will be more important than guided missiles and hydrogen bombs. The communist world knows, too, that what made America great and a leader in the world today are God-given natural resources and our ingenuity and productive capacity to utilize them. If we are to maintain this position, then, we must strive diligently to develop, preserve, and use wisely these vital resources.

Next to air, water is the most necessary resource for human survival. In this crowded world, water looms as a future problem almost as serious as that of food. Water is not only essential for the production of food, but water is industry's most important raw material. It requires up to 110,000 gallons of water to produce a ton of steel and up to 510,000 gallons of water to produce 1,000 yards of woolen cloth. Since 1900 the demand for water in the U.S. has increased sixfold. Population trends indicate that the demand will double by 1980; and by the year 2000, we will be using 900 billion gallons per day—or or 90 percent of the then available total national supply. Water, in the final analysis, is the heart of our industry, our commerce and agriculture; it is the key to the future progress of America and other countries of the world. Water can be our master or our slave, depending upon how wisely we control and utilize it. President Johnson said recently in signing legislation authorizing the Auburn-Folsom South Project in California: "I have never seen a dollar invested anywhere in this nation in water conservation, in multiple-use projects, that in a period of even a decade didn't prove it was a good investment and would pay very high returns on what we had to expend for it."

If gentlemen, through this National Committee on Natural Resources, we can bring about a new awareness—a renaissance of thinking and acting —not only of water but all our resources, then we have discharged our sacred duty and obligation to this and succeeding generations. I thank you.

---

1. Stewart Lee Udall (1920-), engaged in Arizona law practice (1948-1954); U.S. House of Representatives (1954-1960); secretary of the interior (1961-1969). *Who's Who in America, 1972-1973,* 37th ed. (Chicago, 1972).

2. Gifford Pinchot (1865-1946), was an early advocate of the science of forestry in the United States. As the head of the Forest Service under Theodore Roosevelt and William Howard Taft, Pinchot attacked haphazard exploitation of natural resources and championed a program of government regulated scientific manage-

ment designed to provide maximum, nondestructive utilization of resources for future generations. Dumas Malone, ed., *Dictionary of American Biography* (New York, 1935), vol. 16, pp. 135–43.

3. A section of this speech related to the proposed interstate mining compact has been deleted.

4. Earl L. Butz (1909-), member of the faculty and dean of the School of Agriculture, Purdue University (1937-1967); assistant secretary of agriculture during Eisenhower administration; secretary of agriculture during Nixon administration; prior to his appointment by Nixon, Butz had generally opposed high subsidies to farmers, preferring the free play of market forces and the replacement of small farms with large high technology agribusiness as a natural economic development. *Current Biography, 1972,* pp. 65-67.

5. George Arne Borgstrom (1912-), instructor in plant physiology, University of Lund, Sweden (1935-1938); various positions relating to food preservation and nutrition, Sweden (1938-1956); professor of food science and human nutrition, University of Michigan (1956-). *American Men of Science: The Physical and Biological Sciences,* 11th ed. (New York, 1965), p. 501.

STRIP MINING STATEMENT
Frankfort / November 24, 1965

I WANT the Widow Combs and all other Kentuckians whose homes and farms are threatened with destruction by strip and auger mining to know that I am on their side.[1] Our state government is moving by every means which we can lawfully use to protect these people and to protect all Kentuckians from the destruction of homes and property.

We do not believe that the old broad-form deed ought to be construed to permit the ruin of homes, farms, and other property by those types of mining, including strip and auger mining, which are unknown to the people who executed these deeds at the time they were executed.[2] The interpretation of the broad-form deed, under present law, is up to the courts, and there are now pending cases in court which are designed to obtain a reconsideration of the meaning and effect of these deeds. At my request, the attorney general has already intervened in these cases on the side of the homeowners and landowners against the strip and auger mining corporations.

As of today, I am instructing the commissioner of public safety that the personnel of the state police are not to be utilized for the enforcement of civil process in our courts without special permission of the governor in each particular case. The primary functions of the state police are to preserve the public peace, to keep our highways safe, and to enforce the criminal law. Court orders in civil cases are directed primarily, if not exclusively, to sheriffs and constables; the sheriff of any county has legal power to appoint deputies and, if necessary, to enlist a posse to aid him in the performance of his official duty. Only after all possibilities for the enforcement of the orders of civil courts by ordinary means have been exhausted would I approve the use of state police personnel for this purpose. In addition, I urge all citizens of Kentucky and expect all citizens of Kentucky to obey the law. But history has sometimes shown that unyielding insistence upon the enforcement of legal rights by the rich and powerful against the humble people of a community is not always the quickest course of action. These questions will never be settled until they are settled right, and I should like to urge the strip and auger corporations whose activities are provoking and causing these disturbances to desist from further insistence upon their pound of flesh until the courts can reconsider the meaning and scope of the broad-form deed.

In the event that our courts should fully and finally disagree with the legal position which this administration has taken with respect to the broad-form deeds, I shall urge the incoming session of the General Assembly to enact legislation, to the fullest possible constitutional extent, to protect homeowners, farms, and other property owners against destruction by strip and auger mining corporations claiming rights under broad-form deeds.[3]

If tumult, disorder, and violence should prevail in the areas where controversy is now raging, I shall be forced to consider what further steps may be taken by the executive department of our state government to preserve peace and perhaps maintain the status quo until the courts and the legislature can decide these fundamental questions.

---

1. The "widow Combs," Mrs. Ollie Combs of Knott County, became a symbol of opposition to the ravages of strip mining when she was jailed for obstructing strip-mining operations near her home in 1965. The incident was widely publicized, and Mrs. Combs later testified before a committee of the General Assembly considering Governor Breathitt's proposed strip-mining legislation in 1966. *Louisville Courier-Journal,* November 24, 25, 26, 1965.

2. The broad-form deed was a contract commonly entered into by eastern Kentuckians in the late nineteenth and early twentieth centuries through which the landowner assigned the mineral rights to his property to a second party. Mineral rights to land capable of yielding 5,000 to 20,000 tons of coal per acre were commonly sold for fifty cents per acre. The deeds customarily conveyed not only the mineral rights but the right to use the surface lands in any way "convenient or necessary" to the extraction of the minerals. This included the use of the land's

timber and water as well as the right to build or dump mining wastes. The surface owner's interest in the land was rendered secondary in perpetuity to the interest of the holder of the mineral rights. The inferior position of the surface owner was sealed by a clause protecting the broad-form deed holder from liability from damages resulting "directly or indirectly" from mining operations. See Harry M. Caudill, *Night Comes to the Cumberlands* (Boston, 1963), pp. 70-76. See also the *Louisville Courier-Journal,* February 26, 27, 1966.

3. During the 1966 session of the General Assembly Governor Breathitt supported a measure, H.B. 258, which would have limited the rights granted to strip-mining companies under the broad-form deed. Under the proposed legislation the provisions of the deeds would apply only to mining methods practiced at the time the deeds were drawn, thereby effectively excluding strip mining, which was a later means of extraction. The bill originally applied to all mineral deeds, but was limited to coal by amendment in order to secure enough votes to move the bill out of committee. The bill was tabled on February 14, and the Breathitt forces were unable to revive it for a later vote. The bill was defeated by a coalition of Republicans and eastern Kentucky Democrats who, according to the *Courier-Journal,* were subjected to intensive lobbying efforts by the coal industry. The bill also suffered from doubts about its constitutionality.

GOVERNOR'S CONFERENCE ON FORESTRY
Lexington / February 16, 1966

ON taking office two years ago, I pledged to you a partnership for progress between the state administration and all of you interested in promoting the development, wise use, and protection of our natural resources. I meet with you tonight in a spirit of rejoicing and of strong resolve. I rejoice in that not only have we expanded and improved conservation activity on all fronts, but we have strengthened this vital cause with new laws passed by the General Assembly. I resolve that during the next two years we shall —with your cooperation—make the strongest effort Kentucky has ever made to conserve and perpetuate the Commonwealth's forest, land, water, and mineral resources.

The strip-mine bill, now signed into law, is only a part of a package of natural resources proposals being considered at this time by the General Assembly.[1] The proposals revolve around creation of a Water Resources Authority with power to issue revenue bonds, if necessary, to finance construction of storage capacities for water behind federal dams.[2]

Despite our many rivers, lakes, and streams, many communities in our state are faced with water shortages. And the problem will grow as our population expands, as our industry grows. One section of the water resources bill would strengthen existing antilitter laws by adding rivers, lakes, streams, and adjacent banks. Another section of the bill would control pollution of the air from all sources of fumes, dirt, gases, odors, smoke, or dust. While all these proposals are designed for the betterment of our state, we are merely carrying out our sacred duty and obligation to protect the birthright of our future citizens.

For, whether we acknowledge it or not, the realities of American growth and the demands of the American people are recasting American government along new and more exacting lines. For America is, as James Madison prophesied, a system of interacting federalism—and the influence of the states will fluctuate with their responsiveness to the needs of the times and the demands of the people.

It is when the state fails to fulfill its role in such areas as conservation, civil rights, education, enhancing the opportunities for the poor, and others, that the federal government moves into the vacuum. It is when the states are not responsive, are not laboratories of experimentation, do not reach all the people, that the state forfeits its strongest argument for a future. As long as I am governor, I intend to see to it that Kentucky meets its responsibilities—that we act to solve our problems. Some problems we have solved, and others we are attempting to solve, but the list is staggering. I am much more concerned about what must yet be done than I am about what has been done.

As chairman of the Natural Resources Committee of the National Governors' Conference, which is meeting here in Lexington tomorrow, I have directed that a study be made of the states' responsibility in natural resources development.[3] An important part of this study, which is now under way, concerns forestry. In the realm of forest resources development, it is our feeling in Kentucky that the state must provide the primary action, with the federal government taking on a supporting role. This relationship must be maintained, for if it is not, then the leadership of forestry activities will slip rapidly from the hands of our state officials into those of one or more federal agencies.

In the committees' studies, we have outlined some fields of activity in which the state should participate. First is in approved management practices: this phase of forest development has as its objective the placing of a reasonable percent of the private forest land of the state under a minimum acceptable level of management. To accomplish this, Kentucky must be in a position to provide technical forestry assistance to its many small forest-land owners. This assistance must be provided free or at a very nominal fee. It is the state's responsibility to determine what level of management will be recommended under the many and varied site conditions. Whatever the recommendation is, it must have as its objective the increasing of yields to meet the future needs for forest products.

Second is fire protection: the state must provide basic protection to all its forest land. This, I am happy to say, is now being done in Kentucky. Specifically, basic protection is the establishment of an organization which is capable of providing satisfactory protection under expected average bad fire danger, including a nucleus which is capable of rapid expansion and statewide flexibility of operation to successfully meet emergency situations. The makeup of the organization must vary with forest conditions found in different sections of the state. In Kentucky, detection and suppression methods vary greatly from the rugged, heavily forested eastern area to the rolling, sparsely forested Bluegrass area. For example, in eastern Kentucky we rely heavily upon forest-fire lookout towers, while in the less heavily forested areas of central Kentucky we have found that airplanes provide a better means of fire detection.

Third is insect and disease control: the state is fortunate in having authority to carry out adequate control programs. The statutes place in the Division of Forestry the authority and responsibility to control forest pests and infestations which are declared to be a public nuisance, in order to protect and preserve forest resources, enhance the growth and maintenance of forests, promote stability of forest-using industries, aid in fire control by reducing the menace created by dying and dead trees, conserve forest cover on watersheds, and protect recreational, wildlife, and other values of the forests of the Commonwealth.

Since infestations of forest pests do not recognize state lines, the insect and disease detection phase of the program should be established as a cooperative program between the states and the federal government. If such was the case, the several states involved with a common problem would have a basis for coordinating their programs. Emergency control programs should be handled by the states with federal support. The federal government should continue to operate insect and disease laboratories. It is urgent that other states develop adequate laws to allow them to fully handle their forest pest detection and control problems.

Fourth is marketing and utilization: in meeting its responsibility in marketing and utilization, Kentucky must utilize all available sources of assistance. We must depend upon various units of state government to develop new and expanded industries. We must utilize the services of the Extension Service to inform landowners of the difference in value of various grades of logs. We must continue to rely on assistance of the federal government in developing log grades and other research projects. The state must have full responsibility for collecting and disseminating market and price information.

Fifth concerns land purchases: all land should contribute to the economic and social benefit of the community. Where these benefits are not forthcoming under private ownership the responsibility falls to the state. This can be done either by legislation or acquisition. Where the state cannot fulfill these obligations it falls to the federal government to do so. The Division of Forestry now owns or leases seven state forests. These areas are used as demonstrations of what can be done with good management. We in Kentucky must launch a vigorous acquisition program to expand our state forest system. These forests would provide recreation areas as well as management demonstration sites.

Sixth is land use itself: countywide land use planning must be encouraged by the state. The result of such planning will be the full and proper use of the various areas within each county. The state should assist local units of government in planning guidelines.

Seventh is watershed protection: the state should acquire areas at the headwaters of major streams and manage them to protect and improve the watershed values. Where critical watersheds exist the state should have the responsibility to purchase such areas if they cannot be protected under private ownership.

Eighth is research: the state should encourage our colleges and universities to train research personnel. There should be a more critical selection of people who go into research. The federal government should be guided by the states' needs in developing their research program. More emphasis should be placed on the need of state organization. The state should be represented on a review and advisory board for the federal experiment stations serving their state. Management problems of local nature should be the responsibility of our state forestry organizations. The state should try to find answers to local problems through short-term applied research projects.

Ninth and final is information and education: the state should provide guidance for conservation education activities pointed at all levels of education and age groups. And on the subject of education, the University of Kentucky is proceeding with plans for a four-year forestry program. They have recently established a two-year associate degree program in forestry and wood utilization technology.

---

1. For details on the strip-mine bill of 1966, see the section of these papers entitled "Legislative Messages and Statements."

2. For information on the Water Resources Authority, see the section of these papers entitled "Legislative Messages and Statements."

3. In his address to the Midwestern Governors' Conference on February 17, 1966, Governor Breathitt reviewed Kentucky's efforts to protect natural resources

and praised the 1966 strip-mine bill as the most comprehensive in the United States. This address is not included in this volume.

PRESS CONFERENCE
Frankfort / January 3, 1967

THE decision rendered by the Knott Circuit Court is a hallmark ruling that is an important step in providing protection for property owners from strip miners, and strikes at the very heart of this evil long inherent in the old broad-form deed. The court holds that the strip-mine operator is liable for any damage he causes to a property owner's home, land, or improvements thereon. If this decision stands in court, no longer will strip-mine operators have the right to remove coal by any method, including destruction of surface properties, without paying for damages. Heretofore, he could destroy the surface, short of "wanton, arbitrary or malicious conduct."

Beginning with *Buchanan vs. Watson* in 1956, the Kentucky Court of Appeals, in ruling on the broad-form mineral deed, has held that the mineral owner has the right to strip the property and that there is no liability for damage to the surface, absent an arbitrary, wanton, or malicious destruction of the land. I want the Widow Combs and all other Kentuckians whose homes and farms are threatened with destruction by strip and auger mining to know that I am on their side. I intend to continue this fight in the courts, if necessary, to stop this travesty upon property rights. We do not intend to rest.

Last November I asked the state and attorney general to intervene in this *Martin vs. Kentucky Oak Mining Company* court case in Knott County on the side of the aggrieved property owners. Our lawyers have spent many hours and many days working on this case. I want to personally commend them for their work. They are on the right side, and I want them to continue their efforts if it becomes necessary.

FOURTH ANNUAL GOVERNOR'S CONFERENCE ON FORESTRY
Lexington / February 15, 1967

WHEN Gene Butcher told me that the theme of the forestry conference this year would be "Effective Marketing of Kentucky's Forestry Products," I was quite pleased.[1] Improved marketing practices is one of the ways the Commission on Agriculture proposed to increase our farm income to the billion dollar mark.

Realizing the need to explore this field to the utmost, the Processing and Marketing Committee of the Commission on Agriculture held a farm marketing workshop in Louisville last October. Many of the problems facing Kentucky farmers in marketing their products were discussed. These problems suggest many opportunities in improving the efficiency of present marketing systems—probably expansion of present markets—and areas of concern to producers, processors, distributors, and retailers. Many of the marketing problems facing the farmer are similar to those you face in marketing forest products—for example, changes in consumer tastes—restrictive rail rates—foreign imports and exports. These are just a few of the problems you have in common.

We already have scored a major breakthrough last year with announcement of the opening of the WesCor Corporation at Hawesville—the first pulp mill in over 100 years to locate in Kentucky. This $12 million investment is a direct result of an eight-county study in western Kentucky by Spindletop Research. And WesCor is expected to go into production this spring. Also as a result of the Spindletop study, the West Virginia Pulp and Paper Company is considering very seriously another western Kentucky location. And still other pulp and paper mills and fiberboard companies are considering Kentucky locations on the basis of information presented by Spindletop. We now have the greatest interest in Kentucky locations by wood and pulp mills that we ever have had.

In just two years now, forty-four new or expanded wood industries have been added to Kentucky's growing list of manufacturers. These new wood industries have added 2,617 new jobs in the manufacturing phases, and an estimated 3,500 new jobs in the forests themselves. Also, in just two years, production of round wood in the Commonwealth has increased by 36 percent—from 73,515 cords in 1964 to an estimated 100,000 cords last year. The value of last year's round wood production at the mill was $1.4 million. This year, the production of round wood in Kentucky is expected to double to 200,000 cords, and a value of $2.8 million. I should mention, however, that part of this production is in the form of sawmill residue. This increase is a result of the new industries primarily using wood fiber and which have been brought into the state in the last two years.

The Department of Commerce at Frankfort, headed by Commissioner Katherine Peden, deserves praise for the excellent work it has done in assisting existing industry to expand and also in attracting new industry to Kentucky. For example, in the past two years alone, the state Department of Commerce has worked with more than 100 wood industrial prospects. Many of these prospects now are in production and others will be shortly. Of particular interest to you here today, the Commerce Department developed appraisals of plant location opportunities for six different types of wood products. Thus, the department can provide a prospect prompt and accurate answers to his questions. The immediate availability of this information has been immensely helpful in locating new industry in Kentucky.

And I have other encouraging progress of particular interest to report to you today. Some of you may recall that three years ago at the first conference on forestry, I reported the organization of the Commission on Agriculture. The purpose of this commission was to seek ways and means to increase Kentucky farmers' agriculture income to one billion dollars a year. Just last month, the commission, under its able executive director, Hayden Timmons, held a conference in Louisville to review the activities of its various committees.[2] At that time I announced the appointment of Eddie Moore of Hyden as chairman of the forestry committee. He succeeds Barney Tucker. But Barney, because of his wide interest and experience in the field, will chair the promotion committee, at my request.

Farm income in Kentucky set a new record last year—this we already know. Early estimates from agricultural economists at the University of Kentucky place cash receipts at $760 million. And this is a conservative figure. The final total could even be higher. But already, the 1966 figure is 8 percent higher than 1965. Just three years ago, in 1963, cash receipts were only $644 million. So we already have an increase in these three years of $116 million, or an average increase of nearly $39 million a year.

I'm going to review briefly now some of the accomplishments of the various organizations concerned with the conservation of our natural resources. The state Division of Forestry is upgrading its forest fire control and is in the process of rebuilding sixteen of its older wooden fire lookout towers. These are being replaced by new sixty-foot towers. The money for this was included in our recent bond issue. Several of these towers are being moved to new locations to improve the fire detection system. And the recent expansion of Forestry's utilization and marketing section from two to six men will provide increased assistance to landowners, timber operators, and primary wood processors in this important field. The Forestry Division also is in the process of holding a series of information meetings across the state. These meetings are being held to explain to industry, development groups, and other interested people how the material from the recently published Kentucky forestry survey can be used in planning the expansion of existing industry or in attracting new industry to a particular area. For the first time, we have reliable figures by species for each county in the Commonwealth. Information from the survey already has proved invaluable in attracting new forest-based industry to Kentucky.

Much of the Forestry Division's nursery activity during the last year has been directed to its tree improvement program—specifically, selection of superior genetic makeup of timber specie trees as seed sources for improved nursery stock. The shortleaf and loblolly pine-seed orchards at Kentucky Dam were expanded to twenty-two acres. And a new white pine-seed orchard was established at the Morgan County tree nursery. This was done in cooperation with the TVA.

But hardwoods have not been neglected. A cherrybark oak-seed orchard will be established this spring. The hybrid poplar program is being expanded, and a cottonwood cutting orchard is being established, using cuttings from superior trees. Seed production areas are being started—this effort is to obtain seed from a known geographic source. These areas will provide seed from trees of superior quality. All of this is being done to provide Kentucky tree planters with seedlings of desirable quality and growth characteristics. The Forestry Division expects to have eighteen to twenty million seedlings available for distribution to landowners this spring.

I'm also happy to report that this past year, for the first time, the sale of forest products from state land paid the entire cost of the state forest program. We are planning to acquire an additional number of state forests to locate geographically in order to permit all private woodland owners interested in forest management the opportunity of observing firsthand the best-known and latest forestry practices.

The Forestry Division has used to the fullest extent the manpower available under the Work Experience and Training Program—or, as it is more familiarly known, the "happy pappy" program. The men in this program have planted nearly four million seedlings. In addition, these men were responsible for suppressing 75 percent of the fires in the eighteen counties in which they served. So—the availability of these men also helped to conserve a valuable natural resource.

Our Forestry Division recently acquired two new airplanes to replace the ones they had been using the last five years. These planes are used in detecting fires in the less heavily forested portions of the Commonwealth during the spring and fall fire seasons. They also are used in aerial surveys to detect insect and disease outbreaks.

The division's sixty-four-page booklet, "Forestry in Kentucky," has been highly complimented by industry people, by educators, and by laymen. The original printing of 15,000 copies is nearly exhausted, and a reprint is planned.

Still another encouraging item of good progress is that of the Daniel Boone National Forest in its land acquisition program in Clay, Leslie, and Harlan counties. So far this unit has acquired 60,000 acres at a cost of $2,020,000, and it has an additional 11,000 acres under option. These lands are located in the headwaters of the Middle Fork Kentucky River Watershed. This expansion of Forest Service holdings is a tangible implementation of one of twelve points Governor Combs included in his program. I'm talking about the program he presented to the White House Governors Conference during his administration. These points were the foundation for the present Appalachian program in eastern Kentucky. Funds for this expansion I've been talking about were obtained from the Appalachian Commission as part of the Appalachian development program.

On July 1 this year—just four and one-half months from today—this newly acquired forest land will be organized as the Eighth Ranger District of the Daniel Boone National Forest. The old Ford Motor Company headquarters at Peabody is being rehabilitated to serve as the new district headquarters. As soon as this area becomes a new ranger unit, work will start on all phases of forest management, wildlife, and recreation. The area was placed under national forest fire protection last year, and the program will be intensified this year. This purchase by the Daniel Boone unit brings the national forest ownership to approximately 520,000 acres. And all of this land is open to public hunting and general recreation. The federal ownership provides a base of work for public assistance programs based on public employment.

Another activity I should tell you about is planning now under way to develop the recreational potential of Cave Run and Laurel reservoirs. Under an agreement with the Corps of Engineers, the Forest Service will develop and implement a recreational program around these two new reservoirs. The recreational development will include such items as boat-launching ramps, picnic and camping areas, and trails. Part of the actual development will be by private concessioners who will operate such facilities as boat docks. The orderly development of recreational lands around these two reservoirs should provide a terrific influx of tourists.

Human conservation also is vitally important, of course. And the Daniel Boone Forest has been very successful with its two Job Corps camps. The camp at Pine Knot, with 264 enrollees, is the largest rural center in the nation. And the camp at Frenchburg has 120 men. Men from both camps are engaged in conservation and recreation improvement projects on the forest. At the same time, they are improving themselves academically in the classroom.

Recently, we received a $25,000 planning grant from the Economic Development Administration to make a detailed study of the feasibility of building an arboretum in Breathitt County. This arboretum would be devoted to native plants of Kentucky, but it would not be just a unique tourist attraction. It would be an invaluable tool in conservation work for our young people.

So, you see, with your help, we are making progress in all areas of conservation—and in both human and natural resources. I ask you here today to continue the teamwork that not only is bringing us national recognition but, so important on the immediate Kentucky scene, the preservation and development of our God-given natural assets.

---

1. Gene Butcher (1920-   ), a native of Bath County who served in various conservation and forestry positions for the Commonwealth of Kentucky (1950-1968). At the time of his resignation he was a resident of Georgetown, Kentucky. Information provided by Division of Personnel, Frankfort.

2. Welby Hayden Timmons (1926-   ), from Henderson, Kentucky; assistant director and administrative assistant with the Department of Conservation (1951-1953, 1960-1961); administrative assistant to governor's office (1964-1967); at the time of resignation Timmons was a resident of Frankfort. Information provided by Division of Personnel, Frankfort.

STRIP MINING SYMPOSIUM
Owensboro / July 13, 1967

AMERICA is probably more aware today than ever before of the vital importance of conservation, and of the need to protect, develop, and use wisely the treasures of earth and water with which this land has been so greatly blessed. Nothing contributes more materially to our economic strength, to the enrichment of our lives, and to the value of the heritage we will leave our children than the richness of our natural resources. We will be untrue to ourselves and to those who come after us if we do not guard them well.

For these reasons the 1966 session of the Kentucky General Assembly enacted more beneficial natural resources legislation than any other session in the history of the Kentucky legislature. The strip-mining bill, the creation of a Kentucky Water Resources Authority, the water pollution and air pollution measures, and the antilitter law were all significant pieces of legislation.

I am especially proud of the strip-mining bill, which was adopted amid cries of doom for the coal industry from some quarters. The August, 1966, issue of *Coal Age,* a leading industry publication, referred to Kentucky's new law as "the most restrictive reclamation law in the nation." Our position, however, was that the strong bill was responsible legislation and that it would not drive the coal industry out of business. Our position has been verified, as evidenced by the latest figures after only one year of operation under the new law.

Since the new law went into effect nearly 12,000 acres of land have been placed under permit—a figure that is double the 6,000 acres which were stripped in the 1965 fiscal year. At the same time, forty-four new coal operations have been granted permission to strip in Kentucky. Ten of these operations were from out of state. Yet they still decided to move their operations to Kentucky with full knowledge of our comprehensive reclamation law. It is not inconceivable that strip mining has just begun in Kentucky, for there are probably ten million potential acres that possibly could be mined. To date, only about 1 percent of this potential has been disturbed.

On the field trip tomorrow you will be able to see for yourself the results after one year's operation under the new law. I think you will find that the results in western Kentucky have been, in fact, astounding and remarkable. Nearly 5,000 acres have been strip mined and regraded since our law went into effect. The difference in these acres and the former practice of leaving parallel rows of spoil ridges and deep valleys is like comparing night and day.

In mountain-type strip mining, or the contour method, significant reclamation has been accomplished in some areas, but serious problems remain. Perhaps the most serious problem today stems from the Kentucky Court of Appeals' interpretation of the "broad-form" or long-form mineral deed. Thousands of acres in eastern Kentucky are burdened by the effects of the broad-form deed as the law stands today. The typical "broad-form" mineral deed was executed some fifty or sixty years ago and severed the mineral estate from the surface ownership. These deeds normally provide for mining "in any manner necessary or convenient in order to remove the mineral." Moreover, there is usually a clause waiving all liability for damage to the surface in removing the mineral. Obviously, strip mining was not contemplated by the parties when this deed was executed. The first large-scale operations only came to the mountains following World War II.

Yet in 1956 the Kentucky Court of Appeals, in the landmark decision of *Buchanan vs. Watson,* ruled that the "broad-form" deed, even though it contained no reference to strip mining, did allow such a method of mining.[1] Moreover, there was to be no liability for any damage to the surface, absent an "arbitrary, wanton or malicious" destruction of the land. The effect of this decision was to make the mineral owner's claim superior to that of the surface owner. The family who had lived on the land for years, working its soil and improving their home, now resided at the sufferance of the mineral owner, under the threat of the landslides and general destruction of their land.

The "broad-form" mineral deed is not peculiar to Kentucky; it is common throughout the coal areas. What is peculiar, however, is the Kentucky courts' interpretation of the deed. The Kentucky interpretation stands alone among the states and is contrary to the general rule of law. West Virginia, Pennsylvania, Ohio, Colorado, and other states have ruled on similar mineral deeds, but in favor of the landowner. In general, these decisions have held that where the deed is silent or ambiguous on the question of strip mining, then the deed must be read in its entirety, taking into full account the circumstances and mining methods practiced in the area at the time, so as not to attribute an unreasonable interpretation to what the parties intended when the deed was signed.

My position in the "broad-form" deed controversy was made quite clear prior to the last session of the General Assembly. I do not believe that the old broad-form deed ought to be construed to permit the ruin of homes, farms, and other property. Prior to the legislature, I instructed the attorney general's office to intervene in a lawsuit for the purpose of reversing the Kentucky interpretation of the "broad-form" deed as enunciated in the *Buchanan* decision.

This lawsuit, styled *Leroy Martin vs. Kentucky Oak Mining Company* and *Kentucky River Coal Corporation,* was filed in Knott County Circuit Court.[2] The attorney general intervened in the role of "amicus curiae," or "friend of the court," for the purpose of explaining to the court what the rule of law in this matter should be. Last December, Knott Circuit Judge John Chris Cornett ruled that the broad-form deed in question allowed strip mining on the land, but that the coal operator was liable for any damage to the land.[3] Both sides have appealed this decision to the Kentucky Court of Appeals. An early decision is expected when the court begins a new session in September.[4] Thus the Court of Appeals now has the opportunity to reverse the *Buchanan* case and related decisions, and to bring Kentucky law in line with the general rule of law in other states.

But seeking court reversal of the *Buchanan* decision was not my only action to protect the landowners in eastern Kentucky from the onerous effects of the "broad-form" mineral deed. In the last session of the General

Assembly, I requested the drafting of a bill for the benefit of the surface owners. Called the "Widow Combs'" bill by the press, this bill would have provided that where a mineral deed was silent or ambiguous on the question of strip mining, there would be a rebuttable presumption created that such deed did not contemplate strip mining. Thus, the burden of proof would have rested with the mineral owner to prove that strip mining was intended when the deed was signed by the parties. Unfortunately this bill was tabled in the last legislature, but I believe it should be given serious consideration during the coming session of the General Assembly.

On the question of reclamation in the mountain areas, an evaluation of the present law is being made to determine whether they are accomplishing the objectives of the law, particularly on the steep slopes. The regulations today prohibit the creation of a fill bench on slopes above thirty-three degrees. Serious consideration should be given to reducing this provision to slopes of perhaps twenty-eight or thirty degrees.

But let's make one point absolutely clear. You cannot eliminate all of the problems in strip mining in mountains or by the contour method. The challenge to the coal industry is clear. You must do all within your ability to operate not only within the letter of the law, but the spirit as well.

It is important for Kentucky and all states to meet the problems of strip mining. If a state refuses to accept its responsibility in this area, then it is only right that the federal government intervene. At the banquet tonight, Assistant Secretary of the Interior Cordell Moore will brief you on the highlights of the surface-mining report that was given to President Johnson on July 1.[5] The very necessity for such a federal study indicates that the individual states are not accepting their total responsibility in the strip-mining area. I believe it is high time that each state accept the challenge.

Kentucky, Pennsylvania, and West Virginia have shown the lead by adopting outstanding reclamation laws, and Kentucky and Pennsylvania have authorized membership in the Interstate Mining Compact. This compact can be of benefit to both the citizens of the state and the industry as well. I urge all of the states' representatives here today to give serious consideration to joining the Interstate Mining Compact. This compact seeks to establish sensible, workable, fair, and uniform control and reclamation practices in all coal-producing states. This is, actually, the only sensible way to do it. It is the only fair way to do it.

A state trying to control the damages of surface mining is automatically handicapped as long as major coal companies can threaten to move to adjoining states that require no reclamation. Furthermore, it is unfair to compel coal producers on one side of a hill to pay the costs of reclamation —often amounting to several cents a ton—while producers on the other side of the hill, because they are in another state, are required to make no reclamation effort whatever.

But in the long run the greatest unfairness rests on the people who, in the absence of effective reclamation laws, must sooner or later pay the cost of restoring the ravaged land to beauty and usefulness. It is unfair to the people of one state to let the people of a neighboring state silt and pollute the streams running across state lines. In the final analysis, the only fair and reasonable method of controlling this damage is to require the industry that does the damage to correct it. And let me add here that the cost is far less if it is done at the time the mining is completed.

Admittedly, the Interstate Mining Compact is not our only alternative. Powerful forces are already working toward federal control of surface mining. Members of Congress and cabinet officials have become disturbed by the damage done by this industry, and by the failure of the states to meet the challenge that it represents. Control is coming. Make no doubt about it. The only question is whether it shall be federal control or that exercised by the states, through the states by the fair, strict, and uniform regulation made possible by the Interstate Mining Compact. I appeal to you—let us choose the path of mature responsibility. Let's do this job ourselves.

---

1. In *Buchanan vs. Raleigh Watson and Stella Watson* the Kentucky Court of Appeals ruled that the estate of the surface owner was "subservient to the dominate estate of the grantee." Thus the owner of the mineral rights was empowered to use stripping methods as "the only feasible process of extracting coal" regardless of the methods contemplated by the original contracting parties unless the process was used "aggressively, arbitrarily, wantonly, or maliciously." *I.H. Buchanan vs. Raleigh Watson and Stella Watson,* Ky., 290 S.W. 2nd 40.

2. In *Leroy Martin et al. vs. Kentucky Oak Mining Company et al.* Knott County Circuit Court Judge John Chris Cornett ruled that landowners could sue mining companies for damages "to their estate in land, including surface timber, vegetation, water supply, fences, buildings or other improvements thereon" resulting from strip-mining operations even though companies were operating under the provisions of a broad-form deed. Judge Cornett had made a similar ruling in 1955 in *Buchanan vs. Watson,* only to have his decision overturned by the Kentucky Court of Appeals. The plaintiff in *Martin vs. Kentucky Oak Mining Company,* Leroy Martin, was a leading figure in the Appalachian Group to Save the Land and People, an organization formed in 1965 by eastern Kentuckians to protect their lands from the destruction caused by coal stripping. Harry M. Caudill, Whitesburg lawyer and a former member of the Kentucky House of Representatives, acted as Martin's attorney. Caudill had already achieved notoriety as the author of *Night Comes to the Cumberlands,* a "regional biography" of Kentucky's Cumberland plateau which directed national attention to the problems of Appalachia and the ravages of strip mining. Immediately following Cornett's ruling, Breathitt assigned

Attorney General David Schneider and special counsel Edward Prichard to assist Caudill in preparing his case for appeal. *New York Times,* January 15, 1967, and the *Louisville Courier-Journal,* January 4, 1967.

3. John Chris Cornett (1910-), attorney, Hindman, Kentucky. Employed by the Elkhorn Coal Mining Company (1927-1929); teacher, Knott County school system (1929-1940); completed law degree, University of Kentucky (1940); Knott County judge (1942-1946); circuit judge, Knott County (1950-). Hambleton Tapp, ed., *Kentucky Lives* (Hopkinsville, Ky., 1966), p. 106.

4. The court's decision in *Buchanan* (see earlier footnote) remained the basis for the eventual disposition of *Martin* by the Court of Appeals in June of 1968. The opinion of the court stated that Martin's arguments, which turned on the question of the intention of the contractual parties, were weakened by two considerations. First, the landowners received compensation for the mineral rights to their land commensurate with the price of land at the time of sale. Second, though less destructive than strip mining, the mining practices of the day often rendered some lands unsuitable for agriculture. These two factors indicated to the court that the landowner may have been sufficiently aware of the consequences when he sold the mineral rights to his land. Therefore, the precedent established in *Buchanan* had to be followed. *Leroy Martin et al. vs. Kentucky Oak Mining Company et al.,* Ky. 429 S.W. 2nd 395.

5. In his address to the 1967 Kentucky strip mining symposium in Owensboro, Assistant Secretary of the Interior Cordell Moore clearly indicated that the mining industry's general disregard for environmental damage and the state's continued failure to adequately regulate mining practices would necessitate intervention by the federal government. "The ground swell of public concern about strip mining," he explained, "now has swept across the nation," and government at some level would have to respond. As evidence of the government's intentions, Moore cited a report prepared by the Department of Interior which recommended the extension of effective strip-mining controls to every state and the appropriation of $757 million to reclaim stripped-out areas. The threat of federal intervention reaffirmed one of Breathitt's long-standing arguments for effective regulation of strip mining. Concurrently, additional pressures were building from the local end of the political spectrum. At the same symposium addressed by Moore, demonstrators representing the Appalachian Group to Save the Land and the People protested the destruction of eastern Kentucky land and property by strip-mine operations. And while they sought the attention and aid of government, their friends in the mountains of eastern Kentucky employed more direct means to defend their interests. On June 29, Jink Ray and his neighbors surrounded a bulldozer belonging to the Puritan Coal Mining Company and prevented it from beginning strip-mining operations on the mountainside above Ray's land near Island Creek in Pike County. On July 3, Puritan sought a court injunction ordering Ray to cease obstruction of the company's efforts to extract coal which it claimed under a broad-form deed signed in 1887. Each Pike County judge successively disqualified himself from hearing the case, an indication of the local political importance of the case and the public support for Ray's stand in the county. Finally, Judge George O. Bertram of Taylor County accepted the case and, after hearing the arguments and visiting the disputed mining site, issued the injunction requested by Puritan. On the same day

that Judge Bertram issued his ruling, Breathitt visited Island Creek during an inspection tour of eastern Kentucky mining sites and landslide areas. In a meeting with Ray the governor cautioned him not to use violence to protect his property. Apparently, he also promised to come to Ray's aid should Puritan attempt to resume clearing overburden from the coal seam under Ray's land. The next morning the Puritan bulldozer began working its way down the mountain toward Ray's property. Ray rushed a telegram to Breathitt which read: "Bulldozer working—if you intend to help me do it now." Breathitt, acting under the authority granted by the 1966 strip-mining legislation, immediately suspended the Puritan Company's mining permit pending a complete investigation by the Reclamation Division. Ray later remarked in gratitude: "He [Breathitt] did just what he said he was going to do." On August 2 the Reclamation Commission permanently cancelled Puritan's coal mining permit, the first real action under the 1966 law. The commission cited the following findings in justifying its decision: "Because of the inadequate drainage pattern involved, the absence of an adequate filter zone and the proximity of dwelling houses, there is a strong likelihood of damage to persons and property should the operation be allowed to progress on the precipitory slopes under the permit. . . . Moreover experience in the Commonwealth with a similar type of operation upon land with similar overburden shows that landslides and substantial deposition of sediment in the drainage land below cannot feasibly be prevented in the area in question." While the Puritan case established the ability and the interest of the Breathitt administration to limit stripping operations on the steep slopes of eastern Kentucky, the method employed was at best impermanent. Following his July inspection of the area's coal field, however, Breathitt ordered Reclamation Commissioner J.O. Matlick to conduct a study to determine whether existing regulations provided adequate protection for lives and property of the area's inhabitants. In his directive, Breathitt noted a recent Department of Interior study which recommended that strip-mining operations be restricted to mountainsides with slopes of 28 degrees or less. The existing Kentucky regulation allowed mining on 33-degree slopes, a limit approached by the Puritan operation and by the "similar" operations mentioned in the August revocation order. Breathitt's own position was clear from the circumstances surrounding his directive, and as his administration entered its final days it became clear that he intended to establish a conservation policy which would outlast his term of office. On December 7 the Kentucky Reclamation Commission conducted hearings as required by the 1966 Strip Mine Control Act to consider alterations in the regulations governing the industry. The commission proposed to restrict mining to slopes of 28 degrees or less. The strip mine owners asked for a continuance; nevertheless, the commission voted in favor of the tighter restriction. The *New York Times,* citing unnamed sources, described Breathitt's tactic as a means of "boxing in" his successors. Louie Nunn "was strongly supported by strip mine interests" in the November elections, according to the *Times,* and it was doubted that he would promote stringent mining controls during his administration. However, conservationists within the Breathitt administration felt that it would be politically difficult for Nunn to repeal regulations once they were in place. Therefore, Breathitt bequeathed possibly the most stringent strip-mining conservation measures in the country to his Republican successor. *New York Times,* July 16, 18, 19, August 2, December 12, 14, 1967.

SOUTHERN WATER RESOURCES CONFERENCE
Biloxi, Mississippi / July 13, 1967

I AM highly honored to be a part of your discussion of this vital subject —water. I am grateful for the opportunity to talk about a subject that is very close to my heart—natural resources and their development. Without the wise use and development of our water resources we need not be concerned about the other resources. Without adequate supplies of usable water to sustain people, we need not worry about land, minerals, forests, recreation, or wildlife. Next to air, water is our most necessary resource for human survival. In this crowded world, water looms as a future problem almost as serious as that of food. Water is not only essential for the production of food—water is industry's most important raw material. . . .[1]

Every year more than a billion dollars in flood damage still occurs in the nation's upstream watersheds. Sediment damage in these areas costs more than $85 million a year. Every year a billion and a half cubic yards of sediment are deposited in the nation's major reservoirs. This reduces our water supply capacity by an amount equivalent to the annual needs of a city of five and one-half million people—or almost both Los Angeles and Chicago. All of these examples show evidence of the carelessness and selfishness that we must stop and reverse. It is indeed a national problem that cries out for action in each of our states. . . .

Having served as chairman of the Natural Resources Committee of the National Governors' Conference, I am thoroughly convinced that we who have positions of leadership in our states must assume the major responsibility. For if we do not meet our state responsibilities in the conservation of water, we will forfeit this right and duty to the federal government. Our responsibility is to design a long-range, comprehensive master plan for the orderly development, management, and pollution abatement of water resources in our states. This plan should be so coordinated with all federal programs that no duplications occur and full cooperation for the benefit of all can be achieved.

The fifty governors and territorial governors of the National Governors' Conference, at their Los Angeles meeting in 1966, adopted the report of the Natural Resources Committee, which recommended: first, the states should designate one state agency to carry out their responsibilities in comprehensive water resource planning, development, and management; second, the states develop and implement interstate compacts and utilize federal cooperative programs to provide solutions to water problems that cross state borders; third, intrastate water resources be developed on the basis of need within the state; fourth, the states, through the Council of

State Governments, or otherwise, exchange information in the development of water quality criteria and standards; fifth, the states provide basic research data for comprehensive planning and encourage training for careers in water development, research and management; sixth, the states and the federal government continue their efforts to meet an increasing demand for water-oriented outdoor recreation, fully utilizing the federal-state approach to multiple-purpose water resource projects; seventh, exclusive federal control in the planning and development of river basins is not desirable, and states should accept their responsibilities and proper roles in river basin development; and eighth, since dam and reservoir sites are a natural resource, each should be developed to its full potential to meet present and future needs as a multipurpose structure. Therefore, the Congress should revise and broaden its policy relating to the conservation and wise use of the nation's water supply so that water storage to meet expanding municipal, industrial, and recreational needs and other future beneficial uses is established as a primary benefit with the same priority as flood control, navigation, pollution abatement, and low-flow augmentation in establishing project justification. The governors also recommended that federal funds should be appropriated in sufficient amounts to provide adequate water storage capacity for these purposes.

In the limited time I have here tonight I cannot go into detail about each of these proposals, but there is one particular area where I do want to direct my remarks because I feel the matter is of the utmost importance, especially to the southern states. One of the specific beneficial uses referred to in the last recommendation is water for agricultural uses for farming purposes and—now being omitted as a cost benefit factor in federal projects.

As recently as April 4, this year, I wrote the Secretary of Agriculture Orville Freeman that: "We are vitally concerned over what we think is a glaring omission in water resource development planning, on the local as well as the national level, i.e., the omission of reserve water for agricultural development—especially water for future increased irrigation—in reservoirs now being planned and constructed." The Corps of Engineers, as you know, plans construction of dams and reservoirs in accordance with criteria established by the Congress. Currently allowable benefits include flood control, water quality, recreation, and fish and wildlife; also water supply for municipal and industrial growth on a reimbursable basis. But water for irrigation is not allowed as a benefit.

This oversight is particularly important in view of the rapidly expanding role our nation is expected to play in increasing agricultural production to assist in feeding the world. It also is important to the fifteen southern states represented here whose economies depend greatly upon farming.

It is unfortunately true that a stream may be running nearly full during dry periods as a result of reservoir augmentation for pollution abatement and yet not contain one drop of water which can be legally used for irrigation. This fact has bothered our water planning personnel in Kentucky for quite some time, and it has been discussed with other states and with water-oriented representatives of the federal government without any discernible impact. Except for Bureau of Reclamation projects, we cannot discover any agency concerned with this situation, and of course that bureau has no responsibility east of the Mississippi River.

In Kentucky we are working closely and successfully with the Corps of Engineers, the U.S. Department of Agriculture, and with the Department of the Interior on the general problem of water development, but we so far have been unable to find any basis for projecting, planning, or assuring the increased availability of irrigation water commensurate with the probable expansion of requirements.

The modern world is making deep inroads into the available agricultural lands. Due to the world food situation, it is apparent that we must, in the future, grow more food on less land than we do now, and it is just as apparent that the availability of an increasing amount of irrigation water will be a companion necessity. Because a reservoir preempts the site forever and has a minimum life of about fifty years, full utilization of the site is an overriding necessity, and irrigation water requirements must be determined and planned into the reservoir for at least the life of the project.

For the foregoing reasons, I would urge that a project be established in the U.S. Department of Agriculture to provide required planning information which will permit us to determine future irrigation water requirements on a continuing basis. I strongly recommend that Congress take immediate action to revise and broaden its policy relating to the conservation of the nation's water supply to assure a water storage for future agriculture needs. This need should be established by Congress as a primary benefit in determining project costs with the same priority as flood control, navigation, and pollution abatement. And, federal funds should be appropriated to meet this urgent need. Taking the lead in this effort should be the U.S. Department of Agriculture, for it, more than any other federal agency, is responsible for this nation's future food supply.

I know that many of you in the southeastern states have water laws designed to help you develop your water resources. We, in Kentucky, feel fortunate that our 1966 General Assembly, among many other natural resources bills, created a water authority. This water authority is composed of representatives of those state agencies that have major interests in water. The director of the Division of Water in the Department of Natural Resources serves as executive director of the authority. This authority provides the tool necessary to coordinate the activities of the Commonwealth in the development and wise use of public water, not only for the present but for many years ahead. Among its many broad powers the authority may contract with the federal government for the inclusion of additional water supply storage space behind existing or proposed flood control dams or other projects. It may construct, maintain, repair, and operate water resource projects in addition to providing financial assistance. The authority is empowered to promote the beneficial and proper distribution of water throughout the Commonwealth.

The state laws that we have are merely to give us the opportunity to do something in water resources development. The banks of a river may belong to one man, one city or one state, but the waters which flow between these banks must in many cases meet the needs of thousands of men, of many cities, and of several states. This is the reason why the problem of water control cries out for states' actions, states' cooperation, and state standards of water quality.

We in the Southeast have the undeveloped reservoir sites—we have the rainfall and, above all, we have the opportunity to act now to provide for a growth in population, agricultural development, and industrial development much above national averages.

This is the water resources challenge—can we meet it? We have the capacity and our water resources are adequate if we plan to conserve and use them wisely. We're straining now, but in the future we will burst the bonds of all restraint if we do not act now. This is no time for gradualism, no time for halfway measures. Our system of law has always regarded the trustee who is faithless to his trust as the worst of all malefactors. If we fail to take the necessary measures demanded of us by our own responsibility as trustees of the natural resources which Providence has showered upon us with almost reckless generosity, then we shall earn the contempt of those who come after us.

---

1. A section of this speech detailing future water needs has been deleted.

STRIP MINE STATEMENT
Frankfort / September 6, 1967

I HAVE today directed the Department of Natural Resources, effective September 15, to begin notifying the individual landowner when a stripping application request is filed in Frankfort by a coal operator.[1] Heretofore, the landowner had no way of having this information unless he came to Frankfort to inspect the public record or unless contacted by an agent of the coal company. In many cases, his first knowledge that his land was about to be disturbed was when the bulldozer arrived to begin work. This is wrong, and my action will correct this injustice.

I feel, and feel strongly, that any property owner has the right to know in advance that his land may be stripped. The state, in my judgment, has a humane obligation to supply this information and notice. With systematic advance warning, the property owner will have better opportunity to file legal objections if he so desires, to inspect the application proceedings, or to prepare his surface property where necessary for the stripping.

Law now requires oil companies to give coal companies notice when they are about to drill for oil in order to prevent unnecessary disturbance or ruin to a coal seam. I think the property owner has just as much right, if not more, to such notice.

Beginning September 15, the Department of Natural Resources will notify the property owner by registered letter that a strip-mining request is pending. In addition, a public notice will be placed at the courthouse of the county where the land is located.

I recognize that in some cases the ownership of surface property may be complex and difficult to pinpoint. But even in those cases, a conscientious effort will be made by the state to inform the landowner. This step that I've taken today is one more effort on my part to help the little man in eastern Kentucky whose property is threatened by strip-mine operations. In my remaining months in office, I'll continue to do all in my power to protect the landowner from injustices brought about by the old broad-form deed.

---

1. The directive, issued as a memorandum, is in the Natural Resource file, Breathitt papers.

GOVERNOR'S CONSERVATION CONGRESS
Lexington / October 26, 1967

It is gratifying and reassuring to see so many of you here and to observe the great interest that is being displayed by so many of our citizens in the conservation of the natural resources of our state. For four years I've enjoyed working with you in developing programs to preserve and protect our land, our mountains, our water, our air, our forests, our rivers and streams. We have had some stormy times together and some controversial issues, but in the overall picture, we have made great progress.

As I leave office, I want to express to you my deep appreciation for the support and interest you rendered in these efforts. Among you are representatives of many organizations which have been in the very forefront of this battle. Without your support we could have never achieved the success we did. Long after we've departed the scene, history will record, in my judgment, that the 1966 Kentucky General Assembly passed the greatest list of conservation legislation on behalf of our overall environment ever written into our state's law books.

I think all Kentuckians can point with pride to the many accomplishments of the Department of Natural Resources. This department has had an outstanding and dedicated commissioner in Jack Matlick. I'm sure you agree with me that the citizens of Kentucky owe a debt of gratitude to Jack Matlick and to the members of his staff for their dedication and devotion to a program designed to develop and wisely use Kentucky's natural resources, and to provide for citizens of the Commonwealth, now and in the future, a beautiful, prosperous, and productive state.

Kentucky is considered a leader in the field of conservation, and people from throughout this country are constantly asking the state for assistance in developing conservation programs. Those of you in this hall, dedicated and knowledgeable private volunteers in the resource conservation field, are chiefly responsible for this position of leadership.

For example, Kentucky's watershed program is one of the best in the nation and has captured two national titles, the only state to accomplish this feat. The Mud River Watershed in Logan, Butler, Todd, and Muhlenberg counties won in 1964, and the North Fork of the Little River Watershed won in 1967.

The new Kentucky Water Resources Authority, passed by the 1966 legislature, is laying the groundwork for an adequate water supply for the future. This law, which is being studied by many other states, is the most far-sighted and comprehensive of any water legislation passed by any legislature in the history of the Commonwealth.

Kentucky's small lakes development program is a unique method of providing communities with water for municipal, industrial, agricultural, and recreational uses. Since the project was started sixteen lakes, ranging from 5 to 857 acres of water, have been built, most of them created by converting a highway fill into a dam.

Kentucky's forestry program has won numerous awards and, more importantly, saved untold millions of dollars in valuable timber land. A young state employee, Danny Helm of Hustonville, is in the University of Kentucky Hospital tonight suffering from serious burns he obtained yesterday while fighting a forest fire in Casey County.[1] The contribution made by such dedicated people as Danny and the many others who endanger their lives every day in protecting our forests is very important to this state's future.

Kentucky's clean-up and beautification program also has gained national recognition. Kentucky was the first state to receive the National Keep America Beautiful State Award, and last year Laurel County received the national county award for its clean-up and beautification efforts. The importance of this program—which now reaches nearly every one of our 120 counties—cannot be overemphasized. It is important to our economy because both tourists and industry look to clean, well-kept towns and countrysides, to visit and locate industries. The series of antilitter and beautification laws, including the billboard law, the junkyard law, and the updating of the antilitter law in 1966, making littering illegal on all public properties, including water, and on private property without the owner's consent—all of these are important to the beauty of this great state.

Just recently I appointed a wild rivers advisory committee to develop a plan strictly oriented for Kentucky. These clear and free-flowing streams —still relatively free from commercial development—are truly a Kentucky heritage and they offer natural beauty which we should cherish and protect. This committee is in the process of developing criteria for the designation of such rivers so that the conservation views on these unique rivers will be on record for Congress and the U.S. Corps of Engineers in all future planning.

Closely connected to the beauty of our land, our mountains and our streams is the new strip-mine law described by many as the "strongest strip-mine law in the United States." This law, perhaps more than any other single conservation measure or development, demonstrates our determination to protect and conserve our land. It has resulted in lands stripped in western Kentucky being returned to nearly the original contour and stronger regulations on lands being stripped in eastern Kentucky. While Kentucky's new strip-mine law may be the most restrictive in the nation, it is by no means the final solution. Many problems still exist, particularly in the mountains of eastern Kentucky. We are working on those problems now in an effort to find solutions.

At the same time we are applying the pollution brakes on our water and air, thanks to laws passed by the 1966 legislature. Control measures are gathering strength and speed, and it is now possible to predict an end to mounting pollution and a gradual rollback to ever cleaner, purer air and water. It matters not in what direction you turn your eyes here on the home front. The conservation battle is going forward with vigor, with vision, and above all, with an interlocking purpose about it. Resources, wildlife, all the elements of the environment we live in and are part of, are receiving due regard. We have a duty, I feel, and I've tried to demonstrate this duty during my administration with action rather than just talk—to preserve a part of our past to give present and future millions of Kentuckians and Americans a natural and pleasant experience in forests, on streams and lakes, in mountains, and everywhere else where God intended us to be.

Yet I would be remiss if I said the battle has been won. We are living in a rapidly changing world—a nation that is growing in population by leaps and bounds, a nation whose advancing technology is never-ending. If we relax, if we are lulled to sleep, the destruction of our natural resources will come fast and furious. We consider our atmosphere, for example, as something to be taken for granted—it is there and it has the right combination of elements to sustain our lives. But every minute of every hour that we live, as the population increases, we are adding to it many elements that could kill us—in fact, they are killing many people every day in parts of these United States. The very breath of life, particularly in our larger cities, contains the poison of our destruction.

We sometimes forget about the tremendous amount of water this nation and our states and our cities are going to need in the future. We very easily can pollute our water supplies so they are no longer usable.

The mountains of Kentucky and other states have stood for thousands of years. Yet today sophisticated machinery can rip them apart in days. Our technology is a marvelous thing, but our use of it is often shortsighted and extremely dangerous. Our abuse of some of our natural resources today is similar to the management a half century ago of our wildlife and forests. We have learned how to use fish and game without exhausting them, and we have learned to use our forests for shade and shelter yet keep their value sustained for timber. Use of air and water, the preservation of the beauty of our mountains and land—are just as important. We must learn to use them in an intelligent way which will prevent their destruction or harm. We must learn techniques and values of preserving mountain beauty and land or not disturb them at all.

As I leave office, I pledge to continue to work with you to conserve and preserve our natural resources. But I warn you, you cannot lower your guard. In a very few days, the conservationists and the citizens of this state will be voting for your next governor and other public officials. I can tell you from experience that a governor and your elected legislators are very important in seeing to it that our land, our mountains, our streams, our lakes, our forests are protected. A governor can strictly and fairly enforce the laws that are on the books or he can, through lack of concern or political obligations, give them lip service. He can meet the challenges of strip mining and conservation, and I can tell you they will come during the next four years, or he can turn his back on them. I think it is important that you elect men who know conservation, who are experienced in this field, who are fully conscious of their responsibility in protecting our God-given resources. This is a choice that only you can make. Working together, you and Kentucky's next governor will, I hope, continue the march forward in this never-ending struggle to conserve our natural resources.

---

1. Danny Helm (1944-), forest guard injured in fighting a forest fire in Lincoln County, *Louisville Courier-Journal,* October 28, 1967.

BOND ISSUE

KENTUCKY JAYCEE WINTER BOARD MEETING
Frankfort / February 20, 1965

As governor of this Commonwealth, I have recommended to the people a bond issue totaling $176 million. They will register their judgment upon the recommendation in the general election in November of this year.[1] Taxes, debt, and bonds are sensitive matters in this state, as in all states. The people are always, as indeed they should be, vitally interested in the taxes they pay, the expenditure of those taxes in the public good, and the public debt which is contracted and the bonds which are, from time to time, sold as the instrument of that debt. I am well aware of the public's concern with all aspects of taxes and bonds, and I totally approve and share their concern in these matters. When we decided to recommend a general obligation bond proposal to the legislature and the people, I was not unaware of the emotion which has often been attached to public discussion regarding the use of bond financing within the state government and its subdivisions.

Notwithstanding the emotion which has been generated in the past regarding this method of more immediate financing of needed public improvements which could not otherwise be afforded, it was my best judgment, and it remains my best judgment, that resort to a general obligation bond issue at this time is a responsible and compelling solution to some very critical needs of our public agencies and institutions. I have conveyed this judgment to the General Assembly and to the people of this state. I shall, between now and November, continue to emphasize that, in my judgment, these critical and unmet needs of our agencies and institutions make this bond issue desirable and attractive. Its passage in November will represent a renewed commitment on the part of the people to continue the kind of progress which promises a better life for every Kentuckian and a stronger economy for every community.

I do not for one minute believe that we in Kentucky are ready to halt the kind of economic growth and social enrichment which the advances of the last few years have introduced into our state. For the first time in many years Kentucky is aggressively on the march, standing shoulder to shoulder with many of our more affluent sister states, and competing effectively with their advances in education, new roads, welfare services, and agricultural and industrial growth. When Kentucky is mentioned these days, other states no longer frown; they have taken notice of the last few years' progress which we have made. They are impressed as we too are impressed.

For too many years we were permitted to believe that things couldn't be any better for Kentucky. They can be better and they are materially better today. Of the progress we have already made, many thought we couldn't do it. We have done it, and we have not gone bankrupt in the process as many predicted! Nor are we going to go bankrupt! The bonds we are proposing now will not jeopardize the finances of the Commonwealth.

What many people either overlook or ignore is that borrowing money to finance facilities and plants that are needed now, and which will contribute to their own cost, is one of the oldest established principles of the American free enterprise system. Who becomes emotional when American Telephone and Telegraph borrows hundreds of millions of dollars to finance new plant outlays? Who cries "irresponsible" when General Telephone goes into the market with bonds to borrow for needed plant improvements? Who objects to the federal government selling its citizens "savings bonds" as a means of borrowing money to finance the operating costs of the government? Who denies his family a home of their own for thirty years while he saves the money to pay cash for it? Why then, must the state government always have to have these long harangues about borrowing money, as both large corporations and individual families throughout America do daily? Obviously, what creeps into the discussion of the state's borrowing money is more politics than finances.

So far as my administration is concerned, politics is not involved in the question of borrowing the money to complete our interstate road system, and bring other roads up to the standards which today's traffic requires for both time and safety of Kentucky families using them. Politics is not involved in providing dormitory and classroom space for Kentucky youngsters who cannot otherwise have a college education. Politics is not involved in the question of building more public libraries throughout this state. We are charged with administering the affairs of this government. We were chosen by the people to lead in the state for four years. It is not my purpose, nor was it my mandate in the election, to lead this state backwards, or to cause it to stand still. We are committed, and we are mandated, to a course that distinctly leads into a brighter future. My administration will not reverse that course.

Our decision to recommend and seek approval of his bond issue rests foursquare upon my commitment to lead this state as best I can. The needs of our service agencies and institutions are great. The bond issue alone will not solve all their needs. It is the minimum, in our best-considered judgment, which will provide facilities and buildings which cannot responsibly be further delayed. It will provide facilities which Kentucky can use over the next fifty to one hundred years; facilities which will permit our citizens to travel in safety and comfort; facilities in which youngsters will be educated and their lives enriched; facilities in which our citizens and guests to our state may enjoy recreational activities; facilities in which the handicapped and needy may be served; and facilities in which our industrial and agricultural economy can be enhanced.

And all these facilities will be available to the people of Kentucky now and over the next thirty years, while bonds are being retired, and for long years thereafter. Under no circumstance can the state of Kentucky wisely postpone these needed improvements for another thirty years while it saves the money at the rate of a few million dollars a year, and while construction costs continue to increase, and while Kentucky gets bypassed by many elements of modern progress, all because she was saving her money so she could pay cash.

You are all young enough, and close enough to the business community, its practices and habits, that you know well that when the alternative to bond financing is doing without needed plant and capital improvements, bond financing represents a responsible and prudent course. You well know, that whether it is business, or the family, or the government, if your debt is less than two years' income, you are not excessively in debt. You well know that plant investment, which contributes not only to social welfare and progress but also to economic growth and stability, is a wise investment, even if you do have to pay interest for borrowed money, as everyone does in order to have the benefits earlier and longer. One hundred seventy-six million dollars, which this proposed bond issue represents, is less by more than $100 million than next year's General Fund receipts. The total general obligation debt of the Commonwealth, even with this $176 million included, is less than the two-year income which accrues to the state's General Fund. How many families, how many businesses, are in better shape in regard to their debt as it is related to their annual income?

I am perfectly willing, and anxious, to discuss with anyone what I think are the real and basic merits of this bond proposal. I am not willing to engage in superficial and contrived debate as to charges of fiscal irresponsibility, which some elements have already hurled at the proposal. They are untrue, and the people making the charges know full well they are untrue. Their charges are not intended to educate or enlighten. They are, at best, designed only to harass and harangue for some little bit of hoped-for political advantage.

If anyone seriously, and honestly, is concerned about fiscal responsibility being jeopardized by this proposal, then let them seek the advice of the financial and fiscal experts. And I don't mean just those in state government. Let them check with the Wall Street analysts and the brokerage firms and banking firms which deal commercially with such matters. Let them discover the conservative posture of the nation's financial market. Let them learn firsthand that bonds just won't sell beyond that point where credit is excessive and security is not sound, or where the purposes are inappropriate, where there are no safeguards upon the use of the funds and the repayment of the funds.

A lot of people want to treat this bond proposal as "Breathitt's bond issue." That's all right with me. It does represent a carefully considered policy judgment and recommendation of my administration. And there will be no cause for me or my administration ever to apologize for that judgment, or for my commitment to that judgment and the recommendation to the people of this state. However, the proposed bond issue was neither conceived nor designed just to benefit Breathitt. I'll go on being governor, with or without the bond issue. The issue is proposed for the benefit of the government and the agencies and the people of this Commonwealth. It was conceived and designed and proposed solely for their benefit and for their welfare. It's "Kentucky's bond issue." It's the "people's bond issue." Its benefits over the years will accrue not to Breathitt, nor to the Breathitt administration—the benefits will accrue throughout the coming years to the people of Kentucky.

There are certain individuals challenging the wisdom of the proposal on grounds which, in fact, have no bearing on the question which the people must decide. What these few people desire for Kentucky, we do not know. But I am sure of one thing: there can be no greater injustice to the people than to mislead them, to misinform them, to scare them and to alarm them, and to deny them their own best judgment for the singular and selfish purpose of trying to reap some personal and privileged selfish political advantage. This I will never do, whatever the personal consequences to myself or to my future.

The people have the benefit of my best judgment: this bond issue is responsible and prudent; it is needed; we can afford it; and the continuing needs of our children and the economy of this state strongly recommend it. When the good people of this Commonwealth, in their best-considered judgment, render their decision, Ned Breathitt will respect it and will continue to give them the benefit of his best thinking as to the developing needs and opportunities which face this state. The bond proposal is the people's; it's yours. If you want it, for what it means in improvements, you must support it. I can't pass it for you, I can't keep it from passing. I have done what I had to do to keep faith with the people of this state, and now it's up to all the people. I am only your governor—you are the people—and the opportunity is ours.

---

1. The $176 million bond issue was clearly vital to Governor Breathitt's administration. It is not an overstatement to suggest the whole character of his term would have been different without the bond issue. In his campaign for governor he made a firm pledge his administration would enact no additional taxes. His Democratic predecessor and political benefactor, Bert Combs, had secured passage of the existing 3 percent sales tax; and both A.B. Chandler, in the Democratic primary, and Louie B. Nunn, in the general election of 1963, had linked Combs and Breathitt on the tax issue. In a state that voted new taxes as reluctantly as Kentucky, it would have been politically imprudent for the Breathitt administration to seek additional taxes, especially in view of his relationship to Combs. Yet Breathitt wished to continue the initiatives of the Combs administration in road building, state parks, education, and social services. In one area, education, the growth of enrollment in the public schools and the state's institutions of higher education placed greater demands on the Breathitt administration than the Combs administration. Moreover, Breathitt came to office at a time when unprecedented sums were available from the federal government in dollar matching programs. The combination of funding requests and dollar matching opportunities required financial outlays far in excess of current state revenues. The answer was the $176 million bond issue. The bond issue was carefully designed to provide funds for capital improvements only. None of the funds were available for recurring operating costs of government programs. The largest portion of the bond issue, $139 million, was dedicated to highway construction; however, funds for schools, parks, correctional institutions, mental health facilities, lakes, forest fire control towers, libraries, airports, child welfare centers, county health centers, hospitals, laboratories, livestock facilities, and state police facilities were also included. After securing authorization from the 1964 General Assembly to place the bond issue on the ballot November 2, 1965, Governor Breathitt began a personal campaign to assure its passage. He delivered several addresses directly seeking support for the bond issue. The addresses included in this section are representative of those speeches. In addition, he frequently promoted the bond issue when speaking on other topics. Yet Breathitt did not rely on speeches alone to generate support for the bond issue. The Department of Finance provided effective graphic materials to show how each dollar would be spent; the support of dozens of state and local organizations was secured; and citizens committees, representing the state highway districts, were organized. In January, 1965, Lieutenant Governor Harry Lee Waterfield attacked the bond issue proposal as "inherently deceptive" because it provided no new source of income to pay off the bonds. Sometime in the future, he claimed, another administration would be forced to adopt new taxes to pay the Breathitt administra-

tion's growing debt. In February Waterfield proposed that the administration's plan be redrawn to allow voters to decide on a method of repayment. Waterfield was joined by former Governor A.B. "Happy" Chandler in opposition to the bond issue. Despite the opposition, the broad-based support of the bond issue assured its passage in November. When the ballots were counted it carried by a three to one margin. See Department of Finance, *The Bond Issue: A Long Range Public Improvement Program For Kentucky* (Frankfort, Ky., 1965), pp. 1-44. See also "Organizations Endorsing the Bond Issue" and "Highway District Citizens Committees," typescripts in Bond Issue file, Breathitt papers.

BARREN COUNTY COURTHOUSE DEDICATION
Glasgow / May 8, 1965

THIS is a day of rejoicing not only for Barren County—not only for Glasgow—but for all Kentucky because this new, brick courthouse is one more piece of evidence that Kentucky is on the move. Joined together in the brick and mortar of this new structure are countless days and hours of community leadership and teamwork—effort put forth by you, the citizens of Barren County. It stands here as a tribute to your county leaders and to all of you who have worked so hard to make it a reality.

But even more significant is the fact that it blends in with so many other examples of progress you are making in Barren County. Your new industry, your fine schools, the many new businesses and new homes, the new streets and roads, the development of a new lake—all demonstrate a county and its people moving, choosing, planning, working, and dreaming.

It is particularly important, I think, to point out that this beautiful Georgian-style courthouse was constructed without any new direct taxes. As you know, it was paid for through a federal grant, through county funds, and through revenue bonds that will pay for themselves.

Here in Kentucky this November our people will have an opportunity to vote for a similar development program—one that will combine federal and state dollars which will build great monuments of opportunity throughout the Commonwealth—and one that will require no new taxes. I am speaking of the $176 million bond issue that will be on the ballot this fall. Through matching federal dollars, we will be able to build over $860 million in new highways and new facilities—almost a billion dollars in development projects—if the people approve the issue.

And, in my travels across Kentucky, I am finding a ground swell of support for the issue. The vast majority of Kentuckians want to see Kentucky continue to go forward. They want to see us compete with neighboring states and move ahead. They want to see more and better highways, newer and more modern educational facilities, finer and more state parks.

Once the people fully understand the issue, there is no doubt in my mind that they will approve it. It is just a question of getting the facts to the people because Kentuckians always respond properly and wisely when they are given all the facts.

Let me, if I may, give you some of the reasons I hope you will be for this issue. Both in 1956 and 1960 the people of this state approved bond issues. Barren County and Glasgow benefited greatly from those two issues and you will benefit even more from the present one. Funds from the two previous issues have brought Barren County over $2 million worth of highway improvements. This is more than one-third of all the money spent for highway construction in Barren County since 1957. Bond funds helped finance projects on the Glasgow by-pass, the Glasgow-Beckton-Hydro road and Columbia avenue, in addition to preliminary work on Interstate 65. Without bond issues, these projects could not have been accomplished. Funds from these two previous bond issues will expire at the end of this year—there will be no more money—and this is why it is so important that the $176 million bond issue be passed this fall.

The bond issue to be submitted to the voters would help finance such projects as the completion of I-65, which will give you a modern, high-speed, north-south route through Kentucky, and the needed improvement of KY 90 from the Glasgow by-pass to Interstate 65. The Highway Department is presently carrying forth studies to determine the most feasible approach to the improvement of KY 90. Preliminary estimates indicate that it will cost Kentucky well over a half million dollars to match federal funds for a million-dollar-plus project, and the bond issue would supply this. Present schedules call for completion of I-65 in 1967. Kentucky must have adequate financing in order to meet this schedule, and passage of the bond issue will insure the availability of the cost.

Also of prime importance to you is the new state park on the Barren River reservoir. This issue contains $1,750,000 for the construction and development of a new state park. We have already hired an architect—McCullough and Vickel of Louisville—to design the lodge and other facilities. On January 1 of this year, the state obtained a fifty-year lease on 798 acres for this park, and already we've begun draining and ditching the area, which will continue through the summer. I want to see and I know you want to see this new park become a reality just as you've seen this fine, new courthouse become actual.

I have great faith in the future of Kentucky—so much, that I assure you I'll be back, if you invite me, to cut the ribbon on the new lodge of this park. I do not share the view of those who say we should move more slowly. On the contrary, I say the opportunity is here today. We must grab it with both hands. We can and we shall go forward.[1]

---

1. Governor Breathitt made numerous addresses across Kentucky seeking support for the bond issue. His Glasgow speech, in which he identified specific local projects the bond issue would finance, was typical of his speeches to chambers of commerce and service organizations.

FIVE-STATION TELEVISION APPEARANCE
Louisville / September 28, 1965

THIS election day, November 2, we Kentuckians are going to the polls to make a decision on a matter that is very important to all of us—the Kentucky bond issue.[1] This is not a political matter, but rather a personal and economic matter which will affect each and every one of us in Kentucky, young and old alike.

Let me begin by saying that passing this bond issue is just plain good business for us Kentuckians. As you undoubtedly know from your radio, television, and newspaper, all of your civic, state, and business organizations which have considered this bond issue have come out in favor of it. Virtually all of Kentucky's farm groups and labor unions have endorsed it. So have Kentucky's chambers of commerce and professional organizations. Teachers and educators are backing the issue. Republicans, Democrats, and independents alike have come out for it. So this is not a political matter. But it definitely is a matter that is important to the well-being, convenience, and moneymaking potential of every Kentucky citizen. It will affect you, the car owner; or you, the student; or you, the skilled laborer; or you, the businessman, both large and small—vacationer, professional man, farmer, or housewife.

Let's look at what this bond issue is—and what we will gain from it. Basically, states have two ways of getting money. They can borrow—one way is to issue bonds—or they can tax. A state usually issues bonds as a way of borrowing to finance long-term capital improvements. And that is what passage of this bond issue will do. It will allow the Commonwealth of Kentucky to borrow money to finance long-term improvements that you want and need. We could raise the money by levying more taxes. However, neither you nor I want any more taxes. And in this case, a new tax is not necessary.

Now, what does this bond issue provide? What will this borrowed money bring to you and me? Passage of this $176 million bond issue will enable us to build new roads, new schools, new health facilities, and new parks. Communities will get new libraries, child welfare centers, and airport improvements. Small lakes will be constructed at selected sites throughout the state. We will have new forestry facilities; our penal institutions will be modernized. New facilities for agricultural research and market development will be made available.

But how, you may ask, how can we afford to build all these things with only $176 million? The answer is we can't! This is where the federal government's system of matching funds comes in. Let me take time here to explain how this system of federal matching funds works to our benefit, and why we cannot afford to pass them up.

When a state builds highways, for example, the federal government will put up as much as nine dollars for every one dollar put up by the state. The ratio of federal money to state money varies according to the kind of roads we build, but the biggest portion of our road money, by far, comes from the federal government in the form of matching funds. We must take advantage of these matching funds if we want to keep up with other states in the building of all kinds of roads—farm to market roads—primary and secondary highways—interstate routes—and the new Appalachian roads program.

The federal government also puts up matching money to help with construction of college classrooms, new health facilities, and the building of new parks and recreational areas. So, through this bond issue—and after all of these federal funds are figured in and averaged out—Kentucky will spend five dollars for every dollar we put up. When you pass this bond issue, which amounts to $176 million, you will be claiming a total of $632 million in federal matching funds and $52 million from other sources. This will let us meet the needs of our state without new and burdensome taxes. This is a good proposition for us Kentuckians—a proposition we just can't afford to pass up. We must raise that one dollar so we can claim the other four dollars we need.

Look at it this way. States are in a prosperity race. Right now they are all issuing bonds to take advantage of the matching money for highway construction. With a 1972 deadline set on the money by the federal government, this bond issue is Kentucky's last chance to take advantage of massive federal funds that are available. If Kentucky is unable to put up its one dollar, the money already allocated will be given to other states which are ready to proceed. And these increased federal grants cannot be matched by current funds. The money we received from the 1956 and 1960 bond issues will have been used for highways and for other matching programs. Last year we built or improved 1,666 miles of roads with this money. A lot of these were rural roads. Also, last year we doubled the annual allocation for rural roads, raising it to $10 million. As you can see, the money from these two other bond issues has been used wisely, and for the benefit of all Kentuckians.

But, since federal matching funds operate on a first come, first served basis, we must get the rest of our share now before it is too late. If we don't, Kentucky's road building program would come to a halt. College and construction projects would stop. However, if Kentucky voters approve the bond issue, other funds will become available for road construction not on the federal system. In other words, we will have added money to work with. Our performance in the past bears this fact out. Since the first bond issue in 1956, the rural and secondary road fund has increased almost 60 percent. Farm truck ownership is up 24 percent. Land values have increased 7 percent.

We will help our schools through this bond issue. We all know how important education is to our children—to our state. We must provide the right type and amount of education in high schools, vocational schools, colleges and universities, to qualify our children for jobs in modern industry and the professions. College enrollments today are booming as more and more of our young people realize they need more and better education to get the good, well-paying jobs they want. This boom means our colleges and universities will need new classrooms, dormitories, and laboratories to handle this great influx. Will need, did I say? "Need now" are even better words to describe the situation. All of our state colleges and universities are bursting at the seams with increased enrollments. Kentucky must be able to find room and build classrooms for all its students. Very often if a college student goes to another state for an education, he does not return. He finds a job in some other state. This is Kentucky's loss. We need to keep our trained and skilled people to meet the demands that lie ahead.

The college construction program and other education programs which come under this bond issue and will receive money from the federal government will enable Kentucky to get those badly needed classrooms, dormitories, and laboratories. More than $35 million in state and federal funds will be used for the University of Kentucky and nine community colleges at Somerset, Hopkinsville, Hazard-Blackey, Ashland, Covington, Henderson, Cumberland, Elizabethtown, and Prestonsburg. More than $6.5 million will be used for vocational education schools at Hazard, Bowling

Green, Paintsville, Lexington, Owensboro, Jeffersontown, and LaGrange, among others.

Now you and I all know that our state needs new roads. This bond issue we're talking about will get us those new roads and improve old ones. How? Let's consider some figures for a moment. One hundred thirty-nine million dollars of the $176 million in the bond issue will go for the building of new roads. And $597 million of the $632 million we will receive from the federal government will go for the building of primary and secondary roads as well as the new Appalachian system and interstate systems.

Speaking of roads, let's take a moment here to see what we've done up to now and what's ahead. We have a good plan under way that calls for more than one thousand miles of new parkways and interstate highways by 1972. Four hundred seventy miles of this are now open, and 129 miles are under construction.

So, you see, we are making progress. Yet, I believe we must accelerate our effort. The new industry we want to bring into our state needs modern highways. And good highways make it easier to attract tourists who spend money in Kentucky. We must accelerate our effort because, as I said, the federal matching money expires on October 1, 1972. Our state should have its last interstate projects under construction by mid-1970 in order to get all its share of federal funds. This is why we need this bond issue —to get a commitment for our proper share of those federal funds. If we fail to pass the bond issue, the only way we can get federal matching money is to raise taxes, or take money away from the rural and secondary road program—and we must not do either. But with the bond issue, we can get the money to build the roads quickly, using mostly federal money. And we can pay off the bonds as we use the roads.

Now what does this mean to you? By providing new and improved highways, Kentucky drivers can get to where we want to go easier, faster, and safer. On holidays, when there are more cars on the road than usual, this will mean many people who might have become victims of accidents will be able to spend that holiday with friends, relatives, or children. Better roads can also mean more mileage from gasoline and tires, fewer car repair bills.

This bond issue will help our farmers. Since much of our state's wealth depends on what we grow in the country and how fast our farmers can get their tobacco, wheat, milk, or eggs to market, we've got to have the best farm-to-market roads our state can afford. And if we can improve that road to your farm and make your marketplace a few minutes closer and easier to get to—why, then, that's money in your pocket. And if we can make more market places easier to go to that means more places to sell your products. We don't want any farmer to have to pass up a buyer offering a few more cents a bushel because a road is too narrow, too hilly, or too bad to drive a loaded truck on. Other projects which will aid our farmers are planned, also. A million dollars will be set aside to build an animal disease diagnostic laboratory, plus livestock sales and exhibition facilities, at Murray State College and the state fairgrounds.

Another provision of the bond issue, one which will do its share to bring more tourist dollars into the state, will be the addition of new state parks and lakes, and more and better facilities for present parks. Nine million dollars will be spent for parks, including new lodges at Barren River and Barkley Lake, and there will be many other improvements and additions to existing facilities.

While we're talking about vacation fun, camp-outs and other such things, we can't afford to neglect our shut-ins—our people in various hospitals and health centers across the state. These people will be helped by the bond issue, too. So will doctors and nurses who care for them. New local and statewide facilities are to be built for the care of the mentally ill. And with the help of matching money from the federal government, new county health centers and child welfare centers will be built, and others expanded, to meet a serious need. The School for the Blind in Louisville will receive a new manufacturing building where blind patients will be taught new skills so they can earn a living on their own, regardless of their handicap. The School for the Deaf at Danville will receive a new dining hall, as will the School for the Blind. Also, $250,000 will go to the Tuberculosis Commission for new heating and air-conditioning facilities at Hazelwood Hospital in Louisville for a healthier climate in which Kentucky's tuberculosis patients can live and recover.

Our state penal institutions will be modernized through the use of nearly $3 million from the bond issue. Two state forestry camps would be built—new dormitories at the reformatory and penitentiary farms, and renovation of reformatory dormitory and reception centers.

Going back to college and university improvements for a moment, let me give you a quick run-down on some of the projects and buildings which will be put up with money from this bond issue. They include $3 million for the University of Louisville Medical Center and dormitories, and an education building, among others, for Murray State College. Still other projects include a fine arts building and athletic complex at Western Kentucky State College, a science building at Eastern Kentucky State College, new classrooms and dormitories for Morehead State College, and a new men's dormitory and science building for Kentucky State College. In all, education will receive more than $22 million from the bond issue—allowing a total building program of over $95 million.

Other construction improvements called for, outside of the college program, will include many airport improvements as well as three new state police barracks to replace housing now rented or leased.

I know I've been doing a lot of talking about the federal government matching or carrying so much of the expense for many of these projects. Now, we come to a factor that I want you to keep uppermost in your mind. I can't stress it enough. The Commonwealth of Kentucky will lose this federal money if the state matching money is not provided. The bond issue must be passed in order to get the matching money. And while you might feel, as many of us do, that we should not encourage federal involvement in state affairs, the fact is that these federal matching funds represent money we have all contributed in federal taxes. We would be foolhardy not to use this money to which we are rightfully entitled.

And I want to stress this. Kentucky can easily afford this bond issue. Our expanding economy is a strong indicator. Bank deposits are up about 9 percent. Corporate income tax receipts have increased more than 11 percent. New jobs are being developed at a greater-than-ever rate. In 1964 actual investment in new and expanded Kentucky plants was $117 million—more than double the total for 1963. Income from out-of-state visitors has almost doubled in the last eight years. Our debts are being paid on schedule and some ahead of schedule. The Kentucky Turnpike, from Louisville to Elizabethtown, is paying off its bonds and refunding previous payments to the state many years ahead of schedule. Other parkways, financed by revenue bonds, are enjoying increased returns each month. So, you see, issuing bonds is a good business investment. And Kentucky has an enviable position in the bond market, where it enjoys excellent interest rates. But, even with all these gains and advantages, other states have matched Kentucky's gains. Let's look at what some of our neighboring states are doing.

Last May, Ohio voters approved a bond issue calling for $500 million to complete its interstate and primary road system. Approval came by 65 percent of the electorate and eighty-seven of eighty-eight counties approved. Ohio will become the first state in the nation to complete its system. Last November, Ohio voters gave its state administration another vote of approval for $250 million worth of bonds for college and university construction. Ohio's $500 million issue alone will help provide matching money for about $2 billion in future federal funds—giving Ohio a $2.5 billion program over the next five years.

Other neighbors are doing the same thing. Maryland is embarking on a six-year highway program costing more than $525 million. Between 1950 and 1960, Indiana has issued $280 million in highway bonds; Illinois, $479 million; Virginia, $404 million; and West Virginia voters recently approved a program for $200 million, to mention just a few.

What can we learn from this? Our neighbors' actions show that we cannot afford to stand pat on progress we have made up to this time. Kentucky is being challenged! If we fail to meet this challenge, then Kentucky will lose federal funds and, even more importantly, our competitors will forge ahead in the ever growing battle for the tourist dollar and new factories, jobs, and income. We have the choice of falling behind or moving ahead to match strides taken by other states. Let's not miss the boat.

I hope you will vote for the Kentucky bond issue. In so doing you will be casting your vote for the continued growth and prosperity of our state. Prosperity and growth that will bring better roads, better education, better health, and better living for all Kentuckians. Voting "yes" for the Kentucky bond issue at this time will provide for a $60 million capital construction program in Kentucky during the next five years, and no tax increase is required!

Let me remind you again of the many Kentucky organizations who have studied this bond issue and the benfits which it will provide for our people, and who have gone on record in favor of its passage. Civic and business clubs, chambers of commerce, professional and farm groups, labor unions, educators—virtually all are on record in favor of passing this bond issue. We need it. And we need it now!

I foresee a great future ahead for our state. A future of increasing prosperity and well-being for all our people. More industry, better-paying jobs, a richer farm economy—all these benefits await us if we will only dedicate ourselves now to accomplishing them. This requires passing the Kentucky bond issue on November 2. That is why I am asking for your "yes" vote. I am also asking that you talk to your friends and neighbors and urge them to come to the polls and vote "yes" for this bond issue. If you will do this you will perform a great service for yourself and for all Kentuckians, now and in the years to come. Thank you and good night.

---

1. This speech was carried by television stations WLEX in Lexington, WLAC in Nashville, WSAZ in Huntington, WLTV in Bowling Green, and WBIR in Knoxville.

BOND ISSUE FINANCING
Frankfort / October 12, 1965

THERE have been unfounded allegations that the administration has not clearly and completely explained the method and the cost of retiring the indebtedness which the state would incur upon passage of the bond issue.

Two points in particular have been raised: (1) how much will it take to retire the debt? and (2) what pledges of revenue are made from the General Fund and the Road Fund, and do these pledges constitute commitments to raise taxes?

Both sets of queries have been answered by the Department of Finance on numerous occasions. In brief, the debt would require $9.5 million annually for servicing. This includes principal and interest. The General Fund portion would require $2.5 million; the Road Fund portion, $7 million. The computations contain these assumptions: (1) an overall interest rate of 3.25 percent; (2) a period of thirty years in which to retire the bonds; and (3) equal annual payments on the debt (level debt service). The total cost, including financing charges (fiscal agents and legal fees), would therefore be thirty times $9.5 million, or $285 million.

The revenues pledged toward retirement of the debt are clearly outlined in the enabling legislation and in the question as it will appear on the November 2 ballot. The General Fund obligation would be met technically from the constitutionally levied property tax. This pledge is stated, and no requirement to raise the tax is either implied or assumed. The Road Fund obligation would be met from present taxes and fees relating to registration, operation, and use of vehicles on public highways. This pledge requires that such taxes be maintained at such a level required to pay the indebtedness. The pledge being therefore a pledge not to lower the total Road Fund tax below the amount presently.

These are the technical points of the bond issue. Of more importance, however, is the overall relationship of debt to income. In summary, that relationship is capsuled as follows: it will cost Kentucky about $9.5 million each year for a period of thirty years. This $9.5 million annual cost would not start next year. This amount is the maximum annual cost, for both principal and interest, that will apply when all the bonds have been sold. They will not all be sold at one time. Some will likely not be sold for four or five years. Then, the annual cost will level off at about $9.5 million.

The annual debt figure is backed up by the state's annual income from tax sources. This income last year totaled more than $380 million. Without any new or increased taxes, the state's income last year represented an increase of over 9 percent over the previous year. We confidently estimate these increases to continue as Kentucky continues to prosper and grow. By 1970 our income from revenue will exceed $500 million.

Now let's bring these figures together into a meaningful relationship. In five years, if the bond issue is passed, the state's expenditure for debt service will be $9.5 million more per year than it is today. In five years, if the bond issue is passed, the state's income from the present tax sources, and at the present tax rates, will be $120 million more per year than it is today, and revenue will continue to rise by more than 4 percent each year.

This means that the percentage of the state's income which would be dedicated to debt service seven years from now would be less than it is today.

What the raw statistics do not reveal is that the investment which this bond issue represents will assist in the growth of the state's economy to such an extent that the annual requirements of the state's education, health, and welfare programs can be met with less burden on the individual taxpayer.

EDUCATION

KENTUCKY SCHOOL BOARDS ASSOCIATION CONVENTION
Louisville / March 17, 1964

ALTHOUGH I am unable to be with you this morning, I appreciate the opportunity of speaking to you, and I appreciate your indulgence in permitting me to address you in this fashion, which is, I am sure, less than satisfactory to all concerned. I must apologize for not appearing in person, but this is a week that comes to all governors once every two years, during which the last minute press of legislative affairs precludes practically all other activity.[1] I am sorry that it had to occur at the same time as your annual convention.

My inability to be there produces one bright spot as far as the success of your convention is concerned, however. That bright spot is that you will have more time to devote to the message of Dr. Oswald, once my brief remarks are completed. I am sure that if I were there, I would speak longer than I plan to now. And I am equally sure that if Dr. Oswald chooses to take some of the time I would have used, it will add considerably to the luster of your session this morning.

I was gratified to learn of the theme of your convention—"School Board Responsibilities to Children"—and of the many discussions of all the facets and ramifications of this theme that you have scheduled. It is a theme that gets to the very essence of your organization's reason for existence and to the principles that should guide and activate all of us interested in education.

Education is, of course, for all of our society, and a good system of schools profits all citizens. But education must be oriented toward the child, and it must be planned and conducted to meet the requirements of our children. This is a fundamental that I am not sure we always keep sight of as we discuss our needs, our legislation, our theories, our teacher requirements, our financing, our courses of study, our politics. It is a fundamental that it is well to repeat and recognize in a convention such as yours.

Last year campaigning through Kentucky, I outlined what I considered to be some needs of education and my recommendations concerning them. I stressed these needs in terms of what our children deserve and require and—in line with your convention theme—I suppose my campaign speeches could have been entitled, "State Government Responsibilities to Children." I told how I thought some of our responsibilities to our children could be met in the four years ahead by some specific actions to strengthen our educational system. Some of thes actions have already been taken and others are in the process. Let us see what the results are thus far.

First, I thought our children should be provided the very best instruction that we could afford, and I agreed with the Kentucky Education Association and with many other Kentuckians that teachers' salaries would have to be raised in order to attract the best new teachers and retain the best teachers that we now have. The budget that I proposed to the General Assembly provided for the raises that I pledged, and it has passed both houses and become law. Because it is now possible for teachers to make more money teaching in Kentucky, we shall expect our teachers to be better trained, to be more effective—to help us meet our responsibilities to our children.[2]

Good teachers are more likely to keep teaching if they can see opportunities and security in their profession. We have acted to strengthen our teacher retirement system in order to help keep our classrooms supplied with the professional personnel our children require and deserve.[3]

I spoke often last year of the need for improvement in the schooling provided for children who are unable to take their places in regular classrooms because of handicaps. Better facilities at both the School for the Deaf in Danville and the School for the Blind in Louisville were needed, and I listed them as a goal of this administration. Action has been taken to improve both of these institutions. The School for the Deaf will receive money from the emergency fund for badly needed buildings, and both schools will receive funds under the bond issue that I have proposed for submission to the people.

The subject of school dropouts received a lot of discussion during the gubernatorial campaign, and I pledged to make an all-out effort to study the cause of children dropping out of school and to see what could be done to combat it. This does not seem to be a problem peculiarly suited to legislation—our laws seem to be reasonable and clear on the matter of school attendance. This is both an educational and sociological problem, and I hope to meet it as such. I plan a series of meetings on the subject starting this spring, during which I will get the best thinking from educators, sociologists, school board members, social workers, representatives of various government agencies, and all interested citizens on what the best solutions are. I do not intend to leave out of the meetings those most affected by the problem—children of dropout age. I will particularly want to get their thinking and their suggestions.

Financing, it seems, is constantly the major concern as we seek to meet our responsibilities to our children. We have solved a portion of the problem during this session, but there is no school district in Kentucky that does not need more funds. Help on the problem in counties that have cities of the first or second class may come in an amendment that is to be offered in the Senate today to House Bill 2.[4] The amendment would enable any school board in such counties to levy a .5 percent occupational tax for any need of its school system. This amendment would become law next year, and while it is no immediate solution to the financial troubles that beset our schools, it could be helpful in the near future. The amendment, if passed, could go a long way toward easing our problem of double sessions in those districts that now have them and lifting the threat of double sessions in other districts where the amendment would apply.

The educational gains or prospective gains I have mentioned will, I think, prove to be extremely meaningful in Kentucky's overall educational progress. There are many others that we hope to record during the next months and years, and I hope that your organization will be of help—that your theme of meeting your responsibilities to Kentucky children will have concrete results. I hope, further, that it will be recognized and pushed by all organizations and groups interested in the schools of our Commonwealth and in the young people of Kentucky. I wish you all success for your convention and express to you again my regrets at not being able to attend.

---

1. This address was delivered by telephone from Governor Breathitt's office.

2. The National Education Association reported that salaries for Kentucky classroom teachers in 1963-1964 averaged $4,400. The Commonwealth ranked forty-sixth among the fifty states. Only North Dakota, South Carolina, Arkansas, and Mississippi trailed Kentucky. See National Education Association, *Rankings of the States, 1964* (N.P., 1964), p. 20. The budget adopted by the 1964 General Assembly raised teacher salaries $300 the first year of the biennium and $200 the second year.

3. As a result of legislation adopted by the 1964 General Assembly, the state's contribution to the teacher retirement system was increased $2,417,000 to a total of $19,400,000. *Louisville Courier-Journal,* March 22, 1964.

4. House Bill 2, which related to depreciation as a tax deduction, was to be amended to permit school boards in counties with cities of the first and second class to levy an occupational tax of one-half of one percent. The Senate refused to accept

the amendment and the bill passed 31-2. *Acts, 1964,* Chapter 140 (H.B. 2), p. 502, and *Louisville Courier-Journal,* March 20, 1964.

UNIVERSITY OF KENTUCKY ALUMNI
New York, New York / June 1, 1964

FIRST of all, I want to invite you to return to your alma mater and mine—to return next year to help all of us celebrate the centennial. Even as we gather here tonight, meetings are under way in Lexington and in Frankfort to make further plans for the centennial celebration. The big day will be February 22, for it was on that day in 1865 that the university received its charter from the General Assembly.

But I want to urge you to return for still another reason. Big things are happening on the campus. By September of 1964 a great dormitory complex is expected to be ready for new students, a skyscraper complex to house 2,600 undergraduates. A new College of Law is being built. So is a new College of Commerce. And we are getting still other plants—other construction which I will not detail tonight—to care for young Kentuckians and others who look to a growing and great institution to care for their preparation for life.

There is some discussion of additional physical change. There is a belief on the campus, for instance, that the present site of the football stadium is valuable land and should be used for classroom buildings and research facilities. And so, if those plans are developed, we may within this decade move the stadium to another part of the campus.

But physical changes are not the only ones taking place. Next week—on June 12—our dynamic new president will meet with the board of trustees in special session to outline his academic plans for the next ten years. He already has given some broad hints of what he wants to bring about.

He has suggested informally that a new college be established—the University College. All incoming freshmen and sophomores would be enrolled in that school. There they would get a strong background in the liberal arts and in the arts and sciences. And then—when that task is completed, when they have acquired that background—they would go on to select their majors in the College of Engineering, the College of Commerce, the College of Education or of Agriculture. Dr. Oswald has said—

with great truth—that our schools and colleges are producing overtrained but undereducated young men and women.

Dr. Oswald has another plan—a plan fast growing into reality. He believes—and many are in agreement—that the university must do a better job in serving the entire state. And he would do so through a system of community colleges. There, young people, who for one reason or another cannot leave their home, will be able to obtain two years of college training before transferring to the mother campus at Lexington—or to some other school. Already we have such community colleges—two years of work—at Covington, Ashland, Henderson, Cumberland, and Elizabethtown. And several more will shortly be under construction.

This program of community colleges does several things. It allows students to attend college without the outlay of large sums of money for transportation, room and board. The savings would be equivalent to a scholarship of $1,000 a year for each student. And the system will also permit the campus at Lexington to concentrate on upper-class and graduate level work.

So much for the future. Let's discuss what has happened in the past. Perhaps the best measure of a college or university is the products produced. In the new Helen G. King Alumni House (and you should visit it) will be a hall of distinguished alumni. It will house the portraits and biographies of Kentucky alumni who have brought glory to their alma mater through their accomplishments in life. We have given to the nation—the University of Kentucky has—a number of college presidents, presidents of Vassar, Indiana, Mississippi, Virginia Tech, Centre, Georgetown, and many others. We number among our fellow alumni a Pulitzer Prize winner, a Nobel Prize winner. Five of our last seven governors are alumni of the university.[1]

We also bask in the reflected glory of the stars worn on the shoulders of a half-dozen generals and admirals. We number among us presidents of some of the leading American industrial firms. We have atomic scientists and space scientists. And we have nationally known bankers and attorneys and doctors. I could go on to recite other glories, other accomplishments in which we can well take pride.

But let me conclude with this: the University of Kentucky has had a great past. And we look forward to a second century of even greater service. Anything that you can do with your time, or talent, or especially your treasure, will speed the day when the University of Kentucky will take its rightful place among the greatest institutions of higher learning in this land of ours.

---

1. The five governors were Bert T. Combs, A.B. Chandler, Breathitt, Earle Clements, and Keen Johnson.

KENTUCKY EDUCATION ASSOCIATION LEADERSHIP CONFERENCE

Lexington / August 12, 1964

RARELY does the governor of a state have the opportunity to speak to an audience of such powerful influence and extreme importance as is gathered here today. For this privilege and opportunity, I am grateful. I am impressed by this traditional get-together of Kentucky's school people because I think it has contributed greatly to the well-being of our state. I salute you for your past successes, and I am confident that this leadership conference, like your others, has been beneficial to our children and our state's people.

As leaders in the Kentucky Educational Association, it is within your power to see that local schools do not produce students who can recite every word of our Declaration of Independence but who know not the meaning of the document. It is within your power to determine the course of our state and the course of our nation because some say there is a continuous race between catastrophe and education. Therefore, to underestimate the power and influence of the educator in our society today would be folly and unwise.

Nearly 200 years ago the great Edmund Burke, speaking as an Englishman about the American Revolution, said that "a great empire and little minds go ill together."[1] As we think this morning about Kentucky's future and Kentucky's educational problems, we must conclude that "a great state and little minds go ill together." Our progress as a state can be no swifter than our progress in education because the human mind is our fundamental and most precious resource. Today we waste precious resources when the bright youngster, who should have been a skilled chemist or able engineer, must remain a pick-and-shovel worker because he never had a chance to develop his talents.

Two of our educational challenges of 1964 must be: a new quality of excellence in education and an increased effort to attack the school dropout problem. First, we must constantly remember that quality education is the cornerstone to our progress. Kentucky can never reach its full economic potential until we have quality education. That is why we must put education first if we are to put Kentucky first.

This administration has put more dollars into education than has any administration in the history of our Commonwealth. Some $180 million will be spent for education during this academic year—an increase of $19 million over last year, of nearly $2 million more for each month of the school year. Most of this money will enable school teachers throughout Kentucky to have a substantial pay increase during the next two years. I consider this pay increase greatly deserved by those who will receive it and necessary in order to attract and keep good school teachers in our state because the teacher is the very heart of our system.

Yet it remains a fact that dollars and increased salaries can do just so much for better schools. The people of Kentucky expect, and I expect, the quality of our schools to improve as a result of this added money. We must be sure that we are teaching well the subjects which are vital in any area, the basic disciplines, English, math, language, history. Next we must have the flexibility to prepare children according to their abilities to make the most of their opportunities in a rapidly changing world. We must not neglect the area of guidance and counseling. The gifted student, the average student, the slower student, obviously should not receive the same instruction throughout school. We should also consider very critically other courses which are often shallow efforts in many directions. I personally believe that if we teach our children to think, many of these other courses become unnecessary.

I also believe that it is a major responsibility of the teaching profession, as well as other professions, to evaluate the quality of its services. We must have continued research to discover means of objective evaluation of the performance of all professional personnel and their interrelationships for the purpose of improving instruction. I'm also inclined to believe that we should begin some type of recognition for the career teacher—for those teachers who exhibit the additional interest and ability. And, above all, we must work towards a public atmosphere which will show always a respect and concern for the teaching profession.

Our fundamental objective must be quality education—that type of excellence which means we are developing the mind, teaching the child to think for himself, to learn how to keep on learning. As our people become better educated and as our schools improve, more jobs will come to Kentucky because industry is attracted to an educated state. We must remember, and remember always, that those who learn more will earn more.

Our second great challenge for this coming school year, as I see it, is the problem of the school dropout.[2] We made substantial progress last year in keeping more young Kentuckians in school, but our progress was not good enough for self-satisfaction. Thousands of young men and women are still dropping out of school each year—sad reminders that even now, with all we have accomplished in the field of education in recent years, our educational task is far from complete. Young boys and girls throughout our state at this very hour, at this very moment, are pondering over the decision to return to school this fall. We can no more afford to waste the potential of these young people than we can afford to waste our coal, our oil, our water, or our soil.

As automation proceeds, there will be an ever diminishing need for the simpler jobs formerly open to those with limited skills and limited education. Those who lack education and training will find themselves vulnerable and unwanted—a social and economic cancer. A sad fact about the school dropout in Kentucky, according to recent studies, is that about half the boys and girls come from homes whose parents have educational levels of grade six or less. Many of the parents are unemployed or have low incomes. This circle of poverty can be broken only when the children are made to realize that education is their only way out. When they see this fact, the great majority of them will find their way out. I propose that we undertake to sell these boys and girls on the financial value as well as the human value of a good education.

We have in Kentucky some 204 school districts. Yet only 76 school districts presently are making some planned effort to combat the dropout. This is cause for deep concern, for deep alarm. I am confident we can do better, but it is not a task merely for the schools but for the entire community. We must also take a closer look at our schools and find out why they cannot hold more of our young people. Among reasons for withdrawals, according to a study made by the Department of Education for the 1962-63 academic year, was lack of interest—35 percent. Perhaps our secondary education is oriented too much in the direction of preparation for college, and not enough toward those who need vocational skills. Perhaps our vocational education is not tailored sufficiently for the age of automation. No one person knows the answers, but I am convinced that we can meet the challenge.

In view of the alarming dropout situation, I am announcing two initial action steps which the state will undertake. First, the superintendent of public instruction and I have agreed that a long-range, positive, stepped-up, plan to combat the school dropout will be initiated, utilizing present studies and existing personnel in the Department of Education. Second, a series of regional conferences for school officials, under the sponsorship of the Department of Education and my office, will be held to plan for full and effective use of the Economic Opportunity Act of 1964 and the Vocational Education Act of 1963.

Kentucky stands to benefit immeasurably by the "antipoverty bill"—the Economic Opportunity Act—which cleared Congress yesterday and is now ready for the president's signature. The measure will set up a number of programs to educate and vocationally train many of our unemployed people and low-income groups. It will also help solve the dropout problem. Under the act the Department of Education and the area program office, headed by John Whisman, will work closely with local school districts to set up "work-study" programs wherein a student will attend school part-time and work part-time. Another provision of the act enables Kentucky to establish remedial reading programs, tutoring programs, and preschool readiness programs for potential dropouts. Still another benefit of the act is the adult education program which will, in the long run, instill greater appreciation of education among the parents of possible dropouts.

Also of prime importance to Kentucky is the Vocational Education Act, which was passed under the capable leadership of Congressman Carl Perkins, because this bill will provide for the improvement of area trade schools and the establishment of vocational extension schools.[3] These schools will be within the reach of every student because full transportation will be provided from the student's home to and from the schools.

I have touched on two of the major problems that exist in Kentucky's educational system today—quality education and the school dropout—and I have given my comments on what some of the solutions may be. There is no question in my mind that we have made great educational advances during the last few years, that our schools are better than ever—but this is no time for complacency. Working together, we can continue the painful climb up the educational ladder so that our state will become a richer, more stately place in which to live. Once we reach the top of the ladder, then and only then, can we take full satisfaction that the children of Kentucky are getting every educational opportunity they deserve.

---

1. Edmund Burke (1729-1797), eighteenth century English statesman critical of the excess of the French Revolution and British colonial policy. *The Concise Dictionary of National Biography* (London, 1930), pp. 170-71.

2. The superintendent of public instruction reported 19,830 children under age seventeen, but beyond the compulsory attendance age of sixteen, not in school. *Report of the Superintendent of Public Instruction for the Biennium Ending June 30, 1965* (Frankfort, Ky., 1965), p. 317.

3. The Vocational Education Act of 1963 authorized $581 million in fifty-fifty matching grants to states expanding vocational education programs in fiscal years 1964-1967. An additional $150 million was provided for "work-study programs" and $170 million for low interest National Defense Education Act loans. *Congressional Quarterly Weekly Report,* December 20, 1963, pp. 2207-09.

STATEMENT ON EDUCATION
Frankfort / November 9, 1964

I HAVE met today with Dr. Sparks, representatives of the Kentucky Education Association, the school superintendents of Louisville and Jefferson County, and other state officials to discuss a 1966 legislative program for our schools and, in particular, to discuss the financial problem facing the Louisville and Jefferson County schools.[1]

Although the school situation in Jefferson County is acute and immediate, we must keep in mind that the problem there cannot be confined to the borders of Jefferson County. It is one which will spread to other counties and school districts in Kentucky unless we take proper action in the next regular session of the General Assembly. A second-rate school system in any part of our state—and most especially in our largest metropolitan area—is a drag on the earning power, on the economy of all Kentucky.

Kentucky cannot afford to halt or to slow down the march of educational progress—much less to slide backward. Even the dramatic breakthroughs of the past few years must be measured against the forward movement which has been taking place in our sister states—so we need more teachers, better salaries, more buildings. In short, we need more money for our schools because our progress as a state can be no swifter than our progress in education.

We are now drawing up a positive legislative program, in cooperation with the Kentucky Education Association, other school groups and legislators, for presentation to the General Assembly. This session is just a year off. We must prepare a program which will provide money for our schools, but we must also present it to the people, explain the details, mobilize support, and be ready to go with it when the legislature can act. It will take time to sell this program to the people. Therefore, I have no present plans for a special legislative session, but I shall not slam the door.

In regard to the Jefferson County school crisis, let me make it clear that I will talk with any and all leaders in an effort to find a workable solution. I believe very deeply that we must avoid making the schools a partisan matter. It is a problem which requires the best leadership of both parties, mobilized fully and completely behind our school children.

If we are to keep our teachers in Jefferson County, if we are to end double sessions, if we are to improve our quality of schools—we must find more money. We have done more than ever before, but we have not done enough. For this reason, I sympathize with the teachers and children of Jefferson County.

However, I do feel that the teachers have an obligation and a responsibility to remain in the classrooms. They have obligated themselves by contract to do so. It is the children who suffer when our teachers stay away from the schools. I am hopeful that all the teachers of Louisville and Jefferson County will return to the schools tomorrow. Meanwhile, I pledge that we will do our best to bring them help.

This administration has put more money into schools than any administration in the history of our Commonwealth. The 1964 General Assembly voted a budget that provides some $180 million for education during the current fiscal year—an increase of $19 million over last year. Every additional revenue dollar we had, we put into the state's schools. Part of this increase went to Louisville and Jefferson County. I only wish that our financial abilities had been greater so that we could have provided larger increases.

All of us must remember that we live under a government which depends, in the final analysis, on the will of the people. Sometimes it is possible for those in public life to act first and then win the people's approval. Even so, the success of leadership must always rest, in a free society, on the leaders' ability to carry the people with them.

Let me say, to our teachers, in the utmost friendship and concern, that those who cannot persuade the people will not succeed in coercing the people. Our common task is not to bludgeon the people of Louisville, of Jefferson County, or of Kentucky. Rather, we must do a better job in deciding what action is right, and in persuading the people to do what is right.

---

1. Governor Breathitt's statement was in response to a strike by 150–200 Louisville teachers following a November 3 voter rejection of a tax referendum for city schools. The principal issue was salaries. New teachers holding the B.A. degree received $4,400. Teachers with the Masters of Arts plus twenty-four additional hours earned $6,600. The National Education Association threatened sanctions, and representatives of the American Federation of Teachers were in Louisville to assist the strikers. Teachers in Georgia, Oklahoma, and Louisiana were threatening strikes for similar reasons. The crisis was temporarily solved with the emergence of a proposal to raise the property assessment ratio from 38 to 48 percent. The proposal led ultimately to a court challenge of property assessment in Kentucky and the special legislative session of 1965. *Louisville Courier-Journal,* November 3, 7, 9, 10, 11, 15, 16, 1964.

UNIVERSITY OF KENTUCKY LAW ALUMNI BANQUET
Louisville / May 12, 1965

NEARLY two hundred years ago the great Edmund Burke, speaking as an Englishman about the American Revolution, said that "a great empire and little minds go ill together." Tonight as we think about Kentucky's future and Kentucky's problems, we must conclude that "a great state and little minds go ill together."

It is no accident that the great new complexes of the space-age industrial giants are located near, and draw their lifeblood from, the great institutions of higher learning in this country—in Massachusetts, in California, in Huntsville, Alabama, in the North Carolina Research Triangle. The new industries and the growing industries of this age demand not merely well-trained workmen; they demand physicists, chemists, biologists, engineers, mathematicians. This means that Kentucky's economic position in the space age will depend not only on the quantity but on the quality of her higher education.

You and I know that Kentucky has made progress in higher education in recent years. Indeed, our progress has been dramatic. You need only to return to the campus of the University of Kentucky to witness the monuments of this progress. The budget of the 1964 General Assembly provided $57.2 million for the University of Kentucky compared to 1962's $39.2 million budget. All totaled, higher education in Kentucky received $90 million in the 1964 appropriation, compared to $60.3 million in 1962. This additional money has enabled us to have a major breakthrough in this state's program for higher education.

But the demand for more and more dormitory space, more classrooms, more teachers, more laboratories at our universities and colleges is growing because our enrollment figures are skyrocketing.[1] If the Commonwealth of Kentucky intends to fulfill its educational obligation to the people of the state and increase its participation in the leadership of the country, we must make even further far-reaching and comprehensive efforts to increase the capacity of our institutions of higher learning in the next few years. This is necessary not only to satisfy the demand of more people for higher education, but to assure them that they receive the highest quality of instruction that is available.

The University of Kentucky anticipates that by 1980 over 20,000 students will be pursuing a college degree at the Lexington campus and that it will require a doubling of the faculty and staff to maintain the programs of instruction, research, and public service in which these students will be involved. It is further estimated that the system of community colleges which the university has established will be called upon to accommodate over 10,000 students in two-year programs, and that an accompanying large increase in faculty and staff will be required for their instruction.

In 1961 the university initiated a program of long-range physical planning in order to establish in detail the physical facilities necessary to support its educational program through 1980. The results of the planning studies which have been completed to date indicate that it will be necessary to significantly expand the size of the Lexington campus. This expansion in campus size is necessary in order to provide space for the construction of five million square feet of new academic and related facilities and two and one-half million square feet of student residences. Furthermore, it will be necessary to establish additional community colleges in order to accommodate the projected increase in their enrollment, in addition to broadening the program offerings at the existing colleges. It is estimated that a total of 650,000 square feet of new construction will be required to support the community college program over the next fifteen years.

The $176 million bond issue to be voted on in November contains direct allocations of $5,783,000 for the University of Kentucky. However, the $5,783,000 will be supplemented by funds from other sources, including federal grants and revenue bonds, thus giving the univeristy $35 million for capital construction during the next few years. This construction would represent an initial step in the achievement of the university's long-range goals. All totaled, the bond issue would provide $87 million for the University of Kentucky and the University of Louisville and our colleges.

This four-year capital improvement program at the University of Kentucky would provide housing for 2,600 undergraduate students, general classroom and office space, a biological science facility for the College of Arts and Sciences, and a biological science facility for the Agricultural Science Center.

A new community college would be constructed in Ashland to replace presently inadequate facilities, and another in southeastern Kentucky. We will also be able to expand the community college facilities in Covington, Henderson, Cumberland, Elizabethtown, Prestonsburg, Hopkinsville, and Somerset to accommodate the broadening of the educational programs now offered by the institutions. Technical and semiprofessional programs will be included in these expansions. So, you can readily see another reason why the bond issue is extremely important to the future of Kentucky. I hope you will support it.

---

1. In the fall semester of 1965 there were 52,623 students enrolled in Kentucky's public colleges and universities. Of that total 16,944 were enrolled at the University of Kentucky and its community colleges. Kentucky Council on Public Higher Education, "Kentucky College and University Enrollments, December, 1965," p. 28, typescript report in Education file, Breathitt papers.

VOCATIONAL EDUCATION FUNDING
Frankfort / October 13, 1965

I AM happy to announce that the Appalachian Regional Commission has this morning approved a $6,880,000 expansion program for vocational education in eastern Kentucky. The twelve-state commission awarded Kentucky $5,450,000 in federal funds from the Appalachian Regional Development Act and the Vocational Education Act of 1963. The remaining $1,430,000 will be put up by local groups and by the state. The commission approved our application exactly as we submitted it.

Approval of this proposal represents a big forward step for Kentucky. By further uplifting the technical capabilities of our eastern Kentucky people, the overall economic level of the entire area will be raised. This is the first proposal of its type approved by the commission.

Funds approved today will be used to finance the first of a three-phase program for the development of vocational education facilities in Kentucky's Appalachian area. Construction and expansion of four area and twelve local extension facilities will be done during the 1965-67 period. The sixteen first-phase schools are expected to handle up to 4,000 regular daytime high school students each day, and up to 8,000 out-of-school youths and adults in night classes.

When funded, the second phase will construct four more schools in the area during 1967-68, and another eleven schools will be built during the 1968-71 third phase period.

During the first-phase period, nine new facilities will be built in Corbin (total cost, $350,000), Bell County ($300,000), Clay County ($420,000), Letcher County ($400,000), Russell County ($250,000), Lee County ($360,000), Garrard County ($300,000), Montgomery-Bath counties ($300,000), and Martin County ($250,000). The plan will also double, and in some cases triple, the student capacity of vocational education schools in Ashland ($1,500,000), Mayo ($650,000), Somerset ($500,000), Harlan ($500,000), Belfry ($300,000), Jackson ($300,000), and Barbourville ($200,000).

The proposal was drawn up at my request by Kentucky's Area Development Office and the Bureau of Vocational Education of the Kentucky Department of Education. It was presented at a special meeting of the Appalachian Regional Commission which I called during the Southern Governors Conference at Sea Island, Georgia, last month. Because of unusual circumstances I was unable to attend the meeting and asked my special assistant, Mr. John Whisman, to make the presentation in my behalf.

With this approval by the Appalachian Regional Commission, Kentucky reaches the second of three important mileposts through which we are putting into effect a crash expansion of Kentucky's program to furnish vocational education and job training for those who need it. The three major construction elements of this program are from (1) the Vocational Education Act, (2) the Appalachian Regional Commission combined with Vocational Education Act funds and (3) construction funds from the Kentucky bond issue to be voted on November 2, 1965. . . . The result of the three programs combined will triple the number of Kentuckians to whom vocational training is available. If Kentucky voters approve the bond issue—and I believe they will—we plan to complete all three of these major elements of vocational school construction within two years.

GOVERNOR'S CONFERENCE ON LIBRARIES
Louisville / October 28, 1965

It is with real pleasure that I come before you tonight at the second Governor's Conference on Libraries during my administration. The occasion is in many ways an historic one, full of promise of Kentucky's future on the one hand, or possibly full of forebodings of a possible slide downwards, depending on what happens at the polls November 2. As governor of your state, I am committed to improving education and educational facilities for all of Kentucky. Progress in school libraries is evident when we see that over 41 percent of the state's elementary school libraries now have the services of a qualified librarian. Ten years ago there were almost no elementary school libraries, yet it is in the early years of the child that the reading habit is developed. Even more heartening is the fact that 93 percent of all the librarians serving school libraries are now fully qualified in accordance with certification requirements.

A major addition to the University of Kentucky's King Library was constructed in 1963; some 50,000 volumes a year are being added, with greater emphasis on graduate and research materials. Last summer a new agricultural research library was opened. New library services were provided for the new School of Architecture. A reading room was opened in the new College of Commerce. The university's building program can continue if the bond issue passes, providing $783,000 in matching funds for federal and other matching funds in excess of $19,000,000.

Of the nine new community colleges, all are rapidly building library collections for student use. Needs for more library space will be made possible by an extensive building program for each college, if the bond issue passes. Enrollments in these colleges have been much higher than was formerly expected.

At Murray State College an $800,000 addition to the library is under way. The library will be almost doubled in size. The operating budget has increased 20 percent over last year's budget. Increased enrollments require state bond issue funds of almost $1,500,000 to match more than $5 million from federal and other sources for the college.

Morehead State College just completed a new addition to its library, at a cost of $843,000. The operating budget has increased 20 percent. The fast-growing college needs additional buildings from the state bond issue costing $1,630,000.

At Western Kentucky State College the former physical education building has just been completely remodeled for a new library at a cost of $1,500,000. The operating budget has increased over 36 percent in the last year—from $220,000 in 1964-65 to over $303,000 in 1965-66. The state bond issue calls for additional construction to meet growing college needs of $1,880,000—to match almost $6 million from federal and other sources. The new library is aptly named after one of Kentucky's most beloved librarians—Miss Margie Helm.[1]

At Eastern Kentucky State College, the library building is being reconstructed at a cost of some $3,000,000. The operating budget has been increased by more than 65 percent in the last two years. Ten years ago the book budget for the library was $7,000. Last year the library's book budget was $97,000. Growth has been rapid here. An additional $1,880,000 will be provided by the state bond issue to match almost $6,000,000 from federal and other sources.

Kentucky State College's comparatively new Blazer Library will soon be doubled in size. Its operating budget has been increased 100 percent. The demands for a growing and rapidly integrating college in the capital require $1,461,000 from the state bond issue to match almost $2,000,000 from federal and other sources.

The University of Louisville's library has also experienced great growth. The new building was constructed seven years ago, and operating budgets have had to mount regularly since. The state bond issue will bring a much needed $3,000,000 to match $21,000,000 from federal and other sources—for building the new medical and dental complex of buildings, including a central medical sciences library. The city bond issue will provide matching funds for a new life science building and a new college and liberal arts building.

The Louisville Free Public Library system, one of the country's busiest, has long been in dire need of a new main library building. Passage of the city bond issue will assure a long overdue addition costing $4,000,000.

Private and parochial college libraries have not been standing still. They, too, have been making every effort to give better services and to construct many new library buildings. I shall urge the Congress to appropriate in its entirety authorization of funds made for the Higher Education Act, which includes funds to upgrade all colleges and library schools as well.

Special, industrial, and other libraries have experienced greater increases in demands than have ever been experienced in the past.

The Kentucky Department of Libraries faces an overwhelming challenge to develop more and better regional library systems, a strong information referral center, and more services of all kinds for all citizens. A new processing center was constructed this year to serve public regional library systems. Private and parochial school libraries will be served here soon. Later, other libraries may participate. The department's state budget has increased 35 percent during the past two years—to help develop five new regional library systems and to help purchase forty-one new bookmobiles.

Eleven construction or remodeling projects for local libraries have been approved with federal and local funds. Included in these projects are the following:

Henry County Public Library Eminence, Kentucky	$ 83,620.00
Morgan County Public Library (J.F. Kennedy Memorial Library) West Liberty, Kentucky	$ 79,299.70
Nicholas County Public Library Carlisle, Kentucky	$ 92,718.00
Ohio County Public Library Hartford, Kentucky	$128,923.71
Fayette County Public Library Lexington, Kentucky	$ 70,517.36
Letcher County Public Library Whitesburg, Kentucky	$ 20,013.50

Green County Public Library Greensburg, Kentucky	$ 81,295.00
Washington County Public Library Springfield, Kentucky	$ 90,113.00
Union County Public Library Morganfield, Kentucky	$ 62,403.00
Fleming County Public Library Flemingsburg, Kentucky	$ 91,616.00
Monroe County Public Library Tompkinsville, Kentucky	$114,007.00

Six hundred forty-five thousand dollars will be added to this program—for the construction of more new library buildings and to help reduce local matching funds for such buildings—if the bond issue passes.

What you have heard is evidence of sound progress with your tax dollar. It is my opinion that libraries are a vital part of the educational process and therefore all libraries should be improved simultaneously, if all citizens are to reach their full potential for self-development and for service to the state. Let us look forward together and work for a day of planned, willing cooperation at all levels. If we do not plan now for coordinated action, we may find that education, including library service, has become a "many splintered thing." We could easily duplicate services and expenses to a point where we may become engulfed in our own complexities. Let us keep sight of our objectives, which are the citizens of Kentucky. It is easier to build a boy than to mend a man. It will be easy for agencies to accentuate their competitive tendencies. To put it another way: "Don't look back or around; someone may be gaining on you." Please do look around, so that all may gain.

Education and library service involve the whole man; and therefore a knowledge of programs for better health, for the aged, for economic development, for better transportation, for the disadvantaged, for conservation, and for recreation, as well as for instruction, are responsibilities of good librarians. . . .[2]

Kentucky has worked hard at the state level to take full advantage of new federal programs. Many hold great promise for more effective service from libraries. Intelligence, ingenuity, and imagination are needed to see the possibilities. The Elementary and Secondary Education Act will provide help never before experienced—for schools and school libraries. The National Defense Education Act, now broadened to include the humanities, has great possibilities. The Economic Opportunity Act could open doors to a new kind of library and bookmobile service—for the disadvantaged. The Appalachian Regional Development Act, followed by the Public Works and Economic Development Act, may hold promise for further library development. Because of the information explosion and the student explosion as well, the whole country has suddenly waked up to its educational inadequacies. . . .

My administration will continue to reflect my interest in libraries as an important part of the total educational system and the total pattern of economic growth. I shall appoint a committee of librarians and other leaders to study the overall requirements of our citizens for library service. I shall charge this committee with making plans and recommendations for both short-term and long-range improvements in the state. I further charge the Kentucky Library Association with presenting to me a carefully considered list of names representing all types of libraries, as well as trustees, friends of libraries, and other lay citizens for my consideration. These leaders will face a tremendous challenge to work out together a plan for quality library service for every man, woman, and child in the Commonwealth. . . .

Good library service costs money—lots of money. The demands for the best in easy, or preschool, books for very young children are now overwhelming. The Department of Libraries has informed me that the new books, records, and films already provided by the department for bookmobiles and for libraries participating in state regional library systems have created demands for more and more material.

We can be proud of what was done this summer by the Department of Libraries, by regional librarians, and by cooperative-minded local librarians—to help the Head Start programs. Extra books and records were provided by the Department of Libraries, and many regional librarians added an Operation Outreach of their own by visits to participating libraries for Head Start programs. Stories were told, films were shown, records were played. In some, refreshments were provided. Local public and school librarians worked hard together as well to give these youngsters a new outlook on life. Story hours for young school and preschool children have been a part of the public library for years.

The disadvantaged have been served for years by Kentucky's bookmobiles. Sometimes we lost sight of what has been done and is being done by these castles on wheels. Adults as well are now using local and regional libraries as never before. Formerly women were the main borrowers; now businessmen, farmers, and workers are flocking to libraries. School librarians are struggling valiantly to give much better service to all schoolchildren, and to enrich the school curriculum. They must not be forgotten. The recent growth of graduate and research programs in our colleges and in our universities is requiring ever mounting support of better library programs. The growth in demand is here. The growth in support can come, if everyone understands the problem and acts accordingly.

---

1. Margie Helm, born Auburn, Kentucky; A.B., Randolph-Macon College (1916); B.L.S., Pratt Library School (1922); M.A., University of Chicago (1933); teacher, public schools of Virginia and Kentucky (1916-1919); librarian, Western Kentucky State University (1920-1965); head librarian (1923-1965); president, Kentucky Library Association (1928-1930); resident of Bowling Green, Kentucky. Information provided by Penny Harrison, Kentucky Library, Western Kentucky University.

2. Three sections of this speech detailing advantages of the bond issue have been deleted.

LEXINGTON VOCATIONAL TECHNICAL-TRAINING CENTER GROUNDBREAKING
Lexington / November 23, 1965

THESE are the first fruits of the bond issue which you, the people of Kentucky, supported so magnificently in the recent elections. Your foresight, your vision are now to be vindicated.

I shall treat your confidence as an inviolable trust—and I pledge you that the funds which you have entrusted to our administration we shall expend and invest not only with honesty and fidelity, but with a single objective in mind—a growing, dynamic Kentucky, worthy not only of its past heritage but of the fine young men and women whom we must equip to meet the challenges of a complex and changing age.

Last week Henry A. Wallace died.[1] To many of our people, Henry Wallace is only a line or a footnote in their history books. But to some of us who are getting a bit older, Henry Wallace recalls some of the stirring debates and controversies which rocked our nation two decades ago. Henry Wallace made some serious mistakes in his public life, but he also made many contributions to his country. More than twenty years ago Henry Wallace predicted that, with wise management and progressive government, this nation could provide sixty million jobs for its people in the postwar era. Mr. Wallace even wrote a book called *Sixty Million Jobs.* For this prediction, for seeking to establish this goal, Henry Wallace was denounced and scorned as a crackpot. But the fact is that we passed his goal of sixty million jobs more than ten years ago, and are now establishing more ambitious goals, even in the face of an age of automation and cybernation.

Two years ago, I proclaimed as a goal for Kentucky's economy 75,000 new and additional jobs for Kentuckians. For this I, too, was laughed at by some people who said it couldn't be done. Now, in less than two years, we have exceeded this goal by 35,000—a total of 110,000 new jobs in less than two years.

Let me be clear about it. I do not say to you now, and I did not say then, that Ned Breathitt could pass a miracle and create 75,000 new jobs, or 110,000 new jobs, or any number of new jobs. What I said then and what I say now is that, with sound policies in our state government, with progressive programs in our state government, with a growing and prosperous national economy and a great national leadership, with the indispensable cooperation of voluntary groups at the community level—I did say that with all the forces working together, we can eventually provide job opportunities for all our people, opportunities which will let us keep our young people at home, opportunities which will push Kentucky up the economic ladder and give us a future worthy of our past.

Today we meet to break ground for a new vocational school which is both an instrument and symbol of that progress. For more than three years I have preached all over this state the gospel of education—the proposition that, if we are to find jobs for our people, we must fit them for the jobs which are in demand in the age in which we live.

Passage of the bond issue has made possible the building of this $1,500,000 vocational and technical school. Half of the money will come from state government and half from federal funds. The people of twenty counties will look here for training in vocational and technical skills, and the unbelievable growth of this Bluegrass area will receive still another quickening impulse from this school. I express gratitude and tribute to those of you locally who have worked to make this dream a reality—and especially your chamber of commerce.

A moment ago I said that this school and this ceremony are both an instrument and a symbol. We must never forget this symbolic importance of this day—because this day is but the beginning. During the next two years, we shall spend $13 million in building new or greatly expanded area vocational school and extension centers—nine schools and nineteen extension centers.

It is our goal—and we shall reach that goal—to bring modern, up-to-date vocational education within fifteen to twenty-five miles of every Kentuckian, within the next four years. During the coming two years, we shall increase our total expenditures for construction of vocational schools by more than 500 percent. This will result from the cooperation of many forces and many funds—the federal vocations program, the Appalachian programs, the Commonwealth, and local school districts. Let me say that Kentucky, and her Department of Education under the able leadership of E.P. Hilton, has pioneered in developing the concept of the area vocational school, and that our own area program office, ably headed by John Whisman—who is in many ways the creator of our whole Appalachian program—showed the vision and foresight to present this program to the Appalachian Regional Commission, which gave us a grant of nearly $5 million over the next four years.[2]

Many times I have said that our economy is a seamless web. We cannot separate its strands without weakening the fabric of the whole. Of those strands which go to make up the fabric there are many—highways, natural resources, agricultural and industrial planning—but the stoutest strand is and will remain the development of our human resources. That means education—education for jobs, education for citizenship, and education for life.

Let us today renew our dedication to the full development of our human resources—quality education, both vocational and academic, is the keystone in the arch of Kentucky's economic progress.

---

1. Henry A. Wallace (1888-1965), U.S. secretary of agriculture (1933-1941); vice president of the United States (1941-1945). Wallace contributed to such New Deal innovations as the "ever-normal granary" and crop production controls. Following World War II he criticized Truman's Cold War policies and advocated a more conciliatory approach to the Soviet Union, a stand that proved unpopular in the late 1940s. *The National Cyclopedia of American Biography* (New York, 1971), vol. 53, p. 15.

2. Everett P. Hilton (1901-), vocational education instructor, supervisor, director, and bureau head with Division of Vocational Education (1936-1967); born in Webbville, Kentucky, and a resident of Frankfort. Information provided by Division of Personnel, Frankfort.

EDUCATION STATEMENT
Frankfort / February 3, 1966

ON this day the attention of every Kentuckian will be centered, I am sure, upon the importance of education and of our teachers in the life of our state and the future of our young people.[1]

Let me assure you that my attention is centered upon the importance of education and upon the important role of our teachers, not merely on this day but on every day. I am a product, for whatever I may be worth, of Kentucky's school system, as are most of you; and on every occasion when it has become my responsibility to decide what is vital, what must come first in the progress of our Commonwealth, I have sincerely tried to put education first, not merely to please you or to please any particular organization, although I want and need their support, but because I know that without their improved educational effort, everything else that we will try to do for Kentucky will be doomed to failure.

The particular need which has caused the most animated discussion, not to say controversy, in recent weeks, is the finances of education in Kentucky and, in particular, the provision of adequate salaries for our splendid and dedicated teachers. As one who has drawn deeply on the devotion and the intelligence of fine Kentucky teachers, not merely in school but in public life, I know that the teachers of our state need and deserve better pay. This is not merely a matter of justice for the teacher—not merely a matter of adequate compensation for the long years of preparation, for the long hours of service in and out of the school room. More than that, it is a matter of economics. If there are pay scales for teachers which do not nearly approach their adequate level, then we shall not be able to properly equip young men and women who come out of our colleges and universities each year into our educational system.

The problem is not one of recognizing the merits of your case. The problem is one of finding ways and means to meet this need—ways and means to increase the level of compensation for our teachers within the resources which are available at the state level and at the local level.

Many of our teachers' organizations have set as their goal an increase in teachers' salaries of $900 per year, this level to be attained over the coming two-year period. I do not think that any Kentuckian who has studied the facts, who has studied the needs and problems, would see that this figure is in itself unreasonable and that it places too high a value on the services of those in the teaching profession.

In 1963 I was a candidate for governor. I told the educational organization in Kentucky that I would meet their request with reference to the financing of an expanded foundation program in the 1964 budget, providing funds for an increase of $500 per classroom unit for teachers' salaries.

In the 1965 special session, I advocated and led in securing the passage of legislation which would make available additional funds for local school boards despite the rollback in maximum tax rates designed to compensate for increased property assessments.

I insisted upon this legislation because I felt that it was our duty to make available to local school boards additional revenue for the vital needs of education. Under this bill, it will be possible for local school boards to secure $8 million this year and $17 million for each subsequent year of additional money at the local level for education.

In the 1966 budget, I recommended additional increases over the coming two years of $400 per classroom unit for increased teachers' salaries. This was, I felt, the maximum amount of salary increases which we could make available in view of all the needs of our various state programs in accordance with the revenue estimates which had been given me of income for the next biennium under the existing tax structures. These revenue estimates were made as of December 1, 1965.

I am sure that you do not feel that the increases which we have already provided were sufficient. I agree with you; but the problem is how to get the job done. We cannot do it by juggling statistics. We cannot do it by political fakery or by the art of the demagogue. We cannot do it by pretending to cut items of mythical fat from a budget where there is no fat. We cannot do it by creating a fictitious surplus conjured up by the same political mathematicians who said two years ago that our revenue estimates were padded and excessive.

We can only do it by hard study, by hard work and by making conclusive choices. For these reasons, I have appointed a commission to study and report on the needs for financial problems of education—not to report to some future General Assembly, not to report to posterity, but to report to the present General Assembly. In order that I may not be thought to duck or dodge my responsibility, I named myself as chairman of a Commission on Education. Its membership is composed of men and women of wide experience, including representatives from our teachers' organization, including also members of the legislature and leaders from all walks of life.

I am already convinced that the work of the commission will be fruitful, that it will produce results which will be good for our teachers, good for our children, good for our educational system. I am convinced already that the recommendations which will emerge from this type of study will be sounder in the long run, not only for Kentucky, but for you, than if I had simply put a rubber stamp of approval on the recommendations of any particular organization at the time the budget was submitted.

I ask you to trust your leaders who are serving on this commission, and to await the account of its deliberations before making any final judgment as to what can be done to better your load during the coming two years.

I cannot promise you any magic formula, I cannot promise you to please everybody, but I can promise you two things: first, that we shall all do our dead level best to provide for our schools and teachers what they need and deserve; and second, that I shall not evade my responsibility to be the best possible governor both for education and for all of our people. Thank you for giving me this opportunity to talk with you.

1. On January 17, 1966, the Kentucky Education Association scheduled a statewide, one-day teachers' strike to protest the passage of the Breathitt administration budget, which fell short of teachers' educational demands. The new budget provided only $400 for salary increases for teachers over the biennium; the K.E.A. had requested $900. In addition, the K.E.A. argued the budget provided insufficient support for educational facilities. If the government failed to respond the K.E.A. threatened censure by the National Education Association and measures to discourage teachers from working in Kentucky. The K.E.A. suggested an increase in the sales tax to provide the additional revenue to meet their demands; however, Governor Breathitt, citing his 1963 campaign pledge not to raise state taxes, promised to veto such legislation if it passed the General Assembly. He insisted other means be found to finance increases in educational appropriations, and he appointed a special Commission to Help Education to suggest alternative recommendations. The commission was made up of representatives from the legislature, the executive branch, the K.E.A., and school boards. Breathitt appointed himself as chairman; however, the direct supervision of the commission fell to the vice chairman, Dr. Harry M. Sparks, state superintendent of public instruction. The commission examined five possible sources of additional revenue. Four of the alternatives were permissive measures designed to allow local governments to raise the money: a local income tax; a local sales tax; an occupational tax; and the removal of the ceiling on property taxes established during the special legislative session of 1965. The fifth alternative was the establishment of a state monopoly on package liquor sales. The anticipated profits would be allocated primarily for educational improvements, including increased teachers' salaries. However, during the course of the commission's deliberations, testimony from recognized economists indicated that the inflationary growth of the American economy and changes in the corporate tax collection schedules would likely provide the necessary revenue to finance the salary increases. The state liquor monopoly option was therefore rejected in favor of a combination of the more conventional and less politically controversial alternatives. On March 8 the General Assembly passed H.B. 471 which provided for teacher salary increases ranging from $450 to $1,000, depending upon an individual's teaching experience. An additional $24 million was appropriated for this purpose from the General Fund in anticipation of increased tax revenues and earlier collection of corporate income taxes. In order to provide additional funds for school construction and classroom facilities, local school boards were empowered to levy an occupational tax, a 3 percent utilities tax, and a surcharge on state income taxes. *Acts, 1966,* Chapter 24 (H.B. 471), pp. 226-40. See also "Report of the Commission to Help Education," typescript in Education file, Breathitt papers, and *Louisville Courier-Journal,* March 8, 1966.

FOUNDERS DAY CEREMONIES EASTERN KENTUCKY UNIVERSITY

Richmond / March 21, 1966

SIXTY years ago today a great Kentucky governor—J.C.W. Beckham—signed into law a measure that laid the foundation of a great state educational institution.[1] On that day—March 21, 1906—Eastern State Normal School was established.

It marked the beginning of a new era of education here in Richmond and Madison County and eastern Kentucky as well, for higher educational opportunities were made possible for thousands of Kentuckians who might not have had them otherwise. Today we are on the threshold of a new era of higher education here. As governor of the Commonwealth, I am indeed honored to be able to say to you today that from the foundation of the old normal school has developed Eastern Kentucky State University.

The growth of this institution through several phases of educational levels has been slow but sure. It is testimonial of the faith those before us had in us today. It was a faith which met all challenges, and we today are the benefactors of it. But today we are the challenged. A new generation faced by complex problems is our concern—and let me say to you, we already have begun to meet the challenges of the future, to meet the higher educational demands of our young people, by pressing for more and better higher educational facilities, for better standards. We expect Eastern Kentucky State University, along with our other fine colleges and universities, to continue to carry the burden.

If we must pay recognition to past accomplishments—and we must—we cannot overlook the fact that we owe a great deal to a hardy and persevering group of educators who established a university here eighty-nine years ago. That university—known as Central University—was a Southern Presbyterian school; and when the university closed its doors in 1901, the buildings and grounds were later available for the state normal school.

One of those buildings—University Building—is still in use on this campus. This, too, is indicative of the faith those before us had in the future of Richmond and Madison County as a center for higher education. I believe if our forefathers could look upon this sprawling campus and the numerous new modern buildings here they would say we have kept their faith and ideals alive, and we have prospered in that we have built upon those ideals.

Let us briefly assess the past accomplishments. In 1922 Eastern became a four-year teachers college in addition to being a normal school. In 1928 it was accredited by the Southern Association of Colleges and Secondary

Schools. It became solely a teachers college in 1930 and began a graduate program in 1935. In 1948 it became a full-fledged liberal arts college with the right to grant nonprofessional degrees. Since 1959 the enrollment has climbed from 2,900 to nearly 7,000; the faculty doubled; academic programs expanded; and the building construction program has totaled over $35 million. Since 1960 every major facility on this campus has been either constructed or reconstructed.[2]

Indicative of Eastern's extensive building program are the just recently completed twelve-story, air-conditioned dorm for women and an eight-story dorm for men. Already under construction is a $3,300,000 expansion of the John Grant Crabbe Library. A twenty-two story men's dorm and a nine-story dorm for women, for which we will break ground at noon, and numerous other buildings will soon get under construction. Others are being planned, for we are not only building for today but for the future.

What does the future hold? Enrollment here next year is expected to be over 8,000, and by 1970 on-campus enrollment is expected to top 10,000 students. What these figures mean is that the demands for higher education are no longer required by a few but are a necessity for a majority of our young people, if our Commonwealth is to survive in a technological and space-age world. We must and we shall meet the demands upon us year by year and decade after decade.

The people of Kentucky last year overwhelmingly demonstrated by referendum they are willing to meet the needs of their Commonwealth. They approved a $176 million bond issue of which part is being used for higher education purposes. The people have given us their support and we are, to the best of our ability, accomplishing the objectives.

Elevating this institution, and three other regional colleges, to university status is an essential part of our program toward fulfilling the higher educational needs of the future. With this recognition, however, goes much responsibility.

We live in a changing world. Many of the things we see and do today were little thought of only a generation ago, even by the most expert prognosticators. We were aware of change at that time, but few thought it would come so rapidly. The fact that it has come rapidly has presented us with both great opportunities and great problems, unthought of by the students of a few years ago. Both these opportunities and these problems can be dealt with successfully only by flexible minds, by ever enlarging intellect, by ever increasing growth of the human spirit.

It is not the fraternity or sorority or other extracurricular activities, though we may like all this, that make a university truly great. It is not the enrollment figure or the splendor of a building or the number of graduates that give a university status. More so, it is the teachers, the libraries, the laboratories, the atmosphere, the students—these are the products of a great university, the developers of the mind.

Cardinal Newman once described an ideal university as a place where there is a "collison of mind with mind."[3] I hope you do not fear controversy, that you do not shy away from argument—disciplined argument, at any rate. I hope you are not afraid of an ideal foreign to any you might have had yourself. I hope, on the other hand, that you are not afraid to express your own ideas or to stand up for what you consider a just cause.

I hope you are developing an appreciation of the power of knowledge—both what it can do for you personally and how it can propel mankind across new frontiers of achievement and move us toward universal happiness and peace.

I hope you are learning that knowledge must be tempered with understanding if it is to work for mankind properly. While a little knowledge may be a dangerous thing, a great deal of knowledge can be much more dangerous if it is not applied according to the rules and needs of humanity.

I hope your training is awakening in you an appreciation of the great heritage that has been left you by the scholars, the scientists, the poets, the theologians, the saints, the artists, the statesmen who have preceded you on this planet. It is a heritage so rich that it can never be absorbed by any of us, and certainly four years of university training is much too brief a time to sample much of it.

Above all, among the things I hope you are gaining from your experience here at Eastern, is character. By character I mean strength of self that keeps you morally right and that enables you to exercise the restraints that are required by society. But by character I also mean an attitude toward your neighbor or fellow man that forces you to automatically consider him and his needs—that requires you to help make his way a little smoother. The trait is, in a word, "kindness." It is the most powerful force in human association and without it your chemistry and physics, your history and literature—your university degrees—will enable you to progress little toward the goals of personal happiness and service to mankind. So with this recognition, as you can readily see, does go much responsibility.

The decision to name Eastern, Morehead, Murray, and Western universities is partly the result of a two-year study by the best experts in the field of higher education I could find. Two years ago I named these people to a special Commission on Higher Education with the purpose to determine the needs of higher education for a ten-year period. This commission also obtained three other eminent educators to conduct a special eight-month study.[4]

The result of the studies is all too clear. We must continue to run fast—expand and improve our higher education system—if we in Kentucky are to keep pace with the rest of the nation. A greater emphasis must be placed on the graduate levels—and this is one of the compelling reasons why it is necessary to elevate these institutions. We have removed obstacles which would hinder this accomplishment; we have opened the doors to greater opportunities for these institutions to develop research and service programs for their regions which they otherwise would be unable to do.

Most important of all, we have established a nine-member lay council to plan the future growth of the state's system of higher education. It will be a blue-ribbon group, academically oriented, that will strengthen our system of higher education and assure an orderly, efficient, scholarly expansion. We know the accomplishment of a long-range and coordinated program for higher education in Kentucky will not be easy, but it is a program which must succeed. We have made our decision and we shall not fail.

---

1. J.C.W. Beckham (1869-1940), governor of Kentucky (1900-1907). Beckham, as lieutenant governor, completed the term of William Goebel and won a full four-year term in 1903. In 1915 he was elected to the United States Senate; however, he failed in his bid for re-election for a second term. He remained active in Kentucky politics until his death in 1940. Robert A. Powell, *Kentucky Governors* (Danville, Ky., 1976), p. 78.

2. With slight variations, Breathitt's description of the evolution of Eastern Kentucky University characterized the development of Western Kentucky University, Murray State University, and Morehead State University.

3. John Henry Newman (1801-1890), nineteenth century churchman and educator; outlined the aims and principles of an education in *Idea of a University. The Concise Dictionary of National Biography* (London, 1930), pp. 940-41.

4. See Kentucky Commission on Higher Education, "Higher Education in Kentucky, 1965-1975: Recommendations to the Governor of Kentucky for Establishing a Basic Program to meet the State's Higher Education Needs in the Coming Decade," January 7, 1966, typescript in Education file, Breathitt papers. The commission was chaired by Mr. William Abell of Louisville, and its membership was dominated by the presidents of Kentucky's public and private institutions of higher education. The report projected student enrollment in public institutions of higher education to grow from 45,215 "full-time equivalent" students in 1965 to 94,500 in the fall of 1975. The commission recommended: that the four regional colleges expand graduate studies at the master's level in arts and sciences, business administration, education, and other appropriate fields as resources become available; the four regional colleges be designated universities and that Kentucky State College, after expanding its graduate programs, be accorded university status; that the University of Kentucky expand and strengthen its graduate programs at the doctoral and post-doctoral level and that it serve as the principal state institution for statewide research and service programs; that the regional universities develop appropriate research and service programs for their geographical areas; and that the

University of Louisville become a state university. The report made additional recommendations regarding the expansion of undergraduate curricula, community college development, capital construction financing, and tuition policy. Finally, the commission recommended that the Council on Public Higher Education be reconstituted to include nine laymen appointed by the governor, and the presidents of each of the four-year public institutions of higher learning. The recommendation further provided that only those members appointed by the governor could vote, a development opposed by the presidents of the four regional colleges, the president of Kentucky State College, and two other members of the commission. Despite their opposition, Governor Breathitt shortly deprived the presidents of voting privileges on the council.

UNIVERSITY OF KENTUCKY DENTAL SCHOOL GRADUATION

Lexington / May 9, 1966

THIS is indeed a proud and important moment. A proud moment for you, the first graduating class of the University of Kentucky Medical Center College of Dentistry, and an important moment for all the citizens of Kentucky, as you lead a procession of dentists that will improve their health and well-being. On behalf of all Kentuckians I salute you and congratulate you. Today's graduation marks the completion of years of study and work for you, and the beginning of a fruitful and satisfying career of service.

Today also marks the successful completion of twelve years' effort to develop the Medical Center of the University of Kentucky. On June 1, 1954 the Board of Trustees of the University of Kentucky authorized the establishment of a College of Medicine, which was expanded to include dentistry, nursing, and the hospital. Ground was broken on December 10, 1957, and in September of 1962 the first class of the College of Dentistry was admitted.

The results to date have been astounding. You, the first graduating class, are the first dividends on an investment in the future by the people of Kentucky. That investment is a $27 million one—plus staffing and equipment—to develop a medical center of unequalled excellence. The students and faculty of this growing College of Dentistry are proving that this expenditure was a wise investment.

The dentists in Kentucky have long been recognized and respected as important leaders in the Commonwealth. I am delighted that the Kentucky Dental Association will now be strengthened by graduates from this new school. Certainly the need is great. This fine medical center with its three colleges of the health fields was conceived for the purpose of responding to this need.

In the United States there is approximately one dentist for every 1,900 people. There is only one dentist for every 3,000 Kentuckians. Seven counties in the Commonwealth have no dentist at the present time. In at least five counties there is only one dentist, and in several others the ratio is one dentist for every 17,000 people. I hope you will practice in Kentucky.

I am pleased that three of the doctors who are graduating today have received support for their education under the rural scholarship plan sponsored by the state and therefore have agreed to open their offices in rural Kentucky, where the need is greatest. In order to provide greater opportunities in the financing of dental care it is important to note that Kentucky is one of eleven states of the nation which has an active dental service corporation. Through this organization prepayment and dental insurance programs are being developed.

Undoubtedly, however, the most important step which Kentucky has taken in order to improve the dental health of our citizens has been the development of this fine new school with all its modern equipment. Actually, the dental profession has come a long way in the last century—and I, personally, am happy about its achievements. I'd just as soon not have been one of your patients when your only tools were a straight chair, a pair of pliers, a hammer, and a bottle of corn liquor! Again, congratulations to you graduates, and thanks to Dean Morris and his faculty for their leadership.[1]

---

1. Alvin Leonard Morris (1927-), D.D.S., University of Michigan (1951); assistant professor of oral medicine, University of Pennsylvania (1957-1960); professor and dean of the College of Dentistry, University of Kentucky (1961-). *American Men of Science: The Physical and Biological Sciences,* 11th ed. (New York, 1966), p. 3736.

GOVERNOR'S CONFERENCE ON ETV
Frankfort / May 17, 1966

IN Act IV of Shakespeare's *Julius Caesar,* Brutus warns that "we must take the current when it serves or lose our ventures." Somewhat more recently, Gerald Jaggers, editor of the *Kentucky Education Journal,* sounded a similar warning for education.[1] "Crisis will follow crisis," he said, "if we do not keep up to date in the utilization of technological and human resources available to us."

Today the current is running strongly in the direction Gerald suggests—toward the introduction into our educational system of the best in technological resources, particularly those that fully utilize the human resources of the teaching profession. Without question the greatest such technological innovation in education in this century—many say it is the greatest since the invention of movable type—is television put to the service of education.

We have watched educational television develop in the last few years, not only in this country but throughout the world, and we have looked for the current to be favorable to launch it in Kentucky. The time had to be right, for it is no simple matter to introduce so organic a teaching tool into two hundred school systems and a million homes at one time. Brutus said that we must take the current when it serves. The same current, taken at the wrong time, could as easily swamp us as carry us to success.

So we watched and we waited. We observed how other states went about developing ETV systems, and we studied the results to see what approaches were best. We drew up a state plan and then improved it to the point where it was acclaimed by experts as a model for the nation. Our challenge then became to execute that plan so that what we did would be as much a model for the nation as what we planned to do. Our success depended, and still depends, on our readiness.

When the General Assembly met in 1966, I was convinced that the time had come for Kentucky to make its move in ETV. Let me illustrate how far we progressed on the road to readiness between the initial conception under the leadership of Governor Bert Combs in 1960 and this moment of execution.

In 1960, when Kentucky first toyed with the idea of ETV, few of our educators knew anything about it. By 1966, more than half our school districts had gained experience with ETV, most by picking up signals from out of state, many by using the broadcast instruction of Kentucky's pioneering system in Jefferson County. These schools—from Russellville to Ashland, from Daviess County to Harlan County—are now equipped and waiting to receive Kentucky's own ETV programs. Further, every school built in Kentucky in the last three or four years has included conduit for television.

The eagerness of Kentucky's schools to benefit from ETV was well demonstrated when, a year ago, a commercial station in Huntington, West Virginia, broadcast a course in new math for the fifth grade. The program was made possible by the Ashland Oil and Refining Company. During the three months that the series was carried, more than three thousand students and five hundred teachers used it in Kentucky schools from Greenup to Letcher County. This eagerness is perhaps best explained by Hazard school superintendent Roy Eversole, who says simply that in his view, "ETV is the only hope of a rural school to offer courses and instruction comparable to those offered in richer areas."[2]

In 1960 no Kentucky educational organization had really explored ETV, let alone taken a stand on it. By 1966, Kentucky's ETV plan was fully supported by the Kentucky Education Association and its Department of Classroom Teachers, by the Kentucky Association of School Administrators, by the state's institutions of higher education, by the Kentucky State Board of Education, by the Kentucky School Boards Association, and last but very far from least, by the Kentucky Congress of Parents and Teachers.

In 1960 no more than a handful of Kentuckians outside education had any notion about the out-of-school potential of ETV. By 1966 the adult and continuing education benefits of ETV had been thoroughly investigated and endorsed by such business and professional groups as the Kentucky Chamber of Commerce, the Kentucky Medical Association, the Kentucky Broadcasters Asociation, and the Kentucky Hospital Association.

Much of this progress in understanding and preparedness has taken place since 1964, when I included in my executive budget the first full biennial budget for the Kentucky Authority for Educational Television. I said then that I was looking toward activation of the Kentucky ETV Network in 1966, and I am satisfied and pleased that we are now fully ready for that activation. I want to congratulate each of the groups I mentioned, and the many organizations and individuals I won't have time to single out, for their thoughtful efforts to pave the way to effective utilization of this powerful educational tool. I want especially to express my appreciation to the Advisory Committee of the Kentucky Authority for Educational Television, to the staff of the authority, and to the authority members themselves—Roy Owsley, Dick Van Hoose, Don Bale, Harry Sparks, Bob Martin, Pete Mathews, Al Temple, Lyman Ginger, and Marion Gumm—and to the only two other members the authority has had since its beginning: Wendell Butler, who was a member by virtue of being superintendent of public instruction, and Dr. David McLean Greeley, formerly of Harlan but now out of the state.[3]

And I must pay tribute to radio, television, and the press for the magnificent job they have done in the past two years in explaining ETV to the public and thus creating the anticipation which is a prerequisite to effective use.

It is this enthusiasm, this pulling together by all of you in education, in industry, in the professions, which puts Kentucky in the enviable position to see the magic carpet of television carry us to unprecedented progress in education and economic development. I put education and economic development together because they are, in fact, inseparable. If we are going to continue to attract industry to Kentucky, I need hardly tell you that we have to assure a constant supply of well-educated executive talent and of trained and trainable workers.

Educational television will contribute directly and indirectly to this end. It will establish a basic floor of instructional quality for every schoolchild in Kentucky. At the same time, it will offer adult and vocational education ranging from an accelerated attempt to eradicate illiteracy, to specialized training in high-demand skills.

Nor should anyone get the impression that educational television is of value only to the substandard school. The fact is that ETV started out—and proved out—in large cities and in superior school systems—systems which could afford to make already good programs even better. The chief characteristic of the Kentucky ETV system, and the one for which it has received such wide acclaim, is that it will serve not only the cities but every rural school in every remote hamlet in Kentucky. Nor will any Kentucky school have to pay to use the programs broadcast by Kentucky's ETV network. We have guaranteed by our total state approach that the areas of Kentucky which stand in greatest need of ETV support will not be the last to get it. I might add, with some pride, that this philosophy, which was at the core of our thinking from the beginning, has since been adopted by a number of other states.

I am not going to try to describe for you now the many ways in which ETV will prove a boon to Kentucky because we have experts who will do that for you this afternoon. But I want to pledge you this: Kentucky will have the best educational television system in the country. We are not the first to get into ETV—we waited for the right time, the best time, and I am confident that this was the wise course. But now that we are getting into it, we are going first class. For one thing, we cannot afford to do less, especially since we are the focus of national attention. For another, the difference in cost between first class and any other class is small, but the difference in capability and effectiveness would be tremendous.

The Kentucky ETV network, with its twelve transmitters, its ten translators, and its eight production centers, will cost about $8 million—roughly the equivalent of a few miles of superhighway. Of that amount, $2 million will come from federal matching funds—$1 million under the ETV Facilities Act, and $1 million, thanks to the vision of John Whisman in relating ETV to the development of our human resource, will come from the Appalachian Regional Development Act.

Actually this will be an integral part of a three-pronged attack on educational problems in Appalachia. ETV will work hand in glove with the vocational schools and library expansion programs. Miss Margaret Willis will have more to say about that this afternoon.[4] Throughout Kentucky, ETV will be an important adjunct to other training and development programs. Again, you will hear more about that this afternoon.

I can report to you now that we are making excellent progress toward completion of this network within the next twenty-four months, in time to test it out before it goes into use in the schools in September of 1968. The studio at Eastern Kentucky State University is under construction and should be ready this fall. The other state colleges and the University of Kentucky are well along in their studio planning. Sites for the transmitters are being acquired now, and I'll have more to say about that in the next part of our program.

Let me review now the ETV picture as I see it. Educational television is the product of a felt need. It is an educational lifeline at a time of educational crisis. I am not talking about the crisis in school construction—ETV cannot reduce the need for more space. Nor am I talking about the shortage of good teachers—ETV cannot replace one live classroom teacher. As a matter of fact, it takes a good teacher in the classroom to exploit the latent ability of ETV to improve learning. The crisis I am talking about is the crisis of demand. Colleges are demanding better preparation as the competition for placement increases. The knowledge explosion puts tremendous pressure on all the professions, even as it does on teachers, to keep abreast of developments not only in our own but in related fields. Industry demands better trained and more readily trainable workers. This in turn requires a better basic education.

Changing technology demands frequent retraining of workers. There is also a constant demand for abler and better-trained supervisors and middle-management executives. In South Carolina, more than 18,000 supervisory and management personnel in more than 200 plants have received on-the-job training over the state ETV network in the last two years. The courses ranged from business letter writing to creative problem solving. The companies gladly paid the tuition for their employees.

One out of every five American families moved last year, and the rate is increasing. This mobility of the contemporary population demands a basic quality of education for all children so they will have a fair chance to adjust to a new school.

And then there is the demand for more and better driver training to reduce the slaughter on our highways—and you know I feel strongly about this. I am told that driver training is the most expensive single thing a school can teach—except by television, where the parent complements the teacher and uses his own car. The ETV station in Denver, Colorado, reported that of a group of 280 who took its television driving course, 190 took the state test and 180 passed.

Of course, as we unhappily know, this is just a start. For some, a license to drive is also a license to turn into a highway menace. For others, it is a license to be incredibly thoughtless and careless. Here is an area in which television can not only provide initial instruction, but can and should be used for regular continuing education.

Finally, there is the need to expose more of our young children to the broadening world of the arts—to museums and symphonies and outstanding plays. How do you expose a child in a remote Kentucky community to these things? Obviously one answer is by television. But it does much less good to expose the children if you cannot give the parents an opportunity to participate also. That, too, we will do.

Kentucky's ETV programs will go directly into the homes as well as the schools. And television has made better inroads into Kentucky homes than any other modern convenience. In Kentucky's poorest county more than 60 percent of the homes have television sets—and this despite the fact that the nearest station is so far away and reception is so poor that they can count on "snow" all year round. In much of Kentucky, the ETV station will provide the first and only good picture the people have had.

I have touched on many of the things ETV can and will do in Kentucky. They are all important, all desperately needed. And yet I would be satisfied that we were bringing in an educational gusher if educational television could do no more than put a great and commanding presence like Carl Sandburg or Jesse Stuart at the front of a thousand classrooms—if it could do no more than give 10,000 teachers much needed team support—if it could do no more than let 100,000 students gaze on the moving world revealed by an electron microscope.[5] These things it can and will do—not as occasional events, but as a planned part of the learning experience in schools throughout the Commonwealth. I tell you now that our challenge is to make ETV do what it can do, and do it as superbly as we have planned. It is a task we can only accomplish successfully if we all work at it—together.

---

1. Gerald Wilfred Jaggers (1917-), born in Hart County, Kentucky; B.A., University of Kentucky (1938); M.A. (1947); Ph.D., George Peabody College (1949); teacher, public schools of Kentucky (1938-1941, 1945-1946); faculty member, East Tennessee State College (1947-1958); director of publications, Kentucky Education Association (1958-); resident of Frankfort. Telephone interview, March 2, 1981.

2. Roy Grigsby Eversole (1906-), currently a resident of Hazard, Kentucky; B.A., University of Kentucky (1929); M.A. (1942); Perry County teacher (1929-1931); principal, Jackson High School, Jackson, Kentucky (1932-1934); attendance officer, principal, coach, and superintendent, Hazard city schools (1935-1972). Telephone interview, February 4, 1981.

3. Roy Owsley (1908-), field consultant for Kentucky Municipal League (1929-1937); associate director of Washington, D.C., office of the American Municipal Association (1940-1941); consultant to city of Louisville (1948-1952); chairman of board of trustees of Kentucky Health Educational Welfare Research Program, Incorporated (1962-1966); chairman, Kentucky Authority on Educational Television (1962-). *Who's Who in the South and Southwest, 1969-1970,* 11th ed. (Chicago, 1969). Richard Van Hoose (1910-), teacher, Warren County, Kentucky (1933-1937); teacher and coach, Frankfort public schools (1937-1939); principal, Frankfort elementary schools (1939-1943); superintendent of schools, Anchorage (1943-1946); assistant superintendent, Jefferson County (1948-1950); superintendent, Jefferson County (1950-1975). *Who's Who in America, 1978-1979,* 40th ed. (Chicago, 1978). Don C. Bale (1912-), B.A., Campbellsville College; M.A., Western Kentucky State College; elementary and high school teacher, coach and principal, Hart County, Kentucky (1935-1952); assistant superintendent for instruction, Kentucky Department of Education (1952-1977); consultant for Kentucky Educational Television (1977-). Telephone interview, March 2, 1981. Robert Richard Martin (1910-), teacher and principal in Mason and Lee County public schools (1935-1948); auditor, director of finance, and head of business administration and finance, Kentucky Department of Education (1948-1955); superintendent of public instruction (1955-1959); president of Eastern Kentucky University (1960-1976). *Leaders in Education, 1974* (New York, 1974), p. 734. Pete Mathews, associated with radio station WLW in Cincinnati until 1966; associated with WCET-TV, Cincinnati educational television station (1954-1966); member of Kentucky Authority on Educational Television (1962-1966); producer for closed circuit television, U.S. Army Armor Training Center, Fort Knox, Kentucky (1966-). Mathews was a pseudonym; his real name was Manthis Manchikes. *Louisville Courier-Journal,* April 12, 1966. Al Temple (1904-), resident of Bowling Green; board member, Kentucky Authority for Educational Television (1965-1977). Information provided by Division of Personnel, Frankfort. Lyman V. Ginger, Lexington; dean of the College of Adult Extension Education, University of Kentucky (1954-1956); dean of the College of Education, University of Kentucky (1956-1966); superintendent of public instruction (1972-1976). Landis Jones, ed., *The Public Papers of Governor Wendell H. Ford, 1971-1974* (Lexington, Ky., 1978), p. 155. Marion Gumm, resident of Greensburg, Kentucky; member, Kentucky Authority for Educational Television (1964-1971). Information provided by Personnel Division, Frankfort. David Mc-

Lean Greeley (1912-), board member of Kentucky Authority for Educational Television (1962-1964). Information provided by Division of Personnel, Frankfort.

4. Margaret F. Willis (1906-), State librarian (1957-1976); coordinator of the Library Extension Division (1955-1957); head of circulation, Louisville Free Public Library (1944-1955). Landis Jones, ed., *The Public Papers of Governor Wendell H. Ford., 1971-1974* (Lexington, Ky., 1978), p. 133.

5. Carl Sandburg (1878-1967), an important American poet and historian. Sandburg, as a historian, was best known for his five-volume biography of Abraham Lincoln. *Encyclopedia of World Literature in the Twentieth Century* (New York, 1971), pp. 227-28. Jesse Stuart (1907-), a noted Kentucky author of novels, short stories, poetry and autobiographical works. Stuart's work draws heavily upon the "folk wisdom, family legend and community experience" of his Kentucky hill-country background. Frank A. Magill, ed., *Cyclopedia of World Authors* (New York, 1958), pp. 1041-44.

BELLARMINE COLLEGE COMMENCEMENT
Louisville / May 18, 1966

SOMEONE has said: "Shadow and sun—so too our lives are made, here learn how great the sun, how small the shade." I recall this brief bit of verse because I believe it applies to this institution. Bellarmine College, in its short history, has developed a tradition of educating the whole person—of providing spiritual and moral, as well as academic, emphasis on college experience.

This college is led by administrators and faculty with the vision, the philosophy, the learning, and the faith and interest in young people that are the ingredients of a successful college staff. This college, based as it is on solid Christian precepts and supported as it is by a great and dynamic religious denomination, is a natural fortress against the forces of ignorance and prejudice, against the deadening and defiling forces of godlessness.

Bellarmine College is a great credit to Louisville, to this Commonwealth, to the Roman Catholic Church, and to those who have dedicated themselves to its growth and welfare. It, like other church-supported institutions, provides an untold service to the American people—a service too often we take for granted. As you graduates move on into other pursuits, enforced by the knowledge you've gained here, you will remember—"How great the sun"—of Bellarmine.

My best advice to you is to remember always the lessons and examples set before you here. Remember and follow the principles that guide this college. And—for your lifetime—be inspired and guided by the spirit of your alma mater. I would not give you the advice to believe everything you have learned—or think you have learned—here. If this seems inconsistent with what I just said, let me put it another way: believe in the principles you have been taught but retain a reasonable amount of doubt and flexibility of mind. I say this because college is a place to open minds and inspire individual thought. And if you leave here today with a mind dedicated to opinions already formed and closed to all others, college has been a failure for you.

I hope that—on the other hand—college has been a time of awakening for you, a time during which you have created a desire for knowledge and a respect for varying opinions that will stay with you always. If this is true—if the last four years have been for you a time of discovering how much there is to learn, rather than a time for riveting many small facts into an unchanging mind—college has helped you to prepare for success in life.

For you are moving into a rapidly changing and challenging world which best can be described by the Chinese word "crisis" which is composed of two characters, one representing danger and the other, opportunity. The fact that change has come so rapidly has presented us with both great opportunities and great problems, unthought of by the graduates of a few years ago. Both these opportunities and these problems can be dealt with successfully only by flexible minds, by ever enlarging intellects, by ever increasing growth of the human spirit.

Here—at the end of May, 1966—it is not enough to think of answers to today's problems, to think of what tomorrow might bring or even to limit our thoughts to the twentieth century. The twenty-first century is staring us in the face, and many of you who leave here today will experience your most productive and satisfying years after the year 2000.

If it is to be a century that starts off well for mankind, we all have many important tasks facing us, problems that still linger unsolved. You, as the intellectual leaders of your generation, will be called on to help solve those problems within the next few years, and gradually—as the rest of us get older—they will become entirely your problems.

What are some of the tasks that will confront you—tasks that have been worked at by previous generations but that will remain uncompleted?

First of all, you will have to find a way to help men live peacefully together and at the same time retain for all men the rights that go with being created in the image of God. This is a job that has been difficult throughout the long history of mankind. It is a job that is complicated and intensified by increasing populations, rapid transportation, and new sophistication in producing instruments of annihilation.

Incidents—terrible, bloody incidents—like the present one in Viet Nam will continue to happen as long as some men continue to lack either material necessities or human privileges.[1] It will be your job to settle them, but you will be doing a better job if you can prevent them in the first place.

You will have to find a way to feed the increased billions who will inhabit this globe during your lifetime and feed them better than they are now being fed. All our vast stores of food in this country will melt away before the hunger of those we soon will be called on to feed, at the rate the world's population is now growing, and a way to provide the necessary food is still to be found.

You will have the age-old problems of preventing and curing disease. This means making the triumphs of modern medicine available to all, building hospitals that will meet the needs of your day, continuing the training and research on which our curing arts are based.

You will have to provide education for increasingly large numbers of children as our population grows. A larger percentage of that population will be young people, and a smaller percentage will be at the age to hold jobs and support the schools our youth will need. You will be in the job-holding, school-supporting age, and your burden will be significantly greater than that borne by your parents while you were in school.

You will have to develop new ways in which to keep our economy sound, so that no man is denied the right to make a living because of an imbalance or a snarl somewhere in the system. You will have to make our natural resources go further, eliminate practices that waste the bounty of nature, and revive and replenish those resources that can be brought back. Those are only some of the tasks that face you. Those are tasks that have long been with us. I am sure there will be many that are undreamed of today.

Now, what of the opportunities? First, is the new opportunity of longevity. Already nearly 10 percent of our population is over the age of sixty-five. And medical research, if properly encouraged, is on the verge of new breakthroughs in learning the cause and cure of cancer, hardening of the arteries, and other diseases that take their toll in the later years of life. In recent weeks, the cure of heart disease has been greatly encouraged through two successful operations whereby portions of the heart were replaced by mechanical devices. As we conquer disease and hunger, more and more people will live to be sixty-five, seventy-five, and eighty-five.

Second, are the new opportunities in travel and space. Space exploration that unravels the secrets of our universe, a $100 trip to Europe on a 600-passenger plane, civilian travel in space vehicles, and the rule of law and disarmament in space itself—all these lie ahead for this generation.

Third, is the new opportunity in science. The wonders of atomic energy, if properly pursued, promise new miracles in medicine, refrigeration, communication, and power for our homes and factories. The conversion of salt water to fresh water—a project widely neglected in the past—can end forever the need for water for life. We must find ways in the immediate years ahead to obtain an endless supply of food and power from the ocean depths and to replace our dwindling resources of energy from the granite that lies beneath every continent. We have the chance to make life better for our children and our children's children.

Fourth, is the new opportunity for leisure. The coming of automation, the expansion of the labor force, the extension of the life line, the new scientific discoveries, and the speed of modern transportation—all will contribute to the amount of time available to Kentuckians outside of work. What will we do with that time? If we waste our timberland, litter our land, and pollute our streams, we will be denying to ourselves and our children a part of their rightful heritage. If we permit the medium of television to occupy more and more of our time with poorer programs, then we will be failing the public interest in this new opportunity for leisure.

Fifth, is the new opportunity for culture and art. As our leisure time increases, as we enjoy faster and better transportation, as we come in contact with more and more people, we will have a greater opportunity to appreciate the great heritage that has been left us by the scholars, the scientists, the poets, the theologians, the musicians, the artists, the statesmen. It is a heritage so rich that it can never be absorbed completely by any of us—but it is one that we should take every advantage of.

Sixth, is the new opportunity for understanding among men. If we can fulfill our hopes for peace, instead of beating our swords into plowshares, and our spears into pruning hooks, we can convert our bombs into power reactors and our tanks into dams that will electrify this earth and make life better for all mankind. As we Americans get to know individuals better and cast aside skin-deep judgments, as we learn to treat a brother as a brother and a citizen as a citizen, we will live in a stronger, healthier, greater democracy—a life that every American will enjoy better.

Seventh, is the new opportunity for democracy in this world. As more and more of the people of this earth learn the fallacy of communism and appreciate the good life that a democratic government can bring, more and more nations will turn away from dictators and one-party rule. The challenges of poverty, disease, hunger, and land reform, especially in Latin America, are but a few of the struggles that all men will face on this earth during this transformation. We have the chance to bring about the rebirth of freedom in every nation and peace on this planet.

All the opportunities—seven that I have named—are at your feet, graduates. The new opportunities of which I speak call out for pioneers from every walk of life—in your communities, in your schools, in your local and state governments, in your PTAs. Their challenges can be concealed for a little while, but they cannot be ignored, and they cannot be met by a soft complacency, a satisfaction with things as they are, or a commitment to the past.

So, to all of you I say, the opportunity has never been greater for us individually or collectively. For as the Old Testament tells us, this challenge "is not too hard for thee, neither is it far off . . . neither is it beyond the sea." The opportunities of which I speak are not too hard for us, neither are they far off. No one need bring them to us; they are here, both their problems and their advantages, and we must meet their challenges here, in our hearts and our minds.

For as John F. Kennedy said, "We are Americans." That is a proud heart. That is a great privilege, to be a citizen of the United States, and we must meet our responsibilities.[2]

---

1. This was one of the rare occasions Governor Breathitt mentioned Viet Nam in his public addresses. Although the war in Southeast Asia had by 1966 aroused considerable turmoil on college campuses across the United States, opposition to the war among Kentucky college students was little apparent until the administration of Governor Louie B. Nunn.

2. This address is Governor Breathitt's strongest expression of the optimism that characterized both his administration and the mid-1960s.

DR. YOUNG TESTIMONIAL DINNER
Shelbyville / June 8, 1966

UNQUESTIONABLY one of the great leaders in education in Kentucky, and one to whom the state and thousands of students will long be in debt for his leadership in Negro education is Dr. Whitney M. Young.[1] Those among us who have been close to Lincoln Institute and Dr. Young can be proud that he is a native Kentuckian who remained here so that others could benefit from his ability.[2]

Here is a man who never became a dropout, who defied the odds against his reaching the top in his field, and who has applied himself successfully in filling a need for better educational opportunities for Negro youth in Kentucky.

It is his kind of faith in his fellow man, his kind of devotion to his faith and to a cause which has always been a prime mover in the betterment of society. Real, meaningful progress can always be traced to this kind of leadership, and let us hope there are many, many more Dr. Youngs in the world today and tomorrow.

There are many examples of Dr. Young's leadership, but among the best which reveal his obstinate nature to remain with a cause—and one which I believe he can be best justly proud of—came when he rose against the closing of Lincoln Institute in 1935. That was an hour where there appeared to be no reprieve for the doomed institution, when the institution was in debt, had no money and not too many students. Dr. Young, however, refused to accept the verdict.

With friends, Dr. Young asked and received permission to continue with the institution, under no financial obligation to the Board of Trustees. By adopting what they called the "FAITH PLAN," which I can assume meant that with faith there will be a way, Dr. Young marshalled every friend of the institution and put them to work, and in short order they had the most successful recruiting drive completed and the institution debt free.

It is interesting to note that Dr. Young had been with the institution since 1918, as a teacher of engineering, and had just assumed the presidency of the institution when the future for it looked dim. That it survived and remained strong is testimony enough to the value Dr. Young has been to his race and state.

Of course, Lincoln Institute isn't the lone achievement of Dr. Young's life. He ranks as a who's who in many other areas. He was appointed by President Johnson to a citizens committee for implementation of the civil rights law of which he is still a member. He has served on a Commission on Negro Affairs in Kentucky; he has been a member of a Commission on Adult Education in Kentucky; he has been assistant supervisor for Negro Education for the State of Kentucky; he has been on the state Library Commission; he has been a member of the Annual Conference on Education; he has been a member of the Kentucky Development Council; he was appointed a member of the National Budget and Consultation Committee in 1964 and still holds that position; he has served on various educational associations; and he has been cited for outstanding service to the Kentucky 4-H Clubs.

Dr. Young, born at Midway, began his education at Mayo Underwood at Frankfort; he attended Chandler Normal School at Lexington; graduated from Lincoln Institute in 1916; received a B.A. Degree from Louisville Municipal College, an M.A. degree from Fisk University at Nashville, and a doctorate in education from Monrovia College in Africa.

This is part of the success story of Dr. Whitney M. Young, Sr. There is more, for he is the father of three children who are showing marks of character and leadership which have been his during his lifetime. His son, Whitney Young, Jr., is executive director of the National Urban League; his daughter, Arnita Young Boswell, is assistant professor at Chicago University; and another daughter, Eleanor Annice Young, is assistant to the dean of University College, the University of Louisville.

As of June 8 a great era for Lincoln Institute ended, but it is not one to be regarded with sorrow but rather one which is the beginning of even a greater one, for it is an indication we truly are on the way toward greater educational opportunities for all people in Kentucky. This institution will live on and it will continue to contribute to our society. Such an accomplishment can be attributed only to such leaders as Dr. Whitney Young. For Dr. Young will always be a part of Lincoln Institute.

---

1. Dr. Whitney M. Young (1897-1975); resided with his daughter, Dr. Eleanor Young Love, in Louisville until his death in 1975.

2. The 1966 General Assembly directed that Lincoln Institute be converted to a secondary school for exceptionally talented but culturally and economically deprived children of the Commonwealth. *Acts, 1966,* Chapter 112 (H.B. 89), pp. 542-45.

3. Whitney Moore Young, Jr. (1921-1971), B.S., Kentucky State College (1941); M.A., University of Minnesota (1947); attended Harvard University (1960-1961); industrial relations and vocational guidance director, St. Paul Urban League (1947-1950); executive secretary, Omaha Urban League (1950-1953); dean, School of Social Work, Atlanta University (1954-1960); executive director, National Urban League (1961-). *Who's Who in America, 1968-1969,* 35th ed. (Chicago, 1968). Anita J. Boswell (1919-), B.S., Kentucky State College; M.S.W., Atlanta University; advanced certificate in social work, Columbia University School of Social Work; served in a variety of administrative and social service positions; currently associate professor of social service administration, University of Chicago. *Who's Who Among Black Americans, 1977-1978,* 2nd ed. (Northbrook, Ill., 1978). Eleanor Young Love (1922-), born Breckinridge, Kentucky; educated Lincoln Institute; A.B., Kentucky State College (1944); B.L.S., Atlanta University (1946); M.Ed., University of Louisville (1965); Ed.D., University of Illinois (1970); librarian, Florida A. and M. University (1946-1951); librarian, principal, and counselor, Lincoln Institute (1953-1967); assistant dean, University College, University of Louisville (1967-1971); faculty member, Department of Educational Psychology, University of Louisville (1971-). Telephone interview, March 4, 1981.

EASTERN KENTUCKY UNIVERSITY LIBRARY DEDICATION
Richmond / January 6, 1967

IT must be abundantly clear to everyone in Kentucky, at least those who have been following the progress of construction on our colleges and universities through the news media, that we have not been only talking and dreaming of great plans for higher education in Kentucky, but we have been doing something to make those dreams and plans come true. Dreams of bigger things in higher education we had only a few years ago are realities today; and just as our dreams of yesteryear are coming to pass today, our dreams today will assuredly come to pass. This library building, which has undergone reconstruction at a cost of $2.8 million within the past nineteen months, is just one of the many examples of our dreams and plans having come true.

A mere decade ago this project would have warranted headlines by our press throughout Kentucky and justly so, for then any major construction at our colleges and universities was big news. We had not then achieved the breakthrough in providing physical improvements at our colleges and universities that we have today. Here on this campus alone more than $50 million has been expended on construction of new and renovated buildings—classrooms, dormitories, laboratories, and the like. With that kind of money being spent for construction at all of our colleges and universities in that period it may be understandable if our news media fail to view this building as significantly as we who have worked and planned for the future here believe this building to be.

Eastern's new library will be called the John Grant Crabbe Library in honor of the institution's second president, who served from 1910 to 1916. The new library, with its 147,800 square feet of floor space is a far cry from Eastern's first library, a converted building that had been used for storing hay. The new building, too, is four times the size of the building it replaces.

It has not been so long since a former president of Eastern, at dedication of new construction, said he thought what had been built would take care of all Eastern's needs for the foreseeable future. Little did he realize that the enrollment, which seven years ago totaled 2,967, would today reach 7,972.

Eastern has gone far ahead in other things, too. Three years ago, the political science department had only one teacher and a dozen students. Today, this department is staffed by seven educators, five of whom are doctors of philosophy, and has several hundred students. Recently, the regents added twelve new academic programs leading to seven baccalaureate degrees and five at the graduate level.

In doing all we can to bring public higher education to the highest possible plane, construction of other needed buildings is taking place or about to take place here at Eastern. Both the twenty-one story men's dormitory, to be known as Commonwealth Hall, and the nine-story women's dormitory, which will be called Walter's Hall, are nearing completion. The cost of the men's dorm will be $2.3 million and the cost of the women's dorm $2 million. The men's dorm will house 545 students and the women's dorm 404 students.

Well underway at Eastern also, as you all know, is the $3.5 million Moore Science Building. And ground was broken just about three weeks ago for the $1.5 million home economics building. The contract will be awarded Monday. This is not all, of course, as it does not include new dormitories now in the planning stage, an addition to the administration building, and a proposed new maintenance building.

The state of Kentucky, like Eastern, without question, is making vast strides forward in higher education. Kentucky now ranks first in the nation in the percentage increase in state support for public higher education during the past six years, according to Dr. M.M. Chambers of Indiana University.[1]

A study recently completed by Dr. John Fulmer of the University of Kentucky Bureau of Business Research said that the steadily increasing level of education among men over twenty-five years of age is the greatest contributing factor to economic growth in the state.[2] High levels of income have always had a strong relationship to high levels of education, he said, and in present times, the importance of this fact cannot be overestimated. He noted that over a ten-year period, counties like Meade, Martin, and McCracken had increased their level of education as high as 300 percent, 100 percent, and 40 percent respectively. He also said, "Our counties are holding relatively more of their young leadership from a decline in loss by outmigration."

These are signs of progress that demonstrated clearly why a million dollar investment in education is of much more value over the long haul than a million dollar investment in a new steel mill or an automobile factory. (Although we'll take the latter, too.) Education is important not only to our economy, but it is also important to our individual citizens because it will enable them to have a more meaningful, a more useful, a richer, a more wholesome life. The building we dedicate today is important, but what is inside is more important. This new library means Eastern is not only pushing for physical expansion, but what's inside means you are pushing for intellectual expansion.

---

1. Merritt Madison Chambers (1899-   ), teacher and principal, high schools of Ohio (1922-1926); teaching positions at various colleges and universities (1926-1939); visiting professor of higher education, Indiana University (1967). *Who's Who In American Education, 1967-1968,* 23rd ed. (Nashville, Tenn., 1968), p. 139.

2. John Fulmer, director, Bureau of Business Research, University of Kentucky (1964-1968). Information provided by University of Kentucky personnel records office.

KENTUCKY SCHOOL BOARD ASSOCIATION
Louisville / March 14, 1967

WE do not meet here today to discuss the obvious and accepted value or importance of education. I am sure, however, that you have invited me here to discuss some aspects of the partnership we have between local and state bodies concerned with education in Kentucky.

Those of you involved with the administration and financing on the local level, those of us involved with the same on the state level, all face the same basic problems. Of course, we also know that—just as in our homes and businesses—that problem usually seems to converge on one reality, and that stark problem is money. But whether it is money or some other problem, the conduct of education in Kentucky is a partnership. Each partner has a unique and necessary assignment, while sharing the responsibility for the overall enterprise. I would add that the house of education has many rooms and no one need fear that he is being crowded out.

All of us know that with education, as with so many other things, we usually get what we pay for. This is not always true because some people and some material things are overrated or overpaid, and this can be true in education just as in government or in our individual lives and activities. However, a certain amount of money usually buys a predictable quantity or quality.

What we are getting in education—if we look only at money spent—is a mixture of educational offerings. We all know of flourishing schools receiving splendid care in the more affluent communities, and we also know of schools which, by comparison, are inadequate—withering for lack of support. State government's problem is that it cannot wash its hands of this matter and allow laggard communities to stagger about as best they can, nor can it relegate to mediocrity those areas which simply are unable to pay good teachers and build good schools.

I am not suggesting that we cast a mold into which each education unit must fit. I do remind you that it is the state's responsibility and obligation to determine—in the interest of long-run progress and prosperity—a minimum level of quality for all public elementary and secondary schools. A base or guideline must be set for these schools, and it is the state's privilege and problem to make certain that no school falls below it. If your school wishes to rise above that level—so much the better. It is an option which sometimes is not exercised.

Of course, setting a standard statewide for minimum educational quality is easier said than done. The state sets standards for teacher certification, but if we try to establish standards as to the effectiveness with which that certificate is used—where do we begin? The ultimate and perfect solution, of course, would be to evaluate scientifically, with the same accuracy expected of a space missile technician, the finished product—a student's progress.

This cannot be done today—perhaps it may be done someday. If that day comes, maybe a premium will be given schools for producing outstanding products—a premium in the form of cold, hard cash to the school or district which has excelled in performance.

Until that improbable day arrives, perhaps the answer is educational leadership for the educational enterprise. Here, I do not speak of theory, because leadership at the local level also includes what I like to call "practical vision." And practical vision can help make the money we have go further.

Two months ago I addressed a meeting of the University of Kentucky Community College System. At that time, I suggested that they—just as you and I—are always concerned with the problem of money. But, as I pointed out a minute or two ago to you, I also suggested that, although in our public and private lives, money will solve many problems in education, it is only one answer and not the only answer.

Just as in government, the true test of an administrator is not his ability to spend large sums of money—but that he spend those sums, large or small, in the most effective manner possible. No matter how much tax money or how little public money we make available to schools or any other part of public operations, the individual stewardship of responsible administrators, whatever their field, inevitably must be the key to long-range success. It is not always a question of what you have to do with—but, what you do with what you have. As I say, this is equally true in my case and in government, as it is true for school administrators and in education.

Since the first day I entered the legislature in 1952, I have worked to do my part in providing adequate financing for our schools. As governor I have worked, and still am working, to ease this most persistent problem in education. At my request during these four years of my administration, the General Assembly has appropriated $508.6 million for elementary and secondary education, compared to $373 million during the previous four-year administration—an increase of more than $135 million. All of this has been done without increasing state taxes a single dime.

It may interest you to know that the average teacher salary per year in Kentucky in the 1959-60 school year was $3,412. Today that figure has climbed to $5,768 and should reach approximately $6,400 this fall—nearly doubling what it was eight short years ago. This is dramatic progress for a state which has a low per capita income, a state that has had to lift itself up by its own bootstraps.

This school year alone, teachers have received on the average a $576 per year increase paid for by state and local funds which emphasized our partnership. As I stated, it will be even more this fall. When the four years of this administration are finished, the state will have increased teacher salaries on the average by $1,400, compared to $1,100 during the previous administration.

Eight short years ago the state was putting $4.3 million into transportation. Today that figure is doubled, and the total is $8.6 million.

Although millions and millions of dollars of construction are needed today in our schools, as so many of you can testify, we have built under our partnership 4,339 new classrooms since the 1963-64 school year—an average of 1,000 per year and comparable to if not slightly higher than previous years. And we have broadened the permissive tax support base, which in the long run may prove to be the savior of our local schools.

I do not recite our efforts in order to boast of them, or even to take credit for progress I have outlined, because these achievements involve the hard work of many Kentuckians. I mention them only to show that I understand the problem and have understood it for a long time.

As a governor who has only about nine months remaining in his term, as one who has met and discussed the thorny problems of education with many individuals and groups, as one who has initiated several programs for our schools, I would offer you and Kentucky's other educators some advice, for whatever it is worth, on two points on this occasion.

First, I think it is extremely important that you and other groups dedicated to the improvement of our public school system keep the unity that has helped us make so much progress in recent years in education. If a split develops among the powerful education groups, then our total school program will suffer. I would suggest, and suggest strongly, that all groups work together to solve our mutual school problems and present a unified front to the next governor and to the 1968 General Assembly.

Second, I think the school boards of Kentucky need to begin, and begin now, a good public information program—one designed to inform fiscal courts and the citizens of your communities about the financial problems facing your local schools. I know many of you will say we already are doing this. I do not propose that such a program is the final answer. But, I ask: is your present information program good enough? Do the citizens really understand your financial problems? As governor, I have found that Kentuckians generally respond to a situation if they are given the facts, if they understand a problem fully and completely. I cannot overemphasize the importance of such an informative program.

In addition, permit me to briefly discuss two movements which are under way in this nation that could have an important effect on Kentucky's schools in the years ahead. One is the Education Commission of the States, or sometimes referred to as the Compact on Education—an agreement among thirty-eight states which is designed to resolve through interstate cooperation some of the critical problems facing education at all levels. This commission, on which I have the privilege of serving as a member of the steering committee, is set up to spur states into action for the betterment of education.

Presently, the commission has started a series of seven special studies of major problems in education shared by the states. These studies, which are being sponsored by private grants, plus the follow-through and other activities of the commission, hopefully will cause legislatures and governors throughout our nation to take action to increase state activity in education.

The great need for all of us at the state level and at the local level is to make sure we meet our responsibilities in education. If we do not, then we can expect the federal government to move into the vacuum with more and more federal controls. What we need to fear is not the disappearance of states and our local governments, but their increasing irrelevance to the needs of this day. We should not let this happen in education. The commission is designed to make every state more aware of the role it must play in solving its own problems.

The other movement I speak of is the adoption of the so-called Heller Plan by Congress, whereby a percentage of federal funds would be returned to the states without any strings whatsoever attached.[1] As a member of the executive committee of the National Governors' Conference, I sponsored support for such a proposal through a resolution which was adopted by all the governors.

Such a plan, if adopted by Congress, would funnel millions and millions of federal dollars into Kentucky for our General Assembly to appropriate.

A large portion of these funds, I'm sure, would go for education. I would suggest that if you are interested in seeing the Heller Plan become a reality, that you write your congressmen and senators urging their support. This program would be of immense value to Kentucky.

Finally, let us hope that through our state and local partnership in education we can improve the product of that educational system through careful and intelligent use of the funds available, in order that all schools can provide the maximum in good instruction and facilities. A student or graduate's mind and cultural progress cannot be measured by a missile technician's caliper or gauge, but this is usually unnecessary, because individual results—at least—are frequently obvious. I know that none of us doubt that the strength and well-being, even the survival, of our democratic society will be determined primarily by the application of excellence to our educational patterns. Our partnership is faced with great challenges, and I see no reason why we can't meet them.

---

1. The Heller Plan, named for Dr. Walter M. Heller, chairman of the President's Council of Economic Advisors, called for federal revenue sharing with the states. Heller first proposed the plan in 1964. President Johnson, in remarks to the 1966 National Governors Conference, expressed his preference for specific federal grants to the states. The proposal was finally adopted by the Nixon administration in 1972. *Congressional Quarterly Weekly Report,* March 25, 1966, p. 674; January 6, 1967, pp. 8-9; and June 20, 1967, p. 97.

STATEMENT ON VOCATIONAL EDUCATION: MIDWESTERN GOVERNORS CONFERENCE

Lake of the Ozarks, Missouri / August 29, 1967

THE progress and development of any state depends upon its resources—both natural and human. The development of the natural resources to a large extent depends on how well developed the human resources are. People, well informed and progressive, are necessary for the well-being of any state.

In Kentucky in recent years, we have expanded a program for the development of our people. One of the major factors in this development program is education for work. Vocational education is necessary, if a state is to have a supply of well-trained manpower to man and expand present industries and to attract new industries. Vocational education must be able to serve all the people and for all kinds of occupations.

Many of our local school districts are too small to provide a comprehensive vocational education program to meet the manpower needs. For this reason, we in Kentucky have gone into an area vocational school program. This program has earned national recognition from both the U.S. Office of Education and from the national Chamber of Commerce.

Mr. Grant Venn, associate commissioner of the U.S. Office of Education, said at a Senate subcommittee hearing that Kentucky is far ahead of the eleven other states involved in vocational school construction under the two-year-old Appalachian Development Program.[1] He pointed out how our Bureau of Vocational Education, in the Kentucky Department of Education—headed by Mr. E.P. Hilton—was prepared, had a plan ready, and got off to a faster start than the other states. Mr. E.R. Mitchell, a director of the national Chamber of Commerce and chairman of its Human Resources Development Committee, said these kind words about us.[2] "There is no question in our minds that the Commonwealth of Kentucky has done the outstanding job of the nation in vocational education."

State government in Kentucky operates thirteen area vocational schools serving the entire state. These schools provide training in all kinds of occupations for all people—for those with low-level ability as well as those with high-level ability. And many of our newest industries in Kentucky have located near these schools because of the trained manpower available.

These schools serve both youth and adults across local school boundary lines. Vocational education is offered not only in the area schools, but also in our colleges and in our comprehensive high schools. Kentucky's state government now is serving more than 100,000 persons in vocational education. This is an increase of 80 percent in four years—from 60,000 in the fiscal year ending June 30, 1963, to more than 100,000 in the fiscal year which ended just last month.

Our objective has been to provide vocational school facilities within commuting distance of all people in Kentucky. This is not possible through the thirteen area schools alone; therefore, we are building area extension centers, or satellite schools, and attaching them to our area schools. During the past year, twelve satellite schools were operated, ten more are to open next month, and fourteen additional schools either are under construction or will be in the very near future, making a total of forty-nine schools in the Commonwealth.

Our $24 million construction program for vocational education that was launched in 1965 will be completed by next year. It was financed by federal and local money, plus $3.5 million from our state bond issue approved by Kentuckians in 1965. With such a program nearing completion, Kentucky in the next two or three years will have vocational school facilities within commuting distance of all the people in our state.

These schools will be multifold in purpose. During the hours from 8 A.M. to 3 P.M., they will serve as extensions of the comprehensive high schools for vocational education for secondary pupils. From 3 P.M. to 10 or 11 P.M., they will be used to serve the people who have left our regular school program.

Not only do these schools offer preparatory training for job employment; they also will be used to upgrade persons already employed. The facilities are available to handle all kinds of programs. Among these programs are: 1. Training workers for new industries. This can be done either through the Manpower Development and Training Program, or through the regular vocational program. 2. Specialized training for those already employed and who need to be upgraded. 3. Training for persons on welfare or who are unemployed, but who need training to become employable. 4. Training for persons with special problems which require special kinds of training that cannot ordinarily be received in the regular programs.

Area vocational schools permit specialization which is not possible in a comprehensive high school. For instance, in one of our schools, specialized training will be provided for the aeronautics industry (Somerset Area Vocational School). The local airport board for this community has donated the site. We are building a half million dollar facility to provide training specifically for manpower needs in the aeronautics industry. The Kentucky Department of Aeronautics and the Federal Aviation Authority are cooperating in this program. This facility will serve the entire state in the specialty of aeronautics at the present time. However, I have the feeling that it will be necessary to expand this program into other areas later.

Another development in Kentucky now is the planning of facilities for training manpower needed so much for health services below the professional level. Our program for the rehabilitation of inmates at the Kentucky State Reformatory also is moving along. Our State Department of Corrections, State Employment Service, Bureau of Vocational Education, and Bureau of Vocational Rehabilitation are cooperating in the rehabilitation of the prisoners at our state reformatory.

The Bureau of Vocational Rehabilitation, the employment service, and the reformatory personnel select, counsel, and guide those persons who can benefit from vocational training. The local area vocational school provides training in the reformatory for those referred. This training is of the same kind and quality as that offered in the area vocational school itself. This year programs are being offered in eight occupational areas to the inmates.

A construction program is under way which, when completed, will enable the enrollment at the reformatory to double and also will expand the offerings to twelve or more different occupations. In addition, plans include the expansion of this type of program to other correctional institutions as rapidly as facilities can be obtained and personnel trained.

Some specializations, such as data processing, heavy equipment programs, and the like, which require expensive and sophisticated equipment, are not conducted in every school. These are concentrated in a few schools to serve the entire state.

And now, a look at the future. Since population is mobile and many of our people leave all of our states, manpower training is a joint responsibility between the federal government and all states. The solution to many of our economic and social problems lies in the stepped-up program of manpower development and training. Expanding manpower needs in the health programs, in the technical fields, in the service industries, and in all phases of our economy are growing and making it mandatory that both federal government and all states expand these programs.

In Kentucky we have attempted to project our program into the years ahead. Our first problem was to obtain program facilities and equipment. We are well on our way to getting this job done. Our next job is to provide the personnel—qualified and able—to conduct these manpower programs. The third problem is to take those people now unemployed or on welfare programs and who are able bodied and able to take training, and to provide training programs for them so that they may become tax producers rather than tax consumers. This requires the close coordination of our welfare, social, and educational institutions so that there is no overlapping, but a combination of the efforts of all groups toward the development of our manpower resources.

Actually, in looking at the future, in Kentucky and possibly in all states, our biggest problem is providing dormitory facilities for students in our vocational programs—especially those concentrated programs for which the students must live away from home. We in Kentucky have facilities to house the programs, but we do not have facilities to house the students at the concentrated points of study that I have mentioned. As you know, the federal government finances housing programs at the colleges in all of our states. Perhaps the start of an answer to the increasing problem of housing for our vocational students is a resolution by governors to Congress—asking for funds to finance this vocational student housing.

In conclusion, I think it appropriate to reiterate the omnipresent fact in our labor market today of changing times and changing needs. I do not mean simply just the fact of specialization—the idea of specific skills for specific jobs. And I do not mean simply just the certainty of increasing jobless ranks if we do not train the untrained. I do mean the need for retraining even the trained. On the basis of both our own and national studies, we in Kentucky are operating on this policy. Industrial and other labor needs are changing so much, every worker will have to be trained or retrained in his occupation five to seven times during his lifetime.

---

1. Grant Venn (1919-), teacher and guidance director in public schools of Washington (1941-1949); assistant superintendent of schools, Bellvue, Washington (1949-1951); president, Western State College, Gunnison, Colorado (1960-1962); director of field training, Peace Corps (1962-1963); associate commissioner of education, Office of Education, Department of Health, Education and Welfare (1966-). *Who's Who in Government, 1972-1973,* 1st ed. (Chicago, 1972).

2. E.R. Mitchell. No data available.

HEALTH, WELFARE, & PUBLIC SAFETY

CONGRESS ON MENTAL HEALTH
Louisville / May 14, 1964

As is the case so often when I address professional groups, the roster of those who are appearing at this congress today reminds me that when it comes to the subject under discussion I am a nonexpert speaking to a group of experts. It would be difficult for me to contribute to your knowledge of any health subject, and it would be doubly difficult for me to increase your understanding of mental health principles today after you have listened to some of our nation's most knowledgeable men on the subject. I am not here to pretend special knowledge on this subject but to tell you that I have a special interest in it and to express to you the desires, the attitudes, the hopes of your state administration as they relate to the mental health of all Kentuckians. The subject of my speech has been billed as "Mental Health in Kentucky—Past and Future." I think you will agree that this is pretty inclusive, and I want to assure you that I do not intend to cover the subject in its entirety or steal the time that rightfully belongs to the participants in this afternoon's program.

I said I have a special interest in mental health. I have had this interest for some time, and in 1952, as a member of the General Assembly, it was my privilege to help sponsor the bill that created the Kentucky Department of Mental Health.[1] I do not wish to take anything away from the many dedicated persons who gave themselves to the cause of caring for the mentally ill before that time, but I consider this action and the resultant attention and treatment that became available for our mental patients to be a major milestone in our course that we hope leads to eventual provision of adequate care and cure facilities for all Kentuckians with mental illnesses.

Kentucky was one of the first states to establish institutions for the mentally disturbed and in her early history was considered a leader in providing the asylums that were used at that time to keep the mentally ill out of the mainstream of society. Unfortunately, many years later, the same buildings were still being used—and they were still being used as asylums—despite the fact that a great deal of knowledge had been gained about mental illness and principles of treatment had been established. There was no public clamor for the state to create treatment facilities—there was public apathy or, worse, opposition on the part of many [who] thought their mentally disturbed neighbors deserved the tortures they suffered and who were not inclined to pay taxes to help "crazy" people.

There were undoubtedly many understanding and compassionate persons who were ahead of the times in their concept of society's duty to its mentally ill in those early days and, even though they were largely unheeded at the time, we owe them a major debt for keeping alive enough concern to enable us in later years to build a system of mental hospitals out of the old asylums.

I did not mean to imply earlier that successful treatment of Kentucky's mentally ill dates from the time that the Department of Mental Health was established. This was only twelve years ago, and certainly there was treatment prior to that time and had been for many years while the hospitals were considered primarily a welfare function. But the fact remains that creation of the department gave a new emphasis and a new direction to the services rendered and brought our institutions closer to true hospital standards.

When Dr. Frank Gaines was named the first commissioner of mental health, the hospital system was put for the first time under the direction of a psychiatrist.[2] Soon there were psychiatrists on the staffs of all the individual hospitals. Soon there were more nurses, more aides, more social workers with some psychiatric training. Soon there was a regimen of treatment for the majority of patients. New buildings were built. New wards were opened. Restraints were removed. Barriers were torn down. Recreation and training were provided. Eating facilities were improved and food was made more palatable and more nourishing. Much of the stigma formerly attached to mental illness was removed by changes in the laws regarding admission to the hospitals and by changes in terminology relating to patients and their illnesses. The old inmate concept was done away with and patients were encouraged to have company, were allowed visits home. Because of all these things and thanks to vast improvements in drugs and in treatment methods, more patients are now discharged as cured.

I do not wish to make our hospitals of today sound as if they are ideal. Certainly we have a long way to go before they will be ideal, before they will do the job all of us want them to do. But I did want to cite the improvements that have been made and I do want to pay tribute to Dr. Gaines and to his successor, Dr. Harold McPheeters, who is the present commissioner of mental health.[3] I also think the people of Kentucky owe a great debt to those many, many hospital staff members—at all levels—who labor long and hard and under the most trying circumstances to help relieve the suffering of their fellow Kentuckians and restore them to health.

We have made great progress in the last few years, but now I think it is time for another milestone. This milestone would mark the creation of community mental health facilities throughout Kentucky to complement our present system of hospitals, to help make treatment of mental illness more successful, and to help facilitate its prevention. A few years ago such centers would not have been possible. Today, thanks to improved treatment methods, tranquilizers and other medication, they are not only possible but are in existence in many communities and are saving countless patients long hospital visits, travel expenses, weeks and months away from jobs and families, and the disruption in private lives that always results from hospitalization. The patient is spared a long period of orientation in a hospital at the very time that any kind of orientation is the most difficult for him. And he is spared reorientation into his home community when his period of treatment is completed. Because he is close to home, he sees his own doctor, his own clergyman, members of his family, and others who can give him comfort and assistance at the time he needs it most. He can perhaps continue his job while undergoing treatment, thus avoiding the personal financial loss of hospitalization and the public loss created by his joblessness and the need to care for both him and his dependents.

There are many benefits to be gained by the creation of such community facilities, and I am sure that other speakers on today's program will explain them and describe them adequately. This new milestone is not one that we can put behind us immediately. I am sure you are all aware of the fact that the biennial budget that I submitted to the recent session of the General Assembly did not contain all the money that any of us would have liked for mental health—or for most other state services for that matter.

The unfortunate fact is that we do not presently have the financial ability to push many of the programs we would like to push—to provide many of the services we would like to provide. But certainly we can plan, and the Department of Mental Health has planning facilities we need to look to now if we are to build wisely in the future, if we are to make realities of those facilities which can eventually be possible. I hope you will work with the department in its planning for your community. I hope that you, not only as doctors but as community leaders, will take active leadership to help us extend mental health facilities to all parts of our great state.

I hope you will consider them your facilities—treatment centers to help you care for your patients better.

And I cannot resist this opportunity to make the point that one of the most effective ways you can help bring into being these community facilities is to work for passage of the bond issue to come before Kentucky's voters in 1965. The issue contains money which, when supplemented by federal funds, will help us make significant progress on community centers to serve not only the mentally ill but the mentally retarded.

I have spoken of past care for the mentally ill in Kentucky—of how it progressed from the state's merely providing four walls and barred windows to the treatment that is provided today. As we look to the future, I think we can all be heartened by the progress we have made and by technical and medical developments that will make future progress come faster.

As we look to the future, let me assure you that your state administration is dedicated to doing all it can to advance the cause of mental health, both in existing facilities and in the community facilities. Let me solicit your help, the help of all citizens, and the help of private groups and organizations in your hometowns and throughout Kentucky to advance this cause. Together we can make the way easier for many of our unfortunate fellow citizens and we can help solve one of our greatest health problems.

---

1. See "an act relating to a Department of Mental Health and its establishment," *Acts, 1952,* Chapter 50 (S.B. 140), pp. 93-103.

2. Frank McFarland Gaines, Jr. (1916-), physician and psychiatrist, Louisville; M.D., University of Louisville (1941); director of the Division of Hospitals and Mental Hygiene for the Commonwealth of Kentucky (1951-1952); commissioner of the Department of Mental Health, Commonwealth of Kentucky (1952-1957). Hambleton Tapp, ed. *Kentucky Lives* (Hopkinsville, Ky., 1966), pp. 189-90.

3. Harold Lawrence McPheeters (1923-), M.D., University of Louisville (1948); assistant commissioner, Kentucky Department of Mental Health (1955-1957); commissioner of the Department of Mental Health (1957-1964). George W. Robinson, ed., *The Public Papers of Governor Bert T. Combs, 1959-1963* (Lexington, Ky., 1979), p. 140.

KENTUCKY ACTION PROGRAM FOR HIGHWAY SAFETY
Benton / February 9, 1965

AUTOMOBILES and young people have a strong affinity for each other, which is a rather schoolish way of saying that teenagers and cars go together like hamburgers and soft drinks. Many young people have their own automobiles. Others drive the family car when they can soften up their parents. Some teenagers know every nut and bolt and cylinder in their cars and can take them apart and put them back together. Most young drivers are adept with the steering wheel. And so there is not much I can tell you about cars, but I would like to talk upon a related subject: highway safety.

Youth is a time of life when the driving habits of a lifetime are formed. And it is vital to your life and happiness that these habits be good ones. If you're automobile addicts, at least drive so that you'll still be around to see what next year's models look like.

Perhaps you know that more Kentuckians died on highways last year than in any other single year in the history of the Commonwealth. Nine hundred and ten lives were sacrificed on the altar of traffic death. What are the mortar and stones of this grim altar, the ingredients of which it is made? This altar is constructed of a lack of driving principles, of a lack of respect for human life, of a lack of self-discipline. Other lacks go into its construction: sadly lacking are consideration, courtesy, and respect for law on our highways.

The driver who brazenly violates traffic laws and safety principles is an example of these deficiencies. I started to say "a living example," but such a driver may be soon dead. Many of them drive as if they were late for their accident.

We have more cars and more roads, and so some people say it's just natural that we have more accidents. But there is one flaw in this logic: the accident and death rate is increasing twice as fast as highway travel. We are at a crossroads in traffic safety. We can take one way and ignore the carnage, let the smashed automobiles and broken bodies pile up. Or we can take the right way that leads to highway safety, through the cooperation of the people and their government. The specter of tragedy is standing at the crossroads, frantically waving us down the wrong road.

Last year 48,500 persons obeyed this specter and met death on the highways. The National Safety Council predicts 470,000 persons will die in motor accidents during the 1960-70 decade. Of these, 9,400 will die in Kentucky.

Let's turn away from this specter and look for a moment at the Kentucky Action Program for Highway Safety. It was designed by my Coordinating Committee for Highway Safety, working in close harmony with the National Insurance Institute for Highway Safety. Some of these safety needs require legislation.

One phase of our action program, of special interest to students, is driver education in high schools. You deserve to be taught the right driving habits from the start. If you are going to obey all the rules in the complex traffic patterns of today, you have the right to ask that proper driving be made a part of your public school education. The action program also includes an increase in the number of Kentucky State Troopers on our highways. A highway trooper is a handy friend to have around during some unavoidable trouble on the road. The program also asks for periodic inspection of motor vehicles and re-examination of licensed drivers—a fair request that driver and automobile be in safe condition for traffic.

There are other needs in the program which we are filling without legislation. One of these is to improve public information on highway safety. You can help me in this. Pass the word about safe driving throughout your school, pass it from school to school, so that my safety message reaches young drivers all over Marshall County. And then practice what you preach: drive as if your life depends upon it![1]

---

1. North Marshall High School; Benton High School; South Marshall High School. Highway safety was a theme frequently developed by Governor Breathitt in addresses to high school audiences.

GOVERNOR'S OCCUPATIONAL HEALTH AND INDUSTRIAL HYGIENE CONFERENCE

Lexington / March 10, 1965

It gives me a great deal of pleasure to greet you at this, the first occupational health and industrial hygiene conference. The title of this conference might have just as appropriately been "A New Day for Workers' Health in Kentucky." To those of you who have made this conference possible and to those of you who have come from distant places to attend this most important meeting, I want to express my appreciation and willingness to help you achieve our common goals.

We have long recognized the importance of maintaining healthful environments in which to work, just as we have been aware of the importance of pure food, of good water, and of clean air. The provision of all of these necessities is a constant challenge to us and is never to be taken for granted.

In our endeavor to cope with our environment, our best efforts are at times inadequate. We have witnessed the ravages of crippling diseases, the devastation of floods, and slaughter of our citizens on the highways. In all of these matters the combined efforts of specialists of many kinds, including those in private practice, in universities, in industry, and in government have been marshaled to foster better progress. In this fashion, the greatest understanding of such problems may be developed and the best utilization of resources may be made.

In considering any aspect of health, the physician and the nurse immediately come to mind. Their groups are well represented here. The hygienist, the chemist, the engineer, and the safety expert search the environment for those numerous thieves of life and limb which await the unwary.

As the program for this meeting attests, the planning committee has done an excellent job in bringing together a wide variety of talent with the common interest of improving our effectiveness in maintaining the health of the worker. Our purpose, then, is to work together towards this goal.

The timing for this first conference on occupational health and industrial hygiene has special significance. We have engaged an all-out war on unemployment in Kentucky. It is our intention to bring as much industry into the state as possible. We are happy to say that in 1964, 84 new establishments located in Kentucky and 134 others expanded their operations. Since the beginning of this year, 9 new industries and 7 existing ones have added about 2,800 more jobs. Agriculture is receiving much attention, with emphasis being placed on a greater variety of crops and marketing. In short, with the great need for economic improvement of adult Kentuckians and the hosts of youngsters joining the ranks of the employable, it is my intent that these efforts shall be maintained at the highest possible level. It is, therefore, important that adequate attention be given to the health of the labor force, many of whom are learning to do new tasks or who are entering the labor force for the first time. The time is, therefore, favorable for increasing our coverage and improving our effectiveness as regards the health of the worker.

My personal interest in occupational health is by no means new. Prior to my election as governor, I visited with Commissioner Teague and his staff members to learn at first hand what health problems were considered to be important in the field of public health and what was being done to meet these problems.[1] Occupational health was one of those areas covered. I learned that while our facilities and our competence were good, as in many other program areas, more effort is needed.

Then upon my assumption of the governorship I became chief executive of an establishment employing some 20,000 persons. This responsibility has naturally enhanced my awareness of the need for employee health protection. Government as an employer stands to gain greatly from the deliberations of this conference. Efficiency in government suffers from loss of time due to illness and is therefore the concern of all. It is important to the taxpayers of Kentucky that their employees remain healthy and physically fit so they can do the job that they are hired to do.

The inclusion of "Occupational Health in Agriculture" as the subject of a panel discussion this afternoon pleases me greatly. The farmer is often left out of considerations benefiting others because of his geographical isolation, or because of his self-employment, or due to the seasonal nature of his work. While we are striving to increase manufacturing and service employment, the source of income for a large percent of Kentuckians has been and will remain the farm.

One is awed by the great changes which have come to the farm in recent years. Modern machinery and chemistry have transformed the working environment of the farmer as much as or more so than that of the factory worker. It is my hope that discussions here will explore the farm as a site for improved health protection. The farm worker who may be employed on a part-time or seasonal basis often lacks the knowledge necessary for the safe handling of hazardous materials and farm machinery that the more experienced farmer has learned.

Kentucky also has hundreds of migrant laborers who spend from one to two months per year here. We are concerned about these people, not only from the standpoint of occupational health, but also because their state of health affects that of the communities through which they pass and do business.

Health, it seems to me, is like a garment which an individual or a community or even a state or nation wears. The fabric is woven of our personal habits, our working conditions, and our community patterns of living. We can't think of the work place as isolated from the remainder of our environment but rather as an integral part of it.

Accordingly, pollution which comes from the industrial process is often discharged into the atmosphere or stream, and mingles with the contaminants from the chimneys of our homes, from the exhaust pipes of our automobiles, trucks, and buses, from our incinerators and dumps, from the massive spraying of crops, along with airborne infectious agents which we transmit to one another. The housewife who labors at home may, in fact, be exposed to a more harmful atmosphere than her husband who works in a modern, well-controlled plant environment. When we open the front door, the community air enters. We are, in fact, bathed in our common atmosphere continuously.

Obviously, this atmosphere should be maintained in a safe, usable condition wherever we are. It was with this thought in mind that I asked Dr. Russell E. Teague to be our appointed representative for negotiations with the federal government, under the Clean Air Act, to set up a program on air pollution to study the problems of air pollution, its effects upon communities and upon individuals, and to start planning for the conservation of this valuable resource.[2] I am informed that a program is now in progress to carry out this responsibility.

The relationship of health on the job to health in general and, in turn, the impact this has on our economic stability and on the well-being of our family units is obviously of much concern to the community. "Occupational Health in the Community" is therefore a many faceted thing which one of this afternoon's panels will explore in considerable detail.

In several respects this conference is to be considered unique—not just because it is the first of its kind in Kentucky but because of its potential breadth of interest and because of its composition. From a medical point of view, the field, I am told, is vast. The same holds true for all other disciplines represented. The subject of worker health has appeal for the worker, the employer, and the community alike. The benefits derived are profitable to all concerned. This factor alone provides a strong incentive for real accomplishment.

If a suggestion might be admissible it would be that the contents of your papers, your deliberations and your conclusions be recorded in form suitable for distribution to those who would have benefited greatly by this conference had they been here. Your personal communication with members of your professions and organizations will do much to stimulate others to participate in succeeding meetings. Our future success in all major areas of accomplishment depends on the unselfish giving of personal concern and effort beyond the narrow limits of our daily responsibilities. Such consideration is demonstrated by your presence here today. Working together, I am confident we can make our communities and our places of work healthier, cleaner, and safer for ourselves and for our children.

---

1. Russell E. Teague (1905-1972), commissioner, Department of Public Health (1956-1970); born in St. Charles, Kentucky, and a resident of Frankfort. George W. Robinson, ed., *The Public Papers of Governor Bert T. Combs, 1959-1963* (Lexington, Ky., 1979), p. 289. In his comments to the conference, Commissioner Teague emphasized the role of state government in providing leadership in the promotion of industrial health. He also echoed the overall theme of the conferences, one which Governor Breathitt often applied to the areas of federal-state relations: industry must solve the many problems associated with growing industrialization or government would be forced to intervene. *Louisville Courier-Journal,* March 11, 1965.

2. The Clean Air Act of 1963 (H.R. 6518, P.L. 88-206) authorized the expenditure of $95 million over a four-year period to reduce air pollution. The law sought to encourage federal, state, and local cooperation through state legislation, interstate compacts and joint agencies. Extended research programs were to be established and a program of federal grants to state, local, and interstate air pollution control agencies was authorized. *Congressional Quarterly Almanac,* vol. 19 (1963), pp. 236-39.

KENTUCKY HOSPITAL ASSOCIATION CONVENTION
Louisville / March 31, 1965

IT is a pleasure for me to join you this evening in this dinner meeting of your thirty-sixth annual convention. I wish to assure you that this administration is not unaware of the increasingly important role being played by hospitals in the social and economic life of our Commonwealth.

The impressive assets of Kentucky's hospitals today exceed a quarter of a billion dollars. Over 25,000 Kentuckians are employed from day to day in rendering the services which combine to comprise good hospital care, and the annual payroll of hospital personnel in our state approaches $100 million. Actually, it is appropriate that the hospital industry should assume such a sizable segment of our state's resources commitment, for certainly among the very primary of our individual and collective concerns is the matter of personal and community health. On behalf of all Kentuckians, I salute your attainment of another year of traditional service to our Commonwealth. You are certainly deserving of our commendations.

The hospitals with which most Kentuckians are directly acquainted and which account for over 90 percent of the state's hospital admissions are the acute, short-term general hospitals which serve the various communities of our state. At this very moment there are approximately 7,500 Kentuckians in patient status in the state's short-term hospitals. It is to these community service institutions and in line with your convention's theme—"Let's Face the Future"—that I wish to direct my remarks this evening.

As I see it, one of the more acute and immediate problems facing Kentucky hospitals, and of concern to all of us, is that of adequate financing of hospital services. An underfinanced hospital is hampered in its attempts to provide high-quality care to all of its patients, rich and poor. Furthermore, so long as financing is a problem in any part of our state, no hospital will be totally unaffected by it.

But we know that the financial problems of hospitals are most acute in the counties where men work for meager wages and where fathers are unemployed. With the increased attention being given to these areas by the federal government, and with the rapidly developing programs of financing care for the poor and aged groups, I believe that we will continue to see rapid improvement in the immediate future.

The hospital provisions of our own Kentucky Medical Care Program continue to grow.[1] After only four short years, we are purchasing hospital care at a rate of $6,500,000 per year, and paying in full for 85 percent of all hospital stays by welfare recipients. More important, the program is soundly based on reimbursable cost payments, and its planning by the Advisory Council for Medical Assistance is directed toward the eventual full coverage of full reasonable stay for all beneficiaries eligible under law.

Currently before the Congress are legislative proposals which would have immediate and long-range significance to our state efforts at meeting this financing problem. Among other things, they would provide far greater federal support of Kentucky's efforts at care for the indigent and medically indigent by making matching funds available on behalf of new population groups and at a matching ratio more favorable to the state.

Were such a law enacted, which seems likely, the effect would be to greatly expand the potential purchasing power of each state dollar allotted to medical care, and a hoped-for result would be a more uniform and even distribution of our medically indigent funds among all areas and all hospitals. In the meantime, we must do the best we can with what we have and, above all, we cannot afford to fall back at any point. From time to time, stop-gap measures have been required. These must be recognized for what they are; namely, temporary holding actions designed to stave off misfortune until permanent solutions can be implemented.

A more chronic and persistent problem facing our hospitals is the scarcity of essential health personnel. Each day brings new medical advances with their increased demand for trained and experienced personnel—professional, technical, service, and administrative. If anticipated future demand is to be met, we must continue and accelerate our current efforts at expanding programming for the training of all medical and paramedical personnel, especially nurses, technicians, and therapists of all types.

The recruitment of our young people to enter these fields of service must proceed apace with the development of the new programs, and both must be founded in a strong basic educational system within the state. There are no short-cut solutions to this problem. No amount of grant funds can assure a quick alleviation of a health manpower shortage. It will demand the diligent and persistent application of our best efforts, and a mature acknowledgment that we must begin to plan today for tomorrow's needs. I tend to think this personnel problem will ultimately be our most pressing and distressing one, unless we honestly and immediately face the challenge of educational needs.

A third problem area confronting our hospital system is the development of adequate physical facilities. Many of our urban hospitals are in urgent need of modernizing their physical plants, and much of our rural population is still too far removed from the sophisticated complex of services available in our medical centers. We must not allow facility deficiencies to limit the quantity or quality of care available to the public we serve. We must plan for the orderly and rational development of health care facilities throughout the state, and seek to establish among them relationships which will make quality comprehensive hospital care accessible to every Kentuckian in a manner as effective, efficient, and economical as possible. Our needs are too great, and our resources too limited, to permit the luxury of duplication on the one hand and coverage gaps on the other.

I have recently named a new Advisory Council for Health Facilities and charged it with the responsibility not only to advise on construction grants programs, but also to address itself on a continuing basis to this problem of statewide health facilities planning. Efforts at hospital planning, such as they are undertaking, are never easy, and are occasionally quite unpopular, but they are essential if we are to have valid objectives and priorities in our development of facilities.

I trust you will not consider it presumptuous that I mention a fourth task confronting you as hospitals; namely, the challenge of leadership. Kentucky communities are more and more looking to their hospitals for increased leadership in health care matters. Hospitals have become an increasingly crucial element in the strivings for ever better quality of all medical care. So that Kentucky citizens may realize the full benefits of scientific discoveries and advances, our hospitals will continuously face the problem of upgrading the standards of professional performance. In the case of hospitals, this may well take the form of increased emphasis on accreditation. In other cases the pressures for improvement will originate from the organized professions, and this is as it should be.

Legislation may often be an instrument by which higher standards are implemented. For example, I recall that bills affecting the practice of pharmacy and nursing were considered by the 1964 General Assembly. These issues call for the highest level of statesmanship on the part of Kentucky hospitals. By demonstrating an ability to exercise calm and wise judgment, and by basing their actions on the public interest, with which they are by nature closely identified, hospitals can effectively carry out a leadership function upon which the health of our people is so vitally dependent.

Fifth, and finally, we must strive to provide the highest quality hospital care at the lowest possible cost. We must do all we can to prevent the cost of hospital care from outrunning our ability to pay for it. I say this because there is a growing awareness that new or additional hospital facilities should be built on the basis of proven need and that present hospitals and equipment should be utilized as efficiently and economically as possible. We must avoid unnecessary hospital construction and interinstitutional rivalry that results in duplication of services. We do not need a $50,000 machine used once a month when there is similar equipment at a nearby hospital where a loan or service-swapping arrangement can be made. We must avoid unnecessary hospital admissions and unneeded days of stay. As unwarranted use of the hospital increases, so does the cost of hospital insurance rates. We must also keep the rising costs of overhead down through improved purchasing procedures and through the efficient handling of housekeeping and staff services.

All of this can be achieved without detracting from the quality of hospital care provided—in fact, economy and efficiency should improve it. I know that all of you want to help in solving these problems and in doing all you can to keep hospital costs to the patient as low as possible.

It is obvious that the problems facing hospitals are not insignificant. In meeting these problems—as in meeting all the problems that press upon us in the sixties, problems of education, poverty, race relations, highway safety—our task is not light. Our responsibilities are many. But I ask you to remember that a speech was found among Franklin Roosevelt's papers when he died at Warm Springs which he had written but never delivered —and it closed with these words: "The only limit of our realization of tomorrow will be our doubts of today. Let us move forward with strong and active faith."

---

1. The Medical Assistance Act passed by the General Assembly in 1960 was intended to provide medical care for the Commonwealth's indigent citizens. The legislation established the Advisory Council for Medical Assistance, a panel appointed by the governor to collect information and develop plans for implementing the medical care program. Its recommendations were to be conveyed to the Department of Economic Security and the Department of Health, which were responsible for funding the program and defining the services to be offered through it. *Acts, 1960,* Chapter 68 (H.B. 439), pp. 271-78.

PUBLIC HEALTH ASSOCIATION CONVENTION
Louisville / April 20, 1965

It gives me great pleasure to appear before this large group of professional public health workers. My experience with public health activities in Frankfort and my local health department in Christian County gives me a feeling of close familiarity with all of you. It is most impressive to observe the many services you perform in program areas such as maternal and child health, food and water sanitation, health education, nutrition, mental health, control of communicable diseases, and the provision of direct medical care services.

It requires little insight to realize that public health is undergoing a drastic change due to rapid developments in medical sciences, environmental concepts, and social-economic concepts. I can note a few problems involved and you can add to them. You in public health are in the center of this complex development, and let me challenge you to bold decisions, to chart a new course and take a fresh approach.

This year may go down in history as the greatest year the health field has ever experienced. There is unquestionably more federal legislation being enacted than has ever occurred in the past. The Economic Opportunity Act and the Appalachia Act both present significant opportunities for the improvement of health conditions. The new federal water pollution legislation will result in greatly increased activities in this area. The extension of the Hill-Burton Act advanced the potentiality for increased health facilities throughout the state.[1] A bill providing medical care for the aged will be passed this year and will have great impact on health care in Kentucky.[2] The increased federal programs establishing diagnostic and treatment projects for children under the auspices of the Children's Bureau and the Public Health Service are most noteworthy.[3]

As you know, one of my greatest concerns is for improving the economy of Kentuckians. Our plans include making every effort to take advantage of federal programs for better roads, training of our youth, development of tourism and new industry. I believe an improved economy will result in improved health and that—conversely—healthier young people and adults make for increased learning and ability to be productive.

It is important that we have sound federal, state, and local planning so that both the economy of Kentucky and the health of her citizens may be sustained at the highest levels. You have probably observed that there is today a trend toward greater intergovernmental cooperation, consolidated programming, and more emphasis on efficiency. I know that you in public health are already exerting efforts to adjust to this development with the creation of regional health centers throughout the state. Their existence should add measurably to the health and well-being of Kentuckians.

Further on this matter of planning, I have recently named a new Advisory Council for Health Facilities to work with Dr. Teague in giving more careful scrutiny to construction grants and to comprehensive evaluation of state and regional planning mechanisms for health facilities. They will be concerned with the effective location and operation of hospitals, nursing homes, health centers, community mental health centers, and facilities for the mentally retarded.

Many of the developments which I have been mentioning are directly related to the November general obligation bond issue. Kentucky is seriously jeopardized by inadequate funds to keep pace with her needs. Without such funds it will be impossible to take advantage of federal programs which are so necessary to carry on our road construction program, school development, health facilities construction, and numerous other projects so critically needed at this time. With the bond money we will be able to move forward on a number of fronts. For example, the bond issue will make possible the completion of the schools of medicine and dentistry at the University of Louisville. In the past, the University of Louisville has served Kentucky well, but it today needs additional facilities in order to train physicians and dentists, which are in great shortage.

Further, the passage of the bond issue will, in a direct way, be most significant to you in that it will permit continued state participation in the construction of health centers, and, of course, there is no need to go into detail as to the merit of this program with this audience. It should be reiterated that the bond issue will be of considerable concern to you in that because of its contribution to the general improvement of the economy of Kentucky, it will in turn make for improved health for all Kentuckians. I urge each of you to work, between now and next November, for the passage of this critical bond issue.

I would like to pay a special tribute to the splendid job you in the county health departments have done in developing and improving your vaccination programs. In 1954 there were 823 cases of polio reported in Kentucky. In 1963 and 1964 there were none. I understand that local health departments are vigorously working to accomplish the same feat with diphtheria, whooping cough, and typhoid. Because of this record of accomplishment, it gives me pleasure to announce that the state Health Department is presently working out a plan, to be effective May 15, for a mass vaccination program against measles. There has been a tendency to consider measles an uncomfortable but rarely serious disease. In fact, however, measles and resulting complications result in more than 400 deaths a year in the United States, mostly infants and small children. In 1963 there were 13 deaths because of measles in Kentucky.

The most serious complication of measles is encephalitis, which is estimated to occur once in 1,000 cases and which can cause mental crippling, as well as death. It can leave a child mentally damaged for life. Other serious associated effects include pneumonia, which accounts for nine of ten measles deaths; deafness; inflammation within the ear; and the reactivation of arrested tuberculosis.

The dramatic results of new medicines and new methods are opening the way to a fuller and more useful life for all Kentuckians. But, let me hasten to say that illness is still a state problem. There are too few doctors, too few nurses, and too few hospitals.[4] Too few of our handicapped are being rehabilitated—too many rivers are dangerously polluted. Too few of our poor obtain proper and adequate medical service.

Illness knows neither barriers of region or race or religion or creed. It is up to you and me and other citizens—and all our doctors and nurses who work daily to improve the health of our citizens, to make life longer—to meet our critical needs in a manner consistent with our obligation to freedom and our obligation to humanity.

In meeting these problems, as in meeting all the problems that press upon us in the sixties, problems of race relations, education, poverty, housing—our task is not light. Our responsibilities are many. Our critics will always be present. But I ask you to continue the excellent public health progress you are making, and I challenge you to exercise leadership in maintaining pace with the rapidly changing health needs of our people. This way we will build a stronger, healthier Kentucky.

---

1. Congress passed a five-year extension of the Hill-Burton Act in August, 1964. It allocated $1.4 billion for construction of hospitals, nursing homes, and other health facilities in communities which could provide partial matching funds from state and/or local sources. *New York Times,* August 19, 1964.

2. On the strength of his overwhelming electoral victory in 1964 and the large majorities won by Democrats in accompanying congressional elections, President Johnson gained approval of his medicare plan in 1965 (H.R. 6675, P.L. 89-97). Opponents of federally financed health care, led by the American Medical Association and the powerful chairman of the House Ways and Means Committee, Wilbur Mills, had repeatedly blocked related proposals. The bill contained a number of programs. The basic plan committed the federal government to pay a large share of the hospital and nursing home costs for all people sixty-five or older. A supplemental voluntary plan, costing $3 per month covered the costs of doctors' fees. Other sections of the act extended benefits and federal funds available under the Kerr-Mills Act, increased federal funding of child-care programs established by the Social Security Act, and increased social security retirement and disability benefits by 7 percent. The total estimated annual cost of the program was $6.5 billion. *Congressional Quarterly Almanac,* vol. 20 (1965), pp. 236-69.

3. The Children's Bureau was created in 1912 primarily as an investigative agency of the federal government concerned with "all matters related to child life." Title V of the Social Security Act, which the bureau administers, greatly increased its realm of activity. It authorized the bureau to award grants to state and local agencies to provide health services and facilities to children and mothers. Furthermore, the bureau was directed to assist in planning and establishing systems providing welfare services beneficial to children and to administer research and demonstration projects pertinent to its activities. General Services Administration, *U.S. Government Organization Manual, 1965-1966* (Washington, 1966), pp. 365-67.

4. Kentucky contained [99] physicians per 100,000 population in 1965, a ratio which placed it forty-first in the nation. The national average was 153 physicians per 100,000. U.S. Bureau of the Census, *Statistical Abstract of the United States, 1966* (Washington, 1966), p. 67.

KENTUCKY HANDICAPPED ASSOCIATION
Louisville / April 22, 1965

TODAY, as I enjoy the opportunity of recognizing the finest efforts of 1964 in the field of service to the handicapped citizens of Kentucky, I can reflect upon the experience of a young man who once sought the advice of a learned public figure in the field of law. Before encountering the elderly barrister, the young man rehearsed, again and again, the matter they were to discuss—in order to phrase it clearly and distinctly when he met the old counselor. Halfway home from his meeting, the young man suddenly realized that the interview had come and gone. He had come away fully inspired, but had forgotten to mention his problem at all. Suddenly in reflecting upon his oversight, the young man came to this astonishing realization: it was not an answer to a specific problem which he needed so much, although the matter had given him no end of trouble. No, my fellow Kentuckians, what he really needed was not an answer so much as the transmission of a great spirit.

Today I am surrounded by the invincible examples which are borne of great spirits. Several months ago I made this observation in *Performance*, which is the journal of the President's Committee on Employment of the Handicapped: "My attention has been attracted on more occasions than I can count by the excellent work record of persons with some kind of physical handicap," I wrote. "I have come to realize more and more, and especially during and since my term as commissioner of the Kentucky Department of Personnel, that persons with physical handicaps are not disabled when it comes to a desire to be productive and useful to our society. They want to work. They do not ask for sympathy, however much they merit it."

I now say to you that we have not come here today to convince each other that this is a worthy cause. We already know that. We have not joined here today simply to enumerate our own accomplishments in the field of employment or rehabilitation of the handicapped, although great strides have been made. What we have come for today is to pay tribute to those who have set examples for the rest of us to follow. We are here to honor men and women to whom obstacles are challenges, and not insurmountable barriers. In the words of one writer, "Obstacles are those frightful things you see when you take your eyes off the goal." We are here to commend special citizens who have concentrated upon our common goal—the removal of barriers, and the overcoming of handicaps.

How great is the problem which they have faced? By official estimates, 10 percent of our national population are disabled in some way which requires a special effort on their part to walk or move about. There is a great national concern—and a concern which I share fully—about the one person out of five in this country whose life in this land is devoid of hope because of the condition of poverty. Here we face another great truth—that one person out of ten has a physical handicap which prevents or impedes normal functioning in the home or on the job. Let me say to you, in all sincerity, that the question of poverty is not half so great as the problem of having a physical handicap.

And yet, let us examine the record. The records show that in the past two decades all across the nation, in Kentucky and everywhere, in all manner of jobs, handicapped workers have compiled a record of great accomplishment which more than justifies the confidence which their employers have placed in them. This is their answer to the question of hope or despair. They are not daunted when it comes to difficulty. They accept it as a challenge. They rise above it, attaining great heights and setting sound examples for all of us to follow.

There are a number of employers in the audience today, some of whom I will go on to recognize in a few moments. These are the bosses who have found that hiring the handicapped is sound business, and each year brings a greater need for broader recognition of the contributions which our handicapped Kentuckians are eager to make. They are eager for the chance, Mr. Employer, and they will satisfy your needs and answer your curiosity, if you will allow them to do so.

With automation and in the light of rapidly changing factors in the nature of today's jobs, employers are offered new incentives to make use of the special skills which the handicapped are learning through modern vocational rehabilitation.

Actually, the number of jobs which require unimpaired physical faculties, the all-around "jack of all trades" or robust type of person, are growing fewer in number and as a percentage of the total job force. The demands of today's jobs are more for the excellence in quality of human spirit and mind, rather than the sole dependence upon the brute strength of the worker's physique.

In the area of vocational rehabilitation, Kentucky found herself in fiftieth place in the nation in the year 1954. By the time Bert Combs had served a year in office in 1959, we had moved up to thirty-first place. Last year the efforts of the Bureau of Rehabilitation Services elevated Kentucky to thirteenth rank among the states. During 1964 there were about 7,300 of our citizens who received rehabilitation services—a 58 percent increase over the previous year—a record unequalled by any other state in America. In that period of time almost 3,000 Kentuckians with disabilities had been restored to the point that they could become employed. More than 2,000 with handicaps were placed by the Kentucky Employment Service.

The real proof of the pudding, as employers will realize, is the high caliber of work turned out by our handicapped persons who are on the job. Statistics show that handicapped persons take fewer sick days than the average worker, to cite one example. Watch a handicapped person yourself, and you'll see that his efforts can be the equal of anyone's.

Andrew Carnegie once said that the average person puts only 25 percent of his energy and ability into his work.[1] The world takes off its hat to those who put in more than 50 percent of their capacity, and stands on its head for those few-and-far-between souls who devote 100 percent. Mary Pickford, whom some of you here today will remember more clearly than I, once was asked how she had faced so many heartaches and disappointments.[2] She replied, "All the water in the world can't sink a ship unless it gets on the inside."

Between the effort which handicapped Kentuckians put forth and the disappointment which they face daily, we can do no more than to pay them tribute for all that they have done. With full faith, they sail a troubled sea, and with maximum effort they make the impossible seem not really impossible at all.

---

1. Andrew Carnegie (1835-1919), noted nineteenth century American industrialist. Following the sale of his steel company in the 1890s, Carnegie became one of America's most generous philanthropists. *Concise Dictionary of American Biography* (New York, 1964), pp. 144-45.

2. Mary Pickford, stage name for Gladys Marie Smith (1894-   ), American

actress who became a favorite of film audiences in the 1920s. *Who's Who in America, 1962-1963,* 32nd ed. (Chicago, 1962).

FRONTIER NURSES' BENEFIT DINNER
Frankfort / December 2, 1965

TO merely welcome you here and say that we are grateful for your presence sounds completely inadequate when we are gathered for such an important occasion. Our purpose is not only to honor two members of the Frontier Nursing Service who almost gave their lives for the benefit of the people of our state, but in a way to pay tribute to the service itself.

Mrs. Mary Breckinridge, late director of Frontier Nursing Service, in her book *Wide Neighborhoods* describes the beginning of one of the most astounding and selfless health services in the world.[1] On May 28, 1925, the committee for mothers and babies held its first meeting in the assembly room of the Capitol Hotel in Frankfort, Kentucky, to form an organization and to elect its executive officers. This organization was to become the Frontier Nursing Service. Mrs. Mary Breckinridge, whose love for mothers and children led her to dedicate her life to their care, began the preparation for her future at Saint Luke's Hospital School of Nursing in New York City. Following the deaths of her own two children and her work with mothers and children in Europe during World War I, Mrs. Breckinridge dreamed and made preparation for her return to Kentucky.

The Frontier Nursing Service throughout its forty years of service has been a guide and inspiration to the great and the less fortunate, and to all of the developing countries in the world. In 1939 a school for nurse-midwives was established. When the fiftieth class graduates in February of 1966, the school will have prepared 285 qualified nurse-midwives. They are now serving in a number of states, including Alaska, the Philippines, New Guinea, India, Thailand, South Korea, Canada, France, the Middle East, and in parts of Africa and South America.

In the Fortieth Annual Report of the Frontier Nursing Service, we find the following statement: "In the 12 districts operated by the Service from the Hospital, Wendover, and five outpost centers, we attended 10,446 persons in 2,369 families. Of these, 4,506 were children, including 1,934 babies and toddlers. The district nurses paid 23,129 and received 18,596 visits at their nursing centers and at their special clinics. Bedside nursing care was given in their homes to 1,500 sick people. . . . At the request of the State Board of Health, the Frontier Nursing Service gave 4,928 inoculations and vaccines against typhoid, diphtheria, smallpox, whooping cough, polio, and similar diseases."

This does not take into account such things as buying coal for indigent families, buying stoves for those who are destitute, providing groceries for thirty-eight families, and shoes and school clothes for twenty-six children, or providing seed potatoes and garden seed for the families who cannot afford them. These are only a few of the services, other than medical care, provided by the ladies of the Frontier Nursing Service. This typifies the great concern for all the needs of the people of eastern Kentucky by the members of the Frontier Nursing Service. Nurses from throughout the world have wanted to be a part of this outstanding organization.

Eleven years ago Miss Molly Lee, an English nurse trained in midwifery, came to the mountains of eastern Kentucky to be a part of the Frontier Nursing Service. She had planned to resign and return to her native England, and to celebrate this event, her sister, Miss Nora Lee, had arrived for a brief visit before they returned together to their homeland.[2]

On Friday afternoon, July 30, of this year, there occurred the worst tragedy in the history of Frontier Nursing Service. Misses Molly and Nora Lee were visiting a patient who was living about seven miles from Hyden. En route, the jeep struck a homemade land mine which had been planted in the road. Both of the ladies were badly injured. Extreme heroism on the part of Molly was evident when she gave explicit instructions to those who arrived at the scene of the accident as to care for her sister. Both were admitted to the Appalachian Regional Hospital in Harlan. The people of Leslie and surrounding mountain counties, in an expression of love and appreciation to Miss Molly Lee, contributed $1,600 for the care of her and her sister. All debts for care have now been paid. On October 12 they returned to England by air and were admitted to the rehabilitation center in London. Both are making rapid improvement. Molly is beginning her exercises in walking. Nora has excellent vision in one eye and is being fitted for the two artificial legs.

I could go on and on relating the accomplishments and services of this organization to Kentucky and wide areas of the world. But, let me say on behalf of all Kentuckians, we are humbly grateful for its contribution to the health and welfare of the people it so ably serves. And, especially tonight, we are grateful for the sacrifices made by Misses Molly and Nora Lee. It is one of the greatest pleasures of my life to be able to present this check to Mr. Redmond Carroll on behalf of the Lee sisters as a small token of our appreciation to them.[3]

---

1. Mary Breckinridge, *Wide Neighborhoods: A Story of the Frontier Nursing Service* (1952; reprint ed., Lexington, Ky., 1981).

2. For details of the bombing incident, see the *Louisville Courier-Journal,* July 31, 1965.

3. Redmond Carroll (1895-), employed by the Department of Conservation (1953-1961); at the time of his resignation Carroll was a resident of Henderson, Kentucky. Information provided by Division of Personnel, Frankfort.

STATEMENT ON OLD AGE ASSISTANCE
Frankfort / June 9, 1966

IN my budget message presented to the 1966 General Assembly, I announced that effective in January, public assistance benefits to the needy aged would increase by an average of about two dollars per month. I also promised that some additional changes would be placed into effect if the budget was passed and that these would become effective on July 1.

I am now in a position to report to the people of Kentucky that this promise has been kept. The alterations in our state program of old age assistance will mean that an additional three dollar increase will be made to all cases, and that another three dollars will be added in July to public assistance payments for those who elected to take advantage of the supplementary medical insurance program under federal social security. This latter number totals approximately 60,000 Kentuckians.

We are making these changes because of our fundamental belief in the dignity of all individuals, regardless of age, and because experience is showing that older persons naturally have more expenses in the area of medical needs. These same changes will allow Kentucky to move much closer to the actual needs of indigent older persons. The absolute ceilings which had previously been applied to all adult cases, regardless of the extent of the need, will now be removed and we will pay 100 percent of need to adult public assistance cases. Credit for part of this recommendation belongs, of course, to the social work and advisory staff of the Department of Economic Security. But no small measure of thanks is due to the legislature of Kentucky, which had the foresight to adopt our budget bill and the public assistance changes of 1966.[1]

In more concrete terms, the maximum of $87 which was previously applied to the monthly benefits for old-age recipients living alone and the ceiling of $122 per month which affected these persons living with an essential relative, will now be put aside. Instead, an accurate public assistance budget will be used to determine the benefit amount due for old-age assistance cases.

For example, the needs of an elderly person living alone in an urban situation are very apt to exceed $87 per month, and could conceivably amount to $250 or more if he needs nursing or homemaker services from someone outside the home. These changes mean that we will be able to assist such citizens in a way and in an amount never before possible. We are going to be able to assist our elder persons in a much more realistic way.

Further, we will provide more help for older persons who are living in licensed homes for the aged. There are three classifications of such homes, based upon the quality and adequacy of care provided by each home. These same public assistance changes will allow maximum payments to our nursing homes of $120, $103, or $95 monthly per public assistance patient, according to the type of care received. The payments to these homes replace previous ceilings which were three dollars lower. Leaving maximums in force for personal care homes will mean that these agencies will be specifically encouraged to increase the quality of care rendered.

It might be interesting to note that basic and very significant research by the Department of Economic Security has identified a great amount of information about our aged recipients. Nearly two-thirds of these persons are women, because of their longer life spans, lower earning capacities, and more prevalent ineligibility for federal social security payments. Almost 20 percent of these old-age recipients were unable to leave their homes because of physical or mental conditions. Four percent of these were bedfast, and another 5 percent were confined to chairs or wheelchairs.

More than 30 percent of these elderly persons required care from some other person in order to carry on daily life. About 30 percent needed to have some other person within call, and 3 percent of these did not even have anyone available who could meet that need. By the time our recipients reach eighty-five years of age or more almost 70 percent need someone else to help them. Their needs for food, shelter, and other living costs averaged about seventy-five dollars per month by the strictest standards. We can be quite thankful, I believe, that since May of 1965 our public assistance to the needy aged has met virtually 100 percent of these basic requirements up to the maximum payments of $87 or $122 depending upon the presence of an essential person also in need. More than half of the houses of the needy aged were in need of major repair. Almost half are without running water, and less than half could heat their complete home during winter months.

I have cited these facts not so much to point to the needs of our older citizens as to emphasize that the changes in our public assistance program are needed very decidedly. That is why we identified improvements to be made in the appropriations under the budget bill, and that is part of the justification for changing our programs.

Before I conclude this presentation on the needs of our older persons allow me to observe that our state-administered medical care program also meets a very critical need for the aged. As of July 1 there will be some of the most significant changes ever in our medical care program under Title XIX of the federal Social Security Act. These changes, plus the new social security health insurance program for persons aged sixty-five and over, will yield far more adequate health care for the old-age recipient. The medical assistance for the aged program will now be incorporated in a more comprehensive program. There will be a broad scope of services provided by physicians, dentists, hospital inpatient and outpatient care, an expanded drug list and nursing home services, plus several new types of medical services (home health services, outpatient care at community mental health centers, etc.). The "deductibles" and co-insurance of the social security health program will be paid for by our medical care program.

The state will pay: the full amount of the hospitalization insurance deductibles and co-insurance, including the forty dollar inpatient deductible during each spell of illness under hospitalization; the twenty dollar outpatient deductible plus 20 percent co-insurance; the five dollars per day after the twentieth day in an extended care facility, plus the cost of remaining longer than 100 days; the costs of medical services not covered by hospitalization insurance, including care in nursing homes not eligible under hospitalization insurance; care which is not on a posthospital basis from both nursing homes and home health agencies; outpatient hospital services other than diagnostic; and services outside the scope of hospitalization insurance, such as drugs and dental care.

If the recipient over sixty-five elected supplementary medical insurance and pays the three dollar premiums, these are also available: while the Kentucky Medical Assistance Program will not pay the full amount of supplementary medical insurance deductibles, as it does for hospitalization insurance, it will pay any part of such costs which is for services which are within the scope of the program. For example, it will not pay for surgery, but it will pay for physicians' visits at the prices allowable. Those old-age recipients confined to mental and tuberculosis hospitals will receive the personal allowance ordinarily paid to recipients in nursing homes (ten dollars) for the first time beginning July 1. The hospitals will receive vendor payments for their services.

---

1. See "an act relating to the administration of public assistance," *Acts, 1966*, Chapter 134 (H.B. 115), pp. 590-93.

MEDICARE STATEMENT
Frankfort / June 24, 1966

ON July 1, 1966, Kentucky will begin its participation in the comprehensive medical assistance program under Title XIX of the Social Security Act. This program, financed not only by substantial federal assistance but from state funds as well, will bring greatly expanded medical, hospital, nursing care, and other benefits to those who are unable to carry the full financial burden of adequate medical care.

It is unfortunate that on the very threshold of this program in which Kentucky is pioneering, and which will mean so much to the lives and health of thousands of Kentuckians, we should find ourselves involved in a controversy within the medical profession over fees. The question is whether recognized and certified specialists should receive, out of public funds, fees which recognize their special training, additional residency and their qualifications.

Spokesmen for general practitioners contend that this involves a dual fee system, providing higher fees for the specialists in return for services identical to those provided by general practitioners. Other physicians, including some general practitioners and many specialists, contend that the services rendered by specialists are different in character and the fee system which recognizes this difference reveals the present prevailing practice in the medical profession.

This is a technical and not a political issue. It must be resolved by those who have training and experience in medicine and in medical economics. The law has established in Kentucky a governor's Advisory Council for Medical Assistance which includes not merely public officials and distinguished lay citizens, but representatives of all the professions, medical, dentistry, pharmacy, nursing and hospitals which provide services under the medical assistance program. These representatives were chosen by me from nominees submitted by the recognized professional organizations.

The fee schedule, which is now in controversy, was unanimously adopted by the council after a public hearing held on June 13, presided over by Dr. Gaithel Simpson, chairman of the council, past president of the Kentucky Medical Association, a general practitioner and a general surgeon.[1] The council had the advice and assistance of technical committees representing the various professions. The medical committee was composed of five physicians selected by the Kentucky Medical Association, four of whom were general practitioners.

I am in no position to interfere with the autonomy or professional character of the council. In addition, interference by me would result in a delay in the expanded benefits provided for Kentuckians under the Title XIX medical assistance program. I should not take any step which would delay or impede this program which will mean better health for our people and will also provide much needed additional compensation for the hard-working physicians, both general practitioners and specialists, who are participating and providing high-quality services to our medical assistance beneficiaries.

It was suggested by the general practitioners who met with me today that current systems of providing aid for the medically indigent be kept in effect for another month, until August 1, and that the system of fees already announced be reconsidered by the council in a July meeting.

It is impossible to continue present practices and at the same time provide much needed care for many thousands of Kentuckians because present systems of care are being replaced July 1 by Title XIX. The advisory council is a continuing body with the duty of continually reviewing the operation of all aspects of our medical assistance program under Title XIX. The council meets regularly once during each quarter of the year, and it will meet regularly during the quarter which commences July 1, 1966. I am asking the council to hold its regular quarterly meeting as early in July as possible and to invite representatives of the Academy of General Practice and all specialty groups in the medical profession to attend. At this time any group, or any individual, physician, or layman will have an opportunity, as they have always had, to provide argument or information to the council with respect to fee schedules or any other part of this program. I am sure that the distinguished members of this body will also consider these matters in a fair and just manner to the best of their abilities.

Certainly it would be unbecoming in me to appoint such a body and then to reject its conclusions with respect to matters on which I am not professionally expert and with respect to which I have not had an opportunity for long and detailed consideration. Let me make it clear that I am passing no judgment on this issue, am taking no sides, and that my primary interest lies first in meeting the needs of the program beneficiaries, promptly and generously, and secondly in maintaining the integrity of orderly procedure in making decisions of this kind.

---

1. Gaithel L. Simpson (1905-   ), born, Christian County, Kentucky; M.D., University of Louisville (1931); medical practice, Greenville, Kentucky (1932-   ); president of Kentucky Medical Association (1962); service on numerous medical committees in the Commonwealth of Kentucky. Telephone interview, March 2, 1981.

HILL-BURTON STATEMENT
Frankfort / August 10, 1966

TWENTY years ago the Hill-Burton program was launched. This program, one of the most important health acts ever enacted in the United States, is a prime example of federal, state, and local cooperation.

The Hill-Burton program, while providing a significant amount of funds for health facility construction to the various states, has given impetus to much needed areawide planning for health facilities, has stimulated the development of higher construction standards, and has improved the overall operation of health facilities.

Kentucky has benefited greatly from the Hill-Burton program. One hundred eleven communities in Kentucky have Hill-Burton facilities. This represents 240 projects which have received a total of $69,150,000 in federal funds. These projects have provided 7,351 inpatient beds and ninety-seven other health facilities. In Fayette County alone the federal share of Hill-Burton projects totals $12,126,246.44. This includes the construction of the University of Kentucky Medical Center, which was aided by a federal share of $8,683,731.50. In Jefferson County federal Hill-Burton funds total $18,162,678.59. Construction of new facilities and additions to existing ones added a total 2,362 inpatient beds.

The first Hill-Burton project approved in Kentucky was the Logan County Hospital, Russellville, Kentucky. This facility, which opened in January, 1951, provided fifty-two general hospital beds and received approximately $181,000 in federal aid. We have present today Mr. Kenneth Hawthorne, administrator, and Mr. Thomas Lyne, chairman of the board of Logan County Hospital.[1]

The latest Hill-Burton project to be approved in Kentucky was the Western Kentucky Hospital Services Corporation. This project is a very significant example of local cooperation in that seven hospitals have come together to construct and operate a joint laundry, purchasing, and data processing unit. This facility, which is expected to be under construction this fall, will receive approximately one-half million dollars in federal assistance. We also have representatives of this project present today: Mr. Carl Wieler, administrator of Hopkins County Hospital and representative of the hospital corporation and Mayor David Parrish, Madisonville, chairman of the building commission.[2]

---

1. Kenneth G. Hawthorne (1936-   ), hospital administrator, Logan County, Kentucky (1962-1967); previously Hawthorne had served as hospital administra-

tor in Fairbury, Illinois. He became involved in a controversy with the Logan County Fiscal Court and was fired August 29, 1967. The entire Logan County Hospital Board of Trustees resigned in protest of the fiscal court's action. *Louisville Courier-Journal,* August 30, 1967. Thomas Lyne, Sr. (1889-1967), farmer in Logan County; member, Logan County Hospital Board, Federal Land Bank Board. Information provided by Thomas Lyne III.

2. Carl Wieler, no data available. David Andrew Parrish (1899-), born in Madisonville, Kentucky; attended United States Naval Academy; pharmacist in Madisonville (1926-1980); mayor of Madisonville (1948-1976); resident of Madisonville. Telephone interview, March 3, 1981.

KENTUCKY WELFARE ASSOCIATION
Louisville / November 4, 1966

SEVERAL years ago Kentucky launched its own kind of war—a war against backwardness, not only backwardness in its highway program, which was bad enough, but backwardness of its schools, which were worse. Today Kentucky is on the move. New highways are ribboning this state, teacher salaries are beginning to give teachers the dignity they deserve, industry is locating throughout our Commonwealth, unemployment is at an all-time low.

Indeed we are closer to the Kentucky dream to create a society in which every citizen has unfettered opportunity to lift himself and his family to something better than ever before. Among those stricken by poverty, we are seeking the answers for every age with the help of the federal government—from our preschool youngsters to our senior citizens. We are seeking answers for every place of poverty, from the city slums to the hollows in Appalachia.

Civil rights legislation is an essential part of the war on poverty. So is aid to our elementary and secondary schools. So is our highway program. So is medicare. So are our industry hunts. So are our new programs in corrections, in mental health, in health. So are the new undertakings generally called the poverty program—community action, Head Start, the Job Corps, the neighborhood Youth Corps and others.

We are moving into new ground, and there are no blazed trails for us to follow. Some of the approaches we try, especially in our poverty program, may not work out, and you may read about them in blaring headlines. This is bound to happen. Doctors have tried for years to find a cure for cancer, and we are not dismayed that they have not; we simply ask them to try and try again. On the other hand, some of the things we try may work out far better than we expected. We must change or discard those programs which are not making headway, and we must expand those that are.

We have already made a significant impact in our overall development of Kentucky. For example, United States Department of Labor figures show that unemployment is down to 3.3 percent in our state, which is even substantially lower than a year ago. And we have also, I think, begun to identify the major directions in which we must move forward. I would stress four in particular—education, road construction, job development, and the enhancement of human dignity.

The more we examine the facts and figures, the more we confirm what Kentuckians have begun to recognize—that education is, has been, and always will be our soundest and most productive investment as a state. And this is as true in our war on poverty as of every aspect of our life. Perhaps the biggest gain we have scored so far against poverty has been in keeping thousands of young Kentuckians in high school and college, so that they can meet the stricter standards for employment in this technological age.

At the other end of the spectrum, we need to do more to assure an adequate income and care to those who are too old or too handicapped to work. We must do more, too, about jobs for the poor. We must regard the untrained and unemployed not as drags on our state, but as unused resources. Our state needs and wants the services these "wasted Kentuckians" can provide.

Let me cite to you some of the programs, many of them totally familiar to you, where we are moving to improve the lives of our citizenry. Kentucky has been designated, retroactive to the first of July, as the first state in the South and the sixteenth in the nation, to operate a federally approved medical assistance program under Title XIX of the federal Social Security Act. Actually, invisible to the eyes of many members of the general public, our progress in medical care over the past five years has been the parallel of the brilliant record that this state has compiled in the area of building modern highways. This program was begun in 1961 under provisions of the federal laws relating to public assistance and under the Kerr-Mills Act, so that Kentuckians of all ages began to receive indigent medical care and medical aid for the aged.

A look at the size of our expenditures for calendar year 1965 and a comparison with the next two calendar years will give you some idea of the expansion we will undergo in the future. In 1965 we spent $22 million on medical care—and bear in mind that 80 percent of these figures are federal tax funds returned to Kentucky for use—and in the present year the figure for medical assistance is expected to reach $35 million, an increase of $13 million in one year. Calendar year 1967 will see the growth of this medical program reach an estimated $42 million. These amounts are regulated entirely by the amounts, approximately 20 percent, appropriated by the General Assembly of Kentucky in my last biennial budget act. What Kentucky reaps as a reward is based upon our own participation in the medical assistance program.

Today we are offering physician, dental, hospital, pharmaceutical and nursing home services, and are adding home health services and care for the elderly in mental and tuberculosis hospitals. The quantities of care were increased immediately with adoption of the new medical assistance program and our decision to add the three dollar monthly payments for social security supplementary medical insurance to our monthly state public assistance checks.

For the next ten years we expect to see Kentucky building upon this foundation. More important in some ways than the question of quantity of care is the question of quality medical help for our needy citizens. I think that it is entirely to the credit of the medical, dental and related health professions in this state that their leaders have seen the wisdom of working closely with this medical program through the state Medical Advisory Committee, which has aided the economic security and health departments to see what can be done.

By 1975, for example, it is entirely possible that Kentucky will be providing for all Kentuckians who can be classed as medically needy. At the present time, as you may know, we are restricted to medically needy people who are either qualified for public assistance or closely related to one of its existing categories, such as old age, disability, blindness, or family deprivation. There has been a recent stir over a certain kind of case which does not presently qualify for medical assistance, even though there is an unquestioned need involved. By not later than 1975 I believe that this kind of problem will be taken care of by changes in our eligibility requirements.

The national report of the Advisory Committee on Public Welfare has churned up a great deal of interest among all of you, I have been told. This blueprint for social action looks far into the future and covers far more material than I can talk with you about here today. But one thing that I can point to is the recommendation on work and training programs, which began experimentally with the social security amendments of 1962. Beginning in January of 1964 we had in Kentucky a $1 million grant to try out the "unemployed parent" option. Today we have this same approach in nineteen counties of eastern Kentucky under Title V of the Economic Opportunity Act. Economic Security administers this program, and we are seeing every day why the National Advisory Committee recommended that these programs should become a permanent part of our social welfare approach.

Here we see how adult basic education, high school equivalency training, and vocational training can begin to change basically the lives of the poor. At the present time 100 of these fathers every month, on an average, are graduating from the program to accept private employment. These men, mind you, were numbered as being chronic or "hard-core" unemployed, but they are moving toward the mainstream of society today because of the imaginative nature of new public welfare approaches. The good which is being done in our less affluent counties makes a very strong case for continuing this program indefinitely. If you do not believe me, just talk to Mayor Archer or Judge Stumbo at Prestonsburg, or check with Judge Slone in Knott County.[1] They have told our representatives how many miracles have occurred in community services because of the presence of the unemployed father program.

Bridges have been built, streams cleared to reduce flooding, roads built to bring school buses to the hollows where our children had been required to walk for miles just to get to school every day. These are quiet miracles. But even you as social workers and special friends of Kentucky welfare should know more about these success stories.

Community centers are being built or renovated for our people, schools and day care centers repaired and put in working order; even playgrounds are being built for the little ones. And, perhaps, most important of all, the school dropout figure has lowered among the children of these unemployed parents. We are replacing hopelessness with hope in these mountain communities because of some of the aspects of this forward looking program.

Another forward looking movement is the Food Stamp program, which has been authorized for an additional twenty-two Kentucky counties. About ten of these counties are receiving their first food coupons just now, and the remainder will do so in December. This will bring the total number of counties with Food Stamp programs to almost forty, giving this state the largest number of counties, the highest dollar benefit, and perhaps the greatest number of persons benefiting from the program. I should not have to tell social welfare practitioners the value of the Food Stamp program—but certainly this is one more area in which the look is to the future. Our stockpiles of agricultural surpluses are being reduced, and we can expect the U.S. Department of Agriculture to continue to move ahead with the conversion of this segment of the war on poverty to the newer kind of food program. I believe that the future is going to find Kentucky in the forefront of the movement to move ahead with food stamps and away from the giveaway program of commodities.

In child welfare, the state served more than 10,000 children in the fiscal year just ended. It placed a record number of 511 children in adoptive homes. And we are developing new facilities so we can serve even more children in the future—a boys' camp in Boone County and a treatment center for delinquent girls in Jefferson County, which is being built by the Kentucky Federation of Women's Clubs.

An important goal for the future is the establishment of five regional diagnostic centers for delinquents; the first, which will be built with a $400,000 appropriation from the bond issue, will be built in northern Kentucky. We are developing a long-range master plan in mental health that will soon be announced. Among other programs, it will include a major facility, which I plan to get under construction before I leave office, to alleviate overcrowding at our mental institutions. And there are many other programs.

Finally, let me pay a tribute to those of you who make up this association. The services you are giving mankind often go unrewarded. In many cases, it is self-sacrifice on your part. The poor, the aged, the disabled, the unfortunate—they do not have a powerful lobby; you are their lobby. I'm proud that all of you see such service to humanity as an essential part of your responsibility to your state, and to yourselves. John F. Kennedy once said: "When the youngest child alive today has grown to the cares of manhood, our position in the world will be determined first of all by what provisions we make today—for his education, his health, and his opportunities for a good home and a good job and a good life." Therefore, let our state be known not only for its Bluegrass, but for its compassion—not only for its fast horses, but for its creative scholars—not only for its increasing wealth, but for its willingness to share it with those less fortunate. Let us show, in deeds as well as in words, the warm humanity and the spirit of brotherhood which have always characterized Kentucky at its best.

---

1. George P. Archer (1915-1973), physician, Prestonsburg, Kentucky; M.D., University of Louisville (1940); mayor of Prestonsburg (1962-1973); chairman of the area development district (1970-1973). Information provided by Mr. Chalmer H. Frazier. Henry Stumbo (1908-1978), born in McDowell, Kentucky; Floyd County magistrate (1940-1950); county judge (1950-1978). Information provided by Mrs. Henry Stumbo. Merdith Slone (1919-1973), born in Knott County, Kentucky; educated at Caney College, Pippa Passes, Kentucky; magistrate for Knott County (1946-1950); county judge (1950-1954, 1966-1970); sheriff (1954-1958). Information provided by Mrs. Merdith Slone.

CONFERENCE WORKSHOP ON HOUSING
Covington / February 22, 1967

IN the areas of housing and urban development, where we need to step up our efforts, the needs are obvious.[1] There must be an upgrading of areas now occupied by the poor. Additional low- and moderate-income housing, open to nonwhites and whites alike, must be constructed. New areas, outside the central cities, must be open to lower income households. We must demonstrate, for all to see, that the most disadvantaged person when exposed to human renewal, offered equal opportunities, and afforded decent housing in an attractive and adequately serviced setting, becomes a good neighbor. In the process, we will bring relief, confidence, and hope to a large number of people.

The Federal Housing Act of 1965 started a new program for low-income families—the rent supplements. This program will supplement public housing, at the same time that the latter has been expanded and made more flexible. Today in public housing the federal government is leasing existing structures, rehabilitating such structures, and discouraging the planning and construction of large, institutional new projects, which I think is a good approach. And this is occurring in a low-income program which is three times larger than that which existed in 1960.

The Congress last year passed a new and exciting proposal that should help the housing problem. The demonstration cities program, which I strongly supported, will attack whole neighborhoods of blight and slum, rehabilitating the people as well as the residential structures and neighborhood facilities. It will, on a pilot basis, restore (among other areas) some of our slums, providing a pattern that can be applied ultimately to all slum areas and developing the tools for upgrading them to the status of good neighborhoods.

We, who have long analyzed and deplored the slums, now have a potential vehicle to initiate a coordinated, all-out attack upon them. The demonstration cities program is not designed to solve the mammoth slum problem in one bite. But it is designed to, and it will, devise programs and approaches that will revitalize whole neighborhoods and which can be utilized in every city where there are pockets of poverty and neglect. It merits your enthusiastic support.

When I came into office, I named F.E. "Dutch" Lackey, former mayor of Hopkinsville and former president of the Kentucky Municipal League, as director of the Office of Urban Affairs—a new agency which I created because of the growing urban problems.[2] Those of you who are familiar with Dutch know his dedication and enthusiasm for his job. He has helped many mayors and other officials in Kentucky in preparing applications for federal grants since he assumed his new post.

Here and now tonight, I want to tell you that your state government stands ready to be of assistance to you in your efforts to secure better housing. Though the programs are federal, we at the state level can give technical assistance. Mr. Lackey can be of immense help and so can our planning division. I include the latter group because I feel it is extremely important that communities plan ahead in housing development. Our planners can help and they are available if local governments desire their assistance.

Finally, let me pay a tribute to those of you who are attending this conference and who planned it. The services you are giving mankind often go unrewarded. In many cases, it is self-sacrifice on your part. The poor, the aged, the disabled, the unfortunate—they do not have a powerful lobby; you are their lobby. I'm proud that all of you see such service to humanity as an essential part of your responsibility to your state—and to yourselves.

John F. Kennedy once said: "When the youngest child alive today has grown to the cares of manhood, our position in the world will be determined first of all by what provisions we make today—for his education, his health, and his opportunities for a good home and a good job and a good life." Therefore, let our state be known not only for its Bluegrass, but for its compassion—not only for its fast horses, but for its creative scholars —not only for its increasing wealth, but for its willingness to share it with those less fortunate. Let us show, in deeds as well as in words, the warm humanity and the spirit of brotherhood which have always characterized Kentucky at its best.

---

1. A portion of this speech relating to poverty and repetitious of other remarks recorded in these papers has been deleted.

2. Fredrick E. Lackey (1906-), mayor of Hopkinsville (1946-1949, 1958-1966); director of the Office of Local Affairs (1966-1967); currently chairman of the Board, Hopkinsville Broadcasting Company. Information provided by Mrs. Sherry Jeffers.

GOVERNOR'S OCCUPATIONAL HEALTH CONFERENCE

Lexington / April 6, 1967

It is hard for me to realize that two whole years have passed since I last stood before this group and welcomed you to your first Occupational Health Conference. In this short period of time, many things have come to pass which make us proud to be Kentuckians and to live at a time when the betterment of our environment and the improvements of the quality of living, in all aspects of our lives, lie within our grasp. With the improvement in our educational system, our highways, our recreational facilities, our concern for civil rights, the improvement in the protection of our natural resources and our increase in industrial activity—our confidence in Kentucky's future seems well justified.

Yet, I would submit to you that this is but a beginning in the monumental task which lies ahead of us. Equal to the opportunity for betterment is the need for increasing effort and zeal on the part of all of us here in our respective fields of endeavor.

The zeal that this conference has exhibited during the brief two years of its existence, demonstrates clearly the type of effort to which I refer when I speak of a better life for Kentuckians. One can't help but be impressed by the vigor and diversity in growth which this group has experienced since its first meeting.

The role of management in occupational health will, I am sure, have received its due consideration in the progress of this meeting. The importance of management's responsibility cannot be overly stressed. One might just as aptly refer to the role of educational institutions, the role of labor or the role of government in occupational health. These are all members of a team which functions together to enhance each other's effectiveness. It is this responsibility of working together about which I would address a few remarks.

Concern for the total health of our people has been voiced by the president and the Congress and has found expression in medicare, air pollution, auto safety, and other legislation, including comprehensive health planning which has as its objective an all-out attack on disease and impairment which cripples our people and results in great economic loss. This massive attack will seek to enlist the efforts of all resources, including institutions both public and private, voluntary and official agencies, universities and hospitals, industry and labor, as well as private citizens, to work together for the comprehensive solution of health problems. I'm convinced that occupational health, whether administered voluntarily or by government, is a wave of the future. We know that work-related diseases and other physical and mental disorders are on the rise.

However, we do not know enough about what really happens to men and women who handle chemicals, asbestos, petroleum products, plastics, and glass. We do not know enough about the effects on a worker subjected to extremes of heat, cold, noise, or humidity. In all these areas we need to gather information and knowledge. Research is needed by both industry and government. Once the information is available, industry should move quickly and responsibly to correct whatever problems exist. It is when industry fails to be responsive, fails to innovate through experimentation, that industry forfeits certain rights in dealing with the health of employees, and government moves in. Industry must take the lead.

The health of the worker as influenced by the work place is superimposed upon the conditions brought on by adverse factors in the home, in the community, or those brought on by bad personal habits or natural deterioration. These are all punched on the same tape, so to speak, each contributing to the ultimate impairment or breakdown of the individual.

The mere fact of the broad participation of the various disciplines represented here attests to the awareness of the need for a variety of efforts to protect the health of the worker at the work place. No less important is the integration of these efforts with those in the home and in the community. As I have mentioned to you before, the cost of illness is a great drain upon our economy and, along with poor housing, ignorance, and poverty, constitutes a blight upon our society. I would hope that from groups such as this would continue to come the leadership for attacking not only those health problems which are occupational in nature, but the much broader problems which engulf our communities, our large metropolitan areas, and even beyond. Polluted water and air, unnecessary accidents, and waste disposal constitute some of these problems. It is not my intent to change in any way the primary purpose of this group but merely to indicate the broader context within which the deliberations of this meeting fit.

Another fact of which I am ever reminded, is the forfeiture of private or local determination by failure to carry out our responsibilities on a voluntary basis. I have no doubt that if occupational health problems, like other problems, are not solved voluntarily or through the action of local or state government, federal laws will eventually be enacted to extend federal control of health in the work place.

I hope that we as private citizens, as members of management, or as persons in any position of influence may assume the initiative in meeting our respective responsibilities in general and those of occupational health in particular. It is with much gratification and pride that I have been able to briefly address you at this the Third Occupational Health Conference. May I wish you more of the same success which has been evident from your first meeting. The continuation of your efforts should provide inspiration to other groups seeking to improve the quality of life in Kentucky.

MEDICAL CENTER DEDICATION
Inez / April 22, 1967

NEARLY three years ago we undertook in Martin County one of the most extensive health projects ever attempted in the United States. We marshaled and directed every facility at our command toward the eradication of tuberculosis in Inez and Martin County. Today I can report that while we have not totally eliminated this devastating disease from this county, we do have the disease under control, and I believe in time this county will be free of tuberculosis.

As a result of the efforts of the past two years, 1,200 tubercular victims in Martin County are now receiving treatment and another 200 will soon begin receiving treatment. This 14 percent of this county's population would have been a dreadful loss, had we not begun the extensive attack against tuberculosis here nearly three years ago. I can promise you that we at the state level will continue the battle until this county is as nearly free of this disease as humanly possible.

The problem developing here with tuberculosis came to our attention in 1964. I called together the state Tuberculosis Association, the state TB Hospital Commission, the division of Community Medicine of the University of Kentucky Medical Center, and the state Health Department in order to combine their facilities toward control and eradication of tuberculosis here.

This project, begun in 1964, screened and tested this county's entire population of 10,000—first time such a project had ever been attempted in the United States. This was a pilot project. Our success here will determine the future of similar projects for other counties in Kentucky—those which are directed toward eliminating diseases which cripple and devastate entire communities. And, I might add, such a project need not be confined against tuberculosis. Our success here can be extended to other diseases of a community nature. We must and we shall extend our attack against disease using modern techniques and a "total effort" approach. We have made great gains in the field of health, and we shall make more, because we are increasing our capabilities against disease month by month and year by year.

However, we are not here today solely to take note of the effective attack against tuberculosis. We are here to dedicate health facilities which were also part of a goal we set out to accomplish nearly three years ago—facilities which will go far toward the control of tuberculosis and other health problems of this community.

These facilities are an example of what can be accomplished when we at the state, federal, and local levels join in partnership in a common cause. These facilities are a fine tribute to the local leadership here and would not be possible had this project not received the support of the Martin County Development Association and more than $9,000 in local money. We provided an equal amount of state money for expansion of the health department building here and we obtained more than $18,000 under the Hill-Burton Act.

Perhaps as noteworthy as any of your accomplishments is the enlistment of Dr. Ray Wells, who has agreed to share the burden of medical service here which has been shouldered so ably for so many years by Dr. John Ford.[1] I know Dr. Ford has for many years looked forward to this day.

The good working quarters you have provided these physicians show that you do care about health services and are doing something to provide them. We in state government will continue to provide all assistance at our command—and I invite you to seek assistance from the Department of Health and each other appropriate state agency.

Martin County can in time benefit from another pilot health project. That one is being conducted in Leslie County by the Kentucky Department of Health under a federal grant. Our state health officials have discovered health problems which are believed to be extensive throughout eastern Kentucky and have developed economically feasible programs which will lead toward a better health program in rural areas. These programs, like the tuberculosis program conducted here, first seek out the disease, determine the cause, and then attack the disease through both treatment and prevention. I believe you here in Martin County will soon either directly or indirectly benefit from these and other health programs now being tested.

I want you to know that we in state government are as concerned over and motivated toward solving health problems, both physical and mental, as much so as any other problem facing our state. It is from such concern that we have continued to increase state appropriations to meet public health needs. For 1956-57, the state legislature appropriated from the General Fund $2,994,000 for the Department of Health and $6,845,000 for mental health services. Ten years later, 1966-67, the state legislature at my request appropriated $7 million for the Department of Health and $17,800,000 for mental health purposes. These are substantial increases in a ten-year period, and I believe the next legislature will be equally far-sighted.

We have not solved all our health problems and never shall unless we continue to press the attack. We must continue the attack and win the battle because good health is the first essential for a prosperous and happy people.

---

1. Raymond Douglas Wells (1940-), born in Auxier, Kentucky; B.A. University of Kentucky (1962); M.D. (1965); medical practice in Inez, Kentucky (1967-); president, University of Kentucky College of Medicine Alumni Association (1969-1974); president, Martin County Medical Society (1978-). Telephone interview, March 8, 1981. John Ford (1897-1978), born in St. Augustine, Pennsylvania; M.D., College of Physicians and Surgeons, St. Louis, Missouri (1920); medical practice in various east Kentucky and Tennessee communities (1920-1946); medical practice in Inez (1946-1978). Information provided by Mrs. John Ford.

MOSQUITO CONTROL CONFERENCE
Madisonville / May 16, 1967

WE have called this conference today for the purpose of exploring means on how all of us can step up the fight against the mosquito in western Kentucky. This conference is important not only because the mosquito is a pest for the children who play outdoors, for the farmer who works in the field, for our livestock and for the man who labors outside, but it is also important to the economic future of this area. For if we do not take proper actions and tackle this problem in a manner whereby we can be successful, it will grow and grow and grow. We must not let the mosquito menace get so bad that it affects the economic growth of this area. I speak not only of the adverse effect it can have on tourism that pumps millions of dollars into the economy of this area, but also of industrial growth itself. I am thankful we have not reached this point yet. More and more tourists are coming to western Kentucky, and you, better than anyone, know our industrial growth story.

With our abundance of natural beauty in Kentucky—the lakes and the streams, our forests and our land, with the finest state park system in the nation, we have so much to offer people who come to our state. Just as we conserve and protect our natural resources, we also must protect those who want to enjoy the beauty of our state. Camping has become the fastest growing aspect of all tourism. More and more Americans want to camp out. If we are going to take full advantage of this dollar potential, we must continue to make camping comfortable for anyone who comes to Kentucky and desires to live and sleep outdoors.

But even more important is the comfort of the residents of this area. It is sad indeed when children cannot play outdoors for fear of being tormented by mosquitoes. It is sad indeed when livestock die because mosquitoes suffocate them. It is sad indeed when the farmer can't comfortably plow and sow his fields.

The state of Kentucky has now for a number of years been spending a rather large sum of money each year in this area for the sole purpose of spraying mosquitoes. This year alone we've budgeted $79,000 and just recently I signed an emergency grant which allocated $10,000 more to provide additional equipment, chemicals, and personnel. Not only has the Commonwealth been spraying, but even here in Hopkins County your fiscal court, under the leadership of Judge Reid, has purchased an airplane so that the county itself can help out with this problem.[1] We at Frankfort appreciate this local initiative and assistance.

But spraying is not a long-term solution. Its poison lasts only a short time. And some of you probably believe these giant salt marsh mosquitoes just get bigger off the spray. I will not argue with you. What I am trying to say, and I'm sure you agree with me, is that spraying is not the final answer, that we must seek ways to eliminate the mosquito over the long period.

We have at this conference today every level of government represented—federal, state, and local. We've also brought in an expert from another state—Mr. Glenn Stokes, who directs the Jefferson Parish Mosquito Control District in Louisiana.[2] We have asked Mr. Stokes to come to this conference and tell us how they handle similar mosquito problems in his home state. Representing the Tennessee Valley Authority is Mr. G.S. Christopher, who is chief of its Reservoir Ecology Branch, and speaking for the U.S. Public Health Service will be Clyde Fehn, sanitary engineer director of the service's Communicable Disease Center at Atlanta.[3] Also on hand are officials from the Department of Agriculture and the Department of Health at Frankfort.

This is the first time to my knowledge that such a group has been drawn together in western Kentucky for the single purpose of tackling this problem. I do not know what the results will be—we cannot wave a magician's wand and eliminate the problem—but I am hopeful that we will be able to come up with some concrete plans that will lead to long-term solutions. Of one thing I am certain. Your local governments cannot solve the problem by themselves. Neither can Frankfort. Nor can our federal government. All of us at every level must work together to come up with the answers, and that is the primary purpose for this conference.

All of us have a stake in the solution—from those of you who face the problem locally, to those of us who hear about it at Frankfort and have the responsibility of helping Kentuckians, to the federal government which has such a large investment in western Kentucky. I have told you, and you can see by looking at your program, that there will be several speakers. I think they would be the first to admit that they do not have all the answers. They are here to get your ideas as well. So I am hopeful that we will be able to have a very frank and open discussion. We want to hear from you and get your thinking. Together, we can arrive at some solutions.

---

1. Charles Hubert Reid (1908-), born in Henderson County, Kentucky; owner and operator of Reid Funeral Home, Earlington, Kentucky (1929-1968); coroner and county judge, Hopkins County, Kentucky. Information provided by Mrs. Charles Reid.

2. Glenn Maurice Stokes (1938-), born Houston, Texas; B.S., University of Southwestern Louisiana (1961); M.S. University of Nebraska (1962); A.M., Harvard University (1964); director of Jefferson Parish Mosquito Control Department, New Orleans, Louisiana (1965-). Telephone interview, March 9, 1981.

3. Grigsby S. Christopher (1911-), born in Gadsden, Alabama; B.S. in engineering, Auburn University (1933); M.S. in sanitary engineering, Harvard University (1940); employed by the Tennessee Valley Authority (1947-1974); chief of Reservoir Ecology Branch (1952-1974). Telephone interview, March 11, 1981. Clyde Fredrick Fehn (1917-), born Watertown, South Dakota; B.S. in civil engineering, South Dakota State University (1940); M.S., University of Missouri (1947); Center for Disease Control, U.S. Public Health Service, Atlanta, Georgia (1942-1972). Telephone interview, March 1, 1981.

CIVIL RIGHTS

STATEMENT TO RELIGIOUS LEADERS
Frankfort / February 27, 1964

I WELCOME this opportunity to discuss civil rights with you. As ministers, rabbis, and priests you have shown your dedicated and devoted concern to the cause of human liberty through your past efforts and by your appearance here today. You and other religious leaders are to be commended for your efforts to eliminate discrimination against individual citizens. I have an important announcement to make to you. Senator Shelby Kinkead today has introduced a bill in the Senate which prohibits discrimination against individual citizens in public businesses.[1] Representative Norbert Blume and the cosponsors of his bill are supporting a committee substitute identical to the Kinkead bill.[2] This is the bill which I will support.

I am taking action at this time because it now appears that Congress will not act on civil rights during the timetable which I set out in my State of the Commonwealth message on January 7. By introducing the measure now, rather than waiting until the last fifteen days of the session, members of the legislature and the public will have more time to consider the bill. Deliberations and hearings can start at once. I am confident that Congress will pass the civil rights legislation now pending before the United States Senate, probably in April. However, I would rather Kentucky enact civil rights legislation and have the Kentucky Human Rights Commission enforce the provisions than have the federal courts implement the federal public accommodations law. Let me clarify this position by pointing out that the federal legislation has a provision which permits state enforcement of the law if the state has a public accommodations law. That is one reason why I think Kentucky should act now.

I want to commend Senator Kinkead and Representative Blume and the cosponsors of their bills for the courage and justice which they have demonstrated through the leadership they are exemplifying in their respective chambers in the field of civil rights. In the long run, the way of conviction, the way of courage, the way of sacrifice—is the only highway to lasting victory. This is a time to speak the truth, the whole truth, frankly and boldly. As governor of this great Commonwealth, I am guided by a simple formula: to do in all cases, without regard to narrow political considerations, what seems to me to be best for all the people of Kentucky.

Freedom means the supremacy of human rights everywhere, not only in the voting booth, but in public accommodations, too. To deny a man a place to sleep overnight or a place to eat is a denial of basic human dignity. My support goes to those who struggle to gain these rights. We must face the fact that in a complex and highly mobile society, property carries with it power to influence and sometimes to govern the lives and liberties of others. Private property, unregulated and unrestricted, can become both a sword of the oppression of other individuals and a shield for individual liberty. That is why Theodore Roosevelt said, as far back as 1912 when a social revolution was under way among working men, that: "We stand for man." That is why health and safety codes, minimum wages, workmen's compensation, zoning ordinances, and many other regulatory measures have restricted the rights of property whenever property has been used to injure or to degrade human beings. Therefore, I do not believe that the citizens of our state wish to turn a deaf ear to the appeal of nearly 10 percent of our citizenry who want the right to be served in establishments doing a public business.

I believe in the golden rule of doing unto others as you would have them do unto you. Discrimination against individual citizens is a moral issue which affronts the Creator and denies the basic brotherhood which we have affirmed down the centuries in the Declaration of Independence and the Constitution of the United States. The fundamental force for liberty must start in the community, where respect for human beings can make individual freedom possible. For us here, and for us in the months and years to come, the truest homage which we can pay to the fundamental beliefs of our Hebrew-Christian ethic is to exercise these teachings and principles in our communities.

It would not be the first time the church and its leaders in America played a major role in bringing about human reform. One of the most significant developments in this history of religion in our nation was the crusade in the early part of the twentieth century to improve unjust and inhumane working conditions for men, women, and children. Leaders of all faiths called for the abolition of child labor and for the protection of the worker from dangerous machinery, occupational disease, injuries, and mortality. I think the rabbis, ministers, and priests in Kentucky and all of America now have an unprecedented challenge to help a group of human beings achieve complete dignity and full freedom in the image of God. As is evidenced by your being here today, you have accepted the challenge. I challenge all others to accept the challenge.

Events in the field of civil rights have now brought you to new influence and new responsibilities. They will test your courage, your devotion to duty, your concept of morality. But I say to you and your colleagues throughout Kentucky, what we have achieved in liberty because of the fundamental principles of Hebrew-Christian teachings, we shall surpass with your help and your courage.

---

1. Shelby Kinkead (1913-), city commissioner, Lexington, Kentucky (1954-1956); mayor of Lexington (1956-1960); Kentucky state senator (1964-1968). *Who's Who in American Politics, 1971-1972,* 3rd ed. (New York, 1972).

2. Norbert Blume (1922-), Democrat from Louisville; labor representative, president of Teamster Local 783; speaker pro tem (1970), speaker of the house (1972-1974); vice chairman (1971-1974), cochairman (1975), Legislative Research Commission; elected to Kentucky House of Representatives (1964). W. Landis Jones, ed., *The Public Papers of Governor Wendell H. Ford, 1971-1974* (Lexington, Ky., 1978), p. 495.

CIVIL RIGHTS STATEMENT
Frankfort / March 20, 1964

THE fact that the General Assembly has adjourned its regular session without passing a public accommodations bill is a great personal disappointment to me and, I believe, a great defeat for the cause of human rights in Kentucky. This disappointment and this appraisal of the severity of our loss is apparently shared by many other citizens throughout the Commonwealth. I have received a large number of letters and telegrams during the last two or three days requesting that I call a special session of the General Assembly immediately for the purpose of considering public accommodations measures further.

I believe that both houses of the Assembly have made clear their opposition to legislation of this type, and I do not believe that they would be likely to change their positions over the weekend. In my opinion, a special session at this time would only be a financial burden to the state and would move us no closer to the goal we seek of equal rights for all our citizens.

We have not given up our fight, however. We are simply moving it outside the legislative halls for the time being, and I pledge that this administration will continue to exert all efforts to gain the success that simple morality and the promise of democracy decree must be won.

Prospects are good that a federal civil rights bill will be enacted within the next few weeks. When that bill is enacted, I will call the entire membership of the General Assembly, as a group, into conference, and together we will discuss the subject of a public accommodations law. I will try again to persuade them of the necessity of such a law, and I will at this time evaluate the possible success of a special session as I seek support from each member. If, in my judgment, a special session would likely result in the passage of a bill that would effectively outlaw discrimination in places serving the public, I will call the Assembly into session immediately. I hope that the federal bill is passed soon. I hope that members of the legislature will then choose to put Kentucky law on the side of equality for all our citizens.

To those dedicated persons who have fought the fight for equality during this session of the General Assembly—including those who chose to suffer physical pain and deprivation as a demonstration of their beliefs—I commend you for your conduct and your sincerity. To you I reaffirm my pledge of a continued fight and repeat a thought that I expressed last week that no just cause is ever permanently defeated and no question is ever settled until it is settled right. To Shelby Kinkead, to Norbert Blume, to those Kentuckians who have waited out this fight, whether in their homes or in the halls and galleries of the General Assembly, I say, "Keep up your courage. We shall overcome."

MAYORS CONFERENCE
Frankfort / May 15, 1964

IT is a high honor to welcome the leaders of so many of Kentucky's cities to the state Capitol on this significant occasion.[1] I echo Mayor Flynn's words of hospitality and assure you we will do all that is within our power to make your day in Frankfort a pleasant one.[2] I hope that our session this morning may result in greater understanding of one of the greatest problems to trouble our nation during this generation and that because of this meeting many of the communities in Kentucky will be better able to work toward its solution.

The whole issue of assuring equal treatment and equal opportunities for all Americans is one that is causing great concern throughout our nation today and is requiring the time and energy of many of our national and state leaders and hundreds of thousands of our citizens. The right of each individual citizen to make his place in the world unhampered by restrictions based upon race, color, or religious belief and his right to maintain dignity as he seeks his place have been affirmed and reaffirmed through the years in such documents as the Declaration of Independence and the Constitution of the United States and should by now, in this one hundred and eighty-eighth year of our independence, be firmly established and unquestioned.

Yet today we find the Senate of the United States locked in a battle over civil rights that paralyzes it to act on any other bills, a battle that will preclude the passage of much other important legislation this session. Today we find similar deliberative bodies representing many of our cities and states tied up over measures that would not have been necessary if our earlier promises of equality for all persons had been kept. Today we find the law enforcement agencies of many of our states and cities tied down by the threat of demonstrations both for and against the rights that our founding fathers proclaimed for us many years ago.

And we still find meetings such as this to be necessary—meetings which take the energy and the time that you and I as leaders of the people of Kentucky could be devoting to other endeavors to advance the welfare of our state. This dissipation of our talent and capabilities, our time and energy, our emotional strength, and our material and human resources is a national shame and a perversion of our national purpose.

It is an irony of our time that we will probably have some Americans exploring the surface of the moon while other Americans are still engaged in petty argument over who sits next to them to drink a cup of coffee at a drugstore lunch counter. I say to you, let us here in Kentucky get on with the job of providing basic rights to all our people. Let us solve this problem of human rights now and not let the fretting and the fighting continue to sap the vitality of this great state. Let us be done with the problems of prejudice and bigotry and get on with the other problems that face us. Let us complete this chapter of our development and move on to the next.

This morning we are going to exchange information and ideas relating to the role of our cities in promoting human rights, and our discussion is going to center mainly on the rights of individuals to be served in places doing business with the public. It is my firm belief that no citizen should be denied service as long as he is orderly, law-abiding, and able to pay for the goods or services he seeks. This principle is becoming more and more firmly established in Kentucky, and I hope we can soon make it universal.

Let me assure you right now that this meeting has not been called to shift the responsibility of the state in the field of public accommodations to the cities. I still plan to seek legislative action on this matter and still plan to meet with members of the legislature, as soon as the federal civil rights bill is passed, to discuss the possibility of a special session.

But I believe there is much the cities can do and, with most of our larger cities represented here today, any progress we make will benefit a large portion of our population. It would be ideal if we could persuade places that serve the public to open their doors to all persons voluntarily and not have to resort to laws. We will discuss ways to get voluntary compliance, but we will also discuss the legal abilities of cities to pass public accommodations ordinances. A number of cities throughout Kentucky have formed human rights commissions. We will hear from some of them this morning and learn how their commissions have served to improve relations among their citizens. We will also hear from the state Human Rights Commission, a group that helped to set up this meeting and a group that has been of great help to me and to Governor Combs. The state commission has services that are available to all municipalities and can probably help make your jobs a little easier.

I know that you are wondering how the federal civil rights law will affect you and your cities, as it is now written, and how a possible state law would be administered under the federal law and under local ordinances. This, too, will be discussed.

I hope that our meeting today will be conducted and participated in in a spirit of cooperativeness, understanding, and charity—that our discussions will be motivated and guided only by what is good for Kentucky, what is good for our neighbors who look to us for leadership—what is the right thing to do.

I received this week a proclamation on the subject of civil rights written and adopted by the eighth grade class of Christ the King School in Louisville. I would like to quote briefly from it because I think it points out to us our responsibility as leaders as seen by those who will some day follow us in leadership. The proclamation asks for federal civil rights legislation and then says, "We are teenagers who will build America in the future and we deserve freedom from color discrimination. Therefore, we think the present generation should act more sensibly in building our future America."

Let us as leaders not stand accused of not acting "sensibly" in building a strong Kentucky and a strong America. Let us, for the sake of your children and mine, help free them from color discrimination. Let us, for the sake of your children and mine, help free them from the prejudices that have so long plagued us. Let us resolve that they will be free from the bigotry that has so long been our burden.

---

1. The mayors of Kentucky's ninety-four first, second, third, and fourth class cities were invited to Frankfort to discuss civil rights issues. Forty-two mayors attended. The only tangible outcome was a unanimous call for the legislature to pass a civil rights bill regardless of action in Congress. *Louisville Courier-Journal,* May 16, 1964.

2. James Walter Flynn (1925-), born in Frankfort, Kentucky; operator of Packard Automobile Agency, Frankfort (1946-1950); mayor of Frankfort (1962-1968); state adjutant, Kentucky Veterans of Foreign Wars (1969-1973); owner and operator of the Statesman Restaurant, Frankfort. Telephone interview, March 4, 1981.

CONFERENCE ON HUMAN RIGHTS
Louisville / December 16, 1965

IT is a pleasure for me to meet with you tonight and to appear on the same program with Dr. Martin Luther King and so many distinguished leaders in the human rights movement.[1] This meeting climaxes a conference in which the participants, persons representing various occupations and interests from across the state, have been discussing ways of creating and mobilizing support for Kentucky civil rights legislation. You are to be commended for the efforts which you have made and the concern which you have expressed in coming to this meeting.

I come to this meeting because I share your concern. I, too, want to see strong civil rights legislation enacted by the General Assembly this year and, as I have stated previously, I shall put back of this bill every ounce of strength and leadership which I possess. This I pledge.

The issue of civil rights in Kentucky is a moral issue. It is the issue of justice and opportunity for all persons regardless of race, color, religion, or ethnic origin. This issue is as old as the golden rule and as explicit as the Constitution of the United States of America. The hopes and aspirations of a democratic society, with men of good will working together for the common good, will not be achieved until a moral confrontation on the issue of discrimination results in equal rights and opportunities for all Americans, and for all Kentuckians.

We Kentuckians must do our part in bringing about this moral confrontation with unreasonable and irrational discrimination. Every citizen in Kentucky should assume the responsibility of working, and working hard, in the pursuit of the goal of equality of opportunity and the protection of basic human rights. This effort should be made by all citizens, not because of the promise of economic reward or the threat of demonstrations or unrest, but simply because it is right and just that the principle of equality be pursued.

The recent demands of the Negro mass movement in America, the demands of justice, and the demands of morality have produced a federal civil rights law. The civil rights law, passed by Congress in 1964, was the strongest national proclamation of equality for the Negro since the days of Reconstruction, ninety years ago. The 1964 civil rights law was a vital legislative achievement, but it must be recognized that weaknesses were inherent in its coverage and in its implementation procedures. There is much that the state can and must do.

The federal Civil Rights Act emphasizes that its enforcement should be through state agencies which function under state laws compatible with federal statute. The Civil Rights Act in effect says to the state: if you will meet your responsibility to all citizens of your state, then there will be no need for federal officials to come into the state. We plan to meet this responsibility, because it is the job of state government to move, and to move effectively, against the evils of discrimination. State government has a practical and moral responsibility to safeguard the rights and opportunities of all citizens. The late President John Kennedy, in a televised speech to the nation in 1963, commented on this responsibility, saying: "It is time to act in Congress, in the state and local legislative bodies, and above all, in all of our daily lives."

In accord with the state's responsibility which I have outlined, a Kentucky civil rights bill will be introduced early and considered for passage in the 1966 General Assembly. The aim of this legislation is the utilization of the state's efforts and resources in the defense of its citizens from the forces of prejudice and discrimination. This I must do personally because of the moral rightness of the position and because I have a responsibility, as governor, to all the citizens of this Commonwealth.

In general, the Kentucky civil rights act will cover the vital areas of public accommodations and employment, while enabling the Kentucky Commission on Human Rights to bring about compliance through persuasion, where possible, and court enforcement where necessary. We are fortunate to have this commission, which was created in 1960, for it can and should be utilized as a means of protecting citizens from the brutality and degradation of discrimination.

In the area of public accommodations, our state needs to insure, by legislative action, the right of any citizen, regardless of race, to utilize the services of accommodations which are advertised to the public, are dependent upon the public for trade, and are regulated by public license or regulation or supported by government funds. In the 1966 General Assembly, a Kentucky civil rights act will be introduced to cover public accommodations, to prohibit racial discrimination in the services offered by all businesses open to the public.

The coverage of the federal law does not apply to many facilities, such as amusement parks, laundromats, golf courses, or other places of active amusement. The state Commission on Human Rights reports to me that it has encountered discrimination in several types of facilities not covered by the federal law. If a law is to be fair, it should provide uniform coverage. It should apply to all equally. Our legislative proposal would provide the full protection which the state owes to its citizens and would prove to be fairer to Kentucky's businessmen because of its uniform coverage.

The problem of employment discrimination is of great concern to me. Those who do not have a job or those who do not have a good-paying job cannot use many of the places of public accommodation which are now open and will be opened to them. All men want to engage in meaningful work. All men want to help produce the goods and services which our society needs, and all men want to share in the wealth of our great American society. All men have the right to have an opportunity to work and to share in the benefits of American society. The employment section of the Kentucky civil rights act would place all employees and potential employees on an equal basis. Each person would be hired, paid, and promoted on the basis of his individual merit.

The Kentucky Negro, with equal access to job training programs, with the possibility of achieving positions of employment which were previously beyond his reach, and with protection from discrimination in the regular upgrading and promotion process based on merit, can reach a higher earning potential. This higher earning potential can go far in helping to eliminate the degradation of the Negro male, who has often been trapped in employment in a stereotyped, menial, "traditional" situation. We seek to eliminate this degradation by providing legal protection allowing equal access to nonskilled, semiskilled, and skilled positions of employment which, even under the federal civil rights law, are not yet available to Negroes in our own state.

The federal government has only taken a first step in nondiscrimination in employment and leaves much responsibility to the state in this area. Under the federal civil rights law, which will not be fully effective until 1968, over 40 percent, or more than two hundred thousand Kentucky employees will be working in firms not covered by federal nondiscrimination regulations.

We seek to assume the role of responsibility in Kentucky by passing a fair employment practice law with a coverage of significant employers, expanding the limited federal coverage in Kentucky, and providing that the Commission on Human Rights utilize negotiation, conciliation, and court enforcement in the very rare situations where that is needed. As in the case of public accommodations, implementation of the employment law at the state level would prove more feasible than utilizing the enforcement provisions of the federal law.

Under the provisions of the federal Civil Rights Act, if conciliation of a complaint of discrimination is unsuccessful, the aggrieved individual must, in most cases, bring his own federal court suit. We believe that it is unjust for this person to carry the whole burden of ending discrimination. Quite often the person discriminated against does not have the wherewithal to fight discrimination against himself. We believe the state has a responsibility to protect the well-being of all its citizens.

I have briefly summarized the coverage and details of the proposed civil rights legislation. In this legislative effort I ask the nonpartisan support of all Kentuckians, for the issue of civil rights is not a partisan issue, but a human and moral issue. I have pledged my efforts to secure its passage and I ask that you do the same. Our hoped for and badly needed state civil rights legislation will be a springboard from which equal rights and opportunities for all citizens can become a reality. In the words of our president, we have to direct our attention to "help the Negro fulfill the rights which, after the long time of injustice, he is finally able to secure; to move beyond opportunity to achievement; to shatter forever not only the barriers of law and public practice, but the walls which bound the conditions of man by the color of his skin." As Kentuckians desiring to fulfill the inherent promises of our democracy in providing "liberty and justice for all" we can do no less.[2]

---

1. Martin Luther King, Jr. (1929-1968), was the pre-eminent civil rights leader of the 1950s and 1960s. His movement was founded on the tactics of civil disobedience and on the belief that integration was necessary to achieve racial harmony. The Southern Christian Leadership Conference was founded under his leadership in 1957 to direct the struggle against racial segregation and to aid the Negro in securing his political rights. In 1964 King won the Nobel Peace Prize for his achievements. He was assassinated in Memphis, Tennessee, on April 8, 1968. *Current Biography, 1965,* pp. 220-22.

2. At a press conference on December 15, the day before this address was delivered, Governor Breathitt outlined the substance of the civil rights bill he proposed to submit to the 1966 General Assembly. Press release December 15, 1965, Civil Rights file, Breathitt papers.

CIVIL RIGHTS BILL SIGNING
Frankfort / January 27, 1966

FOR me as for thousands of Kentuckians, black and white, "this is the day I oft' have sought and wept because I found it not." Here, in the shadow and beneath the shadow of the Great Emancipator, we proclaim throughout this Commonwealth and to all this nation that all of God's children are free.

We, as Kentuckians, have been challenged by the demands of justice and the principles of our spiritual heritage to carry forward the torch of freedom, equality, and democracy for all citizens. We have been challenged to fulfill the vision of Lincoln and the great unfinished task of American democracy. Equality for all men, rich men, poor men, black men, yellow men, brown men, white men—equality of acceptance, equality of the fullness of humanity—this is the great unfinished task of a free society. We, as Kentuckians, have accepted this challenge and have begun to fulfill, in reality, that "proposition that all men are created equal" by insuring, by law, that all men are treated equally.

It is entirely fitting that Kentucky should be a leader in this vital area. The General Assembly of Kentucky, in this historic legislative act, has produced the broadest and most effective civil rights law produced by any state in the spirit of the federal Civil Rights Act of 1964. Kentucky has also become the first state south of the Ohio River to pass a strong, basic civil rights law. This bill has broader coverage and more effective enforcement powers than the laws of border states and most northern states in the fields of public accomodations and employment. We hope and trust that other southern states will soon follow with legislation which will help to make the "brotherhood of man" a reality in this great nation.

This civil rights act, which I sign today, reflects the aspirations and the struggles of an oppressed people for over three centuries in America.[1] This civil rights act is a symbol of success in the struggle of the Negro in Kentucky. This civil rights act is a moral commitment kept after a hundred years of hope deferred—a promissory note long overdue. The legislators in the 1966 Kentucky General Assembly have met their responsibility in their historic and overwhelming passage of this bill. As I sign this bill, and it becomes law, it becomes the responsibility of every citizen of this Commonwealth to comply with the spirit as well as the letter of the law, and I am confident that Kentuckians will respond with the same magnificent spirit which prevailed in our legislative halls.

This is a strong bill, not a weak one. It outlaws discrimination in public accommodations and in job opportunities. It creates a Human Rights Commission endued with strength and power. But this is only a beginning. Only in the human heart can justice win the final victory. Only in the lives of individual men and women can freedom find ultimate security. We have made that beginning. Many will remember what we have done today. Let history record what we shall do in the long tomorrows where we have ". . . promises to keep, and miles to go before we sleep."[2]

---

1. Kentucky became the first southern state to enact a civil rights bill when Governor Breathitt signed the Kentucky Civil Rights Act of 1966 on January 27. While generally modeled on the federal law of 1964, the Kentucky statute was more inclusive, embracing employers of 8 or more workers as opposed to the immediate federal limit of 100 and eventual federal limit of 25. Employers were prohibited from practicing racial discrimination in hiring, in establishing conditions of employment, and in classification of employees. Labor organizations were also forbidden to discriminate in their membership policies or in practices affecting employment. In addition to equality in the workplace, the act required "full and equal enjoyment" of goods, services, and facilities in "places of public accommodation," as defined in the act. The law contained a disclaimer that no part of the act would require anyone to grant preferential treatment to any group or individual; in other words, "affirmative action" programs. The legislature established the Kentucky Commission on Human Rights to implement the act. The commission was assigned numerous powers and responsibilities: to assist the U.S. Equal Employment Opportunity Commission; to promote creation of local human rights commissions; to receive and act upon complaints of discrimination filed by individuals or groups; to create advisory agencies; and to adopt regulations necessary to enforce the act. The bill also prescribed enforcement procedures. The process began with the receipt of a complaint by an aggrieved group or individual. If the commission found the complaint justified, the first remedy was a conciliation agreement between the conflicting parties which would be monitored periodically by the commission. Should conciliation fail, the commission was empowered to hold full-scale hearings with mandatory testimony and presentation of evidence under oath. Following the hearing, the commission could issue an order to terminate any illegal practices. The commission's orders were subject to judicial enforcement and review by the circuit courts. Cities and counties were also empowered to enforce the act through the adoption of local ordinances and the creation of local human rights commissions. *Acts, 1966,* Chapter 2 (H.B. 2), pp. 43-62.

2. Following the passage of the Kentucky civil rights law Governor Breathitt was among ten prominent American citizens to receive the 1966 Russwurm Award for civil rights contributions. The awards were made by the National Newspaper Publishers Association in memory of John B. Russwurm, founder of the first Negro newspaper in the United States. The organization cited Breathitt for his leadership in passing the "strongest civil rights legislation ever passed by a state." In addition to Breathitt, the award went also to Vice President Hubert H. Humphrey, Mrs. Lyndon B. Johnson, and United States Attorney General Nicholas B. Katzenbach. Breathitt was unable to attend the awards banquet; however, he requested Paul

Oberst to accept for him. Oberst, professor and acting dean of the College of Law at the University of Kentucky, had assisted in drafting the state legislation, was a member of the state Human Rights Commission, and was one of several close associates who lent steadfast support to Breathitt in the civil rights struggle. Press release, June 24, 1966, in Civil Rights file, Breathitt papers and Breathitt interview, June 10, 1980.

LOUISVILLE AND VICINITY MINISTERS MEETING
Louisville / May 16, 1966

It is good to meet with you this morning, to talk with you about our mutual problems, our mutual hopes, our mutual difficulties. Here in Kentucky, we have been making progress, but not enough progress. The Civil Rights Act of 1966 is a major step forward in the unending struggle against racial discrimination. We have put Kentucky on record as the first state south of the Ohio River to put major civil rights legislation on the statute books.

There were those who advised us to confine the state law to a mere local mechanism for enforcing the federal law. Such a proposal would have been a fraud and a humbug, and I rejected it, just as you would have. Consequently, we have gone well beyond the federal law with reference to public accommodations, not only as to local as well as interstate commerce, but with regard to the type of establishment defined as a place of public accommodation. With respect to fair employment, we have covered the overwhelming majority of employers, as the vastly overwhelming majority of employees—90 percent.

We still have before us the job of enforcing the new legislation, of making its promises a reality in the lives and experience of our people. I pledge to you my unreserved support for the work of our Human Rights Commission and of all similar local bodies in carrying out the policies and mandates of the 1966 legislature and of the people of Kentucky.

When I signed, in the shadow of the Great Emancipator's shadow, this new law, I stated that it was not the end but only the beginning of our task. Already, with the ink scarcely dry on the 1966 legislation, we are compelled to struggle on new sectors in the war against injustice.

All of us will, I think, agree that public accommodations, desegregated schools, and many of the other guarantees afforded by our laws and our constitutions cannot come fully alive so long as millions of our fellow citizens are condemned to the ironbound, festering, soul-destroying life of the ghetto—that miserable existence which combines poverty and discrimination into a single, life-denying poison.

Unlike some other forms of discrimination, the ghetto knows no sectional or regional preferences. North, South, East, or West, it works its evil throughout our nation—and it is our job to destroy it. The destruction of the ghetto will symbolize to the revolution of human rights what the fall of the Bastille symbolized in the French Revolution.

I wish that I could tell you that I had the power, or owned the formula, to accomplish the result in a few weeks or a few months. I wish that I could tell you that some one single great act of dedication or purpose would achieve this great goal. Knowing as I do that you and all our brothers are sick to death of that terrible word "later," I must tell you that the diseases of urban life in this nation and this state will yield only to long-term treatment.

But this is no excuse to delay or to postpone our commitment. The time to start is now—and not with a token program, but with a real, long-term commitment to a massive reconstruction of urban life in this nation.

What are the essentials of such a commitment? First, the poverty program must be expanded, and expanded greatly. There will be mistakes, just as there have been mistakes in war. There will be some waste, just as there is a great deal of waste in war. But the basic elements of the program are sound. Head Start must be made available to every child who needs it, all the year round. The Youth Corps must be improved and made available to every young man and woman who needs it. This is the real heart of the battle for educational opportunity. The Community Action Program, with all its difficulties, must remain, for it seeks to make available to our disadvantaged people the greatest of all gifts—the priceless right is true citizenship.[1]

Second, the programs under the Elementary and Secondary Education Act must be refined and expanded.

Third, President Johnson's demonstration cities program must be taken off the drawing board and put into active operation on a scale which will actually bring its benefits into the reach of our urban population.[2] Here, for the first time, is a unified program which treats our slum dwellers and our city dwellers as people, not as obstacles to some federal bulldozer. It is a program which is oriented toward people rather than real estate. It is the greatest hope in more than a generation for a real and unique advance in making life livable for our urban poor. Along with our rent subsidy and teacher corps programs, it gives us a real chance to elevate the quality of urban life. Already I have written Vice President Hubert Humphrey, a former mayor himself, and Urban Affairs Secretary Robert Weaver, asking them to include Louisville in this program should it be approved by Congress.[3]

Fourth, we must also have fair housing legislation to protect our people against discrimination in the sale or rental of real estate. The recent civil rights legislation passed in 1966 by Kentucky makes it possible for cities and counties to pass fair housing ordinances. The federal Congress is considering similar legislation on the federal level—legislation which I hope will pass.

Some of you may be familiar with the recent decision of the California Supreme Court which invalidated the repeal of the California fair housing law. This decision opens up new avenues of legal action which deserve the most careful study by legal authorities. This is but a hasty summary of some of the tasks we face and some of the solutions which we may hopefully attempt. All of us must work together in carrying forward this great cause.

In concluding, let me say to you that this nation is greatly in the debt of the Negro clergy of America for the Christian dimension which they have given to the racial issue in this country. But at the same time I must warn white America that this dimension cannot be taken for granted and used as an excuse to postpone or deny the just claims of our brothers and fellow citizens. But I am confident that somehow, if we give ourselves unstintingly to the work of making justice and brotherhood a living reality, God's grace will bring us to a truer and nobler brotherhood.

---

1. The Community Action Program was designed to provide more and better welfare service for the poor through a combination of local initiative and federal aid in both rural and urban communities. The community action budget for fiscal 1965 totalled $236.7 million and grew to $775 million in fiscal 1967. The budget included national programs such as Head Start, Upward Bound, and neighborhood health centers, as well as funding for locally developed programs covering a wide range of services and human development projects. Community action agencies were established to provide local direction of the program, and the enacting legislation specified that representatives of the poor as well as the more traditional elements of community leadership be included in the agencies. In fiscal 1965, 250 agencies were formed. By fiscal 1967, the number had grown to 1,050. *Congressional Quarterly Weekly Report,* June 16, 1967, pp. 1035-37.

2. The demonstration cities program was aimed at the problems of inferior housing and deteriorating neighborhoods in the nation's cities. Unlike the urban renewal program, which tended to replace slums with expanded business districts and transportation facilities, the demonstration cities program was intended to "establish or maintain a residential character in the area" through a combination of improved housing, new community facilities, and complementary social programs. Like many of the other "Great Society" programs, it called upon local

leadership to initiate its own programs and mobilize local resources in order to receive cooperative federal assistance. *U.S. News and World Report,* February 7, 1966, pp. 55-57.

3. Robert C. Weaver (1907-), was a noted economist, educator, and author. After holding numerous posts in the federal bureaucracy, he became the first Negro cabinet officer in U.S. history when Lyndon Johnson appointed him secretary of Housing and Urban Development in 1966. *Who's Who in America, 1976-1977,* 39th ed. (Chicago, 1976).

DERBY STATEMENT
Frankfort / May 4, 1967

THE Kentucky Derby traditionally has been Kentucky's friendliest, finest hour in the eyes of people throughout the world. This year, as in the past, we plan to continue that tradition and provide the same genuine Kentucky hospitality. To citizens everywhere who enjoy racing, I extend a cordial invitation. I am confident, that despite the open housing problem in Louisville, the afternoon will be peaceful and will come off well. Kentucky has an excellent record of orderly progress in civil rights. Our Commonwealth, in 1966, enacted the most comprehensive civil rights act ever passed by any state south of the Ohio River in the history of this nation. We have, in my judgment, made excellent progress in this sensitive area.

Speaking as one who has helped substantially in advancing civil rights, I cannot believe that the cause of open housing or any other facet of civil rights could be helped by demonstrations at Churchill Downs on Saturday. People go to the Derby to watch the races. They go for a day of pleasure, merriment, food, fellowship, and good humor. They do not go there to be swayed politically or ideologically one way or the other. Demonstrations by proponents or opponents of open housing will have only an adverse effect on their respective causes and will serve no purpose.[1]

Obviously, local and state law enforcement agencies will do whatever is necessary to assure the safety and well-being of those who come to Louisville and Churchill Downs for this great occasion. We have traditionally provided state police and national guardsmen to assist local officials at the Derby. I can assure those who intend to come to Louisville and the Derby that an adequate number of law enforcement personnel will be on hand to see to it that all goes well at the Derby. I have signed the traditional annual order, at the request of Louisville Mayor Kenneth Schmied, and the officials of Churchill Downs, giving our national guardsmen and state police authority to assist local officials.[2] I have instructed General Lloyd, who commands the guard, to provide the necessary personnel to assure a peaceful afternoon and maintain law and order.[3] I also have asked Public Safety Commissioner Glenn Lovern to coordinate his assistance with General Lloyd and see to it that a sufficient number of state troopers are there to serve the same peaceful objective.[4]

---

1. The disorders which threatened to disrupt the 1967 Kentucky Derby began after the Louisville Board of Aldermen rejected an open housing ordinance for the city on April 11, 1967. For the next two weeks, Louisville's South End was racked by violence and racial turmoil as civil rights demonstrators repeatedly clashed with open housing opponents and city police. Over six hundred people were eventually arrested. The demonstrators were sponsored by the Committee on Open Housing, a Louisville civil rights organization led by such notable local figures as the Reverend W.J. Hodge, president of the Louisville chapter of the N.A.A.C.P., the Reverend A.D. Williams King, brother of Dr. Martin Luther King, and the Reverend Leo Lesser. The inability of Louisville Republican party leaders and the various government agencies which dealt with civil rights to reach agreement among themselves exacerbated the difficulties of dealing with the crisis. Finally, at a meeting on April 25, sponsored by the Louisville Urban League and attended by Mayor Kenneth Schmied, Representative William Cowger, the Board of Aldermen, and the local Human Rights Commission, the basis for a "day-to-day truce" with the open housing forces was worked out. An important element in the truce was an announcement by the city's legal offices that through the combined effects of three existing statutes the administration already possessed the authority to enforce open housing within the city. As Derby Day approached, however, members of the Open Housing Committee became suspicious that the city government was not seriously considering their demands, but rather, merely stalling to avoid disruption of the race. Therefore demonstrations were resumed and plans for disrupting the Derby itself were once again discussed. Demonstrators chanted "no housing ordinance, no Derby" as they marched through the South End once again on May 3 and 5 and through downtown Louisville on the fourth. The night before the Derby was to be run, thirty-five demonstrators were arrested for staging a sit-in at Churchill Down's ticket windows. Despite the increased activity, however, a serious rift developed among the leaders of the open housing forces. On March 4, Dr. Martin Luther King arrived in Louisville to add the power of his presence to the open housing forces. In a stormy Friday meeting, Dr. King was instrumental in convincing the more militant elements in the open housing coalition to forego plans to stage demonstrations at Churchill Downs on Saturday, the day of the race. However, when word of the decision was leaked almost immediately to the press, the issue was reopened. Only six hours before the start of the race, Dr. King finally announced that the anticipated demonstration had been cancelled "as a gesture of good faith to refute the claim that we are interested only in disruption for disruption's sake" and because the excessive publicity and predictions of violence which

preceded the proposed demonstrations made rioting a likely possibility. Instead open housing forces conducted a march through downtown Louisville. Given the uncertainty over the plans of the open housing advocates, Breathitt had ordered a large increase in the number of national guardsmen and state troopers on duty at the Derby. Duty which in normal times was considered something of a holiday became serious business. Approximately 2,500 guardsmen, state troopers, and city and county police were on hand to forestall any disruptions of the festivities. *Louisville Courier-Journal,* April 11-May 7, 1967.

2. Kenneth Albert Schmied (1911-), born in Louisville; began political career as an alderman in 1961 and later served as president of the board; elected mayor of Louisville (1965); helped establish the Louisville Commission on Human Relations; served as commissioner of the Louisville Urban Renewal and Community Development Agency. *Who's Who in the South and Southwest, 1969-1970,* 11th ed. (Chicago, 1969).

3. Arthur Young Lloyd (1908-), A.B., Western Kentucky State College (1926); M.A., Vanderbilt (1929), Ph.D. (1934); graduate, Army Command and General Staff School (1957); principal, Webster County High School (1926-1928); instructor in political science, Vanderbilt (1929-1931); associate professor of history and political science, Morehead State Teachers College (1931-1934); director of public assistance, Kentucky Department of Welfare (1936-1942); director, Legislative Research Commission of Kentucky (1948-1956); joined U.S. Army Reserve (1927); served in various capacities and retired as a major general, Army of the United States (1968); adjutant general of Kentucky (1959-1967). *Who's Who in America, 1978-1979,* 40th ed. (Chicago, 1978).

4. Glenn Lovern (1910-), city commissioner, Owensboro, Kentucky (1941-1945); mayor, Owensboro (1945-1949); city manager, Paducah, Kentucky (1953); Kentucky state welfare commissioner (1953-1955); city manager, Sidney, Ohio; Covington, Kentucky; Lexington, Kentucky (1955-1959); commissioner of public safety (1959-1967). George W. Robinson, ed., *The Public Papers of Governor Bert T. Combs, 1959-1963* (Lexington, Ky., 1979), p. 206.

CONSTITUTION REVISION

LOUISVILLE ROTARY CLUB

Louisville / May 13, 1965

KENTUCKIANS are reluctant to alter their constitution.[1] And rightly so. For these changes cannot be redone in the day-to-day decision making process, be it legislative, judicial, or executive. These changes affect the basic rights of the individual, the basic relationships of man-to-man, the basic workings of government and its ability to serve the people. But today we have reached a point where we are hobbled by an instrument loaded with nineteenth century restrictions while we prepare for the twenty-first century.

Presently, we have a real opportunity in the success of the efforts of the Constitution Revision Assembly. This assembly reflects what we have learned, or should have learned, from the recent history of constitutional revision in Kentucky.

We are moving closer to public acceptance of the necessity for revision. On three different occasions steps have been taken to call a convention. The first call in 1931 was defeated by over a three to one vote. The 1947 effort, in which I was interested as a university student, failed by 45,000. The most recent attempt, in 1960, lost by but some 17,000 votes out of 670,000 votes cast on the issue. Each time the margin of defeat has narrowed, while the number of votes cast on the question has risen.

The 1960 proposal was for a limited convention, restricted to twelve areas of the constitution. The Court of Appeals upheld this call for a limited convention, which was designed to allay some of the public apprehension of an unlimited convention.

The 1960 election taught several lessons to those of us who had participated in the effort. First, although the call was limited, the twelve areas were so broad that the people were unsure of the extent of the proposed changes. They had no proposed drafts in hand to consider and judge. And when the people are unsure they have the tendency to vote "no." The second message from 1960 is: do not involve a major constitutional effort with other controversial election issues. In 1960 too many issues were on the ballot. Everyone could not concentrate his attention on all with the same degree of intensity.

I am hopeful, however, that we have hit upon a new method of revision whereby these obstacles can be overcome. In the full glare of publicity, delegates of our present-day Constitution Revision Assembly are discussing the problems of constitutional revision and are hammering out solutions which are acceptable to the people.

The Constitution Revision Assembly is a serious and unique attempt to overcome the failings in past efforts. Foremost we must remember that the assembly is purely advisory. Its work is not binding on anyone. It is a deliberative body created for the purpose of presenting a document for consideration by the General Assembly and ultimately for ratification by the people.

The assembly is acting in the same manner as would a constitutional convention. The full assembly has met five times and will hold its sixth general session in Frankfort on May 20. The full body has organized itself into six committees, with some fifteen to twenty subcommittees working on various constitutional problems, seeking solutions. Under the law creating the assembly, a final report is due prior to the beginning of the 1966 regular session of the legislature.

The Constitution Revision Assembly is approaching the end of the first major phase of its operation—committee consideration of existing sections of the 1891 constitution and committee recommendations for changes in these sections. Public hearings on every subject matter of the charter have been held, and will continue to be held, so that the public expression can be heard. The next phase will be full assembly debate and action on the committee recommendation.

The broad outline of committee thinking is emerging. It will be a conservative approach to the modernization of Kentucky's constitution. The present constitution would be modified to meet the needs of the twentieth century, while at the same time not restricting those who will follow us. Committees, to date, have recommended deletion of sixty-four sections of the 1891 document.

The assembly has decided to take no final action on a particular section until all committee reports are before the assembly. This has resulted in an unevenness in pace and less frequent full assembly sessions. The result of the apparent slowness is not altogether negative. If nothing else, it has overcome the charge that the assembly was a rubber stamp device designed to sanction a secret document already drawn.

Committee reports thus far have contained these basic recommendations. The bill of rights will be retained as set forth in the constitution. The General Assembly will be upgraded. Appointment of the superintendent of public instruction is favored. Local units of government should be less bound by restrictions, should have more adequate means of financing their operations, and should be given more authority to govern their own affairs. A new judicial article based on a unified court system is advocated. Committees have proposed to change the election pattern in some manner so that Kentucky will not have a primary and general election each year; to remove from the constitution the statutory detail relating to corporations; to provide a more flexible method of amending the constitution; to charge the General Assembly with the duty of fixing the compensation of all public officers and employees, the present maximums having been rendered less meaningful by court decisions; to provide for an intermediate court of appeals to speed decisions of cases which now in some instances take years to decide; to staff the courts, as far as possible, with lawyers and to remove these judges from partisan politics; to reduce the number of statewide executive officers required to be elected and to permit them to serve two consecutive terms; and to lengthen the terms of members of the General Assembly and to permit extension of the biennial legislative sessions.

As I previously mentioned, the work of the assembly is not binding on anyone or on any authority. Any proposed draft must be submitted to the General Assembly and to the public. This preparation of a draft prior to a popular vote on the constitutional question is new to Kentucky. It grasps a truth which I believe has been one of the reasons for recent failures. The people are more likely to vote for the calling of the convention if they realize, generally, what type of constitution the convention will present for ratification.

The timing for presentation of the draft remains open and will be discussed by the assembly on May 20. Three avenues are possible. First, a new constitution could be proposed by way of one or two amendments. This would require passage by only one General Assembly and the vote of the people. Second, the 1966 General Assembly could re-enact the unlimited convention call passed at the last session, and a convention could be assembled to ratify a proposed constitution and then submit it to the people. A third possibility is a restricted convention, called for the purpose of considering the draft prepared by the Constitution Revision Assembly. The Court of Appeals has set the precedent for this when it upheld the limited convention call of 1960.

This last approach would require action by the June special session of the General Assembly and repassage of the call by the 1966 General Assembly. If the Constitution Revision Assembly decides that this procedure is sound, I will include it in the June call for an extraordinary session of the General Assembly.

As businessmen and leaders of our largest city, I commend you for taking an active interest in the framing of this new charter. I am confident you can help generate sufficient wisdom and enthusiasm to make a new constitution a reality.

---

1. Governor Breathitt's introductory statements, in which he thanked the Louisville business community for its past support and discussed several state-supported projects that had benefited Louisville and Jefferson County, have been deleted. This speech was Breathitt's first major statement on constitutional revision.

CONSTITUTION REVISION ASSEMBLY
Lexington / April 26, 1966

IT is entirely fitting and proper that this assembly should come here today as the guests and under the auspices of the University of Kentucky.[1] The cause of constitution revision has found sustenance, support, and spiritual nourishment on this campus and from the great minds and hearts of this faculty, in and out of season. It was here, as an undergraduate, that my own enthusiasm for this great cause first caught fire, from men like Tom Clark and Jack Reeves, one of whom has served with eminent usefulness as a member of the assembly and the other of whom has been chosen as its historian.[2]

In the work of the Constitution Revision Assembly, there has been a fruitful fusion of the worlds of thought and action, of theory and practice, which sustains and ennobles the democratic process at its best. All Kentuckians, without respect to geography, without respect to party, without respect to personal or faction loyalty, unite to do honor to the men and women, who for more than two years, have labored to fashion a modern constitution for a modern commonwealth. The work of the assembly has been stamped from the beginning by an approach which was both practical and theoretical—based upon a commendable and entirely workable desire to cling fast to those things which are proved and tested by time, while at the same time adapting old institutions to the needs and requirements of a fast changing era.

You have, for example, retained the ancient principles of our bill of rights in all their strength and vigor. Indeed, you have added to their efficacy by extending cherished protections against invasions of privacy and personal liberty in an electronic age.

You have realized, as do all those who study deeply the workings of our free institutions, that the strength of one branch is the strength of all, and that the weakness of one branch is the weakness of all. You have, I think dramatically and wisely, strengthened our legislature. In so doing, you have not weakened, but rather have strengthened the effectiveness of the executive branch—for in the long run a strong, independent, and well-equipped legislature will add to rather than subtract from the effectiveness of the governor in his leadership. Likewise your work in modernizing our judiciary and removing it from political arenas will strengthen both the legislative and executive branches, and at the same time provide additional and necessary safeguards for the liberty for the individual citizen.

It is perhaps in the area of local government that the proposals of the assembly have aroused the greatest controversy—largely, I think, because of misunderstanding. My own observations have convinced me that it is in this area that constitutional reform is most necessary and offers the greatest hope for future improvement. The issue here is whether local government can survive as a vital factor of our system of free institutions. Just as the failure of the states to meet their responsibilities has speeded the trend toward federal power, so the impenitence of local government—its lack of flexibility, its crippling by constitutional fetters—has speeded the trend toward centralization of power in the state at the expense of the local unit. I am convinced that the recommendation of this assembly would result in more home rule, not less; in greater freedom for local communities, not less; in a more workable method of adapting local institutions to changing needs.

There are those who feel that the proposed constitution will meet its death at the hands of our county officials. This I do not believe. There is nothing in the proposed revision which would threaten the legitimate interest or welfare of our county or local officials. There is nothing in the proposed constitution which would take away the right of local institutions of government to select their own officials or would give the governor a jot or title of power to appoint local officials. For the first time since 1891, sheriffs would be permitted to succeed themselves. Unworkable limitations on the salaries of local officials would be eliminated. I believe, and believe firmly, that our county officials will, if we sweep away misconceptions and misinformation and give them a clear explanation of the new charter, rally to its support. In the last analysis, what is good for the people is good for our county officials, and the courthouses belong to the people.

Once more I applaud this assembly and its members for their labors, and as a citizen I join members of both parties in commending and supporting the proposed revision. As a token of the esteem in which we hold you, I am presenting to each of you the Governor's Medal for distinguished public service. You will receive a certificate today and a medal as soon as they can all be struck. But the best evidence we of Kentucky can offer for our gratitude is to join in a vast, comprehensive, bipartisan effort to ratify this revised constitution. Thus can we do our part in completing the work you have so nobly begun. Thus can we make your contribution a part of the permanent heritage of Kentucky.

---

1. Governor Breathitt had earlier addressed the Constitution Revision Assembly in Frankfort on January 3, 1966. In that speech he noted that two-thirds of the proposed draft had been derived from the 1891 constitution and commended the assembly for its devotion to existing institutions; praised the retention of the bill of rights; paid tribute to the spirit of unity that characterized the assembly's work; and praised the work of former Governor Earle Clements as chairman of the assembly. This speech is not included in these papers.

2. Thomas D. Clark (1903-), notable Kentucky historian; A.B., University of Mississippi (1928); Ph.D., Duke University (1932); faculty member, University of Kentucky (1931-1968); Hallman professor (1965-1968); head of department (1942-1965); distinguished professor of history, Indiana University (1968-1973); distinguished professor, Eastern Kentucky University (1973-); author of numerous books on the American South. *Who's Who in America, 1976-1977,* 39th ed. (Chicago, 1976). John Estill Reeves (1902-1978), A.B., University of Kentucky (1926); M.A. (1938); research associate, Kentucky Legislative Council (1937-1938); executive assistant, Kentucky Department of Revenue (1944-1945); delegate, Kentucky Constitutional Revision Assembly (1964-1966); faculty member in political science, University of Kentucky (1940-1968); author of several works on Kentucky government. *Who's Who in American Politics, 1971-1972,* 3rd ed. (New York, 1972).

STATE CONVENTION OF COUNTY MAGISTRATES AND COMMISSIONERS
Prestonsburg / July 28, 1966

I AM pleased to meet with you at this time, this time of challenge and of opportunity for all Kentuckians. It is particularly a time of challenge and of opportunity for those who hold positions of responsibility. And each of you has held, or is holding, such a position, a position more vital perhaps than those at other levels of government. For no one is closer to the people, more cognizant of their hopes, their desires, their ambitions, and their wants.

We meet at a great period in the development of Kentucky and of the nation. We have achieved new goals together through cooperation. We have been able to set even higher goals. These in turn can be achieved through cooperation, through mutual understanding, through coordination of efforts. They will not be achieved if we dissipate our efforts and resources; if we do not devise and utilize methods to release the creative energies of talent at all levels of government and in every community.

We hear much of "dynamic federalism"; that our system of government will not work unless every unit of government properly works. This I believe is true. Our duty, yours and mine, is to further a dynamic Kentucky to the end that every Kentuckian can be protected in his rights, freed from his wants, and can advance in his own ambitions.

In the last few years, we have been a dynamic Kentucky. We have achieved new goals in education, in social advancement, in economic growth. One of the basic factors necessary to the future advancement is the strengthening of each unit of government. Government is merely the vehicle which gives expression to the desires of the people. The degree to which the talents of government are stifled becomes the measure in which the talents of the people, the individual, are stifled.

On November 8 the people of Kentucky will make a basic decision with respect to permitting local government to become a more vital partner in the emerging new Kentucky. I speak, of course, of the vote on the proposed revision of the constitution. There are provisions of our present constitution which stand in the way of a vital partnership of government, which stand in the way of an efficient utilization of resources and talent to meet the people's desires.

Recognition of constitutional deficiencies is not new. As early as 1924 a really great survey of Kentucky government stressed the need for constitutional revision. On three different occasions in the past, the General Assembly has taken the necessary steps to permit the question to be voted on by the people. The fourth opportunity will come on November 8, as a result of action taken by the 1964 and 1966 General Assemblies.

This present effort was not taken in the dark. It resulted from lessons taken from the past. The votes in 1931, 1947, and 1960 revealed an ever increasing participation by the voters on the question of constitutional revision and an ever increasing proportion of voters in favor of the revision. The 1960 election indicated the advisibility of having the question of revision stand on its own merits, of not having it run with a presidential race, a governor's race, and a bond issue.

The 1966 proposed revision was written by a group of fifty prominent Kentuckians, men and women, Republicans and Democrats, former governors and present senators, lawyers and nonlawyers, businessmen, farmers, educators, and county and city leaders. It was written and debated in the open. All interested parties were invited to, and did, present their views. It was debated in the General Assembly and amended as a result of that fruitful debate.

The 1966 revision has twenty-two years, a generation of effort, behind it, dating from the first action taken by the 1944 General Assembly. It covers the work of the Constitution Review Commission created in 1948 and the work of the Legislative Research Commission since 1958. That the effort has required a generation is not surprising. It fits markedly the pattern of 1891 which was first attempted to be revised in 1877. It fits the pattern of 1850 which was first attempted to be revised in 1837.

The 1966 revision seeks to do several things to permit the talents of 1966 to be exercised within the context of twentieth century Kentucky. First, it retains the workable features of the present constitution, 75 percent of the proposed constitution is the old constitution. Obsolete features peculiar to the 1890s have been deleted—for instance, corporation law has been removed.

The basic guarantees of a free people, of the worth of the individual, are retained in the bill of rights. The guarantees of 1792, 1850, 1891 were not changed at all. They were added to by provisions covering the rights of accused, of witnesses; and the freedom from the invasion of privacy by modern devices.

Another primary consideration was to remove the imbalance in Kentucky's governmental structure; to strengthen the legislature, to unify the court system, and particularly to strengthen local government.

I hope that every one of you—and every Kentuckian—will study the proposed constitution from the standpoint of what is good for Kentucky. To paraphrase the words of President Kennedy, "Ask not what the new constitution can do for you, but what it can do for your Commonwealth."

You here are interested primarily in county government and in the judiciary. Most of you are, either in fact or in legal power, judges; and almost all of you sit upon your local governing bodies.

The judicial article in the revised constitution makes substantial changes in our court structure. So-called inferior courts are consolidated into a district court, which is a constitutional tribunal, headed by a lawyer, but elected by the people. However, unlike the 1891 constitution, the new charter permits the legislature to create new and additional courts if the necessity should arise.

There has been a persistent series of misrepresentations directed against the local government articles of the new constitution. In the beginning, these misstatements were based on lack of information. Time after time these errors have been pointed out. But the misstatements continue. Kentuckians must, therefore, be entitled to wonder whether there is under way a deliberate campaign of untruth sponsored by a small group of men who are thinking only of selfish interest rather than the interest of our children and grandchildren.

The proposed charter gives to local units of government a greater and not a lesser degree of local control than that granted by the 1891 constitution. Local units of government, under the 1966 charter, would be authorized to do all things under home rule which are not specifically denied either by the constitution or by law. Counties may be consolidated, and cities and counties may be consolidated with each other, but only after a vote of the people in the counties affected. Local units of government may adopt any democratic form of government agreeable to their own people. Surely these provisions are progressive, democratic, and flexible, suited to the needs of an increasingly urban era.

Now, let me assure you that there are certain things which the proposed constitution does not do. It does not permit local officials to be appointed by the governor or by anyone else in Frankfort. It specifically guarantees that the chief executive and the legislative body of every city, county, or other local unit of government must be elected by the local voters and by no one else. All local officers must be chosen by local authority—not in Frankfort.

It is true that the proposed constitution does not, as does the 1891 constitution, spell out the title of every local officer and make him a constitutional officer. The present constitutional offices are kept inviolate for the present term and for one additional term. Beyond that, it was felt that changing times and changing circumstances might create a situation where some change in existing county offices would prove wise or necessary—but such a change would only come if the people wanted it. The new constitution preserves and strengthens the liberty of the citizen under our precious bill of rights. The new constitution upgrades and strengthens the legislature as a truly independent branch of government. The new constitution takes our schools out of partisan politics. The new constitution makes it possible for our urban areas to have flexible, responsible, economical government. The new constitution is a bipartisan charter for twentieth century government, without a trace of selfishness. It deserves your support and mine.[1]

---

1. Governor Breathitt made essentially the same speech at Murray State University on August 3, 1966. He added: "The new constitution will save property owners millions of dollars in taxes. For example, we have in Kentucky today approximately $210 million worth of outstanding school bonds at the local level on which taxpayers are paying interest. In addition, county governments have more than $20 million in bonded indebtedness on which they are paying. Because of the antiquated provisions of the present constitution, interest rates are higher on these school and county bonds than they would be under the proposed constitution. Through revision, through adoption of this new constitution, millions and millions of property tax dollars can be saved by lower interest rates. Still another unnecessary cost to government and the taxpayers is the annual elections in Kentucky. Under the proposed constitution, elections would be held only every two years, thus eliminating the costly operation of holding elections each year. This provision alone would save the taxpayers $2 million during a six-year cycle." This speech is not included in these papers.

UNIVERSITY OF LOUISVILLE
Louisville / August 11, 1966

RECENTLY, we are hearing a lot of discussion about the proposed revision to the Constitution of Kentucky. I want to spend a short time outlining for you the more important contrasts and similarities between the old constitution and the new revision. Before doing so, I want to tell you why you will be called on to express your choice at the polls.

The Constitution Revision Assembly was created by the General Assembly—the people's elected representatives. Every living former governor was made a delegate—Republicans and Democrats alike. The remaining delegates were chosen by an appointing authority representing all three branches of state government—legislative, executive, and judicial. . . .[1]

The assembly, without any power except the moral weight of its recommendations, submitted its proposals to the 1966 legislature. That legislature, on a strictly nonpartisan basis, voted to submit the revised constitution to the original source of all power—the people.

As an individual, the most direct way the constitution will touch and concern you is in its personal guarantees of freedom. The bill of rights, the twenty-five basic guarantees of your individual freedom and dignity which have been preserved through Kentucky's first four constitutions, have been incorporated into the revision word for word. For the first time, three additional guarantees have been added to the bill of rights which are not found in the 1891 constitution. The first is the right for anyone to waive indictment. This will speed up trials in criminal cases by allowing the accused to forego indictment by grand jury and go directly to trial. The second is freedom from imprisonment as a material witness. This will prevent the shameful practice of jailing someone who has witnessed but has not committed a crime. The final freedom added to the bill of rights is the freedom from interception of communication. The privacy of each and every citizen will be henceforth protected from snooping and electronic bugging.

Two other guarantees of your freedom from oppression are found in the revision. For the first time, you will be guaranteed an appeal in every law case. You are also protected from administrative action by the government without due process of law. These two legal guarantees together with the additions to the bill of rights will be your insurance that Kentucky will never lose sight of the principle that the citizen must come before the state.

Between the old and the new constitution, the most obvious change is in the length of the new document. The 1891 version has been simplified and culled down from 21,000 to 13,000 words. This should appeal to every nonlawyer in this group. A constitution, after all, should be a basic structure from which to build our laws and government. It must not forever bind us to doing things the way they were done in 1891. Under the old constitution, for example, all state aid for higher education is prohibited except for "maintenance of the Agricultural and Mechanical College." In other words, so far as the present charter is concerned, there is only one institution of higher learning in the Commonwealth—one that no longer exists. This is only one example of the many detailed provisions of the old constitution which are no longer relevant today and which in fact impede progress in this state.

Under the old constitution, the legislature, which should be the strong third branch of government, is much less effective than it should be. It now meets for only about three months out of every twenty-four. In the 1966 General Assembly, your senators and representatives were confronted with 1,142 different bills and resolutions, some as lengthy as 268 pages. It was impossible for them to give the careful, orderly consideration to proposals which is essential to the enactment of better laws for the Commonwealth. The revision will correct this situation to provide for sessions every year. The General Assembly will be a continuing body. Certain committees will be empowered to meet at times other than when the legislature is in session.

The result will be to put state government on an orderly, annual basis. For example, it will no longer be necessary to budget two and a half years in advance of unforeseen events. And the state will be better equipped to take advantage of desirable federal programs. The new constitution will thus give the legislature the opportunity to perform the role for which it exists—to enact better laws for Kentucky.

Another provision in the revision will also strengthen the legislature by giving each house more continuity and competence. Terms of members of the house of representatives will be lengthened to four years, with elections of one half of the members every two years. Terms of senators will be increased to six years. This will soon give Kentucky a more experienced, better-equipped group of lawmakers, and will insure balance of powers in our government.

The new constitution will save Kentuckians millions of dollars in interest on local indebtedness. Under the 1891 constitution, cities, counties, and local school districts are tightly limited in the amount of general obligation bonds which they are allowed to sell. This limitation does not in fact restrict the issuance of bonds, but it does cause higher rates of interest which increase your tax burden.

The new constitution allows local units to borrow money at lower interest rates. This saving will be passed on to you, the local taxpayer in reduced taxes. This new provision, like others, will help insure that local governments in Kentucky will make progress because of the constitution, not in spite of it.

As for the executive department of state government, the new document makes the changes required by new conditions. The executive would be greatly simplified, at least so far as constitutional requirements are concerned. The offices which would still be elective under the new constitution are those of governor, lieutenant governor, attorney general, and auditor of public accounts.

Those local officers who are presently allowed to succeed themselves in office may continue to do so under the new constitution. The General Assembly will be empowered to alter the structure and functioning of the executive branch to meet the changing needs of good government—and this is the most important general effect of the revision in this area: it will allow the executive branch to adapt readily to the needs of the time.

In the field of education, the new document provides a framework for education which will allow Kentucky to make tremendous strides in the training of our young people. The office of superintendent of public instruction will be placed beyond the grasp of factional politics. Instead of the elected superintendent of public instruction which the present constitution requires, the new document provides for the election on a nonpartisan basis of a state board of education. Each part of Kentucky will be guaranteed a voice on the board because the members will be elected from districts. This board will appoint the superintendent. This means that the leadership of our school system will be in a trained educator who takes office on merit rather than on politics.

Our system of courts of justice has been vastly improved by the revision. A formula has been adopted which has proved highly successful in Missouri and has been adopted by Illinois, Michigan, and other progressive states. Anyone who has had to wait two or three years to have a hearing before the Court of Appeals will recognize the obvious benefits in our system of courts. In short, Kentucky will have a three-level system of courts rather than the present two-level system—a system that guarantees an appeal from every decision of a trial court, and a system that will speed up the present two- or three-year wait in our higher court to a matter of months.

Another tremendous savings in dollars and cents will be possible under the new constitution. At present, elections are held every year to fill various local, statewide, and federal posts. Elections for county and state offices under the new document will coincide with federal elections so that voters will have to go to the polls only once every two years. Election expenses will be cut in half. This means that over a six-year period, you the taxpayers will save $2,128,000. And that is a lot of money.

The new constitution will give greater freedom, greater flexibility, and more self-government to our local communities. Your city or county government will be freed from the tight control at Frankfort which the present constitution places upon it. The new document allows each city and county to decide for itself what sort of government it needs, what that government should do, and what officers are needed to do it. This allows local government far more freedom than the present version. Under our 1891 constitution, here is how things are set up: the constitution tells each county exactly what officers are to be elected to run the county government. By this formula the same officers performing the same functions and having the same authority are required for Robertson County, with a population of 2,400, and Jefferson County, with a population of 610,000. Does it make sense to you? Furthermore, under our 1891 constitution, cities and counties must go to Frankfort, hat in hand, to get a solution to their local problems.

Today, we hear more and more about the centralization of power and authority in Washington. What is needed, we hear, is a restoration of a free people's power to govern themselves. This is exactly what the new constitution will give to Kentuckians. No longer will counties be compelled to set up their government the way a group of men in 1891 felt it shoud be set up. No longer will local problems stagnate until the General Assembly gets around to enacting a law to remedy it. In one sentence, expressing confidence in the ability of Kentuckians to run their own affairs with a minimum of state interference, the new constitution grants a broad authority to cities and counties. It says they may: "Create any democratic form of government or perform any functions not denied to them by the Constitution, by law, or by their own charters."

The new constitution requires that the head of your county government, the county judge and the legislative body of county government, the fiscal court or county commission, must be elected and that the unit of local government, the city or county, must have a democratic form of government. All local officials must be chosen locally and cannot be chosen in Frankfort.

The revision also offers a solution to the financial problems of local government. It removes the strait jacket which places increasing burdens on the farmer and homeowner. The 1891 constitution forbids the state to return any tax money to cities or counties unless it is for roads. Under the 1966 constitution, the state will be allowed to return tax monies to the local communities to help meet local needs. This provision will help stop centralization of power in Frankfort.

What the 1891 constitution has done is to freeze a system of local government inherited from medieval England. In many cases, this system has proved to be unworkable, or worse, unneeded. It keeps the people powerless to choose their own form of local government. The new constitution will return this power to the people at home.

Of course, you may find some who wish to perpetuate for all-time this rigid structure of local government whose design the people cannot control. They seem to fear the power of the people to have the local government and the type of local officials the people want. Let me say that any official filling a needed job, one which rightly deserves taxpayers' money to pay the salary, need not fear the new constitution.

Let me re-emphasize the important provisions of the new constitution in regard to the area of local government. First, it will not abolish the county courthouse. To the contrary, the present functions of county judge as leader of county government, or the mayor, as leader of city government, are specifically mentioned in the new document, and such officials must be elected by the people. The fiscal court county commission, or the board of aldermen, whatever it may be called in the locality, is also described in the new constitution and also must be elected, just as under the present constitution.

Lastly, no city or county official will be appointed by anyone in Frankfort. The new constitution specifically says that all other local offices will be filled either by a local election or will be chosen by the county judge and the fiscal court, depending on how the General Assembly or you, the local voters, want to go about choosing their officers.

The draftsmen of the new constitution felt, and I think rightly so, that the power to modify local government to meet local needs must lie in part directly with the people. It is this they have given you. It is up to you whether these newly granted freedoms are to be the guiding light of your government or whether we will draw back from this threshold and remain mired in an unchanging system. The needed reform depends on you.

In summary, this constitution will save you money. It will return local matters to local communities for local solutions. It will improve the administration of justice. It will strengthen sacred guarantees of individual rights. It will modernize the executive branch at Frankfort. It will create a stronger, more effective legislature. It will improve education for your children. It will create a better climate for economic growth in the Commonwealth. It has been drafted by a representative group of distinguished, public-spirited Kentuckians and approved by an enthusiastic legislature. The question in my mind today is not, "Who is for this great constitution for all Kentuckians?" The real question is, "Who can be against it?" Who will oppose this essential step toward a greater and more progressive Commonwealth?

---

1. In deleted remarks Governor Breathitt mentioned several members of the Constitution Revision Assembly. The full membership included Earle C. Clements, chairman, Marlowe W. Cook, vice chairman, James W. Stites, vice chairman, Dee Ashley Akers, secretary, Charles S. Adams, John M. Berry, Paul G. Blazer, George Street Boone, Raymond F. Bossmeyer, T.C. Carroll, James C. Carter, Jr., James A. Cawood, Albert B. Chandler, Oldham Clarke, James M. Collier, Beckham Combs, Bert T. Combs, John S. Cooper, William O. Cowger, Grace A. Cruickshank, Dewey Daniel, Charles Peaslee Farnsley, Robert L. Farris, Edward L. Fossett, Maxey B. Harlin, Edward R. Hays, C.C. Howard, Joe R. Johnson, Jr., Keen Johnson, James W. Lambert, Robert O. Miller, Robert L. Mills, Thruston B. Morton, Louie B. Nunn, Charles H. Parrish, James R. Poston, Edward F. Prichard, Jr., John E. Reeves, Samuel M. Rosenstein, Flem D. Sampson, J. Phil Smith, Jesse Stuart, William L. Sullivan, Rumsey B. Taylor, Sr., Thomas S. Waller, Lawrence W. Wetherby, Simeon S. Willis, William L. Wilson, Phyllis R. Wood, and Gates F. Young. Kentucky Legislative Research Commission. *A Comparison: The Present, The Proposed Kentucky Constitutions* (Frankfort, 1968).

KENTUCKY SAVINGS AND LOAN LEAGUE
Gilbertsville / September 24, 1966

THERE is no sense in kidding ourselves—a constitution, setting forth the basic framework of government, is naturally harder to understand than other issues. But it appears that many people, too many people, are making it much more difficult than it really is by inventing problems that simply are not there. Let me give you an example. People have written to the *Paducah Sun-Democrat,* the *Courier Journal,* and other papers saying that if the revision is accepted, all local officials will be appointed from Frankfort. To show you just how far from the truth this is, let me quote from Article 8. "The chief executive and the members of the legislative bodies of all units of local government shall . . . be elected by the qualified voters thereof for terms no longer than four years; all other officers of units of local government shall be chosen by local authority."

As a lawyer, I have developed a certain skill for interpreting constitutional language. But I cannot find in the language I have quoted, even by the most brutal twisting of these simple phrases, the slightest indication that sheriffs, or county judges, or mayors, or any other local officials will be chosen by anyone other than local people.

I am reminded of the time Abraham Lincoln asked a friend how many legs a dog would have if you called his tail a leg. When the friend replied five, Lincoln said, no—because calling a tail a leg will never make it a leg. This should remind us to keep the distinction between fact and fiction ever in the forefront of our thinking. Lincoln, perhaps more than any other statesman in our nation's history, had the gift for making this distinction. And we Kentuckians need this gift this fall. Because whenever we hear one of the many fictions being spread about the proposed constitutional revision, we must be able to respond with facts.

And let me warn you right now—there are people in this state who are spreading deliberate, malicious falsehoods about the revision. Of course, others are making innocent mistakes about its contents—their error lies in speaking before trying to learn the facts. But both these types of people are spreading fictions; and whatever the source of these fictions, whether innocent mistake or malicious falsehood, we must be quick to expose them for what they are.[1]

Let me add that there are others who know and state the truth about the words of the revision, but who in good faith disagree with the judgment of the Constitution Revision Assembly. And with them, I have no quarrel. My quarrel is with those who continue to call a tail a leg, who spread fiction where the nature of the issue demands that we speak only the truth.

My friends, good government doesn't just happen. The young Americans who die each day in Viet Nam bear a now silent witness to this truth. The least we can do to honor their sacrifice is to make democracy work at home. We make democracy work by telling one another the truth about great public issues—and nothing but the truth.

Now as you know, I am in favor of this revision and strongly so. But earlier in this campaign I intended to stay quiet, to express my support and then to stand aside and let others carry on—for fear that people would think that I had some selfish interest to serve. I remained silent even when views with which I sharply disagreed were circulated—since there are some parts of the revision where reasonable men might in good faith differ in matters of interpretation. When it became apparent that certain completely erroneous statements, like the example I just cited, were being made about its contents, I began to have doubts about my decision to stand aside. But when the charge was made that the Constitution Revision Assembly was communist inspired—well, that was the last straw, the ultimate indignity to the distinguished members who labored for almost two years without any compensation and to the tens of thousands of Kentuckians who count them among their friends.

Then and there, I resolved one thing. If this campaign is to fail—if we and our children are to be subjected to who-knows-how-many-more decades of backward government and inefficient justice—then at least if I had anything to do with it the causes of this failure would not be slander and misinformation—at least the people of this state would know what they are voting about, and equally important, what they are not voting about—at least they would accept or refuse this revision on the basis of the truth about its contents.

And I call upon public-spirited Kentuckians to join me in trying to put the discussion of the revision on the level of fact, to eliminate the fictions. Let me note some of these fictions. There is the incredibly reckless fiction, developed by I know-not-what perverted individuals or groups, that the Constitution Revision Assembly which drafted the revision was a communist-controlled organization and that the new constitution would pave the way for a communist takeover in Kentucky. This slander is unworthy of comment—except to say that if anything will contribute to a communist takeover, it will be our failure to provide democratic government with the constitutional framework it needs to serve the needs of the people—our failure to meet the challenges of change. Communism never succeeds where the institutions of democratic government are given the ability to perform their essential tasks—where the people care enough to make them succeed. And I suppose the ultimate question to be decided on November 8 is whether the people really care.

I have already alluded to another fiction—the false allegation that under the revision local officers will be appointed from Frankfort. And I have quoted the specific section from the document which shows this to be utterly and completely false.

There is yet another fiction—the fiction that in some sense I dictated the contents of this revision. The fact of the matter is, of course, quite to the contrary. It is an insult to the distinguished members of the assembly even to suggest that they would be subject to dictation. And I can think of no more futile a project than to attempt to dictate to people of such independent views as Marlow Cook, Earle Clements, A.B. Chandler, Bill Cowger, and the others who helped write this constitution.[2] And furthermore, my vote was only one of four in the committee designated by the legislature to select the assembly. The others were those of the lieutenant governor, the chief judge of the Court of Appeals, and the Speaker of the house—each of them a man who exercises a completely independent judgment.

This is not the administration's constitution. Many in my administration join me in supporting it for the same reason that I do—it is a good revision and we need it urgently. But a vote for or against the new constitution is not a vote for or against this administration—nor is it a vote for or against any political party. A vote for the new constitution is a vote for that 70 percent of the old which remains as sound today as it was the day in 1891 when it was adopted and it is for the changes which must be made if Kentucky is going to progress. It is a vote for a greater Kentucky for all of us.

There is another fiction related to this last one—that this constitution will give more power to the governor. Again the fact is just the contrary. Under the revision significant power will move from Frankfort to the local units of government—instead of being authorized as now to do only what is expressly or impliedly granted by law, units of local government will be permitted to do all that is not prohibited by law. But equally important on this question is the fact that the legislature will be strengthened. Right now, much of the governor's power results from circumstances beyond his control. It is power that he doesn't want. It is power that results from the fact that the legislature is too weak under our present constitution.

A body which meets only for a few weeks every two years, whose membership turns over after every session, cannot keep itself as well informed as it must in these times. It cannot react quickly and effectively to the problems of the day. And the unwanted power of the governor comes from the fact that since the legislature is weak, he must step in to fill the vacuum if the essential tasks of government are to be executed properly and promptly. Under the revision, the legislature will be able to fulfill its historic role in American constitutional theory.

My friends, these are some of the fictions which are beginning to distort public debate and discussion of the proposed constitutional revision. These are some of the tails that people are calling legs. And I hope that the voters of this Commonwealth will discharge their duty to the future to see the difference between the tails and the legs, the fictions and the facts. I hope that they will use the wisdom of Lincoln in considering this vital issue.

I remain convinced that once the people know about the revision, they will support it as I do. To be sure, if I had the power to do so, I would perhaps not write it word for word the way the Constitution Revision

Assembly did. But I had no hand in drafting it. And in those few instances where I differ with the assembly, I am willing to yield to the judgment of the amost fifty able, experienced, public-spirited citizens who gave twenty-two months of tireless effort to make Kentucky a more perfect Commonwealth. Where my differences are so minor, who am I to say that I am right and those who have such a precise, detailed knowledge of the needed changes are wrong?

Certainly I agree that local government needs to be strengthened in the manner provided by the revision; that the legislature needs to become a more effective instrument of the people's will; that our court system is in desperate need of assistance; that our present system of annual elections causes the waste of enormous sums of money; that school financing is needlessly expensive under the old constitution, involving the waste of millions of dollars each year; and that our bill of rights needs the strengthening additions provided by the revision.

With these judgments of the assembly and with the measures proposed by it to remedy the problems, I am in perfect accord. And therefore I commend the revision to you. And I urge you, and all Kentuckians, to consider the revision carefully. I urge you not to fall victim to the fictions circulated in this campaign. I urge you to make your own independent judgment. And I hope that you will talk to your friends and neighbors. Because the greatest tragedy of this campaign would be if the people heard, not the truth, but only the misinformation spread by some of the opposition and the errors of those who never read the document. I intend to do all that I can to see that this ultimate tragedy does not occur. And you too can help.

---

1. The principal arguments against ratification of the proposed constitution were contained in a feature article published by the *Henderson Gleaner & Journal,* September 18, 1966. Edward T. Prichard, Jr., a Breathitt advisor, argued in favor of revision. Prichard reiterated arguments employed by Breathitt in the speeches in this section. Arguments against revision were presented by Joseph J. Leary, an attorney. Leary found the document wanting in several respects. First, the proposed constitution was drafted by an appointed body rather than an elected one. The document, therefore, was not responsive to the will of the people because the people had no voice in its drafting. Second, a provision allowing the governor to succeed himself was unacceptable because "the cost of mounting a primary campaign against an incumbent governor is so great that there is little likelihood that an incumbent governor would ever be defeated." Third, the proposed four-year terms for members of the House of Representatives and six year terms for members of the Senate were nowhere apparent in American state government. Fourth, annual sessions of the legislature were unnecessary and too expensive. Fifth, that part of the proposed constitution providing "the General Assembly shall have the

power to provide for the government, officers and functions of units of local governments, and to create, alter, consolidate and dissolve them," said Leary, "places the very power of life and death over units of local government smaller than a county in the hands of the General Assembly." Sixth, maximum tax rates fixed by the existing constitution would be fixed by the General Assembly. "The sum and substance of the proposed constitution," Leary asserted, "is to transfer to the state government the traditional supervision and authority of local affairs which heretofore have been regulated by local units of government." Leary's opposition to the proposed constitution was a reasonable, dispassionate statement; however, letters to the editor that appeared in Kentucky newspapers frequently reflected an intense concern that the proposed constitution was either the product of a communist conspiracy or the prelude to a fascist takeover and revealed more absurd attitudes. For examples of this body of opinion, see the *Louisville Courier-Journal,* November 5, 1966. Thelma Stovall, secretary of state, was the highest ranking state official to oppose the revised constitution. In addition to a few scattered citizens groups who organized opposition, the proposed document was opposed by the Kentucky Farm Bureau Federation and most county officials. Marlow Cook, a vice chairman of the Constitutional Revision Assembly, signed the assembly report but campaigned against its adoption. Louie Nunn, a member of the assembly who attended only its first meeting, also opposed the adoption of the new constitution. *Louisville Courier-Journal,* November 10, 1966.

2. Marlow Webster Cook (1926-), attorney from Louisville; member Kentucky House of Representatives (1958-1960); Jefferson County judge (1961-1968); United States Senator (1968-1974). Robert Sexton, ed., *The Public Papers of Governor Louie B. Nunn, 1967-1971* (Lexington, Ky., 1975), p. 185. Albert Benjamin Chandler (1898-), attorney from Versailles; L.L.B., University of Kentucky (1924); elected to Kentucky Senate (1929); lieutenant governor of Kentucky (1931-1935); governor (1935-1939, 1955-1959); U.S. Senator (1939-1942); commissioner of baseball (1945-1951); candidate for governor (1963, 1967). *Who's Who in America, 1978-1979,* 40th ed. (Chicago, 1978). William Owen Cowger (1922-), born, Hastings, Nebraska; mayor of Louisville (1961-1964); U.S. House of Representatives (1967-1970); delegate to Republican National Convention (1968); currently resides in Louisville. *Who's Who in American Politics, 1971-1972,* 3rd ed. (New York, 1971).

ELECTION STATEMENT
Frankfort / November 8, 1966

WHEN, in 1947, nearly two decades ago, I enlisted in the fight for a better constitution, I enlisted for the duration of the war. My enlistment is still in effect. The people have spoken, and every Kentuckian must accept their judgment—cheerfully and in good grace. But no cause is settled until it is settled right. Most of the opponents of the 1966 revision have told the people that they favor revision but oppose certain provisions of the 1966 charter.

In this spirit, I call upon all Kentuckians to join in a renewed study of the revision. I hope that every school, every college, every civic organization will begin the study of both constitutions at length and in depth.

Let those of us who supported the revision give full and fair consideration to every possible improvement in the 1966 draft. I urge sincere opponents to give every full and fair consideration of the same sort. I urge our legislators and other Kentuckians to search every possible means for an acceptable method of revising and submitting another draft to the people. No issue is ever settled until it is settled right. That is what Lincoln said about slavery. That is what I say about a better constitution for Kentucky.[1]

---

1. The proposed constitution was soundly defeated at the polls on November 8, 1966. The final vote was 510,099-140,210 against adoption. It was defeated in every county, normally by margins of 4-1. Strongest support came from Louisville and Jefferson County, where it failed 44,711 to 90,361. *Louisville Courier-Journal,* November 9, 1966. In an editorial published shortly after the election the *Courier-Journal* noted ". . . opponents, some out of ignorance, some for cynical and selfish reasons, managed to plant doubts about the revision in the minds of many voters. Many others obviously had alreaded decided that: 'If you don't know, you should vote no.' The reaction of the voters reflected a preference for the familiar over the unknown, even though the known is admittedly bad. More discouraging, it was evidence again of the traditional distrust of Kentuckians for Kentuckians, a feeling that has divided and handicapped the state for almost a century. It reflected the feeling that the only good Kentuckians are dead Kentuckians, people who lived almost eighty years ago. . . . As a result, Kentucky will continue to be run by the Court of Appeals, which will enable it to evade the constitution, since it cannot abide by it. . . ." The editor doubted that another attempt to revise the constitution would come for many years. Ibid. November 10, 1966.

CORRECTIONS, CRIME, & THE LAW

TASK FORCE ON CRIMINAL JUSTICE
Frankfort / July 17, 1964

I WANT to welcome you to the first meeting of the Task Force on Criminal Justice and express to you my deep appreciation for you giving your time and talents to help solve the dilemma of the poor man in our courts. Your main purpose, as a task force, will be to begin a drive to eliminate distinctions between rich and poor criminal defendants.

I don't need to tell you that some Kentuckians live in a poverty nightmare where it is a struggle merely to exist. These people are not poor because they want to be poor, because they can't learn, or because they are lazy. They are poor because they were born to the wrong parents, in an age of automation, in the wrong racial group, or at a place where opportunity was lacking. We cannot change the poor man's misery overnight, but we can see to it that Kentucky does not unjustly punish in our courts the man who is already serving a life sentence of poverty.

There are three distinct areas in which I have asked you to base your study: bail-bond procedures, state counsel for the needy, and capital punishment. I am hopeful you will begin your work and place your primary attention initially on our bail bond procedures. The practice of depositing money or collateral, better known as bail, is generally a door to pretrial liberty for the rich, to pretrial detention for the poor. Those who can afford bail are free until their trials. For those who cannot afford bail, poverty is, in essence, a punishable offense. They lose their jobs and their families' lives are disrupted. They cannot locate witnesses and attorneys in their behalf, and because of this their chances for acquittal are lowered. They are often treated like already convicted criminals despite our treasured principle that people are presumed innocent until proven guilty.

I think, as part of the task force's study, we should conduct two bail bond pilot project studies—one at the University of Kentucky and one at the University of Louisville—using the law students of both institutions in this effort. I would like for you to look into the minimum cost of such a project and recommend soon some action to me. According to the New York Manhattan bail project, it appears that verified information about a defendant's background is a more reliable criterion on which to release a defendant than is his ability to purchase a bail bond.[1]

Our Kentucky study would enable us to have accurate, factual information on this aspect of pretrial release as well as other points of consideration. If we go ahead with the two projects, you would probably want to conduct them during the 1964-65 academic year. This would enable you to have the information for the completion of your study, which is set for November of 1965. I am sure that during the executive session you will be able to go into this entire matter in more detail. It is now my privilege to present to you William A. Geoghegan of the United States Justice Department.[2]

---

1. The Vera Foundation, a New York based organization founded by Louis Schweitzer in 1961, was a leader in correcting evils associated with bail bonding. Accordingly, it provided New York judges with information relating to a defendant's family ties, employment, and health. The foundation recommended release without bail pending a hearing if data justified that action. See *Saturday Evening Post,* June 20, 1964, pp. 66-67, and *Time,* August 20, 1965, p. 47.

2. William Aloysius Geoghegan (1925-), lawyer and government official; associated with law firm of Geoghegan, Long and Daly, Cincinnati, Ohio (1949-1955), firm of Dinsmore, Shoht, Barrett, Coates and Deupree (1955-1961), partner (1958-1961); assistant deputy attorney general, Department of Justice (1961-1965); partner, Pierson, Ball and Dowd, Washington, D.C. (1965-), *Who's Who in America, 1970-1971,* 36th ed. (Chicago, 1970).

STATEMENT ON CORRECTIONS
Frankfort / November 12, 1964

I HAVE met today with Commissioner Cannon, the wardens of Eddyville State Penitentiary and LaGrange Reformatory, members of the Commission on Corrections and Community Service, and other officials of the Department of Corrections to discuss a positive correctional program and to outline the prison policy of this administration.[1]

Broadly speaking, this administration is dedicated to an overall philosophy of penology based on two principles. First, our job is to lock up the convicted offender and to retain him in a humane manner for the period of time prescribed by judge or jury, subject to probation and parole. Second, our long-range goal must be to give a man something he didn't have before in terms of an understanding of his own problems and skills that will enable him to cope with life outside the prison walls once he is released.

I feel, and feel deeply, that our correctional system would be a total failure if it performed no other task than custody. Of equal importance is rehabilitation. We must teach inmates to read and write, to be carpenters and welders, to be radio and television repairmen. We must teach them useful skills so they can be productive, self-supporting citizens once they return to society. We must counsel with them, try to understand their motives and individual thinking in an effort to reform these men. Not to teach skills and not to attempt to reform them would be foolish and inhumane and costly to our taxpayers, who must foot the bill of every criminal repeater.

Along these lines, I feel, we've made measurable strides during the past year. We now have deputy wardens for treatment in charge of rehabilitation and education in all three institutions—something we didn't have before. We are separating youthful first offenders from the more hardened, sophisticated criminals. We are now offering some medical treatment and psychiatric help, although far, far more needs to be made available. We have made great progress in the probation and parole area. And, we've received splendid cooperation from the University of Kentucky and the University of Louisville on research and study projects.

It is important for those of us who are in charge of this program to keep sight of the fact that a good correctional program is what this administration is committed to and what the people of Kentucky expect. Those conducting our prison programs cannot be blamed for outdated facilities and lack of money, but they can be blamed if they spare any possible effort toward improvement. I do not expect miracles but I do expect all employees to work within the framework of this program and to make personal adjustments if they are necessary.

It is difficult anytime you go through a change in a program, when you modernize outdated methods and programs, not to have administrative problems. Difficulties occurred in the Department of Mental Health and in the Department of Child Welfare when they were upgraded and professionalized. But now that new programs have been established firmly in these departments, problems of administration have been reduced. This is not unusual, and I am hopeful the public will understand that problems which now exist in the Department of Corrections are being worked out.

We cannot be successful in this penology program unless we operate with a single policy administered through a central office. No institution can be independent of another, nor independent of the department's main office or policy in Frankfort. I will not tolerate it any other way. We must work together, and if there are differences of opinion, they should be worked out within the department.

I plan to ask the 1966 General Assembly to appropriate enough money to raise the salaries of our correctional officers at our institutions, and to place them on a five-day week. Presently we have 118 officers at Eddyville, 211 at the reformatory, and eleven at Pewee Valley who would be affected by these changes. Without these officers, we could not operate our institutions because they play a vital role in the overall program. The correctional officer receives $266 a month and works six days a week. Because of this pay and work scale an officer recruiting problem and morale problem have developed in our correctional system. Therefore, it is necessary that we take this action. I am making this recommendation on the advice of Commissioner Cannon, Warden Thomas and Warden Davis, and the Commission on Corrections and Community Service.[2] I am hopeful the legislature will approve this salary increase and change in the work week when it convenes at the next regular session.

I have confidence in Commissioner Cannon and his desire to upgrade and professionalize Kentucky's correctional system. Likewise, I have confidence in the dedication and sincerity of Warden Thomas and Warden Davis. I expect them and all other employees in the Department of Corrections to follow these overall administrative policies which I've outlined. I am certain that, working together, we can have a good correctional program that will be as modern and progressive as any in the country.

---

1. Joseph Gorman Cannon (1925-), case worker, Ohio State Penitentiary (1946-1956); director, treatment services, assistant commissioner, Ohio Division of Corrections (1956-1963); commissioner, Kentucky Department of Corrections (1963-1966). *Who's Who in the South and Southwest, 1971-1972,* 12th ed.(Chicago, 1971).

2. Luther T. Thomas (1903-1965), farmer and automobile dealer, Trigg County (1957-1961); warden, Kentucky State Penitentiary, Eddyville (1961-1965); *Louisville Courier-Journal,* January 21, 1965. David L. Davis (1912-), served as judge, Elliott County, Kentucky, prior to appointment as warden of La Grange by Governor Bert Combs. Differences with Commissioner of Corrections Joseph G. Cannon, relating primarily to employment practices, led to his resignation at La-Grange in July, 1965. Breathitt immediately appointed him to a four-year term on

the state parole board. *Louisville Courier-Journal*, December 31, 1959; July 3, 1965; December 29, 1965.

KENTUCKY COMMONWEALTH ATTORNEYS ASSOCIATION
Covington / December 10, 1964

THERE could not be found a group of persons more distinguished and expert in all facets of criminal law in Kentucky than the one assembled here today. As Commonwealth attorneys, you have been most instrumental in helping upgrade Kentucky's criminal rules of procedure and helping improve and professionalize the Department of Corrections. And I am confident that, during the working sessions of the next two days here in Covington, your collective experience and skills will expose the faults and virtues of other phases in our court system and the way in which the state deals with criminals and those accused of criminal offenses.

We live in a time of growing awareness and responsiveness to the problems of criminal justice. There is an increasing concern among people all over our state who want to insure that the scales of our legal system weigh justice and not wealth.

A number of factors have contributed to this concern. The *Gideon* decision of the Supreme Court, requiring the appointment of counsel for poor defendants in state as well as federal cases, is an important factor.[1] Another factor is the special attention given recently in our news media to that fifth of our citizenry who [are] ill housed, ill clad, and ill fed. Still another is the splendid leadership demonstrated by Attorney General Robert Kennedy in grappling with the poor man problem in our courts.[2] All of this, including books and other court decisions, [has] made us all more aware of the poor man and his relationship with the courts.

But, let me say at the outset that Kentucky is no "Johnny-come-lately" to this problem. For years we have required appointive counsel for the poor in our courts. And, we now have one of the best, if not the best, criminal rules procedure in this country. Let me also make it clear that I regard myself as a fairly tough-minded and hard-nosed citizen. I am 100 percent opposed to coddling any of our criminals, but I am also 100 percent opposed to making any citizen a criminal until he is found to be so by a court.

Hundreds of persons each year in this state who are charged with minor and moderately serious crimes are held in jail awaiting disposition of their cases because they are unable to raise bail in moderate, low, or even nominal amounts. And their neighbors, charged with crimes of the same gravity, sometimes codefendants charged with the same crime, but possessed of insufficient means to secure bail, remain at liberty. These are facts, indisputable facts, unfair, undemocratic, and unhealthy facts. Surely, this alone should command our attention. I need not expand on the many thousands of dollars it costs the taxpayers each year, to support their dependents who are forced onto relief rolls, and the thousands it costs to build bigger jails to lodge the constantly increasing detention population.

In too many cases, one factor determines whether a defendant stays in jail prior to trial. That factor is not guilt or innocence. It is not the nature of the crime. It is not the character of the defendant. That factor, simply, is money. As a result, the professional bondsman, who has made it his impersonal, balance-sheet business to produce the defendant in court, has gradually replaced the friend or relative surety—to an extent where he has virtually taken over the bail posting process in many areas of our state.

Let me make it clear at this point, if I may, I do not advocate the outright scrapping of financially secured bail. I am not prepared now to say that financially secured bail is not appropriate in many cases. But I do believe that hundreds of persons in this state are jailed each year because of inability to raise bail who should be released on parole or on their own recognizance.

So, I have appointed a Task Force on Criminal Justice to look into the entire relationship of the poor man and the courts. I have asked them to make a study of the bail bond procedures in Kentucky and to explore the means by which we might improve our system of counsel for the indigent. The task force also is studying the whole question of capital punishment. We have established bail bond projects at the University of Kentucky and the University of Louisville law schools. The law students, in cooperation with officials in Jefferson County and Fayette County, are carrying out the projects and should be able to report to the task force sometime early next year. It pleases me very much that the students in the two institutions have really put their teeth into the study.

Procedure in the two projects works like this. A person is arrested and taken to jail. If the offense is bailable and the person cannot make bail because he does not have the money, the investigating law student checks the charge and the person's previous criminal record, if any. If the record indicates the person is eligible for release, the student interviews him to determine whether he is a good risk to release without putting up bail. The defendant is asked about his job, whether he supports his family, and other questions. His story is checked by telephone with people involved. If the defendant is still considered a good risk, the information is given to the court with a recommendation that the person be paroled on his own word. When a defendant is so released, project staff members then notify him in writing of the date and location of subsequent court appearances. If the parolee is illiterate, a fact that is recorded in the questionnaire, he is telephoned as well as notified by letter.

It is our belief that such experimentation can help us to improve the administration of justice in our Kentucky courts. It can also provide information and examples of benefit to you, as prosecutors, who must contend with so much greater a share of the problem.[3]

We are now working on a governor's statewide conference on criminal justice to be held sometime in January in Louisville. We will soon announce the date for this conference, and I am hopeful you will be able to attend. This conference will present us—prosecutors, police, judges, lawyers—all of us, a challenge which goes beyond the mechanics or abuses of our bail system. That challenge will extend to the entire relationship of the poor man and the courts. It will be an opportunity for all of us to sit down, to study our procedures, and see to it that Kentucky does not unjustly punish the man who is already serving a life sentence of poverty.

---

1. After two decades of wrestling with the relationship between a defendant's right to counsel and the "fairness" doctrine, in 1963 the Supreme Court ruled that indigents in all felony cases had to be provided an appointed attorney. *Gideon* vs. *Wainwright,* 372 U.S. 335.

2. Robert Francis Kennedy (1925-1968), Massachusetts and New York Democrat; a member of the party's liberal wing and the most influential advisor of President John F. Kennedy, his brother; attorney with the United States Department of Justice (1951-1952); counsel and chief counsel of the United States Permanent Subcommittee on Investigations (1953-1959); attorney general of the United States (1960-1964); United States Senate (1964-1968); candidate for president (1968). Dan and Inez Martin, *Who Was Who in American Politics* (New York, 1974).

3. In a pilot project associated with the Task Force on Criminal Justice, University of Louisville law students performed pretrial investigations of defendants to determine their suitability for release and the appropriateness of Kentucky's existing pretrial detention procedures. *Louisville Courier-Journal,* June 30, 1964.

UNIVERSITY OF LOUISVILLE LAW DAY
Louisville / May 5, 1965

WE meet here today to honor the law. The law of the land, the law of America, has honored us through the years. May we honor it every day we live. I know of no greater subject on which a man may speak, a more sobering or more inspiring subject than the law of our nation. For the meaning of law in our nation rests upon the meaning of our life as a nation.

The law of the land has served one supreme purpose: to give expression and protection to our spiritual heritage proclaiming the worth of the individual, his sanctity and dignity as a creature of God. This has been the historic inspiration and the political motivation of our life as a people. This idea was conceived first in the hearts and minds of the men and women who settled this country. It was later proclaimed for all to read in that great document heralding the advent of a free America—the Declaration of Independence. From the time of that immortal proclamation, followed by the Constitution and the Bill of Rights, the role of law in our history as a people, has forever been to give living testimony to our faith in the individual man, his free destiny and the universal brotherhood of man.

The ultimate realization of these aspirations rests upon more than laws and statutes. It rests upon the compassion, concern, and conscience of each individual for his neighbor, his community, and all mankind. Only in the light of these truths of the spirit do the ideas of liberty, justice, and equality assume clear meaning.

We all know that men are not equal in the sense of being alike; the individuality of each is the very hallmark of each individual's free and different nature and development. But all men are equal as children of God and brothers one to another. It is this recognition of man's very nature, this equality conferring upon all the right of equal opportunity, that our law is dedicated to serve. Freedom under the law does not mean that all must be the same; it includes the right to be different.

The history of freedom in our country has been the history of knocking down the barriers to equal opportunity. One after another they have fallen, and great names in our history record their collapse: the Virginia Statute of Religious Freedom, the Bill of Rights, the Emancipation Proclamation, the Woman's Suffrage Amendment, the 1964 Civil Rights Act, and within a few days the passage of the Federal Voting Act.[1] The record of our progress is a proud one, but it is far from over. We live in a world which has narrowed into a neighborhood before it has broadened into a brotherhood. We cannot rest until we honor in fact as well as word the plain language of the Declaration of Independence. This is our goal. It requires far more than action by government. Laws are never as effective as habits. The fight for equality of all men everywhere must be waged every day in our own souls and consciences, in our schools and in our churches, our homes, and our factories.

Last year I appointed a Task Force on Criminal Justice, whose membership includes Dean Volz and Professor Newman from the university, to study the areas of bail bond procedures, counsel for the indigent, and capital punishment.[2] This task force is currently making this study and will report to me by November 15 of this year on actions that can be taken by our Commonwealth to assure equal and humane justice.

All over the United States there is a growing sentiment to do away with capital punishment because more and more people are realizing, as have practically all professional penologists and criminologists, that this feudal punishment is no deterrent to crime. If their mood is reflected in the letters they write me daily, a large segment of the Kentucky people want capital punishment abolished, too. Sixty-one percent of these letters that have been mailed to me on this subject show opposition to the electric chair. Since the electric chair was placed in operation at Eddyville State Penitentiary in 1911, some 162 men have been electrocuted.[3] Of this number, approximately one-half have been Negroes. A large majority of these 162 had little, if any, financial resources, to employ competent counsel to represent them.

In another development, the United States Supreme Court has been quite consistent and most vocal in its repeated admonitions that every individual is entitled to be represented not only by counsel—but by adequate and competent counsel. Kentucky has been a pioneer in this field, but the time has now come for us to take a new and closer look at our system to make sure we are providing adequate counsel for the poor man in our courts.

We also have countless accused persons in Kentucky who are forced to spend weeks, months, or even a year or more in jail, awaiting the next call of the grand jury or a trial of their case on the merits or the outcome of an appeal. They remain jailed during this period of time solely because they are unable to make a $500, $1,000, or $2,500 bond. This is wrong; it's undemocratic and it ought to be changed.

Several of you here have been working on the University of Louisville bail bond project which will be most helpful to us in making this study and in preparing data to show that many Kentuckians who are charged with minor crimes can be released on their own recognizance. I appreciate your assistance, and I think you are providing a valuable service to the state and all our people.

I believe that it is incumbent that the law of force and influence be replaced with the force and influence of law. I believe that it is imperative that the judicial scales weight justice and not wealth. I believe that if justice is limited to a social, economical, or political class it is no longer justice. I believe that every citizen, not merely a class, is entitled to justice. I believe that justice and power must be brought together in order that what is just may be powerful and whatever is powerful may be just.

The prophet Micah observed that God's first requirement of man is to do justly. We can do no less. We must look to the hour at hand. We cannot rest upon the laurels of yesterday's achievements; neither may we become anxious about tomorrow. For yesterday is but a dream and tomorrow is only a vision. But this hour, this day well spent will help to make our yesterdays a dream of happiness and our tomorrow a vision of hope. May we look well, therefore, to this day!

---

1. Public reaction to the racial strife accompanying a Negro registration drive in Selma, Alabama, spurred the passage of the Voting Rights Act of 1965. President Johnson and congressional supporters of the bill timed their efforts to exploit the favorable circumstances created by the incidents. The key to the act was a "triggering formula" which allowed the attorney general or federal courts to appoint federal voting examiners, who were to determine voter eligibility and protect voting rights in areas where governments (city, county, etc.) were found to be practicing massive racial discrimination in voting registration procedures. The formula established two conditions which had to exist before examiners could be appointed. First, the attorney general was to ascertain that discriminating devices such as literacy tests were being used to restrict registration. Secondly, the formula stipulated that less than 50 percent of the eligible voters in an area were registered or had voted in the 1964 presidential election. The act also suspended literacy and other discriminating voting tests in areas which met the conditions of the triggering formula. The attorney general was also directed to initiate legal proceedings against governmental units which imposed poll taxes, another common discriminating device. *Congressional Quarterly Almanac,* vol. 21 (1965), pp. 533-64. The prospect of massive intervention by the attorney general, the federal courts, and federal examiners into state and local politics provided Governor Breathitt with a strong argument for the adoption of his civil rights proposals by the 1966 General Assembly.

2. Martin Milton Volz (1917-), attorney, admitted to Wisconsin Bar (1940); member, University of Wisconsin Law School faculty (1946-1950); dean, University of Kansas City School of Law (1950-1958); University of Louisville School of Law (1950-); resident of Louisville. *Who's Who in America, 1964-1965,* 33rd ed. (Chicago, 1964). Charles L. Newman (1923-), instructor in sociology, Fairleigh Dickinson College (1950-1951); instructor in sociology and social work, University of North Dakota (1952-1955); assistant professor of social welfare and corrections, Florida State University (1955-1959); director, division of correctional training, Kent School of Social Work, University of Louisville (1959-1962); director, Center for Correctional Training (1962-). *American Men of Science: The*

Social and Behavioral Sciences, 10th ed. (Tempe, Ariz., 1962), p. 793. The task force appointed by Governor Breathitt in June, 1964, included sixteen distinguished Kentuckians. In its report, the task force severely criticized the existing bail bond procedures. Their investigation disclosed that corruption was inherent in the system, with bondsmen paying policemen and magistrates to increase their business. The task force recommended legislation to regulate surety companies and individual bondsmen, and legislation which would authorize judges to release defendants awaiting trial upon payment of a fee much smaller than the usual bond payment. In its report on capital punishment, the task force recognized three alternatives to the existing law: the simple abolition of capital punishment; replacement of the death penalty with a life sentence without parole; or the abolition of the death penalty except in certain closely defined, particularly repugnant, crimes. A majority of the task force supported elimination of the death penalty with the possible exception of murder convictions where a policeman or corrections officer was the victim. The task force examined two alternatives to the existing system of aid to indigent defendants whereby court-appointed counsel received no fees or reimbursement of expenses. However, they could reach no firm conclusions on the comparative merits of a public defender system or a system which would pay private court-appointed attorneys from state funds according to a governmentally determined rate schedule. As a stopgap measure the task force recommended that court-appointed attorneys be reimbursed for costs incurred in conducting an adequate defense. *Louisville Courier-Journal,* June 30, 1964, December 7, 1965, and January 1, 1966.

3. The last man to die in Eddyville's electric chair was Kelley Moss, who was executed on March 2, 1962. Moss was convicted on November 7, 1957, for beating his stepfather to death. He failed to have the verdict set aside in three appeals to the U.S. Supreme Court. Breathitt brought an already strong aversion to capital punishment with him to the governorship. In the 1964 General Assembly he endorsed a bill abolishing the death penalty, but the measure failed. Afterward, he announced a general stay of execution for all condemned state prisoners until he could place the measure before the legislature once again in 1966. At the time of this speech, death sentences hovered over nine men in Kentucky's prisons. *Louisville Courier-Journal,* March 3, 1962.

PRESS CONFERENCE
Louisville / July 19, 1965

I APPEARED before this grand jury today for two equally important reasons.[1] First, I wanted to personally impress upon the members of the grand jury and the commonwealth attorney's office the gravity of the situation in the city of Louisville and in the county of Jefferson with respect to what can only be called "wide-open illegal gambling." In the process of doing this, I gave to the grand jury and to the commonwealth attorney's office specific information and leads that should enable them to conduct their own investigation in this matter for purposes of taking corrective action at the local level. Secondly, I hope my appearance before the grand jury will serve to call attention of all the citizens of Louisville and Jefferson County to the fact that this community has experienced a serious breakdown in local law enforcement that could not have come about except for the failure to enforce the law effectively on the part of both city and county officials.

Prior to coming here today and getting involved in a local situation that should be, and ordinarily is, handled locally, I wrote the mayor of the city of Louisville and the county judge of Jefferson County personal letters in which I called to their attention the serious illegal gambling situation that existed in Louisville and Jefferson County. I wrote these letters the week of April 15. They took no action to correct the situation, and in the case of the county judge, he recently attended a meeting with the leading representatives of the pinball gambling industry in Kentucky. With respect to this meeting, certain details have already become public property. Judge Cook, in a television statement, has freely admitted that he did attend this luncheon meeting.

So far, so good. But we must probe deeper to find the essential truth. I have never stated—and do not now state—that Judge Cook actually listened in on those portions of the conversation in which the pinball kings actually sought to collect specific sums from liquor wholesalers for the purpose of raising a pinball slush fund. I have never stated, and do not believe, that Judge Cook sought or accepted personal bribes from the pinball kings. Marlow and I have been personal friends for years, and I do not charge him with violating the law.

But I do say that the meeting held on May 18 was not a casual social gathering. It was a premeditated, planned gathering for a corrupt and illegal purpose. Judge Cook's attendance was sought for the purpose of lending prestige and strength to the corrupt designs of the pinball kings at the Backdoor Restaurant. Judge Cook is not a simple child to be led about by nurses on apron strings. He knew the business in which the Berhmans were engaged—for it was a matter of public record.[2] He knew who Frank Haddad's clients were—because Frank Haddad and his father are kingpins in his political organizations.[3] He knew that pinball rackets were running wide-open in Louisville because I had told him so in a letter to him in April, and the federal gambling stamp holders and locations were given to him.

It is in the light of these facts that the people must judge whether Marlow Cook's presence at this meeting was a social indiscretion or a departure from proper standards of public conduct. I could call names and detail specific information; however, I have given these names and the information to the grand jury and the commonwealth attorney's office. I believe the best interests of effective law enforcement require me to remain silent concerning those names and information. It is my hope that the grand jury, with the assistance of the commonwealth attorney's office, will make a complete and thorough investigation into gambling operations in this city and county. The attorney general of Kentucky has pledged his full support and cooperation in any investigation he may be asked to assist in. All of our state police and investigative agencies stand ready to do whatever may be asked of them by the grand jury.

To illustrate the seriousness of this problem, I call your attention to the following background. In 1951, as the result of an intensive investigation and hearings conducted by the Kefauver Committee of the United States Senate, the Congress of the United States enacted a law that prohibited transportation across state lines of the so-called one-armed bandit, or slot machine.[4] At the time that law was passed, more than 2,000 slot machines were in day-to-day operation in various cities, towns, and counties in Kentucky. The result of the passage of that act was to precipitate enforcement drives on the part of various state and local law enforcement agencies and the Federal Bureau of Investigation. The one-armed bandit became practically extinct in Kentucky, as well as in many other states in this nation within three years thereafter.

At about the time that the slot machine went out, the gambling industry utilized the scientific advances of the electronics industry to develop a device that was not prohibited by the 1951 federal law because it did not have a drum or reel in it, and did not pay off directly, as was true in the case of the slot machine. This was the Bally Bingo pinball machine. Outwardly, it has the physical appearance of an ordinary amusement pinball machine, but on the inside there is a maze of electronic equipment and wiring whose only purpose is to control the payoffs. Although this type machine does not drop the cash winnings directly into the player's hands, it has a metering device inside the machine that records the "pay-outs" by the bartender or waitress, as the case may be, as accurately as if it did dispense money itself. It will take the player's nickels faster than a slot machine. The player can put as many as 600 nickels into one of these machines prior to shooting a single ball. He can win as many as 600 so-called free plays in a single playing operation and can accumulate up to 999 free games.

A federal judge in a Kansas district court in a case involving a gambling tax on pinball machines found, as a matter of fact, that if a player accumulated 999 free games, it would require him thirty-three hours and eighteen minutes of continuous play to use up the free games game-by-game, and longer than that if he won additional free games in the process.

These type machines are owned and operated by a relatively few companies in Louisville and Jefferson County. They are placed out on location in restaurants, taverns, bars, and other business establishments on a fifty-fifty net profit basis with the proprietors of bars, taverns, and restaurants. After paying for the $250 Federal Gaming Device Tax Stamp, reimbursing the bar or tavern for the cash pay-outs made to winning players, and splitting the cost of "courtesy" fines occasionally assessed in police court against a waitress who has made a payoff, the net profits are divided one-half to the owner-operator of the machine and one-half to the proprietor of the business establishment.

In 1962, Congress recognized that its 1951 law dealing with slot machines was ineffective insofar as the gambling pinball machines were concerned. It therefore enacted a statute which prohibits shipment across state lines of a pinball machine that is designed and manufactured primarily for use in connection with gambling. Last fall, a federal jury in Louisville found that two Bally Bingo pinball machines had been designed and manufactured primarily for use in connection with gambling. This spring the federal court at Louisville entered judgment that those Bally Bingo pinball machines are not excepted from the operation of the 1962 federal law by reason of a Kentucky statute which permits the single coin, limited replay, amusement-type pinball machines to be operated so long as no cash prizes or merchandise are awarded a player.

The pinball gambling device is a more corrupting evil than the one-armed bandit ever was. These devices can be found in drug stores, restaurants, and other places frequented by children that are fourteen, fifteen, and sixteen years of age. They put their lunch monies and their allowances into these machines. I am sure in many cases that children have been caused to steal nickels from their mothers' purses and then later nickels from others in order to play the gambling pinball machines. Some of the pinball distributors in Louisville have made it a practice with respect to so-called hot locations to make cash advances of several thousand dollars to a neighborhood bar or tavern on a payday for a nearby factory in order that money will be available to cash payroll checks, with the expectation that the greater part of the cash will go into the machines and not home to the wives and families of the customers.

I cannot believe that this type of gambling could have been so long continued and widespread in Louisville and Jefferson County without at least the tacit cooperation of city and county officials. And such cooperation did not come about by reason of neglect or incompetency. It has been a cooperation achieved through deliberate choice.

It is my earnest hope that this grand jury, with the assistance of the commonwealth attorney's office and any assistance that may be requested of us at the state level, will be able to find out what persons were responsible for and participated in the operation and tolerance of this widespread illegal gambling, and will determine whether or not a similar situation exists with respect to bookmaking and similar vices, and will take whatever steps are necessary to remove from public office and employment the persons responsible.

Let me say in conclusion that the conditions of which I complain are not the exclusive responsibility of one political party. The pinball racketeers have sought—and found—allies and defenders in the ranks of both political parties. They will play with any and all who give them protection. But my party has purged itself of this moral poison and we intend to keep it clean. I call upon Judge Cook, Mayor Cowger, and their friends to do likewise—to break up the evil alliance between the underworld which is nothing more nor less than a cease-fire treaty between lawbreakers and those sworn to uphold the law.

---

1. Governor Breathitt's appearance before the Jefferson County Grand Jury was closely related to his well-publicized crusade against the lucrative and multiple-play pinball industry, announced in the *Courier-Journal* on April 24, 1965, under the sensational headline "Breathitt Declares War on Pinball Machines." In November, 1964, the U.S. District Court ruled that the multiple-play pinball machine was subject to federal taxation as a gambling device. In April, 1965, the courts declared the machines were gambling devices under Kentucky law as well. These decisions gave Breathitt the legal ammunition he required to attack pinball gambling. The inspiration was provided by Attorney General Robert Kennedy following a conference on criminal justice in January, 1965. Kennedy's description of connections between the gambling industry, of which pinball operations were a significant part, and organized crime in the United States prompted Breathitt to order an investigation by the state police and the Alcoholic Beverage Control Department. The nature and size of the pinball industry in Kentucky which the report revealed, along with recent court decisions, moved Breathitt to issue a call to local officials on April 23 to shut down those machines which were being used for gambling. In his message he noted that the November decision which required owners to purchase federal gambling stamps made offenders easy to identify. Local governments were given thirty days to act before state agencies intervened. On May 28 Breathitt ordered the crackdown, and shortly thereafter the first arrests were made by state police in Frankfort; however, state police could not act in Louisville without a formal request from the city government, and the city resisted state intrusion into local law enforcement activities. Moreover, County Judge Marlow Cook contended that Kentucky law was too vague in defining what constituted a gambling-type pinball machine to allow successful prosecution and that the April district court decision would have no permanent legal standing until the Court of Appeals made

a ruling. Therefore, the pinball industry continued to operate in Louisville and Jefferson County, which contained about one-half of the machines in the state. Governor Breathitt raised serious questions about the reluctance of Jefferson County officials to prosecute pinball operators when he charged on June 29 that Judge Cook had attended a meeting of pinball operators and liquor wholesalers at which a plan to raise money for the defense of pinball interests in Kentucky was discussed. Cook denied the allegations and labeled the charge a cheap political ploy. Louisville and Jefferson County were Republican strongholds, and Breathitt was accused of seeking to improve his party's performance in the 1965 elections by involving the Republican party in a trumped-up scandal. Cook suggested that Breathitt was trying to divert public attention from a then current Democratic scandal, in which the Combs administration was suspected of accepting bribes from the trucking industry. In the letter to Commonwealth Attorney Edwin A. Schroering, Jr., in which he detailed his allegations, Breathitt called for an investigation of the May 18 meeting. A special grand jury was convened in Jefferson County, but again the administration found itself in conflict with local Republican officials. The administration sought to expand the probe's scope into a general investigation of pinball operations in Jefferson County, but Schroering refused the assistance of Paul Huddleston, a special prosecuter appointed by Breathitt, and the presiding judge denied Huddleston's contentions that Kentucky law entitled the state attorney general's office to assume control of the investigation. Indeed, the judge partially sabotaged a concurrent Alcoholic Beverage Control Board investigation into the meeting by forbidding eleven witnesses scheduled to appear before both tribunals to appear before the board. As a result, the grand jury before which Breathitt testified restricted itself to investigating potential illegalities in the alleged May 18 meeting. Breathitt charged that the following men attended the May 18 meeting at the Backdoor Restaurant during which plans were discussed to raise up to $250,000 for the legal defense of pinball interests in Kentucky: (1) Leon Levitch, president of the Southern Liquor Company; (2) I.E. Robinson, sales manager of the Falls City Wholesale Liquor Company; (3) James Hutchinson, sales manager of the Crane Distributing Company (a wholesale liquor distributor); (4) T. Owen Campbell, president of Crane Distributing Company; (5) Frank E. Haddad, Jr., and (6) Leon Shaikun, Louisville attorneys representing the Automatic Amusement Association, a statewide organization of pinball operators; (7) Bernard Berhman, president of B & B Amusement Company, one of the state's largest pinball operators; (8) Robert Berhman, Bernard's brother and secretary-treasurer of B & B; (9) Jack Swarz, a business associate of the Berhmans; and (10) Harry Davis, a Frankfort attorney. The most notable personage allegedly attending the meeting, however, was Marlow W. Cook, the Jefferson County judge and an important figure not only in Jefferson County politics but also in the state Republican party. The grand jury exonerated Cook "of any wrongdoing whatsoever" in connection with the May 18 meeting. While all of the men mentioned in Breathitt's letter to Schroering were at lunch at the restaurant at approximately the same hour, only Robinson and Levitch were there at the invitation of the Berhmans, according to the grand jury report. Furthermore the Berhmans did, indeed, solicit contributions from Robinson, Levitch, Campbell, and Hutchinson; but Cook, Haddad, Shaikun, Davis, Swarz, and Harry Amon (a reporter with the *Courier-Journal*) were eating lunch in a separate room at the time. Though Shaikun was invited into the pinball fund discussion at one point to give an opinion on its legality, the grand jury saw no significant evidence of collusion in the incident. The grand jury concluded with recommendations that a subsequent grand jury investigate the full range of pinball activity in Jefferson County and that the governor call a special legislative session to clarify Kentucky statutes governing pinball machines and their operation. *Louisville Courier-Journal,* April 24, 25, 1965; June 30, 1965; July 16, 22, 1965.

2. Bernard Berhman, president, B & B Amusement Company. Robert Berhman, secretary-treasurer, B & B Amusement Company. *Louisville Courier-Journal,* June 30, 1965.

3. Frank E. Haddad, Jr. (1928-), born in Louisville, Kentucky; L.L.B., University of Louisville (1952); engaged in law practice in Louisville (1952-); president, Louisville Bar Association (1964); president, Kentucky Bar Association (1978). Telephone interview, March 9, 1981.

4. Cary Estes Kefauver (1903-1963), L.L.B., Yale University (1927); U.S. House of Representatives (1939-1949); U.S. Senate (1948-1963); Democratic nominee for vice president (1956); became a national figure in the 1950s as a result of his Senate probe into organized crime in the United States. *Biographical Directory of the American Congress, 1774-1971* (Washington, 1971), p. 1216.

PINBALL MACHINE STATEMENT
Frankfort / February 6, 1966

THE attack made on me yesterday by the pinball gamblers was not unexpected.[1] I am not surprised. I imagine that during the next few days the protests of their lobbyists both privately and publicly at Frankfort will be long, loud, and specious. They will attempt to lull the legislators and the public to accept their so-called amusement machines as simply innocent servants of whimsy. "Just a harmless means of sport and entertainment," they will say. It will be the same arguments the gamblers used in the early 1950s when the state moved to rid itself of the old one-armed bandit slot machines.

However, nothing could be farther [to] the contrary. Pinball gambling is cancerous and widespread in some areas of this state, and like any malignancy, it must be cut out at the roots. Pinball slot machine gambling is a forty million dollar illegal industry in Kentucky that exploits the poor and the young. The bingo-type pinball machine takes in money much faster than the old slot machine. Careful surveillance of one location near an industrial plant in Jefferson County by state police on a recent payday revealed that more than $400 was deposited in four machines in less than eight hours. Ask any schoolboy in Kentucky if payoffs on these machines are common practice. These machines serve no useful purpose, fill no sociological, psychological, aesthetic, or moral need. These machines exist simply for the enrichment of those who own and operate them.

Twenty-seven other states in this country have outlawed the multiple-coin pinball slot machines. The Congress of the United States in 1963 passed anticrime legislation to curb the interstate traffic of these machines. And the U.S. Justice Department selected Louisville, because of the widespread operation there and because Kentucky ranked third among all states in number of machines, to test a legal suit in federal court. The court held in March of 1965 in Louisville that the bingo-type pinball machine was a gambling device per se and illegal. However, a federal court decision is not binding on state courts.

Last summer a Jefferson County grand jury called on the state to pass legislation to clarify our present law and ban the pinball slot machines. Jefferson County Judge Marlow Cook, Commonwealth Attorney Edwin Schroering, and other officials echoed these same sentiments.[2] Mayor Kenneth Schmeid, in his campaign last fall, and Republican and Democratic candidates for the General Assembly also supported state legislation to eradicate this illegal gambling. I am in agreement with their positions and intend to put the full weight of my administration behind passage of Senate Bill 104. As long ago as last July, I called for legislation to ban these machines.

Senate Bill 104, if passed, will re-establish the pinball law as it existed in 1950 and for many years prior to that time, permitting play on single coin machines for amusement only, not gambling.[3] The law, if enacted, will eliminate the metering device which records free games in each machine and will outlaw the multiple coin bingo-type slot machine. The Senate will conduct a committee hearing Tuesday where a demonstration of the bingo-type pinball gambling machine will be conducted. I'm confident that this demonstration will show that these machines are illegal gambling devices and that we ought to ban this activity.

---

1. On February 5, 1966, Leon Shaikun, attorney for the Automatic Amusement Association, issued a statement protesting the introduction of Senate Bill 104 by Senator J.D. Burkman, the majority floor leader. The bill proposed to repeal subsection 5 of *Kentucky Revised Statutes* 436.230, a 1950 statute which exempted free play pinball machines from the legal definition of gambling devices established by a series of Court of Appeals decisions in the 1940s. Shaikun claimed that the bill's introduction contradicted an earlier statement by Breathitt that he would allow the

courts to determine the legality of pinball machines in a case which was then under consideration on appeal. Shaikun went on to defend his clients' pinball operations. The machines, he claimed, were not intended to serve as gambling devices, nor were they controlled by large gambling businesses, and their occasional misuse could be remedied under existing legislation without resort to the extreme measures advocated by the governor. Shaikun concluded by pointing out the inconsistency in the governor's attack on pinball machines while pari-mutuel machines were allowed to operate at the state's racetracks without the least hindrance.

2. Edwin Anthony Schroering, Jr. (1929-), born in Louisville, Kentucky; B.A., University of Louisville (1951); J.D. (1953); assistant U.S. attorney, Western District of Kentucky (1959-1960); assistant county attorney, Jefferson County (1961-1962); commonwealth attorney (1963-1975); law practice in Louisville (1956-). Telephone interview, March 5, 1981.

3. See "an act relating to gambling," *Acts, 1966,* Chapter 5 (S.B. 104), pp. 96-9. Governor Breathitt signed the bill on February 16, 1966. "For me it has been a difficult fight against a big, well-financed, well-organized operation," he said. "To the many legislators who had the courage to stand up against this menace, I commend and express my appreciation." Press release, February 16, 1966, Breathitt papers.

CITIZENS ADVISORY COMMITTEE LUNCHEON
Eddyville Penitentiary
Eddyville / August 4, 1966

I AM sincerely grateful for the interest you evidence in this institution. As interested citizens you provide us wise counsel and direction we need to evaluate our progress and rechart the course to meet present and future needs. We have realized our greatest gains at the penitentiary in the recruitment of better-qualified personnel, and the training and development of personnel who have been with the institution for a period of time.

The most significant personnel changes have consisted of the appointment of a professionally trained warden, in the person of John W. Wingo, and the establishment of a new position of associate warden for treatment.[1] This associate warden's position was filled, until his recent death, by a clinically trained psychologist. We have a candidate for this position, and it is believed that this vacancy will soon be filled to strengthen our rehabilitation program. The transfer of our school principal to associate warden for custody has greatly increased our effectiveness in rehabilitating inmates of this institution.

A qualified training officer has been recruited from the federal Bureau of Prisons, and staff development programs have been established as a result of his joining the staff. In addition to this, a full-time dentist and the services of two physicians have been secured to improve the overall dental and medical service. New teaching positions have been established and filled. New methods of teaching the illiterate offender have been established, in cooperation with Western Kentucky University.

Salaries and recruitment standards for correctional officers have been upgraded. A personnel performance rating system has been established. And, on the first of July, the five-day work week was initiated, as I pledged. Civilian clerks have replaced inmates in the records office.

A comprehensive master disturbance-control plan has been developed. Farm trucks have been equipped with mobile radio units, and each farm detail supervisor is provided with a walkie-talkie set. These preventive measures have greatly reduced the walk-away rate.

Recent new construction includes a sewage disposal plant; a school constructed entirely by inmate labor; a 300,000-gallon water storage tank; and a slaughterhouse.

Architects are now drawing plans for a $500,000 farm dormitory complex which will be under construction later this year. A medical clinic costing $75,000 will also soon be under construction. Both these additions were provided for in the bond issue passed last year.

Cell house number four is presently being renovated and bids are out for renovation of cell house number five, both projects to cost $155,000. At the same time, we are modernizing the lighting system within the compound at a cost of $15,000, and a like amount is being spent to expand the clothing plant of the prison industry. Of the $700,000 that is being spent on projects at this penitentiary, more than $500,000 is being spent to help in the rehabilitation of inmates. . . .[2]

It has been estimated that a life of crime on the average costs the taxpayers $100,000. This is a ghastly sum and points up the importance of rehabilitation, the importance of changing a man from a life of crime to a responsible citizen if it is possible. Along these lines in Kentucky, I feel we are making progress.

The expansion of the clothing plant here is a step in our program to provide full-time purposeful employment to all able-bodied inmates and expand our rehabilitation efforts. The new farm dormitory will provide facilities for ninety men who will work in agriculture, not only to provide food for this institution, but to help them learn the latest farming methods. Though we've made progress, we still have a long way to go, however, to provide enough purposeful employment. I think all of you will agree with me that John Wingo is doing a fine job as warden. He is a real asset to this institution and to this program. I also want to compliment this committee, which is a hardworking group—a group that meets often and contributes much to the overall program.

---

1. John Will Wingo (1913-), teacher, public schools, Graves County, Kentucky (1935-1938); supervisor, U.S. Civilian Conservation Corps, Van Nuys, California (1938-1942); officer and administrator, U.S. Bureau of Prisons, Washington, D.C. (1942-1965); warden, director of institutions and acting commissioner, Kentucky Department of Corrections (1965-). *Who's Who in the South and Southwest, 1971-1972,* 12th ed. (Chicago, 1971).

2. A section of this speech, repetitious of remarks made by Governor Breathitt in his statement on corrections November 12, 1964, has been deleted. That address is included in these papers.

CAMPBELL COUNTY CHAMBER OF COMMERCE
Newport / August 29, 1966

It is my pleasure to announce today that the state will build a Northern Kentucky Regional Diagnostic Center for delinquents on a fifteen-acre site in Boone County parallel to Interstate Highway 75 near the Florence interchange. We have just completed negotiations with Judge Bruce Ferguson and other Boone County citizens for the purchase of this land, which will be obtained from the Boone County Foundation for approximately $ 30,000.[1]

The center, which will be operated by the state Department of Child Welfare, will provide service to seven northern Kentucky counties—Campbell, Boone, Kenton, Pendleton, Grant, Gallatin, and Carroll. Total cost of the project will be $450,000, provided for by the 1965 bond issue. In this center we will determine, after careful study and evaluation, the causes for delinquent young people's behavior and then prescribe rehabilitative treatment. It will be our hope that this treatment will bring about changed behavior, so that when they return to their communities, they will be able to take their respective places as young successful citizens. An advantage of this center will be the ability to permit children placed in it to remain close to their homes and communities, allowing staff members to work closely with their parents and other interested persons.

I believe that the construction of the northern Kentucky center should be the beginning of a long-range program to establish five such reception-diagnostic centers across Kentucky. While it will be impossible to construct these other facilities during the remaining seventeen months of this administration, I am today directing the Department of Child Welfare to proceed immediately with planning on these projects. Once completed, these facilities would give our state a program for delinquent children second to none in this nation.

These regional centers could also provide adequate detention facilities for those counties in Kentucky which lack detention facilities for children and consequently must place boys and girls in common jails. This would enable us to take a big step forward in overcoming this travesty of justice which is, of course, in violation of current statute.

I also want to report that we are proceeding with our plans on the Daniel Boone Boys' Camp near Bellevue, and we hope to have it operational early next year. A total of $185,000 has been set aside in our current budget for renovation and construction of this camp, which will provide residential care and treatment for forty-five young boys between the ages of nine and twelve. The camp will be located at former lock site thirty-eight, which has been awarded to the Commonwealth of Kentucky by the U.S. Corps of Engineers. The lock site has several existing cottages and other facilities which will be converted in such a way as to provide residential care for groups of boys no larger than eight to ten.

Two new buildings, a kitchen and a dormitory-classroom facility, will be constructed. This type of small grouping permits a high level of interaction between staff and children and, in many ways, simulates the living arrangement of a normal family. There is approximately twelve and one-half acres of ground which will lend itself very nicely to recreation and other outdoor activities.

Because of the ages of the boys, a great deal of attention will be given to remedial and special education programs. Arrangements have been worked out by the Department of Child Welfare for the Boone County school system to provide teachers. The funds for these teaching units will be paid for by the Minimum Foundation Program. The classes will be small and geared toward the individual needs of the boys so that they may have the experience of a positive classroom situation. Most of these boys are educational cripples and have truanted and been poorly motivated toward formal school. Admissions and discharges from the facility will be regulated around the regular school year as much as possible.

In addition to the intensive remedial education program, boys will work, eat, and sleep as members of small treatment groups. These groups will meet for special problem solving sessions many times during each week. All boys will have individual counseling, and the families will be involved in treatment and planning on a regular basis. With this total family impact and intensive involvement of the child, this program will take on the aspects of a preventive treatment approach and will alter the deviant, delinquent behavior of the children involved.

With the opening of this camp, the Department of Child Welfare will have in operation four camps serving different age groups. This camp facility provides the type of program that is so necessary for the disturbed or delinquent child or youth. This youth forest camp program will combine with a single continuous impact the preservation and conservation of both our human and natural resources.

---

1. Bruce Stuart Ferguson (1929-), born in Covington, Kentucky, educated University of Kentucky and Villa Madonna College, B.A. (1966); member, board of education, Boone County (1955-1964); county judge executive (1964-). Telephone interview, March 5, 1981.

PRESS RELEASE
Frankfort / September 22, 1966

I HAVE today dismissed Joseph Cannon as commissioner of corrections and named John Wingo, warden of Eddyville State Penitentiary, acting commissioner.

This action follows conversations I have had with Mr. Cannon during the last several weeks in which I expressed dissatisfaction with his conduct of his position. I asked him to submit his resignation and have given him a period of about two months in which to resign. Since Mr. Cannon has chosen not to resign, dismissal has become necessary.[1]

I regret deeply that this is so, but I feel that I have no alternative if Kentucky is going to progress in its penology program. This program is important to all Kentuckians, and I do not intend to jeopardize it any longer by retaining a commissioner who refuses to cooperate with me or with other officials in my administration with whom he is supposed to be working.

This Mr. Cannon has refused to do. He has not only ignored directives from me and from the legislature; he has ignored or tried to ignore the basic rules of administration of state government to the point where his department is a constant source of turmoil for the rest of state government.

I do not believe the people of Kentucky want the continuation of a situation where one of the most important departments of their state government is rendered impotent by the inability of its administrator to live up to his responsibilities.

I pledge to the people of Kentucky that this department will become a strong department and that Kentucky's corrections program will progress. I have great confidence in the ability of Mr. Wingo and appreciate his agreeing to become acting commissioner. We will move as quickly as possible to recruit a permanent man for this job, and I have named a committee to assist in the recruiting. On the committee are Dr. E. Preston Sharp, general secretary, American Corrections Association, Washington, D.C.; Dr. James B. Bennett, head of the Federal Bureau of Prisons; Dr. Paul Oberst, acting dean of the University of Kentucky Law School; Dean Kenneth W. Kindlesperger, of the Kent School of Social Work, University of Louisville; and George Stoll, Louisville, a member of the Commission on Corrections and Community Action.[2]

---

1. According to the *Courier-Journal* Cannon's differences with Governor Breathitt dated from the beginning of the administration. At the news conference announcing the dismissal of Cannon, Breathitt cited several examples of the commissioner's insubordination and lack of cooperation. According to the governor, Cannon had appointed Henry Burns as deputy commissioner, an appointment Breathitt opposed, while the governor was out of state. Burns had failed to act on a resolution passed by the 1966 General Assembly establishing a program to send prisoners into high schools to impress upon teenagers the unfortunate consequences of crime. In addition, Cannon had proved unable to articulate a corrections program sufficiently attractive to generate public and legislative enthusiasm. Finally, the governor suggested Cannon had disregarded merit system procedures. *Louisville Courier-Journal,* September 23, 1965, and *Acts, 1966,* Chapter 44 (HR. 73). p. 366-67.

2. Edward Preston Sharp (1904-   ), criminologist, educator; Ph.D., University of Pittsburgh (1933), various educational positions, Pennsylvania public schools (1926-1945); director, Bureau of Community Work, Pennsylvania Department of Welfare (1945-1948); chief, division of training schools, Pennsylvania Department of Welfare (1948-   ). *Who's Who in America, 1966-1967,* 34th ed. (Chicago, 1966). James V. Bennett (1894-1978), born at Silver Creek, New York: B.A., Brown University (1918); L.L.B., George Washington University, Washington, D.C. (1926); U.S. Army (1917-1918); assistant investigator and management analyst, U.S. Bureau of Efficiency (1919-1930); assistant director, U.S. Bureau of Prisons (1930-1937); director (1937-1964). Information provided by U.S. Bureau of Prisons, Washington, D.C. Paul Oberst (1914-   ), J.D., University of Kentucky (1939); L.L.M., University of Michigan (1941); associated with firm of Ryland, Stinson, Mag and Thomson, Kansas City, Missouri (1941-1942); member of faculty, University of Kentucky Law School (1946-   ); professor and director, civil liberties program, New York University (1959-1961); member, Kentucky Commission on Corrections (1961-1965); Kentucky Commission on Human Rights (1962-1970,

1973-1976). *Who's Who in American Law,* 1st ed. (Chicago, 1977). Kenneth W. Kindelsperger (1914-), B.S., George Williams College (1940); M.S. (1942); D.D.S., Syracuse University (1956); U.S. Navy (1942-1946); lecturer in sociology, Syracuse University (1946-1950); assistant professor of social work and sociology (1950-1957); dean, Kent School of Social Work, University of Louisville (1962-1971). Information provided by University Archives and Records, University of Louisville. George Stoll, no information available.

KENTUCKY STATE REFORMATORY
LaGrange / November 30, 1966

I APPRECIATE the opportunity to meet with you this evening. I want to thank HELP, the sponsoring organization, for extending me this invitation. It is encouraging to me, and I believe it is to our staff members in the Corrections Department, to know that there are many organizations such as HELP within this institution through which the inmates take the initiative to develop their own capabilities toward becoming productive citizens.

You know, until in recent years such organizations as HELP (health, education, leadership, and public relations for self-improvement) were unheard of in penal institutions. And I am happy that Kentucky is among the few states which today foster and encourage such organizations. I am pleased to note that this institution is just one of eleven penal institutions in the country which have a properly chartered junior chamber of commerce chapter. Your participation in organizations of this nature is encouraging in that you have shown a desire for a better life and are willing to make an effort through cooperation with your fellow man to achieve a life more meaningful than was yours before entering here.

As you know, we have many programs within the institution which are designed to help you become better and more productive citizens when you leave here, and we are rapidly developing others. But no matter how well we plan and develop training programs for developing your capabilities, we know we cannot hope to succeed unless you show a genuine interest in improving yourself and taking advantage of what we have to offer.

It is interesting to note that only two years ago we began a treatment program here with only four staff members, and today we have a highly trained staff of fifty-six who are carrying out and expanding these programs. Today, in our education department alone, there are 250 inmates who are taking advantage of training either on a full- or part-time basis, and there are more than 95 percent of the institution's population who are participating in a recreation program.

Education is, I believe, the most significant program here. It is the most important program for society as a whole; our social and economic system is built upon education, so why shouldn't education be the most important function for you here? A fact we must face is that modern man cannot compete in today's complex society unless he can do something well and understand something of the problems before him. As automation proceeds, there will be an ever diminishing need for the simpler jobs formerly open to those with limited skills and little education. Those who lack education will find themselves vulnerable and unwanted—a social and economic cancer.

Therefore, we are laying the utmost emphasis upon vocational training throughout the Commonwealth for those youths so inclined, and we are equally stressing vocational education training here in the belief it will benefit more inmates in the shortest possible time. I can say to you tonight that we intend to double the facilities for vocational education here in the immediate future. Before I leave office next December, I expect to see under construction here a building that will provide training for at least 200 inmates, or twice as much training opportunity as now available. I already have set aside $200,000 in state bond money, and I expect this soon to be supplemented by enough federal funds that will construct a building costing from $300,000 to $400,000.

When completed, this new school will be an extension of the state's area vocational school at Jeffersontown, which soon is to be expanded by an addition costing $600,000. This new school here will be a cooperative project by the Corrections Department, the Department of Education, and the Department of Vocational Rehabilitation.

We intend to tailor the courses offered here for the age of automation so that when inmates leave here they will be properly skilled to take advantage of the existing labor market. Our education program in the Corrections Department already is extensive. One hundred inmates at this institution alone are in vocational training, and sixty-five others who have been paroled from here to our three community guidance centers are also in training.

You know, our community guidance centers, or the half-way house concept, is another phase of prison reform for the betterment of the inmate and one which Kentucky is among a relatively few states to have adopted. And Kentucky is the only state which has obtained federal funds of a $1,079,000 for that purpose. This program, now only a year old, is among those which in time will play a major role in making life more meaningful for convicted offenders. Through this program, courses are being taught in auto mechanics, auto body repair, welding, carpentry, and industrial electricity.

We also are in the process of establishing a continuing in-service training program for all employees which will be implemented during the month of December. These programs will offer instruction in a wide variety of subjects—all designed to improve and upgrade the staff.

The religious program of the institution will continue to be upgraded with the establishment of a religious teaching program utilizing students from Louisville Presbyterian Seminary and Southern Baptist Theological Seminary during the academic year as well as students from other major protestant seminaries during the summer. These students, while serving the need of the inmates, will be receiving clinical pastoral training under joint supervision of the seminary faculty and our own chaplains.

It is hoped that the dental laboratory will shortly be involved in the manufacturing of dentures for other state institutions. We are in the process of obtaining accreditation for our dental laboratory. This program also will serve a dual purpose in that the inmate technicians will be receiving realistic training as well as providing a service to their fellow man.

Arrangements are presently being made with the Bureau of Rehabilitation in order to provide additional services to the inmate body in the area of vocational training, and counseling, for those inmates in need of this type of service prior to their return to the community. These, then, are but a few of our accomplishments and goals. We still have a long way to go to make this truly a rehabilitation institution, but we are headed in the right direction. Philosophies and attitudes toward convicted offenders are changing. Prisons are no longer regarded merely as holding institutions. We recognize the need to provide in those programs which will help the convicted offender become a useful person to himself, his family, and his community.

We believe this can be accomplished, for society is spending a great deal of money and is making a big effort for that purpose. I for one do not believe our many programs for self-improvement here are in vain. You apparently do not either; otherwise more than 250 of you would not have joined such organizations as HELP, the junior chamber of commerce, the AAA, or SPADE (society of personality, adjustment, development, and education).

COMMISSION ON CHILD WELFARE
Frankfort / December 6, 1966

I AM announcing today the first long-range, comprehensive blueprint for the care, treatment and rehabilitation of delinquent youth in Kentucky. The program, a six-year institutional construction plan, is the result of long and careful study by the Department of Child Welfare. With twenty-one new buildings and four renovation projects, it will ultimately provide for the accommodation of over 1,337 children at any one time. The six-year plan is being launched today with the awarding of two contracts for the construction of the Daniel Boone Boys' Camp in Boone County and the Jewel Manor Treatment Center for Girls in Jefferson County.

These and the other new projects included in the six-year plan are Kentucky's response to the growing need for juvenile rehabilitation services. New commitments of juveniles to the Department of Child Welfare rose from 580 in 1960 to 820 a year in 1966. And it is estimated that residential facilities must be developed to accommodate over 1,400 new commitments by 1972. The total population at our present six child welfare facilities averages 850. These institutions were designed to accommodate 550—this is their "rated capacity." Our proposed six-year plan will enable the Commonwealth to handle the new commitment and free itself from inadequate, overcrowded, and antiquated institutions.

Let me point out that we are concentrating our building efforts on institutions for delinquent youth because it is the delinquent who is most urgently in need of institutional care. The Child Welfare Department currently operates one facility for the dependent, neglected, or emotionally disturbed child. But it has been recognized nationwide that the best plan for dependent children, who for the most part do not require institutional care, is a home in a community. Our efforts on behalf of the child who has no problem other than dependency or neglect will be concentrated, therefore, on a vigorously developed home care program.

The construction of Jewel Manor and Daniel Boone Boys' Camp will get under way immediately. The contract for the construction of the Boone Boys' Camp is being awarded today to the William Vaughn Building Company, Inc., Cincinnati, for $287,657. Construction is to be completed within 250 days. The contract for construction of Jewel Manor, to be completed within 340 days, is awarded to E.L. Noe & Sons, Inc., Louisville, for their low bid of $615,656.

Daniel Boone Boys' Camp is being developed for forty-five boys between the ages of nine and twelve, who have been committed to the department as delinquents in need of residential care. It is the fourth such camp for boys in Kentucky. Jewel Manor will be designed to accommodate forty-eight young delinquent girls. The Kentucky Federation of Women's Clubs has agreed to raise approximately $75,000 toward construction costs of Jewel Manor. The state's share will come from proceeds of the 1965 bond issue. Jewel Manor will be Kentucky's first completely separate treatment center for girls. Young girls now are sent from the reception center at Louisville to Kentucky Village near Lexington—our largest and most overcrowded institution for delinquents. Commissioner Harmon, whose knowledge of the field is well recognized, tells me that Jewel Manor will be the best institution for the treatment of delinquent girls in the South.[1]

In keeping with the philosophy that it is best to program and provide facilities easily accessible to courts, communities, and families, we are including in our six-year program a statewide system of regional reception-diagnostic centers. The first such facility—the Northern Kentucky Regional Diagnostic and Detention Center—will cost an estimated $600, 000 and will be designed to house fifty children. Our first choice for a site was near Florence; however, a petition, circulated by some citizens protesting construction there, caused us to change our plans on this. I am today instructing Commissioner Harmon of the Child Welfare Department and Finance Commissioner Felix Joyner to seek a new site for this center.[2] Meanwhile, architectural and other work will proceed so that we will be ready to move immediately when a new site is ready.

In addition to the northern Kentucky center, four other regional diagnostic centers have been planned as part of the six-year program: at Louisville, in western Kentucky, southeastern Kentucky, and eastern Kentucky. No sites have been selected for these yet. The Louisville center will handle about 110 children; the other three are for 50 children each. Target dates for launching construction of these centers are: 1968 for Louisville, 1970 for western Kentucky, 1971 for southeastern Kentucky, and 1972 for eastern Kentucky.

In addition to the Boone County boys' camp, the six-year plan provides for construction of eight additional camps, two to be built in each of the years from 1968 through 1971. The camps will each accommodate forty-five boys of various age groups. When completed, Kentucky will have twelve of these camps, including the present three at Gilbertsville, Woodsbend, and Lake Cumberland.

The boys at these camps are involved in work, education, and group therapy programs. The small population of the camps allows for closer relationships between the staff and the boys, which is the real backbone of our residential treatment.

In addition to the eight new camps, at the Barkley Boys' Camp near Gilbertsville new buildings will be constructed to replace all the old facilities, except for the superintendent's home and one shop building. The

Barkley camp is the oldest of the three existing camps, first constructed in 1956 as a summer camping facility. Replacement of the old buildings is slated to begin in 1969.

The Kentucky Reception Center will also undergo a facelifting. The center is scheduled to be converted to an intensive treatment unit, with work to start in 1968. The renovation will provide security features and programs for fifty boys—those who cannot adequately be cared for elsewhere. This group will include the chronic AWOLers, the youths convicted of aggressive and assaultive behavior, and those considered to be a threat to the community.

Facilities at Kentucky Village will also be renovated. The work is scheduled for 1969. Kentucky Village has a present population averaging about 450. It has the staff to adequately rehabilitate no more than 200 children. The program, after the renovation, would be devoted to those children who need longer-term institutional care than is provided in the camps or elsewhere. The academic and vocational programs at the village would be sharply upgraded, with a variety of small vocational education and academic classes offered.

At the Kentucky Children's Home, currently operating for the dependent, neglected, and emotionally disturbed child, a renovation project will help us convert this facility to use for emotionally disturbed children only.

A new program in child welfare work in Kentucky would be launched with the construction of four halfway houses in 1972. They will be located near the regional diagnostic centers, and each will house about sixteen children recently discharged from other institutions. The halfway houses will help to bridge the gap between the institution and the home, thus aiding the adjustment back to the community. Also scheduled in 1972 are two residential treatment centers, each to house fifty girls aged thirteen to eighteen. They will be modeled after similar programs at Kentucky Village. These centers will help us hold down the population at Kentucky Village, while providing for the expected increase in commitments to the Child Welfare Department.

Our goal, of course, is not just buildings for custodial care of the youngsters who come to us. We have a treatment program in Kentucky, and we have a good treatment program. Our goal is to have the finest facilities available in which to carry this program out. I am convinced that by 1972, when all of these facilities are under way, Kentucky can look forward to the best program for treatment and care of juveniles in the nation.

---

1. Maurice Harmon (1916-   ), born Xenia, Ohio; B.S. Ohio State University; M.A. Western Reserve, Cleveland. Prior to assuming his post as commissioner of child welfare, Harmon served twelve years as supervisor of juvenile rehabilitation

for the state of Washington and director of two training schools for juvenile delinquents in Montana. He served as commissioner of child welfare for Kentucky from 1965-1968. *Louisville Courier-Journal,* July 14, 1965, and February 10, 1968.

2. Felix Joyner (1924-), born in Savannah, Georgia and a resident of Chapel Hill, North Carolina; budget analyst in Department of Finance, head of Division of the Budget, deputy commissioner (1945-1955), administrator of state Health and Welfare Agency (1959-1963); commissioner of finance (1963-1967). George W. Robinson, ed., *The Public Papers of Governor Bert T. Combs, 1959-1963* (Lexington, Ky., 1979), p. 399.

PRESS CONFERENCE
Frankfort / February 16, 1967

I AM today announcing the appointment of Mr. Sture V. Westerberg, a professional penologist with nearly twenty-five years' experience with the federal Bureau of Prisons, as commissioner of corrections.[1] The appointment of Mr. Westerberg is being made after careful and extensive consideration of several applicants by the Commission on Corrections and Community Service, the Department of Personnel, and me in an effort to obtain the services of a highly qualified and competent commissioner. Mr. Westerberg, in my opinion, will provide outstanding leadership to the Department of Corrections so that we will be able to continue the progress we've made in improving our correctional system.

This administration is dedicated to an overall philosophy of penology based on two principles. First, our job is to imprison the convicted offender and retain him in a humane manner for the period of time prescribed by judge or jury, subject to probation and parole. Second, our long-range goal must be to give a man something he did not have before in terms of an understanding of his own problems, plus, if possible, enable him to cope with life outside the prison walls once he is released. I feel, and feel deeply, that our correctional system would be a total failure if it performed no other task than custody.

In Mr. Westerberg we have a man who understands the importance of education and rehabilitation as well as custody in operating our institutions. A large portion of his experience has been involved in supervising education and vocational training programs in our federal prison system. This experience and understanding will enable him to provide valuable leadership in this vital area of successfully restoring an offender to the community as a productive, contributing member of society.

Mr. Westerberg, in his administrative posts, including his assignment as acting warden of the United States Federal Reformatory at Chillicothe, has served effectively and efficiently. He comes highly recommended as an administrator of excellent competence and character. In my own personal interview with him and his family, I found Mr. Westerberg to be highly motivated, knowledgable, and personable. I think he will be a fine asset to our community of state employees. Mr. Westerberg will assume his new duties March 6 with my full support to continue our efforts to upgrade and professionalize Kentucky's correctional system. A good correctional program is what this administration is committed to and what the people of Kentucky expect. . . .[2]

---

1. Sture V. Westerberg (1906-), born in Sweden and educated in Minnesota, Ohio, and Maryland; U.S. Navy (1943-1946); teacher in public schools of Minnesota (1927-1941); supervisor of education, U.S. National Training School for Boys, Washington, D.C. (1942-1943, 1947-1953); supervisor of education, U.S. Federal Reformatory, Petersburg, Virginia (1954-1960); associate warden, U.S. Correctional Institution, Englewood, California (1961-1962); acting warden, U.S. Federal Reformatory, Chillicothe, Ohio (1962-1967); commissioner of corrections, Commonwealth of Kentucky (1967-1969). Biographical statement in Corrections File, Breathitt papers, and Division of Personnel, Frankfort.

2. Governor Breathitt's concluding remarks, in which he expressed appreciation to those individuals who assisted in the selection of Westerberg, have been deleted.

KENTUCKY CRIME COMMISSION
Frankfort / July 5, 1967

I HAVE called you here today to undertake a monumental task. The problems to which I ask you to address yourselves are perplexing and frustrating as any in our society. They affect the lives of more people more intimately and directly than any other that comes to mind. By contemporary law and historic tradition, their solution is the responsibility of governmental institutions, although private organizations cooperate extensively and generously.

You, I, and all others who have assumed public or private responsibilities for securing and maintaining a better way of life for our fellow citizens have reason for doubting the effectiveness of the control system used heretofore, as the problems I refer to multiply, rather than diminish. And I refer, of course, to the complex cluster of problems which both end and begin with criminal behavior. A criminal act is the end of a process. It signifies the failure, pro tanto, of our laws, policies and institutions aimed, in whole or in part, at the prevention of acts forbidden by legislative decree.

The act is also the beginning of a second process, that of law enforcement. It is not in every case, of course, because an enormous volume of criminal activity goes on, unreported and unchallenged. We can now only guess at the volume of unreported crime in Kentucky. And the responsible police and judicial officials are the first to state that law enforcement processes are only partially successful in responding to reported crime.

The situation in our Commonwealth is not as serious as in other more populous and urbanized states. It is, nevertheless, intolerable and growing worse. I could point to some statistics, although these are shamefully incomplete. There is probably no other fundamental social problem in this country about which so few relevant data are known. But statistics, even if perfect, can never reflect what is to me the most important fact about crime—its incalculable toll in terms of human values—the family, the home, freedom from fear, physical and economic well-being, among others.

The deprivations suffered by our people are intolerable. They look to government at all levels for relief, and small wonder some tend to doubt the effectiveness of free democratic institutions when the human toll continues to mount. Government officials, present and future, need your assistance in planning a strategy for the future. This is why I, in behalf of myself, my successors, the General Assembly, the leaders of units of local government and all the people, have called you here today.

My charge to you is to answer two fundamental questions. First, why are our present laws, institutions, policies, and procedures not meeting the challenges of law enforcement and crime prevention? And second, what changes are necessary in order that government and all institutions in our society can fully meet their responsibilities?

I hope and believe that out of your deliberations on these two questions, in all their complexity, will come a viable, intelligent, and effective strategy for a war on crime in Kentucky. I wish to articulate this broad charge with a few points which should serve as guidelines to you. First, your aim should be reasoned, principled, and constructive appraisal and criticism of our laws, institutions, policies, and procedures. The sound elements in our system should be recognized for their merit and thereby strengthened. No element should be taken to task in the interim or annual report unless a better alternative is articulated.

Second, the range of your specific inquiries should be as broad as the problem itself. The ultimate goal is an overall, but articulated, strategy; hence you should treat as many problems as possible. Of course, I recognize that constraints of time limit the number of specific proposals which can be digested before the annual report next July. However, from the nature of the problem and of the commission as constituted, there is good reason to believe that its lifetime will be longer than one year. Hence, it is likely that knowledge even of your incomplete studies will prove to be of invaluable assistance to a future commission.

Third, I direct your attention to the recommendations of the president's Commission on Law Enforcement and Administration of Justice. These contain the current thinking of many of the best-qualified authorities in the nation. As a starting point for your work, I recommend the analysis of these reports in terms of their present or prospective application to the problems of the Commonwealth.

Fourth, bear in mind that every established civil liberty must be given recognition and protection. Identify those present practices which are in derogation of constitutional rights. Insure that every proposal for change can bear close constitutional scrutiny.

Fifth, secure the advice and assistance of every citizen who can make an effective contribution, within the commission's organizational framework.

Sixth, within the reasonable limits of human foresight and advance judgment, try to anticipate the problems of the future, to the extent that they differ from those with us today. What will they be and what can we do to forestall them?

Seventh, call upon the officials of the executive branch of state government whenever they can be of assistance. The door of no one responsible to me as governor is closed to you, provided that all the rights of the public are maintained.

I would like also to take this opportunity, in behalf of the commission, to request the cooperation of all public officials in supplying the information and other assistance, without which the commission cannot hope to act intelligently. I trust that these few guidelines will help define the scope and intent of the commission's work. Your chairman will supplement them in his remarks.

You are a commission of forty members, a number by no means too large in terms of the mission you are asked to accomplish. The state of Michigan, for example, has half again as many members. Coordinated committee work will be a key element in the total program, as Mr. Mills will explain.[1] He and the committee chairmen have assumed extra responsibilities in making each committee, and such joint- and subcommittees as may be established, effective instruments in this undertaking. The executive director and his staff will assume responsibility for communications, the preparations of reports and other papers, meetings, and, with the steering committee of committee chairmen, the preparation of agenda.

In appointing each of you to this body, I have recognized again what has so often been observed before—your leadership in law enforcement and crime prevention in the widely various capacities in which you have served the Commonwealth heretofore. By the same token, I have expressed my hope and belief that you will apply the energies and abilities that distinguish you to one of the most compelling problems of our time.

Thank you for accepting this challenge and coming here today.

---

1. Maubert R. Mills (1925-), attorney from Madisonville, Kentucky; L.L.B., University of Kentucky (1950); commonwealth attorney for 4th judicial district (1958-1970); member, law firm Mills, Mitchell and Turner, Madisonville (1950-). Telephone interview March 3, 1981. Governor Breathitt appointed the commission on June 21, 1967. "The creation of this commission," he said, "is the first step in preparation for the likelihood Congress will pass the Safe Streets and Crime Control Act now before it. If this act passes . . . it will provide $50 million the first year and $350 million the second year in federal grants to states and communities. By moving early . . . I am hopeful Kentucky . . . will get in on the ground floor in qualifying for federal funds." The commission was to make an interim report on December 1, 1967, for use of the next governor and the 1968 General Assembly. Press release, Corrections file, Breathitt papers.

STATE GOVERNMENT

AUTOMOBILE PURCHASE STATEMENT
Frankfort / July 2, 1964

In order to clarify my position on the purchase of ten new automobiles by the state, I feel that I should put the record straight on several matters involving this purchase. First, I feel very strongly that we should adopt a system of uniformity on the purchase of automobiles whenever we can because of economy. I am opposed to buying one car at a time, or maybe two, or even three in one order—all of various makes and models and equipment. I believe we should, whenever possible, combine these purchases in one, larger order and specify the exact standards. For this reason, on January 14, I held up the purchase of five cars which were individually requisitioned.

I believe the state's responsibility is to furnish adequate transportation, in order to carry out official duties, on the most economical basis possible. I therefore asked that medium-price cars be purchased and that all of them be purchased on one order. This made it possible for several dealers to bid on the cars. There is no question in my mind that if we buy cars singly and with various types of equipment, we can always expect a much higher cost to the state. Because of our opposition to this type purchasing, we were able to save the taxpayers several thousand dollars on the purchase of the cars. The list price on the Mercury Monterey purchased is $3,810, including federal tax. Through our revised purchasing methods, we obtained each car for $2,550. I consider this a good bargain made possible through sound, business-like procedures.

Second, five of these ten new cars were routine replacements for old cars that were no longer dependable. The commissioner of agriculture and superintendent of public instruction have had leased vehicles for some time. I approved the purchase of new cars for the other elected officials because I felt all of these officials should be treated equally. Elected officials must serve the entire state and should be provided transportation to more efficiently conduct the duties of their office.

Third, it has been standard procedure for many years that the Highway Department purchase cars and lease them to other agencies. The state's motor pool is located in the Highway Department because this department uses more automobiles than any other agency and is equipped to handle lease arrangements. This procedure is perfectly legal. Also, there is not the slightest question of legality concerning who may purchase automobiles. The law very clearly and specifically says that an automobile may be purchased for any state official providing the purchase is "certified in writing by the Commissioner of Finance, with approval of the Governor. . . ." There also is no constitutional question concerning the highway revenue used to purchase these automobiles. The purchase price for the automobiles was not paid from funds earmarked for road construction by the constitution. Instead, it came from a fund in which miscellaneous receipts are placed.

Fourth, this criticism inspired by members of the opposition party is obviously political.[1] I announced in May that automobiles would be purchased for all the elected state officials and outlined the procedures for the purchase. These same critics raised no question at that time, which was certainly the time to object. Very obviously, their desire is to play politics.

---

1. Governor Breathitt's statement was in response to criticism from Representative Joe Johnson, a Republican from Lexington and a member of the Republican fiscal affairs committee. Johnson requested that Attorney General Robert Mathews block the purchases and threatened to initiate suit himself if Mathews failed to act. The automobiles were purchased from a single dealer following competitive bidding on a lot of ten cars. *Louisville Courier-Journal,* July 1, 1964.

NATIONAL ASSOCIATION OF BUDGET OFFICERS
Lexington / August 6, 1964

WE are honored to have you here in Kentucky for this budget institute. I know you have reaped great benefit from these sessions. And I hope that, in addition to the professional exchanges, the occasion will prove to have been a memorable Kentucky visit for you. We are proud that we could join your national association in sponsoring this week-long activity. We are glad we could share with you our facilities and such public resources as Jim Martin, not, incidentally, a Kentuckian by birth, but significantly, we think, a Kentuckian by choice.[1] We are very proud of him and greatly indebted to his singular record of service to the Commonwealth. Although Kentucky takes a very possessive attitude in regard to him and his talents, we are disposed to sharing him with other states for special events such as this.

It would have been revealing, I'm sure, if I could have slipped in and listened to your sessions this week. Probably any governor would have found them quite revealing. Perhaps we could have learned some of the tricks of budgeting from you. I am sure that professional self-examination of the principles and methods of budgeting must be a stimulating endeavor. Looking at yourselves as budget analysts and budget officers and sharing your work experiences and notions should be of meaningful value to you and your state budget offices in coming months.

Since the week has involved the budget analyst himself looking at the budget analyst and at budgeting, suppose we take a few minutes to let a governor look at the budget analyst and budgeting. After all, governors are interested in budgets, and maybe impressions from my side won't be inappropriate for a budget seminar.

As a rule, I find you budget people to be a rather resourceful lot. You seem versatile enough and adaptable to most all situations. You are responsive and even ingenious. You seem to be familiar with all that's going on in the state government and I'm sure we couldn't for long keep the government together without you. Budget offices seem to be much like governors' offices: they come into contact with every area and activity of the state government. There is obvious affinity between the two. They have the same interests and deal with the same specifics and keep the same long hours; but they do not, and should not, duplicate one another.

Budget people like you are professionals, dedicated to ideals of professional and continuous operation of the government. We governors are the politicians. We do not always see everything the same way you do. Sometimes we don't even go the route you recommend. The policy finally chosen is not always the one you would prefer. When this happens, you are sometimes disappointed and may even sense frustration with a particular policy direction. There are good reasons from our viewpoint when we have to go counter to the budget recommendation. There is the difference that you are the professionals, we are the politicians. Perhaps there is even some comfort in an old administrative proverb that if two people agree all the time, on everything, then one of them is unnecessary.

Now, I know of no state which elects its budget director. Neither do I know of any state which appoints its governor. These two very different sources of authority impose very different types of responsibility and different styles of operation. This system imposes different points of reference and different methods of accountability. It is these differences, I submit, that explain the different ways in which we all view the same subject matter. And these differences of authority, style, and accountability need acknowledgement by both of us. Failure on the part of either to accept as legitimate these very factors which make us different only leads to the frustration of administrative and policy machinery in our governments.

Policy making is not all technical. It is instead, and certainly ought to be, as much political as technical. This is not to say that policy should occur in a technical or factual vacuum, but it does say that political or public policy is inherently a political task. It might be better policy if purely technical, but if good policy need be less democratic than bad policy, which it doesn't, still might it not be incumbent upon us to go with the more democratic policy? I am not suggesting that the technical and political division of the policy function are necessarily exclusive of one another. They are not and neither can function best without the other. Continued and respected divisions within the policy function have advantages for both of us. After all, we have to get elected without you. You could run the government without us. We couldn't run the governments without you, but you couldn't get yourselves appointed without someone getting elected. And so, neither of us could do for very long without the other.

If we observe the legitimate divisions of our singular task, you doing the technical job, we politicians doing the political job, the system will function to the best advantage of the electorate, to whom we are all responsible. You, of necessity, must provide your chief executive with all the facts, the alternatives and their ramifications, the analysis, pinpointing the areas of contention and the possible areas for compromise.

We, of necessity, must finally make the policy decision as we, of necessity, must then live with that decision. If compromises or alternatives are possible, they should be left to the politician. Premature compromises, made in anticipation of expected executive action or preferences, do not gain your chief executive any advantage in difficult situations. Just as the chief executive should not attempt to make his decision prior to the staff work and without the full facts, you should not attempt to anticipate or restrict his field of decision. The minute either of us assumes prerogatives of the other, the entire system for policy can get botched up.

We governors are tempted on occasion to make the policy decision before all the facts get to us, just as I'm sure you are, on occasion, tempted to go ahead and make the policy without waiting for your governor. Either course represents a fundamental violation of the unwritten system, and denies the constituency the best results of the best, collective effort. The specialization within the policy function imposes upon the budget office its staff relationship to the governor, and the staff relationship itself requires the "passion for anonymity" to which your profession adheres.

The authority to analyze the facts, to review and recommend, remains an identifying characteristic of a favored spot within the administrative structure. The proper exercise of this assignment assumes the factor of anonymity, which becomes in fact your finest piece of armor, protecting both you and your chief executive. The single most valuable attribute of budget offices, aside from their technical capacity, has been their institutional ability to move almost unnoticed within the framework of their government in the service of the chief executive. Your relative anonymity gives you a strength which public recognition would dissipate. We governors need this strength of yours because we must exercise our authority in public, and the public exercise of authority can attract pressures and forces which temper and restrain that authority itself.

And so, as you return to your state budget offices, I would admonish you to observe closely your staff relationship to your chief executive, and to guard jealously your passion and habit for anonymity. If you permit either to become endangered, you will jeopardize your value to your governor, as indeed you will weaken his dependence upon your institution. Although the staff relationship and the anonymity have long since become traditional within your profession, I caution you never to let these two fundamental and preeminent principles fall from fashion within your profession.

---

1. The reference is to Dr. James W. Martin. For information on Dr. Martin see page 21.

ECONOMY AND EFFICIENCY COMMISSION
Frankfort / September 8, 1964

In view of the rising and ever demanding needs of the people and the subsequent increasing cost of government, I welcome the help of this commission in our effort to get a dollar's worth of service for every dollar spent out of the public treasury.[1] Accordingly, I have instructed my department heads to cooperate fully and completely with the commission and its staff. You have my blessing for entree into the records and operation of every department and agency in state government.

Our state's resources, financial and otherwise, are limited resources. During the last administration, increasing revenues from a broad-based tax structure have made possible unusual progress. For the remainder of this administration, we must rely for extended progress on that same tax structure. This makes it an absolute necessity for us to use our financial resources in accordance with priorities, efficiency, and economy. We must make every penny count in Kentucky's government. If we waste dollars, then we deprive some child of a better education or postpone the blacktopping of a much needed rural road.

I am asking your commission to examine any area where economies are possible or where changes will provide additional services at the same cost. There are two such areas that I might suggest initially to you today. First, are economies possible in the travel-transportation areas of state government? I think we need to review our travel regulations, our system of auditing travel claims, our use of various means of transportation including state-owned vehicles and the location of personnel who must travel from day-to-day. I would hope that you would recommend to me administrative methods and legislative changes that would make our system more economical.

Second, does the administration of the state's natural resources require reorganization? I would hope that you would review and make recommendations in this area with some of these thoughts in mind. Do the various agencies—fish and wildlife service, agricultural extension, conservation, health, and others—need better coordination among themselves and with other agencies concerned with natural resources? How can this, if required, [be] achieved? Is management of such resource-related activities as the State Fair Board and the Department of Parks based on a sound philosophy? Is the administration geared for producing excellent public service at minimum unit cost?

Let me say that I am, and I am sure the people of Kentucky are, appreciative of your acceptance to serve and give your time to the work of this commission. You are busy people whose time and talents are very valuable. Therefore, on behalf of the citizenry of this state, I thank you for providing this public service.

---

1. The Commission on Economy and Efficiency was established by joint resolution of the General Assembly on February 7, 1964. Breathitt announced its membership on May 13, and the commission began its work on August 16. It was chaired by Senator Shelby Kinkead; other members were Thomas A. Ballantine, Sr., Ben B. Fowler, Walter R. Gattis, Jr., L. Felix Joyner, Pierce Livily, John W. Manning, and John M. Swinford. In its report on travel regulations the commission recommended changes in reimbursement rates and a more restrictive policy on

eligibility. In its report on natural resource management, the commission noted a general confusion of direction and authority and recommended that the governor and the legislature streamline executive organization and establish clear lines of responsibility. The commission also investigated contingency appropriations and policy; the need for state investments legislation; state use of Lincoln Institute facilities; administration of state insurance premium taxes; state procurement of professional services; and the organization and operation of Kentucky government. *Louisville Courier-Journal,* September 9, 1964, and Commission on Economy and Efficiency, *General Report* (Frankfort, 1965).

BANK DEPOSITS STATEMENT
Frankfort / November 24, 1964

I HAVE reviewed with the state treasurer and the commissioner of finance the recommendations of the Commission on Economy and Efficiency, which were delivered to me last Friday. I appreciate their speedy consideration of this problem which I presented to them on November 9.[1]

The commission has recommended that interest charges of 3 percent be assessed on all of the funds deposited by the state treasurer in banks throughout the state. The commission further recommends that such funds as are not invested by the treasurer at a 3 percent rate be removed from his control by the state Investment Commission and invested in United States government securities. The treasurer, the commissioner of finance, and the governor are members of this commission.

I am unable to accept this recommendation in detail, although I agree with the principles underlying the recommendation. I have, therefore, recommended to the treasurer, and he has accepted my recommendation, that two-thirds of the deposits in banks throughout the state begin, as of January 1, to draw interest at the rate of 3 percent, and that the remaining one-third be held by the banks on a demand basis at no interest. We have arrived at this policy for the following reasons. First, it is our opinion that the money should remain in state banks and support the state's economy rather than be placed in government securities. Second, it is our opinion that an interest rate of 3 percent on time deposits is the maximum interest rate at this time which will assure us that the funds can be placed on a statewide basis. Third, it is my opinion, and that of the commissioner of finance, that the final decision as to the amounts which should be deposited on a demand basis is by statute a decision of the state treasurer. The treasurer has advised me that he regards one-third of the funds, as of this time, as the approximate amount which should be held on a demand basis.

Furthermore, it is our conclusion that the policy at which we have arrived will result in net earnings, over the next calendar year, which will equal those which would have been realized had we accepted the recommendations of the commission. We conclude this since the commission recommendation assumes a gradual move to a 3 percent rate on all deposits, and requires administrative costs which will not be necessary under the policy adopted.

---

1. The new policy was expected to produce an average interest of 2 percent on all idle funds as compared to the previous earnings of .56 percent, for a total additional earning of $764,263. At the time the state reported $53,030,000 on deposit in 317 banks throughout Kentucky. *Louisville Courier-Journal,* December 24, 1964.

NATIONAL ASSOCIATION OF RAILROAD AND UTILITIES COMMISSIONERS
Honolulu, Hawaii / December 3, 1964

It is indeed an honor and privilege for me to have the opportunity to appear before this body, and in particular for me, because I have so recently been closely associated with this organization. You will note that I said fellow members of the N.A.R.U.C., as I like to still think of myself as associated with your organization. In the few minutes that I have with you this morning I would like to give you my thoughts about the public service commission as an arm of state government and its importance to the state both on a local level and on the national scene through the able activities of this great organization.

On the local state scene I know of no arm of the state government that is of greater importance to a governor and his administration than his public service commission. You as commissioners are close to the people and, perhaps of even greater importance to the public, is the impact you have on its pocketbook. Your work will affect almost every citizen of the state. The public image that you create will and does have a profound effect on the public image of the state's administration. Public service commissioner is a post that requires the highest of personal integrity, devotion to public service, wisdom, tact, and above all the great common touch.

You are one arm of the state government that comes in close contact with the jurisdiction of the federal commissions empowered to regulate utilities, transportation, and other areas, operating in interstate commerce. It is most important to the states and to the state administrations that your work be of the highest caliber because we in the states can best preserve our right to govern ourselves by doing an outstanding job, one above reproach and criticism. If we meet this responsibility there can be neither reason nor excuse for those who would extend federal control or further their efforts to govern our local affairs from the national level.

In many cases, jurisdiction of federal and state regulation bodies join. Theoretically, one will begin where the other ends, but this line of demarcation of regulation responsibility is not always a clearly defined one. By cooperative study, again through this organization, I visualize that in stating our views and thrashing out our differences in committees we can come up with solutions that are most likely to serve the best public interest. In this way, the collective views of the state will be heard.

Then, too, there are matters clearly defined as under federal jurisdiction that are of paramount interest to the state commissions. I cite, for example, gas transported in interstate commerce, clearly under the jurisdiction of the Federal Power Commission; yet it leaves a profound effect, both as to supply and price, on the services rendered by gas utilities operating under state jurisdiction. In fact, one of the great pipelines extending from the producing fields in the South and Southwest may pass through and supply utilities in many states. Thus one case involving rates on service of such a pipeline would be of interest to those states.

Because of lack of personnel, means or time, many of the state commissions could not be represented adequately at the hearings concerning such a case, and consequently, only the views of those states able to be represented would be placed before the federal commission. This would be a great opportunity for this association, through its committee work, to study such problems and present principles to be used in solving them that would be to the best interest of all of the states involved. Collectively, the states would accomplish what an individual state would find difficult or impossible to do. No doubt the federal commission involved would find such collective work of assistance to it in carrying out its responsibilities.

As regulators of services so closely related to the overall economy of our states, I feel, and feel strongly, that the good public service commissioner must have a long-range view of his state's economic development. In Kentucky, I have asked the public service commissioners to work closely with the commissioner of commerce and other department heads in a coordinated development effort. Not to do so would be harmful to Kentucky's economy because industry, for example, must be dependent on water, power, transportation and those regulations which govern their use. Governmental as well as private programs must be planned and directed toward meeting the needs of our dynamic, changing society. Those who deal with the day-to-day activities of government must look ahead, plan ahead, and lift their eyes to the future.

Viewed from any perspective, the next four score, in fact the next two score, years will bring unprecedented changes. Dr. Peter Goldmark of the Columbia Broadcasting System recently made the following statements: World population, which was three billion in 1960, will be six billion by the year 2000; twelve billion by 2033; twenty-four billion by 2060.[1] The goods and services needed by this population stagger the imagination. On the other hand, scientific advancement in the next forty years is expected to equal that of the past 400. Again the imagination reels.

Let us come a bit closer to home. Here the projection time is shorter, but no less challenging. The Bureau of the Census estimates that U.S. population may reach 272 million by 1980. If this occurs we will have an additional eighty million citizens by that year. This means greatly increased income, greater consumption, and more jobs.

The outlook is bright; the future is challenging. But we must begin to plan for the needs of this much larger society and economy. Much hard work—much foresight—is needed. There are many things we must do if we are to meet essential demands. We must complete and improve our rapidly modernizing highway system. Highways are important arteries of our economic system over which the life blood of many industries move.

The educational system must be improved. Particular attention must be given to making vocational systems responsive to the industrial needs of tomorrow. Needed technical training must be available to meet a rapidly changing technology.

Community facilities, such as sewers and water, must be expanded and increased to meet the needs of eighty million more inhabitants and to serve the greatly increased industrial and business population.

Recreational facilities must be expanded to meet the desires of a much larger population. Cities and counties must begin to plan for this future. Land must be used judiciously. And adequate land simply must be set aside for industrial and business needs.

Work must continue to increase and conserve our water resources. This is critical to the growth of our population and industry. This is true even in Kentucky where we are fortunate to have abundant water.

Organization at state, area, and local levels for social and economic development must be strengthened to cope with the strains and stresses of a much larger, more complex society.

We must be sure that adequate power is available. Future demand for gas must be estimated and plans for supply formulated. We must look at the possible need for transportation and develop plans to provide the necessary rails, roads, trucks, and barges. This sort of future planning must be a closely cooperative public-private effort.

You, as regulators of utilities, railroads, and motor carriers, have a key role in this future. Your regulations and rulings must be of such a nature to stimulate, not stifle, business and industrial growth. However, they must also be fair to the consumer. Your task will not be easy, but it is an essential one. I think we must prove to a watching world that our way of life is the way of the future. The preservation of a balanced, competitive economy is never an easy task. But it should not be made more difficult by unnecessary administrative delays or regulations not in the public interest. Courage—judgment—dedication—honesty—these are the qualities which, with God's help, must guide us on this voyage of extraordinary change and challenge. Our country is great. Our country can be greater.

---

1. Peter Carl Goldmark (1906-), physicist, born in Budapest, Hungary; immigrated to U.S. (1933); chief engineer, television department, Columbia Broadcasting System, New York (1936-1944); director of engineering, research and development (1944-1950); vice president, Engineering, Research and Development Department (1950-). *Who's Who in America, 1966-1967,* 34th ed. (Chicago, 1966).

PERSONAL SERVICE CONTRACTS
Frankfort / January 20, 1965

FOR many years it has been customary for state agencies to engage the services of professional consultants in special tasks for state government.[1] Contracts of this character have been limited to those situations in which it would be too cumbersome and costly to rely upon regular state employees or officials. Such contracts have customarily been entered into on a negotiated basis because professional men and women—lawyers, physicians, psychiatrists, architects, and engineers—have been involved. Professional men do not customarily engage in competitive bidding; indeed, in most professions competitive bidding would result in the expulsion of the bidder from professional organizations and might well result in the loss of professional status.

This administration did not invent the long-established custom of negotiating professional contracts. This system has been in existence for many decades, and it prevails, for the most part, at all levels of government, including the federal government, and in private business. These contracts, fees, and compensation are not set upon the basis of whim, caprice, or favoritism, but upon the basis of professional standards worked out over the years by professional organizations and applicable to professional services of both public and private character. Our minimum fee schedules for legal services, for example, have long been promulgated by the State Board of Bar Commissioners, and the same schedules apply whether the attorney is serving a private client or a public agency.

This system, as I have already stated, was in effect long before I became governor and long before my predecessor, Mr. Combs, became governor. Since becoming governor, I have received no complaints as to the contracts negotiated during my administration. As to matters which took place before my administration—and before the administration of Governor Combs—my knowledge is no greater and my ability to obtain information is no greater than that of any other citizen.

If any person has information to the effect that the negotiation and operation of such contracts has at any time or in any administration resulted in bribery, corruption, or any violation of law, I urge such person to bring this information to the attention of the commonwealth's attorney and the grand jury of Franklin County; and I shall request the attorney general to provide all assistance within his power in the exposure and prosecution of such offenses.

It is my responsibility to see that the business of this state is conducted on a high plane, free from the waste of public funds and in a manner which will guarantee that the taxpayer receives full value for his dollar. Let me say that at no time have I ever required any person doing business with the state to make political contributions or to employ my personal or political friends. At no time have I instructed my department heads, either directly or by implication, to deal only with persons or firms who are politically or personally my friends, or to blacklist my political enemies. Furthermore, I do not believe that my department heads have engaged in such practices.

I recognize that any system of contracting which is not based upon competitive bidding contains the possibility of abuse, and if we can devise a system which can guard against that possibility, I intend to do so. Many weeks ago, long before the recent spate of publicity, the Commission on Economy and Efficiency had begun an investigation of the operation of personal service contracts with an eye to improvement. Information had been requested from several department heads, which they gladly furnished. I am urging the commission to continue its work in this field and to make recommendations for safeguarding such contracts against abuses.

More recently, and since the recent publicity, the chairman of the Legislative Research Commission has demonstrated some interest in these problems. I want to encourage his interest and to cooperate with the commission in every possible way. I therefore urge that both of these bodies make to the General Assembly and to me such constructive and practical suggestions as may occur to them. I particularly suggest that these bodies consider the following possible changes in our present methods of operation:

1. The institution of competitive bidding in service contracts.

2. The establishment of independent review boards in the various departments for the purpose of qualifying proposed contractors, or for the further purpose of passing upon the terms and conditions of such contracts as being in the public interest in all their terms and conditions. Such boards should be composed of recognized, outstanding professional men, not themselves having any contractual relations with the state, and named in consultation with established professional organizations.

I am interested in making our government work better and in giving a fair shake to the taxpayer and to those who want to have a chance to perform needed tasks for state government. I hope that the Commission on Economy and Efficiency and the Legislative Research Commission will give thorough consideration to these and all other proposals for making our contract procedures operate fairly and economically.

I am not interested, and the people of this state are not interested, in making a political circus out of this issue. But I am interested and the people of Kentucky are interested in specific, concrete proposals to put state government on the highest possible plane. In that effort, I propose that we get down to brass tacks—at once.

---

1. The state's criteria for awarding professional service contracts became a sensitive political issue after publication of testimony from a case before the U.S. Court of Claims in Washington involving the methods employed by Tecon Engineering, Brighton Engineering, and Capitol Engineering to obtain state contracts in the 1950s. Lawrence Wetherby, a former governor of Kentucky and a partner in Brighton Engineering since the expiration of his term in 1955, testified that it was "... necessary to be friendly with the administration ..." to win contracts. The administration's friendship could be won in three ways: (1) by contributing money to the governor's campaign; (2) by performing organizational work in the campaign; or (3) by hiring engineering consultants who were political friends of the governor. William H. May testified that he employed each of these methods to obtain business during the terms of Governor A.B. Chandler and Governor Bert Combs.

May had supported Combs in the 1955 gubernatorial primary, and after Combs's opponent, Chandler, became governor, May found that his companies (Brighton and Tecon) were unable to bid on state contracts. In 1957 and 1958 May hired legislators allied with Chandler as a "liaison group" to the administration at a salary of $1,500 a month. Shortly thereafter Brighton and Tecon were actively negotiating for state contracts. May remained a Combs supporter, however. In 1959 he contributed $10,000 to Combs's campaign, extended a $20-25,000 loan, and guaranteed an additional $50-70,000 in bank loans to the campaign. In addition, May hired three of Combs's political supporters during the campaign who, according to the Internal Revenue Service, performed campaign work rather than business-related duties. May also cited a number of instances where employees of the Highway Department were given part-time employment with his companies during the Chandler administration. On January 18, Governor Breathitt and Highway Commissioner Ward issued statements in response to May's testimony. Ward stated that none of the political favors described by May had been either solicited or accepted as a condition for awarding contracts since his term of office began. Likewise, Governor Breathitt stated that his administration did not maintain a list of politically preferred contractors, although he would "hope" that if two companies were equally competent, the "friendly" company should be given consideration, a feeling with which Ward concurred. The governor expressed his disapproval of "moonlighting" by state officials and his belief that the practice was ended by the recent conflict-of-interest law. Neither was he guilty, he stated, of bartering influence for positions with private companies on behalf of political allies. Breathitt acknowledged that his administration did employ lawyers on a political basis, but saw nothing unethical in the practice. Breathitt concluded that nothing in the May testimony warranted an official inquiry. Political circumstances soon forced Breathitt to change his assessment, however. On January 20, Harry Lee Waterfield, acting in his dual capacity as lieutenant governor and chairman of the Legislative Research Commission demanded that all state contracts negotiated with professionals since 1950 be made available to the L.R.C. One week later Waterfield announced a thorough investigation of state contract practices. The L.R.C., he said, would make copies of all state contracts awarded since 1950 and, after review and analysis, release them to the press, the legislature, the governor, and the Commission on Economy and Efficiency. Public hearings would follow, if warranted. Waterfield also criticized the concurrent Commission on Economy and Efficiency study as a possible source of confusion and accused Breathitt of using the commission to distract public attention away from the L.R.C. study. Waterfield said, "I think he's trying to minimize not only what's probably happened but what we're trying to do. . . ." The next day in a speech to the Paducah Rotary Club Waterfield launched a general attack on the Breathitt administration with the theme that Breathitt was creating a deceptive "paper image" for the people of Kentucky. While Waterfield's primary target was the $176 million bond proposal, he also cited the recent revelations concerning professional contracts as evidence of "government by cronies." He alleged that political favoritism had recently reached "fantastic proportions," citing the "indecent haste" with which May's company received contracts for work on the West Kentucky Parkway after Combs's election in 1959 and on the Purchase Parkway after Breathitt's election in 1963. In addition to the Legislative Research Commission and the Commission on Economy and Efficiency studies, Attorney General Matthews directed an investigation of state contract procedures from 1960 to 1965. On February 8, he issued his final report, having found no "irregularities" in the contracts. On the same day Governor Breathitt disclosed the preliminary findings of the Commission on Economy and Efficiency study. The commission reported "substantive administrative improvement in the handling of personal service contracts over the past few months." The commission found competitive bidding to be impractical for professional, technical, and artistic contractors and recommended service quality judgments as the proper criteria for selection. To promote the fairness and accuracy of such judgments the Commission on Economy and Efficiency recommended the establishment of basic standards for each category of work and the creation of advisory committees. Satisfied that the matter had been resolved, Breathitt ordered the Highway Department to resume contracting with engineering consultants. See the *Louisville Courier-Journal,* January 17, 19, 27, 28, and February 9, 1965.

HENDERSON CHAMBER OF COMMERCE
Henderson / February 9, 1965

I AM sure that when I address any gathering in Kentucky I can proceed under the assumption that the members of that group are interested in politics. Politics in our state is a vocation and a way of life to many, an avocation to many more, and at least a popular spectator sport rivaling horse racing and basketball to the remainder of our citizens.

Politics is never out of season in Kentucky. As soon as we conclude one election, the campaign for the next one begins. Only at Derby time and perhaps around Christmas does discussion turn to other topics, and I am sure that if many Kentuckians had their way the Derby horses would have to run in a primary first, and Santa Claus would have to face the electorate before being allowed to make his visit.

I did not come here tonight to make a political speech. I do not believe that meetings of this type are proper forums for political discussion of a partisan or a factional nature. I do not believe that you want to hear such a speech.

I would like, however, to review with you some of the actions that have been taken by your state government within the last few years in the realm of political reform and to discuss some of the measures which I feel must still be taken. I do this because I believe that you, as citizens and as business and professional people making a home and a livelihood in Kentucky, care, and care deeply, about the future of your state. Politics may still be and perhaps will always be "the damnedest in Kentucky," but I believe we are moving steadily along a road that will make public officials more accountable to the people they represent and will make politics—and I use the word here in its most onerous meaning—secondary to performance. I intend to keep us on that road and I intend to ask you from time to time to help us in Frankfort keep to this straight course.

The first in a series of meaningful reforms within the last fifteen years took place when the General Assembly in 1952 passed a registration and purgation law designed to establish the right of individuals to vote and to put a stronger emphasis on residential requirements and on identification at the polls.[1] The heart of the law was a comparative signatures system long advocated by those seeking stronger safeguards against election fraud. This law was sponsored as an administration bill by Governor Lawrence Wetherby, and his administration later beat down attempts to weaken or repeal it.[2]

Voting day safeguards were strengthened further in 1960 when the General Assembly passed a bill making the adoption of voting machines mandatory.[3] Today, thanks to this measure and the sponsorship given it by my predecessor as governor, practically all precincts in Kentucky use machines, and the rest will soon have them.

The same session of the legislature passed a conflict of interest law to keep those employed by the state from taking advantage of their positions by directing state business to themselves or to firms in which they are interested.[4]

Perhaps the most controversial and most widely publicized piece of legislation passed during the last few years to help Kentuckians get the most from their state expenditures was the merit system law passed also in 1960. The idea that an employee should earn his right to work for the state by education, by experience, by examination, and by performance on the job rather than by political influence was not new, and, indeed, many employees had previously been chosen without regard to political affiliation.

But it was only five years ago that a law went into effect requiring competence on the part of all state workers and telling them that if they perform their duties in a satisfactory manner they will not be blown aside by the next shift in political winds.

I believe that the people of Kentucky want their affairs handled by responsible people, and that they want the very best that can be hired, and that they want them to make careers of state service as long as that service is satisfactory. I hope that you believe this too and will help us to continue to strengthen the merit concept in dealing with state personnel.

Another milestone I believe to be important in administering the business of government in Frankfort is the model purchasing act which came into being last year. Under the provisions of this act we are now saving money for Kentucky's taxpayers in the buying of many commodities and materials necessary for the conduct of the programs of state service. Generally speaking, bidding competition is wider, quality of products is maintained, and prices are lower. We will continue to do all that is possible to sharpen our buying practices.

It is necessary in the conduct of state business to call on, from time to time, professional people—lawyers, engineers, architects, doctors and others in the medical profession—to provide services which the state cannot provide with its own personnel. There has been a great deal said recently about contracts for these professional services, about how they are awarded, the fees that are paid, and the services rendered. I welcome this discussion because I think it is helpful periodically to take a look at all practices of government to see if they cannot be improved upon.

We have had good relations with those who provide professional services and the work they have been assigned has generally been skillfully and conscientiously carried out, but I am not willing to say that we cannot do better. For this reason I have asked my Commission on Economy and Efficiency in Government to conduct a study of this whole area of endeavor in order to make absolutely sure that we are getting all we are paying for and that the contracts are being awarded wisely and fairly. The commission has made a preliminary report to me and will continue to conduct its study. I believe that this is another instance of action being taken to improve state services—to assure that performance, not politics, is the number one criterion for doing business with the state.

While we have made much progress within the last few years, there has been one area where reform is needed that all of us have neglected—in fact it has been spoken of only in whispers by political people if it has been mentioned at all. It is a subject which causes candidates to cringe, campaign organizers to run for cover, and the entire electorate to look the other way. Yet it is a subject basic to the system under which our government is operated and basic to the right of free men to choose their leaders. I believe that it is none too soon to bring it into open discussion and to see if something can't be done to solve some of the problems and right some of the injustices involved in this subject. I refer to the whole matter of financing political campaigns and to the unrealistic laws which govern this financing today.

No candidate of either party for statewide major office in recent years would have stood a chance of being elected if he and those who organized his campaign had restricted total expenditures on his behalf to the amount prescribed in the statutes.[5] For this reason, it has become common practice for candidates to be supported by a number of committees which fragment the expenditures into amounts not exceeding those set by law. The candidate does not know what these expenditures are and who has so generously organized and contributed on his behalf because for him to know would be in violation of the law. As long as the candidate can honestly say that money spent by him and his organization proper does not exceed the limits set by law, those around him are free to spend other sums through other organizations to get him elected, and the law is satisfied.

I would like to state tonight what all of you know is true and what all candidates of both political parties for the last several years know is true. I would like to say that $10,000, the present amount, is not a reasonable limitation to set on campaign expenses for a serious candidate for governor. In these days of television and other expensive campaigning methods, it would be easy for a moderately financed candidate to spend that amount in a single week, and one major television performance could use it all.

I do not know what a reasonable limitation on expenses would be, and probably there is no ready source to go to for such information. But I do know that the time has come to look this question straight in the eye and try to find some answers. I do know that the system of financial reporting as it is practiced today, as it must be practiced because of unreasonable and archaic limitations, does nothing to enhance our election process and protect the public for which the laws were written.

I am going to act to correct this situation. Within the next few days I plan to name a committee composed of leaders of both of our political parties to make a study on campaign financing. I will ask them to report their findings to me as soon as they have had opportunity to make an exhaustive study, including information on what practices are followed in our sister states. Along with their findings, I will ask them to make recommendations to me involving two courses of action. First, I will ask them to recommend measures which should be included in new legislation relating to expenditures in a primary or a general election and the reporting of these expenditures. These recommendations will be the basis of legislation I will recommend to the General Assembly next year.[6] Secondly, I will ask this group for recommendations for a basic campaign code to be followed by both parties which will set down rules of conduct which relate to expenses, reporting of expenses, and other campaign subjects which are important to the voters of Kentucky.

I believe that the people of Kentucky are interested in who finances the campaigns of the candidates they are asked to vote for and how much is spent, and that they are entitled to this information. I believe, further, that no candidate should be asked to run under a system that makes violation of the spirit, if not the letter, of the law necessary to his success. I hope that we soon may make some changes in this important area, and I solicit your help and your thinking in bringing them about.

I would like to close with a story that was a favorite of President Kennedy's, one he told a number of times in public speeches: In 1789 the Connecticut House of Representatives was in session when the sky became overcast at 10:00 A.M., and by noon it had darkened to such an extent that the religious men of that era fell on their knees and begged a final blessing before the end came. The members of the house of representatives clamored for immediate adjournment. The Speaker of the house, one Colonel Davenport, silenced the crowd with these words: "The day of Judgement is either approaching or it is not. If it is not, there is no cause for adjournment. If it is, I prefer to be found doing my duty. I wish, therefore, that candles may be brought forth."

In this difficult and dangerous time in the life of our state and our country, a time of challenge and controversy, may we all bring forth candles in the form of understanding, dedication, and hard work, to help illuminate our path, to help find a way to a better Kentucky and a better America.

---

1. The 1952 Registration and Purgation Act changed existing procedures in an attempt to prevent fraudulent voting and manipulation of voting lists for political advantage. See *Acts, 1952,* Chapter 134 (H.B. 95), pp. 329-65.

2. Lawrence Wetherby (1908-   ), born Middletown, Kentucky; L.L.B., University of Louisville College of Law (1929); lieutenant governor of Kentucky (1948-1950); governor (1950-1955); Robert A. Powell, *Kentucky Governors* (Danville, Ky., 1976), p. 102.

3. The purpose of the act was to "eliminate the antiquated manner in which elections are now conducted. . . ." The bill provided for financing the purchase of voting machines by counties through the State Property and Building Commission. *Acts, 1960,* Chapter 128 (H.B. 274), pp. 538-45.

4. The 1960 conflict of interest law prescribed proper standards of conduct and specified and prohibited unethical practices in those areas where the official duties of state government officials and their private financial and business affairs overlapped. For example, no member of the General Assembly was to accept direct or indirect payment for his aid in procuring government contracts, nor could he own more than a 5 percent interest in a company on whose contracts he might be required to vote or with which he might otherwise be concerned in an official capacity. *Acts, 1960,* Chapter 181 (H.B. 444), pp. 846-48.

5. The campaign spending limitations in force in 1965 were established by a 1946 statute. Candidates were limited to the following expenditures: (1) governor —$10,000; (2) at-large state office other than governor—$5,000; (3) state senator —$1,000; (4) state representative—$750; (5) Court of Appeals judge or railroad commissioner—$3,000; circuit judge or commonwealth attorney—$2,500. There

were various limits for candidates in county and city elections ranging from $500 to $5,000. *Kentucky Revised Statutes,* 1963. 123.050.

6. The law proposed by Breathitt and passed by the 1966 General Assembly eliminated the artifically low limits on campaign spending and sought to regulate the reporting and making of campaign contributions. To accomplish this the bill created the Kentucky Registry of Election Finance, a bipartisan, independent agency consisting of five gubernatorial appointees. Candidates were to establish a campaign treasurer and a campaign depository which, along with any separate subunits, were to be filed with the registry. Contributions were to be made through the treasurer or one of his deputies, and any contributions over $100 were to be reported separately along with reports of total contributions and expenditures. Any committee organized on behalf of the candidate was also to be registered with the registry. *Acts, 1966,* Chapter 216 (S.B. 265), pp. 903-13.

NATIONAL LEGISLATIVE CONFERENCE
Portland, Maine / August 17, 1966

TODAY I am here to share a few random observations with you on the future of state government. On an occasion such as this, one is tempted to jump onto some all-or-nothing platform and to make some glowing generalizations about the importance of state government, the difficulties of state government, and the future of state government. The trouble with these all-or-nothing pronouncements is that they are usually compounded equally of foolish hopes and foolish fears.

There are times when it is fashionable to denouce the federal juggernaut and plead for a return to some mythical Eden where the states function in primal innocence and the federal government acts as a rather prim governess whose duty is simply to keep the children from throwing mud pies at each other and to exclude from the playground the naughty boys and girls from the dirty neighborhoods. Then there are other times when it is fashionable to wonder whether the states are obsolete—whether they really fulfill any useful function in this highly organized and increasingly complex society of ours; whether they had better not be replaced by some new regional groupings which fit the facts of modern life more clearly and more nearly than the historic boundaries of our fifty states. On other occasions, it is fashionable to talk as if all the complexities of state and federal relationships could be brought within the four corners of some new formula, "the new federalism," "creative federalism," or some other form of words which, however useful and however well intended, serves as often to obscure as to clarify.

Here in the United States, our federalism had its origins in history, not in theory. At the formation of the American union, we were a largely homogeneous people, though not completely so; and most of the differences which then seemed so great now seem to us so small—the differences between congregationalism and episcopalism, between tobacco planters and subsistence farmers. Nevertheless, those differences, based as they are upon history, upon tradition, upon folklore if you please, have persisted with remarkable strength and remarkable capacity for survival; and I think that any man in public life today who claims to see any real prospect for the obliteration of state boundaries and the elimination of state government ought to have his head examined. Mr. Justice Holmes once said that continuity with the past was not a duty, only a necessity. The truth of this observation is nowhere more firmly proven than in the survival and hardihood of the states in the midst of an unprecedented and ever increasing expansion of federal power.

What we need to fear is not the disappearance of the states, but their increasing irrelevance to the needs of this day. The states will not disappear, but they could become like the vermiform appendix, mere relics and reminders of some former stage in the existence of our society, surviving only as names on a map, traditions at a family reunion, or the easiest way to designate a vacation spot or a post office.

But this is not necessary. Even in an era of expanding federal power there is wide scope for state authority, for state initiative, and for creative contributions by the state in such programs as highway construction, welfare, water pollution, the conservation of our natural resources. The states still control some of those functions of government which are closest to the lives and liberties of our people, such as the administration and enforcement of the criminal law, management of our prisons, and the education of our children. In fact, with all our talk about the welfare state and federal domination, both the federal budget and the federal debt will be a smaller fraction of the national economy than they represented twenty years ago; and state and local budgets and debts represent a substantially larger fraction.

Further, the states have long served as laboratories in the development of governmental programs. Whether successful or not, state efforts highlight problems and possible solutions to them which are often taken over and modified by other states and the national government. For example, North Carolina and Kentucky were conducting their own attempt to break the "cycle of poverty" prior to the national war on poverty. In the field of vocational education and elsewhere, we anticipated some of the Appalachian programs. The Appalachian Act and the Economic Opportunity Act of 1964 incorporated some of our innovations for the national program.

Success depends on the energy with which the states attack their problems. It is when the states fail to fulfill their role in such areas as education, civil rights and liberties, enhancing the opportunities for the poor, and others, that the federal government moves into the vacuum. It is when the states are not responsive, are not laboratories of experimentation, do not reach all the people because they are either oppressive or not representative, that the states forfeit their strongest argument for a future. The fact is that some who have argued loudest and shrillest for states rights have done more to undermine states rights than anyone else in the Union. These few have used the term as a shield against responsible action, rather than the spear of innovative improvement of the lives of their people. There is too quick a tendency to blame the federal government for our own shortcomings and the courts for our own lack of responsibility. The new voting rights bill and the reapportionment decisions should have never been necessary. That they occurred is more a sign of state neglect of duty than federal usurpation of authority.

While we have built a great industrial complex, harnessed our natural resources, made our land ever more productive, and created huge metropolitan giants, we have, again and again, confounded ourselves with social problems which seemingly defy solution. Some problems we have solved, and others we are attempting to solve, but the list is staggering, and many of our solutions have been no more than stopgap measures. But the most compelling argument for continuing and strengthening the role of the states lies not in what has been done, but in what must yet be done.

Education must be one of our primary concerns. We have 50.4 million people currently enrolled in educational institutions and another 5.2 million aged fourteen to twenty-four who either have no high school degree or are not enrolled in school. In only five years our school-age population will jump almost 50 percent, and we will have to provide classrooms, teachers, and equipment for nearly seventy-three million children. At the same time we are providing for this enormous growth—and let me emphasize how little time we have—we must also try to discover why we are failing to reach so many of our young people with today's educational offerings. Making education available is not enough; we must make it relevant.

If we are to be successful in our venture of universal education, it will require every level of government functioning at near peak efficiency. No branch can handle it alone. As long as the revenue sources remain essentially as they are, we will need federal money. But we will need more and more experimentation and innovation. We need creative thinking from every possible source, and it must not be stifled by attempted uniformity projected from Washington.

Education is only one of the vital concerns we face. As the Los Angeles riots demonstrated, we must now begin the arduous and confusing task of fully assimilating minorities into our society.[1] Recent civil rights legislation has broken down many of the barriers, but it will require much state and community action and much time if we are to erase the legacy of the northern ghetto and the southern cotton field. Federal legislation can topple the legal barriers, but state and local action programs are the only ones that can bring about the full understanding that now seems critical to the health of our society. Here, as in education, we need all levels of government functioning as best they can. We need the best thinking from all possible sources; and while our diversity creates different types of problems, it can also spawn the different solutions required.

We are also faced with the problems generated by our increasing urban and suburban growth. Over the last five years our urban population has risen 5 percent annually as a total of the whole population. We have decayed and decaying center cities, traffic-clogged, smoke-polluted, and recreationally barren. Slum clearance and housing challenge the resources of every level of government, and every level must participate if our cities are to remain livable. Here too, we should expect federal participation, but the states must play a drastically increased role, especially in policy planning.

The conservation and wise development of our natural resources—our water, land, and air—is not a Kentucky or Maine problem. It is not an eastern or western problem. It is indeed a national problem that cries out for action in each of our states. Our water need, for example, now stands at 370 billion gallons a day. In 1980—fourteen years from now—our water need will more than double. By the turn of the century it will rise to triple what it is now. Yet already in the Northeast twenty-five million people have felt the quiet devastation of drought. Under its tight grip, reservoirs shriveled, water taps dried out, farm land parched, and crops withered. In New York City some 600,000 tons of soot and fly ash blanket the town in a year. Our sport and commercial fisheries last year counted eighteen million fish killed by water pollution. Hundreds of thousands of fish were killed in Louisiana because of poisons reaching the Mississippi far upstream.

In my home state of Kentucky giant machines last year literally ripped the tops off beautiful mountains so they could get to valuable coal. Elsewhere in Appalachia, acid from mines pollutes thousands of miles of streams, making them useless, lifeless, and ugly. I have seen the hillsides gutted by uncontrolled strip and auger mining, void of their precious timber, their topsoil and vegetation cover washed down the mountains to choke our streams with silt, and their acid waters pouring pollution into our urban drinking supplies and destroying our recreational potential.

Along Lake Erie, which is the main water supply for ten million Americans, pollution closes beaches to our children. New York Harbor's once flourishing shellfish industry is all but dead, the victim of water pollution. In the largest metropolis in the world, eight children last summer fished a watermelon out of the Hudson River, ate it, and contracted typhoid fever.

All of these examples show evidence of the carelessness and selfishness that we must stop and reverse. For if we do not meet our state responsibilities in conservation, we will forfeit this right and duty to the federal government. Make no mistake: the people are aroused to the danger and aware of the need to conserve, restore, and strengthen the natural heritage of America for generations to come. This is a race between the quick and the dead, for nothing less is at stake than the sheer survival of our burgeoning, affluent society.

I think it is time for the states to get to where the people are—and where the problems are. It is time to reassert their historical role in the American experiment. For the states were once the innovators in this country, and they must innovate again. The first antitrust statutes were developed by the states; the first maximum-hours-minimum-wage legislation was developed by the states; the states fashioned the first antidiscrimination statutes, the first child labor laws, the first unemployment insurance.

There are signals on the horizon, I feel, that would indicate that a new day is about to dawn in the states. Fifty-two governors of the states and territories have indicated an interest in a new nationwide compact for the advancement of education. The New England states are striving to put together a joint alliance to act in concert on all kinds of problems that spill over state lines; the water crisis in the Northeast has caused a revitalization of the partnership in the states around the Delaware basin, and has stimulated new initiatives to cure pollution and water wastes. We are at work on a strip mining compact, and the Natural Resources Committee of the National Governors' Conference has been at work.

In many ways the states are getting stronger—they are appropriating more money, improving more services, taking over an increasing share of local costs and functions. Their budgets in the last fifteen years have risen at a tremendous rate and so have the level of their services. There must be a rebirth of state responsibility. The governors and legislators of the states will play the crucial role. Given the choice and the direction, I think that the American people will furnish the tools.[2]

---

1. The reference is to Watts, a black neighborhood in south Los Angeles in which residents looted and burned their community in August, 1965. See William

O'Neill, *Coming Apart: An Informal History of America in the 1960's* (Chicago, 1971), pp. 170-72.

2. Governor Breathitt expressed similar views in addresses to the Southern Governors Conference at Asheville, North Carolina, September 11, 1967, and to the Louisville League of Women Voters in Louisville, May 10, 1967. These addresses are not included in these papers.

DEDICATION OF HISTORICAL MARKERS
Ashland / April 19, 1967

MY overriding concern upon assuming office three years ago was to help Kentucky prepare herself for a greater and more prosperous future. I saw my term as governor as an opportunity to undertake new programs, and expand existing ones, which would be the framework for accelerated growth and development for her citizens. While concentrating on where we can go, I feel it is vital that we recall where we have been. We should retain a lively sense of our history and culture. In a time of change, we should strive to retain the features of our way of life which mark us as Kentuckians and distinguish us from every other state in the Union. Our culture is composed of more than our artists and musicians, our statesmen and military heroes. Every distinctive aspect of our economic, social, political, and artistic heritage should be known and appreciated by our citizens and especially by the young.

There are limitations on direct governmental leadership in the effort to make our past more meaningful to present generations. But we can and have attempted to encourage all citizens interested in this work. The Kentucky Heritage Commission and Kentucky Arts Commission are examples of innovations in this area.

The Kentucky Historical Marker Program is an endeavor of longer standing and of success. A joint undertaking of the Kentucky Historical Society and the Department of Highways, it received its first state funds in the spring of 1962. To date, it has erected 528 markers with public funds and is adding about a hundred more each year. Private donations are an important part of this program. One hundred and ninety markers have been erected with funds from private sources, for a total of 718. The program has been fortunate in its chairman, Mr. W.A. Wentworth, and in enlisting the voluntary efforts of several hundred public-spirited men and women.[1] There is no question that the marker program makes a distinct contribution to the general recognition of our heritage. Hence it is with great pleasure that I have come here today to help dedicate these thirteen new historical markers, commemorating key monuments of our industrial past.

This year Kentucky celebrates the one hundred and seventy-fifth anniversary of her admission to the Union in 1792. But the iron industry here is even older. The first blast furnace in Kentucky was built in what is now Bath County in 1791 and later supplied cannon shot and other munitions to Andrew Jackson's army at New Orleans. Iron had been made in Kentucky in forges even earlier. The Hanging Rock iron region, including Boyd, Carter, and Greenup counties in Kentucky and adjacent parts of Ohio, was the leading iron-producing area of the United States in the middle of the nineteenth century. The local industry began in 1818 with the construction of a furnace at Argillite in Greenup County. A total of ninety-six furnaces were built in the region, thirty of them in Kentucky. Three, all in Kentucky and owned by Armco Steel Corporation, are operative now.

In the 1830s, Kentucky ranked third among the states in iron production. Today, despite the total exhaustion of usable local ores, it still ranks eleventh, and iron and steel manufacturing are a major element in the Commonwealth's industrial base. Armco Steel came to Kentucky in 1921 by purchasing the old Ashland furnace, where we now stand. In recent years it has employed, on the average, more than five thousand people at the Ashland works, with a payroll in excess of $40 million. It spends more than $44 million a year for local goods and services, and pays more than $1 million in local taxes each year. Since it embarked on its expansion program in 1953, it has invested over $200 million in plant facilities in Boyd and Greenup counties.

It is fitting that as the heir and perpetuator of the Hanging Rock iron industry, Armco should have donated to the Kentucky Historical Highway Marker Program funds to provide markers for twenty-six of the furnaces which have been built here; the other four have already been marked with state funds.

Today we are dedicating thirteen markers for these furnaces; Steam, Raccoon, Hunnewell, Pennsylvania, Buena Vista, Star, Laurel, Boone, Kenton, Ashland, Norton, Iron Hill, and Pine Grove, built between 1824 and 1881. Thirteen others will be erected next year. They commemorate Kentucky's continuing industrial progress from her earliest days. Part of the story of that progress can be told by statistics. In twenty-four hours the old Argillite furnace could make two tons of iron. The most successful of the pioneer charcoal furnaces, Bellefonte, three miles from here, operated from 1826 until 1893, produced 3600 tons in a year. By contrast, on March 20 of last year, Armco's Amanda furnace, just to the west of us, produced 4,287 tons, a new world's record for a day's production by a single furnace. Ashland furnace, on this site, was the oldest known operating blast furnace in the world when dismantled in 1962, a distinction now enjoyed by Armco's Norton furnace. This continuing juxtaposition of the old and best with the new and best can be taken as symbolic of Kentucky's industrial progress from Daniel Boone's day to the present.

Our thanks are due to the Armco Steel Corporation for these reminders of our historical past. Our compliments go out as well to all the participants in the Kentucky Highway Historical Marker Program for their continuing success in showing Kentuckians the richness, the depth and variety of our cultural history. I firmly believe that these efforts to increase awareness of our past will help fulfill the promise of our future.

---

1. Walter Allerton Wentworth (1889-1971), born in New Hampshire; B.A., Iowa State University; M.A., Michigan State University; director of public relations, Borden Company, New York (1926-1956); chairman, Frankfort, Kentucky, Municipal Housing Commission (1956-1964); president general of the Sons of the American Revolution (1958-1959); president, Kentucky Historical Society (1960-1961); chairman, Kentucky Historical Society marker program. Information provided by Dr. James Klotter, Kentucky Historical Society.

POLITICS

SECOND OF THE NOMINATION OF LYNDON B. JOHNSON
Atlantic City, New Jersey / August 26, 1964

MR. CHAIRMAN, reverend clergy, my fellow delegates, my fellow Americans, "The World's great age begins anew." So wrote the poet Virgil two thousand years ago, as he foreshadowed an era of Roman greatness.

We are a party of perpetual renewal, a party which has not only seen great visions but made those visions into growing, breathing realities and brought them into the lives of ordinary people. The history of this nation records that the great ages of America have been the ages of Democratic leadership—or of Republican leadership like that of Lincoln and Theodore Roosevelt, which carried the ideal of our party into the ranks of the opposition.

Four years ago young America heard the voice of a young leader, a leader of unique quality who sounded the trumpet call for another great age of national renewal. He asked us to get America moving again. We joined him and moved from strength to strength, from the idea to the reality, from the vision to the accomplishment.

America has moved into a position of undoubted military power—and into a maturity which guarantees the exercise of that power for peace rather than atomic war. The American economy has moved from dead center into an era of renewed vigor. There are now more people at work earning more money and living better lives than ever before in the nation's history.

To strength and prosperity we have joined compassion. Ours is the vision and ours the growing reality of a great society in which the accidents of race and color, parentage and poverty, location and geography, will not be allowed to dim the light of human hope and to cripple the possibilities of human growth.

Just as our party and our country have grown strong through the youthful ideal of self-renewal, so the fates decreed that even John Kennedy's death would be the occasion and inspiration for a national renewal and rededication.

Mr. Valiant-for-Truth in *Pilgrims Progress* said, "My sword I leave to him who can wield it." The mighty arm of Lyndon Johnson has carried the flashing blade of John Kennedy, signaling to an anxious world that the forces of freedom, of compassion, of decency and progress cannot be conquered even by death itself.

John Kennedy started America moving again, and Lyndon Johnson has kept America moving—moving steadily, surely, and at a quickened pace toward the promised land of the Great Society. With fidelity, firmness, and a persuasive power unexcelled in America's political history, Lyndon Johnson has redeemed and is redeeming the pledges and covenants which won the hearts of young Americans in 1960.

There are some Americans in this year of 1964 who scorn our ideal of perpetual renewal, of a ceaseless quest for the Great Society.

For the vision of Lincoln, of Franklin Roosevelt, of Truman, of Kennedy, of Johnson, they would substitute a vision which finds its inspiration not in the better angels of our nature, but in the dark and hopeless corners of the human heart. Theirs is a vision of injustice as a condition decreed by fate; a vision of poverty as man's inevitable lot; a vision of atomic war as just another routine problem.

Between these two visions the American people must choose. Upon their choice may rest the continued existence of mankind. Into whose hands will we entrust the power to decide whether there will be a human race?

For us here—and I believe for all Americans—the choice is clear. We choose the survival of humanity, and the seasoned, steady leadership of Lyndon Baines Johnson.

Lyndon Johnson—as a young man—has known poverty at first hand, has known economic collapse at first hand, and he has known war at first hand. These are the enemies of youth, indeed the enemies of all mankind, and in the battle against these enemies the young people of this nation will enlist for the duration with Lyndon B. Johnson as their commander-in-chief.[1]

---

1. Governor Breathitt was joined in seconding the Johnson nomination by Governor Harold E. Hughes, Iowa; Mayor Robert Wagner, New York City; Mayor Richard Daley, Chicago; Senator Edmund S. Muskie, Maine; and Mrs. Patricia Roberts Harris, Washington, D.C.

JOHN F. KENNEDY MEMORIAL SERVICE
Lexington / November 22, 1964

T.S. ELIOT's play *Murder in the Cathedral,* which I am sure many of you have read, deals with the temptations that beset St. Thomas Becket upon the eve and the occasion of his martyrdom. The last, the greatest, and the subtlest of temptations was the desire to choose a martyr's death as the road to a place in history, as a sop to Becket's own ego and self-righteousness.

We who meet here after a twelvemonth still heavy of heart and distressed of spirit, must beware the temptation which will always beset those of us who shared, as part of his generation, the life and the death of John Fitzgerald Kennedy—and that is the temptation to be maudlin, to be damp, to bathe ourselves in the easy tears of sentimentality. How he would hate all that!

Nothing could more surely betray the spirit of John Kennedy. One of the qualities which set him apart from the generality of leaders was the late president's distaste for the false note, the hollow gesture, the heart worn on the sleeve. He disliked emotion, not because he lacked feeling but because he felt so deeply—and would not cheapen his feelings. He scorned the tub-thumping appeals to patriotism, not because he lacked love of country, but because he loved his country too much to identify her with the caricatures drawn in the commonplaces of political oratory. He was, in many respects, an austere man, and he hid his passions and his emotions under a mask of indifference because he felt that the ultimate test of devotion to one's ideals was in deeds rather than words. If we, then, would be true to the heritage he has left us, we must be reborn of his spirit, not in some one cathartic emotional experience but in the decisions we make each day. What, then, is that spirit?

It is first of all a spirit of deep concern, compassionate concern, practical concern for the dignity, the selfhood, the personality of individual people. For him there was no rest of body, mind, or spirit so long as the accidents of color, of geographical isolation, of economic inheritance and environment, served to isolate or to alienate people from the fullness, the richness, the vast opportunities of life in this nation and in the great family of mankind.

It is also a spirit of realism and detachment. No matter how deeply he might have been involved in causes or struggles, or in the individual ambitions from which even he was not free, John Kennedy never lost his capacity to see the world, the nation, and himself under the honest eye of eternity, from the vantage point of history.

It is, perhaps above all, a spirit of courage—gay courage, courage in the classic and heroic sense, courage which Hemingway has defined as grace under pressure—a willingness to assume the risks of personal and political disaster to keep peace in a groping, divided world and to get on with the unfinished business of a mighty nation.

John Kennedy, in his style, was unique among American presidents. His friend, Benjamin Bradlee, has referred to his "special grace"—Jack Kennedy's feeling for excellence, for quality, for distinction as important elements in our national life.[1] Some have labeled President Kennedy as an intellectual. This is debatable, though he did without doubt possess a first-rate intellect. But it is indisputably true that John Kennedy, as did no president save Jefferson, had a deep, appreciative, and perceptive feeling for the world of the intellect, for the world of the arts, for the world of the poet, the thinker, the creative person. That such a man could become president of the United States, could survive the all too prevalent democratic distrust of the first-rate—this added luster, elegance, and maturity to our nation in the eyes of the world.

In one other respect John Kennedy was rivaled only by Lincoln among our presidents—his astringent, arid sense of humor, not of the uproarious, hilarious, broad variety, but of the sharp, subtle, self-deprecating, scalpel-wielding type.

Experience has taught us that it is dangerous to assign a place in history to any president, or any leader, before time has placed all things in perspective. The tragic and untimely end which assassination brought to his career will always make it hard to assess John Kennedy's place in our history. Already the legend is fighting to overwhelm the man. He is becoming one of those folk heroes whose every memory is scored with emotional, not to say sentimental, overtones and through whom all sorts and conditions of men will find outlets for their own purposes and their own self-justification.

How could it be otherwise? To quote one of his favorite authors, writing of another, "He was blessed with great beauty of person; the gift of winning speech; a mind that mastered readily whatever it cared to master; a magic to draw friends to him; a heart as tender as it was brave. Only one gift was withheld from him—length of years."

For such a one to become the youngest of our elected leaders, and not merely to die in the early morning of achievement, but to die by the act of a young Ishmael without even the cruel justification of serious purposes—we have here all the ingredients of a legend.

Let us today, then, not merely rededicate ourselves to the purposes and the qualities which made him unique and which will, so long as memory endures, attest his greatness. Let us dedicate ourselves to saving John Kennedy from those who would make him a cheap souvenir, a symbol of second-rate sentimentality. Let us remember always that his heroism was in the classic and not the maudlin tradition—and that John Kennedy was above all a man.

The rare possibility of such a leader—a leader cast in the classic, heroic mold—a leader who could express the essence of the democratic faith and yet stand above the mass—a leader rather than an administrator, a bureaucrat, or even a servant of the people—that rare possibility was revealed to us in his life. And yet, a year ago, the very incident which revealed the possibility in a blinding, flashing moment, also took him from us—and the possibility was revealed too late.

In that sense, it is for us to determine what his heritage shall finally be. The grace of his life, the poignancy of his death—these will find their lasting significance by the manner of our accepting his gifts to us. His life and his death are truly what we shall make of them.

They say you were still half symbol,
Being given so little time;
Come, let us take you so, but in this sense;
In that region of possibility you fill
There, still, your bright, incontinent essence
Inclines to its own completion, still
Shapes almost its own actuality, still contrives
Some reason, measure, humor in our lives.

---

1. Benjamin Crowinshield Bradlee (1921-), journalist; A.B., Harvard (1943); reporter, *Washington Post* (1948-1951); press attache, embassy, Paris, France (1951-1953); European correspondent, *Newsweek* magazine (1953-1957); managing editor, *Washington Post* (1965-1968); vice president and executive editor (1968-). *Who's Who in America, 1976-1977,* 39th ed. (Chicago, 1976).

WPSD-TV
Paducah / February 28, 1965

In the operation of all governmental units and branches, including many departments of state government, it is often necessary or advisable for the agency to contract for services with persons or with firms outside of government in order to get necessary work accomplished. This is true, in general, because it would not be possible or economically feasible to keep on government payrolls all the specialists who might be needed from time to time within functions of government.

In our Kentucky state government the list of skills and professions from which the state contracts for services ranges all the way from psychiatry to piano tuning. Included are attorneys, architects, veterinarians, physicians, musicians, social workers, court reporters, dentists, laboratory technicians, dry cleaners, optometrists, artists, auditors, actuaries, and many other persons who by special aptitudes or training can help us conduct state business.

Within the last few weeks there has been much said about personal service contracts, and a number of the contracts now held by the state have been publicized both by communications media and by others. You and I must face the fact that some politicians, in both political parties, are constantly searching for a cheap and easy means to satisfy their own ambitions. These political opportunists are more concerned with future elections than they are with education of our children, building highways, finding jobs for our people, and putting money in the pocket of our farmers. These self-serving men are tearing up the yard in search of long-buried bones which they can dig up and gnaw for political nourishment.

It is important and necessary that the people of Kentucky distinguish between the sincere critics who are interested in improving our procedures and getting the taxpayer full service for his dollar and the expedient politicians who are simply trying to squeeze out a headline for their own selfish purposes. Let me suggest a good way for you to test the sincerity and good faith of these political critics. What suggestions have they made for improving our procedures in the negotiation and administration of personal service contracts, or are they simply interested in headline hunting and political infighting?

I welcome the efforts of all those who are honestly trying to correct abuses and improve our standards of public service. I am the first to admit that we have made mistakes, and that we shall probably make mistakes in the future. The only man who makes no mistakes is the man who does nothing, attempts nothing, accomplishes nothing. And I pledge you that whenever I make a mistake, I shall correct it as promptly and as humbly as human limitations will permit.

But I do not intend to let the forward movement of government in Kentucky be held back by petty political snipers who are interested not in doing a job for Kentucky but in doing a hatchet job on this administration.

Recent publicity by some critics of the present administration in Frankfort seems to be motivated by a desire to convince the public that all contracts the state holds are bad, that the taxpayers are getting cheated whenever a contract is signed. They are criticizing practices that have saved Kentucky millions of dollars in highway right-of-way costs, that have provided medical services for those unable to provide for themselves, that train student nurses, that help control animal diseases, that enhance the wealth of our state by increasing industrial potential, that show the way in the development of recreation areas, that help us plan educational facilities, and that assist in any number of ways to build a greater and better Kentucky.

Recently a past president of the Kentucky Education Association and long-time education leader was subjected to criticism for being under state contract to conduct a study pertaining to our planning for future needs in higher education. He was not allowed to complete the study before criticism set in, and none who offered criticism know to this time how much the state may profit by such a study.

Another Kentucky leader was condemned in some circles for being under contract to maintain high standards in the trotting horse industry, although those in the industry agree that he has helped the industry to prosper and to contribute an increased amount of taxes to the state treasury. In fact, tax revenue has recently increased from $9,586 to $258,000 in 1964 and a predicted $300,000 in 1965.

The right to criticize, at least as far as political and press criticism is concerned, carries with it an obligation to obtain all the facts about what is being criticized and to be objective in criticism. The progress of the state of Kentucky and the welfare of its citizens will not be served by automatically impugning the motives of any individual who is under contract or by questioning the value of his service until all the facts are learned.

It is important to the taxpayers that all contracts be drawn for legitimate public purposes, and it is equally important that all materials and services called for be provided before payment is made. It is my firm intention to see that all contracts do serve a public need and that the agreements entered into are carried out.

I have within the last few days received information from the Department of Finance concerning all contracts now held by the state, and I have asked for additional information on some of them.

I am confident that today Kentucky's taxpayers are getting more for the money they spend on salaries and personal service contracts than at any time in the history of the Commonwealth. This situation is the result of the merit system going into effect under the Combs administration, plus the continuing efforts of my administration to sharpen personnel practices and push contract economies.

This administration, believing that all citizens have a right to know how their money is being spent, and that news people should be assisted in passing this information along, has delivered the press and other media in

Frankfort a full list of personal service contracts. This list contains names, amounts, and the purposes of contracts. It will be brought up-to-date each month and delivered to the press and other media on a regular basis. The departments of state government also stand ready to provide any additional information on contracts that the press, or any citizen, may desire. We have nothing to hide.[1]

---

1. This address was a direct response to a speech made by Lieutenant Governor Harry Lee Waterfield to the Paducah Rotary Club in late January. In that speech Waterfield had suggested the administration's handling of personal service contracts was an example of "government by cronies."

STATEMENT ON SENATE RACES
Frankfort / May 7, 1965

On May 25 both parties will hold their primary elections to choose not only their local officials, but their candidates for membership in both houses of the state legislature. In these primaries the people will select their nominees for all seats in our state Senate. At the outset, let me make one thing clear. To the people of Kentucky, and them alone, belongs the choice of these candidates. Their vote is their own, and under our free form of government no man can take that vote away from them. It is not my intention or my purpose to interfere in the slightest degree with their freedom of choice, or to promote a selfish plan to gain control or domination over the people's representatives.

I do believe, however, that as their employee, their fellow Kentuckian, and as their elected chief executive I have a right, just as would any other citizen, to discuss with them in a fair and friendly way the issues which will face us as Kentuckians during the next two years. I believe that I have a right to point out to them the importance of choosing able, progressive, and dedicated senators and representatives—and the effect of their choice on Kentucky's future progress.

Needless to say, I have no intention of dealing in personalities, or in the muddy waters of factional politics. During the past years, and the past months, Kentuckians have grown sick of selfish factionalism, of ugly talk, of personal abuse and partisan malice. I want, as you do, to keep these discussions on a high, impersonal plane—and I shall confine myself to the great issues which will determine and mold our children's future in this great state.

In the beginning, I must tell you with real regret, there is a basic issue of democracy and free government at stake. That issue has been raised and created by the incumbent lieutenant governor, who demands that he and he alone, without let or hindrance, shall be given the power to appoint all the standing committees of the state Senate.[1] This, in effect, will give to one man, who is not a member of the Senate, the power to choke and throttle progressive legislation if he should so desire. The present lieutenant governor is the only lieutenant governor in more than twenty years to claim such a power.

This power is not given to the lieutenant governor by the constitution. It can only be given him by the rules of the Senate. For this reason it is very important that you find out how the candidates for the Senate in your district stand on this question; shall the Senate select its own committee organization, or shall the lieutenant governor assume the dictatorial power to control the Senate? In 1944 the Senate adopted a rule establishing a committee on committees, composed of members of the Senate, and elected by the Senate—and this committee was given power to choose all Senate committees and refer all bills to appropriate committees. Both majority and minority were represented on this committee. This rule was adopted in a Republican administration, and it continued through the administrations of all lieutenant governors for twenty-two years—except for those years when the present lieutenant governor was in office—1956, 1958, and 1964. In 1964, the first legislative session of my administration, I advised my friends in the Senate to accede to the lieutenant governor's wishes—as an evidence of good faith desire for cooperation.

But we found in 1964 that this power was abused—abused so as to deny the people's representatives the right to discuss and vote on important legislation. Therefore I hope that the people will this year nominate and elect members of the Senate who will stand by the freedom of the Senate to choose and select its own committee organization. The constitution confers upon the lieutenant governor the right to preside over the Senate —but not the right to become the master of the Senate. Let us cherish and maintain the sacred right of our legislative bodies to control their own organization. Unfortunately and without necessity, the lieutenant governor has chosen to do battle on this issue—and he has entered a slate of candidates who are pledged to support his plans for one-man rule. I am sure that many of these candidates are sincere, well-meaning individuals —but they have placed the lieutenant governor's political ambitions above the people's interest and the people's rights.

---

1. The roots of the conflict between Governor Breathitt and Lieutenant Governor Waterfield in the 1965 primaries reach back to the foundations of factional conflict in the Democratic party. Harry Lee Waterfield was a central figure in Kentucky politics and government for over two decades and, as he later wrote, "... tried as hard as anyone could for the (gubernatorial) nomination as many times as any Kentuckian...." From 1938 to 1947 he served in the Kentucky House of Representatives and was chosen its Speaker in 1944 and 1946. He waged his first gubernatorial campaign in 1947, but lost to Earle C. Clements in the Democratic primary. After returning to the House in 1950, Waterfield formed a political alliance with former Governor A.B. "Happy" Chandler, whose policies Waterfield had often opposed as a representative. The two men submerged their former differences in order to do battle with the common foe, the powerful political organization of Clements. The struggle between these two factions and their successors dominated Democratic politics through the early 1960s. The Chandler-Waterfield alliance brought dividends in 1955 as Waterfield won the lieutenant governorship, running on an antiadministration ticket with Chandler in the primary. In 1959 he sought the governorship once again, but was beaten by Chandler's 1955 primary opponent and heir to Clements's political forces, Bert Combs. Chandler and Waterfield joined forces a third time in 1963, but while Chandler lost the gubernatorial nomination to Combs's chosen successor, Edward T. Breathitt, Waterfield easily won the nomination for lieutenant governor. Thus, the Democratic victory in the 1963 general election brought men belonging to opposing factions to the state's top executive offices. Breathitt and Waterfield initially agreed on a harmonious working arrangement. But beginning with the 1964 General Assembly policy differences and their conflicting desires to wield legislative authority overcame cooperative efforts. Waterfield's chief opportunity for exercising influence over legislation lay in his relationship to the Senate. As lieutenant governor he was that body's presiding officer, but, more importantly, Breathitt had agreed that Waterfield should make Senate committee appointments in the 1964 General Assembly as Waterfield had done while he was Chandler's lieutenant governor in 1956 and 1958. This power, along with the extensive political friendships and legislative expertise gained in a long political career, gave Waterfield considerable leverage in the Senate, and therefore, in the actions of the General Assembly. Still, under the state constitution the respective powers of the legislature and the governor were decidedly weighted in the latter's favor. One of the governor's advantages lay in his authority to prepare and submit a budget to the General Assembly, which, since it regularly met for only sixty days every two years, could give the proposed budget only limited scrutiny. Waterfield, among others, hoped to increase the legislature's budgeting influence through Senate Bill 23, which would have established a permanent committee of the House and Senate chosen by party caucus to conduct a continuous study of state finances. The Legislative Research Commission had been expected to serve a similar function, but supporters of Senate Bill 23 contended that the Legislative Research Commission was dominated by the administration and thus did not adequately represent the legislature. Waterfield, one of the original proponents of the Legislative Research Commission, therefore saw the bill as a logical continuation of the struggle for legislative equality. Breathitt saw it differently. The 1964 session was a difficult one for him, and

much of the trouble was encountered in the Senate. The governor balked at the prospect of a "watchdog" committee which would likely contain factional opponents, endanger his programs in the next legislative session, and perhaps provide Waterfield with a platform from which he could launch another gubernatorial campaign in 1967. Therefore, Breathitt's allies in the House killed the Senate bill. Waterfield was furious and publicly criticized the governor. Breathitt, he alleged, had succumbed to factional pressures and repudiated an earlier promise to support the measure. Democratic differences were patched over for the sake of party unity in the November, 1964, elections, but the superficial reconciliation exploded into open political warfare in 1965. In January and February, Waterfield publicly attacked administration spending policies and its management of state contracts. He labeled the administration's $176 million bond proposal "inherently deceptive" and criticized the overall debt levels incurred under Breathitt and his predecessor, Bert Combs. In the same speech Waterfield intimated that lucrative engineering contracts were promised to Breathitt supporters before his election. The open break between Breathitt and Waterfield presaged a legislative battle in the upcoming General Assembly; however, the outcome would largely be decided in the May, 1965, primaries. In ten Senate districts Breathitt and Waterfield backed opposing candidates for the Democratic nomination. Breathitt intended to remove the power to make committee assignments from Waterfield's exclusive authority and place it in a Senate committee or committees which would contain a preponderance of administration supporters. The rules change would require a Senate vote, however, in which the votes cast by the victors in the ten key primary contests could be decisive. The issue, therefore, was clearly drawn in the primary campaigns, with Breathitt aiding those candidates who advocated a committee or committees and Waterfield supporting those in favor of the status quo. The results would be instrumental in determining whether the Breathitt programs would be enacted and which Democratic faction would dominate the party. Of the total of twelve Democratic Senate primary contests, ten included candidates who supported either Breathitt's or Waterfield's position on the Senate committee issue. Breathitt supporters won seven of the elections, thus strengthening the governor's influence in the upcoming 1966 General Assembly. *Louisville Courier-Journal,* February 28, June 14, 15, 1964; February 25, April 25, May 26, 27, and September 5, 1965.

FIRST CONGRESSIONAL DISTRICT JEFFERSON-JACKSON DAY DINNER

Mayfield / May 21, 1966

IT is with more than ordinary pleasure that I appear here tonight. Mayfield is not only the home of my wife and much of her family, but I also have the honor of speaking in my home congressional district—an honor I always enjoy. This is my first speaking appearance at a Democratic dinner since we finished the work of "The Great 66" legislative session. You know the story of that session. It was, unequivocally, one of the best, if not the best, legislative sessions ever held.

It was productive for the quantity of major legislation passed, and even more so for the quality. It was a session for which every Democrat can be proud because it was a Democratic administration and Democratic representatives and senators who led the way and pushed many pieces of progressive legislation through the General Assembly. It passed legislation to help education, to provide equal opportunity for our citizens, to keep this state's economy growing and to keep it strong, to make our highways safer. It passed legislation to preserve natural beauty and to protect and develop our natural resources, to combat crime and illegal gambling, to update our outmoded constitution, to continue and expand a modern highway program.

"The Great 66" passed more important legislation than any session in the recent history of the Commonwealth—legislation to help the ordinary citizen—legislation to better the health of Kentuckians, to fight disease and to provide additional care for the disabled and elderly—including a substantial raise in old-age assistance. And, if you will examine that legislation, all of it, you will find that it contains what we Democrats have fought for over the past thirty years.

We Democrats believe that life can be better. We believe in the pursuit of happiness and we believe that there is no such thing as inevitable ignorance, or inevitable poverty, or inevitable injustice. Of particular significance were the advances made in education. A statewide educational television network that will be in operation in the school year 1968, thirty-three new or expanded vocational schools, three new community colleges, elevation of four state colleges including Murray to university status, initiation of a scholarship program, adoption of an index salary schedule, and higher salaries for teachers. Our teachers will have received during this administration the largest salary increases ever provided during any administration in the history of this Commonwealth—and all this without an increase in our state taxes.

Kentucky's 1966 legislative session commanded attention not only in this state but across the nation. The *Oklahoma City Times* headlined an editorial "Action in Kentucky." The *New York Times* called the session "one of the most productive in history." The *St. Louis Post Dispatch,* the *Cincinnati Post,* the *San Francisco Chronicle,* the Providence, Rhode Island, *Journal,* the *Boston Herald* and even the *London Times* of Britain lauded the Kentucky legislature. I say all this because you and all Democrats can be enormously proud of the performance turned in by the legislature. It is a program the Democratic party can stand on this November and next November.

And you ladies did your part to make it a success. And you are doing your part to strengthen the Democratic party. I'm told that you now have nearly 100 active, hard-working Democratic women's clubs in the state and that your goal, according to your president, Mrs. Helen Garrett, is to have one in every county.[1]

Certainly Kentucky was well represented at the National Campaign Conference for Women in Washington last month with fifty-eight delegates, and your "Alliance for Progress" program to help establish small libraries in Ecuador is commendable and in the best tradition of the Democratic party. It is work and programs like these that will make the Democratic party strong.

As you well know, enthusiasm and seriousness are both essential to effective political organization. Unless there is enthusiasm, spirit, excitement, and a sense of purpose, it is difficult, if not impossible, to involve the enormous numbers of people and enormous energies necessary to wage a successful political campaign when they come around.

As you also know, it is the serious, solid, organization work underlying all the hoopla that helps produce the victory. It is the patient, systematic knocking on doors to find and register voters. It is the careful building of a party structure from precinct to ward, to city or town, to county, congressional, and finally state. It is the ability to fill the hall, to gather the crowd, to carry the campaign message from street to street, from farm to farm.

And it is the ability finally to deliver the vote to the polls, to provide transportation, the baby sitters, the sound trucks, and the telephone calls that bring in the voters the campaign has persuaded.

Most important of all is the program—the party's platform, its concern for people—and the confidence of the people that the candidate will act in their best interest. Fortunately, the Democrats tend to have a wealth of good men and women to choose from, and we have a progressive program both at the state and national levels.

Come this fall, I'm confident, we Democrats will be ready to do battle. At stake is a United States Senate seat—one we can win—and seven congressional posts. I hope that when you leave here tonight you will begin making your plans on how to carry out a most successful fall campaign.

Our party has, for nearly twenty uninterrupted years, met the responsibilities of government in Kentucky; and, for twenty-six of the last thirty-four years, has met the responsibilities of government in the nation. For that record, in state and nation, in domestic and foreign affairs, we have no need—I repeat, no need—for apology.

We come into battle once more, not to explain, not to extenuate, but to proclaim the record and the accomplishments of the great Democratic party. And again, in November 1966 and again in 1967, and again in 1968—again and again and again if you will—we shall say when the strife is o'er, the battle won—"We have met the enemy and they are ours."

---

1. Helen Rickman Garrett, born in Paducah, Kentucky; wife of Kentucky Senator Tom Garrett; active in Democratic party politics; upon Senator Garrett's death in 1979, Mrs. Garrett was appointed to complete his term. Information provided by Carol Garrett.

AMERICAN LEGION STATE CONVENTION
Louisville / July 15, 1966

LAST week we celebrated the 190th anniversary of the adoption, in Philadelphia, by the Continental Congress, of the Declaration of Independence. What a glorious day for the cause of man's freedom. But in celebration of that day we should not, I think, lose sight of the events that followed July 4, 1776. The seat of our government moved in those next months from Philadelphia to Baltimore and then to Philadelphia again; to Lancaster to York and back to Philadelphia; to Princeton to Annapolis to Trenton; to New York City and then to Washington.

The Articles of Confederation were adopted in 1777, but they were not ratified by all the states until 1781. Then, in 1787, delegates from each state were invited to come to Philadelphia on May 14 to draft a constitution. But it was not until May 25 that enough delegates had arrived to start the meeting—twenty-nine in all. Finally, several weeks later, some fifty-five delegates had arrived, representing twelve states. Rhode Island never did send anybody. Finally, by September 15, it was time for a vote on a draft constitution. By then thirteen of the delegates had gone home. The remaining forty-two argued all day, but they reached agreement. Even then, three of the delegates refused to sign. And it was another three years before Rhode Island finally decided to join the Union. Well, it all came to something—although it wasn't until 1865 that we really knew we were in business as one nation.

My point is this: we have to take the long view. It isn't always so easy to do it. Mention, for instance, Viet Nam, and you get a response which makes me think of the lines from Horatius: "Those behind cried forward! And those before cried back."

This morning, I want to take a few of your minutes to talk about the war in Viet Nam and to tell you why I think Viet Nam must be seen in the long view and in the perspective of history. It is an issue that was debated frankly and fully at the National Governors' Conference which I attended last week in Los Angeles. It is an issue on which we were briefed clearly and completely by officials from Washington and by the vice president of the United States. At the conclusion of the discussion, forty-nine governors, including Ned Breathitt of Kentucky, voted to support President Johnson and our fighting men in Viet Nam. There was only one dissenter. Permit me to give you my views on why I think we should stand for our country at this hour.

I believe our present policy in Viet Nam to be part of a coherent, restrained, and responsible bipartisan American foreign policy that has emerged over the past twenty-one years. It is a foreign policy directed toward the building, day-by-day, brick-by-brick, of a world of peaceful nations living together in the spirit of the United Nations Charter. It is a foreign policy that has been successful both in preventing the expansion of communist totalitarianism and of avoiding nuclear war.

During the past twenty-one years, we have met various types of communist aggression. Only the United States has been powerful enough to arrest the plans of the Soviet Union and Red China. Our response after World War II, under President Truman's direction but not without dissent in our own country, was firm yet prudent, strong yet patient. The Russian troops were forced out of Iran. The Truman Doctrine saved Greece and Turkey from the brink of disaster. The Marshall Plan poured economic and military aid to our war-weakened allies in Western Europe. When the Russians blockaded Berlin, America refused to budge. When the communists overran China, Mr. Truman drew the line in the Formosa Straits and backed it up with the world's most powerful navy. When the North Koreans, with prompting from Russia and Red China, launched a massive aggression against the Republic of Korea, Mr. Truman committed American troops to the aid of a beleaguered ally.

Many of his policies were criticized; mistakes were undoubtedly made, but American leaders didn't have much time to make their decisions. In saving Greece from a communist takeover, we knew we were defending governments which were far from democratic by our definition of the word. But had we not acted, Greece would have had no opportunity at all to build a democratic institution under a system of self-government.

I think we can see a parallel today in South Viet Nam. This small nation is not a democracy; no one pretends that it is. But the opportunity is there, the hope of self-government is there—as long as we are willing to give South Viet Nam the same chance our country gave Greece and Turkey and South Korea, as long as we can keep in perspective the long view—the idea that democratic governments are not built overnight, just as our country took many, many painful years to reach stability. In 1954, Adlai Stevenson defined our role in international affairs with these words: "It has fallen to America's lot to organize and lead that portion of the world which adheres to the principle of consent in the ordering of human affairs. It is an assignment we undertook not by choice but by necessity and without prior experience. The burden is without historical parallel and so is the danger, and so is our response."[1]

As Mr. Stevenson inferred, we are the policemen in Asia because there is no one else. The British and French are no longer available. India, Asia's largest democracy, could not build itself sufficiently to become the balance wheel against Chinese aggression. The assignment has become ours. This is why we are fighting in Viet Nam. This is why we must stay there until the aggression against the South has ended.

Harry Truman knew the stakes of world leadership—and today Greece and Turkey are still free, West Berlin is still free, Formosa is still free, South Korea is still free. Dwight Eisenhower knew the stakes, and when he sent the marines to Lebanon he assured the freedom of the entire Middle East from the communist subversion. John F. Kennedy knew the stakes when he again refused to budge from West Berlin and when he told the Russians to get their missiles out of Cuba—or else. And Lyndon Johnson knows the stakes in South Viet Nam.

In this room there may be a hundred different opinions on the conduct of the war in Viet Nam. But this is our struggle, an American struggle, no different from any other struggle we have entered in the cause of freedom and security. Under the Constitution, the president is the man we have delegated to direct foreign policy, and no other. We can be Monday morning quarterbacks, but at the crucial time on Saturday it is the president who must make the decisions. And in my opinion, his decisions are backed by a large majority of the Kentucky people.

Our country seeks but one victory—self-determination for fifteen million South Vietnamese. To seek less would be to abandon these people to the rigid totalitarianism of North Viet Nam. At stake is not merely the independence of the South Vietnamese, but the course of future events in Asia.

I found on my mission to Poland that many Poles feel—just as people from other small countries feel who are under communist domination—

that America is the hope for a rebirth of freedom. This is the leadership of the free world which has fallen our way.

We are fighting in Viet Nam to convince the communists again—as we have before—that the price of aggression comes too high, to convince them that just as nuclear blackmail failed and conventional invasion failed, so-called wars of liberation too will fail.

Today, the making of history lies in our hands to a greater degree than has been afforded to any nation before. We must never lose our perspective in the crisis of the moment. We must exercise American power to help those who cannot defend themselves from aggression—not in arrogance, not in passion, but in sober determination. For as John F. Kennedy said, in that great inaugural address: "Let every nation know, whether it wishes us well or ill, that we shall pay any price, bear any burden, meet any hardship, support any friend, oppose any foe to assure the survival and the success of liberty."

---

1. Adlai Ewing Stevenson (1900-1965), attorney from Illinois; governor of Illinois (1949-1953); Democratic party nominee for president (1952 and 1956); ambassador to the United Nations (1961-1965). Dan and Inez Morris, *Who Was Who in American Politics* (New York, 1974).

FAYETTE COUNTY YOUNG DEMOCRATS
Lexington / July 21, 1966

I HAVE come to Keeneland this evening because I want to talk to you about the most important business facing our Democratic party at this time—the business of electing John Y. Brown to the United States Senate and seven Democratic congressmen.[1] The reasons Kentuckians should vote Democratic in 1966 can be stated in a single sentence. A vote for the Democratic party is a vote for Kentucky, for continued prosperity, and for progress.

We have come a long way in recent years in Kentucky. In education, in road building, in industrial development, in finding jobs—Kentucky is making dramatic progress. You know the story of "The Great 66" legislative session. It was, unequivocally, one of the best, if not the best, legislative sessions ever held. It was productive for the quantity of major legislation passed, and even more so for the quality. It was a session for which every young Democrat can be extraordinarily proud because it was a Democratic administration and Democratic representatives and senators who led the way and pushed many pieces of progressive legislation through the General Assembly.

All of you know who the house majority floor leader was during that session—the Fayette County gentleman who day after day, bill after bill, fought for excellent, progressive legislation to help Kentuckians move our state forward and make life easier for our people.

We know that performance, not promises, is the test not only of an individual but of a political party, too. And we of the Democratic party have kept our promises. We are proud of the new strip-mine law, a law that will stop the devastation and destruction of our mountainsides and rolling farm land. We are proud of the civil rights law; it proclaims that there is no room for second-class citizenship in Kentucky. We are proud of our educational record. More than $2,500 on the average will have been given our teachers in salary raises in eight years. We are proud of our road building record. More highways will have been put under contract this year than ever before in our state's history.

I saw John Y. Brown, as majority floor leader, work for these programs. No one who sat in the gallery will ever forget the eloquent, stirring speeches he made in support of the strip-mine bill and the civil rights legislation. They made all of us think about Kentucky and in which direction we wanted our state to travel. John Y. Brown is a great, inspirational leader, and he's been working to move Kentucky forward all his life.

As a young congressman, he sat at the feet of Franklin Delano Roosevelt and Sam Rayburn.[2] He shared their ideals and learned from these great teachers how to put them into practical effect. As six times a member of the state House of Representatives, he won recognition as one of the ablest leaders who ever served in that body. In great issues of government, his advice is sought and given. To every post he has held, John Y. Brown has dedicated all his great talents and all his abundant energy. He has given every waking hour to the job in hand. John Y. Brown has been a forerunner, a man looking to the future. He has never restricted his mind to a traditional pattern of thought and action.

Many, many years before, long before the 1960 legislature acted, John Y. advocated a sales tax to help the education, health, and welfare of Kentuckians. He fought for a sales tax to move Kentucky forward when few others stood beside him. He fought to give eighteen-year-olds the right to vote in Kentucky and was later a cosponsor of the act that achieved this goal. He fought as a young congressman for funds to create Cumberland National Forest, a forest whose name will be changed to the Daniel Boone National Forest Saturday in ceremonies at London.

His mind has always reflected the flexibility and mobility of activities he faced each day. He's been willing to change and to advocate change when he knew it was for the better. He's never permitted his total interests to be directed into rigid channels because he knows that man will never survive in tomorrow's Kentucky or in next week's America. He is without question the young man's candidate.

John Y. Brown is truly one of Kentucky's great leaders, an unsung hero who in many ways has never gotten the credit due him for the progressive thinking he has provided our state. On the basis of performance, John Y. Brown is well qualified to be the United States senator from Kentucky. He has the courage, the vision, the ability, and the determination to help Kentucky become a greater state. He is in tune with the times, and his leadership is needed.

I hope that between now and November 8 that you will do all in your power to help in his election and the election of seven Democratic congressmen, so we can obtain for our state the proper representation it deserves in Washington.

---

1. John Young Brown (1900-), born in Union County, Kentucky; A.B., Centre College (1921); L.L.B., University of Kentucky (1926); Kentucky House of Representatives (1930-1932, 1953-1954, 1962-1963, 1966-1967); majority floor leader (1966-1967); U.S. House of Representatives (1933-1935); a resident of Lexington, Kentucky. *Biographical Directory of the American Congress, 1774-1971* (Washington, 1971), p. 650.
2. Sam Rayburn (1882-1961), Texas lawyer; member, U.S. House of Representatives (1913-1961); Speaker of the House (1940-1947, 1949-1953, 1955-1961). Dan and Inez Morris, *Who Was Who in American Politics* (New York, 1974).

DEMOCRATIC FUND RAISING DINNER
Jefferson City, Missouri / July 23, 1966

GOVERNOR and Mrs. Hearnes, Lt. Governor Tom Eagleton, Chairman Delton Houtchens, ladies and gentlemen of the great state of Missouri: I come here tonight to join with the good and loyal Democrats of Missouri to pay tribute to a great governor and his charming first lady on this occasion which honors their birthdays.[1] I'm delighted to be here.

You may be interested to know that fourteen of your Missouri governors in the first eighty years of your history, after you achieved statehood in 1820, were born in Kentucky. And, if we can get the Mississippi to meander just a little bit we could add still another since Warren's home is only a good rock's throw from western Kentucky.

The dark and bloody ground of Kentucky and the "Show Me" state of Missouri have long shared close ties dating all the way back to Daniel Boone, whose remains you were most generous to return to us at the middle of the nineteenth century. Not only has your state attracted a large proportion of governors from Kentucky, but some of your ablest congressmen and senators were born in our Commonwealth, too. Men like Senator George Vest and Speaker Champ Clark held the affection of Kentuckians just as they did Missourians.[2] And, of course, we would like to lay claim to the fighter from Independence, that great president, Harry Truman, but the best we can do is claim both his grandparents.

So I come here tonight to bring you greetings from three million Kentuckians, who have strong ties to Missouri, and join with you in celebrating Warren's and Betty's birthdays. I feel right at home.

Warren Hearnes is a personal friend of mine, a young, courageous, hard-working, highly successful chief executive who is greatly respected by his fellow governors. He is not the best horse picker, as he proved last May when he was my guest at the Kentucky Derby, but as most of you probably know, Governor Hearnes is a golfer of some renown. If he can handle the Republicans like he hits a golf ball, then Missouri will be Democratic a long time!

The Hearnes Democratic administration's legislative achievements have received national attention and, for many of us, have served as a stimulus to meet our responsibilities in our own states. You in Missouri have dealt effectively with problems in reapportionment, education, civil rights and many other areas, which is a tribute to the leadership of your able governor and the Democratic party.

Warren Hearnes's background, his ten years as a member of the House of Representatives and his four years as majority floor leader, did much, I'm sure, to prepare him for the office of governor. This experience, this dealing day by day, bill after bill with problems facing a state gives a person a well-founded basis for leadership and knowledge in a wide range of subjects.

We governors who have served our apprenticeship in the legislative body have found that the legislative experience has helped immeasurably in preparing us for executive responsibility. In the expansion of industry, in meeting the needs of senior citizens, in educational progress, Warren Hearnes's legislative and executive leadership have been parts of a continuing, advancing career, devoted to a better life for Missouri's people.

His record as governor speaks for itself—and speaks eloquently. To every post he has held, he has dedicated all his great talents and all his abundant energy. I'm happy to join you here tonight to honor your first family, but I know you Democrats don't need a Kentuckian to come here and tell you that you have an outstanding governor.

We of the Democratic party, since its founding by Jefferson and Jackson, have always been concerned about people and their welfare, just as this concern is coursed through the views of Warren Hearnes. This concern for people, for their education, their health, their security has, through the years in my judgment, separated us from the opposition party.

Democrats like Woodrow Wilson, Franklin Roosevelt, Harry Truman, John Kennedy, and Lyndon Johnson, more than any other individuals in the twentieth century, have symbolized the struggle of men and women in all lands; not merely the struggle against dictatorship, against monstrous and cruel wickedness, but the struggle for a fuller, more spacious life, a life of freedom and opportunity, for all men, everywhere. Through the lives and thought of all of these great leaders run the golden threads of a single political philosophy which is the imperishable heritage of the Democratic party, and, indeed, the very bread of life for all Americans in search of a fighting faith which fits the facts of the twentieth century world.

They believed and we believe: First, that peace in this tormented, divided and confused world is not only possible but necessary; that the world's peoples have a right to be their own masters, to seek their own destinies, and to live free from the threat of atomic annihilation. Second, that this world's wealth, actual and potential, is adequate to support mankind, everywhere, in material comfort, free from the exploitation of economic or political overlords, with opportunity for a decent protection against the hazards of old age, unemployment, and sickness. Third, that every individual has a right, and should have the unfettered opportunity, to make his own place in the world, unhampered by restrictions based upon race, color, or religious belief. This includes the right to vote; the right to work; the right to be educated; the right to live in a convenient and suitable location; the right to eat, lodge, or enjoy entertainment in establishments open to the public; the right to aspire to public office; and the right to worship in the place of his choice. Fourth, that those with whom life and its adversities have dealt harshly—the aged, the handicapped, the crippled, the blind, the sick—that these are entitled to live in comfort and in dignity. Fifth, that our natural resources are a gift from Providence in trust for all men and that they must be developed, used, and conserved—and not wasted or exploited for the benefit of a selfish few. Sixth, that man is created in the image of God—and that governments, peoples, political leaders, and indeed all men stand under God's judgment for the uses to which they put His gifts. That it is the responsibility of governments among men to provide opportunities and institutions through which men may develop to the fullest the talents and capacities with which God has endowed them.

Tonight, though, we meet in a time of danger and difficulty for our Democratic party. It might be easier for me, and for you, to ignore the danger and difficulties which we face. But I, for one, do not believe that we solve our problems by fooling ourselves for awhile, for in the long run we shall not be able to fool either ourselves or the American people. Our best bet, under these conditions, is to follow the prescription of Adlai Stevenson and talk sense to the American people. This is not only honorable to the responsible course of action; it is also the best politics.

This year, we enter into a campaign for the election of members of both houses of the Congress. As we begin the battle, let us see where we are and where we are going, so that we may better discern the proper courses to follow. Two years ago our party won what was perhaps the greatest victory in the history of American politics. Faced with a clear choice between progress and less action, between the responsible and irresponsible policies, the American people made a strong and unmistakable decision. Not only was Lyndon Johnson elected on a titanic wave of votes, but overwhelming Democratic majorities were returned in both houses of Congress.

Our Democratic president and our Democratic Congress have tackled boldly, resolutely, and on the whole, effectively, the tasks which the American people prescribed in the 1964 election. Our economy has continued to grow—business proceeds have expanded to unprecedented heights. Employment has come up, and unemployment has gone down. Despite occasional mistakes, we are seeking to bring one-fifth of a nation, the poor and deprived, into the main stream of our life. We are seeking to make available to every American, regardless of his color, not only the full rights of citizenship, but his fair share in the American heritage, self-respect and material well-being. We are seeking to break up, to restore, to rebuild and to remake, the slum areas, urban and rural, which have confined and imprisoned millions of our fellow citizens in a subhuman, soul-destroying, indecent life. We are working to make both the city and the countryside greener, more beautiful, more livable, and better fitted for a new and difficult era of urban living.

On our policies, on our achievements, on our progressive legislation, we could look forward, I am sure, to a vote of renewed confidence from the American people, were it not for a single dark overhanging shadow of war. There are those who say that it is a political mistake to mention Viet Nam, to mention war in a 1966 campaign to elect Democrats. We can no more ignore the war in Viet Nam that we can ignore any other basic and elemental fact of our national life. Our opponents can afford to ignore Viet Nam, but we cannot. Our opponents can take refuge in evasions, in double talk, and in irresponsible criticism, but we cannot. Our opponents have pinned their hope for the 1966 election on the classic prescription for Republican revival—the unearned political dividends of war.

We know those who would be tempted by appeasement upon withdrawal or by the escalation can and will say that this is Lyndon Johnson's war. To those who are impatient of restraint, who risk incalculable hazards of global conflict, to the bomb bouncer and warmonger, the Republicans can and will say that we would win this war quickly, easily, and cheaply if it were not for Lyndon Johnson's leadership. Having no responsibility, making no decisions, running not as a national party but as a collection of local candidates led by National Chairman Ray Bliss, who frankly advocates policies without principle, which the Republicans are supporting for the best of both worlds—what then is the course which we Democrats must take?[3] We cannot duck the issues. We cannot dissolve into a coalition of political tongs. We must give the same answer which Roosevelt gave to Hitler, which Truman gave to the communists in Korea, and which Kennedy gave to Khrushchev at the time of the missile crisis.

Permit me to read from the winning essay of young William Kirgan, whose writing appears in your Democratic program: "When other nations hesitated to become involved, President Truman, through aid to the Greek patriots, stemmed the tide of communism rushing on southern Europe. His dogged determination, his forthrightness, his fearlessness in the face of criticism make me proud to belong to a party that breeds such men," he says.[4] That same strong belief can be applied to our present policy in Southeast Asia.

We must keep flying both the flag of freedom and the flag of responsibility. We must continue to resist the spread of communist aggression without unleashing the fearsome sources of world war and unlimited destruction. We must stand behind our commander-in-chief. This is not a testing time for Lyndon Johnson. He has made his test—with courage and determination. This is a testing time for us, for the American people. We are being tested, each one of us, to determine whether we can be both brave and patient, both resolute and restrained, in a world where answers are not simple and issues are not easy. As we meet our test, then I am confident that under the leadership of the Democratic party we shall break through the clouds of war in a decent settlement in Southeast Asia, and resume our march toward a free, just, and compassionate society both in America and in the world.

---

1. Warren Eastman Hearnes (1923-), attorney who currently resides in Charleston, Missouri; secretary of state for Missouri (1961-1965); governor of

Missouri (1965-1973). *Who's Who in America, 1976-1977*, 39th ed. (Chicago, 1976). Thomas Francis Eagleton (1929-), attorney general for Missouri (1961-1965); lieutenant governor (1965-1968); U.S. senator from Missouri, (1969-). *Biographical Directory of the American Congress, 1774-1971* (Washington, 1971), p. 893. Delton Louis Houtchens (1918-), prosecuting attorney, Henry County, Missouri (1943-1944); Missouri state representative (1948-1952); member, Personnel Advisory Board of Missouri (1959-1964); state campaign chairman for Warren E. Hearnes (1964). *Who's Who in American Politics, 1971-1972*, 3rd ed. (New York, 1971).

2. George Graham Vest (1830-1904), Missouri lawyer; U.S. Senate (1879-1903). Dan and Inez Morris, *Who Was Who in American Politics* (New York, 1974). James Beauchamp Clark (1850-1921), Missouri Democrat; U.S. House of Representatives (1893-1895, 1897-1921); Speaker of the House (1911-1919). *Biographical Directory of the American Congress, 1774-1971* (Washington, 1971), pp. 742-43.

3. Ray Charles Bliss (1907-), from Ohio and long involved in Republican party politics; member, Republican National Committee (1952-); chairman (1965-1969). *Who's Who in America, 1980-1981*, 41st ed. (Chicago, 1980).

4. William Kirgan, no information available.

METHODIST MEN BANQUET
Lexington / January 31, 1967

A HAUNTING fear always rests upon the mind of any speaker privileged enough to be asked to speak often: if he has certain convictions relative to his life, his future, his job and career, he worries that certain phrases and certain ideas enveloped within the framework of those phrases will be repeated too often.

I have deep and abiding convictions regarding the innate and vital place that morality and Christianity do and should occur in politics. I have stated this belief in varying ways since the day I became a candidate for governor and placed "morality in government" first in my platform. I remember well that day I stood with my hand raised on a cold, wintry December 10th, 1963, and took the oath of office as governor of Kentucky. In that inaugural address I pledged an honest government, honestly operated. Since these words were spoken, more than three years have passed. Since that crisp inaugural day I have not changed my mind that this is what I believe. Nor, have I changed my mind that morality—in every vague and exact sense of its meaning—is needed in all levels of government.

I do not use the term "vague" in context which would imply that moral guidelines are vague. You and I know what morality implies, and we literally know what it means. Basically, there would be no reason for any religion in the world to exist if these religions did not set forth those guidelines and attempt to help us abide by them, and hopefully, achieve them.

I believe that the governor and those who work closely with him set the moral tone of any administration in state government. They are responsible for spending millions and millions of tax dollars and for executing hundreds of laws that regulate business and other private financial affairs. In Kentucky, including the colleges and universities, more than 20,000 employees work under these officials, and they, too, deal with the public in helping execute the laws and in spending the tax money.

Certainly 98 percent or perhaps even 99 percent of the employees involved in state work are beyond approach to any wrongdoing and the same percentage figures would most likely apply to the public who deals with state government on business matters. But in all groups there are a few who will waiver, a few who will bend to temptation, a few who will tempt others to gain favors. It is on this small group of private and public individuals that the governor and those close to him can have the greatest effect. If the governor and his close associates are lax, if they create an atmosphere of immorality, then others in the system will follow suit.

In my administration, employees and officials know that I will not tolerate any wrongdoing. There has not been a single scandal during the thirty-seven months and twenty-one days of this administration, which, I feel, is a tribute to your state government and especially its employees. To the best of our belief, there have been no misdeeds or acts of malfeasance. There have been no misappropriations or unlawful spending of tax money.

I am thankful that I've had a scandal-free administration. But, I knock on wood because you never know what might happen tomorrow. However, there is one thing of which the public can be certain—anyone found guilty of violating the moral code of state government will be prosecuted vigorously and as severely as the law permits, whether it be tomorrow, the next day, or the last day of this administration. And I think all our employees know this fact, too. This is the way I believe government ought to be operated, and I've tried to keep faith with my promises and beliefs. I believe that no responsibility of government is more fundamental than the responsibility of maintaining the highest standards of ethical behavior by those who conduct the public business.

Many times I have expressed regret that some citizens who could help most in the governing of their community, state, or federal governments, hesitate to become involved because they fear that politics and their religion do not mix. Some of those potentially most valuable to us in government even consider the idea so distasteful they will not discuss any relationship between politics and religion. I do not believe this, because I have always defined politics by the classic definition—the "art of governing." For this reason, I not only believe politics and religion do mix; they should mix.

It is a part of our humanity that we do have too many examples of vice, crime, and greed. Taking nothing away from the sociologists, the psychologists, those concerned with crime prevention and its detection and punishment, may I submit to you that these also ultimately depend upon government. Also, that this government is run by the people you elect—call them officeholders or politicians.

Government in this land of ours is another way of saying that you elect politicians—and, I admit, some are more and some are less versed in the art of governing. But, for better or worse, you do elect them, and you can do nothing less after you elect them except trust them. Government is a product of politics in this republic, and I urge you to not just observe their operations, but to participate. It will help Kentucky become a greater state.

As Christians, do you intend to help? You can only help if you become involved in that art of governing sufficiently enough to understand its working. You must become so involved that your abilities and ideas can and will be heard in places of power and the innermost circles of government.

Thomas Paine, an astute political writer who died long before we lived, once observed: "The science of the politician consists in fixing the true point of happiness and freedom. Those men would deserve the gratitude of the ages, who should discover a mode of government that contained the greatest sum of individual happiness, with the least national expense." Thomas Paine not only lived ahead of his time; he thought ahead of his time. What man or woman in government would know better his ultimate aim and purpose in government than a politician who knows well the Golden Rule?

This does not involve party politics. Former President Dwight Eisenhower wrote in his book *Waging Peace* these words: "For certain it is that if every decent person in this nation would arouse his conscience, help elect to public office persons of proved courage and integrity, support vocally and morally his police force, his corps of teachers, the local judges and lawmakers and their governors in state capitals, soon the numerous newspaper accounts of delinquencies and neglect would decline. . . ."

Throughout our communities, state, and nation the winds of change are as obvious today as they have been for more years than any of us in this church today can remember. But, as the years have passed, these winds have blown more strongly and with more lasting effect on our individual and collective futures.

For instance, let us hope that our freedom has grown during these years. If is has not, then it is our own fault. Freedom should have a habit of growing, because there is no more such a thing as "a little bit of freedom" than there is "a little bit of death." If you have doubts, for instance, as to whether your freedom has grown and is growing, remember that the surest way to decide in your own mind, is to lose yourself in something bigger than yourself. I assure you that you will make this discovery in politics and its product, government.

Someone once said there are two basic types of conversations. First, there is the skyscraper conversation where two people merely talk at each other and thereby think they build monuments to themselves. Secondly, there is the bridge-building type within which two people genuinely build foundations to stretch their minds across a gap that separates them. I urge you to become the bridge-building type of conversationalist where politics and government are concerned. But always remember, this will be of little use unless you are practical as far as your participation in politics is concerned. Your effort—and mine—will be blunted or nullified unless the citizens in majority and their elected representatives agree with us, according to the procedures of our modified democracy.

I sincerely hope that all of you will be lobbyists, because lobbyists perform valuable services in providing those of us in government with specialized knowledge. I hope that you will be Christian lobbyists for better government, and through that better government be shapers of better lives for our fellow men in a cleaner society. It will help Kentucky become a greater state. I hope that you will be politicians and learn the art of governing and its complexities if you are to help those of us elected and appointed to try to improve your lives. If you are not satisfied with government on any level, if you do not believe that government is working toward a better heritage for your children, do not criticize.

Participate. It will help Kentucky become a greater state. Criticism for the sake of criticism is not only a sad commentary on our lives today; it is also ineffectual. Let us not keep our criticism only vocal—let us learn the issues, the background and qualifications of candidates, and then take our criticism to the polls. Knowledge of such background and the issues is not only constructive, but makes it effective. Electoral support should always be based upon facts and personal decision, and not because of well-disguised distortion of those facts or lack of knowledge.

Should you decide to participate in politics, you will find there is a penalty. This penalty is a penalty of conscience which, as in many pursuits, urges you to devote overtime to your job in order to accomplish some tasks impossible during the day. It may cost you friendships of long-standing and present you with decisions you would prefer not to make. Material rewards are usually not adequate to compensate for these losses, but payments are there in knowing that to some degree you are an architect and molder of a governmental structure which will improve so many things we mutually are interested in—health, roads, education, and even governmental compassion for less fortunate citizens.

Horace Greeley once received a letter from a woman who said her church was distressed financially.[1] She explained the church continued in this moneyless position despite a series of oyster suppers, grab bags, and box suppers. What, she inquired of Mr. Greeley, would he suggest to keep the struggling church from disbanding? The famous editor's reply was short. He said: "Try religion."

I believe only the brave should be in politics—at least in those governmental places which allow them to make important administrative decisions or fashion policy for that government. I believe their minds should direct that courage wisely, and be enlightened enough to understand the decision they make in its perspective as to the possible impact it will have on many tomorrows, as well as today. In government particularly we should always remember the old Chinese proverb which indicated that a journey of a thousand miles begins with the first step. We need intelligence and morality along each step of such a journey in government, every day, because the future comes one day at a time.

---

1. Horace Greeley (1811-1872), nineteenth century newspaperman and presidential candidate in 1872. *Concise Dictionary of American Biography* (New York, 1964), pp. 366-67.

WEBSTER COUNTY YOUNG DEMOCRATS
Frankfort / April 20, 1967

I AM glad to have this opportunity to welcome the Webster County Young Democrats to Frankfort and to the seat of your state government. It would be improper for me to call this day a partial repayment for the splendid hospitality you gave me when recently I was in your county for State Government Day because this house is your house—it is the people's house—and you and other Kentuckians always are welcome.

Since I've been governor, I've tried to talk to as many high schools as possible, to as many youth groups as possible because the young of Kentucky always provide a stimulating, exciting time. I enjoy speaking to young people. No other group is more receptive to change, no other group is more free of the prejudices that all of us inevitably accumulate during our journey through life.

I believe that young people in Kentucky are responsible, and I like to see them taking part in public affairs. As you know, Kentucky and Georgia are the only two states in the nation which allow eighteen-year-olds to vote. As a member of the legislature in 1954, I voted for the act which placed the question on the ballot for ultimate approval in 1955. I've never regretted my action. Kentucky has been a proving ground for the movement to permit eighteen-year-olds to vote. Because of the right to vote, the young people in Kentucky take a greater interest in their government. They become participants at a time when their minds are open, at a time when they are establishing attitudes and philosophies that will remain with them throughout their life. Democracy is participation—it is voting, working for the candidate of your choice in the precincts and your county, being active in the affairs of the day. Young people in Kentucky have that opportunity, and it creates better citizenship.

I would urge that Congress take action to reduce the voting age to eighteen throughout the nation. If eighteen, nineteen and twenty-year-olds elsewhere manifest the great sense of responsibility shown by young Kentuckians, the result will be of great importance to the future of our country. According to national professional polls, nearly two adults in every three, or some 64 percent, think this age group should be allowed to vote. One reason why many think these young people should be allowed to vote is that "if a person is old enough to fight, he's old enough to vote."[1]

A bipartisan proposal for a constitutional amendment to lower the age is now before Congress. I don't know the attitude of the members of the Kentucky delegation in Congress toward the proposal to reduce the age throughout the land by federal action, but I am inclined to believe that a majority, if not all of them, would vote for the change.

Young people today also are playing significant roles in the advancement of Kentucky. Already, in many areas, in jaycee work, in business, in medicine, in education, in government, in student life—young Kentuckians are now writing, and many thousands more can and will write, chapters in the history of the progress of Kentucky.

In state government, for example, we have approximately 3,500 young people under the age of thirty working—many of them holding important, policy-making positions. At least 600 of these employees have college degrees. In this age area and slightly above, there are doctors helping cure disease, engineers designing roads, social workers helping the less fortunate, and administrators running divisions. I have in my cabinet probably the youngest state insurance commissioner in the nation—Roy Woodall.[2]

And another young man, David Schneider, lawyer for the Department of Natural Resources, has made a lasting contribution to the state as a chief author of the 1966 Strip Mine Act.[3]

I sincerely believe that today young people have a unique opportunity to participate in public service. He, or she, may seek a seat in the General Assembly. He may file for a local office or work for the many bureaus and departments of local, state, and federal governments.

In communities all over this state, young men and women are making valuable contributions to the development of their towns and cities. I see them in jaycee clubs, in news media, in professional work, in industry, in schools, in city halls and courthouses, and in other posts of leadership. A young Kentuckian or American can seize the opportunity as never before to participate in decisions which affect his community, state, and nation not just today, but throughout many generations to come.

Just today an announcement is being made that a brilliant young lady, Myra Tobin of Breckinridge County, is being named assistant research director for the Department of Commerce.[4] Myra was an outstanding student at the University of Kentucky and won there the highest honor that can be bestowed upon a student, the Sullivan Medallion presented to the outstanding woman graduate each year. From there she went on to win a Rotary Foundation Fellowship, in stiff competition with all other students from Kentucky, which enabled her to study for a year in New Zealand.

In my office, my legal aide is only twenty-six years old. A Phi Beta Kappa, Alex Campbell is a graduate of Yale Law School, is from Lexington, and is making a valuable contribution.[5] And there are many others.

I'm so glad to see so many young people from Webster County taking a part in the political affairs of your county. I believe that young people should be active in politics, that they should choose a party and be active in it. The Democratic party of Kentucky is the party which, since I was growing up and became a student at the University of Kentucky, has best expressed my philosophy of good government. And it is the party that has provided me with the means of serving the people of this great state.

An illustrious Democrat, an eminent American statesman, Adlai Stevenson, said this about political parties: "the test of a political party, the acid, final test," is the way it governs a nation. The principle, of course, can be applied to the state as well as to a nation. And if we apply it to the Democratic administration, of which I have had the honor to be a part during these past three years and four months, then surely we must conclude that the Democratic party in Kentucky has stood the "acid, final test" of a political party.

Within the time limits which I have prescribed for myself, it would not be possible to review in any detail these achievements. But briefly I would like to enumerate a few of them. Kentucky has made notable progress in education, from the elementary grades through our colleges and our universities, under this administration. The salaries of school teachers have been raised $1,400 on the average per teacher, which is $300 more than was done in the previous administration. Nearly 4,000 new classrooms have been built. An $8.5 million educational television network to serve all Kentuckians is now under construction and should be ready for the school year of 1968. Since 1960, Kentucky has been first in the nation in its progress in education.

Our record in public higher education is just as impressive. During the past six years, Kentucky has led the nation in percentage increase in funds for higher education. We now have under construction three new community colleges and a $15 million expansion program at the other two-year colleges, and we've elevated four colleges to university status.

More than $600 million was spent on Kentucky's highways of all kinds in the past three years—more than any previous four-year total.

Kentucky's progress in obtaining new industry is truly remarkable. More than 600 firms have announced new industries or expansions in Kentucky during the past three years. More than $800 million has been invested in new plants.

One could go on at great length with the listing. But the story is that we have made progress in just about every facet of the services and functions which state government is expected to provide. Moreover, we have, I think, managed the people's treasury, the money they pay in taxes for the operation of their government, carefully and wisely, with the result that it has not been necessary, during this entire administration, to increase state taxes a single dime.

I am not trying to imply that these are achievements to be credited to any one individual or to any small group of individuals. Certainly they represent the combined efforts of a great many persons, many of them connected with the state government organization, some of them not. Nor am I trying to say that it is the achievement of a single political party. Nonetheless, it is the record of an administration given the power by the people under the banner of the Democratic party. It is, in a way, then, the record of the Democratic party in Kentucky, and I reassert that under the acid and final test of our performance, it is a notable record.

Finally, may I again express to all of you my sincere gratitude for the wonderful hospitality and many kindnesses you showed us when we were guests in your county on that cold, snowy day. Please take that message home with you this afternoon to your people. As a fellow Democrat, I salute you for your interest and your loyalty to the oldest political party in the world.

---

1. This phrase was frequently employed in the struggle to secure the right to vote for younger Americans. The draft that sent eighteen-year-olds to Viet Nam afforded the movement powerful impetus.

2. Roy Woodall (1939-), born in Paducah, Kentucky; B.A. and J.D., University of Kentucky; commissioner of insurance, Commonwealth of Kentucky (1966-1967); member, law firm Wyatt, Grafton and Sloss, Louisville (1967-1972); president, Western Pioneer Life Insurance Company, Louisville (1972-1976); assistant to president, American Life and Accident Insurance Company, Louisville (1976-1980); executive vice president, National Association of Life Companies, Atlanta, Georgia (1980-). Information provided by Department of Insurance, Frankfort.

3. David Schneider (1938-), attorney from Covington, Kentucky; J.D., University of Cincinnati (1963); assistant attorney general for Kentucky (1965-1968); partner, firm of Ziegler and Schneider, Covington (1968-). *Who's Who in American Law*, 1st ed. (Chicago, 1978).

4. Myra L. Tobin (1940-), born in Louisville, Kentucky; B.S., University of Kentucky (1962); M.A., Ohio State University (1965); M.B.A., New York University (1971); assistant to Congressman William Natcher, Washington, D.C. (1965-1966); Kentucky Department of Commerce (1967-1969); employed by Marsh and McLennan, New York, New York (1970-); vice president (1980-). Information provided by Marsh and McLennan.

5. Hugh Alexander Campbell (1941-), born in Lexington, Kentucky; B.A., Yale University (1963); L.L.B. (1966); legal assistant to Governor Breathitt (1966-1967); assistant attorney general for the Commonwealth of Kentucky (1967-1968); Ford Foundation (1968-1969); American Child Centers, Nashville, Tennessee (1969-1970); law firm of Trimble, Soyars and Breathitt, Lexington, Kentucky (1970-1971); private law practice, Louisville (1971-1974); law firm of Tarrant, Combs and Bullitt (1974-1980); law firm of Wyatt, Tarrant and Combs (1980-). Telephone interview, March 10, 1981.

FRANKLIN COUNTY WARD RALLY
Frankfort / October 30, 1967

WE come to the end of one administration and to the beginning of another. For nearly four years we have worked together in tackling the problems which face the government and the people of Kentucky. Not only to you who have worked and are working with me in state government, but to those of you who, as residents of our capital community have always shown a close and intimate concern with state government, I want to express my gratitude—not only for me, not only for Frances and the children, but for all the people of Kentucky.

I believe that we can say, modestly but truly, that the end of this four years will leave Frankfort a better, nobler, and more beautiful community. As the city which we envision takes shape and form in future years, all of us can look back, perhaps nostalgically, but with pleasure and pride on the plans which, working together, we have set in motion.

I have always believed that every person who serves in state government, in whatever capacity, is just as much a part of that government as is the governor or any department head. I believe that every state employee, every public servant, helps to give tone and character to the quality of state government, and that the total result is not the work of just one man or a small group of men, but the result of hard work, of blood, sweat, and tears from thousands of men and women laboring each day to make our state government just a little better than it was the day before. And so, when I tell you that I am proud of our record, I am not speaking of just my record, or Henry Ward's record, although I am proud of those, but of the record which you have helped to make.

It is a record of progress—progress in education, progress in road building, progress in industrial and agricultural advancement, progress in providing a richer and more abundant life, with fuller opportunities for our children. Those who would belittle that progress, those who would deny and distort truth in order to ignore that progress, are not worthy either of Kentucky's great heritage or of Kentucky's greater future.

Our record is not only a record of progress; it is a record of truth and honesty, and that is a record which is yours and not just mine. We have not misled or deceived the people of Kentucky, even when political expediency would have pointed to evasion or falsehood. And perhaps above all, I can say, and in saying it can praise you, that you and I have had a clean administration, free from a single scandal or dishonor.

Of all this, this progress, this truth, this honesty, not only have we been a part, but Henry Ward has been a part—not only those who have served in Frankfort, but those who in their own communities and as private citizens have worked for Kentucky's advancement.

Certainly the name of Henry Ward stands for progress in road building and park building, the two programs for state government with which he has been more closely identified. Certainly Henry Ward stands in the minds of all Kentuckians for blunt candor and for telling the truth. And if there is one radio and television jingle which tells the truth, the whole truth, and nothing but the truth, it is the slogan which states that Henry Ward is as honest as the day is long.

Even Henry's opponent has, in his own way, faced up to this fact, when with a sneer on his face, he referred to Henry Ward as "Mr. Clean." Well, we have always known that politics was an arena of name calling, and I cannot for the life of me think of a better name to earn from a somewhat ill-humored opponent than "Mr. Clean." For the truth is, my friends, that Henry Ward is clean, he's been an important part of a clean administration, he will make a clean governor, and everybody in Kentucky knows it. And that is why, on November 7, "Mr. Clean"—Henry Ward, honest as the day is long—will make a clean sweep in Kentucky's polling places and will serve the people of Kentucky for the next four years with a fidelity and capability which will earn for him the title "Governor Clean."

I do not intend tonight to engage in an exchange of personal compliments with Mr. Ward's opponent. But perhaps, after having been on the receiving end of Mr. Nunn's name calling over a period of years, I may be pardoned for stating the fact that nobody has ever called him "Mr. Clean."[1] And unless he sustains a conversion experience, nobody ever will!

I cannot refrain from pointing out that the respected leaders of Mr. Nunn's own party have pointed the finger of rebuke at Mr. Nunn and the type of campaign which he is accustomed to conduct. I should not, I would not, lower the dignity of the great office of which you have honored me by referring to any candidate as a "liar." But the record shows that the Republican nominee for attorney general referred to Henry Ward's opponent as a "liar" in Louisville on April 20, 1967.[2]

I should not, I would not, refer to the nominee of any great political party as a peddler of hate and purveyor of bigotry, but that was the label which United States Senator John Sherman Cooper applied to the primary campaign of Henry Ward's opponent in Washington on May 20, 1967.

I should not, I would not, refer to a political opponent as a "muckraker," but that is the title which was conferred on Henry Ward's opponent by his own running mate, the Republican candidate for lieutenant governor, in Louisville on April 18, 1967.[3]

I should not, I would not, accuse the nominee of the opposition party of stirring up hatred and prejudice against minority groups, but that is the accusation which was leveled against Mr. Ward's opponent by Congressman Tim Lee Carter in Washington on May 17, 1967.[4]

I repeat to you, these are not my charges. These are not my labels; these are the statements deliberately and solemnly made by the leaders of the Republican party against the man who presumes to sneer at Henry Ward by calling him "Mr. Clean."

There you have it, my friends. There's the record; a record of progress, a record of experience, a record of cleanness and honesty. But not only a record, a candidate; a candidate with a progressive program for Kentucky; a candidate who will lead us to the green pastures of quality education for our children, jobs, expanded payrolls, and better farm income for our people, highways and parks, and all the other measures which will make

Kentucky a Commonwealth of expanding horizons and widening frontiers.

I present him to you now, and I tell you that if you know what's good for Kentucky, if you know what's good for your children, if you know what's good for you and me, then you'll go out with your shirt sleeves rolled up, your muscles flexed, and your hearts and hopes high to elect him governor a week from tomorrow. I present to you "Mr. Clean" himself, your next governor, Henry Ward.

---

1. Louie B. Nunn (1924-) county judge, Barren County (1953-1963); manager of Eisenhower, Cooper, and Morton campaigns (1956); manager of Cooper and Morton campaigns (1960, 1962); governor of Kentucky (1967-1971); resident of Lexington, Kentucky. George W. Robinson, ed., *The Public Papers of Governor Bert T. Combs, 1959-1963* (Lexington, Ky., 1979), p. 428.

2. Lester H. Burns, Jr. (1931-), born Oneida, Kentucky; B.S., Eastern Kentucky State College (1956); L.L.B., University of Kentucky (1959); law practice, Manchester, Kentucky (1959-1963); Republican candidate for attorney general, Commonwealth of Kentucky (1967); commonwealth attorney, 41st judicial district (1963-1970); engaged in practice of law, Somerset, Kentucky (1970-); commonwealth attorney, 28th judicial district (1981-). Telephone interview, March 11, 1981.

3. Thomas B. Ratliff (1926-), born in Heller, Kentucky; graduate of Pikeville College; L.L.B., University of Kentucky (1951); practicing attorney, Pikeville, Kentucky (1951-1963); commonwealth attorney 35th Judicial District (1963-1967); Republican candidate for lieutenant governor of Kentucky (1967). *Louisville Courier-Journal,* November 5, 1967.

4. Tim Lee Carter (1910-), physician from Tompkinsville, Kentucky; M.D., University of Tennessee (1937); member of 89th-94th Congresses from 5th District of Kentucky. *Who's Who in America, 1976-1977,* 39th ed. (Chicago, 1976).

VALEDICTORY

VALEDICTORY ADDRESS
Frankfort / December 12, 1967

FOUR years ago we met here under sorrowful and somber circumstances. The death of a noble leader had turned what would have been a day of rejoicing and pagentry into a quieter day of soul-searching and dedication. A flag at half-staff was a silent reminder of the loss so recently sustained by all Kentuckians and all Americans.

Today, as we assemble for the quadrennial renewal of the process that gives leadership and direction to our Commonwealth, that day, four years past, seems long ago. And yet, measured in the perspective of Kentucky history, it was almost yesterday—scarcely the turning of a page on a calendar.

It is not my assignment nor my purpose today to render an appraisal of the last four years in terms of governmental progress or in terms of the forward movement of Kentucky and Kentuckians. Others will have to determine our success or our failure. The future is the truest evaluator of the present, and it alone will define the importance of what we have done in this brief flicker of time.

It is my purpose—and a welcome duty—to express from a full heart my thanks to my fellow Kentuckians for the chance to serve as their governor and for the loyalty, the help, and the inspiration they have given me. This is also a time of thanksgiving for me in a much more personal sense. I give thanks to Him who guides the lives and destinies of us all for allowing me the health and the strength to serve, for preserving the safety of my family, and for the rich spiritual rewards that come from association with a citizenry devoted and dedicated to their state.

I leave the governorship with no regrets except that in the things we did we might have done better. No man can be completely satisfied with any period of his life or in any effort at achievement. The human spirit is characterized by a desire to do better, to be a greater success even when successful.

The same desire characterizes a unit of government cast in the mold of the human spirit, dedicated to the betterment of humans and to the greater attainment of humans—a democratic government. Thus Kentucky state government looks to ever greater achievement and, as it goes through its normal progression and administrations change, it hopes that each four years will be more productive, more meaningful, more successful than the four that have gone before.

To the administration that has its beginnings today, I say that it is my fervent wish that this hope is realized, that the officials today inaugurated will find the skill, the strength, the imagination to do more than we have done and do better.

I say this not because I think we have in any way been derelict in our duties, deficient in our actions, or because I believe we have not had a good administration. Indeed, I proclaim our accomplishments and, as we close the curtain on our efforts, pay tribute to—and extend the thanks of the Commonwealth to—the thousands of state employees and Kentuckians who have worked with me since 1963.

But the people of Kentucky tomorrow will need more than we have been able to accomplish today. The problems and the opportunities of the next four years will be of a different measure from those of the period this ceremony now brings to a close.

And so I wish the best to those who now assume the leadership. I hope they have the fullest cooperation of all Kentuckians, and I pledge to them what help I can give as a private citizen.

Today will mark a milestone, not merely for me but for him whom you have chosen to succeed me. Only one who has stood where he stands today, who has faced what he will face for the next four years, can be fully aware of the burdens which he will carry or of the responsibilities which he will assume. In his efforts to bear those burdens and to meet those responsibilities, he deserves a fair chance and a compassionate judgment from every Kentuckian, regardless of party. To those of you who adhere to my political faith, I should urge that every proposal which he makes be judged by one standard, and one standard alone: is it good for Kentucky?

And to those of you who have served this administration so faithfully and so well I would only make this observation: the greatest and most lasting monument that could be erected to our efforts and our success is that a succeeding administration build on them, improve on them, and exceed them for the benefit of all our citizens.

Kentucky's young people are its greatest challenge, its greatest resource, and its greatest opportunity. That challenge, that resource, that opportunity transcends mere partisanship, in a very particular sense, inaugurating as we do a governor of one political faith and a lieutenant governor of another. This is a day which calls upon us to rise above the selfish voices of partisanship and factional loyalty, and to sink all our lesser loyalties in the supreme task of building a commonwealth worthy of those young men and women on whom hang the hopes and fears of Kentuckians' future years.

And now I am about to depart to learn a great lesson that has been learned by a long succession of men from Isaac Shelby to Bert Combs. That lesson is: there is nothing more ex- than an ex-governor.

But like the other members of the fraternity of former governors, I will cherish for a lifetime all you have done for me and, as with the others who have gone before, the welfare and continued progress of our beloved Commonwealth will remain uppermost in my heart and mind.

Goodbye to you, dear friends, and to you, Governor Nunn, "Godspeed."

APPENDIX 1
The Breathitt Administration

GOV. EDWARD T. BREATHITT, with youthful vigor and enthusiasm, steered Kentucky into the mainstream of American affairs in his four years in office—the valedictory term to 20 years of Democratic administration in Kentucky.[1]

By precept and example, he led this state in such timely areas as conservation, civil rights, industrial growth, highway safety, educational television, accent on youth, and vocational education.

He ranged far beyond his executive suite in the State Capitol. His were roles of meaningful leadership assigned by the White House, as well as in the National and Southern Conferences of Governors and the Appalachian Regional Commission.

Breathitt was identified by the national press with the new breed of Southern politicians, such men as Terry Sanford of North Carolina, Carl Sanders of Georgia, Richmond Flowers of Alabama, Ramsey Clark of Texas, Warren Hearnes of Missouri, and Robert McNair of South Carolina.

This, the upcoming new coterie of Southern leadership, is unfettered by ties to the old shibboleth of states' rights. It disdains racial segregation as an issue for political preferment. It demonstrates the vision and competence to grapple with realities of the present.

To these men and to other state leaders across the nation, Breathitt dinned this jeremiad without surcease: "If we want to preserve states as sovereign units of government, we have got to face up to our own problems. If we don't, the Federal Government will do it for us and states will become political tombstones in a constitutional graveyard."

On the home front, Breathitt had massive problems to face. A few were too knotty to resolve.

He threw the full weight of his administration behind the proposal of a new state constitution at the November election of 1966, to replace the charter written in 1890-91. The proposition lost in every county in the statewide ratio of 36-to-1.

THE PROPERTY-TAX WRANGLE

In mid-1965 the Court of Appeals ruled that property must be assessed at 100 percent of fair cash value, as required by the Constitution. The mandate had been universally ignored 75 years by the public and officialdom alike, with the results that assessments were down statewide, to the average of 29 percent of fair cash value.

Through an unpredictable quirk in the public mind, Breathitt got blamed for the potential increase in property taxes. In the aftermath, a special session of the legislature in the autumn of 1965 and the regular session of 1966 ended with the school people in frustration and the public still angry.

Breathitt's first session in 1964 was a flop, in no respect an augury of the incisive success of his leadership at the 1966 session. Two years later, at his midterm, he appraised his 1964 failure with these words:

"I felt that once the November election battle was over, all political factions and parties would rally around and help me, and I could be magnanimous. I found out the hard way: You simply have to lead—to assume power and use it properly. It's been a question of growing up to the job."

He failed to obtain repeal of the death penalty in Kentucky law, an issue of deep personal conviction.

And, as titular head of the Democratic Party in Kentucky, his was the chagrin to note that, after the November election of 1966, Republicans were a 5-to-4 majority in the Kentucky delegation to Congress for the first time since the Hoover landslide of 1928.

If foresight enjoyed equal billing with hindsight, this 1966 ascendancy of Republican power and prestige would have been viewed as an augury of the Republican upsurge led last Nov. 7 by Gov. elect Louis B. Nunn. He takes office on Tuesday.

But the hindsight prevailed. Breathitt, as the fifth in an unbroken line of postwar Democratic governors, was heartened to look back on 20 years of dramatic progress:

✓ The state, by voting $516 million of bonded debt in the past 12 years, had financed unprecedented improvements in highways, state parks, and public education.

✓ In addition, self-liquidating revenue bonds of $361 million had financed 444 miles of toll roads built, or now being built, to interstate standards. These, added to the interstate allotment to Kentucky of 735 miles, insure an eventual super-network of nearly 1,200 miles.

✓ The 1948 tax of 2 cents a gallon on gasoline for rural roads, and the 3 percent general sales tax of 1960, eased the state comfortably upward on a wide and balanced front of public services.

FOUNDATION PROGRAM

✓ Twenty years of Democratic administration had conceived, enacted, and provided the basic financing for the foundation program, for the first 12 grades of public education, the greatest single stride forward in this century.

Breathitt and his three predecessors—Bert T. Combs, Albert B. Chandler, and Lawrence W. Wetherby—had guided Kentucky to letter-and-spirit compliance with the Supreme Court's ban against racial discrimination. Kentucky emerged as the bellwether state of the South in this respect.

Notwithstanding these high water marks of a backward state on the way up, the Republican slogan of "time for a change" caught fire. Breathitt's best was not good enough to put it out. Nunn's victory Nov. 7 was bitter as gallwood to Breathitt in particular, and to the Democratic leadership of 20 years in general.

But the credit entries in Breathitt's own four-year journal dilute, if not offset, the debit entry of political defeat at the November polls.

Breathitt was governor through four years of unprecedented prosperity in Kentucky, despite the poverty of Appalachia. Racial disorder never got out of hand in the classic sense of similar turmoil elsewhere. Peace and prosperity prevailed throughout his term.

Breathitt's 1966-68 budget hit $1 billion a year for the first time in the fiscal history of the state. Personal income in Kentucky is reaching $7.6 billion in 1967, up 30 percent from four years ago.

In the four years of his term, 749 industries announced new plants, or expansion of present ones, in Kentucky. The potential here was 57,000 new jobs and $1.126 billion in plant investment. Manufacturing jobs were up 23 percent since 1963, nonagricultural employment up 20 percent.

In 1967, more miles of highway were under construction in Kentucky than in any other state of the nation. Contracts awarded last year totaled $194.5 million.

Due to the new aluminum complex in West Kentucky, the state's sharpest growth since 1963 has been in the metals and related industries. These now account for 40 percent of manufacturing employment in Kentucky.

STATE RANKS 11TH

During his term, the four state colleges at Morehead, Richmond, Bowling Green, and Murray were elevated to the status of regional universities. Student enrollment in state-supported institutions now exceeds 50,000 for an all-time high.

In amount of state money appropriated to the first 12 grades of public education, Kentucky now ranks 11th from the top, and is 13 percent higher than the national average of state support.

Finally, out-of-state tourists are finding Kentucky parks and recreational areas more and more magnetic. They spent $295 million here last year, a gain of $75 million in three years.

The economy of Kentucky drummed a boom-boom in the four-year term of Breathitt, and the tempo was a go-go.

In his speech to the opening joint session of the 1964 Legislature, Breathitt declared:

"The people of Kentucky did not choose me to preside over a caretaker administration, a standstill government. There are no rest stops on the road to progress."

SECONDS LBJ NOMINATION

From that statement it is appropriate to take out of context the phrase "no rest stops," when Breathitt is reviewed as the governor of Kentucky beyond Kentucky.

His first exposure to the nation, via television, occurred Aug. 27, 1964, when he delivered a rousing second to the nomination of Lyndon B. Johnson for President at the Democratic National Convention at Atlantic City. His speech was better than most, and as good as the best, in the earnest, forthright oratorical style of the rising breed of young politicians in both parties of this country.

President Johnson appointed him to the White House commission to explore ways to implement the Civil Rights Act of 1964. The President also appointed him chairman of the White House commission on rural poverty and development. This area, so timely and sensitive, gave Breathitt national exposure several times.

In 1966, the President appointed him to represent this country at the International Trade Fair in Paznan, Poland. He headed the Kentucky delegation to Expo 67 at Montreal for the observance of Kentucky Day there last fall.

The governor was proud, naturally, last August when President Johnson named Miss Katherine Peden, Breathitt's Commissioner of Commerce, as the only woman on the President's Advisory Commission on Civil Disorders.

In 1964 Breathitt was named to the executive committee of the National Governor's Conference. In 1965 he was chairman of the standing committee on natural resources. In 1966 he was chairman of another of the four standing committees, this one on interstate cooperation and regional compacts. He used this position as a sounding board to amplify his conviction that the ultimate, effective regulation of strip mining lies only in compacts between the stripping states.

HOST TO GOVERNORS

In 1965, he was chairman of the highway safety committee of the Southern Governors Conference. He was host to the conference in 1966, at Kentucky Dam State Park.

Breathitt was chairman of the Southern Governors' Conference in 1967, his lame-duck year. The conference at Asheville, N.C., drew national attention to the fact that for the first time, Southern governors came to grips with problems of the states, instead of mourning the fallen milestones in states rights.

Kentucky's massive economic stake in the Ohio River Valley prompted Breathitt in 1965 to obtain for the state a membership in the Midwestern Governors' Conference. And early in 1966 he was host to the mid-winter meeting at Lexington of the Executive Board of the Council of State Governments. He and Adj. Gen. Arthur Y. Lloyd are members of it. That meeting activated interest of the board in Spindletop Research, Inc. That interest, in turn, led to removal of the council from Chicago to a 40-acre tract on Spindletop Farm, adjacent to the research center.

MOST MEMORABLE CONTRIBUTION?

The Council of State Governments staffs 40-odd regional conferences of governors, attorneys general, chief state fiscal officers, and the like. It is the service agency and clearing house for the executive, administrative, and legislative arms of the 50 states.

Time, perhaps, will develop the council's location at Spindletop as the most gracious monument to the Breathitt administration. For this concentration of governmental expertise at Lexington will be a catalyst of inestimable stimulation to research in the graduate school of University of Kentucky, Spindletop, and the Legislative Research Commission service agency of the Kentucky Legislature.

A governor's program is not seen or felt until he processes it through the Legislature. Breathitt, then aged 39 and unaccustomed to power, had little of a program to show after the 1964 session.

Civil rights dominated the scene. In the 38-degree temperature of March 5, 1964, Frankfort's greatest demonstration occurred when Dr. Martin Luther King and Jackie Robinson led 10,000 marchers up Capitol Avenue to the Capitol. In the closing days of the session, 23 demonstrators staged a 104-hour starve-in in the House gallery.

Breathitt backed and filled on a state law forbidding racial discrimination in all places of public accommodation. His thin opposition was not enough to satisfy segregationists, and his thin support did not placate the integrationists. The net result was no law, plus dissatisfaction on both sides of the issue.

That Breathitt was wary of the issue is not hard to rationalize. His mentor and predecessor, Gov. Bert T. Combs, had issued an executive order forbidding racial discrimination in public places licensed by the state. That order almost beat Breathitt in the general election. If Nunn, now the Republican governor-elect, had pushed that issue harder and longer in Western Kentucky, he may have defeated Breathitt in 1963, instead of waiting until 1967 to defeat Henry Ward.

1964 INACTION

The 1964 session tackled but did not resolve Kentucky's archaic and incomprehensible Sunday closing law. It considered, but did not enact compulsory automobile inspection. The session recognized the shambles created by under assessment of property then prevailing, but did nothing about it.

A march on Frankfort by 200 teachers from Louisville and Jefferson County failed to obtain correction of double sessions and crowded classrooms.

Breathitt won one and lost one of his two relatively bold steps at the 1964 session. A $176 million bond issue was approved 3-to-1 at the November election. But the apparatus he obtained for rewriting the 1890-91 State Constitution ended in complete rejection at the November election of 1966.

As he put it, Breathitt had grown up to the job when the 1966 session convened. He asked for and got a spectacular program of social, economic, and political change for Kentucky.

ACCOMMODATIONS LAW

His solid insistence led to enactment of a civil-rights law forbidding racial discrimination in all places of public accommodation, the first such state law south of the Ohio River.

He overcame a strip-mine lobby of formidable power to secure enactment of what is acclaimed as perhaps the nation's strongest code to regulate that industry. He strengthened state law against air and water pollution.

He overcame another lobby to secure a law forbidding multiple-coin slot machines. He took a calculated risk on the political consequences to push for and obtain compulsory automobile inspection to start in 1968.

Under threat of congressional redistricting by federal court if the Legislature failed to reapportion, Breathitt sponsored a realignment of the seven

House districts surprisingly acceptable to Democrats and Republicans alike. This was the plan that cut the Third District down to Louisville and Shively, and added the rest of Jefferson County to the Fourth.

PROGRESS, BUT A LOOPHOLE

He tightened state law governing political contributions and reports of expenditures by candidates. The Legislature repealed the old unrealistic limits in campaign expenditures, but required public reporting of all amounts received in excess of $500.

Practice, however has revealed a major loophole in the law. It permits receipts from fund-raising affairs to be reported in one lump sum, instead of requiring the purchasers of block tickets exceeding $500 to be identified by name.

A statewide one-day walkout by teachers during the 1966 session prodded Breathitt to raise their base pay by $450 to $1,100 in the 1966-68 biennium, depending on experience and training.

This raise got on paper by the expedient of upping revenue estimates by $24 million, then expanding the 1967 budget by $24 million. Revenue collections in 1967 did not justify the hopeful expectations of 1966. So, shortly after the Nov. 7 election Breathitt ordered an across-the-board decrease of $24.1 million in the spending budgeted for 1967-68.

Here is a migraine headache of massive proportions for the incoming Nunn administration. Most of the $24 million the tax structure is not yielding already is embedded in the base salary of public school teachers. Moreover, it is embedded as an item of recurring expense.

HIS OWN APPRAISAL

Breathitt has made his own appraisal of significant contributions his administration made to the common weal. He gives high priority to this listing:

✓ Creation of the nation's first top-quality high school for impoverished pupils of exceptional intellectual potential, now operating with the freshman class at Lincoln School, near Simpsonville.

✓ Establishment, with cooperation of the Tennessee Valley Authority, of the 170,000-acre Land Between the Lakes National Recreational Area, thus completing at Kentucky and Barkley lakes the greatest recreation complex in mid-America.

✓ Final fruition of the long-desired educational television network, a $20 million project now financed and on the eve of full operation.

✓ State cooperation with the governments of Frankfort, Franklin County, and the United States, to achieve the $50 million urban renewal complex in Frankfort, to include a 28-story state office building, federal building, coliseum of Kentucky State College, a new YMCA, and double-deck parking.

✓ Transfer of voting power from educators to laymen on the Council of Public Higher Education.

✓ A new thrust in vocational education, by which workers are trained for specific industries such as aeronautics, mining, and services in food, health, government, electronics, computers, and the like.

One distinction of the Breathitt administration remains to be mentioned. Accent on youth. Perhaps it was due to the governor's own youth, perhaps to the growing ascendancy of youth in politics.

Breathitt's commissioners of insurance, banking, and economic security were younger than 30, scores were at the policy level, and 600 held academic degrees.

It is fairly easy to take blue ribbon and tie the triumphs of state government in four-year bundles, then tag them as the administration of Breathitt, Combs, Chandler, etc. But the trouble of government flows in a steady stream. Old trouble is not cut off on Inauguration Day, to be replaced by new and different trouble. Basic problems tumble irresistably from one administration to the next.

Thus Nunn, the incoming governor, will inherit some beauties from Breathitt.

Breathitt is bequeathing his massive resistance to the property tax as a major source of local school revenue. The resistance is sore and sensitive. To scratch it is to invite revolt.

Nunn inherits repeal of the 10-cent-a-gallon production tax on whisky. Breathitt got the 1966 Legislature to repeal it, to be phased out at 2 cents a gallon a year for five years. It will phase out entirely the fourth year of Nunn's term. By current reckoning, the levy yields around $1 million per penny. Hence Nunn's income will fall $2 million a year for four years.

PINCHES AND PUNCHES

Nunn inherits an insatiable desire for two-year community colleges. If this growth is not brought under orderly control, and soon, the Legislature will be authorizing community colleges with the abandon once shown in declaring roads eligible for state maintenance.

Nunn, with his pledge of no new or higher taxes, inherits the formula of expediency forced upon Breathitt by the same pledge in 1963. Breathitt avoided fiscal chaos by diverting to current expenses the cash income normally earmarked for capital improvement. To close the gap, he obtained voter approval of the $176 million bond issue. Nunn will be pinched and punched toward the same extremity.

Breathitt is bequeathing to Nunn an explosive pressure for substantially more state money than the tax structure is yielding. The pressure is arising from education, Medicaid, health, welfare, conservation, public safety, and the competition of private enterprise for the salaried skills required to operate the $1 billion-a-year apparatus of state government.

SCHOOL FINANCE IN BIND

Nunn inherits the patchwork Breathitt contrived in desperation during the public panic following the 1965 mandate of the Court of Appeals that property must be assessed at fair cash value. The patchwork has caught public school finance in an insufferable bind.

Breathitt and the Legislature tried to alleviate the panic with this sort of arrangement. The school tax of $1.50 is to be rolled back in proportion to the rise in assessment so that as much revenue will be realized from the rolled-back rates as the $1.50 produced in 1965.

Except that: One 10 percent raise will be allowed in 1966, and another 10 percent in 1967. Except that if local voters approve, one of three supplementary school taxes can be levied—a ½ of 1 percent occupational tax, a 20 percent surtax on income tax, or a 3 percent tax on utility bills.

And now, on the eve of the 1968-69 school year, local revenue is limited to a 1965 dollar figure. Both 10 percent raises have been levied. Before 1965 there was one tax rate ($1.50) and 199 assessments; [now there is one] assessment (theoretically, 100 percent) and 199 tax rates.

But the 199 tax rates are frozen to produce the 1965 yield in dollars. The bind is desperate. The desperation will be compounded if teachers secure from the 1968 Legislature the right of collective bargaining. For, until Nunn comes up with a plan, there is no legal way to expand the potential of local school revenue. To expose property to such expansion is to invite disaster.

In a nutshell, then, Breathitt is passing to Nunn the hard decision as to whether the 3 percent sales tax shall be applied to services, or raised to 4 percent.

Politically, Breathitt came to office as scared as a rabbit in open season. For he had barely won it. His comfort was scant, indeed; the 13,055-vote margin by which he bested Nunn in 1963 is the second lowest majority on record in the state.

And he is leaving office the victim of one political legend and one historical fact. The legend is: No highway commissioner can be elected governor. Thomas S. Rhea tried it in 1935, J. Lyter Donaldson in 1943, and Henry Ward in 1967. Three up, three down. The historical fact is: Since the Democratic Party split in two factions in 1896, no one faction has survived for more than two consecutive terms. Ward's election, of course, would have extended to 12 years the factional tenure that Combs began in 1959.

FACTIONALISM RENEWED

Breathitt coped with factionalism throughout his term, and came as near as any Democratic governor to achieving party unity. But by term's end it had cropped up anew for another four years of party disunity.

Since 1935, one faction had centered around the political personality of Chandler, twice governor and twice a defeated candidate in primaries for the same office—in 1963 and again in 1967.

High in the Chandler faction was Harry Lee Waterfield, lieutenant governor in Chandler's second term, 1955-59; his running mate in the 1963 primary and, being nominated, the lieutenant governor under Breathitt in 1963-67.

Ten candidates aspired for the nomination in the Democratic primary last May. Ward was in it as the governor's choice, Chandler was in it as the symbol of the fading faction bearing his name; Waterfield was in it as an open opponent to Ward and Chandler alike.

CHANDLER BACKS NUNN

The returns seemed to have dealt a bonecrushing defeat to Democratic factionalism: Ward, 206,000, Chandler 111,500, Waterfield, 42,000; seven others combined, 35,000.

But Chandler declared publicly for Nunn three weeks before the election Nov. 7, and campaigned for him openly. Thus he established himself again as titular head of his faction, in position to claim credit for Nunn's election, in position to enhance his factional stature with whatever fruits accrue from a political coalition publicly announced and openly supported.

But Waterfield is out of the picture. And to Breathitt, as governor, must go the credit for clipping his factional wings.

The Breathitt-Waterfield ticket that came to office in 1963 symbolized what might have been a genuine fusion of the two factions. But it did not work that way. The governor and lieutenant governor functioned under terms of an uneasy truce during the 1964 Legislature. But it was open hostility between them at the special session of 1965.

BREATHITT CONTROLLED SENATE

The 1966 session found them squared off—Waterfield in his corner as the anti-administration candidate for governor in 1967, Breathitt in his corner ready and able to use total power to nominate the candidate of his choice. And the latter turned out to be Ward.

So Breathitt, not Waterfield as president of the Senate, controlled the 1966 Senate. Hence Waterfield's star already had fallen when he entered the 1967 primary in open hostility to Chandler and Ward alike. The poor third he played to Chandler's poor second put the quietus to Waterfield's role in factional politics.

But what of Breathitt's political future? Not enough potential can be seen to justify the remotest of speculation. It suffices to say he is settling down to civil life. He is moving back to his old home in Hopkinsville, there to re-enter his old law firm of Trimble, Soyars & Breathitt as a working partner.

---

1. This review of the Breathitt administration entitled "The Breathitt Years. 'You Have to Lead,' " by Allan Trout, appeared in the *Louisville Courier-Journal* on December 10, 1967. The *Courier-Journal* gave permission to reprint it here provided the article was not altered.

APPENDIX 2
Calendar of Governor Breathitt's Speeches

INAUGURAL ADDRESS, Frankfort, December 10, 1963*

STATE OF THE COMMONWEALTH MESSAGE, Frankfort, January 7, 1964*

BOWLING GREEN–WARREN COUNTY CHAMBER OF COMMERCE, Bowling Green, January 15, 1964*

KENTUCKY SOCIETY DINNER, Washington, D.C., January 18, 1964

EXECUTIVE BUDGET MESSAGE TO THE GENERAL ASSEMBLY, Frankfort, February 10, 1964*

KENTUCKY COOPERATIVE COUNCIL, Lexington, February 11, 1964*

STATEMENT TO THE HOUSE OF REPRESENTATIVES, Frankfort, February 25, 1964*

STATEMENT TO RELIGIOUS LEADERS, Frankfort, February 27, 1964*

CAPITAL CONSTRUCTION MESSAGE TO THE GENERAL ASSEMBLY, Frankfort, March 9, 1964*

PUBLIC ACCOMMODATIONS BILL MESSAGE TO THE HOUSE OF REPRESENTATIVES, Frankfort, March 10, 1964*

KENTUCKY HIGHWAY CONFERENCE, Lexington, March 11, 1964*

KENTUCKY SCHOOL BOARDS ASSOCIATION CONVENTION, Louisville, March 17, 1964*

F.T.C. HEARING, Washington, D.C., March 18, 1964

CIVIL RIGHTS STATEMENT, Frankfort, March 20, 1964*

PRESS CONFERENCE—REVIEW OF 1964 GENERAL ASSEMBLY, Frankfort, March 20, 1964*

KENTUCKY DENTAL ASSOCIATION LUNCHEON, Louisville, April 6, 1964

SPINDLETOP REMARKS, Lexington, April 8, 1964

COVINGTON-KENTON-BOONE COUNTY CHAMBER OF COMMERCE, Covington, April 9, 1964

KENTUCKY CHAMBER OF COMMERCE, Louisville, April 14, 1964

CAMPBELL COUNTY CHAMBER OF COMMERCE, Newport, April 15, 1964

CENTRAL KENTUCKY TURNPIKE GROUNDBREAKING, Bardstown, April 16, 1964

*Address is included in this volume.

AMERICAN BRIDGE, TUNNEL, AND TURNPIKE ASSOCIATION, French Lick, Indiana, April 19, 1964*

INDUSTRIAL DEVELOPMENT, Detroit, Michigan, April 22, 1964

GOVERNOR'S CONFERENCE ON LIBRARIES, Frankfort, May 8, 1964

GOVERNOR'S APPRECIATION DAY, Danville, May 11, 1964

U.S. DEPARTMENT OF INTERIOR NORTH CENTRAL FIELD MEETING, Whitesburg, May 13, 1964*

CONGRESS ON MENTAL HEALTH, Louisville, May 14, 1964*

MAYORS CONFERENCE, Frankfort, May 15, 1964*

MERIT SCHOLARSHIP LUNCHEON, Frankfort, May 15, 1964

EASTERN STATE COLLEGE ALL-SPORTS BANQUET, Richmond, May 18, 1964

NATIONAL ASSOCIATION OF BANK WOMEN, Hopkinsville, May 23, 1964

MOREHEAD STATE COLLEGE COMMENCEMENT, Morehead, May 25, 1964

KENTUCKY DAY, New York, New York, June 1, 1964

UNIVERSITY OF KENTUCKY ALUMNI, New York, New York, June 1, 1964*

BOARD OF DIRECTORS, FIRST NATIONAL CITY BANK, New York, New York, June 2, 1964

CHEMICAL BANK NEW YORK TRUST COMPANY, New York, New York, June 3, 1964*

HIGHWAY AWARD CEREMONY, Frankfort, June 15, 1964

AGRICULTURE DEVELOPMENT COMMISSION, Frankfort, June 17, 1964

MAYORS AND JUDGES CONFERENCE, Frankfort, June 22, 1964

DEDICATION OF NEW HEMLOCK LODGE, Natural Bridge State Park, June 24, 1964*

ECONOMIC DEVELOPMENT COMMISSION, Frankfort, June 28, 1964

AUTOMOBILE PURCHASE STATEMENT, Frankfort, July 2, 1964*

DEDICATION OF DAIRY CENTER, COLDSTREAM FARM-U.K., Lexington, July 7, 1964

GOVERNOR'S COUNCIL ON PHYSICAL FITNESS, Frankfort, July 8, 1964

STATEWIDE NEWS CONFERENCE, Frankfort, July 10, 1964

NATIONAL RETAIL HARDWARE ASSOCIATION, New York, New York, July 14, 1964

SOUTHEASTERN COMMUNITY DEVELOPMENT ASSOCIATION, Lexington, July 15, 1964

TASK FORCE ON CRIMINAL JUSTICE, Frankfort, July 17, 1964*

LEGISLATIVE MEETING, Frankfort, July 20, 1964*

KENTUCKY JUNIOR CHAMBER OF COMMERCE, Frankfort, July 24, 1964

HARVEY ALUMINUM COMPANY GROUNDBREAKING, Owensboro, July 25, 1964

LOUISVILLE BUSINESS LEADERS, Louisville, July 31, 1964

EASTERN KENTUCKY DEVELOPMENT MEETING, Ashland, August 3, 1964*

NATIONAL ASSOCIATION OF BUDGET OFFICERS, Lexington, August 6, 1964*

KENTUCKY EDUCATION ASSOCIATION LEADERSHIP CONFERENCE, Lexington, August 12, 1964*

ECONOMIC OPPORTUNITY ACT, Frankfort, August 13, 1964

BUCKHORN LODGE, Hazard, August 14, 1964

GOVERNOR'S CONFERENCE ON PHYSICAL FITNESS, Louisville, August 17, 1964

SECOND OF THE NOMINATION OF LYNDON B. JOHNSON, Atlantic City, New Jersey, August 26, 1964*

HOPKINSVILLE COMMUNITY COLLEGE, Hopkinsville, September 2, 1964

KENTUCKY SCHOOL FOR THE BLIND, Louisville, September 3, 1964

NEWPORT-CAMPBELL CHAMBER OF COMMERCE, Newport, September 4, 1964

UNIVERSITY OF KENTUCKY COMMUNITY COLLEGE, Elizabethtown, September 8, 1964

ECONOMY AND EFFICIENCY COMMISSION, Frankfort, September 8, 1964*

SOUTHERN RAILWAY LUNCHEON, Lexington, September 9, 1964

PERSHING RIFLES ADDRESS, Lexington, September 10, 1964

DOWNTOWN KIWANIS CLUB, Paducah, September 17, 1964

LONE OAK HIGH SCHOOL, Paducah, September 17, 1964

SOMERSET COLLEGE GROUNDBREAKING, Somerset, September 18, 1964

LUNCHEON PRECEDING DEDICATION OF JOHN SHERMAN COOPER POWER PLANT, Burnside, September 22, 1964

GREATER CINCINNATI AIRPORT, Covington, September 28, 1964*

BURLEY DARK-LEAF EXPORT CONVENTION, Gilbertsville, September 28, 1964*

KENTUCKY DEVELOPMENT COMMITTEE, Jenny Wiley State Park, October 1, 1964

LESLIE COUNTY HIGH SCHOOL, Hyden, October 1, 1964

UPPER CUMBERLAND EDUCATION ASSOCIATION, Barbourville, October 2, 1964

TOLLESBORO CIVIC CLUB, Tollesboro, October 5, 1964

INTER-AMERICAN MUNICIPAL CONGRESS, Louisville, October 5, 1964

KENTUCKY AGRICULTURE DEVELOPMENT COMMISSION, Frankfort, October 6, 1964

COMMUNITY LUNCHEON, Cadiz, October 7, 1964

CONSERVATION CONGRESS, Louisville, October 15, 1964*

SPINDLETOP RESEARCH ANNUAL MEETING, Lexington, October 21, 1964*

U.S. 68 RIBBON CUTTING, Campbellsville, October 22, 1964

EASTERN STATE COLLEGE, Richmond, October 23, 1964

KENTUCKY STATE COLLEGE DORMS, Frankfort, October 23, 1964

COMMUNITY MEETING, Elizabethtown, October 29, 1964

HIGHWAY 31-W RIBBON CUTTING CEREMONY, Radcliff, October 29, 1964

STATEMENT ON EDUCATION, Frankfort, November 9, 1964*

KENTUCKY ASSOCIATION OF INSURANCE AGENTS, Louisville, November 10, 1964

STATEMENT ON CORRECTIONS, Frankfort, November 12, 1964*

KENTUCKY FARM BUREAU CONVENTION, Louisville, November 16, 1964

KENTUCKY BANKERS ASSOCIATION, Louisville, November 17, 1964*

KENTUCKY BARBERS' ASSOCIATION, Louisville, November 17, 1964

JOHN F. KENNEDY MEMORIAL SERVICE, Lexington, November 22, 1964*

STATE POLICE POST MEETING, Frankfort, November 23, 1964

BANK DEPOSITS STATEMENT, Frankfort, November 24, 1964*

NATIONAL ASSOCIATION OF RAILROAD AND UTILITIES COMMISSIONERS, Honolulu, Hawaii, December 3, 1964*

THE ECONOMIC OPPORTUNITY PROGRAM IN KENTUCKY, Frankfort, December 9, 1964*

KENTUCKY COMMONWEALTH ATTORNEYS ASSOCIATION, Covington, December 10, 1964*

GOVERNOR'S COMMISSION ON AGRICULTURE, Frankfort, December 14, 1964

LOUISVILLE CHAMBER OF COMMERCE, Louisville, January 1, 1965

KENTUCKY SOUTHERN BAPTIST CHURCH, Louisville, January 5, 1965

SOMERSET DEMOCRATIC WOMEN'S CLUB, Somerset, January 12, 1965

KENTUCKY COAL INDUSTRY LUNCHEON, Frankfort, January 14, 1965

JEFFERSONTOWN POST OFFICE, Jeffersontown, January 16, 1965

LIBERTY BANK AND TRUST COMPANY, Jeffersontown, January 16, 1965

PERSONAL SERVICE CONTRACTS, Frankfort, January 20, 1965*

REGIONAL CONFERENCE ON BAIL AND RIGHT TO COUNSEL, Louisville, January 22, 1965

HOPKINSVILLE-CHRISTIAN COUNTY CHAMBER OF COMMERCE, Hopkinsville, January 25, 1965

1964 PROFESSIONAL TROPHY AWARD LUNCHEON OF THE SOCIETY OF INDUSTRIAL REALTORS, Houston, Texas, January 29, 1965*

INTRODUCTION OF ORVILLE FREEMAN, Louisville, February 3, 1965

GOVERNOR'S CONFERENCE ON AGRICULTURE, Louisville, February 3, 1965

INTRODUCTION OF BUFORD ELLINGTON, Louisville, February 4, 1965

LOUISVILLE'S CINEMA ONE AND TWO, Louisville, February 4, 1965

GOVERNOR'S PRAYER BREAKFAST, Frankfort, February 5, 1965

KENTUCKY ACTION PROGRAM FOR HIGHWAY SAFETY, Benton, February 9, 1965*

HENDERSON CHAMBER OF COMMERCE, Henderson, February 9, 1965*

KENTUCKY INDUSTRY APPRECIATION LUNCHEON, Louisville, February 15, 1965

DAWSON SPRINGS INDUSTRIAL APPRECIATION DINNER, Dawson Springs, February 18, 1965

GOVERNOR'S CONFERENCE ON FORESTRY, Lexington, February 18, 1965*

KENTUCKY JAYCEE WINTER BOARD MEETING, Frankfort, February 20, 1965*

PADUCAH CITY HALL DEDICATION, Paducah, February 28, 1965

WPSD-TV, Paducah, February 28, 1965*

ECONOMIC OPPORTUNITY ACT, Frankfort, March 3, 1965

GOVERNOR'S OCCUPATIONAL HEALTH AND INDUSTRIAL HYGIENE CONFERENCE, Lexington, March 10, 1965*

KENTUCKY DAIRY PRODUCTS ASSOCIATION, Louisville, March 15, 1965*

KENTUCKY SCHOOL BOARD ASSOCIATION, Louisville, March 15, 1965

KENTUCKY BUSINESS AND PROFESSIONAL WOMEN'S CLUBS ASSOCIATION, Louisville, March 16, 1965

ECONOMIC DEVELOPMENT SEMINAR, Gilbertsville, March 17, 1965

INTERCOLLEGIATE PRESS ASSOCIATION BANQUET, Lexington, March 19, 1965

FRANKLIN-SIMPSON HIGH SCHOOL, Franklin, March 23, 1965

FRANKLIN CHAMBER OF COMMERCE, Franklin, March 23, 1965

KENTUCKY YOUNG FARMERS ASSOCIATION, Mt. Sterling, March 25, 1965

STATEWIDE STUDENT CONGRESS, Frankfort, March 27, 1965

JEFFERSON COUNTY YOUNG DEMOCRATS MEETING, Louisville, March 29, 1965

GOVERNOR'S COMMISSION ON AGRICULTURE, Lexington, March 31, 1965

KENTUCKY HOSPITAL ASSOCIATION CONVENTION, Louisville, March 31, 1965*

ADULT FARMERS GRADUATION, Hopkinsville, April 2, 1965

THE KENTUCKY YOUTH ASSEMBLY, Frankfort, April 2, 1965

THE KENTUCKY PERSONNEL AND GUIDANCE ASSOCIATION, Louisville, April 3, 1965

KENTUCKY PERSONNEL AND GUIDANCE ASSOCIATION, Louisville, April 6, 1965

LUNCHEON FOR STATE TROOPERS, Frankfort, April 7, 1965

DANIEL BOONE CHAPTER ASSOCIATION OF THE U.S. ARMY, Elizabethtown, April 8, 1965

KENTUCKY CHAMBER OF COMMERCE, Owensboro, April 12, 1965

BETA GAMMA SIGMA HONORARY, Lexington, April 13, 1965

CORBIN ROTARY CLUB, Corbin, April 15, 1965

UNION COLLEGE CONVOCATION, Barbourville, April 15, 1965

BOURBON COUNTY SOIL CONSERVATION DINNER, Paris, April 15, 1965*

POST OFFICE DEDICATION, Hopkinsville, April 16, 1965

COMMENTS TO THE GOVERNORS OF THE APPALACHIAN STATES, Washington, D.C., April 19, 1965*

A CONFERENCE ON THE CHILD AND THE GREAT SOCIETY, Louisville, April 19, 1965

KENTUCKY CHAMBER OF COMMERCE, Owensboro, April 20, 1965

PUBLIC HEALTH ASSOCIATION CONVENTION, Louisville, April 20, 1965*

KENTUCKY FARM PRESS AND RADIO ASSOCIATION, Louisville, April 20, 1965

JESSAMINE COUNTY COURTHOUSE DEDICATION, Nicholasville, April 21, 1965

THE METROPOLITAN KIWANIS CLUB, Louisville, April 22, 1965

ALL-AMERICA CITY AWARD BANQUET, Hopkinsville, April 22, 1965

KENTUCKY HANDICAPPED ASSOCIATION, Louisville, April 22, 1965*

BRECKINRIDGE COUNTY HIGH SCHOOL BASKETBALL BANQUET, Hardinsburg, April 26, 1965

KENTUCKY FARM PRODUCTS WEEK, Frankfort, April 27, 1965*

LABORATORY DEDICATION, PUBLIC SERVICE COMMISSION, Lexington, April 28, 1965*

JUNIOR CHAMBER OF COMMERCE ANNUAL BANQUET, Winchester, May 3, 1965

COLUMBIA MUNICIPAL BUILDING DEDICATION, Columbia, May 4, 1965

UNIVERSITY OF LOUISVILLE LAW DAY, Louisville, May 5, 1965*

STATEMENT ON SENATE RACES, Frankfort, May 7, 1965*

KENTUCKY PETROLEUM CONVENTION, Gilbertsville, May 7, 1965*

BARREN COUNTY COURTHOUSE DEDICATION, Glasgow, May 8, 1965*

JEFFERSON-JACKSON DAY DINNER, Aurora, May 8, 1965

NATIONAL CONFERENCE ON MILK SHIPMENT, Louisville, May 11, 1965

UNIVERSITY OF KENTUCKY LAW ALUMNI BANQUET, Louisville, May 12, 1965*

LINCOLN HERITAGE TRAIL MEETING, Louisville, May 12, 1965

KENTUCKY STATE BAR ASSOCIATION, Louisville, May 13, 1965

LOUISVILLE ROTARY CLUB, Louisville, May 13, 1965*

COMMUNITY LUNCHEON, Princeton, May 14, 1965

MESSENGER BUILDING DEDICATION, Madisonville, May 14, 1965

KENTUCKY AUTOMOBILE DEALERS ASSOCIATION, Frankfort, May 17, 1965

KENTUCKY SEED DEALERS ASSOCIATION, Louisville, May 20, 1965*

A.O. SMITH PLANT, Mount Sterling, May 21, 1965

STATE ELKS CONVENTION, Hopkinsville, May 22, 1965

KENTUCKY FEDERATION OF WOMEN'S CLUBS, Louisville, May 26, 1965

KENTUCKY WESLEYAN COMMENCEMENT, Owensboro, May 30, 1965

CHRISTIAN COUNTY HIGH SCHOOL, Hopkinsville, May 31, 1965

GOVERNOR'S COMMISSION ON AGRICULTURE, Frankfort, June 1, 1965

JUNE DAIRY MONTH KICKOFF LUNCHEON, Frankfort, June 2, 1965

KENTUCKY SCHOOL FOR THE BLIND, Louisville, June 2, 1965

KENTUCKY PRESS ASSOCIATION, Gilbertsville, June 5, 1965

APPALACHIAN REGIONAL COMMISSION, Washington, D.C., June 7, 1965*

HIGHWAY CONSTRUCTION STATEMENT, Frankfort, June 9, 1965*

NATIONAL NEWSPAPER PUBLISHERS ASSOCIATION, Louisville, June 17, 1965

NATIONAL ASSOCIATION OF STUDENT COUNCILS, Lexington, June 21, 1965

SYMPOSIUM ON STRIP-MINE RECLAMATION, Lexington, June 23, 1965

POKE SALLET FESTIVAL, Harlan, June 30, 1965

GROUNDBREAKING KY 15, Isom, July 6, 1965*

NATIONAL CAMPERS ASSOCIATION, Bowling Green, July 15, 1965

PRESS CONFERENCE, Louisville, July 19, 1965*

AFL-CIO GREATER LABOR COUNCIL, Louisville, July 20, 1965

NATIONAL GOVERNORS CONFERENCE, Minneapolis, Minn., July 26, 1965*

KENTUCKY AUTOMOTIVE WHOLESALERS ASSOCIATION, Louisville, August 16, 1965

STATE FIREMEN'S ASSOCIATION, Frankfort, August 17, 1965

MASON COUNTY PROJECT, Maysville, August 19, 1965

SPECIAL LEGISLATIVE SESSION, Frankfort, August 23, 1965*

Admiral's Picnic, Frankfort, August 29, 1965

National Catholic College Fraternity, Louisville, September 1, 1965

Press Conference on Amendment to House Bill 1, Frankfort, September 1, 1965*

University of Kentucky Community College, Hopkinsville, September 9, 1965

House Bill 1 Signing, Frankfort, September 16, 1965*

Industrial Dinner, Carrollton, September 27, 1965

Boone County Chamber of Commerce, Burlington, September 28, 1965

Five-Station Television Appearance, Louisville, September 28, 1965*

Kentucky League of Women Voters, Frankfort, September 29, 1965

Kentucky Society of Civil Engineers, Frankfort, September 30, 1965

U.S. 119 Highway Groundbreaking, Baxter, Harlan County, September 30, 1965*

Dedication of the Excello Shirt Company Plant, Middlesboro, September 30, 1965

University of Kentucky Commerce Building Dedication, Lexington, September 30, 1965

Statement on Highways, Fulton, October 1, 1965

Pennsylvania Reclamation Association, Butler, Pennsylvania, October 7, 1965

Farm City Banquet, Ashland, October 11, 1965

Bond Issue Financing, Frankfort, October 12, 1965*

Vocational Education Funding, Frankfort, October 13, 1965*

Fifth Annual Conservation Congress, Louisville, October 14, 1965*

70th Annual Meeting Ohio Valley Improvement Association, Cincinnati, Ohio, October 20, 1965

13th Annual Meeting Kentucky Rural Health Conference, Hopkinsville, October 21, 1965

Safety Coordinating Committee, Frankfort, October 22, 1965

Southern Industrial Development Council, Louisville, October 25, 1965*

KENTUCKY BANKERS ASSOCIATION CONVENTION, Brown Hotel, Louisville, October 26, 1965

GOVERNOR'S CONFERENCE ON LIBRARIES, Louisville, October 28, 1965*

KENTUCKY ASSOCIATION OF CHIROPRACTORS MEETING, Lexington, October 29, 1965

KENTUCKY COAL OPERATORS ASSOCIATION MEETING, Lexington, October 29, 1965

NATURAL RESOURCES COMMITTEE OF THE NATIONAL GOVERNORS CONFERENCE, St. Louis, Missouri, November 4, 1965*

VETERANS' DAY MARCH, Frankfort, November 11, 1965

UNIVERSITY OF KENTUCKY CENTENNIAL "K" BANQUET, Lexington, November 11, 1965

CABINET MEETING, Frankfort, November 16, 1965

KENTUCKY RETAIL FARM EQUIPMENT ASSOCIATION, Louisville, November 22, 1965

NORTH FORK LITTLE RIVER WATERSHED, Hopkinsville, November 22, 1965

BARKLEY CENTENNIAL CONVOCATION, Lexington, November 23, 1965

LEXINGTON VOCATIONAL TECHNICAL-TRAINING CENTER GROUND-BREAKING, Lexington, November 23, 1965*

INTRODUCTION OF GOVERNOR GEORGE ROMNEY, Louisville, November 24, 1965

STRIP MINING STATEMENT, Frankfort, November 24, 1965*

THOMAS JEFFERSON HIGH SCHOOL, Louisville, November 29, 1965

STATE FAIRGROUNDS LUNCHEON, Louisville, November 29, 1965

AEC TEAM BRIEFING, Louisville, November 30, 1965*

FRONTIER NURSES' BENEFIT DINNER, Frankfort, December 2, 1965*

STATE SAVINGS BOND DRIVE DINNER, Frankfort, December 3, 1965

PRELEGISLATIVE SESSION, Gilbertsville, December 6, 1965*

CONFERENCE ON HUMAN RIGHTS, Louisville, December 16, 1965*

KENTUCKY MENTAL HEALTH ASSOCIATION, Louisville, December 17, 1965

TELEVISION NEWS CONFERENCE, Frankfort, December 19, 1965

SCOUT CAMP FUND RAISING KICKOFF, Owensboro, December 21, 1965

LOUISVILLE CHAMBER OF COMMERCE, Louisville, January 1, 1966*

Constitutional Revision Assembly, Frankfort, January 3, 1966

State of the Commonwealth Message, Frankfort, January 4, 1966*

American Horse Show Convention, Lexington, January 14, 1966

State Manpower Conference, Louisville, January 25, 1966

Civil Rights Bill Signing, Frankfort, January 27, 1966*

Silver Anniversary Award, Frankfort, January 28, 1966

Education Statement, Frankfort, February 3, 1966*

Pinball Machine Statement, Frankfort, February 6, 1966*

March: Egg Month Kickoff Breakfast, Frankfort, February 8, 1966

National Farm Machinery Show, Louisville, February 15, 1966*

Governor's Conference on Forestry, Lexington, February 16, 1966*

Kentucky Travel Council, Louisville, February 16, 1966*

National Governors Conference Committee on Natural Resources, Lexington, February 17, 1966

Midwestern Governors Conference on Water Resources and Pollution, Lexington, February 17, 1966

Address to Joint Session of the 1966 Legislature, Frankfort, February 23, 1966*

Natural Resources Bills Signing, Frankfort, March 8, 1966

Founders Day Ceremonies, Richmond, March 21, 1966*

Morehead State College Recognition Dinner, Morehead, March 22, 1966

Safety Bill Signings, Frankfort, March 24, 1966

Governor's Industry Appreciation Luncheon, Louisville, April 11, 1966

World Convention of Methodist Bishops, Louisville, April 13, 1966

Traffic Court Conference, Frankfort, April 13, 1966

Statewide Television Press Conference, Frankfort, April 18, 1966

Cleanup and Beautification Conference, Louisville, April 18, 1966

National Conference of Christians and Jews, Inc., Louisville, April 19, 1966

Kentucky Mothers Association, Frankfort, April 20, 1966

Murray State College Recognition Day, Murray, April 21, 1966

HIGHWAY STATEMENT, Murray, April 21, 1966

CALLOWAY COUNTY AGRICULTURAL COUNCIL, Murray, April 21, 1966

OPENING REMARKS, Las Vegas, Nevada, April 24, 1966

CONSTITUTION REVISION ASSEMBLY, Lexington, April 26, 1966*

CORRECTIONS, Frankfort, April 29, 1966

SCOUT-O-RAMA OPENING, Louisville, April 29, 1966

INDUSTRIAL STATEMENT, Frankfort, April 29, 1966

ROTARY YOUTH CONFERENCE, Lexington, April 30, 1966

SHELBY COUNTY HIGH SCHOOL BANQUET, Shelbyville, May 3, 1966

FRANKLIN COUNTY LAW DAY, Frankfort, May 5, 1966

BETTER ROADS COUNCIL, Frankfort, May 6, 1966

UNIVERSITY OF KENTUCKY DENTAL SCHOOL GRADUATION, Lexington, May 9, 1966*

UNITED CHURCH WOMEN, Lexington, May 9, 1966

STATE RURAL SAFETY CONFERENCE, Louisville, May 10, 1966

YOUTH OPPORTUNITY CENTER OPENING, Louisville, May 10, 1966

GOLF COURSE OPENING, Lawrenceburg, May 11, 1966

SPINDLETOP OFFICE OPENING, Washington, D.C., May 12, 1966

LOUISVILLE AND VICINITY MINISTERS MEETING, Louisville, May 16, 1966*

GOVERNOR'S CONFERENCE ON ETV, Frankfort, May 17, 1966*

STATEWIDE TELEVISION NEWS CONFERENCE, Frankfort, May 18, 1966

BELLARMINE COLLEGE COMMENCEMENT, Louisville, May 18, 1966*

FIRST CONGRESSIONAL DISTRICT JEFFERSON-JACKSON DAY DINNER, Mayfield, May 21, 1966*

CIVIC LUNCHEON, Elkton, May 25, 1966

STATE BAR ASSOCIATION CONVENTION, Louisville, May 26, 1966

MARSHALL UNIVERSITY COMMENCEMENT ADDRESS, Huntington, West Virginia, May 29, 1966

KENTUCKY MILITARY INSTITUTE COMMENCEMENT, Lyndon, May 29, 1966

HOPKINSVILLE HIGH SCHOOL COMMENCEMENT, Hopkinsville, June 2, 1966

DR. YOUNG TESTIMONIAL DINNER, Shelbyville, June 8, 1966*

Southern Association of Workmen's Compensation Administration, Louisville, June 8, 1966

Statement on Old Age Assistance, Frankfort, June 9, 1966*

International Trade Fair, Poznan, Poland, June 15, 1966

Midwestern Governors Conference, Cincinnati, Ohio, June 22, 1966

Vocational School Groundbreaking, Bowling Green, June 23, 1966

Medicare Statement, Frankfort, June 24, 1966*

Tobacco Association of the United States, White Sulphur Springs, West Virginia, June 27, 1966*

OBO Workshop Banquet, Frankfort, June 28, 1966*

Poke Sallet Festival, Harlan, June 29, 1966

RECC Headquarters Groundbreaking, Winchester, June 29, 1966

Crank's Creek Dam and Lake, Harlan, June 29, 1966

Rotunda Remarks, Frankfort, June 30, 1966

Crucible Steel Company, Elizabethtown, June 30, 1966

Plant Dedication, Elizabethtown, June 30, 1966

Natural Resources Committee Report, National Governors' Conference, Los Angeles, California, July 7, 1966

American Legion State Convention, Louisville, July 15, 1966*

Construction Statement, Frankfort, July 20, 1966

Fayette County Young Democrats, Lexington, July 21, 1966*

Barkley Park Statement, Fort Campbell, July 23, 1966*

Democratic Fund Raising Dinner, Jefferson City, Missouri, July 23, 1966*

Vocational Education Conference, Lexington, July 25, 1966

Martin County Courthouse, Inez, July 28, 1966

Area Development Meeting, Prestonsburg, July 28, 1966*

Governor's Day, Breaks Interstate Park, Pikeville, July 28, 1966

State Convention of County Magistrates and Commissioners, Prestonsburg, July 28, 1966*

Library Dedication, Owensboro, July 30, 1966

Introduction of Frank Clement, Gilbertsville, August 1, 1966

MURRAY STATE UNIVERSITY, Murray, August 3, 1966

CITIZENS ADVISORY COMMITTEE LUNCHEON, Eddyville, August 4, 1966*

AREA DEVELOPMENT MEETING, Gilbertsville, August 5, 1966

ABERDEEN ANGUS FUTURITY, Lexington, August 9, 1966

KEA LEADERSHIP CONVENTION, Frankfort, August 10, 1966

HILL-BURTON STATEMENT, Frankfort, August 10, 1966*

UNIVERSITY OF LOUISVILLE, Louisville, August 11, 1966*

AREA DEVELOPMENT MEETING, Falls of Rough, August 12, 1966

HARVEY ALUMINUM DEDICATION, Lewisport, August 12, 1966*

HIGHWAY BOOSTERS LUNCHEON, Owensboro, August 12, 1966

BERKLEY DAVIS TESTIMONIAL DINNER, Owensboro, August 13, 1966

GOVERNOR'S COMMISSION ON AGRICULTURE MEETING, Owensboro, August 13, 1966

AREA DEVELOPMENT MEETING, Somerset, August 15, 1966

KENTUCKY AUTOMOTIVE WHOLESALERS ASSOCIATION, Lexington, August 15, 1966

NATIONAL LEGISLATIVE CONFERENCE, Portland, Maine, August 17, 1966*

STATE FAIR OPENING, Louisville, August 18, 1966

BARKLEY DAM DEDICATION, Gilbertsville, August 20, 1966*

LAKE BARKLEY STATE PARK, Cadiz, August 24, 1966

GROUNDBREAKING CEREMONY ROCKWELL-STANDARD CORPORATION, Winchester, August 25, 1966

MAYORS CONFERENCE, Frankfort, August 26, 1966

CAMPBELL COUNTY CHAMBER OF COMMERCE, Newport, August 29, 1966*

175TH ANNIVERSARY, Frankfort, August 30, 1966

PURCHASE PARKWAY GROUNDBREAKING, Mayfield, August 30, 1966*

KENTUCKY BANKERS ASSOCIATION, Louisville, September 13, 1966

VOCATIONAL SCHOOLS JEFFERSON COUNTY, Frankfort, September 16, 1966

SOUTHERN GOVERNORS CONFERENCE, Gilbertsville, September 19, 1966

DEMOCRATIC CAMPAIGN OPENING, Lexington, September 22, 1966

PRESS RELEASE, Frankfort, September 22, 1966*

State Young Democrats Convention, Owensboro, September 23, 1966

Kentucky Savings and Loan League, Gilbertsville, September 24, 1966*

National Association of Postmasters, Louisville, September 25, 1966

Kentucky Coop Council, Frankfort, September 26, 1966

Kentucky Chamber of Commerce Tour, Bardstown, September 27, 1966

Kentucky Chamber of Commerce Tour, Elizabethtown, September 27, 1966*

Kentucky Chamber of Commerce Tour, Hodgenville, September 27, 1966

Kentucky Chamber of Commerce Tour, Minfordville, September 27, 1966

Kentucky Chamber of Commerce Tour, Mammoth Cave, September 27, 1966

Kentucky Chamber of Commerce Tour, Glasgow, September 27, 1966

Kentucky Chamber of Commerce Tour, Scottsville, September 27, 1966

Kentucky Chamber of Commerce Tour, Franklin, September 27, 1966

Kentucky Chamber of Commerce Tour, Bowling Green, September 27, 1966

Kentucky Chamber of Commerce Tour, Russellville, September 28, 1966

Kentucky Chamber of Commerce Tour, Guthrie, September 28, 1966

Kentucky Chamber of Commerce Tour, Elkton, September 28, 1966

Kentucky Chamber of Commerce Tour, Hopkinsville, September 28, 1966

Kentucky Chamber of Commerce Tour, Madisonville, September 29, 1966

Kentucky Chamber of Commerce Tour, Owensboro, September 29, 1966

KENTUCKY CHAMBER OF COMMERCE TOUR, Henderson, September 29, 1966

KENTUCKY JAYCEES GOVERNMENT SEMINAR, Frankfort, October 1, 1966

TENNESSEE YOUNG DEMOCRAT CONVENTION, Nashville, Tennessee, October 1, 1966

UNIVERSITY OF KENTUCKY LAW STUDENTS, Lexington, October 3, 1966

FARM MARKETING WORKSHOP, Louisville, October 4, 1966

AMBER WHITE BRIDGE DEDICATION, Bowling Green, October 6, 1966

AREA DEVELOPMENT MEETING, Bowling Green, October 6, 1966

INTRODUCTION OF GOVERNOR JOHN B. CONNALLY, Louisville, October 7, 1966

KENTUCKY SCIENCE AND TECHNOLOGY ADVISORY COUNCIL, Frankfort, October 10, 1966*

KENTUCKY SCHOOL PRINCIPALS ASSOCIATION, Louisville, October 10, 1966

PADUCAH ROTARY CLUB, Paducah, October 12, 1966

EMERGENCY RESOURCE MANAGEMENT TEST EXERCISE, Frankfort, October 13, 1966

SEARS STORE DEDICATION, Frankfort, October 13, 1966

SARGENT SHRIVER INTRODUCTION, Gilbertsville, October 14, 1966

KENTUCKY CHIROPRACTORS ASSOCIATION, Owensboro, October 14, 1966

HOPKINSVILLE TEACHERS ASSOCIATION, Hopkinsville, October 18, 1966

ROTARY AND KIWANIS CLUBS, Hopkinsville, October 18, 1966

KENTUCKY MASONS-GRAND LODGE, Louisville, October 18, 1966

KENTUCKY WHOLESALE GROCERS, Lexington, October 21, 1966

HOOVER BALL AND BEARING COMPANY, Cadiz, October 23, 1966

PENNYRILE PARKWAY GROUNDBREAKING, Hopkinsville, October 25, 1966*

KENTUCKY BROADCASTERS ASSOCIATION, Gilbertsville, October 25, 1966

TRANSYLVANIA CONVOCATION, Lexington, October 26, 1966

Introduction of Governor Roger Branigin, Louisville, October 27, 1966

U.S. Civil Defense Council, Louisville, October 27, 1966

Sixth Annual Conservation Congress, Louisville, October 27, 1966

Kentucky Welfare Association, Louisville, November 4, 1966*

N.F.O. Convention, Hodgenville, November 5, 1966

Election Statement, Frankfort, November 8, 1966*

Kentucky State Faculty Housing Groundbreaking, Frankfort, November 11, 1966

Kentucky Highway Conference, Lexington, November 15, 1966

Third Annual Kentucky Science and Industry Procurement Conference, Louisville, November 17, 1966

Highway Progress in Eastern Kentucky, Hazard, November 21, 1966

Hazard Vocational School, Hazard, November 21, 1966

Interstate 75 Dedication, Richmond, November 23, 1966*

Kentucky State Reformatory, LaGrange, November 30, 1966*

Louisa Carpet Mills, Louisa, December 2, 1966

Paul Priddy Dinner, Louisville, December 3, 1966

University of Kentucky Agriculture Extension Conference, Lexington, December 5, 1966*

Commission on Child Welfare, Frankfort, December 6, 1966*

Statement on the Death of Paul Blazer, Frankfort, December 9, 1966

National Advisory Commission on Rural Poverty, Louisville, December 17, 1966*

Southern Regional Highway Safety Conference, New Orleans, Louisiana, December 19, 1966*

Vocational School, Lebanon, December 20, 1966

Cabinet Meeting, Frankfort, December 21, 1966

1966 Economic Development Statement, Frankfort, December 31, 1966*

Press Conference, Frankfort, January 3, 1967*

Kentucky Agricultural Cooperative Council, Lexington, January 5, 1967

EASTERN KENTUCKY UNIVERSITY LIBRARY DEDICATION, Richmond, January 6, 1967*

BUFFALO TRACE LIBRARY, Carlisle, January 7, 1967

WATER DISTRICT ASSOCIATION, Louisville, January 16, 1967

STATE OFFICE BUILDING AUDITORIUM, Frankfort, January 17, 1967

U-KATS, Lexington, January 17, 1967

LOUISVILLE JAYCEES AWARDS BANQUET, Louisville, January 19, 1967

VOCATIONAL SCHOOL DEDICATION, Eddyville, January 24, 1967

SOCIETY OF INDUSTRIAL REALTORS AWARD, Frankfort, January 25, 1967

GOVERNOR'S CONFERENCE ON AGRICULTURE, Louisville, January 25, 1967*

DANVILLE CHAMBER OF COMMERCE, Danville, January 26, 1967

MEETING WITH SECRETARIES, Frankfort, January 27, 1967

FRANKLIN COUNTY YOUNG DEMOCRATS, Frankfort, January 30, 1967

METHODIST MEN BANQUET, Lexington, January 31, 1967*

AGRICULTURAL STABILIZATION AND CONSERVATION SERVICE CONVENTION, Louisville, January 31, 1967

KENTUCKY CHAMBER OF COMMERCE COMMUNITY DEVELOPMENT FORUM AND AWARDS PROGRAM, Louisville, January 31, 1967

RECOGNITION OF APPALACHIAN INDUSTRIES, Frankfort, February 2, 1967*

DEDICATION OF PUBLIC ASSISTANCE BUILDING, Jackson, February 6, 1967*

TRI-CITY YMCA BANQUET, Florence, February 9, 1967

LINCOLN BIRTHDAY OBSERVANCE, Frankfort, February 13, 1967

NATIONAL PRECAST CONCRETE ASSOCIATION, Louisville, February 14, 1967

FRASER CHILD DIAGNOSTIC AND EVALUATION CENTER, Louisville, February 14, 1967

KENTUCKY TRAVEL CONFERENCE, Louisville, February 15, 1967*

NATIONAL FARM MACHINERY SHOW, Louisville, February 15, 1967

FOURTH ANNUAL GOVERNOR'S CONFERENCE ON FORESTRY, Lexington, February 15, 1967*

PRESS CONFERENCE, Frankfort, February 16, 1967*

Farm Awards Luncheon, Louisville, February 18, 1967

Vocational Education Honors Luncheon, Frankfort, February 20, 1967

Industry Appreciation Week 1967, Louisville, February 21, 1967

State Savings Bond Drive, Louisville, February 21, 1967

Conference Workshop on Housing, Covington, February 22, 1967*

Garrard County Library, Lancaster, February 22, 1967

Press Conference, Frankfort, February 24, 1967*

Education Television Statement, Frankfort, February 28, 1967

Mayors Conference, Frankfort, March 9, 1967

Louisville Personnel Association, Louisville, March 13, 1967

Kentucky School Board Association, Louisville, March 14, 1967*

Murray Chamber of Commerce, Murray, March 23, 1967

Kentucky Chapter of Public Personnel Association, Frankfort, March 27, 1967

Dr. Wilson Inauguration, Wilmore, March 28, 1967

Boone County Courthouse Annex Dedication, Burlington, March 29, 1967

Northern Kentucky Planning Council, Newport, March 29, 1967

Central City Dinner, Central City, March 30, 1967

Carborundum Company Dedication, Hickman, March 30, 1967*

North Marshall All-Sports Banquet, Benton, March 31, 1967

Youth in Politics Assembly, Prestonsburg, April 6, 1967

Governor's Occupational Health Conference, Lexington, April 6, 1967*

University of Kentucky Engineering Building, Lexington, April 8, 1967

Press Conference Firestone Plant for Bowling Green, Frankfort, April 13, 1967

Tri-State Council of Boy Scouts, Ashland, April 19, 1967

Kiwanis Club, Ashland, April 19, 1967

Dedication of Historical Markers, Ashland, April 19, 1967*

Vocational School Dedication, Ashland, April 19, 1967

Deed Presentation, Covington, April 19, 1967

UNIVERSITY OF KENTUCKY AIR FORCE RESERVE OFFICERS TRAINING CORPS, Lexington, April 20, 1967

WEBSTER COUNTY YOUNG DEMOCRATS, Frankfort, April 20, 1967*

STATEMENT OF FARM POLICY, Decatur, Indiana, April 20, 1967

MEDICAL CENTER DEDICATION, Inez, April 22, 1967*

LIBRARY DEDICATION, Campton, April 25, 1967

DEDICATION—DOW CORNING CORPORATION, Carrollton, April 27, 1967

JAMESTOWN LIBRARY, Jamestown, April 30, 1967

NATIONAL ADVISORY COMMISSION ON RURAL POVERTY, Natural Bridge State Park, May 3, 1967*

DERBY STATEMENT, Frankfort, May 4, 1967*

LOUISVILLE LEAGUE OF WOMEN VOTERS, Louisville, May 10, 1967

LEXINGTON COUNCIL OF JEWISH WOMEN, Lexington, May 11, 1967

MOSQUITO CONTROL CONFERENCE, Madisonville, May 16, 1967*

CAMP BRECKINRIDGE JOB CORPS GRADUATION, Morganfield, May 17, 1967

MUHLENBURG COUNTY VOCATIONAL SCHOOL DEDICATION, Powderly, May 19, 1967

WESCOR DEDICATION, Hawesville, May 19, 1967

MOUNT CARMEL HIGH SCHOOL COMMENCEMENT, Jackson, May 25, 1967

DEDICATION OF BUILDINGS AT KENTUCKY SCHOOL FOR THE DEAF, Danville, May 26, 1967

HIGHWAY STATEMENT, Frankfort, May 26, 1967*

APPRECIATION DINNER FOR WEST VIRGINIA PULP AND PAPER COMPANY, Wickliffe, May 31, 1967

LOUISVILLE ROTARY CLUB, Louisville, June 1, 1967

FUTURE FARMERS OF AMERICA STATE CONVENTION, Louisville, June 1, 1967

WORLD'S FAIR—BUSINESS MEN'S LUNCHEON, Montreal, Canada, June 2, 1967

THE LEAGUE OF KENTUCKY SPORTSMEN, Covington, June 9, 1967*

LOUISVILLE CHAMBER OF COMMERCE, Louisville, June 13, 1967

EDUCATIONAL T.V. CORNERSTONE LAYING, Lexington, June 21, 1967

NATIONAL ASSOCIATION OF STATE CIVIL DEFENSE DIRECTORS, Lexington, June 21, 1967

FORT THOMAS CENTENNIAL, Fort Thomas, June 27, 1967

MAYO VOCATIONAL SCHOOL COMMENCEMENT, Paintsville, June 29, 1967

JUSTICE REED INTRODUCTION, Brooksville, June 29, 1967

AID STATEMENT, Frankfort, June 30, 1967

20TH ANNUAL BLACKBERRY FESTIVAL, Carlisle, July 3, 1967

KENTUCKY CRIME COMMISSION, Frankfort, July 5, 1967*

STURGIS FLOODWALL, Sturgis, July 8, 1967

FARM PRESS AND RADIO ASSOCIATION OF KENTUCKY, Frankfort, July 10, 1967

STRIP MINING SYMPOSIUM, Owensboro, July 13, 1967*

SOUTHERN WATER RESOURCES CONFERENCE, Biloxi, Mississippi, July 13, 1967*

ECONOMIC DEVELOPMENT COMMISSION MEETING, Frankfort, July 18, 1967

ST. MATTHEWS DEDICATION, St. Matthews, July 19, 1967

KENTUCKY JUNIOR HEREFORD ASSOCIATION, Bremen, July 20, 1967

FRANK DUVENECK MEMORIAL GALLERY, Covington, July 21, 1967

YOUNG KENTUCKIANS ADVISORY COMMISSION, Frankfort, August 3, 1967

AMERICAN ABERDEEN ANGUS BREEDERS FUTURITY, Lexington, August 7, 1967

JOINT MEETING OF STATE PLANNING AGENCIES AND NATIONAL ASSOCIATION OF STATE BUDGET OFFICERS, Lexington, August 7, 1967

BURLEY BELT CONFERENCE BANQUET, Lexington, August 9, 1967

ESSEX WIRE COMPANY DEDICATION, Paducah, August 10, 1967

MERIT SCHOLARSHIP LUNCHEON, Frankfort, August 15, 1967

OPENING REMARKS OF THE 1967 KENTUCKY STATE FAIR, Louisville, August 17, 1967

NAAS BANKERS, Louisville, August 17, 1967

NATIONAL RURAL SOCIOLOGICAL SOCIETY, San Francisco, California, August 27, 1967*

STATEMENT ON HIGHWAY DEVELOPMENT CONCEPT, MIDWESTERN GOVERNORS CONFERENCE, Lake of the Ozarks, Missouri, August 28, 1967*

STATEMENT ON VOCATIONAL EDUCATION, MIDWESTERN GOVERNORS CONFERENCE, Lake of the Ozarks, Missouri, August 29, 1967*

URBAN DEVELOPMENT, MIDWESTERN GOVERNORS CONFERENCE, Lake of the Ozarks, Missouri, August 29, 1967

LOGAN HELMS-WOODFORD COUNTIES LIBRARY, Versailles, September 5, 1967

STRIP MINE STATEMENT, Frankfort, September 6, 1967*

SOCIETY OF AMERICAN TRAVEL WRITERS CONVENTION, Louisville, September 7, 1967

SOUTHERN GOVERNORS CONFERENCE, Asheville, North Carolina, September 11, 1967

REDEDICATION OF JOHN BREATHITT MARKER, Russellville, September 16, 1967

REDEDICATION OF JEFFERSON DAVIS MONUMENT STATE SHRINE, Fairview, September 16, 1967

EMERGENCY RESCUE CONFERENCE, Frankfort, September 20, 1967

STATE GOVERNMENT FOR A DAY, Carrollton, September 21, 1967

PRESS CONFERENCE ON POVERTY, New York, New York, September 22, 1967

INDUSTRIAL APPRECIATION LUNCHEON, New York, New York, September 22, 1967*

KENTUCKY CHAMBER OF COMMERCE TOUR, Paintsville, September 26, 1967

KENTUCKY CHAMBER OF COMMERCE TOUR, Salyersville, September 26, 1967

KENTUCKY CHAMBER OF COMMERCE TOUR, Prestonsburg, September 26, 1967

KENTUCKY CHAMBER OF COMMERCE TOUR, Winchester, September 26, 1967

KENTUCKY CHAMBER OF COMMERCE TOUR, Pikeville, September 27, 1967

KENTUCKY CHAMBER OF COMMERCE TOUR, Elkhorn City, September 27, 1967

KENTUCKY CHAMBER OF COMMERCE TOUR, Breaks Interstate Park, September 27, 1967

KENTUCKY CHAMBER OF COMMERCE TOUR, Shelby Gap, September 27, 1967

KENTUCKY CHAMBER OF COMMERCE TOUR, Whitesburg, September 27, 1967

KENTUCKY CHAMBER OF COMMERCE TOUR, Hazard, September 27, 1967

KENTUCKY ASSOCIATION OF SOIL CONSERVATION DISTRICTS, Gilbertsville, September 28, 1967

KENTUCKY CHAMBER OF COMMERCE TOUR, Beattyville, September 28, 1967

5TH ANNUAL INTERNATIONAL BANANA FESTIVAL, Fulton, September 29, 1967

KENTUCKY CHAMBER OF COMMERCE TOUR, Richmond, September 29, 1967

KENTUCKY COOPERATIVE COUNCIL LUNCHEON, Louisville, October 2, 1967

KENTUCKY ECONOMIC DEVELOPMENT COMMISSION, Gilbertsville, October 4, 1967*

SILVER ANTELOPE AWARD LUNCHEON, Louisville, October 12, 1967

WKU BUILDINGS DEDICATION, Bowling Green, October 13, 1967

GOVERNOR'S CONSERVATION CONGRESS, Lexington, October 26, 1967*

KENTUCKY 15 HIGHWAY, Hazard, October 27, 1967

6TH ANNUAL CONSERVATION CONGRESS, Louisville, October 27, 1967

FRANKLIN COUNTY WARD RALLY, Frankfort, October 30, 1967*

UNIVERSITY OF KENTUCKY COMMUNITY COLLEGE, Maysville, November 15, 1967

VEST-LINDSEY HOUSE RESTORATION, Frankfort, November 16, 1967

ANIMAL DISEASE DIAGNOSTIC LABORATORY, Hopkinsville, November 30, 1967

DEDICATION OF STATE OFFICE BUILDING, Hopkinsville, November 30, 1967

INTERSTATE 24 GROUNDBREAKING, Eddyville, December 6, 1967*

VALEDICTORY ADDRESS, Frankfort, December 12, 1967*

INDEX

www.ingramcontent.com/pod-product-compliance
Lightning Source LLC
LaVergne TN
LVHW040202080826
844660LV00001B/79

* 9 7 8 0 8 1 3 1 0 6 0 3 8 *